# AN INTRODUCTION TO STATISTICAL CONCEPTS

SECOND EDITION

Richard G. Lomax
*The Ohio State University*

Routledge
Taylor & Francis Group
New York   London

Routledge is an imprint of the
Taylor & Francis Group, an informa business

Routledge
Taylor & Francis Group
270 Madison Avenue
New York, NY 10016

Routledge
Taylor & Francis Group
2 Park Square
Milton Park, Abingdon
Oxon OX14 4RN

©2007 by Taylor & Francis Group, LLC
Routledge is an imprint of Taylor & Francis Group, an Informa business
Originally published by Lawrence Erlbaum Associates
Reprinted in 2009 by Routledge
Cover design by Tomai Maridou

Printed in the United States of America on acid-free paper
10 9 8 7 6 5 4
International Standard Book Number-13: 978-0-8058-5739-9 (Hardcover)

**CREDITS**
Tables fournd in the Appendix have been reprinted from the following sources: Tables 1, 2, 3, 4, 5, & 6 from Pearson, E.S. & Hartley, H.O. (1966), *Biometricka Tables for Statisticians,* respectively Tables 1, 12, 8, 18, 14, & 47 by permission of Oxford University Press; Table 7 from Dunnett, C. W. (1955), a multiple comparison procedure for comparing several treatments with a control, *Journal of the American Statistical Association*, 50, 1096-1121, by permission of the American Statistical Association, and from Dunnett, C. W. (1964), New tables for multiple comparisons with a control, ***Biometrics***, *20*, 482-491, by permission of the Biometric Society; Table 8 from Games, P. A. (1977), An improved t table for simultaneous control of g contrasts, *Journal of the American Statistical Association*, 72, 531-534, by permission of the American Statistical Association; Table 9 from Harter, H. L. (1960), Tables of range and studentized range, *Annals of Mathematical Statistics*, 31, 1122-1147, by permission of the Institute of Mathematical Statistics; Table 10 from Bryant, J. L. & Paulson, A. S. (1976), An extension of Tukey's method of multiple comparisons to experimental designs with random concomitant variables, *Biometrika*, 63, 631-638, by permission of Oxford University Press.

**Library of Congress Cataloging-in-Publication Data**

Catalog record is available from the Library of Congress

**Visit the Taylor & Francis Web site at**
**http://www.taylorandfrancis.com**

**and the Routledge Web site at**
**http://www.routledge.com**

*This book is dedicated to
my family and to all of
my former students.*

# CONTENTS

PREFACE      ix

1   INTRODUCTION      1
     What is the value of statistics?      3
     Brief introduction to the history of statistics      5
     General statistical definitions      5
     Types of variables      7
     Scales of measurement      8
     Summary      12

2   DATA REPRESENTATION      16
     Tabular display of distributions      18
     Graphical display of distributions      23
     Percentiles      29
     SPSS      33
     Summary      34

3   UNIVARIATE POPULATION PARAMETERS AND SAMPLE STATISTICS      39
     Summation notation      40
     Measures of central tendency      41
     Measures of dispersion      45
     SPSS      53
     Summary      55

4   THE NORMAL DISTRIBUTION AND STANDARD SCORES                              59
        The normal distribution                                             60
        Standard scores                                                     65
        Skewness and kurtosis statistics                                    68
        SPSS                                                                72
        Summary                                                             73

5   INTRODUCTION TO PROBABILITY AND SAMPLE STATISTICS                       77
        Brief introduction to probability                                   78
        Sampling and estimation                                             81
        Summary                                                             87

6   INTRODUCTION TO HYPOTHESIS TESTING: INFERENCES ABOUT A SINGLE MEAN      92
        Types of hypotheses                                                 93
        Types of decision errors                                            95
        Level of significance ($\alpha$)                                    98
        Overview of steps in the decision-making process                   100
        Inferences about $\mu$ when $\sigma$ is known                      101
        Type II error ($\beta$) and power ($1 - \beta$)                    105
        Statistical versus practical significance                          108
        Inferences about $\mu$ when $\sigma$ is unknown                    109
        SPSS                                                               113
        Summary                                                            114

7   INFERENCES ABOUT THE DIFFERENCE BETWEEN TWO MEANS                      119
        New concepts                                                       120
        Inferences about two independent means                            122
        Inferences about two dependent means                              129
        SPSS                                                               133
        Summary                                                            134

8   INFERENCES ABOUT PROPORTIONS                                           140
        Inferences about proportions involving the normal distribution     141
        Inferences about proportions involving the chi-square distribution  151
        SPSS                                                               156
        Summary                                                            158

9   INFERENCES ABOUT VARIANCES                                             162
        New concepts                                                       163
        Inferences about a single variance                                164
        Inferences about two dependent variances                          166
        Inferences about two or more independent variances
        (homogeneity of variance tests)                                   168
        SPSS                                                               172
        Summary                                                            173

**10** Bivariate Measures of Association 176

Scatterplot 177

Covariance 179

Pearson product-moment correlation coefficient 182

Inferences about the Pearson product-moment correlation coefficient 183

Some issues regarding correlations 186

Other measures of association 188

SPSS 191

Summary 192

**11** One-Factor Analysis of Variance—Fixed-Effects Model 196

Characteristics of the one-factor ANOVA model 198

The layout of the data 200

ANOVA theory 201

The ANOVA model 206

Assumptions and violation of assumptions 210

The unequal $n$'s or unbalanced design 213

Alternative ANOVA procedures 213

SPSS 215

Summary 217

**12** Multiple Comparison Procedures 222

Concepts of multiple comparison procedures 224

Selected multiple comparison procedures 228

SPSS 241

Summary 242

**13** Factorial Analysis of Variance—Fixed-Effects Model 247

The two-factor ANOVA model 249

Three-factor and higher-order ANOVA 265

Factorial ANOVA with unequal $n$'s 267

SPSS 268

Summary 269

**14** Introduction to Analysis of Covariance: The One-Factor
Fixed-Effects Model With a Single Covariate 277

Characteristics of the model 278

The layout of the data 281

The ANCOVA model 281

The ANCOVA summary table 282

Partitioning the sums of squares 283

Adjusted means and related procedures 283

Assumptions and violation of assumptions 286

An example                                                                  289
ANCOVA without randomization                                                292
More complex ANCOVA models                                                  293
Nonparametric ANCOVA procedures                                             293
SPSS                                                                        293
Summary                                                                     294

15   RANDOM- AND MIXED-EFFECTS ANALYSIS OF VARIANCE MODELS                   301
The one-factor random-effects model                                         303
The two-factor random-effects model                                         306
The two-factor mixed-effects model                                          309
The one-factor repeated measures design                                     313
The two-factor split-plot or mixed design                                   319
SPSS                                                                        325
Summary                                                                     331

16   HIERARCHICAL AND RANDOMIZED BLOCK ANALYSIS OF VARIANCE MODELS           335
The two-factor hierarchical model                                           336
The two-factor randomized block design for $n = 1$                          343
The two-factor randomized block design for $n > 1$                          350
The Friedman test                                                           350
Comparison of various ANOVA models                                          351
SPSS                                                                        353
Summary                                                                     357

17   SIMPLE LINEAR REGRESSION                                                361
The concepts of simple linear regression                                    362
The population simple linear regression model                               364
The sample simple linear regression model                                   365
SPSS                                                                        381
Summary                                                                     383

18   MULTIPLE REGRESSION                                                     387
Partial and semipartial correlations                                        388
Multiple linear regression                                                  390
Other regression models                                                     403
SPSS                                                                        408
What's next?                                                                408
Summary                                                                     410

REFERENCES                                                                  415
APPENDIX TABLES                                                             425
ANSWERS                                                                     449
INDEX                                                                       463

# PREFACE

## APPROACH

I know, I know! I've heard it a million times before. When you hear someone at a party mention the word **statistics** or **statistician**, you probably say "I hate statistics" and turn the other cheek. In the more than 25 years I have been in the field of statistics, I can only recall four or five times when someone did not have that reaction. Enough is enough. With the help of this text, the "I hate statistics" slogan will become a distant figment of your imagination.

As the title suggests, this text is designed for a course in statistics for students in education and the behavioral sciences. We begin with the most basic introduction to statistics in the first chapter and proceed through intermediate statistics. Unlike many other statistics textbooks, this book includes topics that are comprehensive enough for either a single course or a two-course sequence (e.g., nonparametric procedures, modern alternative procedures, advanced analysis of variance and regression models). The text is designed for you to become a better-prepared researcher and a more intelligent consumer of research. I do not assume that you have extensive or recent training in mathematics. Many of you have only had algebra, some more than 20 years ago. I also do not assume that you have ever had a statistics course. Rest assured, you will do fine.

I believe that a text should serve as an effective instructional tool. You should find this text to be more than a reference book; you might actually use it to learn statistics (what an oxymoron, that a statistics book can actually teach something). This text is not a theoretical statistics book, nor is it a cookbook on computing statistics, or a statistical software manual. Recipes have to be memorized, consequently you tend not to understand how or why you obtain the desired product. As well, knowing how to run a statistics package without understanding the concepts or the output is not particularly useful. Thus concepts drive the field of statistics.

## GOALS AND CONTENT COVERAGE

My goals for this text are lofty, but the effort and its effects will be worthwhile. First, the text provides a comprehensive coverage of topics that could be included in an undergraduate or graduate one- or two-course sequence in statistics. The text is flexible enough so that instructors can select those topics that they desire to cover as they deem relevant in their particular discipline. In other words, chapters and sections of chapters from this text can be included in a statistics course as the instructor sees fit. Most of the popular as well as many of the lesser-known procedures and models are described in the text. A particular feature is a thorough and up-to-date discussion of assumptions, the effects of their violation, and how to deal with their violation.

The first five chapters of the text cover basic descriptive statistics, including ways of representing data graphically, statistical measures which describe a set of data, the normal distribution and other types of standard scores, and an introduction to probability and sampling. The remainder of the text covers different inferential statistics. In chapters 6 through 10 we deal with different inferential tests involving means (e.g., $t$ tests), proportions, variances, and correlations. In chapters 11 through 16, all of the basic analysis of variance (ANOVA) models are considered. Finally, in chapters 17 and 18 we examine various regression models.

Second, the text communicates a conceptual, intuitive understanding of statistics, which requires only a rudimentary knowledge of basic algebra, and emphasizes the important concepts in statistics. The most effective way to learn statistics is through the conceptual approach. Statistical concepts tend to be easy to learn because (a) concepts can be simply stated, (b) concepts can be made relevant thorough the use of real-life examples, (c) the same concepts are shared by many procedures, and (d) concepts can be related to one another.

This text will help you to reach these goals. The following indicators will provide some feedback as to how you are doing. First, there will be a noticeable change in your attitude towards statistics. Thus one outcome is for you to feel that "statistics isn't half bad," or "this stuff is OK." Second, you will feel comfortable using statistics in your own work. Finally, you will begin to "see the light." You will know when you have reached this highest stage of statistics development when suddenly, in the middle of the night, you wake up from a dream and say "now I get it." In other words, you will begin to think statistics rather than think of ways to get out of doing statistics.

## PEDAGOGICAL TOOLS

The text contains several important pedagogical features to allow you to attain these goals. First, each chapter begins with an outline (so you can anticipate what will be covered), and a list of key concepts (which you will need to really understand what you are doing). Second, realistic examples from education and the behavioral sciences are used to illustrate the concepts and procedures covered in each chapter. Each of these examples includes an examination of the various procedures and necessary assumptions, running SPSS and developing an APA style write-up, as well as tables, figures, and SPSS output to assist you. Third, the text is based on the conceptual approach. That is, material is covered so that you obtain a good understanding of statistical concepts. If you know the concepts, then you know statistics. Finally, each chapter ends with two sets of problems, computational and conceptual. Pay particular attention to the conceptual problems as they provide the best assessment of your understanding of the concepts in the chapter. I strongly suggest using the example data sets and the computational problems for additional practice through available statistics software. This will serve to reinforce the concepts covered. Answers to the odd-numbered problems are given at the end of the book.

## NEW TO THE SECOND EDITION

A number of changes have been made in the second edition based on the suggestions of reviewers, instructors, and students. These improvements have been made in order to better achieve the goals of the text. The changes include the following: (a) sections have been added to most chapters on SPSS, which includes input, output, and APA style write-ups using the example dataset; (b) a CD has been inserted into the text with every dataset used in the text (i.e., both chapter examples and end of chapter problems) in SPSS format; (c) more information on confidence intervals, effect size measures, and power has been added; (d) the sequence of the regression and ANOVA chapters has been altered to provide a better conceptual flow to the text and so that the ANOVA and regression chapters are as independent as possible; (e) additional regression models have been added; (f) computations have been minimized so that more space is available for the discussion of concepts and statistical software; (g) additional end of chapter problems have been added, including more realistic examples as well as interpretive problems; (h) content throughout the book has been updated since the previous edition and numerous additional references have been provided; and (i) an Instructor's Resource CD containing all of the solutions to the end of chapter problems, statistical humor, and other instructional materials is free to adoptees.

## ACKNOWLEDGMENTS

There are many individuals whose assistance enabled the completion of this book. First, I would like to thank the following individuals whom I studied statistics and research design with at the University of Pittsburgh: Jamie Algina, Lloyd Bond, Jim Carlson, Bill Cooley, Harry Hsu, Lou Pingel, Charles Stegman, and Neil Timm. Next, numerous colleagues have played an important role in my personal and professional life as a statistician. Rather than include an admittedly incomplete listing, I just say "thank you" to all of you. You know who you are.

Thanks also to all of the wonderful people at Lawrence Erlbaum Associates, in particular, to Ray O'Connell for inspiring this project back in 1986 when I began writing the second course text, and to Debra Riegert for supporting the development of subsequent texts and editions. I am most appreciative of the insightful suggestions provided by the reviewers of this text, Tim Konold (University of Virginia), L. Suzanne Dancer (University of Texas at Austin), Douglas Maynart (SUNY, New Paltz) and Patrick Markey (Villanova University). A special thank you to all of the terrific students that I have had the pleasure of teaching at the University of Pittsburgh, the University of Illinois—Chicago, Louisiana State University, Boston College, Northern Illinois University, the University of Alabama, and The Ohio State University. For all of your efforts, and the many lights that you have seen and shared with me, this book is for you. I am most grateful to my family, in particular, to Lea and Kristen. It is because of your love and understanding that I was able to cope with such a major project. Thank you one and all.

—RGL

# 1

# INTRODUCTION

## Chapter Outline

1. What is the value of statistics?
2. Brief introduction to the history of statistics
3. General statistical definitions
4. Types of variables
5. Scales of measurement
    Nominal measurement scale
    Ordinal measurement scale
    Interval measurement scale
    Ratio measurement scale

## Key Concepts

1. General statistical concepts
    Population
    Parameter
    Sample
    Statistic
    Descriptive statistics
    Inferential statistics
2. Variable-related concepts
    Variable
    Constant

Discrete variables
Continuous variables
Dichotomous variables
3.    Measurement scale concepts
Measurement
Nominal
Ordinal
Interval
Ratio

I want to welcome you to the wonderful world of statistics. More than ever, statistics are everywhere. Listen to the weather report and you hear about the measurement of variables such as temperature, rainfall, barometric pressure, and humidity. Watch a sporting event and you hear about batting averages, percentage of free throws completed, and total rushing yardage. Read the financial page and you can track the Dow Jones average, the Gross National Product, and bank interest rates. Turn to the entertainment section to see movie ratings, movie revenue, or the top ten best-selling novels. These are just a few examples of statistics that surround you in every aspect of your life.

Although you may be thinking that statistics is not the most enjoyable subject on the planet, by the end of this text you will (a) have a more positive attitude about statistics, (b) feel more comfortable using statistics, and thus be more likely to perform your own quantitative data analyses, and (c) certainly know much more about statistics than you do now. But be forewarned; the road to statistical independence is not easy. However, I will serve as your guide along the way. When the going gets tough, I will be there to help you with advice and numerous examples and problems. Using the powers of logic, mathematical reasoning, and statistical concept knowledge, I will help you arrive at an appropriate solution to the statistical problem at hand.

Some students begin their first statistic class with some anxiety. This could be caused by not having had a quantitative course for some time, apprehension built up by delaying taking statistics, a poor past instructor or course, or less than adequate past success. Let me offer a few suggestions along these lines. First, this is not a math class or text. If you want one of those, then you need to walk over to the math department. This is a course and text on the application of statistics to education and the behavioral sciences. Second, the philosophy of the text is on the understanding of concepts rather than on the derivation of statistical formulas. It is more important to understand concepts than to derive or memorize various and sundry formulas. If you understand the concepts, you can always look up the formulas if need be. If you don't understand the concepts, then knowing the formulas will only allow you to operate in a cookbook mode without really understanding what you are doing. Third, the calculator and computer are your friends. These devices are tools that allow you to complete the necessary computations and obtain the results of interest. If you are performing hand computations, find a calculator that you are comfortable with; it need not have 800 functions, as the four basic operations, sum and square root functions are sufficient (my personal calculator is one of those little credit card calculators, although I often use the calculator on my computer). If you are using a statistical software program, find one that you are comfortable with (most instructors will have you using a program such as SPSS, SAS, or Statistica). In this text we use SPSS to illustrate statistical applications. Finally, this text will take you from raw data to results using realistic examples. These can then be followed up using the problems at the end of each chapter. Thus you will not be on your own, but will have the text, a computer/calculator, as well as your course and instructor, to help guide you.

The intent and philosophy of this text is to be conceptual and intuitive in nature. Thus the text does not require a high level of mathematics, but rather emphasizes the important concepts in statistics. Most statistical concepts really are fairly easy to learn because (a) concepts can be simply stated, (b) concepts can be related to real-life examples, (c) many of the same concepts run through much of statistics, and therefore (d) many concepts can be related.

In this introductory chapter, we describe the most basic statistical concepts. We begin with the question, "What is the value of statistics?" We then look at a brief history of statistics by mentioning a few of the more important and interesting statisticians. Then we consider the concepts of population, parameter, sample, and statistic, descriptive and inferential statistics, types of variables, and scales of measurement. Our objectives are that by the end of this chapter, you will (a) have a better sense of why statistics are necessary, (b) see that statisticians are an interesting group of people, and (c) have an understanding of several basic statistical concepts.

## 1.1 WHAT IS THE VALUE OF STATISTICS?

Let us start off with a reasonable rhetorical question: why do we need statistics? In other words, what is the value of statistics, either in your research or in your everyday life? As a way of thinking about these questions, consider the following headlines, which have probably appeared in your local newspaper.

### Cigarette-Smoking Causes Cancer— Tobacco Industry Denies Charges

A study conducted at Ivy-Covered University Medical School, recently published in the *New England Journal of Medicine*, has definitively shown that cigarette-smoking causes cancer. In interviews with 100 randomly-selected smokers and non-smokers over 50 years of age, 30% of the smokers have developed some form of cancer, while only 10% of the non-smokers have cancer. "The higher percentage of smokers with cancer in our study clearly indicates that cigarettes cause cancer," said Dr. Jason P. Smythe. On the contrary, "this study doesn't even suggest that cigarettes cause cancer," said tobacco lobbyist Cecil B. Hacker. "Who knows how these folks got cancer; maybe it is caused by the aging process or by the method in which individuals were selected for the interviews," Mr. Hacker went on to say.

## North Carolina Congressional Districts Gerrymandered— African-Americans Slighted

A study conducted at the National Center for Legal Research indicates that congressional districts in the state of North Carolina have been gerrymandered to minimize the impact of the African-American vote. "From our research, it is clear that the districts are apportioned in a racially-biased fashion. Otherwise, how could there be no single district in the entire state which has a majority of African-American citizens when over 50% of the state's population is African-American. The districting system absolutely has to be changed," said Dr. I. M. Researcher. A spokesman for The American Bar Association countered with the statement "according to a decision rendered by the United States Supreme Court in 1999 (No. 98-85), intent or motive must be shown for racial bias to be shown in the creation of congressional districts. The decision states a 'facially neutral law . . . warrants strict scrutiny only if it can be proved that the law was motivated by a racial purpose or object.' The data in this study do not show intent or motive. To imply that these data indicate racial bias is preposterous."

## Global Warming—Myth According to the President

Research conducted at the National Center for Global Warming (NCGW) has shown the negative consequences of global warming on the planet Earth. As summarized by Dr. Noble Pryze, "our studies at NCGW clearly demonstrate that if global warming is not halted in the next 20 years, the effects on all aspects of our environment and climateology will be catastrophic." A different view is held by U.S. President Harold W. Tree. He stated in a recent address that "the scientific community has not convinced him that global warming even exists. Why should our administration spend millions of dollars on an issue that has not been shown to be a real concern?"

How is one to make sense of the studies described by these headlines? How is one to decide which side of the issue these data support, so as to take an intellectual stand? In other words, do the interview data clearly indicate that cigarette smoking causes cancer? Do the congressional district percentages of African-Americans necessarily imply that there is racial bias? Have scientists convinced us that global warming is a problem? These studies are examples of situations where the appropriate use of statistics is clearly necessary. Statistics will provide us with an intellectually acceptable method for making decisions in such matters. For instance, a certain type of research, statistical analysis, and set of results are all necessary to make causal inferences about cigarette smoking. Another type of research, statistical analysis, and set of results are all necessary to lead one to confidently state that the districting system is racially biased or not, or that global warming needs to be dealt with. The bottom line is that the purpose of statistics, and thus of this text, is to provide you with the tools to make important decisions in an appropriate and confident manner. You won't have to trust a statement made by some so-called expert on an issue, which may or may not have any empirical basis or validity; you can make your own judgements based on the statistical analyses of data. For you the value of statistics can include (a) the ability to read and critique articles in both professional journals and in the popular press, and (b) the ability to conduct statistical analyses for your own research (e.g., thesis or dissertation).

## 1.2    BRIEF INTRODUCTION TO THE HISTORY OF STATISTICS

As a way of getting to know the topic of statistics, I want to briefly introduce you to a few famous statisticians. The purpose of this section is not to provide a comprehensive history of statistics, as those already exist (e.g., Pearson, 1978; Stigler, 1986; Heyde, Seneta, Crepel, Fienberg & Gani, 2001). Rather, the purpose of this section is to show that famous statisticians are not only interesting, but are human beings just like you and me.

One of the fathers of probability (see chap. 5) is acknowledged to be Blaise Pascal from the late 1600s. One of Pascal's contributions was that he worked out the probabilities for each dice roll in the game of craps, enabling his friend, a member of royalty, to become a consistent winner. He also developed Pascal's triangle which you may remember from your early mathematics education. The statistical development of the normal or bell-shaped curve (see chap. 4) is interesting. For many years, this development was attributed to Karl Friedrich Gauss (early 1800s) and was actually known for some time as the Gaussian curve. Later historians found that Abraham DeMoivre actually developed the normal curve in the 1730s. As statistics was not thought of as a true academic discipline until the late 1800s, people like Pascal and DeMoivre were consulted by the wealthy on odds about games of chance and by insurance underwriters to determine mortality rates.

Karl Pearson is one of the most famous statisticians to date (late 1800s to early 1900s). Among his many accomplishments is the Pearson product-moment correlation coefficient still in use today (see chap. 10). You may know of Florence Nightingale (1820–1910) as an important figure in the field of nursing. However, you may not know of her importance in the field of statistics. Nightingale believed that statistics and theology were linked and that by studying statistics we might come to understand God's laws.

A quite interesting statistical personality is William Sealy Gossett, who was employed by the Guinness Brewery in Ireland. The brewery wanted to select a sample of people from Dublin in 1906 for purposes of taste testing. Gossett was asked how large a sample was needed in order to make an accurate inference about the entire population (see next section). The brewery would not let Gossett publish any of his findings under his own name, so he used the pseudonym of Student. Today the $t$ distribution is still known as Student's $t$ distribution. Sir Ronald A. Fisher is another of the most famous statisticians of all time. Working in the early 1900s Fisher introduced the analysis of variance (see chaps. 11–16) and Fisher's $z$ transformation for correlations (see chap. 10). In fact, the major statistic in the analysis of variance is referred to as the $F$ ratio in honor of Fisher. These individuals represent only a fraction of the many famous and interesting statisticians over the years. For further information about these and other statisticians, I suggest you consult references such as Pearson (1978), Stigler (1986), and Heyde, et al. (2001), which consist of many interesting stories about statisticians.

## 1.3    GENERAL STATISTICAL DEFINITIONS

In this section we define some of the most basic concepts in statistics. Included here are definitions and examples of the following concepts: population, parameter, sample, statistic, descriptive statistics, and inferential statistics.

The first four concepts are tied together, so we discuss them together. A **population** is defined as consisting of all members of a well-defined group. A population may be large in scope, such as when a population is defined as all of the employees of IBM worldwide. A population may be small in scope, such as when a population is defined as all of the IBM employees at the building on Main Street in Atlanta. Thus, a population could be large or small in scope. The key is that the population is well defined such that one could determine specifically who all of the members of the group are and then information or data could be collected from all such members. Thus, if our population is defined as all members working in a particular office building, then our study would consist of collecting data from all employees in that building.

A **parameter** is defined as a characteristic of a population. For instance, parameters of our office building example might be the number of individuals who work in that building (e.g., 154), the average salary of those individuals (e.g., $49,569), and the range of ages of those individuals (e.g., 21 to 68 years of age). When we think about characteristics of a population we are thinking about **population parameters**. Those two terms are often linked together.

A **sample** is defined as consisting of a subset of a population. A sample may be large in scope, such as when a population is defined as all of the employees of IBM worldwide and 20% of those individuals are included in the sample. A sample may be small in scope, such as when a population is defined as all of the IBM employees at the building on Main Street in Atlanta and 10% of those individuals are included in the sample. Thus, a sample could be large or small in scope and consist of any portion of the population. The key is that the sample consists of some, but not all, of the members of the population; that is, anywhere from one individual to all but one individual from the population is included in the sample. Thus, if our population is defined as all members working in the IBM building on Main Street in Atlanta, then our study would consist of collecting data from a sample of some of the employees in that building.

A **statistic** is defined as a characteristic of a sample. For instance, statistics of our office building example might be the number of individuals who work in the building that we sampled (e.g., 77), the average salary of those individuals (e.g., $54,090), and the range of ages of those individuals (e.g., 25 to 62 years of age). Notice that the statistics of a sample need not be equal to the parameters of a population (more about this in chap. 5). When we think about characteristics of a sample we are thinking about **sample statistics**. Those two terms are often linked together. Thus we have population parameters and sample statistics, but no other combinations of those terms exist. The field has become known as statistics simply because we are almost always dealing with sample statistics because population data are rarely obtained.

The final two concepts are also tied together and thus considered together. The field of statistics is generally divided into two types of statistics, descriptive statistics and inferential statistics. **Descriptive statistics** are defined as techniques which allow us to tabulate, summarize and depict a collection of data in an abbreviated fashion. In other words, the purpose of descriptive statistics is to allow us to talk about (or describe) a collection of data without having to look at the entire collection. For example, say I have just collected a set of data from 100,000 graduate students on various characteristics (e.g., height, weight, gender, grade point average, aptitude test scores). If you were to ask me about the data, I could do one of two things. On the one hand, I could carry around the entire collection of data everywhere I go and when someone asks me about the data, simply say "Here is the data; take a look at them yourself." On the other hand, I could summarize the data in an abbreviated fashion and when someone asks me about the data, simply say "Here is a table and a graph about the data; they summarize the entire collection." So, rather than viewing 100,000 sheets of paper, perhaps I would only have to view two sheets of paper. Since statistics is largely a system of communicating information, descriptive statistics are considerably more useful to a consumer than an entire collection of data. Descriptive statistics are discussed in chapters 2 through 4.

**Inferential statistics** are defined as techniques which allow us to employ inductive reasoning to infer the properties of an entire group or collection of individuals, a population, from a small number of those individuals, a sample. In other words, the purpose of inferential statistics is to allow us to collect data from a sample of individuals and then infer the properties of that sample back to the population of individuals. In case you have forgotten about logic, inductive reasoning is where you infer from the specific (here the sample) to the general (here the population). For example, say I have just collected a set of sample data from 5,000 of the population of 100,000 graduate students on various characteristics (e.g., height, weight, gender, grade point average, aptitude test scores). If you were to ask me about the data, I could compute various sample statistics and then infer with some confidence that these would be similar to the population parameters. In other words, this allows me to collect data from a subset of the population, yet still make inferential statements about the population without collecting data from the entire population. So, rather than collecting data from all 100,000 graduate students in the population, I could collect data on a sample of 5,000 students.

As another example, Gossett (a.k.a. Student) was asked to conduct a taste test of Guinness beer for a sample of Dublin residents. Because the brewery could not afford to do this with the entire population, Gossett collected data from a sample and was able to make an inference from these sample results back to the population. A discussion of inferential statistics begins in chapter 5. In summary, the field of statistics is roughly divided into descriptive statistics and inferential statistics. Note, however, that many further distinctions are made among the types of statistics, but more about that later.

## 1.4 TYPES OF VARIABLES

There are several terms we need to define about variables. First, it might be useful to define the term variable. A **variable** is defined as any characteristic of persons or things that is observed to take on different values. In other words, the values for a particular characteristic vary across the individuals observed. For example, the annual salary of the families in your neighborhood varies because not every family earns the same annual salary. One family might earn $50,000 while the family right next door might earn $65,000. Thus, the annual family salary is a variable because it varies across families.

In contrast, a **constant** is defined as any characteristic of persons or things that is observed to take on only a single value. In other words, the values for a particular characteristic are the same for all individuals observed. For example, every family in your neighborhood has a lawn. Although the nature of the lawns may vary, everyone has a lawn. Thus, whether a family has a lawn in your neighborhood is a constant.

There are three specific types of variables that need to be defined, discrete variables, continuous variables, and dichotomous variables. A **discrete variable** is defined as a variable that can only take on certain values. For example, the number of children in a family can only take on certain values. Many values are not possible, such as negative values (e.g., the Joneses cannot have $-2$ children), decimal values (e.g., the Smiths cannot have 2.2 children), and large values (e.g., the Kings cannot have 400 children). In contrast, a **continuous variable** is defined as a variable that can take on any value within a certain range, given a precise enough measurement instrument. For example, the distance between two cities can be any value greater than zero, even measured down to the inch or millimeter. Two cities can be right next to one another or they can be across the galaxy. Finally, a **dichotomous variable** is defined as a variable that can take on only one of two values. For example, gender is a variable that can only take on the values of male or female and is often coded numerically as 0 (e.g., for males) or 1 (e.g., for females). Thus a dichotomous variable is a special restricted case of a discrete variable. Here are a few additional examples of the three types of variables. Other discrete variables include political party affiliation (Republican $= 1$, Democrat $= 2$, independent $= 3$), religious affiliation (e.g., Methodist $= 1$, Baptist $= 2$, Roman Catholic $= 3$, etc.), course letter grade (A $= 4$, B $= 3$, C $= 2$, D $= 1$, F $= 0$), and number of CDs owned (no decimals possible). Other continuous variables include salary (from zero to billions in dollars and cents), age (from zero up, in millisecond increments), height, weight, and time. Other dichotomous variables include pass/fail, true/false, living/dead, and smoker/non-smoker. Variable type is often important in terms of selecting an appropriate statistic, as shown later.

## 1.5    SCALES OF MEASUREMENT

Another concept useful for selecting an appropriate statistic is the scale of measurement of the variables. First, however, we define **measurement** as the assignment of numerical values to persons or things according to explicit rules. For example, how do we measure a person's weight? Well, there are rules that individuals commonly follow. Currently weight is measured on some sort of balance or scale in pounds or grams. In the old days weight was measured by different rules, such as the number of stones or gold coins. These explicit rules were developed so that there was a standardized and generally agreed upon method of measuring weight. Thus if you weighted 10 stones in Coventry, England, then that meant the same as 10 stones in Liverpool, England.

In 1951 the psychologist S.S. Stevens developed four types of measurement scales that could be used for assigning these numerical values. In other words, the type of rule used was related to the measurement scale. The four types of measurement scales are the nominal, ordinal, interval, and ratio scales. They are presented in order of increasing complexity and of increasing information (remembering the acronym NOIR might be helpful).

### 1.5.1    Nominal Measurement Scale

The simplest scale of measurement is the **nominal scale**. Here individuals or objects are classified into categories so that all of those in a single category are equivalent with respect to the characteristic being measured. For example, the country of birth of an individual is a nominally scaled variable. Everyone born in France is equivalent with respect to this variable, whereas two people born in different countries (e.g., France and Australia) are not equivalent with respect to this variable. The categories are qualitative in nature, not quantitative.

Categories are typically given names or numbers. For our example, the country name would be an obvious choice for categories, although numbers could also be assigned to each country (e.g., Brazil = 5, India = 34). The numbers do not represent the amount of the attribute possessed. An individual born in India does not possess any more of the "country of birth origin" attribute than an individual born in Brazil (which would not make sense anyway). The numbers merely identify to which category an individual or object belongs. The categories are also mutually exclusive. That is, an individual can belong to one and only one category, such as a person being born in only one country.

The statistics of a nominal scale variable are quite simple as they can only be based on counting. For example, we can talk about the number of people born in each country by counting up the total number of births. The only mathematical property that the nominal scale possesses is that of equality versus inequality. In other words, two individuals are either in the same category (equal) or in different categories (unequal). For the country of birth origin variable, we can either use the country name or assign numerical values to each country. We might perhaps assign each country a number alphabetically from 1 to 150. If two individuals were born in country 19, Denmark, then they are equal with respect to this characteristic. If one individual was born in country 19, Denmark, and another individual was born in country 22, Estonia, then they are unequal with respect to this characteristic. Again, these particular numerical values are meaningless and could arbitrarily be any values. They only serve to keep the categories distinct from one another. Many other numerical values could be assigned for these countries and still maintain the equality versus inequality property. For example, Denmark could easily be categorized as 119 and Estonia as 122 with no change in information. Other examples of nominal scale variables include hair color, eye color, neighborhood, gender, ethnic background, religious affiliation, political party affiliation, type of life insurance owned (e.g., term, whole life), blood type, psychological clinical diagnosis, Social Security number, and type of headache medication prescribed. The term nominal is derived from "giving a name."

## 1.5.2 Ordinal Measurement Scale

The next most complex scale of measurement is the **ordinal scale**. Ordinal measurement is determined by the relative size or position of individuals or objects with respect to the characteristic being measured. That is, the individuals or objects are rank ordered according to the amount of the characteristic that they possess. For example, say a high school graduating class had 250 students. Students could then be assigned class ranks according to their academic performance (e.g., grade point average) in high school. The student ranked 1 in the class had the highest relative performance and the student ranked 250 had the lowest relative performance.

However, equal differences between the ranks do not imply equal distance in terms of the characteristic being measured. For example, the students ranked 1 and 2 in the class may have a different distance in terms of actual academic performance than the students ranked 249 and 250, even though both pairs of students differ by a rank of 1. In other words, here a rank difference of 1 does not imply the same actual performance distance. The pairs of students may be very, very close or be quite distant from one another. As a result of equal differences not implying equal distances, the statistics that we can use are limited due to these unequal intervals. The ordinal scale then, consists of two mathematical properties: equality versus inequality again; and if two individuals or objects are unequal, then we can determine greater than or less than. That is, if two individuals have different class ranks, then we can determine which student had a greater or lesser class rank. Although the greater than or less than property is evident, an ordinal scale cannot tell us how much greater than or less than because of the unequal intervals. Thus the student ranked 250 could be farther away from student 249 than the student ranked 2 from student 1.

When we have untied ranks, as shown in Table 1.1, assigning ranks is straightforward. What do we do if there are tied ranks? For example, suppose there are two students with the same grade point average of 3.8 as given in Table 1.1. How do we assign them into class ranks? It is clear that they have to be assigned the same rank, as that would be the only fair method. However, there are at least two methods for dealing with tied ranks. One method would be to assign each of them a rank of 2 as that is the next available rank. However, there are two problems with that method. First, the sum of the ranks for the same number of scores would be different depending on whether there were ties or not. Statistically this is not a satisfactory solution. Second, what rank would the next student having the 3.6 grade point average be given, a rank of 3 or 4?

The second and preferred method is to take the average of the available ranks and assign that value to each of the tied individuals. Thus the two persons tied at a grade point average of 3.8 have as available ranks 2 and 3. Both would then be assigned the average rank of 2.5. Also the three persons tied at a grade point average of 3.0 have as available ranks 5, 6, and 7. These all would be assigned the average rank of 6. You also see in the table that with this method the sum of the ranks for 7 scores is always equal to 28, regardless of the number of ties. Statistically this is a satisfactory solution and the one we prefer, whether we are using a statistical software package or hand computations. Other examples of ordinal scale variables include course letter grades, order of finish in the Boston Marathon, socioeconomic status, hardness of minerals (1 = softest to 10 = hardest), faculty rank (assistant, associate, and full professor), student class (freshman, sophomore, junior, senior, graduate student), ranking on a personality trait (e.g.,

**TABLE 1.1**
Untied Ranks and Tied Ranks for Ordinal Data

| Untied Ranks | | Tied Ranks | |
|---|---|---|---|
| *Grade Point Average* | *Rank* | *Grade Point Average* | *Rank* |
| 4.0 | 1 | 4.0 | 1 |
| 3.9 | 2 | 3.8 | 2.5 |
| 3.8 | 3 | 3.8 | 2.5 |
| 3.6 | 4 | 3.6 | 4 |
| 3.2 | 5 | 3.0 | 6 |
| 3.0 | 6 | 3.0 | 6 |
| 2.7 | 7 | 3.0 | 6 |
| | Sum = 28 | | Sum = 28 |

extreme intrinsic to extreme extrinsic motivation), and military rank. The term ordinal is derived from "ordering" individuals or objects.

### 1.5.3  Interval Measurement Scale

The next most complex scale of measurement is the **interval scale.** An interval scale is one where individuals or objects can be ordered, and equal differences between the values do imply equal distance in terms of the characteristic being measured. That is, order and distance relationships are meaningful. However, there is no absolute zero point. Absolute zero, if it exists, implies the total absence of the property being measured. The zero point of an interval scale, if it exists, is arbitrary and does not reflect the total absence of the property being measured. Here the zero point merely serves as a placeholder. For example, suppose that I gave you the final exam in advanced statistics right now. If you were to be so unlucky as to obtain a score of 0, this score does not imply a total lack of knowledge of statistics. It would merely reflect the fact that your statistics knowledge is not that advanced yet. You do have some knowledge of statistics, but just at an introductory level in terms of the topics covered so far.

Take as an example the Fahrenheit temperature scale, which has a freezing point of 32 degrees. A temperature of zero is not the total absence of heat, just a point slightly colder than 1 degree and slightly warmer than $-1$ degree. In terms of the equal distance notion, consider the following example. Say that we have two pairs of Fahrenheit temperatures, the first pair being 55 and 60 degrees and the second pair being 25 and 30 degrees. The difference of 5 degrees is the same for both pairs and is also the same everywhere along the Fahrenheit scale. Thus every 5 degree interval is an equal interval. However, we cannot say that 60 degrees is twice as warm as 30 degrees, as there is no absolute zero. In other words, we cannot form true ratios of values (i.e., $60/30 = 2$). This property only exists for the ratio scale of measurement. The interval scale has as mathematical properties equality versus inequality, greater than or less than if unequal, and equal intervals. Other examples of interval scale variables include the Centigrade temperature scale, calendar time, restaurant ratings by the health department (on a 100-point scale), year (since 1 A.D.), and arguably, many educational and psychological assessment devices (although statisticians have been debating this one for many years; for example, on occasion there is a fine line between whether an assessment is measured along the ordinal or the interval scale).

### 1.5.4  Ratio Measurement Scale

The most complex scale of measurement is the **ratio scale**. A ratio scale has all of the properties of the interval scale, plus an absolute zero point exists. Here a measurement of 0 indicates a total absence of the property being measured. Due to an absolute zero point existing, true ratios of values can be formed which actually reflect ratios in the amounts of the characteristic being measured.

For example, the height of individuals is a ratio scale variable. There is an absolute zero point of zero height. We can also form ratios such that 6'0" Sam is twice as tall as his 3'0" daughter Samantha. The ratio scale of measurement is not observed frequently in education and the behavioral sciences, with certain exceptions. Motor performance variables (e.g., speed in the

**TABLE 1.2**
Summary of the Scales of Measurement

| Scale | Characteristics | Examples |
|---|---|---|
| Nominal | Classify into categories; categories are given names or numbers, but the numbers are arbitrary; mathematical property—equal versus unequal | Hair or eye color, ethnic background, neighborhood, gender, country of birth, Social Security number, type of life insurance, religious or political affiliation, blood type, clinical diagnosis |
| Ordinal | Rank-ordered according to relative size or position; mathematical properties—(1) equal versus unequal, (2) if unequal, then greater than or less than | Letter grades, order of finish in race, class rank, SES, hardness of minerals, faculty rank, student class, military rank, rank on personality trait |
| Interval | Rank-ordered and equal differences between values imply equal distances in the attribute; mathematical properties—(1) equal versus unequal, (2) if unequal, then greater than or less than, (3) equal intervals | Temperature, calendar time, most assessment devices, year, restaurant ratings |
| Ratio | Rank-ordered, equal intervals, absolute zero allows ratios to be formed; mathematical properties—(1) equal versus unequal, (2) if unequal, then greater than or less than, (3) equal intervals, (4) absolute zero | Speed in 100-meter dash, height, weight, age, distance driven, elapsed time, pulse rate, blood pressure, calorie consumption |

100-meter dash, distance driven in 24 hours), elapsed time, calorie consumption, and physiological characteristics (e.g., weight, height, age, pulse rate, blood pressure) are ratio scale measures. A summary of the measurement scales, their characteristics, and some examples are given in Table 1.2.

## 1.6   SUMMARY

In this chapter an introduction to statistics was given. First we discussed the value and need for knowledge about statistics and how it assists in decision making. Next, a few of the more colorful and interesting statisticians of the past were mentioned. Then, we defined the following general statistical terms: population, parameter, sample, statistic, descriptive statistics, and inferential statistics. We then defined variable-related terms including variables, constants, discrete variables, continuous variables, and dichotomous variables. Finally, we examined the four classic types of measurement scales, nominal, ordinal, interval, and ratio. By now you should have met the following objectives: (a) have a better sense of why statistics are necessary; (b) see that statisticians are an interesting group of people; and (c) have an understanding of the basic statistical concepts of population, parameter, sample, and statistic, descriptive and inferential statistics, types of variables, and scales of measurement. The next chapter begins to address some of the details of descriptive statistics when we consider how to represent data in terms of tables and graphs. In other words, rather than carrying our data around with us everywhere we go, we examine ways to display data in tabular and graphical forms to foster communication.

## PROBLEMS

### Conceptual Problems

1. For interval level variables, which of the following properties does not apply?
   a. Jim is two units greater than Sally
   b. Jim is greater than Sally
   c. Jim is twice as good as Sally
   d. Jim differs from Sally

2. Which of the following properties is appropriate for ordinal, but not for nominal variables?
   a. Sue differs from John
   b. Sue is greater than John
   c. Sue is ten units greater than John
   d. Sue is twice as good as John

3. Which scale of measurement is implied by the following statement: "Jill's score is three times greater than Eric's score?"
   a. Nominal
   b. Ordinal
   c. Interval
   d. Ratio

4. Which scale of measurement is implied by the following statement: "Bubba had the highest score?"
   a. Nominal
   b. Ordinal
   c. Interval
   d. Ratio

5. Kristen has an IQ of 120. I assert that Kristen is 20% more intelligent than the average person having an IQ of 100. Am I correct?

6. Population is to parameter as sample is to statistic. True or false?

7. Every characteristic of a sample of 100 persons constitutes a variable. True or false?

8. A dichotomous variable is also a discrete variable. True or false?

9. The amount of time spent studying in one week for a population of students is an inferential statistic. True or false?

10. For ordinal level variables, which of the following properties does not apply?
    a. IBM differs from Apple
    b. IBM is greater than Apple
    c. IBM is two units greater than Apple
    d. all of the above properties apply

11. A sample of 50 students take an exam and the instructor decides to give the top 5 scores a bonus of 5 points. Compared to the original set of scores (no bonus), I assert that the ranks of the new set of scores (including bonus) will be exactly the same. Am I correct?

12. Johnny and Buffy have class ranks of 5 and 6. Ingrid and Toomas have class ranks of 55 and 56. I assert that the GPAs of Johnny and Buffy are the same distance apart as are the GPAs of Ingrid and Toomas. Am I correct?

## Computational Problems

1. Rank the following values of the number of CDs owned, assigning rank 1 to the largest value:

   10    15    12    8    20    17    5    21    3    19

2. Rank the following values of the number of credits earned, assigning rank 1 to the largest value:

   10    16    10    8    19    16    5    21    3    19

## Interpretive Problem

Consider the following actual class survey:

1. What is your gender?
2. What is your height in inches?
3. What is your shoe size (length)?
4. Do you smoke?
5. Are you left- or right-handed? Your mother? Your father?
6. How much did you spend at your last hair appointment (including tip)?
7. How many CDs do you own?
8. What was your quantitative GRE score?

9. What is your current GPA?
10. On average, how much exercise do you get per week (in hours)?
11. On a 5 point scale, what is your political view (1 = very liberal, 3 = moderate, 5 = very conservative)?
12. On average, how many hours of TV do you watch per week?
13. How many cups of coffee did you drink yesterday?
14. How many hours did you sleep last night?
15. On average, how many alcoholic drinks do you have per week?
16. Can you tell the difference between Pepsi and Coke?
17. What is the natural color of your hair (black, blonde, brown, red, other)?
18. What is the natural color of your eyes (black, blue, brown, green, other)?
19. How far do you live from this campus (in miles)?
20. On average, how many books do you read for pleasure each month?
21. On average, how many hours do you study per week?
22. Which question on this survey is the most interesting to you? The least interesting?

## Possible Activities:

1. For each item, determine the most likely scale of measurement (NOIR) and the type of variable (continuous, discrete, dichotomous).

2. Collect data from a sample of individuals. In subsequent chapters you will be asked to analyze this data for different procedures.

Note: An actual sample dataset using this survey is contained on the CD (SPSS file: survey1) and is utilized in later chapters.

CHAPTER

# 2

# DATA REPRESENTATION

## Chapter Outline

1. Tabular display of distributions
   Frequency distributions
   Cumulative frequency distributions
   Relative frequency distributions
   Cumulative relative frequency distributions
2. Graphical display of distributions
   Bar graph
   Histogram
   Frequency polygon
   Cumulative frequency polygon
   Shapes of frequency distributions
   Stem-and-leaf display
3. Percentiles
   Percentiles
   Quartiles
   Percentile Ranks
   Box-and-whisker plot
4. SPSS

## Key Concepts

1.    Frequencies, cumulative frequencies, relative frequencies, and cumulative relative frequencies
2.    Ungrouped and grouped frequency distributions
3.    Sample size
4.    Real limits and intervals
5.    Frequency polygons
6.    Normal, symmetric, and skewed frequency distributions
7.    Percentiles, quartiles and percentile ranks

In the first chapter we introduced the wonderful world of statistics. There we discussed the value of statistics, met a few of the more interesting statisticians, and defined several basic statistical concepts. The concepts included population, parameter, sample and statistic, descriptive and inferential statistics, types of variables, and scales of measurement. In this chapter we begin our examination of descriptive statistics, which we previously defined as techniques that allow us to tabulate, summarize, and depict a collection of data in an abbreviated fashion. We used the example of collecting data from 100,000 graduate students on various characteristics (e.g., height, weight, gender, grade point average, aptitude test scores). Rather than having to carry around the entire collection of data in order to respond to questions, we mentioned that you could summarize the data in an abbreviated fashion through the use of tables and graphs. This way we could communicate features of the data through a few tables or figures without having to carry around the entire data set.

This chapter deals with the details of the construction of tables and figures for purposes of describing data. Specifically, we first consider the following types of tables: frequency distributions (ungrouped and grouped), cumulative frequency distributions, relative frequency distributions, and cumulative relative frequency distributions. Next we look at the following types of figures: bar graph, histogram, frequency polygon, cumulative frequency polygon, and stem-and-leaf display. We also discuss common shapes of frequency distributions. Finally we examine the use of percentiles, quartiles, percentile ranks, and box-and-whisker plots. Concepts to be discussed include frequencies, cumulative frequencies, relative frequencies, and cumulative relative frequencies, ungrouped and grouped frequency distributions, sample size, real limits and intervals, frequency polygons, normal, symmetric, and skewed frequency distributions, and percentiles, quartiles and percentile ranks. Our objectives are that by the end of this chapter, you will be able to (1) construct and interpret statistical tables, (2) construct and interpret statistical graphs, and (3) compute and interpret percentile-related information.

## 2.1   TABULAR DISPLAY OF DISTRIBUTIONS

In this section we consider ways in which data can be represented in the form of tables. More specifically, we are interested in how the data for a single variable can be represented (the representation of data for multiple variables is covered in later chapters). The methods described here include frequency distributions (both ungrouped and grouped), cumulative frequency distributions, relative frequency distributions, and cumulative relative frequency distributions.

### 2.1.1   Frequency Distributions

Let us use an example set of data in this chapter to illustrate ways in which data can be represented. I have selected a small data set for purposes of simplicity, although datasets are typically larger in size. Note that there is a larger dataset (based on the survey from the chap. 1 interpretive problem) utilized in the end of chapter problems and available on the CD as "survey1." As shown in Table 2.1, the data consist of a sample of 25 students' scores on a statistics quiz, where the maximum score is 20 points. If a colleague asked a question about this data, again a response could be, "Take a look at the data yourself." This would not be very satisfactory to the colleague, as the person would have to eyeball the data to answer his or her question. Alternatively, one could present the data in the form of a table so that questions could be more easily answered. One question might be: Which score occurred most frequently? In other words, what score occurred more than any other score? Other questions might be: Which scores were the highest and lowest scores in the class? Where do most of the scores tend to fall? In other words, how well did the students tend to do as a class? These and other questions can be easily answered by looking at a **frequency distribution**.

Let us first look at how an **ungrouped frequency distribution** can be constructed for these and other data. By following these steps, we develop the ungrouped frequency distribution as shown in Table 2.2. The first step is the arrange the unique scores on a list from the highest score to the lowest score. The highest score is 20 and the lowest is 9. Even though scores such as 15 were observed more than once, the value of 15 is only entered in this column once. This is what we mean by unique. Note that if the score of 15 was not observed, it could still be entered as a value in the table to serve as a placeholder within the distribution of scores observed. We label this column as "raw score" or "$X$," as shown by the first column in the table. **Raw scores** are a set of scores in their original form; that is, the scores have not been altered or transformed in any way. $X$ is often used in statistics to denote a variable, so you see $X$ quite a bit in this text.

The second step is to determine for each unique score the number of times it was observed. We label this second column as "frequency" or by the abbreviation "$f$." The frequency column

TABLE 2.1
Statistics Quiz Data

| | | | | | | | | | | | |
|---|---|---|---|---|---|---|---|---|---|---|---|
| 9 | 11 | 20 | 15 | 19 | 10 | 19 | 18 | 14 | 12 | 17 | 11 |
| 13 | 16 | 17 | 19 | 18 | 17 | 13 | 17 | 15 | 18 | 17 | 19 |
| 15 | | | | | | | | | | | |

**TABLE 2.2**
Ungrouped Frequency Distribution of Statistics Quiz Data

| X | f | cf | rf | crf |
|---|---|----|----|----|
| 20 | 1 | 25 | .04 | 1.00 |
| 19 | 4 | 24 | .16 | .96 |
| 18 | 3 | 20 | .12 | .80 |
| 17 | 5 | 17 | .20 | .68 |
| 16 | 1 | 12 | .04 | .48 |
| 15 | 3 | 11 | .12 | .44 |
| 14 | 1 | 8 | .04 | .32 |
| 13 | 2 | 7 | .08 | .28 |
| 12 | 1 | 5 | .04 | .20 |
| 11 | 2 | 4 | .08 | .16 |
| 10 | 1 | 2 | .04 | .08 |
| 9 | 1 | 1 | .04 | .04 |
| | n = 25 | | 1.00 | |

tells us how many times or how frequently each unique score was observed. For instance, the score of 20 was only observed one time whereas the score of 17 was observed five times. Now we have some information with which to answer the questions of our colleague. The most frequently observed score is 17, the lowest score is 9, the highest score is 20, and scores tended to be closer to 20 (the highest score) than to 9 (the lowest score).

Two other concepts need to be introduced that are included in Table 2.2. The first concept is **sample size**. At the bottom of the second column you see $n = 25$. From now on, $n$ will be used to denote sample size, that is, the total number of scores obtained for the sample. Thus, because 25 scores were obtained here, then $n = 25$.

The second concept is related to **real limits** and **intervals**. Although the scores obtained for this data set happened to be whole numbers, not fractions or decimals, we still need a system that will cover that possibility. For example, what would we do if a student obtained a score of 18.25? One option would be to list that as another unique score, which would probably be more confusing than useful. A second option would be to include it with one of the other unique scores somehow; this is our option of choice. The system that all researchers use to cover the possibility of any score being obtained is through the concepts of real limits and intervals. Each value of $X$ in Table 2.2 can be thought of as being the midpoint of an interval. Each interval has an upper and a lower real limit. The upper real limit of an interval is halfway between the midpoint of the interval under consideration and the midpoint of the interval above it. For example, the value of 18 represents the midpoint of an interval. The next higher interval has a midpoint of 19. Therefore the upper real limit of the interval containing 18 would be 18.5, halfway between 18 and 19. The lower real limit of an interval is halfway between the midpoint of the interval under consideration and the midpoint of the interval below it. Following the example interval of 18 again, the next lower interval has a midpoint of 17. Therefore the lower real limit of the interval containing 18 would be 17.5, halfway between 18 and 17. Thus the interval of 18 has 18.5 as an upper real limit and 17.5 as a lower real limit. Other intervals have their upper and lower real limits as well.

Notice that adjacent intervals (i.e., those next to one another) touch at their respective real limits. For example, the 18 interval has 18.5 as its upper real limit and the 19 interval has 18.5 as its lower real limit. This implies that any possible score that occurs can be placed into some interval and no score can fall between two intervals. So if someone obtains a score of 18.25, that will be covered in the 18 interval. The only limitation to this procedure is that because adjacent intervals must touch in order to deal with every possible score, what do we do when a score falls precisely where two intervals touch at their real limits (e.g., at 18.5)? There are two possible solutions. The first solution is to assign the score to one interval or another based on some rule. For instance, we could randomly assign such scores to one interval or the other by flipping a coin. Alternatively, we could arbitrarily assign such scores always into either the higher or lower of the two intervals. The second solution is to construct intervals such that the number of values falling at the real limits is minimized. For example, say that most of the scores occur at .5 (e.g., 15.5, 16.5, 17.5, etc.). We could construct the intervals with .5 as the midpoint and .0 as the real limits. Thus the 15.5 interval would have 15.5 as the midpoint, 16.0 as the upper real limit, and 15.0 as the lower real limit.

Finally, the **width** of an interval is defined as the difference between the upper and lower real limits of an interval. We can denote this as $w = URL - LRL$, where $w$ is interval width, and $URL$ and $LRL$ are the upper and lower real limits, respectively. In the case of our example interval again, we see that $w = URL - LRL = 18.5 - 17.5 = 1.0$. For Table 2.2, then, all intervals have the same interval width of 1.0. For each interval we have a midpoint, a lower real limit that is one-half unit below the midpoint, and an upper real limit that is one-half unit above the midpoint. In general, we want all of the intervals to have the same width for consistency as well as for equal interval reasons. The only exception might be if the topmost or bottommost intervals were above a certain value (e.g., greater than 20) or below a certain value (e.g., less than 9), respectively.

A frequency distribution with an interval width of 1.0 is often referred to as an **ungrouped frequency distribution**, as the intervals have not been grouped together. Does the interval width always have to be equal to 1.0? The answer, of course, is no. We could group intervals together and form what is often referred to as a **grouped frequency distribution**. For our example data, we can construct a grouped frequency distribution with an interval width of 2.0, as shown in Table 2.3. The highest interval now contains the scores of 19 and 20, the second interval the scores of 17 and 18, and so on down to the lowest interval with the scores of 9 and 10. Correspondingly, the highest interval contains a frequency of 5, the second interval a frequency of 8, and the lowest interval a frequency of 2. All we have really done is collapse the intervals from Table 2.2, where interval width was 1.0, into the intervals of width 2.0 as shown in Table 2.3. If we take, for example, the interval containing the scores of 17 and 18, then the midpoint of the interval is 17.5, the $URL$ is 18.5, the $LRL$ is 16.5, and thus $w = 2.0$. The interval width could actually be any value, including .20 or 100, depending on what best suits the data.

How does one determine what the proper interval width should be? If there are many frequencies for each score and less than 15 or 20 intervals, then an ungrouped frequency distribution with an interval width of 1 is appropriate. If there are either minimal frequencies per score

**TABLE 2.3**
Grouped Frequency Distribution of Statistics Quiz Data

| X | f |
|---|---|
| 19 – 20 | 5 |
| 17 – 18 | 8 |
| 15 – 16 | 4 |
| 13 – 14 | 3 |
| 11 – 12 | 3 |
| 9 – 10 | 2 |
| | n = 25 |

(say 1 or 2) or a large number of unique scores (say more than 20), then a grouped frequency distribution with some other interval width is appropriate. For a first example, say that there are 100 unique scores ranging from 0 to 200. An ungrouped frequency distribution would not really summarize the data very well, as the table would be quite large. The reader would have to eyeball the table and actually do some quick grouping in his or her head so as to gain any information about the data. An interval width of perhaps 10 to 15 would be more useful. In a second example, say that there are only 20 unique scores ranging from 0 to 30, but each score occurs only once or twice. An ungrouped frequency distribution would not be very useful here either, as the reader would again have to collapse intervals in his or her head. Here an interval width of perhaps 2 to 5 would be appropriate.

Ultimately, deciding on the interval width, and thus, the number of intervals, becomes a trade-off between good communication of the data and the amount of information contained in the table. As interval width increases, more and more information is lost from the original data. For the example where scores range from 0 to 200 and using an interval width of 10, some precision in the 15 scores contained in the 30–39 interval is lost. In other words, the reader would not know from the frequency distribution where in that interval the 15 scores actually fall. If you want that information (you may not), you would need to return to the original data. At the same time, an ungrouped frequency distribution for that data would not have much of a message for the reader. Ultimately the decisive factor is the adequacy with which information is communicated to the reader. The nature of the interval grouping comes down to whatever form best represents the data. With today's powerful statistical computer software, it is easy for the researcher to try several different interval widths before deciding which one works best for a particular set of data. Note also that the frequency distribution can be used with variables of any measurement scale, from nominal (e.g., the frequencies for eye color of a group of children) to ratio (e.g., the frequencies for the height of a group of adults).

### 2.1.2   Cumulative Frequency Distributions

A second type of frequency distribution is known as the **cumulative frequency distribution**. For the example data, this is depicted in the third column of Table 2.2 and labeled as "*cf.*"

Simply put, the number of cumulative frequencies for a particular interval is the number of scores contained in that interval and all of the intervals below. Thus the 9 interval contains one frequency and there are no frequencies below that interval, so the cumulative frequency is simply 1. The 10 interval contains one frequency and there is one frequency below, so the cumulative frequency is 2. The 11 interval contains two frequencies and there are two frequencies below; thus the cumulative frequency is 4. Then four people had scores in the 11 interval and below. One way to think about determining the cumulative frequency column is to take the frequency column and accumulate upward (i.e., from the bottom up, yielding 1, 1 + 1 = 2, 1 + 1 + 2 = 4, etc.). Just as a check, the $cf$ in the highest interval should be equal to $n$, the number of scores in the sample, 25 in this case. Note also that the cumulative frequency distribution can be used with variables of any measurement scale from ordinal (e.g., the number of students receiving a B or less) to ratio (e.g., the number of adults that are 5′7″ or less).

### 2.1.3    Relative Frequency Distributions

A third type of frequency distribution is known as the **relative frequency distribution**. For the example data, this is shown in the fourth column of Table 2.2 and labeled as "$rf$." Relative frequency is simply the percentage of scores contained in an interval. Computationally, $rf = f / n$. For example, the percentage of scores occurring in the 17 interval is computed as $rf = 5/25 = .20$. Relative frequencies take sample size into account allowing us to make statements about the number of individuals in an interval relative to the total sample. Thus rather than stating that 5 individuals had scores in the 17 interval, we could say that 20% of the scores were in that interval. In the popular press, relative frequencies (which they call percentages) are quite often reported in tables without the frequencies. Note that the sum of the relative frequencies should be 1.00 (or 100%) within rounding error. Also note that the relative frequency distribution can be used with variables of any measurement scale, from nominal (e.g., the percent of children with blue eye color) to ratio (e.g., the percent of adults that are 5′7″).

### 2.1.4    Cumulative Relative Frequency Distributions

A fourth and final type of frequency distribution is known as the **cumulative relative frequency distribution**. For the example data this is depicted in the fifth column of Table 2.2 and labeled as "$crf$." The number of cumulative relative frequencies for a particular interval is the percentage of scores in that interval and below. Thus the 9 interval has a relative frequency of .04 and there are no relative frequencies below that interval, so the cumulative relative frequency is simply .04. The 10 interval has a relative frequency of .04 and the relative frequencies below that interval are .04, so the cumulative relative frequency is .08. The 11 interval has a relative frequency of .08 and the relative frequencies below that interval total .08, so the cumulative relative frequency is .16. Thus 16% of the people had scores in the 11 interval and below. One way to think about determining the cumulative relative frequency column is to take the relative frequency column and accumulate upward (i.e., from the bottom up, yielding .04, .04 + .04 = .08, .04 + .04 + .08 = .16, etc.). Just as a check, the $crf$ in the highest interval should be equal to 1.0, within rounding error, just as the sum of the relative frequencies is equal to 1.0. Also note that the cumulative relative frequency distribution can be used with variables of any measurement scale from ordinal (e.g., the percent of students receiving a B or less) to ratio (e.g., the percent of adults that are 5′7″ or less).

## 2.2 GRAPHICAL DISPLAY OF DISTRIBUTIONS

In this section we consider several types of graphs for viewing the distribution of scores. Again, we are still interested in how the data for a single variable can be represented, but now in a graphical display rather than a tabular display. The methods described here include the bar graph, histogram, frequency, relative frequency, cumulative frequency and cumulative relative frequency polygons, and stem-and-leaf display, as well as common shapes of distributions.

### 2.2.1 Bar Graph

A popular method used for displaying nominal scale data in graphical form is the **bar graph**. As an example, say that we have data on the eye color of a sample of 20 children. Ten children are blue-eyed, six are brown-eyed, three are green-eyed, and one is black-eyed. Note that this is a discrete variable rather than a continuous variable. A bar graph for this data is shown in Figure 2.1 (SPSS generated). The horizontal axis, going from left to right on the page, is often referred to in statistics as the $X$ axis (for variable $X$). On the $X$ axis of Figure 2.1, we have labeled the different eye colors that occurred. The order of the colors is not relevant. The vertical axis, going from bottom to top on the page, is often referred to in statistics as the $Y$ axis (the $Y$ label will

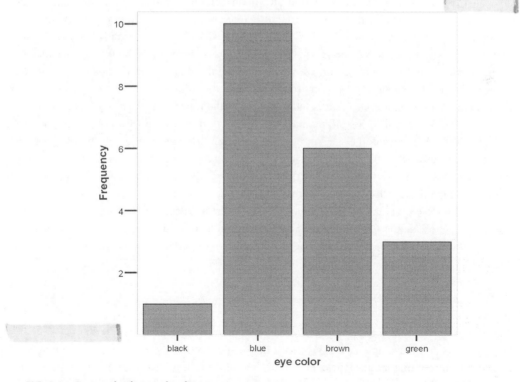

FIG. 2.1   Bar graph of eye-color data.

be more relevant in later chapters when we have a second variable $Y$). On the $Y$ axis of Figure 2.1, we have labeled the number of frequencies that are necessary for this data. Finally a bar is drawn for each eye color where the height of the bar denotes the number of frequencies for that particular eye color. For example, the height of the bar for the blue-eyed category is 10 frequencies. Thus we see in the graph which eye color is most popular in this sample (i.e., blue) and which eye color occurs least (i.e., black).

Note that the bars are separated by some space and do not touch one another, reflecting the nature of nominal data being discrete. As there are no intervals or real limits here, we do not want the bars to touch one another. One could also plot relative frequencies on the $Y$ axis to reflect the percentage of children in the sample who belong to each category of eye color. Here we would see that 50% of the children had blue eyes, 30% brown eyes, 15% green eyes, and 5% black eyes. Another method for displaying nominal data graphically is the pie chart, where the pie is divided into slices whose sizes correspond to the frequencies or relative frequencies of each category. However, for numerous reasons (e.g., contains little information when there are few categories; is unreadable when there are many categories; visually assessing the sizes of each slice is difficult at best) the pie chart is statistically problematic such that Tufte (1992) states, "the only worse design than a pie chart is several of them" (p. 178). The bar graph is the recommended graphic for nominal data.

## 2.2.2   Histogram

A method somewhat similar to the bar graph appropriate for data that are not nominal is the histogram. Because the data are continuous, the main difference of the histogram is that the bars touch one another, much like intervals touching one another as real limits. An example of a histogram for the statistics quiz data is shown in Figure 2.2 (SPSS generated). As you can see, along the $X$ axis we plot the values of the variable $X$ and along the $Y$ axis the frequencies for each interval. The height of the bar again corresponds to the number of frequencies for a particular value of $X$. This figure represents an ungrouped histogram as the interval size is 1. That is, along the $X$ axis the midpoint of each bar is the midpoint of the interval, the bar begins on the left at the lower real limit of the interval, the bar ends on the right at the upper real limit, and the bar is 1 unit wide. If we wanted to use an interval size of 2, for example, using the grouped frequency distribution in Table 2.3, then we could construct a grouped histogram in the same way; the differences would be that the bars would be 2 units wide, and the height of the bars would obviously change. Try this one on your own for practice.

One could also plot relative frequencies on the $Y$ axis to reflect the percentage of students in the sample whose scores fell into a particular interval. In reality, all that we have to change is the scale of the $Y$ axis. The height of the bars would remain the same. For this particular data set, each frequency corresponds to a relative frequency of .04.

## 2.2.3   Frequency Polygon

Another graphical method appropriate for data that are not nominal is the frequency polygon. A polygon is defined simply as a many-sided figure. The frequency polygon is set up in a fashion similar to the histogram. However, rather than plotting a bar for each interval, points are plotted for each interval and then connected together as shown in Figure 2.3 (SPSS generated).

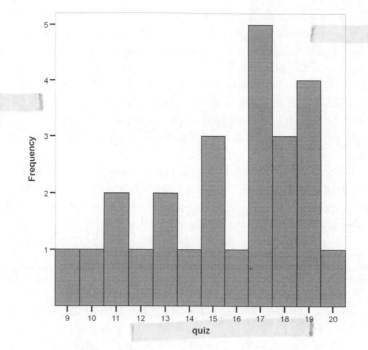

FIG. 2.2  Histogram of statistics quiz data.

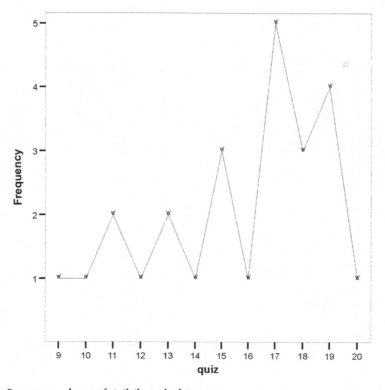

FIG. 2.3  Frequency polygon of statistics quiz data.

The axes are the same as with the histogram. A point is plotted at the intersection (or coordinates) of **the midpoint** of each interval along the $X$ axis and the frequency for that interval along the $Y$ axis. Thus for the 15 interval, a point is plotted at the midpoint of the interval 15.0 and for 3 frequencies. Once the points are plotted for each interval, we "connect the dots."

One could also plot relative frequencies on the $Y$ axis to reflect the percentage of students in the sample whose scores fell into a particular interval. This is known as the **relative frequency polygon**. As with the histogram, all we have to change is the scale of the $Y$ axis. The position of the polygon would remain the same. For this particular data set, each frequency corresponds to a relative frequency of .04.

Note also that because the histogram and frequency polygon each contain the exact same information, Figures 2.2 and 2.3 can be superimposed on one another. If you did this you would see that the points of the frequency polygon are plotted at the top of each bar of the histogram. There is no advantage of the histogram or frequency polygon over the other; however, the histogram is more frequently used due to its availability in all statistical software.

### 2.2.4   Cumulative Frequency Polygon

Cumulative frequencies of data that are not nominal can also be displayed in the form of a polygon, known as the **cumulative frequency polygon** (sometimes referred to as the **ogive curve**). As shown in Figure 2.4 (SPSS generated), the differences between the frequency

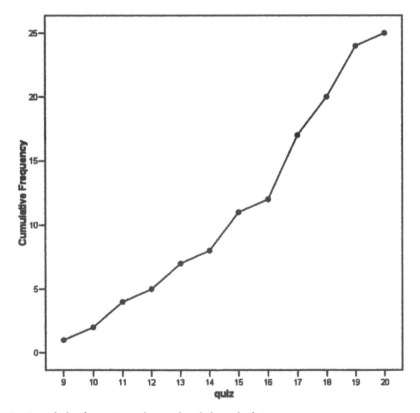

FIG. 2.4   Cumulative frequency polygon of statistics quiz data.

polygon and the cumulative frequency polygon are that the cumulative frequency polygon (a) involves plotting cumulative frequencies along the $Y$ axis, (b) the points should be plotted **at the upper real limit** of each interval (although SPSS plots the points at the interval mid-points), and (c) the polygon cannot be closed on the right-hand side.

Let us discuss each of these differences. First, the $Y$ axis represents the cumulative frequencies from the cumulative frequency distribution. The $X$ axis is the usual set of raw scores. Second, to reflect the cumulative nature of this type frequency, the points must be plotted at the upper real limit of each interval. For example, the cumulative frequency for the 16 interval is 12, indicating that there are 12 scores in that interval and below. Finally, the polygon cannot be closed on the right-hand side. Notice that as you move from left to right in the cumulative frequency polygon, the height of the points always increases or stays the same. For example, there is an increase in cumulative frequency from the 16 to the 17 interval as 5 new frequencies are included. Beyond the 20 interval the number of cumulative frequencies remains at 25 as no new frequencies are included.

One could also plot cumulative relative frequencies on the $Y$ axis to reflect the percentage of students in the sample whose scores fell into a particular interval and below. This is known as the **cumulative relative frequency polygon.** All we have to change is the scale of the $Y$ axis to cumulative relative frequency. The position of the polygon would remain the same. For this particular data set, each cumulative frequency corresponds to a cumulative relative frequency of .04. Thus a cumulative relative frequency polygon of the example data would look exactly like Figure 2.4, except on the $Y$ axis we plot cumulative relative frequencies ranging from 0 to 1.

## 2.2.5 Shapes of Frequency Distributions

There are several common shapes of frequency distributions that you are likely to encounter, as shown in Figure 2.5. These are briefly described here and more fully in later chapters. Figure 2.5(a) is a **normal distribution** (or bell-shaped curve) where most of the scores are in the center of the distribution with fewer higher and lower scores. The normal distribution plays a large role in statistics, both for descriptive statistics (as we show beginning in chap. 4), and particularly as an assumption for many inferential statistics (as we show beginning in chap. 6). This distribution is also known as **symmetric** because if we divide the distribution into two equal halves vertically, the left-half is a mirror image of the right-half (see chap. 4). Figure 2.5(b) is **a positively skewed** distribution where most of the scores are fairly low and there are a few higher scores (see chap. 4). Figure 2.5(c) is a **negatively skewed** distribution where most of the scores are fairly high and there are a few lower scores (see chap. 4). Skewed distributions are not symmetric as the left half is not a mirror image of the right half.

## 2.2.6 Stem-and-Leaf Display

A refined form of the grouped frequency distribution is the **stem-and-leaf display,** developed by John Tukey (1977). This is shown in Figure 2.6 (SPSS generated) for the example data. The stem-and-leaf display was originally developed to be constructed on a typewriter using lines and numbers in a minimal amount of space. In a way the stem-and-leaf display looks like a grouped type of histogram on its side. The vertical value on the left is the **stem** and, in this example, represents all but the last digit (i.e., the tens digit). The **leaf** represents, in this example, the

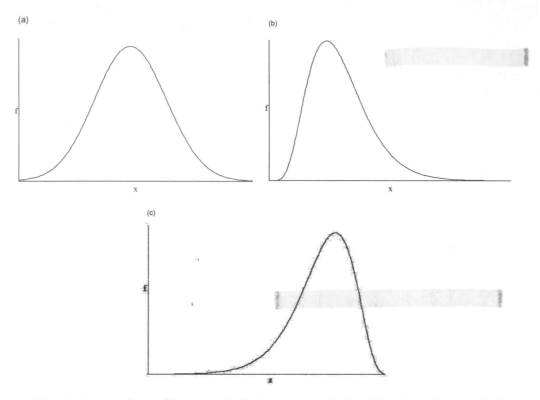

**FIG. 2.5    Common shapes of frequency distributions: (a) Normal. (b) Positively skewed. (c) Negatively skewed.**

```
quiz Stem-and-Leaf Plot

    Frequency      Stem &  Leaf

         1.00        0 .  9
         7.00        1 .  0112334
        16.00        1 .  5556777778889999
         1.00        2 .  0

    Stem width:      10.0
    Each leaf:       1 case(s)
```

**FIG. 2.6    Stem-and-leaf display of statistics quiz data.**

remaining digit of each score (i.e., the units digit). Note that SPSS has grouped values in increments of five. For example, the second line indicates that there are 7 scores from 10 to 14; thus "1 0" means that there is one frequency for the score of 10. From the stem-and-leaf display one can determine every one of the raw scores; this is not possible with a typical grouped frequency distribution (i.e., no information is lost in a stem-and-leaf display). However, with a large sample the display can become rather unwieldy. Consider what a stem-and-leaf display would look like for 100,000 GRE scores!

In summary, this section included the most basic types of statistical graphics, although more advanced graphics are described in later chapters. Note, however, that there are a number of publications on how to properly display graphics, that is, "how to do graphics right." While a detailed discussion of statistical graphics is beyond the scope of this text, the following publications are recommended: Chambers, Cleveland, Kleiner and Tukey (1983), Schmid (1983), Wainer (e.g., 1984, 1992, 2000), Tufte (1992), Cleveland (1993), Wallgren, Wallgren, Persson, Jorner and Haaland (1996), Robbins (2004), and Wilkinson (2005).

## 2.3 PERCENTILES

In this section we consider several concepts and the necessary computations for the area of percentiles, including percentiles, quartiles, percentile ranks, and the box-and-whisker plot. For instance, you might be interested in determining what percentage of the distribution of the GRE-Quantitative subtest fell below a score of 600 or in what score divides the distribution of the GRE-Quantitative subtest into two equal halves.

### 2.3.1 Percentiles

Let us define a **percentile** as that score below which a certain percentage of the distribution lies. For instance, you may be interested in that score below which 50% of the distribution of the GRE-Quantitative subscale lies. Say that this score is computed as 480; then this would mean that 50% of the scores fell below a score of 480. Because percentiles are scores, they are continuous values and can take on any value of those possible. The 30th percentile could be, for example, the score of 387.6750. For notational purposes, a percentile will be known as $P_i$, where the $i$ subscript denotes the particular percentile of interest, between 0 and 100. Thus the 30th percentile for the previous example would be denoted as $P_{30} = 387.6750$.

Let us now consider how percentiles are computed. The formula for computing the $P_i$ percentile is

$$P_i = LRL + \left( \frac{i\% (n) - cf}{f} \right) w \qquad (1)$$

where $LRL$ is the lower real limit of the interval containing $P_i$, $i\%$ is the percentile desired (expressed as a proportion from 0 to 1), $n$ is the sample size, $cf$ is the cumulative frequency up to but not including the interval containing $P_i$ (known as $cf$ below), $f$ is the frequency of the interval containing $P_i$, and $w$ is the interval width.

As an example, consider computing the 25th percentile. This would correspond to that score below which 25% of the distribution falls. For the example data in the form presented in Table 2.2, using equation (1) we compute $P_{25}$ as follows:

$$P_{25} = 12.5 + \left( \frac{25\% (25) - 5}{2} \right) 1 = 12.5 + 0.6250 = 13.1250$$

Conceptually, this is how the equation works. First we have to determine what interval contains the percentile of interest. This is easily done by looking in the $crf$ column of the frequency distribution for the interval that contains a $crf$ of .25 somewhere within the interval. We see that for the 13 interval the $crf = .28$, which means that the interval spans a $crf$ of .20 (the $URL$ of the 12 interval) up to .28 (the $URL$ of the 13 interval), and thus contains .25. The next highest interval of 14 takes us from a *crf* of .28 up to a *crf* of .32 and thus is too large for this particular percentile. The next lowest interval of 12 takes us from a *crf* of .16 up to a *crf* of .20 and thus is too small. The *LRL* of 12.5 indicates that $P_{25}$ is at least 12.5. The rest of the equation adds some positive amount to the *LRL*.

Next we have to determine how far into that interval we need to go in order to reach the desired percentile. We take *i* percent of *n*, or in this case 25% of the sample size of 25, which is 6.25. So we need to go one-fourth of the way into the distribution, or 6.25 scores, to reach the 25th percentile. Another way to think about this is, because the scores have been rank-ordered from lowest (bottom of the frequency distribution) to highest (top of the frequency distribution), we need to go 25%, or 6.25 scores, into the distribution from the bottom to reach the 25th percentile. We then subtract out all cumulative frequencies below the interval we are looking in, where *cf* below = 5. Again we just want to determine how far into this interval we need to go and thus we subtract out all of the frequencies below this interval, or *cf* below. The numerator then becomes 6.25 − 5 = 1.25. Then we divide by the number of frequencies in the interval containing the percentile we are looking for. This forms the ratio of how far into the interval we go. In this case, we needed to go 1.25 scores into the interval and the interval contains 2 scores; thus the ratio is 1.25/2 = .625. In other words, we need to go .625 units into the interval to reach the desired percentile. Now that we know how far into the interval to go, we need to weigh this by the width of the interval. Here we need to go 1.25 scores into an interval containing 2 scores that is 1 unit wide, and thus we go .625 units into the interval [(1.25/2) 1 = .625]. If the interval width was instead 10, then 1.25 scores into the interval would be equal to 6.25 units.

Consider two more worked examples to try on your own, either through statistical software or by hand. The 50th percentile, $P_{50}$, is

$$P_{50} = 16.5 + \left( \frac{50\% \, (25) - 12}{5} \right) 1 = 16.5 + 0.1000 = 16.6000$$

and the 75th percentile, $P_{75}$, is

$$P_{75} = 17.5 + \left( \frac{75\% \, (25) - 17}{3} \right) 1 = 17.5 + 0.5833 = 18.0833$$

We have only examined a few example percentiles of the many possibilities that exist. For example, we could also have determined $P_{55.5}$ or even $P_{99.5}$. Thus we could determine any percentile, in whole numbers or decimals, between 0 and 100. Next we examine three particular percentiles that are often of interest, the quartiles.

### 2.3.2   Quartiles

One way of dividing a distribution into equal groups that is frequently used is **quartiles**. This is done by dividing a distribution into fourths or quartiles where there are four equal groups, each containing 25% of the scores. In the previous examples, we determined $P_{25}$, $P_{50}$, and $P_{75}$, which divided the distribution into four equal groups, from 0 to 25, from 25 to 50, from 50 to 75, and from 75 to 100. Thus the quartiles are special cases of percentiles. A different notation, however, is often used for these particular percentiles where we denote $P_{25}$ as $Q_1$, $P_{50}$ as $Q_2$, and $P_{75}$ as $Q_3$. The $Q$'s then represent the quartiles.

An interesting aspect of quartiles is that they can be used to determine whether a distribution of scores is skewed positively or negatively. This is done by comparing the values of the quartiles as follows. If $(Q_3 - Q_2) > (Q_2 - Q_1)$, then the distribution of scores is positively skewed as the scores are more spread out at the high end of the distribution and more bunched up at the low end of the distribution (remember the shapes of the distributions from Fig. 2.5). If $(Q_3 - Q_2) < (Q_2 - Q_1)$, then the distribution of scores is negatively skewed as the scores are more spread out at the low end of the distribution and more bunched up at the high end of the distribution. If $(Q_3 - Q_2) = (Q_2 - Q_1)$, then the distribution of scores is obviously not skewed, but is symmetric (see chap. 4). For the example data $(Q_3 - Q_2) = 1.4833$ and $(Q_2 - Q_1) = 3.4750$; thus $(Q_3 - Q_2) < (Q_2 - Q_1)$ and we know that the distribution is negatively skewed. This should already have been evident from examining the frequency distribution in Fig. 2.3 as scores are more spread out at the low end of the distribution and more bunched up at the high end. Examining the quartiles is a simple method for getting a general sense of the skewness of a distribution of scores.

### 2.3.3  Percentile Ranks

Let us define a **percentile rank** as the percentage of a distribution of scores that falls below a certain score. For instance, you may be interested in the percentage of scores of the GRE-Quantitative subscale that falls below the score of 480. Say that the percentile rank for the score of 480 is computed to be 50; then this would mean that 50% of the scores fell below a score of 480. If this sounds familiar, it should. The 50th percentile was previously stated to be 480. Thus we have logically determined that the percentile rank of 480 is 50. This is because percentile and percentile rank are actually opposite sides of the same coin. Many are confused by this and equate percentiles and percentile ranks; however, they are related but different concepts. Recall earlier we said that percentiles were scores. Percentile ranks are percentages, as they are continuous values and can take on any value from 0 to 100. The score of 400 can have a percentile rank of 42.6750. For notational purposes, a percentile rank will be known as $PR(P_i)$, where $P_i$ is the particular score whose percentile rank, $PR$, you wish to determine. Thus the percentile rank of the score 400 would be denoted as $PR(400) = 42.6750$. In other words, about 43% of the distribution falls below the score of 400.

Let us now consider how percentile ranks are computed. The formula for computing the $PR(P_i)$ percentile rank is

$$PR(P_i) = \frac{cf + \dfrac{f(P_i - LRL)}{w}}{n} \times 100\% \qquad (2)$$

where $PR(P_i)$ indicates that we are looking for the percentile rank $PR$ of the score $P_i$, $cf$ is the cumulative frequency up to but not including the interval containing $PR(P_i)$ (again known as $cf$ below), $f$ is the frequency of the interval containing $PR(P_i)$, $LRL$ is the lower real limit of the interval containing $PR(P_i)$, $w$ is the interval width, $n$ is the sample size, and finally we multiply by 100% to place the percentile rank on a scale from 0 to 100 (and also to remind us that the percentile rank is a percentage).

As an example, consider computing the percentile rank for the score of 17. This would correspond to the percentage of the distribution that falls below a score of 17. For the example data again, using equation (2) we compute $PR(17)$ as follows:

$$PR(17) = \frac{12 + \dfrac{5(17 - 16.5)}{1}}{25} \times 100\% = \left(\frac{12 + 2.5}{25}\right) \times 100\% = 58.00\% \qquad (2A)$$

Conceptually, this is how the equation works. First we have to determine what interval contains the percentile rank of interest. This is easily done because we already know the score is 17 and we simply look in the interval containing 17. The $cf$ below the 17 interval is 12 and $n$ is 25. Thus we know that we need to go at least 12/25 of the way into the distribution, or 48%, to obtain the desired percentile rank. We know that $P_i = 17$ and the $LRL$ of that interval is 16.5. There are 5 frequencies in that interval, so we need to go 2.5 scores into the interval to obtain the proper percentile rank. In other words, because 17 is the midpoint of an interval with width of 1, we need to go halfway or 2.5/5 of the way into the interval to obtain the percentile rank. In the end, we need to go 14.5/25 of the way into the distribution to obtain our percentile rank, which translates to 58%.

As another example, we have already determined that $P_{50} = 16.6000$. Therefore, you should be able to determine on your own that $PR(16.6000) = 50\%$. This verifies that percentiles and percentile ranks are two sides of the same coin. The computation of percentiles identifies a specific score, and you start with the score to determine the score's percentile rank. You can further verify this by determining that $PR(13.1250) = 25.00\%$ and $PR(18.0833) = 75.00\%$. Next we consider the box-and-whisker plot, where quartiles and percentiles are used graphically to depict a distribution of scores.

## 2.3.4   Box-and-Whisker Plot

A simplified form of the frequency distribution is the box-and-whisker plot, developed by John Tukey (1977). This is shown in Fig. 2.7 (SPSS generated) for the example data. The box-and-whisker plot was originally developed to be constructed on a typewriter using lines in a minimal amount of space. The box in the center of the figure displays the middle 50% of the distribution of scores. The left-hand edge or hinge of the box represents the 25th percentile (or $Q_1$). The right-hand edge or hinge of the box represents the 75th percentile (or $Q_3$). The middle vertical line in the box represents the 50th percentile (or $Q_2$). The lines extending from the box are known as the whiskers. The purpose of the whiskers is to display data outside of the middle 50%. The left-hand whisker can extend down to the lowest score (as is the case with SPSS), or to the 5th or the 10th percentile (by other means), to display more extreme low scores, and the right-hand whisker correspondingly can extend up to the highest score (SPSS), or to the 95th or 90th percentile (elsewhere), to display more extreme high scores. The choice of where to extend the whiskers is the preference of the researcher and/or the software. Scores that fall beyond the end of the whiskers, known as outliers due to their extremeness relative to the bulk of the distribution, are often displayed by dots. Box-and-whisker plots can be used

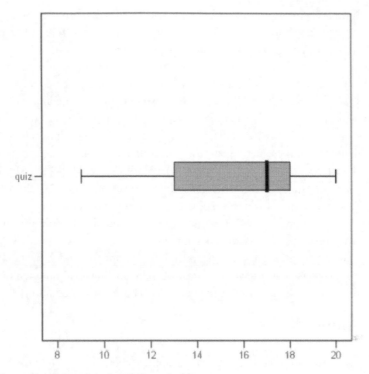

FIG. 2.7   Box-and-whisker plot of statistics quiz data.

to examine such things as skewness (through the quartiles), outliers, and where most of the scores tend to fall.

## 2.4   SPSS

The purpose of this section is to briefly consider applications of SPSS for the topics covered in this chapter, and also to develop an APA-like paragraph summarizing the sample dataset. In terms of the types of tables discussed in this chapter, in SPSS go to the "Analyze" pulldown, into "Descriptive Statistics", and then into "Frequencies". Check on "Display frequency tables" and you will be able to generate a table of freqencies, relative frequencies, and cumulative relative frequencies. If you check on the "Statistics" options box, you can obtain quartiles and selected percentiles (although be sure to check the box for "Values are group midpoints" for reasonable accuracy). However, it should be noted that these values are not always are precise as those from the formula given earlier in this chapter. If you check on the "Charts" options box, you can see bar charts, and histograms, and can plot either frequencies or percentages (relative frequencies). Thus the "Frequencies" program enables you to do much of what this chapter has covered. In addition, stem-and-leaf plots are available in the "Explore" program.

In terms of other ways of generating the types of graphical displays from this chapter, go into the "Graphs" pulldown. The "Histogram" program will generate the same histogram as the "Frequencies" program already mentioned. Use the "Boxplot" program for box-and-whisker plots, and click on the "summaries of separate variables" button. There is also a "Bar charts" program;

click on the "summaries for groups of cases" button, where several types of plots are available, including "number of cases" for frequencies, "cumulative sum" for cumulative frequencies, and "percentiles." Frequency polygons can be found using the "Line" program, and click on the "summaries for groups of cases" button. The best program in SPSS for generating all sorts of graphs is the "Interactive" program. This program allows you to display bar graphs, line graphs, boxplots, and histograms, among many possibilities. You can also plot either frequencies ("count") or relative frequencies ("percent"). The best feature of the "Interactive" program is that you have tremendous control over all aspects of the graphics (e.g., titles, colors, points, scales) and it has the most options available. For presentation purposes, this is the program to use, and the program that was used to generate every figure in this chapter (except for Figure 2.5, which SPSS cannot do).

Here is an example paragraph of results from the statistics quiz data. As shown in Table 2.2 and Figure 2.2, scores ranged from 9 to 20, with more students achieving a score of 17 than any other score (20%). From Figure 2.2 we also know that the distribution of scores was negatively skewed, with the bulk of the scores being at the high end. Skewness is also evident from the quartiles not being equally spaced. Thus, overall the sample of students tended to do rather well on this particular quiz (must have been the awesome teaching), although a few low scores should be troubling (as 20% did not pass the quiz and need some remediation).

## 2.5   SUMMARY

In this chapter we considered both tabular and graphical methods for representing data. First we discussed the tabular display of distributions in terms of frequency distributions (ungrouped and grouped), cumulative frequency distributions, relative frequency distributions, and cumulative relative frequency distributions. Next, we examined various methods for depicting data graphically, including bar graphs, histograms (ungrouped and grouped), frequency polygons, cumulative frequency polygons, shapes of distributions, and stem-and-leaf displays. Then, concepts and procedures related to percentiles were covered, including percentiles, quartiles, percentile ranks, and box-and-whisker plots. Finally, an overview of SPSS for these procedures was included as well as a summary writeup of the quiz dataset. At this point you should have met the following objectives: (a) be able to construct and interpret statistical tables, (b) be able to construct and interpret statistical graphs, and (c) be able to compute and interpret percentile-related information. In the next chapter we address the major population parameters and sample statistics useful for looking at a single variable. In particular, we are concerned with measures of central tendency and measures of dispersion.

## PROBLEMS

### Conceptual Problems

1.   For a distribution where the 50th percentile is 100, what is the percentile rank of 100?

     a.   0

     b.   .50

     c.   50

     d.   100

2. Which of the following frequency distributions will generate the same relative frequency distribution?

| X | f | Y | f | Z | f |
|---|---|---|---|---|---|
| 100 | 2 | 100 | 6 | 100 | 8 |
| 99 | 5 | 99 | 15 | 99 | 18 |
| 98 | 8 | 98 | 24 | 98 | 28 |
| 97 | 5 | 97 | 15 | 97 | 18 |
| 96 | 2 | 96 | 6 | 96 | 8 |

   a. *X* and *Y* only

   b. *X* and *Z* only

   c. *Y* and *Z* only

   d. *X, Y,* and *Z*

   e. none of the above

3. Which of the following frequency distributions will generate the same cumulative relative frequency distribution?

| X | f | Y | f | Z | f |
|---|---|---|---|---|---|
| 100 | 2 | 100 | 6 | 100 | 8 |
| 99 | 5 | 99 | 15 | 99 | 18 |
| 98 | 8 | 98 | 24 | 98 | 28 |
| 97 | 5 | 97 | 15 | 97 | 18 |
| 96 | 2 | 96 | 6 | 96 | 8 |

   a. *X* and *Y* only

   b. *X* and *Z* only

   c. *Y* and *Z* only

   d. *X, Y,* and *Z*

   e. none of the above

4. In a histogram, 48% of the area lies below the score whose percentile rank is 52. True or false?

5. Among the following, the preferred method of graphing data pertaining to the ethnicity of a sample would be

   a. a histogram

   b. a frequency polygon

   c. a cumulative frequency polygon

   d. a bar graph

6. The proportion of scores between $Q_1$ and $Q_3$ may be less than .50. True or false?

7.  The values of $Q_1$, $Q_2$, and $Q_3$ in a positively skewed population distribution are calculated. What is the expected relationship between $(Q_2 - Q_1)$ and $(Q_3 - Q_2)$?

    a.  $(Q_2 - Q_1)$ is greater than $(Q_3 - Q_2)$

    b.  $(Q_2 - Q_1)$ is equal to $(Q_3 - Q_2)$

    c.  $(Q_2 - Q_1)$ is less than $(Q_3 - Q_2)$

    d.  cannot be determined without examining the data.

8.  If the percentile rank of a score of 72, is 65, we may say that 35% of the scores exceed 72. True or false?

9.  In a negatively skewed distribution, the proportion of scores between $Q_1$ and $Q_2$ is less than .25. True or false?

10. A group of 200 sixth-grade students was given a standardized test and obtained scores ranging from 42 to 88. If the scores tended to "bunch up" in the low 80s, the shape of the distribution would be

    a.  symmetrical

    b.  positively skewed

    c.  negatively skewed

    d.  normal

11. Among the following, the preferred method of graphing data to pertaining to the eye color of a sample would be

    a.  a bar graph

    b.  a frequency polygon

    c.  a cumulative frequency polygon

    d.  a relative frequency polygon

12. If $Q_2 = 60$, then what is $P_{50}$?

    a.  50

    b.  60

    c.  95

    d.  cannot be determined with the information provided

13. With the same data and using an interval width of 1, the frequency polygon and histogram will display the same information. True or false?

14. A researcher develops a histogram based on an interval width of 2. Can she reconstruct the raw scores using only this histogram? Yes or No?

15. $Q_2 = 50$ for a positively skewed variable and $Q_2 = 50$ for a negatively skewed variable. I assert that $Q_1$ will not necessarily be the same for both variables. Am I correct?

## Computational Problems

1. The following scores were obtained from a statistics exam.

| | | | | | | | | | |
|---|---|---|---|---|---|---|---|---|---|
| 47 | 50 | 47 | 49 | 46 | 41 | 47 | 46 | 48 | 44 |
| 46 | 47 | 45 | 48 | 45 | 46 | 50 | 47 | 43 | 48 |
| 47 | 45 | 43 | 46 | 47 | 47 | 43 | 46 | 42 | 47 |
| 49 | 44 | 44 | 50 | 41 | 45 | 47 | 44 | 46 | 45 |
| 42 | 47 | 44 | 48 | 49 | 43 | 45 | 49 | 49 | 46 |

Using an interval size of 1, construct or compute each of the following:
   a. frequency distribution
   b. cumulative frequency distribution
   c. relative frequency distribution
   d. cumulative relative frequency distribution
   e. histogram and frequency polygon
   f. cumulative frequency polygon
   g. quartiles
   h. $P_{10}$ and $P_{90}$
   i. $PR(41)$ and $PR(49.5)$
   j. box-and-whisker plot
   k. stem-and-leaf display

2. A **sample** distribution of variable $X$ is as follows:

| $X$ | $f$ |
|---|---|
| 10 | 2 |
| 9 | 1 |
| 8 | 4 |
| 7 | 3 |
| 6 | 4 |
| 5 | 8 |
| 4 | 5 |
| 3 | 2 |
| 2 | 1 |

Calculate or draw each of the following for the **sample** distribution of $X$:
   a. $Q_1$
   b. $Q_2$
   c. $Q_3$
   d. $P_{44.5}$

     e.   *PR*(7.0)

     f.   box-and-whisker plot

     g.   histogram (ungrouped)

## Interpretive Problem

Select two variables from the survey1 dataset on the CD, one that is nominal and one that is not.

    1.   Construct the relevant tables and figures to get an understanding of each variable.

    2.   Write a paragraph which summarizes the findings for each variable.

CHAPTER

# 3

# UNIVARIATE POPULATION PARAMETERS AND SAMPLE STATISTICS

**Chapter Outline**

1. Summation notation
2. Measures of central tendency
    The mode
    The median
    The mean
3. Measures of dispersion
    The range (exclusive and inclusive)
    *H* spread
    Deviational measures
4. SPSS

**Key Concepts**

1. Summation
2. Central tendency
3. Outliers
4. Dispersion
5. Exclusive versus inclusive range
6. Deviation scores
7. Bias

In the second chapter we began our discussion of descriptive statistics previously defined as techniques which allow us to tabulate, summarize, and depict a collection of data in an abbreviated fashion. There we considered various methods for representing data for purposes of communicating something to the reader or audience. In particular we were concerned with ways of representing data in an abbreviated fashion through both tables and figures.

In this chapter we delve more into the field of descriptive statistics in terms of three general topics. First, we examine summation notation, which is important for much of the chapter, and to some extent, the remainder of the text. Second, measures of central tendency allow us to boil down a set of scores into a single value, which somehow represents the entire set. The most commonly used measures of central tendency are the mode, median, and mean. Finally, measures of dispersion provide us with information about the extent to which the set of scores varies—in other words, whether the scores are spread out quite a bit or are pretty much the same. The most commonly used measures of dispersion are the range (exclusive and inclusive ranges), $H$ spread, and variance and standard deviation. Concepts to be discussed include summation, central tendency, outliers, dispersion, exclusive versus inclusive range, deviation scores and bias. Our objectives are that by the end of this chapter, you will be able to (a) understand and utilize summation notation, (b) compute and interpret the three commonly used measures of central tendency, and (c) compute and interpret different measures of dispersion.

## 3.1   SUMMATION NOTATION

Many areas of statistics, including many methods of descriptive and inferential statistics, require the use of summation notation. Say we have collected heart rate scores from 100 students. Many statistics require us to develop "sums" or "totals" in different ways. For example, what is the simple sum or total of all 100 heart rate scores? Summation is not only quite tedious to do computationally by hand, but we also need a system of notation to communicate how we have conducted this summation process. This section describes such a notational system.

For simplicity let us utilize a small set of scores, keeping in mind that this system can be used for a set of scores of any size. Specifically, we have a set of 5 scores or ages, 7, 11, 18, 20, 24. Recall from chapter 2 the use of $X$ to denote a variable. Here we define $X_i$ as the score for variable $X$ for a particular individual or object $i$. The $i$ subscript serves to identify one individual or object from another. These scores would then be denoted as follows: $X_1 = 7$, $X_2 = 11$, $X_3 = 18$, $X_4 = 20$, $X_5 = 24$. With 5 scores, then $i = 1, 2, 3, 4, 5$. However, with a large set of scores this notation can become quite unwieldly, so as shorthand we abbreviate this as $i = 1, ..., 5$, meaning that $X$ ranges or goes from $i = 1$ to $i = 5$. To summarize thus far, $X_1 = 7$ means that for variable $X$ and individual 1, the value of the variable is 7. In other words, individual 1 is 7 years of age.

Next we need a system of notation to denote the summation or total of a set of scores. The standard notation everyone uses is $\sum_{i=a}^{b} X_i$ where $\Sigma$ is the Greek capital letter sigma and merely means "the sum of," $X_i$ is the variable we are summing across, $i = a$ indicates that $a$ is the lower limit (or beginning) of the summation, and $b$ indicates the upper limit (or end) of the summation.

For our example set of scores, the sum of all of the scores would be denoted as $\sum_{i=1}^{5} X_i$ in shorthand version and as $\sum_{i=1}^{5} X_i = X_1 + X_2 + X_3 + X_4 + X_5$ in longhand version. For the example data, the sum of all of the scores is computed as follows:

$$\sum_{i=1}^{5} X_i = X_1 + X_2 + X_3 + X_4 + X_5 = 7 + 11 + 18 + 20 + 24 = 80$$

Thus the sum of the age variable across all 5 individuals is 80.

For large sets of values the longhand version is rather tedious and thus the shorthand version is almost exclusively used. A general form of the longhand version is as follows:

$$\sum_{i=a}^{b} X_i = X_a + X_{a+1} + \cdots + X_{b-1} + X_b.$$

The ellipse notation (i.e., ...) indicates that there are as many values in between the two values on either side of the ellipse as are necessary. The ellipse notation is then just shorthand for "there are some values in between here." The most frequently used values for $a$ and $b$ with sample data are $a = 1$ and $b = n$. Thus the most frequently used summation notation for sample data is $\sum_{i=1}^{n} X_i$.

## 3.2 MEASURES OF CENTRAL TENDENCY

One method for summarizing a set of scores is to construct a single index or value that can somehow be used to represent the entire collection of scores. In this section we consider the three most popular indices, known as measures of central tendency. Although other indices exist, the most popular ones are the mode, the median, and the mean.

### 3.2.1 The Mode

The simplest method to use for measuring central tendency is the mode. The mode is defined as that value in a distribution of scores that occurs most frequently. Consider the example frequency distributions of the number of hours of TV watched per week, as shown in Table 3.1. In distribution (a) the mode is easy to determine, as the 8 interval contains the most scores, 3 (i.e., the mode number of hours of TV watched is 8). In distribution (b) the mode is a bit more complicated as two adjacent intervals each contain the most scores; that is, the 8- and 9-hour intervals each contain 3 scores. Strictly speaking, this distribution is bimodal, that is, containing two modes at 8 and at 9. This is my personal preference for reporting this particular situation. However, because the two modes are in adjacent intervals, some individuals make an arbitrary decision to average these intervals and report the mode as 8.5.

Distribution (c) is also bimodal; however, here the two modes at 7 and 11 hours are not in adjacent intervals. Thus one cannot justify taking the average of these intervals, as the average of 9 hours is not representative of the most frequently occurring score. The score of 9 occurs less than any other score observed. I recommend reporting both modes here as well. Obviously there are other possible situations for the mode (e.g., trimodal distribution), but these examples cover

**TABLE 3.1**
Example Frequency Distributions

| X | f (a) | f (b) | f (c) |
|---|-------|-------|-------|
| 12 | 0 | 0 | 2 |
| 11 | 0 | 1 | 3 |
| 10 | 1 | 2 | 2 |
| 9 | 2 | 3 | 1 |
| 8 | 3 | 3 | 2 |
| 7 | 2 | 2 | 3 |
| 6 | 1 | 1 | 2 |

**TABLE 3.2**
Frequency Distribution of Statistics Quiz Data

| X | f | cf | rf | crf |
|---|---|----|----|----|
| 20 | 1 | 25 | .04 | 1.00 |
| 19 | 4 | 24 | .16 | .96 |
| 18 | 3 | 20 | .12 | .80 |
| 17 | 5 | 17 | .20 | .68 |
| 16 | 1 | 12 | .04 | .48 |
| 15 | 3 | 11 | .12 | .44 |
| 14 | 1 | 8 | .04 | .32 |
| 13 | 2 | 7 | .08 | .28 |
| 12 | 1 | 5 | .04 | .20 |
| 11 | 2 | 4 | .08 | .16 |
| 10 | 1 | 2 | .04 | .08 |
| 9 | 1 | 1 | .04 | .04 |
|  | $n = 25$ |  | 1.00 |  |

the basics. As one further example, the example data on the statistics quiz from chapter 2 are shown in Table 3.2 and are used to illustrate the methods in this chapter. The mode is equal to 17 because that interval contains more scores (5) than any other interval. Note also that the mode is determined in precisely the same way whether we are talking about the population mode (i.e., the population parameter) or the sample mode (i.e., the sample statistic).

Let us turn to a discussion of the general characteristics of the mode, as well as whether a particular characteristic is an advantage or a disadvantage in a statistical sense. The first characteristic of the mode is it is simple to obtain. The mode is often used as a quick-and-dirty method for reporting central tendency. This is an obvious advantage. The second characteristic is the mode does not always have a unique value. We saw this in distributions (b) and (c) of Table 3.1. This is generally a disadvantage, as we initially stated we wanted a single index that could be used to represent the collection of scores. The mode cannot guarantee a single index.

Third, the mode is not a function of all of the scores in the distribution, and this is generally a disadvantage. The mode is strictly determined by which score or interval contains the most frequencies. In distribution (a), as long as the other intervals have fewer frequencies than the 8 interval, then the mode will always be 8. That is, if the 8 interval contains 3 scores and all of the other intervals contain less that 3 scores, then the mode will be 8. The number of frequencies for the remaining intervals is not relevant as long as it is less than 3. Also, the location or value of the other scores is not taken into account.

The fourth characteristic of the mode is that it is difficult to deal with mathematically. For example, the mode tends not to be very stable from one sample to another, especially with small samples. We could have two nearly identical samples except for one score, which can alter the mode. For example, in distribution (a) if a second similar sample contains the same scores except that an 8 is replaced with a 7, then the mode is changed from 8 to 7. Thus changing a single score can change the mode, and this is considered to be a disadvantage. A fifth and final characteristic is the mode can be used with any type of measurement scale, from nominal to ratio.

## 3.2.2  The Median

A second measure of central tendency represents a concept that you are already familiar with. The **median** is that score that divides a distribution of scores into two equal parts. In other words, half of the scores fall below the median and half of the scores fall above the median. We already know this from chapter 2 as the 50th percentile or $Q_2$. The formula for computing the median is

$$Median = LRL + \left( \frac{50\%(n) - cf}{f} \right) w \qquad (1)$$

where the notation is the same as previously described in chapter 2. Just as a reminder, $LRL$ is the lower real limit of the interval containing the median, 50% is the percentile desired, $n$ is the sample size, $cf$ is the cumulative frequency up to but not including the interval containing the median ($cf$ below), $f$ is the frequency of the interval containing the median, and $w$ is the interval width. For the example quiz data, the median is computed as follows.

$$Median = 16.5 + \left( \frac{50\%(25) - 12}{5} \right) 1 = 16.5 + 0.1000 = 16.6000$$

Occasionally you will run into simple distributions of scores where the median is easy to point out. If you have an odd number of untied scores, then the median is the middle-ranked score. For the scores of 1, 3, 7, 11, and 21, the median is 7 (e.g., number of CDs owned). If you have an even number of untied scores, then the median is the average of the two middle-ranked scores. For the scores of 1, 3, 5, 11, 21, and 32, the two middle scores are 5 and 11, and thus the median is the average of 8 CDs. In most other situations where there are tied scores, the median is not as simple to locate and equation (1) is necessary. Note also that the median is computed in precisely the same way whether we are talking about the population median (i.e., the population parameter) or the sample median (i.e., the sample statistic).

The general characteristics of the median are as follows. First, the median is not influenced by extreme scores (scores far away from the middle of the distribution are known as outliers). Because the median is defined conceptually as the middle score, the actual size of an extreme score is not relevant. For the example quiz data, imagine that the extreme score of 9 was somehow actually 0. The median would still be 16.6, as half of the scores are still above this value and half below. Because the extreme score under consideration here still remained below the 50th percentile, the median was not altered. This characteristic is an advantage, particularly when extreme scores are observed. As another example using salary data, say that all but one of the individual salaries is below $100,000 and the median is $50,000. The remaining extreme observation has a salary of $5,000,000. The median is not affected by this millionaire. That individual is simply treated as every other observation above the median, no more or no less than, say, the salary of $65,000.

A second characteristic is the median is not a function of all of the scores. Because we already know that the median is not influenced by extreme scores, we know that the median does not take such scores into account. Another way to think about this is to examine equation (1) for the median. The equation only deals with information for the interval containing the median. The specific information for the remaining intervals is not relevant so long as we are looking in the median-contained interval. We could, for instance, take the top 25% of the scores and make them even more extreme (say we add 10 bonus points to the top quiz scores). The median would remain unchanged. As you probably surmised, this characteristic is generally thought to be a disadvantage. If you really think about the first two characteristics, no measure could possibly possess both. That is, if a measure is a function of all of the scores, then extreme scores must also be taken into account. If a measure does not take extreme scores into account, like the median, then it cannot be a function of all of the scores.

A third characteristic is the median is difficult to deal with mathematically, a disadvantage as with the mode. The median is somewhat unstable from sample to sample, especially with small samples. As a fourth characteristic, the median always has a unique value, another advantage. This is unlike the mode, which does not always have a unique value. Finally, the fifth characteristic of the median is that it can be used with all types of measurement scales except the nominal. Nominal data cannot be ranked, and thus percentiles and the median are inappropriate.

### 3.2.3   The Mean

The final measure of central tendency to be considered is the mean, sometimes known as the arithmetic mean or "average" (although the term average is used rather loosely by laypeople). Statistically we define the mean as the sum of all of the scores divided by the number of scores. Thought of in those terms, you have been computing the mean for many years, and may not have even known it.

The population mean is denoted by $\mu$ (Greek letter mu) and computed as follows:

$$\mu = \frac{\sum_{i=1}^{N} X_i}{N}$$

For sample data, the sample mean is denoted by $\overline{X}$ (read "X bar") and computed as follows:

$$\overline{X} = \frac{\sum_{i=1}^{n} X_i}{n}$$

For the example quiz data, the sample mean is computed as follows:

$$\overline{X} = \frac{\sum_{i=1}^{n} X_i}{n} = \frac{389}{25} = 15.5600$$

Here are the general characteristics of the mean. First, the mean is a function of every score, a definite advantage in terms of a measure of central tendency representing all of the data. If you look at the numerator of the mean, you see that all of the scores are clearly taken into account in the sum. The second characteristic of the mean is it is influenced by extreme scores. Because the numerator sum takes all of the scores into account, it also includes the extreme scores, which is a disadvantage. Let us return for a moment to a previous example of salary data where all but one of the individuals has an annual salary under $100,000, and the one outlier is making $5,000,000. Because this one value is so extreme, the mean will be greatly influenced. In fact, the mean will fall somewhere between the second highest salary and the millionaire, which does not represent well any of the collection of scores.

Third, the mean always has a unique value, another advantage. Fourth, the mean is easy to deal with mathematically. The mean is the most stable measure of central tendency from sample to sample, and because of that is the measure most often used in inferential statistics (as we show in later chapters). Finally, the fifth characteristic of the mean is that it is only appropriate for interval and ratio measurement scales. This is because the mean implicitly assumes equal intervals, which of course the nominal and ordinal scales do not possess. To summarize the measures of central tendency then:

1. The mode is the only appropriate measure for nominal data.
2. The median and mode are both appropriate for ordinal data (and conceptually the median fits the ordinal scale as both deal with ranked scores).
3. All three measures are appropriate for interval and ratio data.

## 3.3 MEASURES OF DISPERSION

In the previous section we discussed one method for summarizing a collection of scores, the measures of central tendency. The central tendency measures are useful for describing a collection of scores in terms of a single index or score (except the mode for distributions that are not unimodal). However, what do they tell us about the distribution of scores? Consider the following example. If we know that a sample has a mean of 50, what do we know about the distribution of scores? Can we infer from the mean what the distribution looks like? Are most of the scores fairly close to the mean of 50, or are they spread out quite a bit? Perhaps most of the scores are within 2 points of the mean. Perhaps most are within 10 points of the mean. Perhaps most are within 50 points of the mean. Do we know? The answer, of course, is that the mean provides us with no information about what the distribution of scores looks like, and any of the possibilities mentioned, and many others, can occur. The same goes if we only know the mode or the median.

Another method for summarizing a set of scores is to construct an index or value that can be used to describe the amount of variability of the collection of scores. In other words, we need measures that can be used to determine whether the scores fall fairly close to the central tendency measure, are fairly well spread out, or are somewhere in between. In this section we consider the four most popular such indices, which are known as **measures of dispersion** (i.e., the extent to which the scores are dispersed or spread out). Although other indices exist, the most popular ones are the range (exclusive and inclusive), $H$ spread, the variance, and the standard deviation.

### 3.3.1   The Range

The simplest measure of dispersion is the **range**. The term range is one that is in common use outside of statistical circles, so you have some familiarity with it already. For instance, you are at the mall shopping for a new pair of shoes. You find six stores have the same pair of shoes that you really like, but the prices vary somewhat. At this point you might actually make the statement "the price for these shoes ranges from \$59 to \$75." In a way you are talking about the range.

Let us be more specific as to how the range is measured. In fact, there are actually two different definitions of the range, which we consider now. The **exclusive range** is defined as the difference between the largest and smallest scores in a collection of scores. For notational purposes, the exclusive range ($ER$) is shown as $ER = X_{max} - X_{min}$, where $X_{max}$ is the largest or maximum score obtained, and $X_{min}$ is the smallest or minimum score obtained. For the shoe example then, $ER = X_{max} - X_{min} = 75 - 59 = 16$. In other words, the actual exclusive range of the scores is 16 because the price varies from 59 to 75 (in dollar units).

A limitation of the exclusive range is that it fails to account for the width of the intervals being used. For example, if we use an interval width of one dollar, then the 59 interval really has 59.5 as the upper real limit and 58.5 as the lower real limit. If the least expensive shoe is \$58.95, then the exclusive range covering from \$59 to \$75 actually **excludes** the least expensive shoe. Hence the term **exclusive range** means that scores can be excluded from this range. The same would go for a shoe priced at \$75.25, as it would fall outside of the exclusive range at the maximum end of the distribution.

Because of this limitation, a second definition of the range was developed, known as the **inclusive range**. As you might surmise, the inclusive range takes into account the interval width so that all scores are **included** in the range. The inclusive range is defined as the difference between the upper real limit of the interval containing the largest score and the lower real limit of the interval containing the smallest score in a collection of scores. For notational purposes, the inclusive range ($IR$) is shown as $IR = URL$ of $X_{max} - LRL$ of $X_{min}$. If you think about it, what we are actually doing is extending the range by one-half of an interval at each extreme, half an interval width at the maximum value and half an interval width at the minimum value. In notational form $IR = ER + w$. For the shoe example, using an interval width of 1, then $IR = URL$ of $X_{max} - LRL$ of $X_{min} = 75.5 - 58.5 = 17$. In other words, the actual inclusive range of the scores is 17 (in dollar units). If the interval width was instead 2, then we would add 1 unit to each extreme rather than the .5 unit that we previously added to each extreme. The inclusive range would instead be 18. For the example quiz data, note that the exclusive range is 11 and the inclusive range is 12.

Finally, we need to examine the general characteristics of the range (they are the same for both definitions of the range). First, the range is simple to compute, which is a definite advantage. One can look at a collection of data and almost immediately, even without a computer or calculator, determine the range.

The second characteristic is the range is influenced by extreme scores, a disadvantage. Because the range is computed from the two most extreme scores, this characteristic is quite obvious. This might be a problem, for instance, if all of the salary data range from $10,000 to $95,000 except for one individual with a salary of $5,000,000. Without this outlier the exclusive range is $85,000. With the outlier the exclusive range is $4,990,000. Thus the millionaire's salary has a drastic impact on the range.

Third, the range is only a function of two scores, another disadvantage. Obviously the range is computed from the largest and smallest scores and thus is only a function of those two scores. The spread of the distribution of scores between those two extreme scores is not at all taken into account. In other words, for the same maximum ($5,000,000) and minimum ($10,000) salaries, the range is the same whether the salaries are mostly near the maximum salary, near the minimum salary, or spread out evenly. The fourth and final characteristic is the range is unstable from sample to sample, another disadvantage. Say a second sample of salary data yielded the exact same data except for the maximum salary now being a less extreme $100,000. The range is now dramatically different. Also, in statistics we tend to worry about measures that are not stable from sample to sample, as that implies the results are not very reliable.

### 3.3.2 *H* Spread

The next measure of dispersion is $H$ spread, a variation on the range measure with one major exception. Although the range relies upon the two extreme scores, resulting in certain disadvantages, $H$ spread relies upon the difference between the third and first quartiles. To be more specific, *H* spread is defined as $Q_3 - Q_1$, the simple difference between the third and first quartiles. The term $H$ spread was developed by Tukey (1977), $H$ being short for hinge, and is also known as the interquartile range.

For the example statistics quiz data, we already determined in chapter 2 that $Q_3 = 18.0833$ and $Q_1 = 13.1250$. Therefore, $H = Q_3 - Q_1 = 18.0833 - 13.1250 = 4.9583$. $H$ measures the range of the middle 50% of the distribution. The larger the value, the greater is the spread in the middle of the distribution. The size or magnitude of any of the range measures takes on more meaning when making comparisons across samples. For example, you might find with salary data that the range of salaries for middle management is smaller than the range of salaries for upper management.

What are the characteristics of $H$ spread? The first characteristic is $H$ is unaffected by extreme scores, an advantage. Because we are looking at the difference between the third and first quartiles, extreme observations will be outside of this range. Second, $H$ is not a function of every score, a disadvantage. The precise placement of where scores fall above $Q_3$, below $Q_1$, and between $Q_3$ and $Q_1$ is not relevant. All that matters is that 25% of the scores fall below $Q_1$,

25% fall above $Q_3$, and 50% fall between $Q_3$ and $Q_1$. Thus $H$ is not a function of very many of the scores at all, just those right around $Q_3$ and $Q_1$. Third, and finally, $H$ is not very stable from sample to sample, another disadvantage especially in terms of inferential statistics and one's ability to be confident about a sample estimate of a population parameter.

### 3.3.3   Deviational Measures

In this section we examine deviation scores, population variance and standard deviation, and sample variance and standard deviation, all methods that deal with deviation from the mean.

**Deviation Scores.**   In the last category of measures of dispersion are those that deal with deviations from the mean. Let us define a **deviation score** as the difference between a particular raw score and the mean of the collection of scores (population or sample, either will work). For population data, we define a deviation as $d_i = X_i - \mu$. In other words, we can compute the deviation from the mean for each individual or object. Consider the credit card data set as shown in Table 3.3. To make matters simple, we only have a small population of data, five scores to be exact. The first column lists the raw scores or the number of credit cards owned for five individuals and, at the bottom of the column, indicates the sum ($\Sigma = 30$), population size ($N = 5$), and population mean ($\mu = 6.0$). The second column provides the deviation scores for each observation from the population mean and, at the bottom of the column, indicates the sum of the deviation scores, denoted by

$$\sum_{i=1}^{N} (X_i - \mu)$$

From the second column we see that two of the observations have positive deviation scores as their raw score is above the mean, one observation has a zero deviation score as that raw score is at the mean, and two other observations have negative deviation scores as their raw score is

TABLE 3.3
Credit Card Data Set

| $X$ | $X - \mu$ | $(X - \mu)^2$ |
|---|---|---|
| 10 | 4 | 16 |
| 8 | 2 | 4 |
| 6 | 0 | 0 |
| 5 | $-1$ | 1 |
| 1 | $-5$ | 25 |
| $\Sigma = 30$ | $\Sigma = 0$ | $\Sigma = 46$ |
| $N = 5$ | | |
| $\mu = 6$ | | |

below the mean. However, when we sum the deviation scores we obtain a value of zero. This will always be the case as follows:

$$\sum_{i=1}^{N}(X_i - \mu) = 0$$

The positive deviation scores will exactly offset the negative deviation scores. Thus any measure involving simple deviation scores will be useless in that the sum of the deviation scores will always be zero, regardless of the spread of the scores.

What other alternatives are there for developing a deviational measure that will yield a sum other than zero? One alternative is to take the absolute value of the deviation scores (i.e., where the sign is ignored). Unfortunately, however, this is not very useful mathematically in terms of deriving other statistics, such as inferential statistics. As a result, this deviational measure is rarely used in statistics.

**Population Variance and Standard Deviation.** So far we found the sum of the deviations and the sum of the absolute deviations not to be very useful in terms of describing the spread of the scores from the mean. What other alternative might be useful? As shown in the third column of Table 3.3, one could square the deviation scores to remove the sign problem. The sum of the squared deviations is shown at the bottom of the column as $\Sigma = 46$ and denoted as

$$\sum_{i=1}^{N}(X_i - \mu)^2$$

As you might suspect, with more scores the sum of the squared deviations will increase. So we have to weight the sum by the number of observations in the population. This yields a deviational measure known as the **population variance**, which is denoted as $\sigma^2$ (lower-case Greek letter sigma) and computed by

$$\sigma^2 = \frac{\sum_{i=1}^{N}(X_i - \mu)^2}{N}$$

For the credit card example, the population variance $\sigma^2 = 46/5 = 9.2$. We refer to this particular formula for the population variance as the **definitional formula**, as conceptually that is how we define the variance. Conceptually, the variance is a measure of the area of a distribution. That is, the more spread out the scores, the more area or space the distribution takes up and the larger is the variance. The variance has nice mathematical properties and is useful for deriving other statistics, such as inferential statistics.

The **computational formula** for the population variance is

$$\sigma^2 = \frac{N\sum_{i=1}^{N}X_i^2 - \left(\sum_{i=1}^{N}X_i\right)^2}{N^2}$$

This method is computationally easier to deal with than the definitional formula. Imagine if you had a population of 100 scores. Using hand computations, the definitional formula would take considerably more time than the computational formula. With the computer this is a moot point, obviously. But if you do have to compute the population variance by hand, then the easiest formula to use is the computational one.

Exactly how does this formula work? For the first summation in the numerator, we square each score first, then sum across the squared scores in the end. For the second summation in the numerator, we sum across the scores first, then square the summed scores in the end. Thus these two quantities are computed in much different ways and generally yield different values. Let us return to the credit card data set and see if the computational formula actually yields the same value for $\sigma^2$ as the definitional formula did earlier ($\sigma^2 = 9.2$). The computational formula shows $\sigma^2$ to be

$$\sigma^2 = \frac{N\sum_{i=1}^{N} X_i^2 - \left(\sum_{i=1}^{N} X_i\right)^2}{N^2} = \frac{5(226) - (30)^2}{(5)^2} = \frac{1130 - 900}{25} = 9.2000$$

which is precisely what we computed previously.

A few individuals are a bit bothered about the variance for the following reason (neither of us, of course). Say you are measuring the height of children in inches. The raw scores are measured in terms of inches, the mean is measured in terms of inches, but the variance is measured in terms of inches squared. Squaring the scale is bothersome to some. To generate a deviational measure in the original scale of inches, we can take the square root of the variance. This is known as the **standard deviation** and is the final measure of dispersion we discuss. The population standard deviation is defined as the positive square root of the population variance and is denoted by $\sigma$ (i.e., $\sigma = +\sqrt{\sigma^2}$). The standard deviation, then, is measured in the original scale of inches. For the credit card data, the standard deviation is computed as follows:

$$\sigma = +\sqrt{\sigma^2} = +\sqrt{9.2} = 3.0332$$

What are the major characteristics of the population variance and standard deviation? First, the variance and standard deviation are a function of every score, an advantage. An examination of either the definitional or computational formula for the variance (and standard deviation as well) indicates that all of the scores are taken into account, unlike the range or $H$ spread. Second, therefore the variance and standard deviation are affected by extreme scores, a disadvantage. As we said earlier, if a measure takes all of the scores into account, then it must take into account the extreme scores as well. Thus, a child much taller than all of the rest of the children will dramatically increase the variance, as the area or size of the distribution will be much more spread out. Another way to think about this is the size of the deviation score for such an outlier will be large, and then it will be squared, and then summed with the rest of the deviation scores. Thus an outlier can really increase the variance. Also it is always a good idea when using the computer to verify your data. A data entry error can cause an outlier and therefore a larger variance (e.g., that child coded as 700 inches tall instead of 70 will surely inflate your variance).

Third, the variance and standard deviation are only appropriate for interval and ratio measurement scales. Like the mean, this is due to the implicit requirement of equal intervals. A fourth and final characteristic of the variance and standard deviation is they are quite useful for deriving other statistics, particularly in inferential statistics, another advantage. In fact, chapter 9 is all about making inferences about variances, and many other inferential statistics make assumptions about the variance. Thus the variance is quite important as a measure of dispersion.

It is also interesting to compare the measures of central tendency with the measures of dispersion, as they do share some important characteristics. The mode and the range share certain characteristics. Both only take some of the data into account, are simple to compute, are unstable from sample to sample, and can be used for all measurement scales. The median shares certain characteristics with $H$ spread. These are not influenced by extreme scores, are not a function of every score, are difficult to deal with mathematically, and can be used with all measurement scales except the nominal scale. The mean shares many characteristics with the variance and standard deviation. These all are a function of every score, are influenced by extreme scores, are useful for deriving other statistics, and are only appropriate for interval and ratio measurement scales.

In the final section of the chapter, we take a look at the sample variance and standard deviation and how they are computed for large samples of data (i.e., larger than our credit card data set).

**Sample Variance and Standard Deviation.**    Most of the time we are interested in computing the sample variance and standard deviation; we also often have large samples of data with multiple frequencies for many of the scores. Here we consider these last aspects of the measures of dispersion. Recall when we computed the sample statistics of central tendency. The computations were exactly the same as with the population parameters (although the notation for the population and sample means was different). There are also no differences between the sample and population values for the range, or $H$ spread. However, there is a difference between the sample and population values for the variance and standard deviation, as we see next.

Recall the definitional formula for the population variance as follows:

$$\sigma^2 = \frac{\sum_{i=1}^{N}(X_i - \mu)^2}{N}$$

Why not just take this equation and convert everything to sample statistics? In other words, we could simply change $N$ to $n$ and $\mu$ to $\overline{X}$. What could be wrong with that? The answer is, there is a problem preventing us from converting everything over to sample statistics.

Here is the problem. First, the sample mean $\overline{X}$ may not be exactly equal to the population mean $\mu$. In fact, for most samples, the sample mean will be somewhat different from the population mean. Second, we cannot use the population mean anyway as it is unknown. Instead, we have to substitute the sample mean into the equation (i.e., the sample mean $\overline{X}$ is the sample estimate for the population mean $\mu$). Because the sample mean is different from the population mean, the deviations will all be affected. Also, the sample variance that would be obtained in this fashion would be a biased estimate of the population variance. In statistics, bias means that something is systematically off. In this case, the sample variance obtained in this manner would be systematically too small.

In order to obtain an unbiased sample estimate of the population variance, the following adjustments have to be made in the definitional and computational formulas, respectively:

$$s^2 = \frac{\sum\limits_{i=1}^{n}(X_i - \overline{X})^2}{n-1}$$

$$s^2 = \frac{n\sum\limits_{i=1}^{n}X_i^2 - \left(\sum\limits_{i=1}^{n}X_i\right)^2}{n(n-1)}$$

In terms of the notation, $s^2$ is the **sample variance**, $n$ has been substituted for $N$, and $\overline{X}$ has been substituted for $\mu$. These are relatively minor and expected changes. The major change is in the denominator, where instead of $N$ for the definitional formula we have $n-1$, and instead of $N^2$ for the computational formula we have $n(n-1)$. This turns out to be the correction early statisticians discovered was necessary to obtain an unbiased estimate of the population variance.

It should be noted that (a) when sample size is relatively large (e.g., $n = 1000$), the correction will be quite small; and (b) when sample size is relatively small (e.g., $n = 5$), the correction will be quite a bit larger. One suggestion is that when computing the variance on a calculator or computer, you might want to be aware of whether the sample or population variance is being computed as it can make a difference (typically the sample variance is computed). The sample standard deviation is denoted by $s$ and computed as the positive square root of the sample variance $s^2$ (i.e., $s = +\sqrt{s^2}$ ).

For our example statistics quiz data, we have multiple frequencies for many of the raw scores which need to be taken into account. A simple procedure for dealing with this situation when using hand computations is shown in Table 3.4. Here we see that in the third and fifth columns the scores and squared scores are multiplied by their respective frequencies. This allows us to take into account, for example, that the score of 19 occurred four times. Note for the fifth column that the frequencies are not squared; only the scores are squared. At the bottom of the third and fifth columns are the sums we need to compute the parameters of interest.

The computations are as follows. We compute the sample mean to be

$$\overline{X} = \frac{\sum\limits_{i=1}^{n}fX_i}{n} = \frac{389}{25} = 15.5600$$

The sample variance is computed to be

$$s^2 = \frac{n\sum\limits_{i=1}^{n}fX_i^2 - \left(\sum\limits_{i=1}^{n}fX_i\right)^2}{n(n-1)} = \frac{25(6,293) - (389)^2}{25(24)} = \frac{157,325 - 151,321}{600} = \frac{6004}{600} = 10.0067$$

Therefore the sample standard deviation is

$$s = +\sqrt{s^2} = +\sqrt{10.0067} = 3.1633$$

**TABLE 3.4**
Sums for Statistics Quiz Data

| $X$ | $f$ | $fX$ | $X^2$ | $fX^2$ |
|-----|-----|------|-------|--------|
| 20 | 1 | 20 | 400 | 400 |
| 19 | 4 | 76 | 361 | 1444 |
| 18 | 3 | 54 | 324 | 972 |
| 17 | 5 | 85 | 289 | 1445 |
| 16 | 1 | 16 | 256 | 256 |
| 15 | 3 | 45 | 225 | 675 |
| 14 | 1 | 14 | 196 | 196 |
| 13 | 2 | 26 | 169 | 338 |
| 12 | 1 | 12 | 144 | 144 |
| 11 | 2 | 22 | 121 | 242 |
| 10 | 1 | 10 | 100 | 100 |
| 9 | 1 | 9 | 81 | 81 |
| | $n = 25$ | $\Sigma = 389$ | | $\Sigma = 6293$ |

## 3.4   SPSS

The purpose of this section is to see what SPSS has to offer in terms of measures of central tendency and dispersion, and also to present an APA paragraph on the example quiz data results. In fact, SPSS provides us with many different ways to obtain such measures. The three programs that I have found to be most useful are as follows. The first program is to go to the "Analyze" pulldown, into "Descriptive Statistics," and then into "Explore." Click the variable of interest (e.g., quiz) into the "Dependent List" box, then click on the "Statistics" button. A new box called "Explore: Statistics" will come up and simply check the "Descriptives" box. This will automatically generate the mean, median (approximate), variance, standard deviation, minimum, maximum, exclusive range, and interquartile range ($H$) (plus skewness and kurtosis to be covered in chapter 4). The output from this is shown in the top panel of Table 3.5.

The second program to consider is also in the "Analyze" pulldown, so go to "Descriptive Statistics," and then into "Descriptives." Click the variable of interest (e.g., quiz) into the "Variable(s)" box, then click on the "Options" button. A new box called "Descriptives: Options" will come up and simply check the statistics that you want. This will allow you to obtain the mean, variance, standard deviation, minimum, maximum, and exclusive range. The output from this is shown in the middle panel of Table 3.5.

The final program to consider is also under the "Analyze" pulldown, go to "Descriptive Statistics," and then into "Frequencies." Click the variable of interest (e.g., quiz) into the "Variable(s)" box, then click on the "Statistics" button. A new box called "Frequencies: Statistics" will come up and simply check the statistics that you want. Here you can obtain the mean, median (approximate), mode, variance, standard deviation, minimum, maximum, and exclusive range. The output from this is shown in the bottom panel of Table 3.5.

**TABLE 3.5**
SPSS Results for Statistics Quiz Data

*Descriptives*

| | | | Statistic |
|---|---|---|---|
| quiz | | Mean | 15.56 |
| | | Median | 17 |
| | | Variance | 10.007 |
| | | Std. Deviation | 3.1633 |
| | | Minimum | 9 |
| | | Maximum | 20 |
| | | Range | 11 |
| | | Interquartile Range | 5 |
| | | Skewness | −0.598 |
| | | Kurtosis | −0.741 |

*Descriptive Statistics*

| | N | Range | Minimum | Maximum | Mean | Std. Deviation | Variance |
|---|---|---|---|---|---|---|---|
| quiz | 25 | 11.0 | 9.0 | 20.0 | 15.560 | 3.1633 | 10.007 |
| Valid N (listwise) | 25 | | | | | | |

*Statistics*

| | *quiz* | | |
|---|---|---|---|
| N | Valid | 25 | |
| | Missing | 0 | |
| Mean | | 15.560 | |
| Median | | 16.333[a] | |
| Mode | | 17.0 | |
| Std. Deviation | | 3.1633 | |
| Variance | | 10.007 | |
| Range | | 11.0 | |
| Minimum | | 9.0 | |
| Maximum | | 20.0 | |

[a]Calculated from grouped data.

Here is an example paragraph of results from the statistics quiz data. As shown in Table 3.5, scores ranged from 9 to 20. The mean was 15.56, the median (approximate) was 17.00 (or 16.33 when calculated from grouped data), and the mode was 17.0. Thus the scores tended to be at the high end of the scale. The exclusive range was 11, $H$ spread (interquartile range) was 5.0, the variance was 10.007, and the standard deviation was 3.1633. From this we can tell that the scores tended to be quite variable. For example, the middle 50% of the scores had a range of 5 ($H$ spread) indicating that there was a reasonable spread of scores around the median. Thus despite a high "average" score, there were some low performing students as well. These results are consistent with those described in section 2.4.

## 3.5   SUMMARY

In this chapter we continued our exploration of descriptive statistics by considering some basic univariate population parameters and sample statistics. First we examined summation notation which is necessary in many areas of statistics. Next we looked at the most commonly used measures of central tendency, the mode, the median, and the mean. The final section of the chapter dealt with the most commonly used measures of dispersion. Here we discussed the range (both exclusive and inclusive ranges), $H$ spread, and the population variance and standard deviation, as well as the sample variance and standard deviation. At this point you should have met the following objectives: (a) be able to understand and utilize summation notation, (b) be able to compute and interpret the three commonly-used measures of central tendency, and (c) be able to compute and interpret different measures of dispersion. In the next chapter we will have a more extended discussion of the normal distribution (previously introduced in chap. 2), as well as the use of standard scores as an alternative to raw scores.

## PROBLEMS

### Conceptual Problems

1.  Adding just one or two extreme scores to the low end of a large distribution of scores will have a greater effect on
    a.  $Q$ than the variance.
    b.  the variance than $Q$.
    c.  the mode than the median.
    d.  none of the above will be affected.

2.  The variance of a distribution of scores
    a.  is always one.
    b.  may be any number, negative, zero, or positive.
    c.  may be any number greater than zero.
    d.  may be any number equal to or greater than zero.

3.  A 20 item statistics test was graded using the following procedure: a correct response is scored $+1$, a blank response is scored 0, and an incorrect response is scored $-1$.

The highest possible score is $+20$; the lowest score possible is $-20$. Since the variance of the test scores for the class was $-3$, we conclude that

    a.   the class did very poorly on the test.

    b.   the test was too difficult for the class.

    c.   some students received negative scores.

    d.   a computational error certainly was made.

4.    Adding just one or two extreme scores to the high end of a large distribution of scores will have a greater effect on

    a.   the mode than the median.

    b.   the median than the mode.

    c.   the mean than the median.

    d.   none of the above will be affected.

5.    In a negatively skewed distribution, the proportion of scores between $Q_1$ and the median is less than .25. True or False?

6.    Median is to ordinal as mode is to nominal. True or False?

7.    I assert that it is appropriate to utilize the mean in dealing with class rank data. Am I correct?

8.    For a perfectly symmetrical distribution of data, the mean, median, and mode are calculated. I assert that the values of all three measures are necessarily equal. Am I correct?

9.    In a distribution of 100 scores, the top ten examinees received an additional bonus of 5 points. Compared to the original median, I assert that the median of the new (revised) distribution will be the same. Am I correct?

10.    A collection of eight scores was collected and the variance was found to be 0. I assert that a computational error must have been made. Am I correct?

11.    Using the same data ($n = 10$), Researcher A computes the sample variance and Researcher B computes the population variance. The values are found to differ by more than rounding error. I assert that a computational error must have been made. Am I correct?

12.    For a set of 10 test scores, which of the following values will be different for the sample statistic and population parameter?

    a.   the mean

    b.   $H$

    c.   range

    d.   variance

13.    Median is to $H$ as mean is to standard deviation. True or false?

14. The inclusive range will be greater than the exclusive range for any data. True or false?

15. For a set of IQ test scores, the median was computed to be 95 and $Q_1$ to be 100. I assert that the statistician is to be commended for their work. Am I correct?

## Computational Problems

1. For the population data in Computational Problem 1 of Chapter 2, and again assuming an interval width of 1, compute the following:
    a. Mode
    b. Median
    c. Mean
    d. Exclusive and inclusive range
    e. *H* spread
    f. Variance and standard deviation

2. Given a negatively skewed distribution with a mean of 10, a variance of 81, and $N = 500$, what is the numerical value of

$$\sum_{i=1}^{N}(X_i - \mu)?$$

3. For the sample data in Computational Problem 2 of Chapter 2, and again assuming an interval width of 1, compute the following:
    a. Mode
    b. Median
    c. Mean
    d. Exclusive and inclusive range
    e. *H* spread
    f. Variance and standard deviation

4. A sample of 30 test scores are as follows.

| X | f |
|----|---|
| 20 | 1 |
| 19 | 0 |
| 18 | 2 |
| 17 | 0 |
| 16 | 0 |
| 15 | 3 |
| 14 | 0 |
| 13 | 0 |
| 12 | 9 |

|    |   |
|----|---|
| 11 | 7 |
| 10 | 3 |
| 9  | 4 |
| 8  | 1 |

Compute each of the following statistics.

    a.  Mode

    b.  Median

    c.  Mean

    d.  Exclusive and inclusive range

    e.  $H$ spread

    f.  Variance and standard deviation

5.   Without doing any computations, which of the following distributions has the largest variance?

| $X$ | $f$ | $Y$ | $f$ | $Z$ | $f$ |
|-----|-----|-----|-----|-----|-----|
| 20  | 6   | 20  | 4   | 20  | 2   |
| 19  | 7   | 19  | 7   | 19  | 7   |
| 18  | 9   | 18  | 11  | 18  | 13  |
| 17  | 9   | 17  | 11  | 17  | 13  |
| 16  | 7   | 16  | 7   | 16  | 7   |
| 15  | 6   | 15  | 4   | 15  | 2   |

## Interpretive Problem

Select one interval or ratio variable from the survey1 dataset on the CD.

1.   Calculate all of the measures of central tendency and dispersion discussed in this chapter.

2.   Write a paragraph which summarizes the findings.

# 4

# THE NORMAL DISTRIBUTION AND STANDARD SCORES

## Chapter Outline

1. The normal distribution
     History
     Characteristics
2. Standard scores
     $z$ scores
     Other types of standard scores
3. Skewness and kurtosis statistics
     Symmetry
     Skewness
     Kurtosis

## Key Concepts

1. Normal distribution (family of distributions, unit normal distribution, area under the curve, points of inflection, asymptotic curve)
2. Standard scores ($z$, CEEB, $T$, IQ)
3. Symmetry
4. Skewness (positively skewed, negatively skewed)
5. Kurtosis (leptokurtic, platykurtic, mesokurtic)
6. Moments around the mean

In the third chapter we continued our discussion of descriptive statistics, previously defined as techniques that allow us to tabulate, summarize, and depict a collection of data in an abbreviated fashion. There we considered the following three topics: summation notation (method for summing a set of scores), measures of central tendency (measures for boiling down a set of scores into a single value used to represent the data), and measures of dispersion (measures dealing with the extent to which a collection of scores vary).

In this chapter we delve more into the field of descriptive statistics in terms of three additional topics. First, we consider the most commonly used distributional shape, the normal distribution. Although in this chaper we discuss the major characteristics of the normal distribution and how it is used descriptively, in later chapters we see how the normal distribution is used inferentially as an assumption for certain statistical tests. Second, several types of standard scores are considered. To this point we have looked at raw scores and deviation scores. Here we consider scores that are often easier to interpret, known as standard scores. Finally, we examine two other measures useful for describing a collection of data, namely, skewness and kurtosis. As we show shortly, skewness refers to the lack of symmetry of a distribution of scores and kurtosis refers to the peakedness of a distribution of scores. Concepts to be discussed include the normal distribution (i.e., family of distributions, unit normal distribution, area under the curve, points of inflection, asymptotic curve), standard scores (e.g., $z$, CEEB, $T$, IQ), symmetry, skewness (positively skewed, negatively skewed), kurtosis (leptokurtic, platykurtic, mesokurtic), and moments around the mean. Our objectives are that by the end of this chapter, you will be able to (a) understand the normal distribution and utilize the normal table, (b) compute and interpret different types of standard scores, particularly $z$ scores, and (c) understand and interpret skewness and kurtosis statistics.

## 4.1    THE NORMAL DISTRIBUTION

Recall from chapter 2 that there are several commonly seen distributions. The most commonly observed and used distribution is the normal distribution. It has many uses both in descriptive and inferential statistics, as we show. In this section, we discuss the history of the normal distribution and the major characteristics of the normal distribution.

### 4.1.1    History

Let us first consider a brief history of the normal distribution. From the time that data were collected and distributions examined, a particular bell-shaped distribution occurred quite often for many variables in many disciplines (e.g., many physical, cognitive, physiological, and motor attributes). This has come to be known as the **normal distribution**. Back in the 1700s, mathematicians were called on to develop an equation that could be used to approximate the normal distribution. If such an equation could be found, then the probability associated with any point on the curve could be determined, and the amount of space or area under any portion of the curve could also be determined. For example, one might want to know what the probability of being taller than 6′2″ would be for a male, given that height is normally shaped for each gender. Until the 1920s the development of this equation was commonly attributed to Karl Friedrich Gauss. Until that time this distribution was known as the Gaussian curve. However, in the 1920s Karl Pearson found this equation in an earlier article written by Abraham DeMoivre in 1733 and renamed the curve as the normal distribution. Today the normal distribution is obviously attributed to DeMoivre.

### 4.1.2 Characteristics

There are seven important characteristics of the normal distribution. Because the normal distribution occurs frequently, features of the distribution are standard across all normal distributions. This "standard curve" allows us to make comparisons across two or more normal distributions as well as look at areas under the curve, as becomes evident.

**Standard Curve.** First, the normal distribution is a standard curve because it is always (a) symmetric around the mean, (b) unimodal, and (c) bell-shaped. As shown in Fig. 4.1, if we split the distribution in half at the mean $\mu$, the left-hand half (below the mean) is the mirror image of the right-hand half (above the mean). Also, the normal distribution has only one mode and the general shape of the distribution is bell-shaped (some even call it the bell-shaped curve). Given these conditions, the mean, median, and mode will always be equal to one another for any normal distribution.

**Family of Curves.** Second, there is no single normal distribution, but rather the normal distribution is a family of curves. For instance, one particular normal curve has a mean of 100 and a variance of 225 (standard deviation of 15). This normal curve is exemplified by the Wechsler intelligence scales. Another specific normal curve has a mean of 50 and a variance of 100 (standard deviation of 10). This normal curve is used with most behavior rating scales. In fact, there are an infinite number of normal curves, one for every distinct pair of values for the mean and variance. Every member of the family of normal curves has the same characteristics; however,

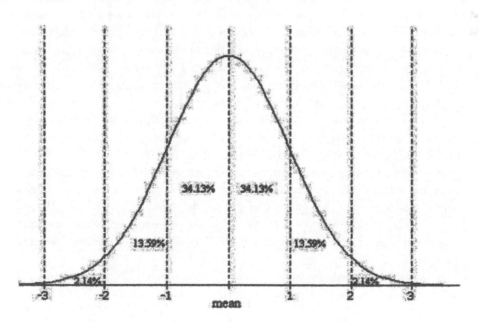

FIG. 4.1   The normal distribution.

the scale of $X$, the mean of $X$, and the variance of $X$ can differ across different variables and/or populations.

To keep the members of the family distinct, we use the following notation. If the variable $X$ is normally distributed, we write $X \sim N(\mu, \sigma^2)$. This is read as "$X$ is distributed normally with population mean $\mu$ and population variance $\sigma^2$." This is the general notation; for notation specific to a particular normal distribution, the mean and variance values are given. For our examples, the Wechsler intelligence scales are denoted by $X \sim N(100, 225)$, whereas the behavior rating scales are denoted by $X \sim N(50, 100)$.

**Unit Normal Distribution.** Third, there is one particular member of the family of normal curves that deserves additional attention. This member has a mean of 0 and a variance (and standard deviation) of 1, and thus is denoted by $X \sim N(0, 1)$. This is known as the **unit normal distribution** (unit referring to the variance of 1) or as the **standard unit normal distribution**. On a related matter, let us define a $z$ score as follows:

$$z_i = \frac{(X_i - \mu)}{\sigma}$$

The numerator of this equation is actually a deviation score, previously described in chapter 3. This indicates how far above or below the mean an individual's score falls. When we divide the deviation from the mean by the standard deviation, this indicates how many deviations above or below the mean an individual's score falls. If one individual has a $z$ score of $+1.00$, then the person falls one standard deviation above the mean. If another individual has a $z$ score of $-2.00$, then that person falls two standard deviations below the mean. There is more to say about this as we move along in this section.

**Area.** The fourth characteristic of the normal distribution is the ability to determine any area under the curve. Specifically, we can determine the area above any value, the area below any value, or the area between any two values under the curve. Let us chat about what we mean by area here. If you return to Fig. 4.1, areas for different portions of the curve are listed. Here area is defined as the percentage or amount of space of a distribution, either above a certain score, below a certain score, or between two different scores. For example, we see that the area between the mean and one standard deviation above the mean is 34.13%. In other words, roughly a third of the entire distribution falls into that region. The entire area under the curve then represents 100%, and smaller portions of the curve represent somewhat less than that.

For example, say you wanted to know what percentage of adults had an IQ score over 120, or what percentage of adults had an IQ score under 107, or what percentage of adults had an IQ score between 107 and 120. How can we compute these areas under the curve? A table of the unit normal distribution has been developed for this purpose. Although similar tables could also be developed for every member of the normal family of curves, these are unnecessary, as any normal distribution can be converted to a unit normal distribution. The unit normal table is given in Appendix Table 1.

Turn to the table now and familiarize yourself with its contents. The first column simply lists the values of $z$. Note that the values of $z$ only range from 0 to 4.0. This is so for two reasons. First, values above 4.0 are rather unlikely, as the area under that portion of the curve is negligible (less than .003%). Second, values below 0 are not really necessary in the table, as the normal distribution is symmetric around the mean of 0. Thus, that portion of the table would be redundant and is not shown here (we show how to deal with this situation for some example problems in a bit).

The second column gives the area below the value of $z$. In other words, the area between that value of $z$ and the most extreme left-hand portion of the curve [i.e., $-\infty$ (negative infinity) on the negative or left-hand side of zero]. So if we wanted to know what the area was below $z = +1.00$, we would look in the first column under $z = 1.00$ and then look in the second column to find the area of .8413. More examples are considered later in this section.

**Transformation to Unit Normal Distribution.** A fifth characteristic is any normally distributed variable, regardless of the mean and variance, can be converted into a unit normally distributed variable. Thus our Wechsler intelligence scales as denoted by $X \sim N(100, 225)$ can be converted into $z \sim N(0, 1)$. Conceptually this transformation is done by moving the curve along the $X$ axis until it is centered at a mean of 0 (by subtracting out the original mean) and then by stretching or compressing the distribution until it has a variance of 1. This allows us to make the same interpretation about any individual's score on any variable. If $z = +1.00$, then for **any** variable this implies that the individual falls one standard deviation above the mean.

This also allows us to make comparisons between two different individuals or across two different variables. If we wanted to make comparisons between two different individuals on the same variable $X$, then rather than comparing their individual raw scores, $X_1$ and $X_2$, we could compare their individual $z$ scores, $z_1$ and $z_2$, where

$$z_1 = \frac{X_1 - \mu}{\sigma}$$

and

$$z_2 = \frac{X_2 - \mu}{\sigma}$$

This is the reason we only need the unit normal distribution table to determine areas under the curve rather than a table for every member of the normal distribution family. In another situation we may want to compare scores on the Wechsler intelligence scales [$X \sim N(100, 225)$] to scores on behavior rating scales [$X \sim N(50, 100)$] for the same individual. We would convert to $z$ scores again for two variables, and then direct comparisons could be made.

**Constant Relationship with Standard Deviation.** The sixth characteristic is that the normal distribution has a constant relationship with the standard deviation. Consider Fig. 4.1 again. Along the $X$ axis we see values represented in standard deviation increments. In particular, from left to right, the values shown are three, two, and one standard deviation units below the mean; the mean; and one, two, and three standard deviation units above the mean. Under the curve, we see the percentage of scores that are under different portions of the curve. For example, the area between the mean and one standard deviation above or below the mean is 34.13%. The area between one standard deviation and two standard deviations is 13.59%, the area between two and three standard deviations is 2.14%, and the area beyond three standard deviations is .13%.

In addition, three other areas are often of interest. The area within one standard deviation of the mean, from one standard deviation below the mean to one standard deviation above the mean, is approximately 68% (or roughly two thirds of the distribution). The area within two standard deviations of the mean, from two standard deviations below the mean to two standard deviations above the mean, is approximately 95%. The area within three standard deviations of the mean, from three standard deviations below the mean to three standard deviations above the mean, is approximately 99%. In other words, most scores will be within two or three standard deviations of the mean for any normal curve.

**Points of Inflection and Asymptotic Curve.** The seventh and final characteristic of the normal distribution is as follows. The **points of inflection** are where the curve changes from sloping down (concave) to sloping up (convex). These points occur precisely at one standard deviation unit above and below the mean. This is more a matter of mathematical elegance than a statistical application. The curve also never touches the $X$ axis. That is, the curve continues to slope ever-downward toward more extreme scores, and approaches, but never quite touches, the $X$ axis. The curve is referred to here as being **asymptotic**.

**Examples.** Now for the long-awaited examples for finding area using the unit normal distribution. These examples require the use of Appendix Table 1. My personal preference is to draw a picture of the normal curve so that the proper area is determined. First let us consider three examples of finding the area below a certain value of $z$. To determine the value below $z = -2.50$, we draw a picture as shown in Fig. 4.2 (a). We draw a vertical line at the value of $z$, then shade in the area we want to find. Because the shaded region is relatively small, we know the area must be considerably smaller than .50. In the unit normal table we already know negative values of $z$ are not included. However, because the normal distribution is symmetric, we look up the area below $+2.50$ and find the value of .9938. We subtract this from 1.0000 and find the value of .0062 or .62%, a very small area indeed.

How do we determine the area below $z = 0$? As shown in Fig. 4.2 (b), we already know from reading this section that the area has to be .5000 or one half of the total area under the curve. However, let us look in the table again for area below $z = 0$ and we find the area is .5000. How do we determine the area below $z = 1.00$? As shown in Fig. 4.2 (c), this region exists on both sides of zero and actually constitutes two smaller areas, the first area below 0 and the second area between 0 and 1. For this example we use the table directly and find the value of .8413. I leave you with two other problems to solve on your own. First, what is the area below $z = 0.50$ (answer: .6915)? Second, what is the area below $z = 1.96$ (answer: .9750)?

Because the unit normal distribution is symmetric, finding the area above a certain value of $z$ is solved in a similar fashion as the area below a certain value of $z$. We need not devote any attention to that particular situation. However, how do we determine the area between two values of $z$? This is a little different and needs some additional discussion. Consider as an example finding the area between $z = -2.50$ and $z = 1.00$, as depicted in Fig. 4.2 (d). Here we see that the shaded region consists of two smaller areas, the area between the mean and $-2.50$ and the area between the mean and 1.00. Using the table again, we find the area below 1.00 is .8413 and the area below $-2.50$ is .0062. Thus the shaded region is the difference as computed by $.8413 - .0062 = .8351$. On your own, determine the area between $z = -1.27$ and $z = 0.50$ (answer: .5895).

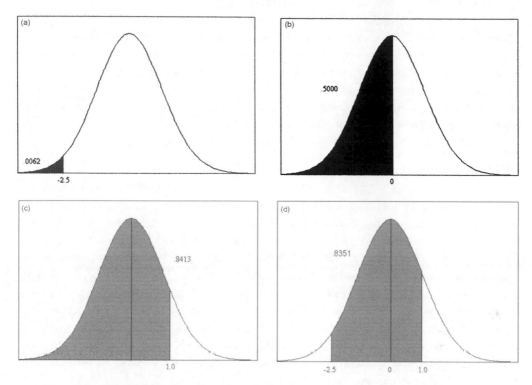

FIG. 4.2   Examples of area under the unit normal distribution: (a) Area below $z = -2.5$. (b) Area below $z = 0$. (c) Area below $z = 1.0$. (d) Area between $z = -2.5$ and $z = 1.0$.

Finally, what if we wanted to determine areas under the curve for values of $X$ rather than $z$? The answer here is simple, as you might have guessed. First we convert the value of $X$ to a $z$ score; then we use the unit normal table to determine the area. Because the normal curve is standard for all members of the family of normal curves, the scale of the variable, $X$ or $z$, is irrelevant in terms of determining such areas. In the next section we deal more with such transformations.

## 4.2   STANDARD SCORES

We have already devoted considerable attention to $z$ scores, which are one type of standard score. In this section we describe an application of $z$ scores leading up to a discussion of other types of standard scores. As we show, the major purpose of standard scores is to place scores on the same standard scale so that comparisions can be made across individuals and/or variables. Without some standard scale, comparions across individuals and/or variables would be difficult to make. Examples are coming right up.

### 4.2.1   z Scores

A child comes home from school with the results of two tests taken that day. On the math test she receives a score of 75 and on the social studies test she receives a score of 60. As a parent, the natural question to ask is "Which performance was the stronger one?" No information about any of the following is available: maximum score possible, mean of the class (or any other central tendency measure), or standard deviation of the class (or any other dispersion measure). It is possible that the two tests had a different number of possible points, different means, and/or different standard deviations. How can we possibly answer our question?

The answer, of course, is to use $z$ scores if the data are assumed to be normally distributed, once the relevant information is obtained. Let us take a minor digression before we return to answer our question in more detail. Recall that

$$z_i = \frac{X_i - \mu_X}{\sigma_X}$$

where the $X$ subscript has been added to the mean and standard deviation for purposes of clarifying which variable is being considered. If the variable $X$ is the number of items correct on a test, then the numerator is the deviation of a student's raw score from the class mean (i.e., the numerator is a deviation score as previously defined in chap. 3), measured in terms of items correct, and the denominator is the standard deviation of the class, measured in terms of items correct. Because both the numerator and denominator are measured in terms of items correct, the resultant $z$ score is measured in terms of no units (as the units of the numerator and denominator essentially cancel out). As $z$ scores have no units, this allows us to compare two different raw score variables with different scales, means, and/or standard deviations. By converting our two variables to $z$ scores, the transformed variables are now on the same $z$ score scale with a mean of 0, and a variance and standard deviation of 1.

Let us return to our previous situation where the math test score is 75 and the social studies test score is 60. In addition, we are provided with information that the standard deviation for the math test is 15 and the standard deviation for the social studies test is 10. Consider the following three examples. In the first example, the means are 60 for the math test and 50 for the social studies test. The $z$ scores are then computed as follows:

$$z_{math} = \frac{75 - 60}{15} = 1.0 \qquad z_{ss} = \frac{60 - 50}{10} = 1.0$$

The conclusion for the first example is that the performance on both tests is the same; that is, the child scored one standard deviation above the mean for both tests.

In the second example, the means are 60 for the math test and 40 for the social studies test. The $z$ scores are then computed as follows:

$$z_{math} = \frac{75 - 60}{15} = 1.0 \qquad z_{ss} = \frac{60 - 40}{10} = 2.0$$

The conclusion for the second example is that performance is better on the social studies test; that is, the child scored two standard deviations above the mean for the social studies test and only one standard deviation above the mean for the math test.

In the third example, the means are 60 for the math test and 70 for the social studies test. The $z$ scores are then computed as follows:

$$z_{math} = \frac{75 - 60}{15} = 1.0 \qquad z_{ss} = \frac{60 - 70}{10} = -1.0$$

The conclusion for the third example is that performance is better on the math test; that is, the child scored one standard deviation above the mean for the math test and one standard deviation below the mean for the social studies test. These examples serve to illustrate a few of the many possibilities, depending on the particular combinations of raw score, mean, and standard deviation for each variable.

Let us conclude this section by mentioning the major characteristics of $z$ scores. The first characteristic is that $z$ scores provide us with comparable distributions, as we just saw in the previous examples. Second, $z$ scores take into account the entire distribution of raw scores. All raw scores can be converted to $z$ scores such that every raw score will have a corresponding $z$ score. Third, we can evaluate an individual's performance relative to the scores in the distribution. For example, saying that an individual's score is one standard deviation above the mean is a measure of relative performance. This implies that approximately 84% of the scores will fall below the performance of that individual. Finally, negative values (i.e., below 0) and decimal values (e.g., $z = 1.55$) are obviously possible (and will most certainly occur) with $z$ scores. On the average, about half of the $z$ scores for any distribution will be negative and some decimal values are quite likely. This last characteristic is bothersome to some individuals and has led to the development of other types of standard scores, as described in the next section.

### 4.2.2   Other Types of Standard Scores

Over the years, standard scores besides $z$ scores have been developed, either to alleviate the concern over negative and/or decimal values associated with $z$ scores, or to obtain a particular mean and standard deviation. Let us examine three common examples. The first additional standard score is known as the CEEB (College Entrance Examination Board) score. This standard score is used in exams such as the SAT and the GRE. The subtests for these exams all have a mean of 500 and a standard deviation of 100. A second additional standard score is known as the $T$ score and is used in tests such as most behavior rating scales, as previously mentioned. The $T$ scores have a mean of 50 and a standard deviation of 10. A third additional standard score is known as the IQ score and is used in the Wechsler intelligence scales. The IQ score has a mean of 100 and a standard deviation of 15 (the Stanford-Binet intelligence scales have a mean of 100 and a standard deviation of 16).

Say we want to develop our own type of standard score, where we determine in advance the mean and standard deviation. How would that be done? As the equation for $z$ scores is

$$z_i = \frac{X_i - \mu_X}{\sigma_X}$$

then algebraically it can be shown that

$$X_i = \mu_X + \sigma_X z_i$$

If, for example, we want to develop our own "stat" standardized score, then the following equation would be used:

$$stat_i = \mu_{stat} + \sigma_{stat}\, z_i$$

where stat$_i$ is the "stat" standardized score for a particular individual, $\mu_{\text{stat}}$ is the desired mean of the "stat" distribution, and $\sigma_{\text{stat}}$ is the desired standard deviation of the "stat" distribution. If we want to have a mean of 10 and a standard deviation of 2, then our equation becomes

$$stat_i = 10 + 2\, z_i$$

We would then have the computer simply plug in a $z$ score and compute an individual's "stat" score. Thus a $z$ score of 1.0 would yield a "stat" standardized score of 12.0.

Consider a realistic example where we have a raw score variable we want to transform into a standard score, and we want to control the mean and standard deviation. For example, we have statistics midterm raw scores with 225 points possible. We want to develop a standard score with a mean of 50 and a standard deviation of 5. We also have scores on other variables that are on different scales with different means and different standard deviations (e.g., statistics final exam scores worth 175 points, a set of 20 lab assignments worth a total of 200 points, a statistics performance assessment worth 100 points). We can standardize each of those variables by placing them on the same scale with the same mean and same standard deviation, thereby allowing comparisons across variables. This is precisely the rationale used by testing companies and researchers when they develop standard scores. In short, from $z$ scores we can develop a CEEB, $T$, IQ, "stat," or any other type of standard score.

## 4.3   SKEWNESS AND KURTOSIS STATISTICS

In previous chapters we discussed the distributional concepts of symmetry, skewness, central tendency, and dispersion. In this section we more closely define symmetry as well as the statistics commonly used to measure skewness and kurtosis.

### 4.3.1   Symmetry

Conceptually we define a distribution as being **symmetric** if when we divide the distribution precisely in half, the left-hand half is a mirror image of the right-hand half. That is, the distribution above the mean is a mirror image of the distribution below the mean. To put it another way, a distribution is **symmetric around the mean** if for every score $q$ units below the mean there is a corresponding score $q$ units above the mean.

Two examples of symmetric distributions are shown in Fig. 4.3. In Fig. 4.3 (a), we have a normal distribution, which is clearly symmetric around the mean. In Fig. 4.3 (b), we have a symmetric distribution that is bimodal, unlike the previous example. From these and other numerous examples, we can make the following two conclusions. First, if a distribution is symmetric, then the mean is equal to the median. Second, if a distribution is symmetric and unimodal, then the mean, median, and mode are all equal. This indicates we can determine whether a distribution is symmetric by comparing the measures of central tendency.

### 4.3.2   Skewness

We define **skewness** as the extent to which a distribution of scores deviates from perfect symmetry. This is important as perfectly symmetrical distributions rarely occur with actual sample

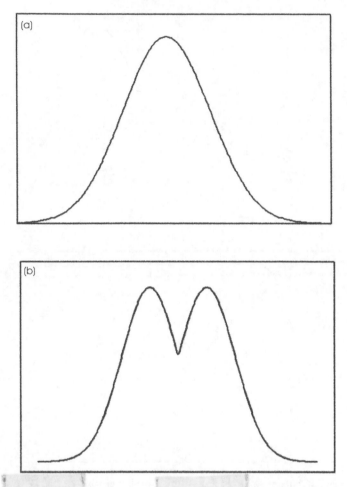

**FIG. 4.3  Symmetric distributions: (a) Normal distribution. (b) Bimodal distribution.**

data. A skewed distribution is known as being asymmetrical. As shown in Fig. 4.4, there are two general types of skewness, distributions that are negatively skewed as in Fig. 4.4 (a), and those that are positively skewed as in Fig. 4.4 (b). Negatively skewed distributions, which are skewed to the left, occur when most of the scores are toward the high end of the distribution and only a few scores are toward the low end. If you make a fist with your thumb pointing to the left (skewed to the left), you have graphically defined a negatively skewed distribution. For a negatively skewed distribution, we also find the following: mode > median > mean. This indicates that we can determine whether a distribution is negatively skewed by comparing the measures of central tendency.

Positively skewed distributions, which are skewed to the right, occur when most of the scores are toward the low end of the distribution and only a few scores are toward the high end. If you make a fist with your thumb pointing to the right (skewed to the right), you have graphically defined a positively skewed distribution. For a positively skewed distribution, we also find the following: mode < median < mean. This indicates that we can determine whether a distribution is positively skewed by comparing the measures of central tendency.

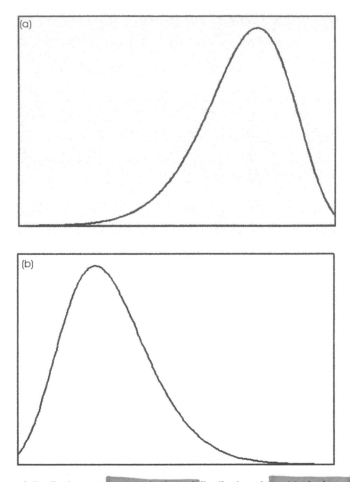

**FIG. 4.4** Skewed distributions: (a) Negatively skewed distribution. (b) Positively skewed distribution.

The most commonly used measure of skewness is known as $\gamma_1$, which is mathematically defined as

$$\gamma_1 = \frac{\sum_{i=1}^{N} z_i^3}{N}$$

where we take the $z$ score for each individual, cube it, sum across all $N$ individuals, and then divide by the number of individuals $N$. This measure is available in nearly all computer packages, so hand computations are not necessary. The characteristics of this measure of skewness are as follows: (a) a perfectly symmetrical distribution has a skewness value of 0, (b) the range of values for the skewness statistic is approximately from $-3$ to $+3$, (c) negatively skewed distributions have negative skewness values, and (d) positively skewed distributions have positive skewness values.

### 4.3.3 Kurtosis

Kurtosis is the fourth and final property of a distribution (often referred to as the moments around the mean). These properties are central tendency (first moment), dispersion (second moment), skewness (third moment), and kurtosis (fourth moment). Kurtosis is conceptually defined as the "peakedness" of a distribution (kurtosis is Greek for peakedness). Some distributions are rather flat and others have a rather sharp peak. Specifically, there are three general types of peakedness, as shown in Fig. 4.5. A distribution that is very peaked is known as leptokurtic ("lepto" meaning slender or narrow) [Fig. 4.5 (a)]. A distribution that is relatively flat is known as platykurtic ("platy" meaning flat or broad) [Fig. 4.5 (b)]. A distribution that is somewhere in between is known as mesokurtic ("meso" meaning intermediate) [Fig. 4.5 (c)].

The most commonly used measure of kurtosis is known as $\gamma_2$, which is mathematically defined as

$$\gamma_2 = \frac{\sum_{i=1}^{N} z_i^4}{N} - 3$$

where we take the $z$ score for each individual, take it to the fourth power (being the fourth moment), sum across all $N$ individuals, divide by the number of individuals $N$, and then subtract 3. This measure is available in nearly all computer packages, so hand computations are not necessary. The characteristics of this measure of kurtosis are as follows: (a) a perfectly

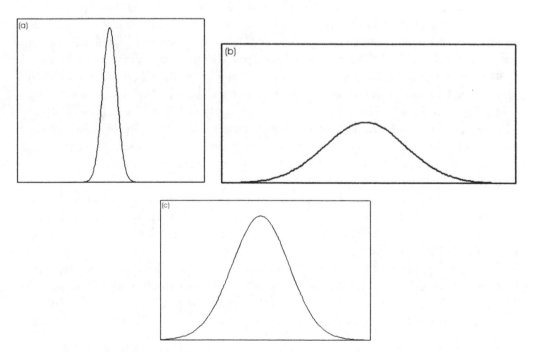

**FIG. 4.5** Distributions of different kurtoses: (a) Leptokurtic distribution. (b) Platykurtic distribution. (c) Mesokurtic distribution.

mesokurtic distribution, which would be a normal distribution, has a kurtosis value of 0 (the 3 was subtracted in the equation to yield a value of 0 rather than 3), (b) platykurtic distributions have negative kurtosis values (being flat rather than peaked), and (c) leptokurtic distributions have positive kurtosis values (being peaked). Skewness and kurtosis statistics are useful for the following two reasons: (a) as descriptive statistics used to describe the shape of a distribution of scores, and (b) in inferential statistics, which often assume a normal distribution, so the researcher has some indication of whether the assumption has been met (more about this beginning in chap. 6).

## 4.4   SPSS

Here we review what SPSS has to offer for the normal distribution and standard scores, and we also present an APA paragraph on the example quiz data results. SPSS provides us with several options. The following four programs have proven to be quite useful. The first program is to go to the "Analyze" pulldown, into "Descriptive Statistics," and then into "Explore." Click the variable of interest (e.g., quiz) into the "Dependent List" box, then click on the "Statistics" button. A new box called "Explore: Statistics" will come up and simply check the "Descriptives" box. This will automatically generate the skewness and kurtosis values, as well as the measures of central tendency and dispersion covered in chapter 3. The output from this was previously shown in the top panel of Table 3.5.

The second program to consider is also in the "Analyze" pulldown, so go to "Descriptive Statistics," and then into "Descriptives." Click the variable of interest (e.g., quiz) into the "Variable(s)" box. If you want to obtain $z$ scores for each individual, check the "Save standardized values as variables" box. This will insert a new variable into your dataset for subsequent analysis. Then click on the "Options" button. A new box called "Descriptives: Options" will come up and simply check the statistics that you want. This will allow you to obtain the skewness and kurtosis values, as well as the measures of central tendency and dispersion from chapter 3.

The third program to consider is also under the "Analyze" pulldown, go to "Descriptive Statistics," and then into "Frequencies." Click the variable of interest (e.g., quiz) into the "Variable(s)" box, then click on the "Statistics" button. A new box called "Frequencies: Statistics" will come up and simply check the statistics that you want. Here you can obtain the skewness and kurtosis values, as well as the measures of central tendency and dispersion in chapter 3. If you click on the "Charts" button, you can also obtain a histogram with a normal curve overlay by clicking the "Histogram" radio button and checking the "With normal curve" box. This output is shown in Fig. 4.6. Two other programs also yield a histogram with a normal curve overlay. The first is under the "Graphs" pulldown in the "Histogram" program. The second is under the "Graphs" pulldown, then into "Interactive", and finally into the "Histogram" program. Both work just like the "Frequencies" program described above.

A fourth program that comes in handy is for transforming variables, such as creating a standardized version of a variable. Go to the "Transform" pulldown and then into "Compute." The "Target Variable" is the name of the new variable you are creating and the "Numeric Expression" box is where you insert the commands of which original variable to transform and how to transform it.

Here is an example paragraph of results for the statistics quiz data. As shown in the top panel of Table 3.5, the skewness value is $-.598$ and the kurtosis value is $-.741$. The histogram

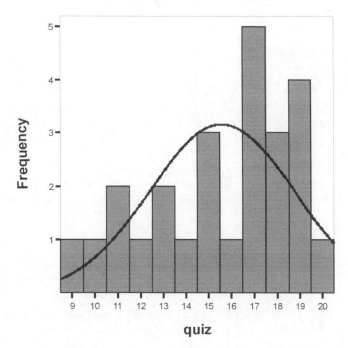

**FIG. 4.6    SPSS histogram of statistics quiz data with normal distribution overlay.**

with a normal curve overlay is depicted in Fig. 4.6. Taken together, these results indicate that the quiz scores are reasonably normally distributed. There is a slight negative skew such that there are more scores at the high end of the distribution than a typical normal distribution. There is also a slight negative kurtosis indicating that the distribution was slightly flatter than a normal distribution, with a few more extreme scores at the low end of the distribution. Thus we consider this to be a reasonable approximation to the normal curve.

## 4.5    SUMMARY

In this chapter we continued our exploration of descriptive statistics by considering an important distribution, the normal distribution, standard scores, and other characteristics of a distribution of scores. First we discussed the normal distribution, with its history and important characteristics. In addition, the unit normal table was introduced and used to determine various areas under the curve. Next we examined different types of standard scores, in particular $z$ scores, as well as CEEB scores, $T$ scores, and IQ scores. The final section of the chapter included a detailed description of symmetry, skewness, and kurtosis. The different types of skewness and kurtosis were defined and depicted. At this point you should have met the following objectives: (a) be able to understand the normal distribution and utilize the normal table; (b) be able to compute and interpret different types of standard scores, particularly $z$ scores; and (c) be able to understand and interpret skewness and kurtosis statistics. In the next chapter we move toward inferential statistics through an introductory discussion of probability as well as a more detailed discussion of sampling and estimation.

## PROBLEMS

### Conceptual Problems

1. For which of the following distributions will the skewness value be zero?
    a. $N(0,1)$
    b. $N(0,2)$
    c. $N(10,50)$
    d. all of the above

2. For which of the following distributions will the kurtosis value be zero?
    a. $N(0,1)$
    b. $N(0,2)$
    c. $N(10,50)$
    d. all of the above

3. A set of 400 scores is approximately normally distributed with a mean of 65 and a standard deviation of 4.5. Approximately 95% of the scores would fall between
    a. 60.5 and 69.5.
    b. 56 and 74.
    c. 51.5 and 78.5.
    d. 64.775 and 65.225.

4. What is the percentile rank of 60 in the distribution of $N(60,100)$?
    a. 10
    b. 50
    c. 60
    d. 100

5. Which of the following parameters can be found on the $X$ axis for a frequency polygon of a population distribution?
    a. skewness
    b. median
    c. kurtosis
    d. $Q$

6. The skewness value is calculated for a set of data and is found to be equal to $+2.75$. This indicates that the distribution of scores is
    a. highly negatively skewed.
    b. slightly negatively skewed.
    c. symmetrical.
    d. slightly positively skewed.
    e. highly positively skewed.

7. The kurtosis value is calculated for a set of data and is found to be equal to $+2.75$. This indicates that the distribution of scores is

    a. mesokurtic.

    b. platykurtic.

    c. leptokurtic.

    d. cannot be determined

8. For a normal distribution, all percentiles above the 50th must yield positive $z$ scores. True or false?

9. If one knows the raw score, the mean, and the $z$ score, then one can calculate the value of the standard deviation. True or false?

10. In a normal distribution, a $z$ score of 1.0 has a percentile rank of 34. True or false?

11. The mean of a normal distribution of scores is always 1. True or false?

12. If in a distribution of 200 IQ scores, the mean is considerably above the median, then the distribution is

    a. negatively skewed

    b. symmetrical

    c. positively skewed

    d. bimodal

13. For which of the following distributions will the kurtosis value be greatest?

| $A$ | $f$ | $B$ | $f$ | $C$ | $f$ | $D$ | $f$ |
|-----|-----|-----|-----|-----|-----|-----|-----|
| 15 | 3 | 15 | 4 | 15 | 1 | 15 | 1 |
| 14 | 4 | 14 | 4 | 14 | 3 | 14 | 5 |
| 13 | 6 | 13 | 4 | 13 | 12 | 13 | 8 |
| 12 | 4 | 12 | 4 | 12 | 3 | 12 | 5 |
| 11 | 3 | 11 | 4 | 11 | 1 | 11 | 1 |

    a. distribution A

    b. distribution B

    c. distribution C

    d. distribution D

14. The distribution of variable $X$ has a mean of 10 and is positively skewed. The distribution of variable $Y$ has the same mean of 10 and is negatively skewed. I assert that the medians for the two variables must also be the same. Am I correct?

15. The variance of $z$ scores is always equal to the variance of the raw scores for the same variable. True or false?

16. The mode has the largest value of the central tendency measures in a positively skewed distribution. True or false?

17. Which of the following represents the highest performance in a normal distribution?

    a.   $P_{90}$

    b.   $z = +1.00$

    c.   $Q_3$

    d.   IQ = 115

18. Suzie Smith came home with two test scores, $z = +1$ in math and $z = -1$ in biology. For which test did Suzie perform better?

## Computational Problems

1. Give the numerical value for each of the following descriptions concerning normal distributions by referring to the table for $N(0,1)$.

    a.   The proportion of the area below $z = -1.66$

    b.   The proportion of the area between $z = -1.03$ and $z = +1.03$

    c.   The 5th percentile of $N(20,36)$

    d.   The 99th percentile of $N(30,49)$

    e.   The percentile rank of the score 25 in $N(20,36)$

    f.   The percentile rank of the score 24.5 in $N(30,49)$

    g.   The proportion of the area in $N(36,64)$ between the scores of 18 and 42

2. Give the numerical value for each of the following descriptions concerning normal distributions by referring to the table for $N(0,1)$.

    a.   The proportion of the area below $z = -.80$

    b.   The proportion of the area between $z = -1.49$ and $z = +1.49$

    c.   The 2.5th percentile of $N(50,81)$

    d.   The 50th percentile of $N(40,64)$

    e.   The percentile rank of the score 45 in $N(50,81)$

    f.   The percentile rank of the score 53 in $N(50,81)$

    g.   The proportion of the area in $N(36,64)$ between the scores of 19.7 and 45.1

## Interpretive Problem

Select one interval or ratio variable from the survey1 dataset on the CD (e.g., one idea is to select the same variable you selected for the interpretive problem from chap. 3).

1. Calculate the measures of central tendency, dispersion, skewness, and kurtosis.

2. Write a paragraph which summarizes the findings, particularly commenting on the distributional shape.

# 5

# INTRODUCTION TO PROBABILITY AND SAMPLE STATISTICS

## Chapter Outline

1.  Brief introduction to probability
    Importance of probability
    Definition of probability
    Intuition versus probability
2.  Sampling and estimation
    Simple random sampling
    Estimation of population parameters and sampling distributions

## Key Concepts

1.  Probability
2.  Inferential statistics
3.  Simple random sampling (with and without replacement)
4.  Sampling distribution of the mean
5.  Variance and standard error of the mean (sampling error)
6.  Confidence intervals (point vs. interval estimation)
7.  Central limit theorem

In the fourth chapter we extended our discussion of descriptive statistics. There we considered the following three general topics: the normal distribution, standard scores, and skewness and kurtosis. In this chapter we begin to move from descriptive statistics into inferential statistics. The two basic topics described in this chapter are probability, and sampling and estimation. First, as a brief introduction to probability, we discuss the importance of probability in statistics, define probability in a conceptual and computational sense, as well as the notion of intuition versus probability. Second, under sampling and estimation, we formally move into inferential statistics by considering the following topics: simple random sampling (as well as other types of sampling), and estimation of population parameters and sampling distributions. Concepts to be discussed include probability, inferential statistics, simple random sampling (with and without replacement), sampling distribution of the mean, variance and standard error of the mean (sampling error), confidence intervals (point vs. interval estimation), and central limit theorem. Our objectives are that by the end of this chapter, you will be able to (a) understand the most basic concepts of probability; (b) understand and conduct simple random sampling; and (c) understand, compute, and interpret the results from the estimation of population parameters via a sample.

## 5.1    BRIEF INTRODUCTION TO PROBABILITY

The area of probability became important and began to be developed during the Middle Ages (17th and 18th centuries), when royalty and other well-to-do gamblers consulted with mathematicians for advice on games of chance. For example, in poker if you hold 2 jacks, what are your chances of drawing a third jack? Or in craps, what is the chance of rolling a "7" with two dice? During that time, probability was also used for more practical purposes, such as to help determine life expectancy to underwrite life insurance policies. Considerable development in probability has obviously taken place since that time. In this section, we discuss the importance of probability, provide a definition of probability, and consider the notion of intuition versus probability. Although there is much more to the topic of probability, here we simply discuss those aspects of probability necessary for the remainder of the text. For additional information on probability, take a look at texts by Rudas (2004), or Tijms (2004).

### 5.1.1    Importance of Probability

Let us first consider why probability is important in statistics. A researcher is out collecting some sample data from a group of individuals (e.g., students, parents, teachers, voters, corporations, animals, etc.). Some descriptive statistics are generated from the sample data. Say the sample mean, $\overline{X}$, is computed for several variables (e.g., amount of study time, grade point average, confidence in a political candidate, widget sales, animal food consumption). To what extent can we generalize from these sample statistics to their corresponding population parameters? For example, if the mean amount of study time per week for a given sample of graduate students is $\overline{X} = 10$ hours, to what extent are we able to generalize to the population of graduate students on the value of the population mean $\mu$?

As we see, beginning in this chapter, inferential statistics involve one making an inference about population parameters from sample statistics. We would like to know (a) how much uncertainty exists in our sample statistics, as well as (b) how much confidence to place in our sample statistics. These questions can be addressed by assigning a probability value to an inference. As we show beginning in chapter 6, probability can also be used to make statements about areas under a distribution of scores (e.g., the normal distribution). First, however, we need to provide a definition of probability.

## 5.1.2 Definition of Probability

In order to more easily define probability, consider a simple example of rolling a six-sided die (as there are dice with different numbers of sides). Each of the six sides, of course, has anywhere from one to six dots. Each side has a different number of dots. What is the probability of rolling a "4?" Conceptually there are six possible outcomes or events that can occur. One can also determine how many times a specific outcome or event actually can occur. These two concepts are used to define and compute the probability of a particular outcome or event by

$$p(A) = \frac{S}{T}$$

where $p(A)$ is the probability that outcome or event $A$ will occur, $S$ is the number of times that the specific outcome or event $A$ can occur, and $T$ is the total number of outcomes or events possible. Thus, for our example, the probability of rolling a "4" is determined by

$$p(4) = \frac{S}{T} = \frac{1}{6}$$

This assumes, however, that the die is unbiased, which means that the die is fair and that the probability of obtaining any of the six outcomes is the same. For a fair, unbiased die, the probability of obtaining any outcome is $\frac{1}{6}$. Gamblers have been known to possess an unfair, biased die such that the probability of obtaining a particular outcome is different from $\frac{1}{6}$ (e.g., to cheat their opponent).

Consider one other classic probability example. Imagine you have an urn (or other container). Inside of the urn and out of view are a total of nine balls, six of the balls being red (event $A$), and the other three balls being green (event $B$). Your task is to draw one ball out of the urn (without looking) and then observe its color. The probability of each of these two events occurring on the first draw is as follows:

$$p(A) = \frac{S}{T} = \frac{6}{9} = \frac{2}{3}$$

$$p(B) = \frac{S}{T} = \frac{3}{9} = \frac{1}{3}$$

Thus the probability of drawing a red ball is $\frac{2}{3}$ and the probability of drawing a green ball is $\frac{1}{3}$.

Two notions become evident in thinking about these examples. First, the sum of the probabilities for all distinct or independent events is precisely 1. In other words, if we take each distinct event and compute its probability, then the sum of those probabilities must be equal to one so as to account for all possible outcomes. Second, the probability of any given event (a) cannot exceed one, and (b) cannot be less than zero. Part (a) should be obvious in that the sum of the probabilities for all events cannot exceed one, and therefore the probability of any one event cannot exceed one either (it makes no sense to talk about an event occurring more than all of the time). An event would have a probability of one if no other event can possibly occur, such as the probability that you are currently breathing. For part (b) no event can have a negative probability (it makes no sense to talk about an event occurring less than never); however, an event could have a zero probability if the event can never occur. For instance, in our urn example, one could never draw a purple ball.

### 5.1.3    Intuition Versus Probability

At this point you are probably thinking that probability is an interesting topic. However, without extensive training to think in a probabilistic fashion, people tend to let their intuition guide them. This is all well and good, except that intuition can often guide you to a different conclusion than probability. Let us examine two classic examples to illustrate this dilemma. The first classic example is known as the "birthday problem." Imagine you are in a room of 23 people. You ask each person to write down their birthday (month and day) on a piece of paper. What do you think is the probability that in a room of 23 people at least two will have the same birthday?

Assume first that we are dealing with 365 different possible birthdays, where leap year (February 29) is not considered. Also assume the sample of 23 people is randomly drawn from some population of people. Taken together, this implies that each of the 365 different possible birthdays has the same probability (i.e., 1/365). An intuitive thinker might have the following thought processing. "There are 365 different birthdays in a year and there are 23 people in the sample. Therefore the probability of two people having the same birthday must be close to zero." I try this on my introductory students each semester and their guesses are usually around zero.

Intuition has led us astray and we have not used the proper thought processing. True, there are 365 days and 23 people. However, the question really deals with pairs of people. There is a fairly large number of different possible pairs of people (i.e., person 1 with 2, 1 with 3, etc., for a total of 253 different pairs of people). All we need is for one pair to have the same birthday. While the probability computations are a little complex, the probability that two or more individuals will have the same birthday in a group of 23 is equal to .507. That's right, about half of the time a group of 23 people will have 2 or more with the same birthday. My introductory class typically has between 20 and 35 students. More often than not, I am able to find 2 students with the same birthday. One semester I wrote each birthday on the board so that students could see the data. The first two students selected actually had the same birthday, so my point was very quickly shown. What was the probability of that event occurring?

The second classic example is the "gambler's fallacy," sometimes referred to as the "law of averages." This works for any game of chance, so imagine you are flipping a coin. Obviously there are two possible outcomes from a coin flip, heads and tails. Assume the coin is fair and unbiased such that the probability of flipping a head is the same as flipping a tail, that is, .5. After flipping the coin nine times, you have observed a tail every time. What is the probability of obtaining a head on the next flip?

An intuitive thinker might have the following thought processing. "I have just observed a tail each of the last nine flips. According to the law of averages, the probability of observing a head on the next flip must be near certainty. The probability must be nearly one." I also try this on my introductory students every semester and their guesses are almost always near one.

Intuition has led us astray once again as we have not used the proper thought processing. True, we have just observed nine consecutive tails. However, the question really deals with the probability of the 10th flip being a head, not the probability of obtaining 10 consecutive tails. The probability of a head is always .5 with a fair, unbiased coin. The coin has no memory; thus the probability of tossing a head after nine consecutive tails is the same as the probability of tossing a head after nine consecutive heads, .5. In technical terms, the probabilities of each event (each toss) are independent of one another. In other words, the probability of flipping a head is the same regardless of the preceding flips. This is not the same as the probability of tossing 10 consecutive heads, which is rather small (approximately .0010). So when you are gambling at the casino and have lost the last nine games, do not believe that you are guaranteed to win the next game. You can just as easily lose game 10 as you did game 1. The same goes if you have won a number of games. You can just as easily win the next game as you did game 1. To some extent, the casinos count on their customers playing the gambler's fallacy to make a profit.

## 5.2   SAMPLING AND ESTIMATION

In chapter 3 we spent some time discussing sample statistics, including the measures of central tendency and dispersion. In this section we expand upon that discussion by defining inferential statistics, describing different types of sampling, and then moving into the implications of such sampling in terms of estimation and sampling distributions.

Consider the situation where we have a population of graduate students. Population parameters (characteristics of a population) could be determined, such as the population size $N$, the population mean $\mu$, the population variance $\sigma^2$, and the population standard deviation $\sigma$. Through some method of sampling, we then take a sample of students from this population. Sample statistics (characteristics of a sample) could be determined, such as the sample size $n$, the sample mean $\overline{X}$, the sample variance $s^2$, and the sample standard deviation $s$.

How often do we actually ever deal with population data? Except when dealing with very small, well-defined populations, we almost never deal with population data. The main reason for this is cost, in terms of time, personnel, and economics. This means then that we are almost always dealing with sample data. With descriptive statistics, dealing with sample data is very straightforward, and we only need make sure we are using the appropriate sample statistic equation. However, what if we want to take a sample statistic and make some generalization about its relevant population parameter? For example, you have computed a sample mean on grade point average (GPA) of $\overline{X} = 3.25$ for a sample of 25 graduate students at State University. You would like to make some generalization from this sample mean to the population mean $\mu$ at State University. How do we do this? To what extent can we make such a generalization? How confident are we that this sample mean represents the population mean?

This brings us to the field of inferential statistics. We define **inferential statistics** as statistics that allow us to make an inference or generalization from a sample to the population. In terms of reasoning, inductive reasoning is used to infer from the specific (the sample) to the general (the population). Thus inferential statistics is the answer to all of our preceding questions about generalizing from sample statistics to population parameters. In the remainder of this section, and in much of the remainder of this text, we take up the details of inferential statistics for many different procedures.

### 5.2.1 Simple Random Sampling

There are several different ways in which a sample can be drawn from a population. In this section we introduce simple random sampling, which is a commonly used type of sampling and which is also assumed for many inferential statistics (beginning in chap. 6). Simple random sampling is defined as the process of selecting sample observations from a population so that each observation has an equal and independent probability of being selected. If the sampling process is truly random, then (a) each observation in the population has an equal chance of being included in the sample, and (b) each observation selected into the sample is independent of (or not affected by) every other selection. Thus a volunteer or "street-corner" sample would not meet the first condition because members of the population who do not frequent that particular street corner have no chance of being included in the sample. In addition, if the selection of spouses required the corresponding selection of their respective mates, then the second condition would not be met. For example, if the selection of Mr. Joe Smith III also required the selection of his wife, then these two selections are not independent of one another. Because we selected Mr. Joe Smith III, we must also therefore select his wife. Note that through independent sampling it is possible for Mr. Smith and his wife to both be sampled, but is not required. Thus, independence implies that each observation is selected without regard to any other observation sampled.

Simple Random Sampling With Replacement.    There are two specific types of simple random sampling. Simple random sampling with replacement is conducted as follows. The first observation is selected from the population into the sample and that observation is then replaced back into the population. The second observation is selected and then replaced in the population. This continues until a sample of the desired size is obtained. The key here is that each observation sampled is placed back into the population and could be selected again.

This scenario makes sense in certain applications and not in others. For example, return to our coin flipping example where we now want to flip a coin 100 times (i.e., a sample size of 100). How does this operate in the context of sampling? We flip the coin (e.g., heads) and record the result. This "head" becomes the first observation in our sample. This observation is then placed back into the population. Then a second observation is made and is placed back into the population. This continues until our sample size requirement of 100 is reached. In this particular scenario we always sample with replacement, and we automatically do so even if we have never heard of sampling with replacement. If no replacement took place, then we could only ever have a sample size of two, one "head" and one "tail."

Simple Random Sampling Without Replacement.    In other scenarios, sampling with replacement does not make sense. For example, say we are conducting a poll for the next major election by randomly selecting 100 students (the sample) at a local university (the population). As each student is selected into the sample, they are removed and cannot be sampled again. It simply would make no sense if our sample of 100 students only contained 78 different students due to replacement (as some students were polled more than once). Our polling example represents the other type of simple random sampling, this time without replacement. Simple random sampling without replacement is conducted in a similar fashion except that once an observation is selected for inclusion in the sample, it is not replaced and cannot be selected a second time.

**Other Types of Sampling.**    There are several other types of sampling. These other types of sampling include convenient sampling (i.e., volunteer or "street-corner" sampling previously mentioned), systematic sampling (e.g., select every 10th observation from the population into the sample), cluster sampling (i.e., sample groups or clusters of observations and include all members of the selected clusters in the sample), stratified sampling (i.e., sampling within subgroups or strata to ensure adequate representation of each strata), and multistage sampling (e.g., stratify at one stage and randomly sample at another stage). These types of sampling are beyond the scope of this text, and the interested reader is referred to sampling texts such as Sudman (1976), Kalton (1983), Jaeger (1984), Fink (1995), or Levy (1999).

## 5.2.2    Estimation of Population Parameters and Sampling Distributions

Take as an example the situation where we select one random sample of $n$ females (e.g., $n = 20$), measure their weight, and then compute the mean weight of the sample. We find the mean of this first sample to be 102 pounds and denote it by $\overline{X}_1 = 102$, where the subscript identifies the first sample. This one sample mean is known as a point estimate of the population mean $\mu$, as it is simply one value or point. We can then proceed to collect weight data from a second sample of $n$ females and find that $\overline{X}_2 = 110$. Next we collect weight data from a third sample of $n$ females and find that $\overline{X}_3 = 119$. Imagine that we go on to collect such data from many other samples of size $n$ and compute a sample mean for each of those samples.

**Sampling Distribution of the Mean.**    At this point we have a collection of sample means, which we can use to construct a frequency distribution of sample means. This frequency distribution is formally known as the **sampling distribution of the mean**. To better illustrate this new distribution, let us take a very small population from which we can take many samples. Here we define our population of observations as follows: 1, 2, 3, 5, 9. As the entire population is known here, we can better illustrate the important underlying concepts. We can determine that the population mean $\mu_X = 4$ and the population variance $\sigma_X^2 = 8$, where $X$ indicates the variable we are referring to. Let us first take all possible samples from this population of size 2 (i.e., $n = 2$) with replacement. As there are only five observations, there will be 25 possible samples as shown in the upper portion of Table 5.1, called "Samples." Each entry represents the two observations for a particular sample. For instance, in row 1 and column 4, we see 1,5. This indicates that the first observation is a 1 and the second observation is a 5. If sampling was done without replacement, then the diagonal of the table from upper left to lower right would not exist. For instance, a 1,1 sample could not be selected if sampling without replacement.

Now that we have all possible samples of size 2, let us compute the sample means for each of the 25 samples. The sample means are shown in the middle portion of Table 5.1, called "Sample means." Just eyeballing the table, we see the means range from 1 to 9 with numerous different values in between. We then compute the mean of the 25 sample means to be 4, as shown in the bottom portion of Table 5.1, called "Mean of the sample means."

This is a matter for some discussion, so consider the following three points. First, the distribution of $\overline{X}$ for all possible samples of size $n$ is known as the sampling distribution of the mean. Second, the mean of the sampling distribution of the mean for all possible samples of size $n$ is equal to $\mu_{\overline{X}}$. As the mean of the sampling distribution of the mean is denoted by $\mu_{\overline{X}}$ (the mean of the $\overline{X}$s), then we see for the example that $\mu_{\overline{X}} = \mu_X = 4$. The mean of the sampling distribu-

**TABLE 5.1**

All Possible Samples and Sample Means for $n = 2$ From the Population of 1, 2, 3, 5, 9

| First Observation | Second Observation | | | | |
|---|---|---|---|---|---|
| | *1* | *2* | *3* | *5* | *9* |
| Samples | | | | | |
| 1 | 1,1 | 1,2 | 1,3 | 1,5 | 1,9 |
| 2 | 2,1 | 2,2 | 2,3 | 2,5 | 2,9 |
| 3 | 3,1 | 3,2 | 3,3 | 3,5 | 3,9 |
| 5 | 5,1 | 5,2 | 5,3 | 5,5 | 5,9 |
| 9 | 9,1 | 9,2 | 9,3 | 9,5 | 9,9 |
| Sample means | | | | | |
| 1 | 1.0 | 1.5 | 2.0 | 3.0 | 5.0 |
| 2 | 1.5 | 2.0 | 2.5 | 3.5 | 5.5 |
| 3 | 2.0 | 2.5 | 3.0 | 4.0 | 6.0 |
| 5 | 3.0 | 3.5 | 4.0 | 5.0 | 7.0 |
| 9 | 5.0 | 5.5 | 6.0 | 7.0 | 9.0 |

Mean of the sample means:

$$\mu_{\bar{X}} = \frac{\sum \bar{X}}{number\ of\ samples} = \frac{100}{25} = 4.0$$

Variance of the sample means:

$$\sigma^2_{\bar{X}} = \frac{(number\ of\ samples)\sum \bar{X}^2 - \left(\sum \bar{X}\right)^2}{(number\ of\ samples)^2} = \frac{25(500) - 10,000}{(25)^2} = 4.0$$

tion of the mean will always be equal to the population mean. Third, we define **sampling error** in this context as the difference (or deviation) between a particular sample mean and the population mean, denoted as $\bar{X} - \mu_X$. A positive sampling error indicates a sample mean greater than the population mean, where the sample mean is known as an **overestimate** of the population mean. A zero sampling error indicates a sample mean exactly equal to the population mean. A negative sampling error indicates a sample mean less than the population mean, where the sample mean is known as an **underestimate** of the population mean.

**Variance Error of the Mean.** Now that we have a measure of the mean of the sampling distribution of the mean, let us consider the variance of this distribution. We define the variance of the sampling distribution of the mean, known as the **variance error of the mean**, as $\sigma^2_{\bar{X}}$. This will provide us with a dispersion measure of the extent to which the sample means vary and will also provide some indication of the confidence we can place in a particular sample mean. The variance error of the mean is computed as

$$\sigma^2_{\bar{X}} = \frac{\sigma^2_X}{n}$$

where $\sigma^2_X$ is the population variance of $X$ and $n$ is the sample size. For the example, we have already determined that $\sigma^2_X = 8$ and that $n = 2$; therefore,

$$\sigma^2_{\bar{X}} = \frac{\sigma^2_X}{n} = \frac{8}{2} = 4$$

This is verified in the bottom portion of Table 5.1, called "Variance of the sample means," where the variance error is computed from the collection of sample means.

What will happen if we increase the size of the sample? If we increase the sample size to $n = 4$, then the variance error is reduced to 2. Thus we see that as the size of the sample $n$ increases, the magnitude of the sampling error decreases. Why? Conceptually, as sample size increases, we are sampling a larger portion of the population. In doing so, we are also obtaining a sample that is likely more representative of the population. In addition, the larger the sample size, the less likely it is to obtain a sample mean that is far from the population mean. Thus, as sample size increases, we hone in closer and closer to the population mean and have less and less sampling error.

For example, say we are sampling from a voting district with a population of 5,000 voters. A survey is developed to assess how satisfied the district voters are with their local state representative. Assume the survey generates a 100-point satisfaction scale. First we determine that the population mean satisfaction is 75. Next we take samples of different sizes. For a sample size of 1, we find sample means that range from 0 to 100 (i.e., each mean really only represents a single observation). For a sample size of 10, we find sample means that range from 50 to 95. For a sample size of 100, we find sample means that range from 70 to 80. We see then that as sample size increases, our sample means become closer and closer to the population mean, and the variability of those sample means becomes smaller and smaller.

**Standard Error of the Mean.**   We can also compute the standard deviation of the sampling distribution of the mean, known as the **standard error of the mean,** by

$$\sigma_{\bar{X}} = \frac{\sigma_X}{\sqrt{n}}$$

Thus for the example we have

$$\sigma_{\bar{X}} = \frac{\sigma_X}{\sqrt{n}} = \frac{2.8284}{\sqrt{2}} = 2$$

Because the applied researcher typically does not know the population variance, the population variance error of the mean and the population standard error of the mean can be estimated by

$$s^2_{\bar{X}} = \frac{s^2_X}{n}$$

and

$$s_{\bar{X}} = \frac{s_X}{\sqrt{n}}$$

respectively.

**Confidence Intervals.** Thus far we have illustrated how a sample mean is a **point estimate** of the population mean and how a variance error gives us some sense of the variability among the sample means. Putting these concepts together, we can also build an **interval estimate** for the population mean to give us a sense of how confident we are in our particular sample mean. We can form a **confidence interval** around a particular sample mean as follows. As we learned in chapter 4, for a normal distribution 68% of the distribution falls within one standard deviation of the mean. A 68% confidence interval (CI) of a sample mean can be formed as follows:

$$68\% \, \text{CI} = \bar{X} \pm \sigma_{\bar{X}}$$

Conceptually this means that if we form 68% confidence intervals for 100 sample means, then 68 of those 100 intervals would contain or include the population mean. Because the applied researcher typically only has one sample mean and does not know the population mean, he or she has no way of knowing if this one confidence interval actually contains the population mean or not. If one wanted to be more confident in a sample mean, then a 90% CI, a 95% CI, or a 99% CI could be formed as follows:

$$90\% \, \text{CI} = \bar{X} \pm 1.645 \, \sigma_{\bar{X}}$$

$$95\% \, \text{CI} = \bar{X} \pm 1.96 \, \sigma_{\bar{X}}$$

$$99\% \, \text{CI} = \bar{X} \pm 2.5758 \, \sigma_{\bar{X}}$$

Thus for the 90% CI, the population mean will be contained in 90 out of 100 CIs; for the 95% CI, the population mean will be contained in 95 out of 100 CIs; and for the 99% CI, the population mean will be contained in 99 out of 100 CIs. The values of 1.645, 1.96, and 2.5758 are areas that come from the standard unit normal distribution table (Appendix Table 1) and indicate the width of the confidence interval. Wider confidence intervals, such as the 99% CI, enable greater confidence. For example, with a sample mean of 70 and a standard error of the mean of 3, the following confidence intervals result: 68% CI = (67, 73) [i.e., ranging from 67 to 73]; 90% CI = (65.065, 74.935); 95% CI = (64.12, 75.88); and 99% CI = (62.2726, 77.7274).

In general, a confidence interval for any level of confidence (i.e., *XX*% CI) can be computed by the following general formula:

$$XX\% \, \text{CI} = \bar{X} \pm z_{cv} \, \sigma_{\bar{X}}$$

where $z_{cv}$ is the critical value taken from the standard unit normal distribution table for that particular level of confidence, and the other values are as before.

**Central Limit Theorem.** In our discussion of confidence intervals, we used the normal distribution to help determine the width of the intervals. Many inferential statistics assume the population distribution is normal in shape. Because we are looking at sampling distributions in this chapter, does the shape of the original population distribution have any relationship to the sampling distribution of the mean we obtain? For example, if the population distribution is nonnormal, what form does the sampling distribution of the mean take? There is a nice concept, known as the **central limit theorem**, to assist us here. The central limit theorem states that as sample size $n$ increases, the sampling distribution of the mean from a random sample of size $n$ more closely approximates a normal distribution. If the population distribution is normal in shape, then the sampling distribution of the mean is also normal in shape. If the population distribution is not normal in shape, then the sampling distribution of the mean becomes more nearly normal as sample size increases. This concept is graphically depicted in Fig. 5.1.

The top row of the figure depicts two population distributions, the left one being normal and the right one being positively skewed. The remaining rows are for the various sampling distributions, depending on the sample size. The second row shows the sampling distributions of the mean for $n = 1$. Note that these sampling distributions look precisely like the population distributions, as each observation is literally a sample mean. The next row gives the sampling distributions for $n = 2$, and we see for the skewed population that the sampling distribution is slightly less skewed. This is because the more extreme observations are now being averaged in with less extreme observations, yielding less extreme means. For $n = 4$ the sampling distribution in the skewed case is even less skewed than for $n = 2$. Eventually we reach the $n = 25$ sampling distribution, where the sampling distribution for the skewed case is nearly normal and nearly matches the sampling distribution for the normal case. This will occur for other nonnormal population distributions as well (e.g., negatively skewed). The morale of the story here is a good one. If the population distribution is nonnormal, this will have minimal effect on the sampling distribution of the mean except for rather small samples. This can come into play with inferential statistics when the assumption of normality is not satisfied, as we see in later chapters.

## 5.3 SUMMARY

In this chapter we began to move from descriptive statistics to the realm of inferential statistics. The two main topics we considered were probability, and sampling and estimation. First we briefly introduced probability by looking at the importance of probability in statistics, defining probability, and comparing conclusions often reached by intuition versus probability. The second topic involved sampling and estimation, a topic we return to in several subsequent chapters. In the sampling section we defined and described simple random sampling, both with and without replacement, and briefly outlined other types of sampling. In the estimation section, we examined the sampling distribution of the mean, the variance and standard error of the mean, confidence intervals around the mean, and the central limit theorem. At this point you should have met the following objectives: (a) be able to understand the most basic concepts of probability, (b) be able to understand and conduct simple random sampling, and (c) be able to understand, compute, and interpret the results from the estimation of population parameters via a sample. In the next chapter we formally discuss our first inferential statistics situation, testing hypotheses about a single mean.

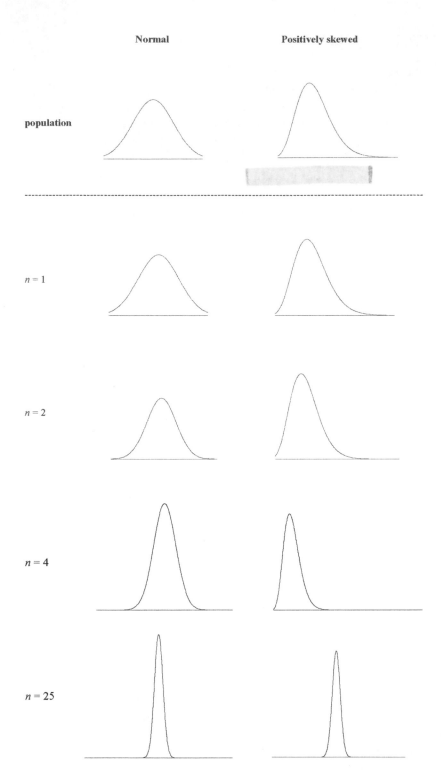

FIG. 5.1    Central limit theorem for normal and positively skewed population distributions.

## PROBLEMS

### Conceptual Problems

1.  The standard error of the mean is the
    a.  standard deviation of a sample distribution.
    b.  standard deviation of the population distribution.
    c.  standard deviation of the sampling distribution of the mean.
    d.  mean of the sampling distribution of the standard deviation.

2.  An unbiased six-sided die is tossed on two consecutive trials and the first toss results in a "2." What is the probability that a "2" will result on the second toss?
    a.  less than $\frac{1}{6}$
    b.  $\frac{1}{6}$
    c.  more than $\frac{1}{6}$
    d.  cannot be determined

3.  An urn contains 9 balls: 3 green, 4 red, and 2 blue. The probability that a ball selected at random is blue is equal to
    a.  $\frac{2}{9}$.
    b.  $\frac{5}{9}$.
    c.  $\frac{6}{9}$.
    d.  $\frac{7}{9}$.

4.  Sampling error is
    a.  the amount by which a sample mean is greater than the population mean.
    b.  the amount of difference between a sample statistic and a population parameter.
    c.  the standard deviation divided by the square root of $n$.
    d.  when the sample is not drawn randomly.

5.  The central limit theorem states that
    a.  the means of many random samples from a population will be normally distributed.
    b.  the raw scores of many natural events will be normally distributed.
    c.  $z$ scores will be normally distributed.
    d.  none of the above

6.  For a normal population, the variance of the sampling distribution of the mean increases as sample size increases. True or false?

7.  All other things being equal, as the sample size increases, the standard error of a statistic decreases. True or false?

8.  I assert that the 95% CI has a larger range than the 99% CI for the same parameter using the same data. Am I correct?

9.   I assert that the mean and median of any random sample drawn from a symmetric population distribution will be equal. Am I correct?

10.  A random sample is to be drawn from a symmetric population with mean 100 and variance 225. I assert that the sample mean is more likely to have a value larger than 105 if the sample size is 16 than if the sample size is 25. Am I correct?

11.  A gambler is playing a card game where the known probability of winning is .40 (win 40% of the time). The gambler has just lost 10 consecutive hands. What is the probability of the gambler winning the next hand?

a.   less than .40

b.   equal to .40

c.   greater than .40

d.   cannot be determined without observing the gambler

12.  The probability of being selected into a sample is the same for every individual in the population for the convenient method of sampling. True or false?

13.  Sampling error increases with larger samples. True or false?

14.  If a population distribution is highly positively skewed, then the distribution of the sample means for samples of size 500 will be

a.   highly negatively skewed

b.   highly positively skewed

c.   approximately normally distributed

d.   cannot be determined without further information

## Computational Problems

1.   The population distribution of variable $X$, number of pets owned, consists of the five values of 1, 4, 5, 7, and 8.

a.   Calculate the values of the population mean and variance.

b.   List all possible samples of size 2 where samples are drawn with replacement.

c.   Calculate the values of the mean and variance of the sampling distribution of the mean.

2.   The following is a random sampling distribution of the mean number of children for samples of size 3, where samples are drawn with replacement.

| Sample mean | $f$ |
|---|---|
| 5 | 1 |
| 4 | 2 |
| 3 | 4 |
| 2 | 2 |
| 1 | 1 |

      a.   What is the population mean?

      b.   What is the population variance?

      c.   What is the mean of the sampling distribution of the mean?

      d.   What is the variance error of the mean?

3. In a study of the entire student body of a large university, if the standard error of the mean is 20 for $n = 16$, what must the sample size be to reduce the standard error to 5?

4. A random sample of 13 statistics texts had a mean number of pages of 685 and a standard deviation of 42. First calculate the standard error of the mean. Then calculate the 95% CI for the mean length of statistics texts.

## Interpretive Problem

Take a six-sided die, where the population values are obviously 1, 2, 3, 4, 5, and 6. Take 20 samples, each of size 2 (e.g., every two rolls is one sample). For each sample calculate the mean. Then determine the mean of the sampling distribution of the mean and the variance error of the mean. Compare your results to those of your colleagues.

# 6

# INTRODUCTION TO HYPOTHESIS TESTING: INFERENCES ABOUT A SINGLE MEAN

## Chapter Outline

1.  Types of hypotheses
2.  Types of decision errors
    Example decision-making situation
    Decision-making table
3.  Level of significance ($\alpha$)
4.  Overview of steps in the decision-making process
5.  Inferences about $\mu$ when $\sigma$ is known
    The $z$ test
    An example
    Constructing confidence intervals around the mean
6.  Type II error ($\alpha$) and power ($1 - \beta$)
    The full decision-making context
    Power determinants
7.  Statistical versus practical significance
8.  Inferences about $\mu$ when $\sigma$ is unknown
    A new test statistic $t$
    The $t$ distribution
    The $t$ test
    An example
9.  SPSS

## Key Concepts

1. Null or statistical hypothesis versus scientific or research hypothesis
2. Type I error ($\alpha$), type II error ($\beta$), and power ($1 - \beta$)
3. Two-tailed versus one-tailed alternative hypotheses
4. Critical regions and critical values
5. $z$ test statistic
6. Confidence interval around the mean
7. $t$ test statistic
8. $t$ distribution, degrees of freedom, and table of $t$ distributions

In chapter 5 we began to move into the realm of inferential statistics. There we considered the following general topics: probability, sampling, and estimation. In this chapter we move totally into the domain of inferential statistics, where the concepts involved in probability, sampling, and estimation can be implemented. The overarching theme of the chapter is the use of a statistical test to make inferences about a single mean. In order to properly cover this inferential test, a number of basic foundational concepts are described in this chapter. Many of these concepts are utilized throughout the remainder of this text. The topics described include the following: types of hypotheses; types of decision errors; level of significance ($\alpha$); overview of steps in the decision-making process; inferences about $\mu$ when $\sigma$ is known; Type II error ($\beta$) and power ($1 - \beta$); statistical versus practical significance; and inferences about $\mu$ when $\sigma$ is unknown. Concepts to be discussed include the following: null or statistical hypothesis versus scientific or research hypothesis; Type I error ($\alpha$), Type II error ($\beta$), and power ($1 - \beta$); two-tailed versus one-tailed alternative hypotheses; critical regions and critical values; $z$ test statistic; confidence interval around the mean; $t$ test statistic; and $t$ distribution, degrees of freedom, and table of $t$ distributions. Our objectives are that by the end of this chapter, you will be able to (a) understand the basic concepts of hypothesis testing; (b) utilize the normal and $t$ tables; and (c) understand, compute, and interpret the results from the $z$ test, $t$ test, and confidence interval procedures.

## 6.1 TYPES OF HYPOTHESES

Hypothesis testing is a decision-making process where two possible decisions are weighed in a statistical fashion. In a way this is much like any other decision involving two possibilities, such as whether to carry an umbrella with you today or not. In statistical decision-making, the two possible decisions are known as hypotheses. Sample data are then used to help us select one of these decisions. The two types of hypotheses competing against one another are known as the

**null** or **statistical hypothesis**, denoted by $H_0$, and the **scientific** or **research hypothesis**, denoted by $H_1$.

The null or statistical hypothesis is a statement about the value of an unknown population parameter. One example $H_0$ might be the population mean IQ score is 100, which we denote as

$$H_0 : \mu = 100 \quad or \quad H_0 : \mu - 100 = 0$$

The version on the left is the more traditional form of the null hypothesis involving a single mean. However, the version on the right makes clear to the reader why the term "null" is appropriate. That is, there is no difference or a "null" difference between the population mean and the hypothesized mean value of 100. In general, the hypothesized mean value is denoted by $\mu_0$ (here $\mu_0 = 100$). Another $H_0$ might be the statistics exam population means are the same for male and female students, which we denote as

$$H_0 : \mu_1 - \mu_2 = 0$$

where $\mu_1$ is the population mean for males and $\mu_2$ is the population mean for females. Here there is no difference or a "null" difference between the two population means. The test of the difference between two means is presented in chapter 7. As we move through subsequent chapters, we become familiar with null hypotheses that involve other population parameters such as proportions, variances, and correlations.

The null hypothesis is basically set up by the researcher as a "straw-man," with the idea being to try to reject the null hypothesis in favor of our own personal scientific or research hypothesis. In other words, the scientific hypothesis is what we believe the outcome of the study will be, based on previous theory and research. Thus we are trying to "knock down" the "straw-man" null hypothesis and find evidence in favor of our scientific hypothesis. The scientific hypotheses $H_1$ for our two examples are

$$H_1 : \mu \neq 100 \quad or \quad H_1 : \mu - 100 \neq 0$$

and

$$H_1 : \mu_1 - \mu_2 \neq 0$$

Based on the sample data, hypothesis testing involves making a decision as to whether the null or the research hypothesis is supported. Because we are dealing with sample statistics in our decision-making process, and trying to make an inference back to the population parameter(s), there is always some risk of making an incorrect decision. In other words, the sample data might lead us to make a decision that is not consistent with the population. We might decide to take an umbrella and it does not rain, or we might decide to leave the umbrella at home and it rains. Thus, as in any decision, the possibility always exists that an incorrect decision may be made. This uncertainty is due to sampling error, which we will see can be described by a probability statement. That is, because the decision is made based on sample data, the sample may not be very representative of the population and therefore leads us to an incorrect decision. If we had population data, we would always make the correct decision about a population parameter. Because we usually do not, we use inferential statistics to help make decisions from sample data and infer those results back to the population. The nature of such decision errors and the probabilities we can attribute to them are described in the next section.

## 6.2 TYPES OF DECISION ERRORS

In this section we consider more specifically the types of decision errors that might be made in the decision-making process. First an example decision-making situation is presented. This is followed by a decision-making table whereby the types of decision errors are easily depicted.

### 6.2.1 Example Decision-Making Situation

Let me propose an example decision-making situation using an adult intelligence instrument. It is known somehow that the population standard deviation of the instrument is 15 (i.e., $\sigma^2 = 225$, $\sigma = 15$). In the real world it is rare that the population standard deviation is known, and we return to reality later in the chapter when the basic concepts have been covered. But for now, assume that we know the population standard deviation. Our null and alternative hypotheses, respectively, are as follows:

$$H_0 : \mu = 100 \quad or \quad H_0 : \mu - 100 = 0$$
$$H_1 : \mu \neq 100 \quad or \quad H_1 : \mu - 100 \neq 0$$

Thus we are interested in testing whether the population mean for the intelligence instrument is equal to 100, our hypothesized mean value, or not equal to 100.

Next we take several random samples of individuals from the adult population. We find for our first sample $\overline{Y}_1 = 105$ (i.e., denoting the mean for sample 1). Eyeballing the information for sample 1, the sample mean is one third of a standard deviation above the hypothesized value [i.e., by computing a $z$ score of $(105 - 100)/15 = .3333$], so our conclusion would probably be, fail to reject $H_0$. In other words, if the population mean actually is 100, then we believe that one is quite likely to observe a sample mean of 105. Thus our decision for sample 1 is, fail to reject $H_0$; however, there is some likelihood or probability that our decision is incorrect.

We take a second sample and find $\overline{Y}_2 = 115$ (i.e., denoting the mean for sample 2). Eyeballing the information for sample 2, the sample mean is one standard deviation above the hypothesized value [i.e., $z = (115 - 100)/15 = 1.0000$], so our conclusion would probably be, fail to reject $H_0$. In other words, if the population mean actually is 100, then we believe that it is somewhat likely to observe a sample mean of 115. Thus our decision for sample 2 is, fail to reject $H_0$. However, there is an even greater likelihood or probability that our decision is incorrect than was the case for sample 1; this is because the sample mean is further away from the hypothesized value.

We take a third sample and find $\overline{Y}_3 = 190$ (i.e., denoting the mean for sample 3). Eyeballing the information for sample 3, the sample mean is six standard deviations above the hypothesized value [i.e., $z = (190 - 100)/15 = 6.0000$], so our conclusion would probably be, reject $H_0$. In other words, if the population mean actually is 100, then we believe that it is quite unlikely to observe a sample mean of 190. Thus our decision for sample 3 is to reject $H_0$; however, there is some small likelihood or probability that our decision is incorrect.

## 6.2.2   Decision-Making Table

Let us consider Table 6.1 as a mechanism for sorting out the possible outcomes in the statistical decision-making process. The table consists of the general case and a specific case. First, in part (a) of the table, we have the possible outcomes for the general case. For the state of nature or reality (i.e., how things really are in the population), there are two distinct possibilities as depicted by the rows of the table. Either $H_0$ is indeed true or $H_0$ is indeed false. In other words, according to the real-world conditions in the population, either $H_0$ is actually true or $H_0$ is actually false. Admittedly, we usually do not know what the state of nature truly is; however, it does exist in the population data. It is the state of nature that we are trying to best approximate when making a statistical decision based on sample data.

For our statistical decision, there are two distinct possibilities as depicted by the columns of the table. Either we fail to reject $H_0$ or we reject $H_0$. In other words, based on our sample data, we either fail to reject $H_0$ or reject $H_0$. As our goal is usually to reject $H_0$ in favor of our research hypothesis, I prefer the term **fail to reject** rather than **accept**. **Accept** implies you are willing to throw out your research hypothesis and admit defeat based on one sample. **Fail to reject** implies you still have some hope for your research hypothesis, despite evidence from a single sample to the contrary.

**TABLE 6.1**
Statistical Decision Table

*(a) General Case*

| | Decision | |
| State of Nature (reality) | Fail to reject $H_0$ | Reject $H_0$ |
| --- | --- | --- |
| $H_0$ is true | Correct decision $(1 - \alpha)$ | Type I error $(\alpha)$ |
| $H_0$ is false | Type II error $(\beta)$ | Correct decision $(1 - \beta) = $ power |

*(b) Example Rain Case*

| | Decision | |
| State of Nature (reality) | Fail to reject $H_0$ (don't carry umbrella) | Reject $H_0$ (carry umbrella) |
| --- | --- | --- |
| $H_0$ is true (no rain) | Correct decision (no umbrella needed) $(1 - \alpha)$ | Type I error (look silly) $(\alpha)$ |
| $H_0$ is false (rains) | Type II error (get wet) $(\beta)$ | Correct decision (stay dry) $(1 - \beta) = $ power |

If we look inside of the table, we see four different outcomes, based on a combination of our statistical decision and the state of nature. Consider the first row of the table where $H_0$ is in actuality true. First, if $H_0$ is true and we fail to reject $H_0$, then we have made a correct decision; that is, we have correctly failed to reject a true $H_0$. The probability of this first outcome is known as $1 - \alpha$ (alpha). Second, if $H_0$ is true and we reject $H_0$, then we have made a decision error known as a Type I error. That is, we have incorrectly rejected a true $H_0$. Our sample data has led us to a different conclusion than the population data would have. The probability of this second outcome is known as $\alpha$. Therefore if $H_0$ is actually true, then our sample data lead us to one of two conclusions, either we correctly fail to reject $H_0$, or we incorrectly reject $H_0$. The sum of the probabilities for these two outcomes when $H_0$ is true is equal to 1 [i.e., $(1 - \alpha) + \alpha = 1$].

Consider now the second row of the table where $H_0$ is in actuality false. First, if $H_0$ is really false and we fail to reject $H_0$, then we have made a decision error known as a Type II error. That is, we have incorrectly failed to reject a false $H_0$. Our sample data has led us to a different conclusion than the population data would have. The probability of this outcome is known as $\beta$ (beta). Second, if $H_0$ is really false and we reject $H_0$, then we have made a correct decision; that is, we have correctly rejected a false $H_0$. The probability of this second outcome is known as power or $1 - \beta$ (to be more fully discussed later in this chapter). Therefore if $H_0$ is actually false, then our sample data lead us to one of two conclusions, either we incorrectly fail to reject $H_0$, or we correctly reject $H_0$. The sum of the probabilities for these two outcomes when $H_0$ is false is equal to 1 [i.e., $\beta + (1 - \beta) = 1$].

As an application of this table, consider the following specific case, as shown in part (b) of Table 6.1. We wish to test the following hypotheses about whether or not it will rain tomorrow.

$$H_0: \text{ no rain tomorrow}$$

$$H_1: \text{ rains tomorrow}$$

We collect some sample data from a prior year for the same month and day, and go to make our statistical decision. Our two possible statistical decisions are (a) we do not believe it will rain tomorrow and therefore do not bring an umbrella with us, or (b) we do believe it will rain tomorrow and therefore do bring an umbrella.

Again there are four potential outcomes. First, if $H_0$ is really true (no rain) and we do not carry an umbrella, then we have made a correct decision as no umbrella is necessary (probability $= 1 - \alpha$). Second, if $H_0$ is really true (no rain) and we carry an umbrella, then we have made a Type I error as we look silly carrying that umbrella around all day (probability $= \alpha$). Third, if $H_0$ is really false (rains) and we do not carry an umbrella, then we have made a Type II error and we get wet (probability $= \beta$). Fourth, if $H_0$ is really false (rains) and we carry an umbrella, then we have made the correct decision as the umbrella keeps us dry (probability $= 1 - \beta$).

Let me make two concluding statements about the decision table. First, one can never prove the truth or falsity of $H_0$ in a single study. One only gathers evidence in favor of or in opposition to the null hypothesis. Something is proven in research when an entire collection of studies or evidence reaches the same conclusion time and time again. Scientific proof is difficult to achieve in the social and behavioral sciences, and we should not use the term **prove** or **proof** loosely. As researchers, we gather multiple pieces of evidence that eventually lead to the development of one or more theories. When a theory is shown to be unequivocally true (i.e., in all cases), then proof has been established.

Second, let us consider the decision errors in a different light. One can totally eliminate the possibility of a Type I error by deciding to never reject $H_0$. That is, if we always fail to reject $H_0$ (don't ever carry umbrella), then we can never make a Type I error (look silly with unnecessary umbrella). Although this sounds well and good, such a strategy totally takes the decision-making power out of our hands. With this strategy we do not even need to collect any sample data, as we have already decided to never reject $H_0$.

One can totally eliminate the possibility of a Type II error by deciding to always reject $H_0$. That is, if we always reject $H_0$ (always carry umbrella), then we can never make a Type II error (get wet without umbrella). Although this also sounds well and good, such a strategy totally takes the decision-making power out of our hands. With this strategy we do not even need to collect any sample data as we have already decided to always reject $H_0$. Taken together, one can never totally eliminate the possibility of both a Type I and a Type II error. No matter what decision we make, there is always some possibility of making a Type I and/or a Type II error.

## 6.3   LEVEL OF SIGNIFICANCE ($\alpha$)

We have already stated that a Type I error occurs when the decision is to reject $H_0$ when in fact $H_0$ is actually true. We defined the probability of a Type I error as $\alpha$. We now examine $\alpha$ as a basis for helping us make statistical decisions. Recall from a previous example that the null and alternative hypotheses, respectively, are as follows.

$$H_0: \mu = 100 \quad or \quad H_0: \mu - 100 = 0$$
$$H_1: \mu \neq 100 \quad or \quad H_1: \mu - 100 \neq 0$$

We need a mechanism for deciding how far away a sample mean needs to be from the hypothesized mean value of $\mu_0 = 100$ in order to reject $H_0$. In other words, at a certain point or distance away from 100, we will decide to reject $H_0$. We use $\alpha$ to determine that point for us, where in this context $\alpha$ is known as the level of significance. Figure 6.1 (a) shows a sampling distribution of the mean where the hypothesized value $\mu_0$ is depicted at the center of the distribution. Toward both tails of the distribution, we see two shaded regions known as the critical regions or regions of rejection. The combined areas of the two shaded regions is equal to $\alpha$, and thus the area of either the upper or the lower tail critical region is equal to $\alpha/2$ (i.e., we split $\alpha$ in half). If the sample mean is far enough away from $\mu_0$ that it falls into either critical region, then our statistical decision is to reject $H_0$. In this case our decision is to reject $H_0$ at the $\alpha$ level of significance. If, however, the sample mean is close enough to $\mu_0$ that it falls into the unshaded region (i.e., not into either critical region), then our statistical decision is to fail to reject $H_0$. The precise points at which the critical regions are divided from the unshaded region are known as the critical values. Determining critical values is discussed later in this chapter.

Note that under the alternative hypothesis $H_1$, we are willing to reject $H_0$ when the sample mean is either significantly greater than or significantly less than the hypothesized mean value $\mu_0$. This particular alternative hypothesis is known as a **nondirectional alternative hypothesis**, as no direction is implied with respect to the hypothesized value. That is, we will reject the null hypothesis in favor of the alternative hypothesis in either direction, either above or below the hypothesized mean value. This also results in what is known as a **two-tailed test of significance** in that we are willing to reject the null hypothesis in either tail or critical region.

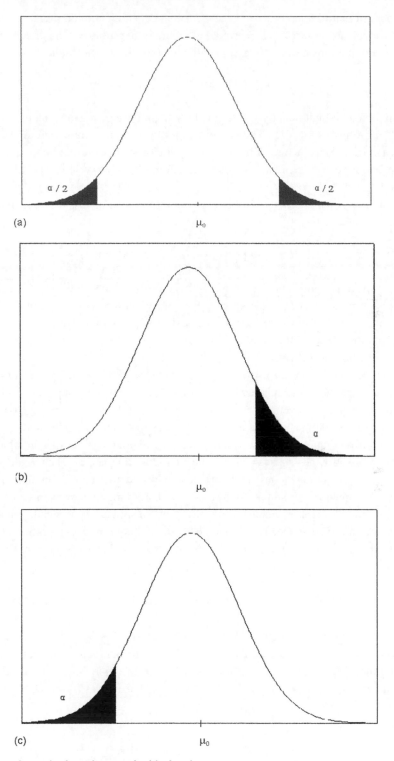

**FIG. 6.1 Alternative hypotheses and critical regions.**

Two other alternative hypotheses are also possible, depending on the researcher's scientific hypothesis, which are known as a **directional alternative hypothesis**. One directional alternative is that the population mean is greater than the hypothesized mean value, as denoted by

$$H_1: \mu > 100 \quad or \quad H_1: \mu - 100 > 0$$

If the sample mean is significantly greater than the hypothesized mean value of 100, then our statistical decision is to reject $H_0$. The entire region of rejection is contained in the upper tail, with an area of $\alpha$, known as a **one-tailed test of significance**. If, however, the sample mean falls into the unshaded region, then our statistical decision is to fail to reject $H_0$. This situation is depicted in Fig. 6.1 (b).

A second directional alternative is that the population mean is less than the hypothesized mean value, as denoted by

$$H_1: \mu < 100 \quad or \quad H_1: \mu - 100 < 0$$

If the sample mean is significantly less than the hypothesized mean value of 100, then our statistical decision is to reject $H_0$. The entire region of rejection is contained in the lower tail, with an area of $\alpha$, also known as a **one-tailed test of significance**. If, however, the sample mean falls into the unshaded region, then our statistical decision is to fail to reject $H_0$. This situation is depicted in Fig. 6.1 (c).

There is some potential for misuse of the different alternatives, which I consider to be an ethical matter. For example, a researcher conducts a one-tailed test with an upper tail critical region, and fails to reject $H_0$. However, the researcher notices that the sample mean is considerably below the hypothesized mean value and then decides to change the alternative hypothesis to either a nondirectional test or a one-tailed test in the other tail. This is unethical, as the researcher has looked at the data and changed the alternative hypothesis. The morale of the story is this. If there is previous and consistent empirical evidence to use a specific directional alternative hypothesis, then you should do so. If, however, there is minimal or inconsistent empirical evidence to use a specific directional alternative, then you should not. Instead, you should use a nondirectional alternative. Once you have decided which alternative hypothesis to go with, then you need to stick with it for the duration of the statistical decision. If you find contrary evidence, then report it, but do not change the alternative in midstream.

## 6.4   OVERVIEW OF STEPS IN THE DECISION-MAKING PROCESS

Before we get into the specific details of conducting the test of a single mean, I want to discuss the basic steps for any inferential test. The first step in the decision-making process is to state the null and alternative hypotheses. Recall from our previous example that the null and nondirectional alternative hypotheses, respectively, for a two-tailed test are as follows:

$$H_0: \mu = 100 \quad or \quad H_0: \mu - 100 = 0$$
$$H_1: \mu \neq 100 \quad or \quad H_1: \mu - 100 \neq 0$$

One could also choose one of the other directional alternative hypotheses described previously.

The second step in the decision-making process is to select a level of significance $\alpha$. There are two considerations to make in terms of selecting a level of significance. One consideration is the cost associated with making a Type I error, which is what $\alpha$ really is. If there is a relatively high cost associated with a Type I error—for example, such that lives are lost, as in the medical profession—then one would want to select a relatively small level of significance (e.g., .01 or smaller). If there is a relatively low cost associated with a Type I error—for example, such that children have to eat the second-rated candy rather than the first—then one would want to select a larger level of significance (e.g., .05 or larger). Costs are not always known, however. A second consideration is the level of significance commonly used in your field of study. In many disciplines the .05 level of significance has become the standard (although no one seems to have a really good rationale). This is true in many of the social and behavioral sciences. Thus, you would do well to consult the published literature in your field to see if some standard is commonly used and to consider it for your own research.

The third step in the decision-making process is to compute the sample mean $\overline{Y}$ and compare it to the hypothesized value $\mu_0$. This allows us to determine the size of the difference between $\overline{Y}$ and $\mu_0$, and subsequently the probability associated with the difference. The larger the difference, the more likely it is that the sample mean really differs from the hypothesized mean value and the larger the probability associated with the difference.

The fourth and final step in the decision-making process is to make a statistical decision regarding the null hypothesis $H_0$. That is, a decision is made whether to reject $H_0$ or to fail to reject $H_0$. If the difference between the sample mean and the hypothesized value is large enough relative to the critical value, then our decision is to reject $H_0$. If the difference between the sample mean and the hypothesized value is not large enough relative to the critical value, then our decision is to fail to reject $H_0$. This is the basic four-step process for any inferential test. The specific details for the test of a single mean are given in the following section.

## 6.5   INFERENCES ABOUT $\mu$ WHEN $\sigma$ IS KNOWN

In this section we examine how hypotheses about a single mean are conducted when the population standard deviation is known. Specifically we consider the $z$ test, an example illustrating use of the $z$ test, and how to construct a confidence interval around the mean.

### 6.5.1   The $z$ Test

Recall from chapter 4 the definition of a $z$ score as

$$z = \frac{Y_i - \mu}{\sigma_Y}$$

where $Y_i$ is the score on variable $Y$ for individual $i$, $\mu$ is the population mean for variable $Y$, and $\sigma_Y$ is the population standard deviation for variable $Y$. The $z$ score is used to tell us how many standard deviation units an individual's score is from the mean.

In the context of this chapter, however, we are concerned with the extent to which a sample mean differs from some hypothesized mean value. We can construct a variation of the $z$ score for testing hypotheses about a single mean. In this situation we are concerned with the sampling distribution of the mean (introduced in chap. 5), so the equation must reflect means rather than raw scores. Our $z$ score equation for testing hypotheses about a single mean becomes

$$z = \frac{\overline{Y} - \mu_0}{\sigma_{\overline{Y}}}$$

where $\overline{Y}$ is the sample mean for variable $Y$, $\mu_0$ is the hypothesized mean value for variable $Y$, and $\sigma_{\overline{Y}}$ is the population standard error of the mean for variable $Y$. From chapter 5, recall the population standard error of the mean $\sigma_{\overline{Y}}$ is computed by

$$\sigma_{\overline{Y}} = \frac{\sigma_Y}{\sqrt{n}}$$

where $\sigma_Y$ is the population standard deviation for variable $Y$ and $n$ is sample size. Thus the numerator of the $z$ score equation is the difference between the sample mean and the hypothesized value of the mean, and the denominator is the standard error of the mean. What we are really determining here is how many standard deviation (or standard error) units the sample mean is from the hypothesized mean. Henceforth, we call this variation of the $z$ score the **test statistic for the test of a single mean**, also known as the $z$ **test**. This is the first of several test statistics we describe in this text; every inferential test requires some test statistic for purposes of testing hypotheses.

We need to make a statistical assumption regarding this hypothesis testing situation. We assume that $z$ is normally distributed with a mean of 0 and a standard deviation of 1. This is written statistically as $z \sim N(0, 1)$ following the notation we developed in chapter 4. Thus, the assumption is that $z$ follows the unit normal distribution. An examination of our test statistic $z$ reveals that only the sample mean can vary from sample to sample. The hypothesized value and the standard error of the mean are constant for every sample of size $n$ from the same population.

In order to make a statistical decision, the critical regions need to be defined. As the test statistic is $z$ and we have assumed normality, then the relevant theoretical distribution to compare the test statistic to is the unit normal distribution. We previously discussed this distribution in chapter 4, and the table of values is given in Appendix Table 1. If the alternative hypothesis is nondirectional, then there would be two critical regions, one in the upper tail and one in the lower tail. Here we would split the area of the critical region, known as $\alpha$, in two. If the alternative hypothesis is directional, then there would only be one critical region, either in the upper tail or in the lower tail, depending on which direction one is willing to reject $H_0$.

## 6.5.2  An Example

Let us illustrate use of this inferential test through an example. We are interested in testing whether the population of undergraduate students from Awesome State University (ASU) has a mean intelligence test score different from the hypothesized mean value of $\mu_0 = 100$. A nondirectional alternative hypothesis is of interest as we simply want to know if this population has a mean intelligence different from the hypothesized value, either greater than or less than. Thus, the null and alternative hypotheses can be written respectively as follows:

$$H_0: \mu = 100 \quad or \quad H_0: \mu - 100 = 0$$

$$H_1: \mu \neq 100 \quad or \quad H_1: \mu - 100 \neq 0$$

A sample mean of $\overline{Y} = 103$ is observed for a sample of $n = 100$ ASU undergraduate students. From the development of this intelligence test, we know that the theoretical population standard deviation is $\sigma_Y = 15$. The standard level of significance in this field is the .05 level; thus, we perform our significance test at $\alpha = .05$. First we compute the standard error of the mean by

$$\sigma_{\overline{Y}} = \frac{\sigma_Y}{\sqrt{n}} = \frac{15}{\sqrt{100}} = 1.5000$$

Second, we compute the test statistic $z$ as

$$z = \frac{\overline{Y} - \mu_0}{\sigma_{\overline{Y}}} = \frac{103 - 100}{1.5000} = 2.0000$$

Next, we look up the critical values from the unit normal distribution in Appendix Table 1. Since $\alpha = .05$ and we are conducting a nondirectional test, we need to find critical values for the upper and lower tails, where the area of each of the two critical regions is equal to .025. From the unit normal table we find these critical values to be $+1.96$ (area above $= .025$) and $-1.96$ (area below $= .025$). Finally, we make our statistical decision by comparing the test statistic $z$ to these critical values. As shown in Fig. 6.2, the test statistic $z = 2$ falls into the upper tail critical region, just slightly larger than the upper tail critical value of $+1.96$. Our decision is to reject

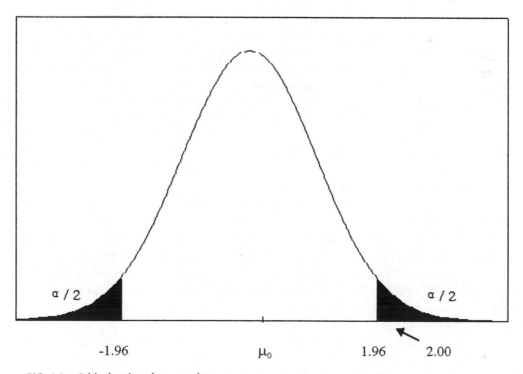

**FIG. 6.2   Critical regions for example.**

$H_0$ and conclude that the ASU population from which the sample was selected has a mean intelligence score different from the hypothesized mean of 100 at the .05 level of significance.

A more precise way of thinking about the same process is to determine the **exact probability** of observing a sample mean that differs from the hypothesized mean value. From the unit normal table, the area above $z = 2$ is equal to .0228. Therefore the area below $z = -2$ is also equal to .0228. Thus the probability $p$ of observing a sample mean of 2 or more standard errors from the hypothesized mean value of 100, in either direction, is $p = 2(.0228) = .0456$. As this exact probability is smaller than our level of significance $\alpha = .05$, we reject $H_0$. Thus there are two approaches to dealing with probability. One approach is a decision based solely on the critical values. Either we reject or fail to reject $H_0$ at a given $\alpha$ level, but no other information is provided. The other approach is a decision based on comparing exact probability to the given $\alpha$ level. Either we reject or fail to reject $H_0$, but we also have information available about the closeness or confidence in that decision.

For this example, the findings in a manuscript would be reported either as $z = 2(p < .05)$, or as $z = 2(p = .0456)$. Obviously the conclusion is the same with either approach; it is just a matter of how the results are reported. Most statistical computer programs, including SPSS, report the exact probability so that the reader can make a decision based on their own selected level of significance. These programs do not provide the critical value(s), which are only found in the appendices of statistics textbooks.

### 6.5.3   Constructing Confidence Intervals Around the Mean

Recall our discussion from chapter 5 on confidence intervals (CI). Confidence intervals are often quite useful in inferential statistics for providing the researcher with an interval estimate of a population parameter. Although the sample mean gives us a point estimate of a population mean, a confidence interval gives us an interval estimate of a population mean and allows us to determine the accuracy of the sample mean. For the inferential test of a single mean, a confidence interval around the sample mean $\overline{Y}$ is formed from

$$\overline{Y} \pm z_{cv}\, \sigma_{\overline{Y}}$$

where $z_{cv}$ is the critical value from the unit normal distribution and $\sigma_{\overline{Y}}$ is the population standard error of the mean.

Confidence intervals are generally only formed for nondirectional or two-tailed tests as shown in the equation. A confidence interval will generate a lower and an upper limit. If the hypothesized mean value falls within the lower and upper limits, then we would fail to reject $H_0$. In other words, if the hypothesized mean is contained in (or falls within) the confidence interval around the sample mean, then we conclude that the sample mean and the hypothesized mean are not significantly different and that the sample mean could have come from a population with the hypothesized mean. If the hypothesized mean value falls outside the limits of the interval, then we would reject $H_0$. Here we conclude that it is unlikely that the sample mean could have come from a population with the hypothesized mean.

One way to think about CIs is as follows. Imagine we take 100 random samples of the same sample size $n$, compute each sample mean, and then construct each 95% confidence interval. Then we can say that 95% of these CIs will contain the population parameter and 5% will not.

In short, 95% of similarly constructed CIs will contain the population parameter. It should also be mentioned that at a particular level of significance, one will always obtain the same statistical decision with both the hypothesis test and the confidence interval. The two procedures use precisely the same values. The hypothesis test is based on a point estimate; the CI is based on an interval estimate providing the researcher with a little more information.

For the ASU example situation, the 95% CI would be computed by

$$\overline{Y} \pm z_{cv}\ \sigma_{\overline{Y}} = 103 \pm 1.96\,(1.5) = 103 \pm 2.94 = (100.06, 105.94)$$

Thus, the 95% confidence interval ranges from 100.06 to 105.94. Because the interval does not contain the hypothesized mean value of 100, we reject $H_0$. Thus, it is quite unlikely that our sample mean could have come from a population distribution with a mean of 100.

## 6.6   TYPE II ERROR ($\beta$) AND POWER ($1 - \beta$)

In this section we complete our discussion of Type II error ($\beta$) and power ($1 - \beta$). First we return to our rain example and discuss the entire decision-making context. Then we describe the factors which determine power.

### 6.6.1   The Full Decision-Making Context

Previously we defined Type II error as the probability of failing to reject $H_0$ when $H_0$ is really false. In other words, in reality $H_0$ is false, yet we made a decision error and did not reject $H_0$. The probability associated with a Type II error is denoted by $\beta$. Power is a related concept and is defined as the probability of rejecting $H_0$ when $H_0$ is really false. In other words, in reality $H_0$ is false, and we made the correct decision to reject $H_0$. The probability associated with power is denoted by $1 - \beta$. Let us return to our "rain" example to describe Type I and Type II error and power more completely.

The full decision-making context for the "rain" example is given in Fig. 6.3. The distribution on the left-hand side of the figure is the sampling distribution when $H_0$ is true, meaning in reality it does not rain. The vertical line represents the critical value for deciding whether to carry an umbrella or not. To the left of the vertical line we do not carry an umbrella, and to the right side of the vertical line we do carry an umbrella. For the no-rain sampling distribution on the left, there are two possibilities. First, we do not carry an umbrella and it does not rain. This is the unshaded portion under the no-rain sampling distribution to the left of the vertical line. This is a correct decision, and the probability associated with this decision is $1 - \alpha$. Second, we do carry an umbrella and it does not rain. This is the shaded portion under the no-rain sampling distribution to the right of the vertical line. This is an incorrect decision, a Type I error, and the probability associated with this decision is $\alpha/2$ in either the upper or lower tail and $\alpha$ collectively.

The distribution on the right-hand side of the figure is the sampling distribution when $H_0$ is false, meaning in reality it does rain. For the rain sampling distribution, there are two possibilities. First, we do carry an umbrella and it does rain. This is the unshaded portion under the rain sampling distribution to the right of the vertical line. This is a correct decision and the probability associated with this decision is $1 - \beta$ or power. Second, we do not carry an umbrella and it does rain. This is the shaded portion under the rain sampling distribution to the left of

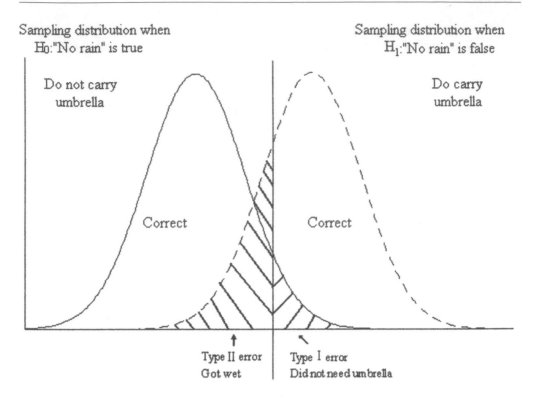

Sampling distribution when
H₀:"No rain" is true

Sampling distribution when
H₁:"No rain" is false

**FIG. 6.3    Sampling distributions for the rain case.**

the vertical line. This is an incorrect decision, a Type II error, and the probability associated with this decision is $\beta$.

As a second illustration, consider again the example intelligence test situation. This situation is depicted in Fig. 6.4. The distribution on the left-hand side of the figure is the sampling distribution of $\overline{Y}$ when $H_0$ is true, meaning in reality $\mu = 100$. The vertical line represents the critical value for deciding whether to reject the null hypothesis or not. To the left of the vertical line we do not reject $H_0$ and to the right of the vertical line we reject $H_0$. For the $H_0$ is true sampling distribution on the left, there are two possibilities. First, we do not reject $H_0$ and $H_0$ is really true. This is the unshaded portion under the $H_0$ is true sampling distribution to the left of the vertical line. This is a correct decision and the probability associated with this decision is $1 - \alpha$. Second, we reject $H_0$ and $H_0$ is true. This is the shaded portion under the $H_0$ is true sampling distribution to the right of the vertical line. This is an incorrect decision, a Type I error, and the probability associated with this decision is $\alpha/2$ in either the upper or lower tail and $\alpha$ collectively.

The distribution on the right-hand side of the figure is the sampling distribution when $H_0$ is false, and in particular, when $H_1: \mu = 115$ is true. This is a specific sampling distribution when $H_0$ is false, and other possible sampling distributions can also be examined (e.g., $\mu = 85, 110$, etc.). For the $H_1: \mu = 115$ is true sampling distribution, there are two possibilities. First, we do reject $H_0$, $H_0$ is really false, and $H_1: \mu = 115$ is really true. This is the unshaded portion under the $H_1: \mu = 115$ is true sampling distribution to the right of the vertical line. This is a correct decision, and the probability associated with this decision is $1 - \beta$ or power. Second, we

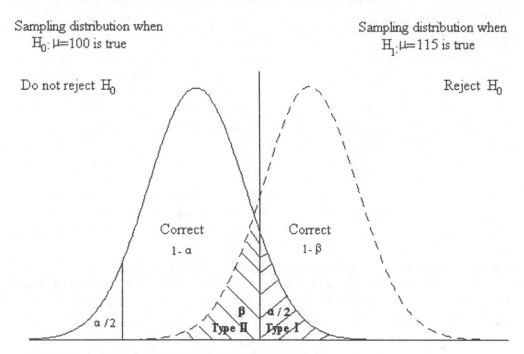

**FIG. 6.4    Sampling distributions for the intelligence test case.**

do not reject $H_0$, $H_0$ is really false, and $H_1$: $\mu = 115$ is really true. This is the shaded portion under the $H_1$: $\mu = 115$ is true sampling distribution to the left of the vertical line. This is an incorrect decision, a Type II error, and the probability associated with this decision is $\beta$.

## 6.6.2    Power Determinants

Power is determined by five different factors. First, power is determined by the level of significance $\alpha$. As $\alpha$ increases, power increases. Thus, if $\alpha$ increases from .05 to .10, then power will increase. This would occur in Fig. 6.4 if the vertical line were shifted to the left. This would increase the $\alpha$ level and also increase power. This factor is under the control of the researcher.

Second, power is determined by sample size. As sample size $n$ increase, power increases. Thus, if sample size increases, meaning we have a sample that consists of a larger proportion of the population, this will cause the standard error of the mean to decrease, as there is less sampling error with larger samples. This would also result in the vertical line being moved to the left. This factor is also under the control of the researcher. In addition, because a larger sample yields a smaller standard error, it will be easier to reject $H_0$ (all else being equal), and the confidence intervals generated will also be narrower.

Third, power is determined by the size of the population standard deviation $\sigma$. Although not under the researcher's control, as $\sigma$ increases, power decreases. Thus if $\sigma$ increases meaning the variability in the population is larger, this will cause the standard error of the mean to increase as there is more sampling error with larger variability. This would result in the vertical line being moved to the right.

Fourth, power is determined by the difference between the true population mean $\mu$ and the hypothesized mean value $\mu_0$. Although not always under the researcher's control (only in true experiments as described in chap. 14), as the difference between the true population mean and the hypothesized mean value increases, power increases. Thus if the difference between the true population mean and the hypothesized mean value is large, it will be easier to correctly reject $H_0$. This would result in greater separation between the two sampling distributions. In other words, the entire $H_1$ is true sampling distribution would be shifted to the right.

Finally, power is determined by whether we conduct a one- or a two-tailed test. There is greater power in a one-tailed test, such as when $\mu > 100$, than in a two-tailed test. In a one-tailed test the vertical line will be shifted to the left. This factor is under the researcher's control.

Power has become of much greater interest and concern to the applied researcher in recent years. We begin by distinguishing between **a priori power**, when power is determined as a study is being planned (i.e., prior to the study), and **post hoc power**, when power is determined after the study has been conducted.

For a priori power, if you want to insure a certain amount of power in a study, then you can determine what sample size would be needed to achieve such a level of power. This requires the input of characteristics such as $\alpha$, $n$, $\sigma$, the difference between $\mu$ and $\mu_0$, and one- versus two-tailed test (or alternatively one could determine power given each of those characteristics). This can be done by either using statistical software [such as Power and Precision, Ex-Sample, or a CD provided with the Murphy & Myors (2004) text], or by using tables [the most definitive collection of tables being in Cohen (1988)].

For post hoc power (also called observed power), most statistical software packages will compute this as part of the analysis for many types of inferential statistics (e.g., SPSS, SAS, STATGRAPHICS). However, even though post hoc power is routinely reported in some journals, it has been found to have some flaws. For example, Hoenig and Heisey (2001) concluded that it should not be used to aid in interpreting nonsignificant results. They found that low power may indicate a small effect (e.g., a small mean difference) rather than an underpowered study. Thus increasing sample size may not make much of a difference. Yuan and Maxwell (2005) found that observed power is almost always biased (too high or too low), except when true power is .50. Thus we do not recommend the sole use of post hoc power to determine sample size in the next study; rather it is recommended that CIs be used in addition to post hoc power.

## 6.7   STATISTICAL VERSUS PRACTICAL SIGNIFICANCE

We have discussed the inferential test of a single mean in terms of statistical significance. However, are statistically significant results always practically significant? In other words, if a result is statistically significant, should we make a big deal out of this result in a practical sense? Consider again the simple example where the null and alternative hypotheses are as follows.

$$H_0: \mu = 100 \quad or \quad H_0: \mu - 100 = 0$$
$$H_1: \mu \neq 100 \quad or \quad H_1: \mu - 100 \neq 0$$

A sample mean intelligence test score of $\overline{Y} = 101$ is observed for a sample size of $n = 2,000$ and a known population standard deviation of $\sigma_Y = 15$. If we perform the test at the .01 level of significance, we find we are able to reject $H_0$ even though the observed mean is only one unit away from the hypothesized mean value. The reason is, because the sample size is rather large, a rather small standard error of the mean is computed ($\sigma_{\overline{Y}} = 0.3354$), and we thus reject $H_0$ as the test statistic ($z = 2.9815$) exceeds the critical value ($z = 2.5758$).

Should we make a big deal out of an intelligence test sample mean that is one unit away from the hypothesized mean intelligence? The answer is: Maybe not. If we gather enough sample data, any small difference, no matter how small, can wind up being statistically significant. Thus larger samples are more likely to yield statistically significant results. Practical significance is not entirely a statistical matter. It is also a matter for the substantive field under investigation. Thus the meaningfulness of a small difference is for the substantive area to determine. All that inferential statistics can really determine is statistical significance. However, we should always keep practical significance in mind when interpreting our findings.

In recent years, a major debate has been ongoing in the statistical community about the role of significance testing. The debate centers around whether null hypothesis significance testing (NHST) best suits the needs of researchers. At one extreme, some argue that NHST is fine as is. At the other extreme, others argue that NHST should be totally abandoned. In the middle, yet others argue that NHST should be supplemented with measures of effect size. In this text I have taken the middle road believing that more information is a better choice.

Let us formally introduce the notion of effect size. While there are a number of different measures of effect size, the most commonly used measure is Cohen's $\delta$ (delta) or $d$ (1988). For the population case of the one-sample mean test, Cohen's delta is computed as follows:

$$\delta = \frac{\mu - \mu_0}{\sigma}$$

For the corresponding sample case, Cohen's $d$ is computed as follows:

$$d = \frac{\overline{Y} - \mu_0}{s}$$

For the one-sample mean test $d$ indicates how many standard deviations the sample mean is from the hypothesized mean. Thus if $d = 1.0$, the sample mean is one standard deviation away from the hypothesized mean. Cohen has proposed the following subjective standards as a convention for interpreting $d$: small effect size, $d = .2$; medium effect size, $d = .5$; large effect size, $d = .8$.

While a complete discussion of these issues is beyond this text, further information on effect sizes can be seen in special sections of *Educational & Psychological Measurement* (April 2001; August 2001) and Grissom and Kim (2005), while additional material on NHST can be viewed in Harlow, Mulaik, and Steiger (1997) and a special section of *Educational & Psychological Measurement* (October 2000).

## 6.8   INFERENCES ABOUT $\mu$ WHEN $\sigma$ IS UNKNOWN

We have already considered the inferential test involving a single mean when the population standard deviation $\sigma$ is known. However, rarely is $\sigma$ known to the applied researcher. When $\sigma$ is unknown, then the $z$ test previously discussed is no longer appropriate. In this section we consider the following: the test statistic for inferences about the mean when the population standard deviation is unknown, the $t$ distribution, the $t$ test, and an example using the $t$ test.

## 6.8.1   A New Test Statistic $t$

What is the applied researcher to do then when $\sigma$ is unknown? The answer is to estimate $\sigma$ by the sample standard deviation $s$. This changes the standard error of the mean to be

$$s_{\bar{Y}} = \frac{s_Y}{\sqrt{n}}$$

Now we are estimating two population parameters, $\mu_Y$ is being estimated by $\bar{Y}$, and $\sigma_Y$ is being estimated by $s_Y$. Both $\bar{Y}$ and $s_Y$ can vary from sample to sample. Thus, although the sampling error of the mean is taken into account explicitly in the $z$ test, we also need to take into account the sampling error of the standard deviation, which the $z$ test does not at all consider.

We now develop a new inferential test for the situation where $\sigma$ is unknown. The test statistic is known as the $t$ **test** and is computed as follows:

$$t = \frac{\bar{Y} - \mu_0}{s_{\bar{Y}}}$$

The $t$ test was developed by William Sealy Gossett, also known by the pseudonym Student, previously mentioned in chapter 1. The unit normal distribution cannot be used here for the unknown $\sigma$ situation. A different theoretical distribution must be used for determining critical values for the $t$ test, known as the $t$ **distribution**.

## 6.8.2   The $t$ Distribution

The $t$ distribution is the theoretical distribution used for determining the critical values of the $t$ test. Like the normal distribution, the $t$ distribution is actually a family of distributions. There is a different $t$ distribution for each value of degrees of freedom. However, before we look more closely at the $t$ distribution, some discussion of the **degrees of freedom** concept is necessary.

As an example, say we know a sample mean $\bar{Y} = 6$ for a sample size of $n = 5$. How many of those five observed scores are free to vary? The answer is, four scores are free to vary. If the four known scores are 2, 4, 6, and 8 and the mean is 6, then the remaining score must be 10. The remaining score is not free to vary, but is already totally determined. This is because

$$\bar{Y} = \frac{\sum_{i=1}^{n} Y_i}{n} = \frac{\sum_{i=1}^{5} Y_i}{5} = \frac{2 + 4 + 6 + 8 + Y_5}{5} = 6$$

where the sum in the numerator must be 30, and $Y_5$ must be 10. Therefore, the number of degrees of freedom is equal to 4 in this particular case, and $n - 1$ in general. For the $t$ test being considered here, we specify the degrees of freedom as $v = n - 1$ ($v$ is the Greek letter "nu"). We use $v$ often in statistics to denote some type of degrees of freedom.

Another way to think about degrees of freedom is we know the sum of the deviations $= 0$. For example, if $n = 10$, there are 10 deviations. Once the mean is known, only nine of the deviations are free to vary. A final way to think about this is that, in general, $df = (n - \#$ of restrictions$)$. For the one-sample $t$ test, because the population variance is unknown, we have to estimate it resulting in one restriction. Thus $df = (n - 1)$ for this particular inferential test.

Several members of the family of $t$ distributions are shown in Fig. 6.5. The distribution for $v = 1$ has thicker tails than the unit normal distribution and a shorter peak. This indicates that there is considerable sampling error of the sample standard deviation with only 2 observations (as $v = 2 - 1 = 1$). For $v = 5$, the tails are thinner and the peak is taller than for $v = 1$. As the degrees of freedom increase, the $t$ distribution becomes more nearly normal. For $v = \infty$ (i.e., infinity), the $t$ distribution is precisely the unit normal distribution.

A few important characteristics of the $t$ distribution are worth mentioning. First, like the unit normal distribution, the mean of any $t$ distribution is 0, and the $t$ distribution is symmetric and unimodal. Second, unlike the unit normal distribution, which has a variance of 1, the variance of a $t$ distribution is equal to

$$\sigma^2 = \frac{v}{v - 2} \quad \text{for } v > 2$$

Thus, the variance of a $t$ distribution is somewhat greater 1, but approaches 1 as $v$ increases.

The table for the $t$ distribution is given in Appendix Table 2. In looking at the table, each column header has two values. The top value is the significance level for a one-tailed test, denoted by $\alpha_1$. Thus, if you were doing a one-tailed test at the .05 level of significance, you want to look in the second column of numbers. The bottom value is the significance level for a two-tailed test, denoted by $\alpha_2$. Thus, if you were doing a two-tailed test at the .05 level of significance, you want to look in the third column of numbers. The rows of the table denote the various degrees of freedom $v$. Thus, if $v = 10$, meaning $n = 11$, you want to look in the 10th row of numbers. If $v = 10$ for $\alpha_1 = .05$, the tabled value is 1.812. This value represents the 95th percentile point in a $t$ distribution with 10 degrees of freedom. This is because the table only presents the upper tail percentiles. As the $t$ distribution is symmetric around 0, the lower tail percentiles are the same values except for a change in sign. The 5th percentile for 10 degrees of freedom then is $-1.812$. If $v = 120$ for $\alpha_1 = .05$, the tabled value is 1.658. Thus, as sample size and degrees of freedom increase, the value of $t$ decreases. This makes it easier to reject the null hypothesis when sample size is large.

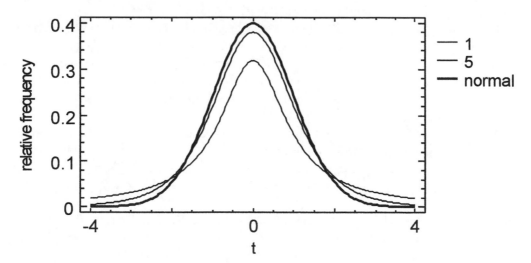

FIG. 6.5    Several members of the family of $t$ distributions.

### 6.8.3   The $t$ Test

Now that we have covered the theoretical distribution underlying the test of a single mean for an unknown $\sigma$, we can go ahead and look at the inferential test. First, the null and alternative hypotheses for the $t$ test are written in the same fashion as for the $z$ test presented earlier. Thus, for a two-tailed test we have

$$H_0: \mu = \mu_0 \quad or \quad H_0: \mu - \mu_0 = 0$$
$$H_1: \mu \neq \mu_0 \quad or \quad H_1: \mu - \mu_0 \neq 0$$

as before. The test statistic $t$ is written as

$$t = \frac{\overline{Y} - \mu_0}{s_{\overline{Y}}}$$

In order to use the theoretical $t$ distribution to determine critical values, we must assume that $Y_i \sim N(\mu, \sigma^2)$. In other words, we assume that the population of scores on $Y$ is normally distributed with some population mean $\mu$ and some population variance $\sigma^2$. The only real assumption then is normality of the population. Conventional research has shown that the $t$ test is very robust to nonnormality for a two-tailed test except for very small samples (e.g., $n < 5$). The $t$ test is not as robust to nonnormality for a one-tailed test, even for samples as large as 40 or more (e.g., Noreen, 1989; Wilcox, 1993). Recall from chapter 5 on the central limit theorem that when sample size increases the sampling distribution of the mean becomes more nearly normal. As the shape of a population distribution may be unknown, conservatively one would do better to conduct a two-tailed test when sample size is small, unless some normality evidence is available. However, recent research (e.g., Basu & DasGupta, 1995; Wilcox, 1997; Wilcox, 2003) suggests that small departures from normality can inflate the standard error of the mean (as the standard deviation is larger). This can reduce power and also affect control over Type I error. Thus a cavalier attitude about ignoring nonnormality may not be the best approach, and if nonnormality is an issue, other procedures, such as the Kolmogorov-Smirnov one-sample test, be considered.

The critical values are obtained from the $t$ table in Appendix Table 2, where you take into account the $\alpha$ level, whether the test is one- or two-tailed, and the degrees of freedom $v = n - 1$. If the test statistic falls into a critical region, as defined by the critical values, then our conclusion is to reject $H_0$. If the test statistic does not fall into a critical region, then our conclusion is fail to reject $H_0$. For the $t$ test the critical values depend on sample size, whereas for the $z$ test the critical values do not.

As was the case for the $z$ test, for the $t$ test a confidence interval for $\mu_0$ can be developed. The $(1 - \alpha)\%$ confidence interval is formed from

$$\overline{Y} \pm t_{cv} \, s_{\overline{Y}}$$

where $t_{cv}$ is the critical value from the $t$ table. If the hypothesized mean value $\mu_0$ is not contained in the interval, then our conclusion is to reject $H_0$. If the hypothesized mean value $\mu_0$ is contained in the interval, then our conclusion is fail to reject $H_0$. The confidence interval procedure for the $t$ test then is comparable to that for the $z$ test.

### 6.8.4   An Example

Let us consider an example of the entire $t$ test process. A hockey coach wanted to determine whether the mean skating speed of his team differed from the hypothesized league mean speed of 12 seconds. The hypotheses are developed as a two-tailed test and written as follows:

$$H_0: \mu = 12 \quad or \quad H_0: \mu - 12 = 0$$
$$H_1: \mu \neq 12 \quad or \quad H_1: \mu - 12 \neq 0$$

Skating speed around the rink was timed for each of 16 players (data are given in Table 6.2 and on the CD as chap6data). The mean speed of the team was $\overline{Y} = 10$ seconds with a standard deviation of $s_Y = 1.7889$ seconds. The standard error of the mean is then computed as

$$s_{\overline{Y}} = \frac{s_Y}{\sqrt{n}} = \frac{1.7889}{\sqrt{16}} = 0.4472$$

We wish to conduct a $t$ test at $\alpha = .01$, where we compute the test statistic $t$ as

$$t = \frac{\overline{Y} - \mu_0}{s_{\overline{Y}}} = \frac{10 - 12}{0.4472} = -4.4722$$

We turn to the $t$ table in Appendix Table 2 and look up the critical values for $\alpha_2 = .01$ and for $v = 15$ degrees of freedom. The critical values are $+2.947$, which defines the upper tail critical region, and $-2.947$, which defines the lower tail critical region. As the test statistic $t$ falls into the lower tail critical region (i.e., the test statistic is less than the lower tail critical value), our decision is to reject $H_0$ and conclude that the mean skating speed of this team is significantly different from the hypothesized league mean speed at the .01 level of significance. A 99% confidence interval can be computed as

$$\overline{Y} \pm t_{cv}\, s_{\overline{Y}} = 10 \pm 2.947(0.4472) = 10 \pm (1.3179) = (8.6821, 11.3179)$$

As the confidence interval does not contain the hypothesized mean value of 12, our conclusion is to again reject $H_0$.

### 6.9   SPSS

Here we consider what SPSS has to offer in the way of testing hypotheses about a single mean, and also present the results of the example in an APA paragraph. As with most statistical software, the $t$ test is included, but the $z$ test is not. In order to conduct the one-sample $t$ test, go to the "Analyze" pulldown, into "Compare Means," and then into the "One-Sample T Test" procedure. Click the variable of interest (e.g., time) into the "Test Variable(s)" box. At the bottom right of the screen is a box for "Test Value," where you indicate the hypothesized value (e.g., 12). The output for the Skating example is provided in Table 6.2.

What follows is an example paragraph of results for the skating data. As depicted in Table 6.2, based on a sample of 16 skaters, there was a mean time of 10 seconds, and a standard deviation of 1.7889 seconds. When compared against the hypothesized mean of 12 seconds, the one-

**TABLE 6.2**
SPSS Output for Skating Example

Raw data:    8, 12, 9, 7, 8, 10, 9, 11, 13.5, 8.5, 10.5, 9.5, 11.5, 12.5, 9.5, 10.5

*One-Sample Statistics*

|      | N  | Mean    | Std. Deviation | Std. Error Mean |
|------|-----|---------|----------------|-----------------|
| Time | 16 | 10.0000 | 1.7889         | .4472           |

*One-Sample Test*

| | *Test Value = 12* | | | |
|------|----------|-----|----------------|-----------------|
|      | t        | df  | Sig. (2-tailed) | Mean Difference |
| time | −4.4721  | 15  | .000           | −2.0000         |

sample *t* test was shown to be statistically significant ($t = -4.72$, $df = 15$, $p < .001$). Therefore the null hypothesis that the team average time would be 12 seconds was rejected, as the sample mean skating time for this particular team was statisticially different from the hypothesized mean skating time of the league.

## 6.10   SUMMARY

In this chapter we considered our first inferential testing situation, testing hypotheses about a single mean. A number of topics and new concepts were discussed. First we introduced the types of hypotheses utilized in inferential statistics, that is, the null or statistical hypothesis versus the scientific or research hypothesis. Second, we moved on to the types of decision errors (i.e., Type I and Type II errors) as depicted by the decision table and illustrated by the rain example. Third, the level of significance was introduced as well as the types of alternative hypotheses (i.e., nondirectional vs. directional alternative hypotheses). Fourth, an overview of the steps in the decision-making process of inferential statistics was given. Fifth, we examined the *z* test, which is the inferential test about a single mean when the population standard deviation is known. This was followed by a more formal description of Type II error and power. We then discussed the notion of statistical significance versus practical significance. Finally, we considered the *t* test, which is the inferential test about a single mean when the population standard deviation is unknown. At this point you should have met the following objectives: (a) be able to understand the basic concepts of hypothesis testing, (b) be able to utilize the normal and *t* tables, and (c) be able to understand, compute, and interpret the results from the *z* test, *t* test, and confidence interval procedures. Many of the concepts in this chapter carry over into other inferential tests. In the next chapter we discuss inferential tests involving the difference between two means. Other inferential tests will be considered in subsequent chapters.

## PROBLEMS

### Conceptual Problems

1.  In hypothesis testing, the probability of failing to reject $H_0$ when $H_0$ is false is denoted by
    a.  $\alpha$
    b.  $1 - \alpha$
    c.  $\beta$
    d.  $1 - \beta$

2.  When testing the hypothesis

$$H_0: \mu = 100$$
$$H_1: \mu < 100$$

at the .05 level of significance with the $t$ test, the region of rejection is in
    a.  the upper tail
    b.  the lower tail
    c.  both the upper and lower tails
    d.  cannot be determined

3.  The probability of making a Type II error when rejecting $H_0$ at the .05 level of significance is
    a.  0
    b.  .05
    c.  between .05 and .95
    d.  .95

4.  If the 90% CI does not include the value for the parameter being estimated in $H_0$, then
    a.  $H_0$ cannot be rejected at the .10 level
    b.  $H_0$ can be rejected at the .10 level
    c.  a Type I error has been made
    d.  a Type II error has been made

5.  Other things being equal, which of the values of $t$ given next is least likely to result when $H_0$ is true, for a two-tailed test?
    a.  2.67
    b.  1.00
    c.  0.00
    d.  $-1.96$
    e.  $-2.70$

6.  The fundamental difference between the $z$ test and the $t$ test for testing hypotheses about a population mean is that

    a.   only $z$ assumes the population distribution be normal

    b.   $z$ is a two-tailed test whereas $t$ is one-tailed

    c.   only $t$ becomes more powerful as sample size increases

    d.   only $z$ requires the population variance be known

7.  If one fails to reject a true $H_0$, one is making a Type I error. True or False?

8.  When testing the hypothesis

$$H_0: \mu = 295$$

$$H_1: \mu < 295$$

at the .01 level of significance with the $t$ test, I observe a sample mean of 301. I assert that, if I calculate the test statistic and compare it to the $t$ distribution with $n - 1$ degrees of freedom, it is possible to reject $H_0$. Am I correct?

9.  If the sample mean exceeds the hypothesized mean by 200 points, I assert that $H_0$ can be rejected. Am I correct?

10. I assert that $H_0$ can be rejected with 100% confidence if the sample consists of the entire population. Am I correct?

11. I assert that the 95% CI has a larger range than the 99% CI for a population mean using the same data. Am I correct?

12. I assert that the critical value of $z$, for a test of a single mean, will increase as sample size increases. Am I correct?

13. The mean of the $t$ distribution increases as degrees of freedom increase? True or false?

14. It is possible that the results of a one-sample $t$ test and corresponding CI will differ for the same data set and level of significance. True or false?

15. The width of the 95% CI does not depend on the sample mean. True or false?

16. The null hypothesis is a numerical statement about

    a.   an unknown parameter

    b.   a known parameter

    c.   an unknown statistic

    d.   a known statistic

## Computational Problems

1. Using the same data and the same method of analysis, the following hypotheses are tested about whether mean height is 72 inches.

$$H_0: \mu = 72$$
$$H_1: \mu \neq 72$$

Researcher A uses the .05 level of significance and Researcher B uses the .01 level of significance.
   a. If Researcher A rejects $H_0$, what is the conclusion of Researcher B?
   b. If Researcher B rejects $H_0$, what is the conclusion of Researcher A?
   c. If Researcher A fails to reject $H_0$, what is the conclusion of Researcher B?
   d. If Researcher B fails to reject $H_0$, what is the conclusion of Researcher A?

2. Give a numerical value for each of the following descriptions by referring to the $t$ table.
   a. the percentile rank of $t_5 = 1.476$
   b. the percentile rank of $t_{10} = 3.169$
   c. the percentile rank of $t_{21} = 2.518$
   d. the mean of the distribution of $t_{23}$
   e. the median of the distribution of $t_{23}$
   f. the variance of the distribution of $t_{23}$
   g. the 90th percentile of the distribution of $t_{27}$

3. The following random sample of weekly student expenses is obtained from a normally distributed population of undergraduate students with unknown parameters:

| 68 | 56 | 76 | 75 | 62 | 81 | 72 | 69 | 91 | 84 |
|----|----|----|----|----|----|----|----|----|----|
| 49 | 75 | 69 | 59 | 70 | 53 | 65 | 78 | 71 | 87 |
| 71 | 74 | 66 | 65 | 64 |    |    |    |    |    |

   a. Test the following hypothesis at the .05 level of significance:

$$H_0: \mu = 74$$
$$H_1: \mu \neq 74$$

   b. Construct a 95% confidence interval.

4. In the population it is hypothesized that flags have a mean usable life of 100 days. Twenty-five flags are flown in the city of Tuscaloosa and are found to have a sample mean usable life of 200 days with a standard deviation of 216 days. Does the sample mean in Tuscaloosa differ from that of the population mean?
   a. Conduct a two-tailed $t$ test at the .01 level of significance.
   b. Construct a 99% confidence interval

## Interpretive Problem

1. Using item 7 from the Statsurvey dataset on the CD, use SPSS to conduct a *t* test to determine whether the mean number of compact disks owned is significantly different from 25, at the .05 level of significance. Then write a paragraph describing your results.

# 7

# INFERENCES ABOUT THE DIFFERENCE BETWEEN TWO MEANS

## Chapter Outline

1.  New concepts
    Independent versus dependent samples
    Hypotheses
2.  Inferences about two independent means
    The independent *t* test
    The Welch *t'* test
    Recommendations
3.  Inferences about two dependent means
    The dependent *t* test
    Recommendations

## Key Concepts

1.  Independent versus dependent samples
2.  Sampling distribution of the difference between two means
3.  Standard error of the difference between two means
4.  Parametric versus nonparametric tests

In chapter 6 we introduced hypothesis testing and ultimately considered our first inferential statistic, the one-sample $t$ test. There we examined the following general topics: types of hypotheses, types of decision errors, level of significance, steps in the decision-making process, inferences about a single mean when the population standard deviation is known (the $z$ test), power, statistical versus practical significance, and inferences about a single mean when the population standard deviation is unknown (the $t$ test).

In this chapter we consider inferential tests involving the difference between two means. In other words, our research question is the extent to which two sample means are statistically different and, by inference, the extent to which their respective population means are different. Several inferential tests are covered in this chapter, depending on whether the two samples are selected in an independent or dependent manner, and on whether the statistical assumptions are met. More specifically, the topics described include the following inferential tests: for two independent samples—the independent $t$ test, the Welch $t'$ test, and briefly the Mann-Whitney-Wilcoxon test; and for two dependent samples—the dependent $t$ test and briefly the Wilcoxon signed ranks test.

We use many of the foundational concepts previously covered in chapter 6. New concepts to be discussed include the following: independent versus dependent samples; the sampling distribution of the difference between two means; and the standard error of the difference between two means. Our objectives are that by the end of this chapter, you will be able to: (a) understand the basic concepts underlying the inferential tests of two means, (b) select the appropriate test, and (c) compute and interpret the results from the appropriate test.

## 7.1   NEW CONCEPTS

Before we proceed to inferential tests of the difference between two means, a few new concepts need to be introduced. The new concepts are the difference between the selection of independent samples and dependent samples, the hypotheses to be tested, and the sampling distribution of the difference between two means.

### 7.1.1   Independent Versus Dependent Samples

The first concept to address is to make a distinction between the selection of **independent samples** and **dependent samples**. Two samples are **independent** when the method of sample selection is such that those individuals selected for sample 1 do not have any relationship to those individuals selected for sample 2. In other words, the selection of individuals to be included in the two samples are unrelated or uncorrelated such that they have absolutely nothing to do with one another. You might think of the samples as being selected totally separate from one another. Because the individuals in the two samples are independent of one another, their scores on the dependent variable $Y$ should also be independent of one another. The independence condition leads us to consider, for example, the **independent samples $t$ test**.

Two samples are **dependent** when the method of sample selection is such that those individuals selected for sample 1 do have a relationship to those individuals selected for sample 2. In other words, the selections of individuals to be included in the two samples are related or correlated. You might think of the samples as being selected simultaneously such that there are actually pairs of individuals. Consider the following two typical examples. First, if the same individuals are measured at two points in time, such as during a pretest and a posttest, then we have two dependent samples. The scores on $Y$ at time 1 will be correlated with the scores on $Y$ at time 2 because the same individuals are assessed at both time points. Second, if husband-and-wife pairs are selected, then we have two dependent samples. That is, if a particular wife is selected for the study, then her corresponding husband is also automatically selected. In both examples we have natural pairs of individuals or scores. The dependence condition leads us to consider the **dependent samples $t$ test**, alternatively known as the **correlated samples $t$ test** or the **paired samples $t$ test**. As we show in this chapter, whether the samples are independent or dependent determines the appropriate inferential test.

## 7.1.2   Hypotheses

The hypotheses to be evaluated for detecting a difference between two means are as follows. The null hypothesis $H_0$ is that there is no difference between the two population means, which we denote as

$$H_0: \mu_1 - \mu_2 = 0$$

where $\mu_1$ is the population mean for sample 1 and $\mu_2$ is the population mean for sample 2. Here there is no difference or a "null" difference between the two population means. The non-directional scientific or alternative hypothesis $H_1$ is that there is a difference between the two population means, which we denote as

$$H_1: \mu_1 - \mu_2 \neq 0$$

The null hypothesis $H_0$ will be rejected here in favor of the alternative hypothesis $H_1$ if the population means are different. As we have not specified a direction on $H_1$, we are willing to reject either if $\mu_1$ is greater than $\mu_2$ or if $\mu_1$ is less than $\mu_2$. This alternative hypothesis results in a two-tailed test.

Directional alternative hypotheses can also be tested if we believe $\mu_1$ is greater than $\mu_2$, denoted as

$$H_1: \mu_1 - \mu_2 > 0$$

or if we believe $\mu_1$ is less than $\mu_2$, denoted as

$$H_1: \mu_1 - \mu_2 < 0$$

These two alternative hypotheses each result in a one-tailed test.

The underlying sampling distribution for these tests is known as the **sampling distribution of the difference between two means**. This makes sense, as the hypotheses examine the extent to which two sample means differ. The mean of this sampling distribution is zero, as that is the hypothesized difference between the two population means $\mu_1 - \mu_2$. The more the two sample means differ, the more likely we are to reject the null hypothesis. As we show later, the test statistics in this chapter all deal in some way with the difference between the two means and with the standard error (or standard deviation) of the difference between two means.

## 7.2   INFERENCES ABOUT TWO INDEPENDENT MEANS

In this section, three inferential tests of the difference between two independent means are described: the independent $t$ test, the Welch $t'$ test, and briefly the Mann-Whitney-Wilcoxon test. The section concludes with a list of recommendations.

### 7.2.1   The Independent $t$ Test

First, we need to determine the conditions under which the independent $t$ test is appropriate. In part, this has to do with the statistical assumptions associated with the test itself. The assumptions of the test are that the scores on the dependent variable $Y$ (a) are normally distributed in each of the two populations, (b) have equal population variances (known as homogeneity of variance or homoscedasticity), and (c) are independent. When these assumptions are not met, other procedures may be more appropriate, as we show later.

The test statistic is known as $t$ and is denoted by

$$ t = \frac{\overline{Y}_1 - \overline{Y}_2}{s_{\overline{Y}_1 - \overline{Y}_2}} $$

where $\overline{Y}_1$ and $\overline{Y}_2$ are the means for sample 1 and sample 2, respectively, and $s_{\overline{Y}_1 - \overline{Y}_2}$ is the **standard error of the difference between two means**. This standard error is the standard deviation of the sampling distribution of the difference between two means and is computed as

$$ s_{\overline{Y}_1 - \overline{Y}_2} = s_p \sqrt{\frac{1}{n_1} + \frac{1}{n_2}} $$

where $s_p$ is the pooled standard deviation computed as

$$ s_p = \sqrt{\frac{(n_1 - 1) s_1^2 + (n_2 - 1)s_2^2}{n_1 + n_2 - 2}} $$

and where $s_1^2$ and $s_2^2$ are the sample variances for groups 1 and 2, respectively, and $n_1$ and $n_2$ are the sample sizes for groups 1 and 2, respectively. Conceptually, the standard error $s_{\overline{Y}_1 - \overline{Y}_2}$ is a pooled standard deviation weighted by the two sample sizes; more specifically, the two sample variances are weighted by their respective sample sizes and then pooled. This is conceptually similar to the standard error for the one sample $t$ test, which you will recall from chapter 6 as

$$ s_{\overline{Y}} = \frac{s_Y}{\sqrt{n}} $$

where we also have a standard deviation weighted by sample size. If the sample variances are not equal, as the test assumes, then you can see why we might not want to take a pooled or weighted average (i.e., as it would not represent well the individual sample variances).

The test statistic $t$ is then compared to a critical value(s) from the $t$ distribution. For a two-tailed test, from Appendix Table 2 we would use the appropriate $\alpha_2$ column depending on the desired level of significance and the appropriate row depending on the degrees of freedom.

The degrees of freedom for this test are $n_1 + n_2 - 2$. Conceptually, we lose one degree of freedom from each sample for estimating the population variances (i.e., there are two restrictions along the lines of what was discussed in chapter 6). The critical values are denoted as $\pm_{\alpha_2} t_{n_1 + n_2 - 2}$. If the test statistic falls into either critical region, then we reject $H_0$; otherwise, we fail to reject $H_0$.

For a one-tailed test, from Appendix Table 2 we would use the appropriate $\alpha_1$ column depending on the desired level of significance and the appropriate row depending on the degrees of freedom. The degrees of freedom are again $n_1 + n_2 - 2$. The critical value is denoted as $+_{\alpha_1} t_{n_1 + n_2 - 2}$ for the alternative hypothesis $H_1$: $\mu_1 - \mu_2 > 0$ and as $-_{\alpha_1} t_{n_1 + n_2 - 2}$ for the alternative hypothesis $H_1$: $\mu_1 - \mu_2 < 0$. If the test statistic $t$ falls into the appropriate critical region, then we reject $H_0$; otherwise, we fail to reject $H_0$.

For the two-tailed test, a $(1 - \alpha)\%$ confidence interval can also be examined. The confidence interval is formed as follows:

$$(\overline{Y}_1 - \overline{Y}_2) \pm_{a_2} t_{n_1 + n_2 - 2} (s_{\overline{Y}_1 - \overline{Y}_2})$$

If the confidence interval contains the hypothesized mean difference of 0, then the conclusion is to fail to reject $H_0$; otherwise, we reject $H_0$. The interpretation and use of CIs is similar to that of the one-sample test described in chapter 6. Imagine we take 100 random samples from each of two populations and construct 95% CIs. Then 95% of the CIs will contain the true population mean difference $\mu_1 - \mu_2$ and 5% will not. In short, 95% of similarly constructed CIs will contain the true population mean difference.

Next we extend Cohen's (1988) sample measure of effect size $d$ from chapter 6 to the two independent sample situation. Here we compute $d$ as follows:

$$d = \frac{\overline{Y}_1 - \overline{Y}_2}{s_p}$$

Thus effect size is measured in standard deviation units, and again we use Cohen's proposed subjective standards for interpreting $d$: small effect size, $d = .2$; medium effect size, $d = .5$; large effect size, $d = .8$. Conceptually this is similar to $d$ in the one-sample case from chapter 6.

Let us consider an example where the independent $t$ test is implemented. In our example, samples of 8 female and 12 male middle-age adults are randomly and independently sampled from the populations of female and male middle-age adults, respectively. Each individual is given a cholesterol test through a standard blood sample. The null hypothesis to be tested is that males and females have equal cholesterol levels. The alternative hypothesis is males and females will not have equal cholesterol levels, thus necessitating a nondirectional or two-tailed test. The raw data and summary statistics are presented in Table 7.1. For the female sample (sample 1) the mean and variance are 185.0000 and 364.2857, respectively, and for the male sample (sample 2) the mean and variance are 215.0000 and 913.6363, respectively.

In order to compute the test statistic $t$, we first need to determine the standard error of the difference between the two means. The pooled standard deviation is computed as

$$s_p = \sqrt{\frac{(n_1 - 1) s_1^2 + (n_2 - 1) s_2^2}{n_1 + n_2 - 2}} = \sqrt{\frac{(8 - 1) 364.2857 + (12 - 1) 913.6363}{8 + 12 - 2}} = 26.4575$$

**TABLE 7.1**

Cholesterol Data for Independent Samples

|  | Female (Sample 1) | Male (Sample 2) |
|---|---|---|
|  | 205 | 245 |
|  | 160 | 170 |
|  | 170 | 180 |
|  | 180 | 190 |
|  | 190 | 200 |
|  | 200 | 210 |
|  | 210 | 220 |
|  | 165 | 230 |
|  |  | 240 |
|  |  | 250 |
|  |  | 260 |
|  |  | 185 |
| Mean: | 185.0000 | 215.0000 |
| Variance: | 364.2857 | 913.6363 |

and the standard error of the difference between two means is computed as

$$s_{\bar{Y}_1 - \bar{Y}_2} = s_p \sqrt{\frac{1}{n_1} + \frac{1}{n_2}} = 26.4575 \sqrt{\frac{1}{8} + \frac{1}{12}} = 12.0752$$

The test statistic $t$ can then be computed as

$$t = \frac{\bar{Y}_1 - \bar{Y}_2}{s_{\bar{Y}_1 - \bar{Y}_2}} = \frac{185.0000 - 215.0000}{12.0752} = -2.4844$$

The next step is to use Appendix Table 2 to determine the critical values. As there are 18 degrees of freedom ($n_1 + n_2 - 2 = 8 + 12 - 2 = 18$), using $\alpha = .05$ and a two-tailed or nondirectional test, we find the critical values using the appropriate $\alpha_2$ column to be $+2.101$ and $-2.101$. As the test statistic falls beyond the critical values as shown in Fig. 7.1, we therefore reject the null hypothesis that the means are equal in favor of the nondirectional alternative that the means are not equal. Thus we conclude that the mean cholesterol levels for males and females are not equal at the .05 level of significance (denoted by $p < .05$).

The 95% confidence interval can also be examined. For the cholesterol example, the confidence interval is formed as follows:

$$(\bar{Y}_1 - \bar{Y}_2) \pm_{\alpha_2} t_{n_1 + n_2 - 2}(s_{\bar{Y}_1 - \bar{Y}_2}) = (185.0000 - 215.0000) \pm 2.101(12.0752)$$
$$= -30.000 \pm 25.3700 = (-55.3700, -4.6300)$$

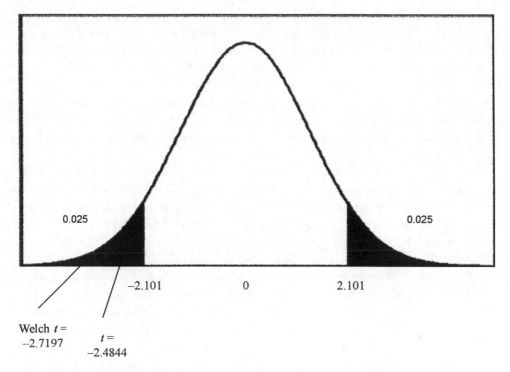

FIG. 7.1    Critical regions for the cholesterol example.

As the confidence interval does not contain the hypothesized mean difference value of zero, then we would again reject the null hypothesis and conclude that the mean gender difference was not equal to zero at the .05 level of significance ($p < .05$).

The effect size is computed as follows:

$$d = \frac{\overline{Y}_1 - \overline{Y}_2}{s_p} = \frac{185.0000 - 215.0000}{26.4575} = 1.1339$$

According to Cohen's recommended subjective standards, this would certainly be a rather large effect size, as the difference between the two sample means is larger than one standard deviation.

Let us return to the assumptions of normality, independence, and homogeneity of variance. The normality assumption is made because we are dealing with a parametric inferential test. **Parametric tests** assume a particular underlying theoretical population distribution, in this case, the normal distribution. **Nonparametric tests** do not assume a particular underlying theoretical population distribution.

Conventional wisdom tells us the following about nonnormality. When the normality assumption is violated with the independent $t$ test, the effects on Type I and Type II errors are minimal when using a two-tailed test (e.g., Glass, Peckham, & Sanders, 1972; Sawilowsky & Blair, 1992). When using a one-tailed test, violation of the normality assumption is minimal for samples larger than 10 and disappears for samples of at least 20 (Tiku & Singh, 1981; Sawilowsky & Blair, 1992). The simplest methods for detecting violation of the normality assumption are graphical methods, such as stem-and-leaf plots, box plots, or histograms, or statistical procedures such as the Shapiro-Wilk test (1965). However, more recent research by Wilcox (2003) indicates that power for both the independent $t$ and Welch's $t'$ can be reduced even for slight departures from normality, with outliers also contributing to the problem. Wilcox recommends several procedures not readily available and beyond the scope of this text (bootstrap methods; trimmed means; medians). Keep in mind, though, that the independent $t$ test is fairly robust to nonnormality in most situations.

The independence assumption is also necessary for this particular test. If the independence assumption is not met, then probability statements about the Type I and Type II errors will not be accurate; in other words, the probability of a Type I or Type II error may be increased as a result of the assumption not being met. Zimmerman (1997) found that Type I error was affected even for relatively small relations or correlations between the samples (i.e., even as small as .10 or .20). In general, the assumption can be met by (a) keeping the assignment of individuals to groups separate through the design of the experiment, and (b) keeping the individuals separate from one another through experimental control so that the scores on the dependent variable $Y$ for sample 1 do not influence the scores for sample 2. Zimmerman also stated that independence can be violated for supposedly independent samples due to some type of matching in the design of the experiment (e.g., matched pairs based on gender, age, and weight). If the observations are not independent, then the dependent $t$ test, discussed further in the chapter, may be appropriate.

Of potentially more serious concern is violation of the homogeneity of variance assumption. Research has shown that the effect of heterogeneity is minimal when the sizes of the two samples, $n_1$ and $n_2$, are equal; this is not the case when the sample sizes are not equal. When the larger variance is associated with the smaller sample size (e.g., group 1 has the larger variance and the smaller $n$), then the actual $\alpha$ level is larger than the nominal $\alpha$ level. In other words, if you set $\alpha$ at .05, then you are not really conducting the test at the .05 level, but at some larger value. When the larger variance is associated with the larger sample size (e.g., group 1 has the larger variance and the larger $n$), then the actual $\alpha$ level is smaller than the nominal $\alpha$ level. In other words, if you set $\alpha$ at .05, then you are not really conducting the test at the .05 level, but at some smaller value.

One can use statistical tests to detect violation of the homogeneity of variance assumption, although the most commonly used tests are somewhat problematic. These tests include Hartley's $F_{max}$ test (for equal $n$s, but sensitive to nonnormality; it is the unequal $n$s situation that we are concerned with anyway), Cochran's test (for equal $n$s, but even more sensitive to nonnormality than Hartley's test; concerned with unequal $n$s situation anyway), the Levene test (for equal $n$s, but sensitive to nonnormality; concerned with unequal $n$s situation anyway) (available in SPSS), the Bartlett test (for unequal $n$s, but very sensitive to nonnormality), the Box-Scheffe'-Anderson test (for unequal $n$s, fairly robust to nonnormality), and the Browne-Forsythe test (for unequal $n$s, more robust to nonnormality than the Box-Scheffe'-Anderson test and therefore recommended). When the variances are unequal and the sample sizes are unequal, the usual method to use as an alternative to the independent $t$ test is the Welch $t'$ test described in the next section. Inferential tests for evaluating homogeneity of variance are considered in chapter 9.

## 7.2.2 The Welch $t'$ Test

The Welch $t'$ test is usually appropriate when the population variances are unequal and the sample sizes are unequal. The Welch test assumes that the scores on the dependent variable $Y$ (a) are normally distributed in each of the two populations, and (b) are independent.

The test statistic is known as $t'$ and is denoted by

$$t' = \frac{\overline{Y}_1 - \overline{Y}_2}{s_{\overline{Y}_1 - \overline{Y}_2}} = \frac{\overline{Y}_1 - \overline{Y}_2}{\sqrt{s_{\overline{Y}_1}^2 + s_{\overline{Y}_2}^2}}$$

where $\overline{Y}_1$ and $\overline{Y}_2$ are the means for samples 1 and 2, respectively, and $s_{\overline{Y}_1}$ and $s_{\overline{Y}_2}$ are the variance errors of the means for samples 1 and 2, respectively. Here we see that the denominator of this test statistic is conceptually similar to the one-sample $t$ and the independent $t$ test statistics. The variance errors of the mean are computed for each group by

$$s_{\overline{Y}_1}^2 = \frac{s_1^2}{n_1}$$

$$s_{\overline{Y}_2}^2 = \frac{s_2^2}{n_2}$$

where $s_1^2$ and $s_2^2$ are the sample variances for groups 1 and 2, respectively. The square root of the variance error of the mean is the standard error of the mean (i.e., $s_{\overline{Y}_1}$ and $s_{\overline{Y}_2}$). Thus we see that rather than take a pooled or weighted average of the two sample variances as we did with the independent $t$ test, the two sample variances are treated separately with Welch's test.

The test statistic $t'$ is then compared to a critical value(s) from the $t$ distribution in Appendix Table 2. We again use the appropriate $\alpha$ column depending on the desired level of significance and whether the test is one- or two-tailed (i.e., $\alpha_1$ and $\alpha_2$), and the appropriate row for the degrees of freedom. The degrees of freedom for this test are a bit more complicated than the independent $t$ test. The degrees of freedom are adjusted from $n_1 + n_2 - 2$ in the independent $t$ test to the following value for Welch's test:

$$\nu = \frac{\left( s_{\overline{Y}_1}^2 + s_{\overline{Y}_2}^2 \right)^2}{\dfrac{\left( s_{\overline{Y}_1}^2 \right)^2}{n_1 - 1} + \dfrac{\left( s_{\overline{Y}_2}^2 \right)^2}{n_2 - 1}}$$

The degrees of freedom $\nu$ are approximated by rounding to the nearest whole number prior to using the table. If the test statistic falls into a critical region, then we reject $H_0$; otherwise, we fail to reject $H_0$.

For the two-tailed test, a $(1 - \alpha)\%$ confidence interval can also be examined. The confidence interval is formed as follows:

$$\left( \overline{Y}_1 - \overline{Y}_2 \right) \pm_{\alpha_2} t_\nu \left( s_{\overline{Y}_1 - \overline{Y}_2} \right)$$

If the confidence interval contains the hypothesized mean difference of zero, then the conclusion is to fail to reject $H_0$; otherwise, we reject $H_0$. Thus interpretation of this CI is the same as with the independent $t$ test.

Consider again the example cholesterol data where the sample variances were somewhat different and the sample sizes were different. The variance errors of the mean are computed for each sample as follows.

$$s_{\bar{Y}_1}^2 = \frac{s_1^2}{n_1} = \frac{364.2857}{8} = 45.5357$$

$$s_{\bar{Y}_2}^2 = \frac{s_2^2}{n_2} = \frac{913.6363}{12} = 76.1364$$

The $t'$ test statistic is computed as

$$t' = \frac{\bar{Y}_1 - \bar{Y}_2}{\sqrt{s_{\bar{Y}_1}^2 + s_{\bar{Y}_2}^2}} = \frac{185.0000 - 215.0000}{\sqrt{45.5357 + 76.1364}} = \frac{-30.0000}{11.0305} = -2.7197$$

Finally, the degrees of freedom $\nu$ are determined to be

$$\nu = \frac{\left(s_{\bar{Y}_1}^2 + s_{\bar{Y}_2}^2\right)^2}{\dfrac{\left(s_{\bar{Y}_1}^2\right)^2}{n_1 - 1} + \dfrac{\left(s_{\bar{Y}_2}^2\right)^2}{n_2 - 1}} = \frac{(45.5357 + 76.1364)^2}{\dfrac{(45.5357)^2}{8 - 1} + \dfrac{(76.1364)^2}{12 - 1}} = 17.9838$$

which is rounded to 18, the nearest whole number. The degrees of freedom remain 18 as they were for the independent $t$ test, and thus the critical values are still $+2.101$ and $-2.101$. As the test statistic falls beyond the critical values as shown in Fig. 7.1, we therefore reject the null hypothesis that the means are equal in favor of the alternative that the means are not equal. Thus, as with the independent $t$ test, with the Welch $t'$ test we conclude that the mean cholesterol levels for males and females are not equal at the .05 level of significance. In this particular example, then, we see that the unequal sample variances and unequal sample sizes did not alter the outcome when comparing the independent $t$ test result with the Welch $t'$ test result.

Finally, the 95% confidence interval can be examined. For the example, the confidence interval is formed as follows:

$$(\bar{Y}_1 - \bar{Y}_2) \pm_{\alpha 2} t_\nu \, (s_{\bar{Y}_1 - \bar{Y}_2}) = (185.0000 - 215.0000) \pm 2.101 \, (11.0305)$$
$$= -30.000 \pm 23.1751 = (-53.1751, -6.8249)$$

As the confidence interval does not contain the hypothesized mean difference value of zero, then we would again reject the null hypothesis and conclude that the mean gender difference was not equal to zero at the .05 level of significance ($p < .05$).

### 7.2.3 Recommendations

The following four recommendations are made regarding the two independent samples case. Although there is not total consensus in the field, our recommendations take into account, as much as possible, the available research and statistical software. First, if the normality assumption is satisfied, the following recommendations are made: (a) the independent $t$ test is recommended when the homogeneity of variance assumption is met; (b) the independent $t$ test is recommended when the homogeneity of variance assumption is not met when there are an equal number of observations in the samples; and (c) the Welch $t'$ test is recommended when the homogeneity of variance assumption is not met when there are an unequal number of observations in the samples.

Second, if the normality assumption is not satisfied, the following recommendations are made: (a) the independent $t$ test using ranked scores (Conover & Iman, 1981), rather than raw scores, is recommended when the homogeneity of variance assumption is met; and (b) the Welch $t'$ test using ranked scores is recommended when the homogeneity of variance assumption is not met, regardless of whether there are an equal number of observations in the samples. Here you rank order the observations from highest to lowest regardless of group membership, then conduct the appropriate $t$ test on the ranked scores rather than on the raw scores.

Third, the dependent $t$ test is recommended when the independence assumption is not met, as described later in this chapter. Fourth, the nonparametric Mann-Whitney-Wilcoxon test is not recommended. Among the disadvantages of this test are that (a) the critical values are not extensively tabled, (b) tied ranks can affect the results and no optimal procedure has yet been developed (Wilcox, 1996), and (c) Type I error appears to be inflated regardless of the status of the assumptions (Zimmerman, 2003). For these reasons the Mann-Whitney-Wilcoxon test is not further described here. Note that most major statistical packages, including SPSS, have options for conducting the independent $t$ test, the Welch $t'$ test, and the Mann-Whitney-Wilcoxon test. Alternatively, one could conduct the Kruskal-Wallis nonparametric one-factor analysis of variance, which is also based on ranked data, and which is appropriate for comparing the means of two or more groups. This test is considered more fully in chapter 11.

## 7.3   INFERENCES ABOUT TWO DEPENDENT MEANS

In this section, two inferential tests of the difference between two dependent means are described, the dependent $t$ test and briefly the Wilcoxon signed ranks test. The section concludes with a list of recommendations.

### 7.3.1   The Dependent $t$ Test

First, we need to determine the conditions under which the dependent $t$ test is appropriate. In part, this has to do with the statistical assumption associated with the test itself. The assumption of the test is that the scores on the dependent variable $Y$ are normally distributed in each of the two populations. Like the independent $t$ test, the dependent $t$ test is reasonably robust to violation of the normality assumption, as we show later.

Although there are several methods for computing the test statistic $t$, the most direct method and the one most closely aligned conceptually with the one-sample $t$ test is as follows:

$$t = \frac{\bar{d}}{s_{\bar{d}}}$$

where $\bar{d}$ is the mean difference, and $s_{\bar{d}}$ is the standard error of the mean difference. Conceptually this test statistic looks just like the one-sample $t$ test statistic, except now the notation has been changed to denote that we are dealing with difference scores.

The standard error of the mean difference is computed by

$$s_{\bar{d}} = \frac{s_d}{\sqrt{n}}$$

where $s_d$ is the standard deviation of the difference scores (i.e., like any other standard deviation only this one is computed from the difference scores rather than raw scores), and $n$ is the total number of pairs. Conceptually this standard error looks just like the standard error for the one-sample $t$ test. If we were doing hand computations, we would compute a difference score for each pair of scores (i.e., $Y_1 - Y_2$). For example, if sample 1 were wives and sample 2 were their husbands, then we would calculate a difference score for each couple. From this set of difference scores, we then compute the mean of the difference scores $\bar{d}$ and standard deviation of the difference scores $s_d$. This leads us directly into the computation of the $t$ test statistic. Note that although there are $n$ scores in sample 1, $n$ scores in sample 2, and thus $2n$ total scores, there are only $n$ difference scores, which is what the analysis is based upon.

The test statistic $t$ is then compared with a critical value(s) from the $t$ distribution. For a two-tailed test, from Appendix Table 2 we would use the appropriate $\alpha_2$ column depending on the desired level of significance and the appropriate row depending on the degrees of freedom. The degrees of freedom for this test are $n - 1$. Conceptually we lose one degree of freedom from the number of differences (or pairs) because we are estimating the population variance (or standard deviation) of the difference. Thus there is one restriction along the lines of our discussion of degrees of freedom in chapter 6. The critical values are denoted as $\pm_{\alpha_2} t_{n-1}$. If the test statistic falls into either critical region, then we reject $H_0$; otherwise, we fail to reject $H_0$.

For a one-tailed test, from Appendix Table 2 we would use the appropriate $\alpha_1$ column depending on the desired level of significance and the appropriate row depending on the degrees of freedom. The degrees of freedom are again $n - 1$. The critical value is denoted as $+_{\alpha_1} t_{n-1}$ for the alternative hypothesis $H_1: \mu_1 - \mu_2 > 0$ and as $-_{\alpha_1} t_{n-1}$ for the alternative hypothesis $H_1: \mu_1 - \mu_2 < 0$. If the test statistic $t$ falls into the appropriate critical region, then we reject $H_0$; otherwise, we fail to reject $H_0$.

For the two-tailed test, a $(1 - \alpha)\%$ confidence interval can also be examined. The confidence interval is formed as follows:

$$(\bar{d}) \pm_{\alpha_2} t_{n-1} (s_{\bar{d}})$$

If the confidence interval contains the hypothesized mean difference of 0, then the conclusion is fail to reject $H_0$; otherwise, we reject $H_0$. The interpretation of these confidence intervals is the same as those previously discussed for the one-sample $t$ and the independent $t$.

The effect size can be measured using Cohen's (1988) $d$ computed as follows:

$$Cohen's\ d = \frac{\bar{d}}{s_d}$$

where Cohen's $d$ is simply used to distinguish among the various uses of $d$. Interpretation of the value of $d$ would be the same as for the one-sample $t$ and the independent $t$ previously discussed.

Let us consider an example for purposes of illustrating the dependent $t$-test. Ten swimmers participated in an intensive 2-month training program. Prior to the program, each swimmer was timed during a 50-meter freestyle event. Following the program, the same swimmers were timed in the 50-meter freestyle event again. This is a classic pretest-posttest design. For illustrative purposes, we will conduct a two-tailed test, although a case might also be made for a one-tailed test as well (conducting a two-tailed test allows us to examine the confidence interval for purposes of illustration). The raw scores, the difference scores, and the mean and standard deviation of the difference scores are shown in Table 7.2. The pretest mean time was 64.0000 seconds and the posttest mean time was 59.0000 seconds.

First we compute the standard error of the mean difference as

$$s_{\bar{d}} = \frac{s_d}{\sqrt{n}} = \frac{2.1602}{\sqrt{10}} = 0.6831$$

Next the test statistic $t$ is computed as

$$t = \frac{\bar{d}}{s_{\bar{d}}} = \frac{5.0000}{0.6831} = 7.3196$$

The next step is to use Appendix Table 2 to determine the critical values. As there are 9 degrees of freedom ($n - 1 = 10 - 1 = 9$), using $\alpha = .05$ and a two-tailed or nondirectional test, we find the critical values using the appropriate $\alpha_2$ column to be $+2.262$ and $-2.262$. As the test statistic falls beyond the critical values, as shown in Fig. 7.2, we reject the null hypothesis that the means are equal in favor of the nondirectional alternative that the means are not equal. Thus, we conclude that the mean swimming performance changed from pretest to posttest at the .05 level of significance ($p < .05$).

## TABLE 7.2
Swimming Data for Dependent Samples

| Swimmer | Pretest | Posttest | Difference (d) |
|---------|---------|----------|----------------|
| 1       | 58      | 54       | 4              |
| 2       | 62      | 57       | 5              |
| 3       | 60      | 54       | 6              |
| 4       | 61      | 56       | 5              |
| 5       | 63      | 61       | 2              |
| 6       | 65      | 59       | 6              |
| 7       | 66      | 64       | 2              |
| 8       | 69      | 62       | 7              |
| 9       | 64      | 60       | 4              |
| 10      | 72      | 63       | 9              |
| | $\bar{d} = 5.0000$ | $s_d = 2.1602$ | |

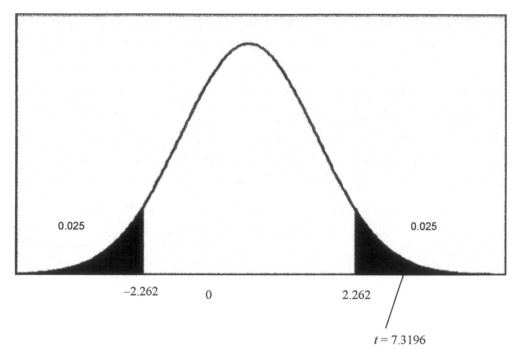

FIG. 7.2    Critical regions for the swimming example.

The 95% confidence interval is computed to be

$$(\bar{d}) \pm_{\alpha_2} t_{n-1} (S_{\bar{d}}) = 5.0000 \pm 2.262(0.6831) = 5.0000 \pm 1.5452 = (3.4548, 6.5452)$$

As the confidence interval does not contain the hypothesized mean difference value of zero, we would again reject the null hypothesis and conclude that the mean pretest − postttest difference was not equal to zero at the .05 level of significance ($p < .05$).

The effect size is computed to be

$$Cohen's \; d = \frac{\bar{d}}{s_d} = \frac{5.0000}{2.1602} = 2.3146$$

which is approximately two and a third standard deviations, a rather large effect size according to Cohen's subjective standard.

### 7.3.2    Recommendations

The following three recommendations are made regarding the two dependent samples case. First, the dependent $t$ test is recommended when the normality assumption is met. Second, the dependent $t$ test using ranks (Conover & Iman, 1981) is recommended when the normality assumption is not met. Here you rank order the difference scores from highest to lowest, then conduct the test on the ranked scores rather than on the difference scores. However, more recent research by Wilcox (2003) indicates that power for the dependent $t$ can be reduced even for slight departures from normality. Wilcox recommends several procedures not readily available and beyond the scope of this text (bootstrap methods; trimmed means; medians; Stein's method). Keep in mind, though, that the dependent $t$ test is fairly robust to nonnormality in most situations.

Third, the nonparametric Wilcoxon signed ranks test is recommended when the data are non-normal with extreme outliers (one or a few observations that behave quite differently from the rest). However, among the disadvantages of this test are that (a) the critical values are not exten-sively tabled and two different tables exist depending on sample size, and (b) tied ranks can affect the results and no optimal procedure has yet been developed (Wilcox, 1996). For these reasons the details of the Wilcoxon signed ranks test are not described here. Note that most major statistical packages, including SPSS, include options for conducting the dependent $t$ test and the Wilcoxon signed ranks test. Alternatively, one could conduct the Friedman nonpara-metric one-factor analysis of variance, also based on ranked data, and which is appropriate for comparing two or more dependent samples. This test is considered more fully in chapter 15.

## 7.4   SPSS

As we have done in previous chapters, here we consider the use of SPSS for the example datasets as well as write an APA style paragraph describing the results. In order to conduct an independent $t$ test, your dataset needs to include a dependent variable $Y$ (e.g., cholesterol) as well as a grouping variable (e.g., gender). Go to the "Analyze" pulldown, into "Compare Means," and then into the "Independent-Samples T Test" procedure. Click the dependent variable (e.g., cho-lesterol) into the "Test Variable(s)" box, and click the grouping variable (e.g., gender) into the "Grouping Variable" box. Now the "Define Groups" option box is active, so click on that to determine which two groups to analyze. Where it says "Group 1" type in the value designated for your first group (e.g., 1), and where it says "Group 2" type in the value designed for your sec-ond group (e.g., 2). Click on "Continue" to return to the original dialog box and then click on "OK" to run the analysis. The output is shown in Table 7.3. The top box gives different descrip-tive statistics for each group, while the bottom box gives the results of the requested proce-dure. There you see that three different inferential tests are automatically provided, Levene's test of the homogeneity of variance assumption, the independent $t$ test (which SPSS calls "Equal variances assumed"), and the Welch $t'$ test (which SPSS calls "Equal variances not assumed").

Here is an example paragraph describing the results of the independent $t$ test for the choles-terol example. As shown in Table 7.3, cholesterol data were gathered from samples of 8 females and 12 males, with a female sample mean of 185 and a male sample mean of 215. According to Levene's test, the homogeneity of variance assumption was satisfied ($F = 3.2007, p = .090$). The independent $t$ test indicated that the cholesterol means were statistically significant ($t = -2.4842, df = 18, p = .023$). Thus the null hypothesis that the cholesterol means were the same by gender was rejected at the .05 level of significance. Parenthetically, notice that the results of the Welch $t'$ test were the same as for the independent $t$ test (Welch $t' = -2.7197$, rounded $df = 18, p = .014$).

To conduct a dependent $t$ test, your dataset needs to include the two variables whose means you wish to compare (e.g., pretest and posttest). Go to the "Analyze" pulldown, into "Compare Means," and then into the "Paired-Samples T Test" procedure. Click both variables (e.g., pretest

**TABLE 7.3**
SPSS Results for Independent *t* Test

*Group Statistics*

|        | gender | N  | Mean     | Std. Deviation | Std. Error Mean |
|--------|--------|----|----------|----------------|-----------------|
| choles | female | 8  | 185.0000 | 19.0863        | 6.7480          |
|        | male   | 12 | 215.0000 | 30.2264        | 8.7256          |

*Independent Samples Test*

|        |                             | Levene's Test for Equality of Variances | | t-test for Equality of Means | | | | |
|--------|-----------------------------|--------|------|---------|--------|------------------|--------------------|----------------------|
|        |                             | F      | Sig. | t       | df     | Sig. (2-tailed)  | Mean Difference    | Std. Error Difference |
| choles | Equal variances assumed     | 3.2007 | .090 | −2.4842 | 18     | .023             | −30.0000           | 12.0761              |
|        | Equal variances not assumed |        |      | −2.7197 | 17.984 | .014             | −30.0000           | 11.0305              |

and posttest) into the "Paired Variables" box. Both variables should now appear in the box, for example, as "pretest—posttest." Then click on "OK" to run the analysis. The output appears in Table 7.4, where again the top box provides descriptive statistics and the bottom box gives the results of the procedure.

What follows is an example paragraph of the results of the dependent *t* test for the swimming example. From Table 7.4 we see that pretest and posttest data were collected from a sample of 10 swimmers, with a pretest mean of 64 seconds and a posttest mean of 59 seconds. Thus swimming times decreased from pretest to posttest. The dependent *t* test was conducted to determine statistical significance, and indicated that the pretest and posttest means were statistically different ($t = 7.3193$, $df = 9$, $p < .001$). Thus the null hypothesis that the freestyle swimming means were the same at both points in time was rejected at the .001 level of significance.

Finally, it should be noted that SPSS does not provide power or effect size information for any of the procedures in this chapter. Effect size, using Cohen's (1988) *d*, can be easily computed by hand from the SPSS results. *A priori* power can be determined using specialized software (e.g., Power and Precision, Ex-Sample) or power tables (e.g., Cohen, 1988). *Post hoc* power can be determined from the exact significance level given by SPSS for a two-tailed test.

## 7.5   SUMMARY

In this chapter we considered a second inferential testing situation, testing hypotheses about the difference between two means. Several inferential tests and new concepts were discussed.

**TABLE 7.4**

SPSS Results for Dependent $t$ Test

*Paired Samples Statistics*

|  |  | Mean | N | Std. Deviation | Std. Error Mean |
|---|---|---|---|---|---|
| Pair | pretest | 64.0000 | 10 | 4.2164 | 1.3333 |
| 1 | posttest | 59.0000 | 10 | 3.6209 | 1.1450 |

*Paired Samples Test*

*Paired Differences*

|  | Mean | Std. Deviation | Std. Error Mean | 95% Confidence Interval of the Difference Lower | Upper | t | df | Sig. (2-tailed) |
|---|---|---|---|---|---|---|---|---|
| Pair 1 pretest-posttest | 5.0000 | 2.1602 | .6831 | 3.4547 | 6.5453 | 7.3193 | 9 | .000 |

The new concepts introduced were independent versus dependent samples, the sampling distribution of the difference between two means, the standard error of the difference between two means, and parametric versus nonparametric tests. We then moved on to describe the following three inferential tests for determining the difference between two independent means: the independent $t$ test, the Welch $t'$ test, and briefly the Mann-Whitney-Wilcoxon test. The following two tests for determining the difference between two dependent means were considered: the dependent $t$ test, and briefly the Wilcoxon signed ranks test. In addition, examples were presented for each of the $t$ tests, and recommendations were made as to when each test is most appropriate. At this point you should have met the following objectives: (a) be able to understand the basic concepts underlying the inferential tests of two means, (b) be able to select the appropriate test, and (c) be able to compute and interpret the results from the appropriate test. In the next chapter we discuss inferential tests involving proportions. Other inferential tests are covered in subsequent chapters.

## PROBLEMS

### Conceptual Problems

1. We test the hypothesis

$$H_0: \mu_1 - \mu_2 = 0$$
$$H_1: \mu_1 - \mu_2 \neq 0$$

at the .05 level of significance and $H_0$ is rejected. Assuming all assumptions are met and $H_0$ is true, the probability of committing a Type I error is

    a.   0

    b.   0.05

    c.   between .05 and .95

    d.   0.95

    e.   1.00

2.   When $H_0$ is true, the difference between two independent sample means is a function of

    a.   degrees of freedom

    b.   the standard error

    c.   the sampling distribution

    d.   sampling error

3.   The denominator of the independent $t$ test is known as the standard error of the difference between two means, and may be defined as

    a.   the difference between the two group means

    b.   the amount by which the difference between the two group means differs from the population mean

    c.   the standard deviation of the sampling distribution of the difference between two means

    d.   all of the above

    e.   none of the above

4.   In the independent $t$ test, the homoscedasticity assumption states that

    a.   the two population means are equal

    b.   the two population variances are equal

    c.   the two sample means are equal

    d.   the two sample variances are equal

5.   Sampling error increases with larger samples. True or false?

6.   At a given level of significance, it is possible that the significance test and the confidence interval results will differ for the same data set. True or false?

7.   I assert the critical value of $t$ required for statistical significance is smaller (in absolute value or ignoring the sign) when using a directional rather than a nondirectional test. Am I correct?

8.   If a 95% CI from an independent $t$ test ranges from $-.13$ to $+1.67$, I assert that the null hypothesis would not be rejected at the .05 level of significance. Am I correct?

9. A group of 15 females was compared to a group of 25 males with respect to intelligence. To test if the sample sizes are significantly different, which of the following tests would you use?

    a. independent $t$ test

    b. dependent $t$ test

    c. $z$ test

    d. none of the above

10. The number of degrees of freedom for an independent $t$ test with 15 females and 25 males is 40. True or false?

11. I assert that the critical value of $t$, for a test of two dependent means, will increase as the samples become larger. Am I correct?

12. Which of the following is NOT an assumption of the independent t test?

    a. normality

    b. independence

    c. equal sample sizes

    d. homogeneity

## Computational Problems

1. The following two independent samples of older and younger adults were measured on a attitude towards violence test:

| *Sample 1 (older adult) data:* | | | | | | *Sample 2 (younger adult) data:* | | | | |
|---|---|---|---|---|---|---|---|---|---|---|
| 42 | 36 | 47 | 35 | 46 | | 45 | 50 | 57 | 58 | 43 |
| 37 | 52 | 44 | 47 | 51 | | 52 | 43 | 60 | 41 | 49 |
| 56 | 54 | 55 | 50 | 40 | | 44 | 51 | 49 | 55 | 56 |
| 40 | 46 | 41 | | | | | | | | |

    a. Test the following hypothesis at the .05 level of significance.

$$H_0: \mu_1 - \mu_2 = 0$$
$$H_1: \mu_1 - \mu_2 \neq 0$$

    b. Construct a 95% CI.

2. The following two independent samples of male and female undergraduate students were measured on an English literature quiz:

| *Sample 1 (male) data:* | | | | | | *Sample 2 (female) data:* | | | | |
|---|---|---|---|---|---|---|---|---|---|---|
| 5 | 7 | 8 | 10 | 11 | | 9 | 9 | 11 | 13 | 15 |
| 11 | 13 | 15 | | | | 18 | 19 | 20 | | |

    a.   Test the following hypothesis at the .05 level of significance.

$$H_0: \mu_1 - \mu_2 = 0$$
$$H_1: \mu_1 - \mu_2 \neq 0$$

    b.   Construct a 95% CI.

3.   The following is a random sample of paired values of weight measured before (time 1) and after (time 2) a weight-reduction program:

| Pair | 1 | 2 |
|------|-----|-----|
| 1 | 127 | 130 |
| 2 | 126 | 124 |
| 3 | 129 | 135 |
| 4 | 123 | 127 |
| 5 | 124 | 127 |
| 6 | 129 | 128 |
| 7 | 132 | 136 |
| 8 | 125 | 130 |
| 9 | 135 | 131 |
| 10 | 126 | 128 |

    a.   Test the following hypothesis at the .05 level of significance.

$$H_0: \mu_1 - \mu_2 = 0$$
$$H_1: \mu_1 - \mu_2 \neq 0$$

    b.   Construct a 95% CI.

4.   The following is a random sample of scores on an attitude toward abortion scale for husband (sample 1) and wife (sample 2) pairs:

| Pair | 1 | 2 |
|------|---|----|
| 1 | 1 | 3 |
| 2 | 2 | 3 |
| 3 | 4 | 6 |
| 4 | 4 | 5 |
| 5 | 5 | 7 |
| 6 | 7 | 8 |
| 7 | 7 | 9 |
| 8 | 8 | 10 |

    a.   Test the following hypothesis at the .05 level of significance.

$$H_0: \mu_1 - \mu_2 = 0$$
$$H_1: \mu_1 - \mu_2 \neq 0$$

    b.   Construct a 95% CI.

5.  For two dependent samples, test the hypothesis below at the .05 level of significance.

$$H_0: \mu_1 - \mu_2 = 0$$
$$H_1: \mu_1 - \mu_2 > 0$$

Sample statistics: $n = 121$; $\bar{d} = 10$; $s_d = 45$.

## Interpretive Problem

Using the statistics survey dataset from the CD, use SPSS to conduct an independent $t$ test, where gender is the grouping variable and the dependent variable is a variable of interest to you. Then write an APA type paragraph describing the results.

# 8

# INFERENCES ABOUT PROPORTIONS

## Chapter Outline

1. Inferences about proportions involving the normal distribution
    Introduction
    Inferences about a single proportion
    Inferences about two independent proportions
    Inferences about two dependent proportions
2. Inferences about proportions involving the chi-square distribution
    Introduction
    The chi-square goodness-of-fit test
    The chi-square test of association
3. SPSS

## Key Concepts

1. Proportion
2. Sampling distribution and standard error of a proportion
3. Contingency table
4. Chi-square distribution
5. Observed versus expected proportions

In chapters 6 and 7 we considered testing inferences about means, first for a single mean (chap. 6) and then for two means (chap. 7). The major concepts discussed in those two chapters included the following: types of hypotheses, types of decision errors, level of significance, power, confidence intervals, effect sizes, sampling distributions involving the mean, standard errors involving the mean, inferences about a single mean, inferences about the difference between two independent means, and inferences about the difference between two dependent means. In this chapter we consider inferential tests involving proportions. We define a **proportion** as the percentage of scores falling into particular categories. Thus the tests described in this chapter deal with variables that are categorical in nature and thus are nominal variables (see chap. 1), or have been collapsed from higher level variables into nominal variables (e.g., high and low scorers on an achievement test).

Research questions to be asked of proportions include the following examples.

1. Is the quarter in my hand a fair or biased coin; in other words, over repeated samples, is the proportion of heads equal to .50 or not?

2. Is there a difference between the proportions of Republicans and Democrats who support the local school bond issue?

3. Is there a relationship between ethnicity (e.g., African-American, Caucasian) and type of criminal offense (e.g., petty theft, rape, murder); in other words, is the proportion of one ethnic group different from another in terms of the types of crimes committed?

Several inferential tests are covered in this chapter, depending on (a) whether there are one or two samples, (b) whether the two samples are selected in an independent or dependent manner, and (c) whether there are one or more categorical variables. More specifically, the topics described include the following inferential tests: testing whether a single proportion is different from a hypothesized value; testing whether two independent proportions are different; testing whether two dependent proportions are different; and the chi-square goodness-of-fit test and chi-square test of association. We use many of the foundational concepts previously covered in chapters 6 and 7. New concepts to be discussed include the following: proportion; sampling distribution and standard error of a proportion; contingency table; chi-square distribution; and observed versus expected frequencies. Our objectives are that by the end of this chapter, you will be able to (a) understand the basic concepts underlying tests of proportions, (b) select the appropriate test, and (c) compute and interpret the results from the appropriate test.

## 8.1 INFERENCES ABOUT PROPORTIONS INVOLVING THE NORMAL DISTRIBUTION

This section deals with concepts and procedures for testing inferences about proportions that involve the normal distribution. Following a discussion of the concepts related to tests of proportions, inferential tests are presented for situations when there is a single proportion, two independent proportions, and two dependent proportions.

### 8.1.1 Introduction

Let us examine in greater detail the concepts related to tests of proportions. First, a **proportion** represents the percentage of individuals or objects that fall into a particular category. For instance, the proportion of individuals who support a particular political candidate might be of interest. Thus the variable here is a dichotomous, categorical, nominal variable, as there are only two categories represented, support or do not support the candidate.

For notational purposes, we define the **population proportion** $\pi$ (pi) as

$$\pi = \frac{f}{N}$$

where $f$ is the number of frequencies in the population who fall into the category of interest (e.g., the number of individuals who support the candidate), and $N$ is the total number of individuals in the population. For example, if the population consists of 100 individuals and 58 support the candidate, then $\pi = .58$. If the proportion is multiplied by 100%, this yields the percentage of individuals in the population who support the candidate, which in the example would be 58%. At the same time, $1 - \pi$ represents the population proportion of individuals who do not support the candidate, which for this example would be $1 - .58 = .42$. If this is multiplied by 100%, this yields the percentage of individuals in the population who do not support the candidate, which in the example would be 42%.

In a fashion, the population proportion is conceptually similar to the population mean if the category of interest (support of candidate) is coded as 1 and the other category (not support) is coded as 0. In the case of the example with 100 individuals, there are 58 individuals coded 1, 42 individuals coded 0, and therefore the mean would be .58. To this point then we have $\pi$ representing the population proportion of individuals supporting the candidate and $1 - \pi$ representing the population proportion of individuals not supporting the candidate.

The **population variance of a proportion** can also be determined by $\sigma^2 = \pi(1 - \pi)$ and thus the population standard deviation of a proportion is $\sigma = \sqrt{\pi(1 - \pi)}$. These provide us with measures of variability that represent the extent to which the individuals in the population vary in their support of the candidate. For the example population then, the variance is computed to be $\sigma^2 = \pi(1 - \pi) = .58(1 - .58) = .58(.42) = .2436$ and the standard deviation is $\sigma = \sqrt{\pi(1 - \pi)} = \sqrt{.58(1 - .58)} = \sqrt{.58(.42)} = .4936$.

For the population, we now have the population proportion (or mean), the population variance, and the population standard deviation. The next step is to discuss the corresponding sample statistics for the proportion. The **sample proportion** $p$ is defined as

$$p = \frac{f}{n}$$

where $f$ is the number of frequencies in the sample that fall into the category of interest (e.g., the number of individuals who support the candidate), and $n$ is the total number of individuals in the sample. The sample proportion $p$ is thus a sample estimate of the population proportion $\pi$. One way we can estimate the population variance is by $s^2 = p(1 - p)$ and the population standard deviation of a proportion can be estimated by $s = \sqrt{p(1 - p)}$

The next concept to discuss is the sampling distribution of the proportion. This is comparable to the sampling distribution of the mean discussed in chapter 5. If one were to take many samples, and for each sample compute the sample proportion $p$, then we could generate a distribution of $p$. This is known as the **sampling distribution of the proportion**. For example, imagine that we take 50 samples of size 100 and determine the proportion for each sample. That is, we would have 50 different sample proportions each based on 100 observations. If we construct a frequency distribution of these 50 proportions, this is actually the sampling distribution of the proportion.

In theory, the sample proportions for this example could range from .00 to 1.00, given that there are 100 observations in each sample. One could also examine the variability of these 50 sample proportions. That is, we might be interested in the extent to which the sample proportions vary. We might have, for one example, most of the sample proportions falling near the mean proportion of .60. This would indicate for the candidate data that (a) the samples generally support the candidate, as the average proportion is .60, and (b) the support for the candidate is fairly consistent across samples, as the sample proportions tend to fall close to .60. Alternatively, in a second example, we might find the sample proportions varying quite a bit around the mean of .60, say ranging from .20 to .80. This would indicate that (a) the samples generally support the candidate again, as the average proportion is .60, and (b) the support for the candidate is not very consistent across samples, leading one to believe that some groups support the candidate and others do not.

The variability of the sampling distribution of the proportion can be determined as follows. The population variance of the sampling distribution of the proportion is known as the **variance error of the proportion**, denoted by $\sigma_p^2$ The variance error is computed as

$$\sigma_p^2 = \frac{\pi\left(1 - \pi\right)}{n}$$

where $\pi$ is again the population proportion and $n$ is sample size (i.e., the number of observations in a single sample). The population standard deviation of the sampling distribution of the proportion is known as the **standard error of the proportion**, denoted by $\sigma_p$. The standard error is computed as

$$\sigma_p = \sqrt{\frac{\pi\left(1 - \pi\right)}{n}}$$

This situation is quite comparable to the sampling distribution of the mean discussed in chapter 5. There we had the variance error and standard error of the mean as measures of the variability of the sample means.

Technically speaking, the binomial distribution is the exact sampling distribution for the proportion; **binomial** here refers to a categorical variable with two possible categories, which is certainly the situation here. However, except for rather small samples, the normal distribution is a reasonable approximation to the binomial distribution and is therefore typically used. The reason we can rely on the normal distribution is due to the central limit theorem, previously discussed in chapter 5. For proportions, the central limit theorem states that as sample size $n$ increases, the sampling distribution of the proportion from a random sample of size $n$ more closely approximates a normal distribution. If the population distribution is normal in shape, then the sampling distribution of the proportion is also normal in shape. If the population distribution is not normal in shape, then the sampling distribution of the proportion becomes more nearly normal as sample size increases. As previously shown in Fig. 5.1 in the context of the mean, the bottom line is that if the population is nonnormal, this will have a minimal effect on the sampling distribution of the proportion except for rather small samples.

Because most of the time the applied researcher only has access to a single sample, the population variance error and standard error of the proportion must be estimated. The sample variance error of the proportion is denoted by $s_p^2$ and computed as

$$s_p^2 = \frac{p(1-p)}{n}$$

where $p$ is again the sample proportion and $n$ is sample size. The sample standard error of the proportion is denoted by $s_p$ and computed as

$$s_p = \sqrt{\frac{p(1-p)}{n}}$$

### 8.1.2    Inferences About a Single Proportion

In the first inferential testing situation for proportions, the researcher would like to know whether the population proportion is equal to some hypothesized proportion or not. This is comparable to the one-sample $t$ test described in chapter 6 where a population mean was compared against some hypothesized mean. First, the hypotheses to be evaluated for detecting whether a population proportion differs from a hypothesized proportion are as follows. The null hypothesis $H_0$ is that there is no difference between the population proportion $\pi$ and the hypothesized proportion $\pi_0$, which we denote as

$$H_0: \pi = \pi_0$$

Here there is no difference or a "null" difference between the population proportion and the hypothesized proportion. For example, if we are seeking to determine whether the quarter you are flipping is a biased coin or not, then a reasonable hypothesized value would be .50, as an unbiased coin should yield "heads" about 50% of the time.

The nondirectional, scientific or alternative hypothesis $H_1$ is that there is a difference between the population proportion $\pi$ and the hypothesized proportion $\pi_0$, which we denote as

$$H_1: \pi \neq \pi_0$$

The null hypothesis $H_0$ will be rejected here in favor of the alternative hypothesis $H_1$ if the population proportion is different from the hypothesized proportion. As we have not specified a direction on $H_1$, we are willing to reject $H_0$ either if $\pi$ is greater than $\pi_0$ or if $\pi$ is less than $\pi_0$. This alternative hypothesis results in a two-tailed test. Directional alternative hypotheses can also be tested if we believe either that $\pi$ is greater than $\pi_0$ or that $\pi$ is less than $\pi_0$. In either case, the more the resulting sample proportion differs from the hypothesized proportion, the more likely we are to reject the null hypothesis.

It is assumed that the sample is randomly drawn from the population and that the normal distribution is the appropriate sampling distribution. The next step is to compute the test statistic $z$ as

$$z = \frac{p - \pi_0}{s_p} = \frac{p - \pi_0}{\sqrt{\dfrac{\pi_0 \left(1 - \pi_0\right)}{n}}}$$

The test statistic $z$ is then compared to a critical value(s) from the unit normal distribution. For a two-tailed test, the critical values are denoted as $\pm_{\alpha/2} z$ and are found in Appendix Table 1. If the test statistic $z$ falls into either critical region, then we reject $H_0$; otherwise, we fail to reject $H_0$. For a one-tailed test, the critical value is denoted as $+_{\alpha} z$ for the alternative hypothesis $H_1 : \pi > \pi_0$ and as $-_{\alpha} z$ for the alternative hypothesis $H_1 : \pi < \pi_0$. If the test statistic $z$ falls into the appropriate critical region, we reject $H_0$; otherwise, we fail to reject $H_0$.

For the two-tailed test, a $(1 - \alpha)\%$ confidence interval can also be examined. The confidence interval is formed as follows:

$$p \pm_{1 - \alpha/2} z(s_p)$$

If the confidence interval contains the hypothesized proportion $\pi_0$, then the conclusion is to fail to reject $H_0$; otherwise, we reject $H_0$. Simulation research has shown that this confidence interval procedure works fine for small samples when the sample proportion is near .50; that is, the normal distribution is a reasonable approximation in this situation. However, as the sample proportion moves closer to 0 or 1, larger samples are required for the normal distribution to be reasonably approximate. Alternative approaches have been developed that appear to be more widely applicable. The interested reader is referred to Ghosh (1979) and Wilcox (1996).

Several points should be noted about each of the $z$ tests for proportions developed in this chapter. First, the interpretation of confidence intervals described in this chapter is the same as those in chapter 7. Second, Cohen's (1988) measure of effect size for proportion tests using $z$ is known as $h$. Unfortunately, $h$ involves the use of arcsin transformations of the proportions, which is beyond the scope of this test. In addition, standard statistical software, such as SPSS, do not compute measures of effect size for any of these tests.

Let us consider an example to illustrate use of the test of a single proportion. Suppose a researcher conducts a survey in a city that is voting on whether or not to have an elected school board. Based on informal conversations with a small number of influential citizens, the researcher is led to hypothesize that 50% of the voters are in favor of an elected school board. Through use of a scientific poll, the researcher would like to know whether the population proportion is different from this hypothesized value; thus a nondirectional, two-tailed alternative hypothesis is utilized. If the null hypothesis is rejected, this would indicate that scientific polls of larger samples yield different results and are important in this situation. If the null hypothesis is not rejected, this would indicate that informal conversations with a small sample are just as accurate as a scientific larger-sized sample.

A random sample of 100 voters is taken and 60 indicate their support of an elected school board (i.e., $p = .60$). In an effort to minimize the Type I error rate, the significance level is set at $\alpha = .01$. The test statistic $z$ is computed as

$$z = \frac{p - \pi_0}{\sqrt{\dfrac{\pi_0(1 - \pi_0)}{n}}} = \frac{.60 - .50}{\sqrt{\dfrac{.50(1 - .50)}{100}}} = \frac{.10}{\sqrt{\dfrac{.50(.50)}{100}}} = \frac{.10}{.0500} = 2.0000$$

Note that the final value for the denominator is the standard error of the proportion (i.e., $s_p = .0500$), which we will need for computing the confidence interval. From the Appendix Table 1, we determine the critical values to be $\pm_{\alpha/2}z = \pm_{.005}z = \pm2.5758$. As the test statistic does not exceed the critical values and thus fails to fall into a critical region, our decision is to fail to reject $H_0$. Our conclusion then is that the accuracy of the scientific poll is not any different from the hypothesized value of .50 as determined informally.

The 99% confidence interval for the example would be computed as follows:

$$p \pm_{\alpha/2} z(s_p) = .60 \pm 2.5758(.0500) = .60 \pm .1288 = (.4712, .7288)$$

Because the confidence interval does contain the hypothesized value of .50, our conclusion is to fail to reject $H_0$. The conclusion derived from the test statistic is always consistent with the conclusion derived from the confidence interval.

### 8.1.3 Inferences About Two Independent Proportions

In our second inferential testing situation for proportions, the researcher would like to know whether the population proportion for one group is different from the population proportion for a second independent group. This is comparable to the independent $t$ test described in chapter 7 where one population mean was compared to a second independent population mean. Once again we have two independently drawn samples, as discussed in chapter 7.

First, the hypotheses to be evaluated for detecting whether two independent population proportions differ are as follows. The null hypothesis $H_0$ is that there is no difference between the two population proportions $\pi_1$ and $\pi_2$, which we denote as

$$H_0: \pi_1 - \pi_2 = 0$$

Here there is no difference or a "null" difference between the two population proportions. For example, we may be seeking to determine whether the proportion of Democratic Senators who support gun control is equal to the proportion of Republican Senators who support gun control.

The nondirectional, scientific or alternative hypothesis $H_1$ is that there is a difference between the population proportions $\pi_1$ and $\pi_2$, which we denote as

$$H_1: \pi_1 - \pi_2 \neq 0$$

The null hypothesis $H_0$ will be rejected here in favor of the alternative hypothesis $H_1$ if the population proportions are different. As we have not specified a direction on $H_1$, we are willing to reject either if $\pi_1$ is greater than $\pi_2$ or if $\pi_1$ is less than $\pi_2$. This alternative hypothesis results in a two-tailed test. Directional alternative hypotheses can also be tested if we believe either that $\pi_1$ is greater than $\pi_2$ or that $\pi_1$ is less than $\pi_2$. In either case, the more the resulting sample proportions differ from one another, the more likely we are to reject the null hypothesis.

It is assumed that the two samples are independently and randomly drawn from their respective populations and that the normal distribution is the appropriate sampling distribution. The next step is to compute the test statistic $z$ as

$$z = \frac{p_1 - p_2}{s_{p_1 - p_2}} = \frac{p_1 - p_2}{\sqrt{p(1-p)\left(\dfrac{1}{n_1} + \dfrac{1}{n_2}\right)}}$$

where $n_1$ and $n_2$ are the sample sizes for samples 1 and 2 respectively, and

$$p = \frac{f_1 + f_2}{n_1 + n_2}$$

where $f_1$ and $f_2$ are the number of observed frequencies for samples 1 and 2 respectively. The denominator of the $z$ test statistic $s_{p_1 - p_2}$ is known as the **standard error of the difference between two proportions**. This test statistic is conceptually similar to the test statistic for the independent $t$ test.

The test statistic $z$ is then compared to a critical value(s) from the unit normal distribution. For a two-tailed test, the critical values are denoted as $\pm_{\alpha/2}z$ and are found in Appendix Table 1. If the test statistic $z$ falls into either critical region, then we reject $H_0$; otherwise, we fail to reject $H_0$. For a one-tailed test, the critical value is denoted as $+_{\alpha}z$ for the alternative hypothesis $H_1$: $\pi_1 - \pi_2 > 0$ and as $-_{\alpha}z$ for the alternative hypothesis $H_1$: $\pi_1 - \pi_2 < 0$. If the test statistic $z$ falls into the appropriate critical region, then we reject $H_0$; otherwise, we fail to reject $H_0$. It should be noted that other alternatives to this test have been proposed (e.g., Storer & Kim, 1990).

For the two-tailed test, a $(1 - \alpha)\%$ confidence interval can also be examined. The confidence interval is formed as follows:

$$(p_1 - p_2) \pm_{\alpha/2} z\, (s_{p_1 - p_2})$$

If the confidence interval contains zero, then the conclusion is to fail to reject $H_0$; otherwise, we reject $H_0$. Alternative methods are described by Beal (1987) and Coe and Tamhane (1993).

Let us consider an example to illustrate use of the test of two independent proportions. Suppose a researcher is taste-testing a new chocolate candy ("chocolate yummies") and wants to know the extent to which individuals would likely purchase the product. As taste in candy may be different for adults versus children, a study is conducted where independent samples of adults and children are given "chocolate yummies" to eat and asked whether they would buy them or not. The researcher would like to know whether the population proportion of individuals who would purchase "chocolate yummies" is different for adults and children. Thus a nondirectional, two-tailed alternative hypothesis is utilized. If the null hypothesis is rejected, this would indicate that interest in purchasing the product is different in the two groups, and this might result in different marketing and packaging strategies for each group. If the null hypothesis is not rejected, then this would indicate the product is equally of interest to both adults and children, and different marketing and packaging strategies are not necessary.

A random sample of 100 children (sample 1) and a random sample of 100 adults (sample 2) are independently selected. Each individual consumes the product and indicates whether or not he or she would purchase it. Sixty-eight of the children and 54 of the adults state they would purchase "chocolate yummies" if they were available. The level of significance is set at $\alpha = .05$. The test statistic $z$ is computed as follows. We know that $n_1 = 100$, $n_2 = 100$, $f_1 = 68$, $f_2 = 54$, $p_1 = .68$, and $p_2 = .54$. We compute $p$ to be

$$p = \frac{f_1 + f_2}{n_1 + n_2} = \frac{68 + 54}{100 + 100} = \frac{122}{200} = .6100$$

This allows us to compute the test statistic $z$ as

$$z = \frac{p_1 - p_2}{\sqrt{p(1-p)\left(\dfrac{1}{n_1} + \dfrac{1}{n_2}\right)}}$$

$$= \frac{.6800 - .5400}{\sqrt{(.6100)(1 - .6100)\left(\dfrac{1}{100} + \dfrac{1}{100}\right)}} = \frac{.1400}{\sqrt{(.6100)(.3900)(.0200)}} = \frac{.1400}{.0690} = 2.0290$$

The denominator of the $z$ test statistic, $s_{p_1 - p_2} = .0690$, is the standard error of the difference between two proportions, which we will need for computing the confidence interval.

The test statistic $z$ is then compared to the critical values from the unit normal distribution. As this is a two-tailed test, the critical values are denoted as $\pm_{\alpha/2} z$ and are found in Appendix Table 1 to be $\pm_{\alpha/2} z = \pm_{.025} z = \pm 1.9600$. As the test statistic $z$ falls into the upper tail critical region, we reject $H_0$ and conclude that the adults and children are not equally interested in the product.

Finally, we can compute the 95% confidence interval as follows:

$$(p_1 - p_2) \pm_{\alpha/2} z (s_{p_1 - p_2})$$
$$= (.6800 - .5400) \pm 1.9600 (.0690) = (.1400) \pm (.1352) = (.0048, .2752)$$

Because the confidence interval does not include zero, we would again reject $H_0$ and conclude that the adults and children are not equally interested in the product. As previously stated, the conclusion derived from the test statistic is always consistent with the conclusion derived from the confidence interval.

### 8.1.4  Inferences About Two Dependent Proportions

In our third inferential testing situation for proportions, the researcher would like to know whether the population proportion for one group is different from the population proportion for a second dependent group. This is comparable to the dependent $t$ test described in chapter 7 where one population mean was compared to a second dependent population mean. Once again we have two dependently drawn samples as discussed in chapter 7. For example, we may have a pretest-posttest situation where a comparison of proportions over time for the same individuals is conducted. Alternatively, we may have pairs of individuals (e.g., spouses, twins, brother-sister) for which a comparison of proportions is of interest.

First, the hypotheses to be evaluated for detecting whether two dependent population proportions differ are as follows. The null hypothesis $H_0$ is that there is no difference between the two population proportions $\pi_1$ and $\pi_2$, which we denote as

$$H_0: \pi_1 - \pi_2 = 0$$

Here there is no difference or a "null" difference between the two population proportions. For example, a political analyst may be interested in determining whether the approval rating of the President is the same just prior to and immediately following his annual State of the Union address (i.e., a pretest-posttest situation). As a second example, a marriage counselor wants to know whether husbands and wives equally favor a particular training program designed to enhance their relationship (i.e., a couples situation).

The nondirectional, scientific or alternative hypothesis $H_1$ is that there is a difference between the population proportions $\pi_1$ and $\pi_2$, which we denote as

$$H_1: \pi_1 - \pi_2 \neq 0$$

The null hypothesis $H_0$ will be rejected here in favor of the alternative hypothesis $H_1$ if the population proportions are different. As we have not specified a direction on $H_1$, we are willing to reject either if $\pi_1$ is greater than $\pi_2$ or if $\pi_1$ is less than $\pi_2$. This alternative hypothesis results in a two-tailed test. Directional alternative hypotheses can also be tested if we believe either that $\pi_1$ is greater than $\pi_2$ or that $\pi_1$ is less than $\pi_2$. The more the resulting sample proportions differ from one another, the more likely we are to reject the null hypothesis.

Before we examine the test statistic, let us consider a table in which the proportions are often presented. As shown in Table 8.1, the **contingency table** lists proportions for each of the different possible outcomes. The columns indicate the proportions for sample 1. The left column contains those proportions related to the "unfavorable" condition (or disagree or no, depending on the situation), and the right column those proportions related to the "favorable" condition (or agree or yes, depending on the situation). At the bottom of the columns are the marginal proportions shown for the "unfavorable" condition, denoted by $1 - p_1$, and for the "favorable" condition, denoted by $p_1$. The rows indicate the proportions for sample 2. The top row contains those proportions for the "favorable" condition, and the bottom row contains those proportions for the "unfavorable" condition. To the right of the rows are the marginal proportions shown for the "favorable" condition, denoted by $p_2$, and for the "unfavorable" condition, denoted by $1 - p_2$.

Within the box of the table are the proportions for the different combinations of conditions across the two samples. The upper left-hand cell is the proportion of observations that are "unfavorable" in sample 1 and "favorable" in sample 2 (i.e., dissimilar across samples), denoted by $a$. The upper right-hand cell is the proportion of observations who are "favorable" in sample 1 and "favorable" in sample 2 (i.e., similar across samples), denoted by $b$. The lower left-hand cell is the proportion of observations who are "unfavorable" in sample 1 and "unfavorable" in sample 2 (i.e., similar across samples), denoted by $c$. The lower right-hand cell is the proportion of observations who are "favorable" in sample 1 and "unfavorable" in sample 2 (i.e., dissimilar across samples), denoted by $d$.

**TABLE 8.1**

Contingency Table for Two Samples

| Sample 2 | Sample 1 | | |
| | *"Unfavorable"* | *"Favorable"* | |
| --- | --- | --- | --- |
| "Favorable" | $a$ | $b$ | $p_2$ |
| "Unfavorable" | $c$ | $d$ | $1 - p_2$ |
| | $1 - p_1$ | $p_1$ | |

It is assumed that the two samples are randomly drawn from their respective populations and that the normal distribution is the appropriate sampling distribution. The next step is to compute the test statistic $z$ as

$$z = \frac{p_1 - p_2}{s_{p_1 - p_2}} = \frac{p_1 - p_2}{\sqrt{\dfrac{d + a}{n}}}$$

where $n$ is the total number of pairs. The denominator of the $z$ test statistic $s_{p_1 - p_2}$ is again known as the standard error of the difference between two proportions. This test statistic is conceptually similar to the test statistic for the dependent $t$ test.

The test statistic $z$ is then compared to a critical value(s) from the unit normal distribution. For a two-tailed test, the critical values are denoted as $\pm_{\alpha/2}z$ and are found in Appendix Table 1. If the test statistic $z$ falls into either critical region, then we reject $H_0$; otherwise, we fail to reject $H_0$. For a one-tailed test, the critical value is denoted as $+_{\alpha}z$ for the alternative hypothesis $H_1: \pi_1 - \pi_2 > 0$ and as $-_{\alpha}z$ for the alternative hypothesis $H_1: \pi_1 - \pi_2 < 0$. If the test statistic $z$ falls into the appropriate critical region, then we reject $H_0$; otherwise, we fail to reject $H_0$. It should be noted that other alternatives to this test have been proposed (e.g., the chi-square test as described in the following section). Unfortunately, the $z$ test does not yield an acceptable confidence interval procedure.

Let us consider an example to illustrate use of the test of two dependent proportions. Suppose a medical researcher is interested in whether husbands and wives agree on the effectiveness of a new headache medication "No-Head." A random sample of 100 husband-wife couples were selected and asked to try "No-Head" for two months. At the end of two months, each individual was asked whether the medication was effective or not at reducing headache pain. The researcher wants to know whether the medication is differentially effective for husbands and wives. Thus a nondirectional, two-tailed alternative hypothesis is utilized.

The resulting proportions are presented as a contingency table in Table 8.2. The level of significance is set at $\alpha = .05$. The test statistic $z$ is computed as follows:

$$z = \frac{p_1 - p_2}{s_{p_1 - p_2}} = \frac{p_1 - p_2}{\sqrt{\dfrac{d + a}{n}}} = \frac{(.4000 - .6500)}{\sqrt{\dfrac{.1500 + .4000}{100}}} = \frac{-.2500}{.0742} = -3.3693$$

**TABLE 8.2**
Contingency Table for Headache Example

| | Husband Sample | | |
| --- | --- | --- | --- |
| *Wife Sample* | *"Ineffective"* | *"Effective"* | |
| "Effective" | $a = .40$ | $b = .25$ | $p_2 = .65$ |
| "Ineffective" | $c = .20$ | $d = .15$ | $1 - p_2 = .35$ |
| | $1 - p_1 = .60$ | $p_1 = .40$ | |

The test statistic $z$ is then compared to the critical values from the unit normal distribution. As this is a two-tailed test, the critical values are denoted as $\pm_{\alpha/2}z$ and are found in Appendix Table 1 to be $\pm_{\alpha/2}z = \pm_{.025}z = \pm1.9600$. As the test statistic $z$ falls into the lower tail critical region, we reject $H_0$ and conclude that the husbands and wives do not believe equally in the effectiveness of "No-Head."

## 8.2 INFERENCES ABOUT PROPORTIONS INVOLVING THE CHI-SQUARE DISTRIBUTION

This section deals with concepts and procedures for testing inferences about proportions that involve the chi-square distribution. Following a discussion of the chi-square distribution relevant to tests of proportions, inferential tests are presented for the chi-square goodness-of-fit test and the chi-square test of association.

### 8.2.1 Introduction

The previous tests of proportions in this chapter were based on the normal distribution, whereas the tests of proportions in the remainder of the chapter are based on the **chi-square distribution**. Thus we need to become familiar with this new distribution. Like the normal and $t$ distributions, the chi-square distribution is really a family of distributions. Also, like the $t$ distribution, the chi-square distribution family members depend on the number of degrees of freedom represented. For example, the chi-square distribution for one degree of freedom is denoted by $\chi_1^2$ as shown in Fig. 8.1. This particular chi-square distribution is especially positively skewed and leptokurtic (sharp peak).

The figure also describes graphically the distributions for $\chi_5^2$ and $\chi_{10}^2$. As you can see in the figure, as the degrees of freedom increase, the distribution becomes less skewed and less leptokurtic; in fact, the distribution becomes more nearly normal in shape as the number of degrees of freedom increase. For extremely large degrees of freedom, the chi-square distribution is approximately normal. In general we denote a particular chi-square distribution with $\nu$ degrees of freedom as $\chi_\nu^2$. The mean of any chi-square distribution is $\nu$, the mode is $\nu - 2$ when $\nu$ is at least 2, and the variance is $2\nu$. The value of chi-square ranges from zero to positive infinity. A table of different percentile values for many chi-square distributions is given in Appendix Table 3. This table is utilized in the following two chi-square tests.

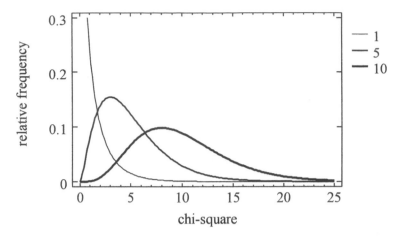

FIG. 8.1    Several members of the family of the chi-square distribution.

## 8.2.2    The Chi-square Goodness-of-fit Test

The first test to consider is the **chi-square goodness-of-fit test**. This test is used to determine whether the observed proportions in two or more categories of a categorical variable differ from what we would expect *a priori*. For example, a researcher is interested in whether the current undergraduate student-body at Ivy-Covered University (ICU) are majoring in disciplines according to an *a priori* or expected set of proportions. Based on research at the national level, the expected proportions of undergraduate college majors are as follows: .20 Education; .40 Arts and Sciences; .10 Communication; and .30 Business. In a random sample of 100 undergraduates at ICU, the observed proportions are as follows: .25 Education; .50 Arts and Sciences; .10 Communication; and .15 Business. Thus the researcher would like to know whether the sample proportions observed at ICU fit the expected national proportions. In essence, the chi-square goodness-of-fit test is used for a single categorical variable.

The **observed proportions** are denoted by $p_j$, where $p$ represents a sample proportion and $j$ represents a particular category (e.g., Education majors), where $j = 1, ..., J$ categories. The **expected proportions** are denoted by $\pi_j$, where $\pi$ represents an expected proportion and $j$ represents a particular category. The null and alternative hypotheses are denoted as follows:

$$H_0: (p_j - \pi_j) = 0 \text{ for all } j$$
$$H_1: (p_j - \pi_j) \neq 0 \text{ for all } j$$

The test statistic is a chi-square and is computed by

$$\chi^2 = n \sum_{j=1}^{J} \frac{(p_j - \pi_j)^2}{\pi_j}$$

where $n$ is the size of the sample. The test statistic is compared to a critical value from the chi-square table (Appendix Table 3) $_\alpha\chi^2_\nu$, where $\nu = J - 1$. The degrees of freedom are one less than the number of total categories $J$, because the proportions must total to 1.00; thus only $J - 1$ are free to vary.

If the test statistic is larger than the critical value, then the null hypothesis is rejected in favor of the alternative. This would indicate that the observed and expected proportions were not equal for all categories. The larger the differences between one or more observed and expected proportions, the larger the value of the test statistic and the more likely it is to reject the null hypothesis. Otherwise, we would fail to reject the null hypothesis, indicating that the observed and expected proportions were approximately equal for all categories.

If the null hypothesis is rejected, one may wish to determine which sample proportions are different from their respective expected proportions. Here we recommend you conduct tests of a single proportion as described in the preceding section. If you would like to control the experiment-wise Type I error rate across a set of such tests, then the Bonferroni method is recommended where the $\alpha$ level is divided up among the number of tests conducted. For example, with an overall $\alpha = .05$ and five categories, one would conduct five tests of a single proportion each at the .01 level of $\alpha$.

Several points should be noted about each of the chi-square tests of proportions developed in this chapter. First, there are no confidence interval procedures. Second, Cohen's (1988) measure of effect size for the chi-square tests of proportions is known as $w$. Unfortunately, $w$ is not provided in standard statistical software, such as SPSS. However, other measures of effect size, such as correlations and measures of association, are commonly reported. These include the contingency coefficient $C$, phi, Cramer's $V$, among many that are available. As an example, from $C$ we can compute Cohen's $w$ as follows:

$$w = \sqrt{\frac{C^2}{1 - C^2}}$$

Cohen's recommended subjective standard for interpreting $w$ is as follows: small effect size, $w = .10$; medium effect size, $w = .30$; large effect size, $w = .50$. See Cohen (1988) for further details.

Let us return to the example and conduct the chi-square goodness-of-fit test. The test statistic is computed as

$$\chi^2 = n \sum_{j=1}^{J} \frac{(p_j - \pi_j)^2}{\pi_j}$$

$$= 100 \sum_{j=1}^{4} \left[ \frac{(.25 - .20)^2}{.20} + \frac{(.50 - .40)^2}{.40} + \frac{(.10 - .10)^2}{.10} + \frac{(.15 - .30)^2}{.30} \right]$$

$$= 100 \sum_{j=1}^{4} (.0125 + .0250 + .0000 + .0750) = 100 (.1125) = 11.2500$$

The test statistic is compared to the critical value, from Appendix Table 3, of $_{.05}\chi_3^2 = 7.8147$. Because the test statistic is larger than the critical value, we reject the null hypothesis and conclude that the sample proportions from ICU are different from the expected proportions at the national level. Follow-up tests for each category could also be conducted, as shown in the preceding section.

## 8.2.3   The Chi-square Test of Association

The second test to consider is the **chi-square test of association**. This test is equivalent to the chi-square test of independence and the chi-square test of homogeneity, which are not further discussed. The chi-square test of association incorporates both of these tests (e.g., Glass & Hopkins, 1996). The chi-square test of association is used to determine whether there is an association between two or more categorical variables. Our discussion is, for the most part, restricted to the two variable situation where each variable has two or more categories. The chi-square test of association is the logical extension to the chi-square goodness-of-fit test, which is concerned with one categorical variable. Unlike the chi-square goodness-of-fit test where the expected proportions are known *a priori*, for the chi-square test of association the expected proportions are not known *a priori*, but must be estimated from the sample data.

For example, suppose a researcher is interested in whether there is an association between level of education and stance on a proposed amendment to legalize gambling. Thus one categorical variable is level of education with the categories being (1) less than a high school education, (2) high school graduate, (3) undergraduate degree, and (4) graduate school degree. The other categorical variable is stance on the gambling amendment with the categories being (1) in favor of the gambling bill, and (2) opposed to the gambling bill. The null hypothesis is that there is no association between level of education and stance on gambling, whereas the alternative hypothesis is that there is some association between level of education and stance on gambling. The alternative would be supported if individuals at one level of education felt differently about the bill than individuals at another level of education.

The data are shown in Table 8.3, known as a **contingency table**. As there are two categorical variables, we have a two-way or two-dimensional contingency table. Each combination of the two variables is known as a **cell**. For example, the cell for row 1, favor bill, and column 2, high school graduate, is denoted as cell 12, the first value referring to the row and the second value to the column. Thus, the first subscript indicates the particular row $r$ and the second subscript indicates the particular column $c$. The row subscript ranges from $r = 1, ..., R$ and the column subscript

### TABLE 8.3
Contingency Table for Gambling Example

| Stance on Gambling | Less Than High School | High School | Under- graduate | Graduate | |
|---|---|---|---|---|---|
| | *Level of Education* | | | | |
| "Favor" | $n_{11} = 16$ | $n_{12} = 13$ | $n_{13} = 10$ | $n_{14} = 5$ | $n_{1.} = 44$ |
| | $p_{11} = .80$ | $p_{12} = .65$ | $p_{13} = .50$ | $p_{14} = .25$ | $p_{1.} = .55$ |
| "Opposed" | $n_{21} = 4$ | $n_{22} = 7$ | $n_{23} = 10$ | $n_{24} = 15$ | $n_{2.} = 36$ |
| | $p_{21} = .20$ | $p_{22} = .35$ | $p_{23} = .50$ | $p_{24} = .75$ | $p_{2.} = .45$ |
| | $n_{.1} = 20$ | $n_{.2} = 20$ | $n_{.3} = 20$ | $n_{.4} = 20$ | $n_{..} = 80$ |

ranges from $c = 1, ..., C$, where $R$ is the last row and $C$ is the last column. This example contains a total of 8 cells, 2 rows times 4 columns, denoted by $R \times C = 2 \times 4 = 8$.

Each cell in the table contains two pieces of information, the number of observations in that cell and the observed proportion in that cell. For cell 12, there are 13 observations denoted by $n_{12} = 13$ and an observed proportion of .65 denoted by $p_{12} = .65$. The observed proportion is computed by taking the number of observations in a cell and dividing by the number of observations in the column. Thus for the 12 cell, 13 of the 20 high school graduates favor the bill or $13/20 = .65$. The column information is given at the bottom of each column, known as the **column marginals**. Here we are given the number of observations in a column, denoted by $n_{.c}$, where the "." indicates we have summed across rows and $c$ indicates the particular column. For column 2, there are 20 observations denoted by $n_{.2} = 20$.

There is also row information contained at the end of each row, known as the **row marginals**. Two values are listed in the row marginals. First, the number of observations in a row is denoted by $n_{r.}$, where $r$ indicates the particular row and the "." indicates we have summed across the columns. Second, the expected proportion for a specific row is denoted by $\pi_{r.}$, where again $r$ indicates the particular row and the "." indicates we have summed across the columns. The expected proportion for a particular row is computed by taking the number of observations in that row $n_{r.}$ and dividing by the number of total observations $n_{..}$. Note that the total number of observations is given in the lower right-hand portion of the figure and denoted as $n_{..} = 80$. Thus for the first row, the expected proportion is computed as $\pi_{1.} = n_{1.}/n_{..} = 44/80 = .55$.

The null and alternative hypotheses can be written as follows:

$$H_0: (p_{rc} - \pi_{r.}) = 0 \text{ for all cells}$$

$$H_1: (p_{rc} - \pi_{r.}) \neq 0 \text{ for all cells}$$

The test statistic is a chi-square and is computed by

$$\chi^2 = \sum_{r=1}^{R} \sum_{c=1}^{C} n_{.c} \frac{(p_{rc} - \pi_{r.})^2}{\pi_{r.}}$$

The test statistic is compared to a critical value from the chi-square table (Appendix Table 3) $_{\alpha}\chi^2_{\nu}$, where $\nu = (R - 1)(C - 1)$. That is, the degrees of freedom are one less than the number of rows times one less than the number of columns.

If the test statistic is larger than the critical value, then the null hypothesis is rejected in favor of the alternative. This would indicate that the observed and expected proportions were not equal across cells such that the two categorical variables have some association. The larger the differences between the observed and expected proportions, the larger the value of the test statistic and the more likely it is to reject the null hypothesis. Otherwise, we would fail to reject the null hypothesis, indicating that the observed and expected proportions were approximately equal, such that the two categorical variables have no association.

If the null hypothesis is rejected, then one may wish to determine for which combination of categories the sample proportions are different from their respective expected proportions. Here we recommend you construct 2×2 contingency tables as subsets of the larger table and conduct chi-square tests of association. If you would like to control the experiment-wise Type I error rate across the set of tests, then the Bonferroni method is recommended where the $\alpha$ level is divided up among the number of tests conducted. For example, with $\alpha = .05$ and five $2\times2$ tables, one would conduct five tests each at the .01 level of $\alpha$. Finally, it should be noted that we have only considered two-way contingency tables here. Multiway contingency tables can also be constructed and the chi-square test of association utilized to determine whether there is an association among several categorical variables.

Let us complete the analysis of the example data. The test statistic is computed as

$$\chi^2 = \sum_{r=1}^{R} \sum_{c=1}^{C} n_{.c} \frac{(p_{rc} - \pi_{r.})^2}{\pi_{r.}}$$

$$= 20\frac{(.80 - .55)^2}{.55} + 20\frac{(.20 - .45)^2}{.45} + 20\frac{(.65 - .55)^2}{.55} + 20\frac{(.35 - .45)^2}{.45} +$$

$$20\frac{(.50 - .55)^2}{.55} + 20\frac{(.50 - .45)^2}{.45} + 20\frac{(.25 - .55)^2}{.55} + 20\frac{(.75 - 45)^2}{.45}$$

$$= 2.2727 + 2.7778 + 0.3636 + 0.4444 + 0.0909 + 0.1111 + 3.2727 + 4.0000 = 13.3332$$

The test statistic is compared to the critical value, from Appendix Table 3, of $_{.05}\chi_3^2 = 7.8147$. Because the test statistic is larger than the critical value, we reject the null hypothesis and conclude that there is an association between level of education and stance on the gambling bill. In other words, peoples' stance on gambling is not the same for all levels of education. The cells with the largest contribution to the test statistic give some indication where the observed and expected proportions differ the most. Here the first and fourth columns have the largest contributions to the test statistic and have the greatest differences between the observed and expected proportions; these would be of interest in a $2\times2$ follow-up test.

## 8.3    SPSS

Once again we consider the use of SPSS for the example datasets as well as write an APA style paragraph describing the results. While SPSS does not have any of the $z$ procedures described in the first part of this chapter, it is capable of conducting both of the chi-square procedures covered in the second part of this chapter. To conduct the chi-square goodness-of-fit test, your dataset needs to include a single variable (e.g., major). Go to the "Analyze" pulldown, into "Nonparametric Tests," and then into the "Chi-Square" procedure. Click the variable (e.g., major) into the "Test Variable List" box. In the lower righthand portion of the screen is a section for "Expected Values." The default is to conduct the analysis with the expected values equal for each category, clicking the radio button "All categories equal." Much of the time you will want to use different expected values, so then you click on the "Values" radio button. Enter each expected value in the box to the right of "Values," in the same order as the categories (e.g., first the value for category 1, then 2, etc.), and click on the add button each time. This sets up an expected value for each category. Then click on "OK" to run the analysis. The output is shown in Table 8.4. The top box gives the observed and expected frequencies for each category, while the bottom box gives the chi-square value, degrees of freedom, and significance value.

**TABLE 8.4**
SPSS Results for Undergraduate Majors Example

*Major*

|  | *Observed N* | *Expected N* |
|---|---|---|
| 1.00 | 25 | 20.0 |
| 2.00 | 50 | 40.0 |
| 3.00 | 10 | 10.0 |
| 4.00 | 15 | 30.0 |
| Total | 100 | |

*Test Statistics*

|  | *Major* |
|---|---|
| Chi-Square[a] | 11.250 |
| df | 3 |
| Asymp. Sig. | .010 |

[a]0 cells (.0%) have expected frequencies less than 5. The minimum expected cell frequency is 10.0.

Now for an example paragraph detailing the results of the chi-square goodness-of-fit test for the undergraduate major example. As shown in Table 8.4, there is a significant difference between the proportion of undergraduate majors at ICU and those nationally ($\chi^2 = 11.250$, $df = 3$, $p = .010$). Thus the null hypothesis that the proportions of undergraduate majors at ICU parallel those expected at the national level was rejected at the .05 level of significance. A follow-up test could be conducted on those categories where the disparity is the greatest; here the greatest difference was for category 4, business, followed by category 2, arts and sciences.

To conduct a chi-square test of association, your dataset needs to include the two variables whose frequencies you wish to associate (e.g., education level and gambling stance). Go to the "Analyze" pulldown, into "Descriptive Statistics," and then into the "Crosstabs" procedure. Click one variable into the "Row(s)" box and the other into the "Column(s)" box [e.g., here we used gambling (1 = support and 0 = not support) as the "Row" variable, and level of education (1 = less than high school, 2 = high school, 3 = undergraduate, 4 = graduate) as the "Column" variable]. If you click on the "Statistics" box, you can choose various measures of association (be sure to check chi-square). Click on the "Cells" box to obtain different "Counts" and "Percentages" to be generated (I asked for "Observed Counts" and "Column Percentages"). Finally, click on the "Format" box to determine which order, "Ascending" or "Descending," you want the row values presented in the contingency table (I asked for descending, such that row 1 was gambling = 1 and row 2 was gambling = 0). Then click on "OK" to run the analysis. The output appears in Table 8.5, where the top box provides the contingency table (i.e., counts and percentages) and the bottom box gives the results of the procedure.

**TABLE 8.5**
SPSS Results for Gambling Example

*gamble ∗ education Crosstabulation*

|  |  |  | education | | | | |
| --- | --- | --- | --- | --- | --- | --- | --- |
|  |  |  | *1.00* | *2.00* | *3.00* | *4.00* | *Total* |
| gamble | 1.00 | Count | 16 | 13 | 10 | 5 | 44 |
|  |  | % within education | 80.0% | 65.0% | 50.0% | 25.0% | 55.0% |
|  | .00 | Count | 4 | 7 | 10 | 15 | 36 |
|  |  | % within education | 20.0% | 35.0% | 50.0% | 75.0% | 45.0% |
| Total |  | Count | 20 | 20 | 20 | 20 | 80 |
|  |  | % within education | 100.0% | 100.0% | 100.0% | 100.0% | 100.0% |

*Chi-Square Tests*

|  | *Value* | *df* | *Asymp. Sig. (2-sided)* |
| --- | --- | --- | --- |
| Pearson Chi-Sqare | 13.333[a] | 3 | .004 |

[a]0 cells (.0%) have expected count less than 5. The minimum expected count is 9.00.

Next we see an example paragraph of the results of the chi-square test of association for the gambling example. From Table 8.5 we can see from the row marginals that 55% of the individuals overall support gambling. However, lower levels of education have a much higher percentage of support, while the highest level of education has a much lower percentage of support. Thus there appears to be an association or relationship between gambling and level of education. This is subsequently supported statistically from the chi-square test ($\chi^2 = 13.333$, $df = 3$, $p = .004$). Thus the null hypothesis that there is no association between stance on gambling and level of education was rejected at the .01 level of significance. A follow-up test could be conducted on subsets of categories where the association appears to be the greatest (e.g., just looking at gambling for the highest and lowest levels of education).

Finally, it should be noted that SPSS does not provide power or effect size information for any of the procedures in this chapter. Effect size, using Cohen's (1988) *h* or *w*, can be easily computed by hand from the SPSS results. *A priori* power can be determined using specialized software (e.g., Power and Precision, Ex-Sample) or power tables (e.g., Cohen, 1988). *Post hoc* power can be determined from the exact significance level given by SPSS for a two-tailed test.

## 8.4   SUMMARY

In this chapter we described a third inferential testing situation, testing hypotheses about proportions. Several inferential tests and new concepts were discussed. The new concepts introduced were proportions, sampling distribution and standard error of a proportion, contingency table, chi-square distribution, and observed versus expected frequencies. The inferential tests described involving the normal distribution were tests of a single proportion, of two independent proportions, and of two dependent proportions. These tests are parallel to the tests of one or two means previously discussed in chapters 6 and 7. The inferential tests described involving the chi-square distribution were the chi-square goodness-of-fit test and the chi-square test of association. In addition, examples were presented for each of these tests. At this point you should have met the following objectives: (a) be able to understand the basic concepts underlying tests of proportions, (b) be able to select the appropriate test, and (c) be able to compute and interpret the results from the appropriate test. In chapter 9 we discuss inferential tests involving variances.

## PROBLEMS

### Conceptual Problems

1. How many degrees of freedom are there in a 5×7 contingency table when the chi-square test of association is used?

   a. 12
   b. 24
   c. 30
   d. 35

2. The more that two independent sample proportions differ, all else being equal, the smaller the $z$ test statistic. True or false?

3. The null hypothesis is a numerical statement about an unknown parameter. True or false?

4. In testing the null hypothesis that the proportion is .50, the critical value of $z$ increases as degrees of freedom increase. True or false?

5. A consultant found a sample proportion of individuals favoring the legalization of drugs to be $-.50$. I assert that a test of whether that sample proportion is different from 0 would be rejected. Am I correct?

6. Suppose I wish to test the following hypothesis at the .10 level of significance:

$$H_0: \pi = .60$$
$$H_1: \pi > .60$$

   A sample proportion of .15 is observed. I assert if I conduct the $z$ test that it is possible to reject the null hypotheis. Am I correct?

7. When the chi-square test statistic for a test of association is less than the corresponding critical value, I assert that I should reject the null hypothesis. Am I correct?

8. Other things being equal, the larger the sample size, the smaller the value of $s_p$. True or false?

9.  In the chi-square test of association, as the difference between the observed and expected proportions increases,

    a.  the critical value for chi-square increases.

    b.  the critical value for chi-square decreases.

    c.  the likelihood of rejecting the null hypothesis decreases.

    d.  the likelihood of rejecting the null hypothesis increases.

10. When the hypothesized value of the population proportion lies outside of the confidence interval around a single sample proportion, I assert that the researcher should reject the null hypothesis. Am I correct?

## Computational Problems

1.  For a random sample of 40 widgets produced by the Acme Widget Company, 30 successes and 10 failures are observed. Test the following hypotheses at the .05 level of significance:

$$H_0: \pi = .60$$
$$H_1: \pi \neq .60$$

2.  The following data are calculated for two independent random samples of male and female teenagers, respectively, on whether they expect to attend graduate school: $n_1 = 48, p_1 = 18/48, n_2 = 52, p_2 = 33/52$. Test the following hypotheses at the .05 level of significance:

$$H_0: \pi_1 - \pi_2 = 0$$
$$H_1: \pi_1 - \pi_2 \neq 0$$

3.  The following frequencies of successes and failures are obtained for two dependent random samples measured at the pretest and posttest of a weight training program:

|          | Pretest |         |
| -------- | ------- | ------- |
| Posttest | Success | Failure |
| Failure  | 18      | 30      |
| Success  | 33      | 19      |

Test the following hypotheses at the .05 level of significance:

$$H_0: \pi_1 - \pi_2 = 0$$
$$H_1: \pi_1 - \pi_2 \neq 0$$

4.  A chi-square goodness-of-fit test is to be conducted with six categories of professions to determine whether the sample proportions of those supporting the current govern-

ment differ from *a priori* national proportions. The chi-square test statistic is equal to 16.00. Determine the result of this test by looking up the critical value and making a statistical decision, using $\alpha = .01$.

5. A random sample of 30 voters were classified according to their general political beliefs (liberal vs. conservative) and also according to whether they voted for or against the incumbent representative in their town. The results were placed into the following contingency table:

|  | *Liberal* | *Conservative* |
| --- | --- | --- |
| Yes | 10 | 5 |
| No | 5 | 10 |

Use the chi-square test of association to determine whether political belief is independent of voting behavior at the .05 level of significance.

## Interpretive Problem

There are numerous ways to use the statistics survey dataset from the CD as there are several categorical variables. Here are some examples for the tests described in this chapter.

a. Conduct a test of a single proportion: is the sample proportion of females equal to .50?

b. Conduct a test of two independent proportions: is there a difference between the sample proportion of females who are right-handed and the sample proportion of males who are right-handed?

c. Conduct a test of two dependent proportions: is there a difference between the sample proportion of student's mothers who are right-handed and the sample proportion of student's fathers who are right-handed?

d. Conduct a chi-square goodness-of-fit test: do the sample proportions for the political view categories differ from their expected proportions (very liberal = .10, liberal = .15, middle of the road = .50, conservative = .15, very conservative = .10)?

e. Conduct a chi-square test of association: is there an association between political view and gender?

# 9

# INFERENCES ABOUT VARIANCES

## Chapter Outline

1.  New concepts
2.  Inferences about a single variance
3.  Inferences about two dependent variances
4.  Inferences about two or more independent variances (homogeneity of variance tests)
    Traditional tests
    The Brown-Forsythe procedure
    The O'Brien procedure

## Key Concepts

1.  Sampling distributions of the variance
2.  The $F$ distribution
3.  Homogeneity of variance tests

In the previous three chapters we looked at testing inferences about means (chaps. 6 and 7) and about proportions (chap. 8). In this chapter we examine inferential tests involving variances. Tests of variances are useful in two applications, (a) as an inferential test, and (b) as a test of the homogeneity of variance assumption. First, a researcher may want to perform inferential tests on variances for their own sake, in the same fashion that we described the one- and two-sample $t$ tests on means. For example, we may want to assess whether the variance of undergraduates at Ivy-Covered University on an intelligence measure is the same as the theoretically-derived variance of 225 (from when the test was developed and normed). In other words, is the variance at a particular university greater than or less than 225? As another example, we may want to determine whether the variances on an intelligence measure are consistent across two or more groups; for example, is the variance of the intelligence measure at Ivy-Covered University different from that at Podunk University?

Second, for some procedures such as the independent $t$ test (chap. 7) and the analysis of variance (chap. 11), it is assumed that the variances for two or more independent samples are equal (known as the homogeneity of variance assumption). Thus, we may want to use an inferential test of variances to assess whether this assumption has been violated or not. The following inferential tests of variances are covered in this chapter: testing whether a single variance is different from a hypothesized value; testing whether two dependent variances are different; and testing whether two or more independent variances are different. We utilize many of the foundational concepts previously covered in chapters 6, 7, and 8. New concepts to be discussed include the following: the sampling distributions of the variance; the $F$ distribution; and homogeneity of variance tests. Our objectives are that by the end of this chapter, you will be able to (a) understand the basic concepts underlying tests of variances, (b) select the appropriate test, and (c) compute and interpret the results from the appropriate test.

## 9.1   NEW CONCEPTS

This section deals with concepts for testing inferences about variances, in particular, the sampling distributions underlying such tests. Subsequent sections deal with several inferential tests of variances. Although the sampling distribution of the mean is a normal distribution (chaps. 6 and 7), and the sampling distribution of a proportion is either a normal or chi-square distribution (chap. 8), the **sampling distribution of a variance** is either a chi-square distribution for a single variance, a $t$ distribution for two dependent variances, or an $F$ distribution for two or more independent variances. Although we have already discussed the $t$ distribution in chapter 6 and the chi-square distribution in chapter 8, we need to discuss the $F$ distribution (named in honor of the famous statistician R. A. Fisher) in some detail here.

Like the normal, $t$ and chi-square distributions, the **$F$ distribution** is really a family of distributions. Also, like the $t$ and chi-square distributions, the $F$ distribution family members depend on the number of degrees of freedom represented. Unlike any previously discussed distribution, the $F$ distribution family members actually depend on a combination of two different degrees of freedom, one for the numerator and one for the denominator. The reason is that the $F$ distribution is a ratio of two chi-square variables. To be more precise, $F$ with $v_1$ degrees of freedom for the numerator and $v_2$ degrees of freedom for the denominator is actually a ratio of the following chi-square variables:

$$F_{v_1, v_2} = \frac{\chi^2_{v_1} / v_1}{\chi^2_{v_2} / v_2}$$

For example, the $F$ distribution for 1 degree of freedom numerator and 10 degrees of freedom denominator is denoted by $F_{1,10}$. The $F$ distribution is generally positively skewed and leptokurtic in shape (like the chi-square distribution) and has a mean of $v_2/(v_2 - 2)$ when $v_2 > 2$. A few examples of the $F$ distribution are shown in Fig. 9.1 for the following pairs of degrees of freedom (i.e., numerator, denominator): $F_{10,10}$; $F_{20,20}$; $F_{40,40}$.

Critical values for several levels of $\alpha$ of the $F$ distribution at various combinations of degrees of freedom are given in Appendix Table 4. The numerator degrees of freedom are given in the columns of the table ($v_1$) and the denominator degrees of freedom are shown in the rows of the table ($v_2$). Only the upper-tail critical values are given in the table (e.g., percentiles of .90, .95, .99 for $\alpha = .10, .05, .01$, respectively). The reason is that most inferential tests involving the $F$ distribution are one-tailed tests using the upper-tail critical region. Thus to find the upper-tail critical value for $_{.05}F_{1,10}$, we look on the second page of the table ($\alpha = .05$), in the first column of values on that page for $v_1 = 1$, and where it intersects with the 10th row of values for $v_2 = 10$. There you should find $_{.05}F_{1,10} = 4.96$.

## 9.2   INFERENCES ABOUT A SINGLE VARIANCE

In our initial inferential testing situation for variances, the researcher would like to know whether the population variance is equal to some hypothesized variance or not. First, the

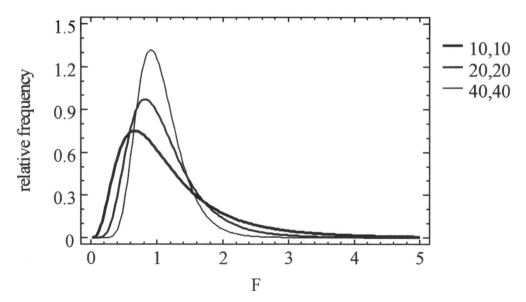

**FIG. 9.1   Several members of the family of *F* distributions.**

hypotheses to be evaluated for detecting whether a population variance differs from a hypothesized variance are as follows. The null hypothesis $H_0$ is that there is no difference between the population variance $\sigma^2$ and the hypothesized variance $\sigma_0^2$, which we denote as

$$H_0: \sigma^2 = \sigma_0^2$$

Here there is no difference or a "null" difference between the population variance and the hypothesized variance. For example, if we are seeking to determine whether the variance on an intelligence measure at Ivy-Covered University is different from the overall adult population, then a reasonable hypothesized value would be 225, as this is the theoretically derived variance for the adult population.

The nondirectional, scientific or alternative hypothesis $H_1$ is that there is a difference between the population variance $\sigma^2$ and the hypothesized variance $\sigma_0^2$, which we denote as

$$H_1: \sigma^2 \neq \sigma_0^2$$

The null hypothesis $H_0$ will be rejected here in favor of the alternative hypothesis $H_1$ if the population variance is different from the hypothesized variance. As we have not specified a direction on $H_1$, we are willing to reject either if $\sigma^2$ is greater than $\sigma_0^2$ or if $\sigma^2$ is less than $\sigma_0^2$. This alternative hypothesis results in a two-tailed test. Directional alternative hypotheses can also be tested if we believe either that $\sigma^2$ is greater than $\sigma_0^2$ or that $\sigma^2$ is less than $\sigma_0^2$. In either case, the more the resulting sample variance differs from the hypothesized variance, the more likely we are to reject the null hypothesis.

It is assumed that the sample is randomly drawn from the population and that the population of scores is normally distributed. The next step is to compute the test statistic $\chi^2$ as

$$\chi^2 = \frac{\nu s^2}{\sigma_0^2}$$

where $s^2$ is the sample variance and $\nu = n - 1$. The test statistic $\chi^2$ is then compared to a critical value(s) from the chi-square distribution. For a two-tailed test, the critical values are denoted as $_{\alpha/2}\chi_\nu^2$ and $_{1-\alpha/2}\chi_\nu^2$ and are found in Appendix Table 3. If the test statistic $\chi^2$ falls into either critical region, then we reject $H_0$; otherwise, we fail to reject $H_0$. For a one-tailed test, the critical value is denoted as $_\alpha\chi_\nu^2$ for the alternative hypothesis $H_1: \sigma^2 < \sigma_0^2$ and as $_{1-\alpha}\chi_\nu^2$ for the alternative hypothesis $H_1: \sigma^2 > \sigma_0^2$. If the test statistic $\chi^2$ falls into the appropriate critical region, then we reject $H_0$; otherwise, we fail to reject $H_0$. It has been noted by statisticians such as Wilcox (1996) that the chi-square distribution does not perform adequately when sampling from a nonnormal distribution, as the actual Type I error rate can differ greatly from the nominal $\alpha$ level (the level set by the researcher). However, Wilcox stated "it appears that a completely satisfactory solution does not yet exist, although many attempts have been made to find one" (p. 85).

For the two-tailed test, a $(1 - \alpha)\%$ confidence interval can also be examined and is formed as follows. The lower limit of the confidence interval is

$$\frac{\nu s^2}{_{1-\alpha/2}\chi_\nu^2}$$

whereas the upper limit of the confidence interval is

$$\frac{v\, s^2}{_{\alpha/2}\chi_v^2}$$

If the confidence interval contains the hypothesized value $\sigma_0^2$, then the conclusion is to fail to reject $H_0$; otherwise, we reject $H_0$.

Now for an example to illustrate use of the test of a single variance. A researcher at the esteemed Ivy-Covered University is interested in determining whether the population variance in intelligence at the university is different from the norm-developed hypothesized variance of 225. Thus, a nondirectional, two-tailed alternative hypothesis is utilized. If the null hypothesis is rejected, this would indicate that the intelligence level at Ivy-Covered University is more or less diverse or variable than the norm. If the null hypothesis is not rejected, this would indicate that the intelligence level at Ivy-Covered University is as equally diverse or variable as the norm.

The researcher takes a random sample of 101 undergraduates from throughout the university and computes a sample variance of 149. The test statistic $\chi^2$ is computed as

$$\chi^2 = \frac{v\, s^2}{\sigma_0^2} = \frac{100\,(149)}{225} = 66.2222$$

From the Appendix Table 3, and using an $\alpha$ level of .05, we determine the critical values to be $_{.025}\chi_{100}^2 = 74.2219$ and $_{.975}\chi_{100}^2 = 129.561$. As the test statistic does exceed one of the critical values by falling into the lower-tail critical region (i.e., $66.2222 < 74.2219$), our decision is to reject $H_0$. Our conclusion then is that the variance of the undergraduates at Ivy-Covered University is different from the hypothesized value of 225.

The 95% confidence interval for the example is computed as follows. The lower limit of the confidence interval is

$$\frac{v\, s^2}{_{1-\alpha/2}\chi_v^2} = \frac{100\,(149)}{129.561} = 115.0037$$

and the upper limit of the confidence interval is

$$\frac{v\, s^2}{_{\alpha/2}\chi_v^2} = \frac{100\,(149)}{74.2219} = 200.7494$$

As the limits of the confidence interval (i.e., 115.0037, 200.7494) do not contain the hypothesized variance of 225, the conclusion is to reject $H_0$. As always, the confidence interval procedure leads us to the same conclusion as the hypothesis testing procedure for the same $\alpha$ level.

## 9.3 INFERENCES ABOUT TWO DEPENDENT VARIANCES

In our second inferential testing situation for variances, the researcher would like to know whether the population variance for one group is different from the population variance for a second dependent group. This is comparable to the dependent $t$ test described in chapter 7 where one population mean was compared to a second dependent population mean. Once again we have two dependently drawn samples.

First, the hypotheses to be evaluated for detecting whether two dependent population variances differ are as follows. The null hypothesis $H_0$ is that there is no difference between the two population variances $\sigma_1^2$ and $\sigma_2^2$, which we denote as

$$H_0: \sigma_1^2 - \sigma_2^2 = 0$$

Here there is no difference or a "null" difference between the two population variances. For example, we may be seeking to determine whether the variance of husbands' incomes is equal to the variance of their wives' incomes. Thus the husband and wife samples are drawn as couples in pairs or dependently, rather than individually or independently.

The nondirectional, scientific or alternative hypothesis $H_1$ is that there is a difference between the population variances $\sigma_1^2$ and $\sigma_2^2$, which we denote as

$$H_1: \sigma_1^2 - \sigma_2^2 \neq 0$$

The null hypothesis $H_0$ is rejected here in favor of the alternative hypothesis $H_1$ if the population variances are different. As we have not specified a direction on $H_1$, we are willing to reject either if $\sigma_1^2$ is greater than $\sigma_2^2$ or if $\sigma_1^2$ is less than $\sigma_2^2$. This alternative hypothesis results in a two-tailed test. Directional alternative hypotheses can also be tested if we believe either that $\sigma_1^2$ is greater than $\sigma_2^2$ or that $\sigma_1^2$ is less than $\sigma_2^2$. In either case, the more the resulting sample variances differ from one another, the more likely we are to reject the null hypothesis.

It is assumed that the two samples are dependently and randomly drawn from their respective populations, that both populations are normal in shape, and that the $t$ distribution is the appropriate sampling distribution. The next step is to compute the test statistic $t$ as

$$t = \frac{s_1^2 - s_2^2}{2s_1 s_2 \sqrt{\dfrac{1 - r_{12}^2}{v}}}$$

where $s_1^2$ and $s_2^2$ are the sample variances for samples 1 and 2 respectively, $s_1$ and $s_2$ are the sample standard deviations for samples 1 and 2 respectively, $r_{12}$ is the correlation between the scores from sample 1 and sample 2 (which is then squared), and $v$ is the number of degrees of freedom, $v = n - 2$, $n$ being the number of paired observations (not the number of total observations). Although correlations are not formally discussed until chapter 10, conceptually the correlation is a measure of the relationship between two variables. This test statistic is conceptually somewhat similar to the test statistic for the dependent $t$ test.

The test statistic $t$ is then compared to a critical value(s) from the $t$ distribution. For a two-tailed test, the critical values are denoted as $\pm_{\alpha_2} t_v$ and are found in Appendix Table 2. If the test statistic $t$ falls into either critical region, then we reject $H_0$; otherwise, we fail to reject $H_0$. For a one-tailed test, the critical value is denoted as $+_{\alpha_1} t_v$ for the alternative hypothesis $H_1: \sigma_1^2 - \sigma_2^2 > 0$ and as $-_{\alpha_1} t_v$ for the alternative hypothesis $H_1: \sigma_1^2 - \sigma_2^2 < 0$. If the test statistic $t$ falls into the appropriate critical region, then we reject $H_0$; otherwise, we fail to reject $H_0$. It is thought that this test is not particularly robust to nonnormality (Wilcox, 1987). As a result, other procedures have been developed that are thought to be more robust. However, little in the way of empirical results is known at this time. Some of the new procedures can also be used for testing inferences involving the equality of two or more dependent variances. In addition, note that acceptable confidence interval procedures are not currently available.

Let us consider an example to illustrate use of the test of two dependent variances. A researcher is interested in whether there is greater variation in achievement test scores at the end of the first grade as compared with the beginning of the first grade. Thus a directional, one-tailed alternative hypothesis is utilized. If the null hypothesis is rejected, this would indicate that first graders' achievement test scores are more variable at the end of the year than at the beginning of the year. If the null hypothesis is not rejected, this would indicate that first graders' achievement test scores have approximately the same variance at both the end of the year and at the beginning of the year.

A random sample of 62 first-grade children is selected and given the same achievement test at the beginning of the school year (September) and at the end of the school year (April). Thus the same students are tested twice with the same instrument, thereby resulting in dependent samples at time 1 and time 2. The level of significance is set at $\alpha = .01$. The test statistic $t$ is computed as follows. We determine that $n = 62$, $\nu = 60$, $s_1^2 = 100$, $s_1 = 10$, $s_2^2 = 169$, $s_2 = 13$, and $r_{12} = .80$. We compute the test statistic $t$ to be

$$t = \frac{s_1^2 - s_2^2}{2 s_1 s_2 \sqrt{\dfrac{1 - r_{12}^2}{\nu}}} = \frac{100 - 169}{2\,(10)\,13 \sqrt{\dfrac{1 - .64}{60}}} = -3.4261$$

The test statistic $t$ is then compared to the critical value from the $t$ distribution. As this is a one-tailed test, the critical value is denoted as $-_{\alpha_1} t_\nu$ and is found in Appendix Table 2 to be $-_{.01} t_{60} = -2.390$. The test statistic $t$ falls into the lower-tail critical region, as it is less than the critical value (i.e., $-3.4261 < -2.390$), so we reject $H_0$ and conclude that the variance in achievement test scores increases from September to April.

## 9.4   INFERENCES ABOUT TWO OR MORE INDEPENDENT VARIANCES (HOMOGENEITY OF VARIANCE TESTS)

In our third and final inferential testing situation for variances, the researcher would like to know whether the population variance for one group is different from the population variance for one or more other independent groups. In this section we first describe the somewhat cloudy situation that exists for the traditional tests. Then we provide details on two recommended tests, the Brown—Forsythe procedure and the O'Brien procedure.

### 9.4.1   Traditional Tests

One of the more heavily studied inferential testing situations in recent years has been for testing whether differences exist among two or more independent group variances. These tests are often referred to as **homogeneity of variance tests**. Here we briefly discuss the more traditional tests and their associated problems. In the sections that follow, we then recommend two of the "better" tests.

Several tests have traditionally been used to test for the equality of independent variances. An early simple test for two independent variances is to form a ratio of the two sample variances, which yields the following $F$ test statistic:

$$F = \frac{s_1^2}{s_2^2}$$

This $F$ ratio test assumes that the two populations are normally distributed. However, it is known that the $F$ ratio test is not very robust to violation of the normality assumption, except for when the sample sizes are equal (i.e., $n_1 = n_2$). In addition, the $F$ ratio test can only be used for the two-group situation.

Subsequently, more general tests were developed to cover the multiple-group situation. One such popular test is Hartley's $F_{max}$ test (developed in 1950), which is simply a more general version of the $F$ ratio test just described. The test statistic for Hartley's $F_{max}$ test is

$$F_{max} = \frac{s^2_{largest}}{s^2_{smallest}}$$

where $s^2_{largest}$ is the largest variance in the set of variances and $s^2_{smallest}$ is the smallest variance in the set. Hartley's $F_{max}$ test assumes normal population distributions and requires equal sample sizes. We also know that Hartley's $F_{max}$ test is not very robust to violation of the normality assumption. Cochran's $C$ test (developed in 1941) is also an $F$ test statistic computed by taking the ratio of the largest variance to the sum of all of the variances. Cochran's $C$ test also assumes normality, requires equal sample sizes, and has been found to be even less robust to nonnormality than Hartley's $F_{max}$ test. As we see in chapter 11 for the analysis of variance, it is when we have unequal sample sizes that unequal variances is a problem; for these reasons none of these tests can be recommended, which is the same situation we encountered with the independent $t$ test.

Bartlett's $\chi^2$ test (developed in 1937) does not have the stringent requirement of equal sample sizes; however, it does still assume normality. Bartlett's test is very sensitive to nonnormality and is therefore not recommended either. Since 1950 the development of homogeneity tests has proliferated, with the goal being to find a test that is fairly robust to nonnormality. Seemingly as each new test was developed, later research would show that the test was not very robust. Today there are well over 60 such tests available for examining homogeneity of variance [e.g., a bootstrap method developed by Wilcox (2002)]. Rather than engage in a protracted discussion of these tests and their associated limitations, we simply present two tests that have been shown to be most robust to nonnormality in several recent studies. These are the Brown-Forsythe procedure and the O'Brien procedure. Unfortunately, neither of these tests is available in the major statistical packages (e.g., SPSS), which only include some of the problematic tests previously described.

### 9.4.2 The Brown-Forsythe Procedure

The Brown-Forsythe procedure is a variation of the Levene test developed in 1960. The Levene test is essentially an analysis of variance on the transformed variable

$$Z_{ij} = |Y_{ij} - \overline{Y}_{.j}|$$

where $i$ designates the $i^{th}$ observation in group $j$, and where $Z_{ij}$ is computed for each individual by taking their score $Y_{ij}$, subtracting from it the group mean $\overline{Y}_{.j}$ (the "." indicating we have averaged across all $i$ observations in group $j$) and then taking the absolute value (i.e., by removing the sign). Unfortunately, the Levene test is not very robust to nonnormality except when sample sizes are equal.

Developed in 1974, the Brown-Forsythe procedure has been shown to be quite robust to non-normality in numerous studies (e.g., Olejnik & Algina, 1987; Ramsey, 1994). Based on this and other research, the Brown-Forsythe procedure is recommended for leptokurtic distributions (i.e., those with sharp peaks) (in terms of being robust to nonnormality, and providing adequate Type I error protection and excellent power). In the next section we describe the O'Brien procedure, which is recommended for other distributions (i.e., mesokurtic and platykurtic distributions). In cases where you are unsure of which procedure to use, Algina, Blair, and Combs (1995) recommend using a maximum procedure, where both tests are conducted and the procedure with the maximum test statistic is selected.

Let us now examine in detail the Brown-Forsythe procedure. The null hypothesis is that $H_0$: $\sigma_1^2 = \sigma_2^2 = ... = \sigma_J^2$ and the alternative hypothesis is that not all of the population group variances are the same. The Brown-Forsythe procedure is essentially an analysis of variance on the transformed variable

$$Z_{ij} = |Y_{ij} - Md_{.j}|$$

which is computed for each individual by taking their score $Y_{ij}$, subtracting from it the group median $Md_{.j}$, and then taking the absolute value (i.e., by removing the sign).

The test statistic is an $F$ and is computed by

$$F = \frac{\sum_{j=1}^{J} n_j \left(\overline{Z}_{.j} - \overline{Z}_{..}\right)^2 / (J-1)}{\sum_{i=1}^{n_j} \sum_{j=1}^{J} \left(Z_{ij} - \overline{Z}_{.j}\right)^2 / (N-J)}$$

where $n_j$ designates the number of observations in group $j$, $J$ is the number of groups (such that $j$ ranges from 1 to $J$), $\overline{Z}_{.j}$ is the mean for group $j$ (computed by taking the sum of the observations in group $j$ and dividing by the number of observations in group $j$, which is $n_j$), and $\overline{Z}_{..}$ is the overall mean regardless of group membership (computed by taking the sum of all of the observations across all groups and dividing by the total number of observations $N$). The test statistic $F$ is compared against a critical value from the $F$ table (Appendix Table 4) with $J - 1$ degrees of freedom in the numerator and $N - J$ degrees of freedom in the denominator, denoted by $_\alpha F_{J-1, N-J}$. If the test statistic is greater than the critical value, we reject $H_0$; otherwise, we fail to reject $H_0$.

An example using the Brown-Forsythe procedure is certainly in order now. Three different groups of children, below-average, average, and above-average readers, play a computer game. The scores on the dependent variable $Y$ are their total points from the game. We are interested in whether the variances for the three student groups are equal or not. The example data and computations are given in Table 9.1. First we compute the median for each group, then compute the deviation from the median for each individual to obtain the transformed $Z$ values. Then the transformed $Z$ values are used to compute the $F$ test statistic.

The test statistic $F = 1.6388$ is compared against the critical value for $\alpha = .05$ of $_{.05}F_{2,9} = 4.26$. As the test statistic is smaller than the critical value (i.e., $1.6388 < 4.26$), we fail to reject the null hypothesis and conclude that the three student groups do not have different variances.

**TABLE 9.1**
Example Using the Brown-Forsythe and O'Brien Procedures

| Group 1 | | | Group 2 | | | Group 3 | | | | |
|---|---|---|---|---|---|---|---|---|---|---|
| Y | Z | r | Y | Z | r | Y | Z | r | | |
| 6 | 4 | 124.2499 | 9 | 4 | 143 | 10 | 8 | 704 | | |
| 8 | 2 | 14.2499 | 12 | 1 | −7 | 16 | 2 | −16 | | |
| 12 | 2 | 34.2499 | 14 | 1 | −7 | 20 | 2 | −96 | | |
| 13 | 3 | 89.2499 | 17 | 4 | 143 | 30 | 12 | 1104 | | |
| Md | $\bar{Z}$ | $\bar{r}$ | Md | $\bar{Z}$ | $\bar{r}$ | Md | $\bar{Z}$ | $\bar{r}$ | Overall $\bar{Z}$ | Overall $\bar{r}$ |
| 10 | 2.75 | 65.4999 | 13 | 2.50 | 68 | 18 | 6 | 424 | 3.75 | 185.8333 |

Computations for the Brown-Forsythe procedure:

$$F = \frac{\sum_{j=1}^{J} n_j\,(\bar{Z}_{.j} - \bar{Z}_{..})^2/(J-1)}{\sum_{i=1}^{n_j}\sum_{j=1}^{J} (Z_{ij} - \bar{Z}_{.j})^2/(N-J)} = \frac{\left[4(2.75 - 3.75)^2 + 4(2.50 - 3.75)^2 + 4(6 - 3.75)^2\right]/2}{\left[(4 - 2.75)^2 + (2 - 2.75)^2 + \ldots + (12 - 6)^2\right]/9} = 1.6388$$

Computations for the O'Brien procedure:

Sample means: $\bar{Y}_1 = 9.75$, $\bar{Y}_2 = 13.0$, $\bar{Y}_3 = 19.0$
Sample variances: $s_1^2 = 10.9167$, $s_2^2 = 11.3333$, $s_3^2 = 70.6667$
Example computation for $r_{ij}$:

$$r_{11} = \frac{(n_j - 1.5)\,n_j\,(Y_{ij} - \bar{Y}_{.j})^2 - .5 s_j^2\,(n_j - 1)}{(n_j - 1)(n_j - 2)} = \frac{(4 - 1.5)\,4\,(6 - 9.75)^2 - .5\,(10.9167)(4 - 1)}{(4 - 1)(4 - 2)} = 124.2499$$

Test statistic:

$$F = \frac{\sum_{j=1}^{J} n_j\,(\bar{r}_{.j} - \bar{r}_{..})^2/(J-1)}{\sum_{i=1}^{n_j}\sum_{j=1}^{J} (r_{ij} - \bar{r}_{.j})^2/(N-J)}$$

$$= \frac{\left[4(65.4999 - 185.8333)^2 + 4(68 - 185.8333)^2 + 4(424 - 185.8333)^2\right]/2}{\left[(124.2499 - 65.4999)^2 + (14.2499 - 65.4999)^2 + \ldots + (1,104 - 424)^2\right]/9} = 1.4799$$

### 9.4.3   The O'Brien Procedure

The final test to consider in this chapter is the O'Brien procedure. While the Brown—Forsythe procedure is recommended for leptokurtic distributions, the O'Brien procedure is recommended for other distributions (i.e., mesokurtic and platykurtic distributions). Let us now examine in detail the O'Brien procedure. The null hypothesis is again that $H_0$: $\sigma_1^2 = \sigma_2^2 = ... = \sigma_J^2$, and the alternative hypothesis is that not all of the population group variances are the same.

The O'Brien procedure is essentially an analysis of variance on a different transformed variable

$$r_{ij} = \frac{(n_j - 1.5)\, n_j\, (Y_{ij} - \overline{Y}_{.j})^2 - .5\, s_j^2\, (n_j - 1)}{(n_j - 1)(n_j - 2)}$$

which is computed for each individual, where $n_j$ is the size of group $j$, $\overline{Y}_{.j}$ is the mean for group $j$, and $s_j^2$ is the sample variance for group $j$.

The test statistic is an $F$ and is computed by

$$F = \frac{\displaystyle\sum_{j=1}^{J} n_j\, (\overline{r}_{.j} - \overline{r}_{..})^2\, /\, (J-1)}{\displaystyle\sum_{i=1}^{n_j}\sum_{j=1}^{J} (r_{ij} - \overline{r}_{.j})^2\, /\, (N-J)}$$

where $n_j$ designates the number of observations in group $j$, $J$ is the number of groups (such that $j$ ranges from 1 to $J$), $\overline{r}_{.j}$ is the mean for group $j$ (computed by taking the sum of the observations in group $j$ and dividing by the number of observations in group $j$, which is $n_j$), and $\overline{r}_{..}$ is the overall mean regardless of group membership (computed by taking the sum of all of the observations across all groups and dividing by the total number of observations $N$). The test statistic $F$ is compared against a critical value from the $F$ table (Appendix Table 4) with $J - 1$ degrees of freedom in the numerator and $N - J$ degrees of freedom in the denominator, denoted by $_\alpha F_{J-1,N-J}$. If the test statistic is greater than the critical value, then we reject $H_0$; otherwise, we fail to reject $H_0$.

Let us return to the example in Table 9.1 and consider the results of the O'Brien procedure. From the computations shown in the table, the test statistic $F = 1.4799$ is compared against the critical value for $\alpha = .05$ of $_{.05}F_{2,9} = 4.26$. As the test statistic is smaller than the critical value (i.e., $1.4799 < 4.26$), we fail to reject the null hypothesis and conclude that the three student groups do not have different variances.

### 9.5   SPSS

Unfortunately there is not much to report on tests of variances for SPSS. There are no tests available for inferences about a single variance, or for inferences about two dependent variances. For inferences about independent variances, SPSS does provide Levene's test as part of the "Independent T Test" procedure (previously discussed in chap. 7), and as part of the "One Way ANOVA" and "Univariate ANOVA" procedures (to be discussed in chap. 11). Given our previous concerns with Levene's test, use it with caution. There is also little information published in the literature on power and effect sizes for tests of variances.

Consider an example paragraph for one of the tests described in this chapter, more specifically, testing inferences about two dependent variances. A sample of 62 first-grade children was given the same achievement test at the beginning (September) and end (April) of the same academic year. The variance in September was found to be 100, while the variance in April was 169. There was a significant increase in the dependent variances from September to April (one-tailed $t = -3.4261$, $df = 60$, $p < .05$). Thus the null hypothesis that the variances would be equal at the beginning and end of the first grade was rejected at the .05 level of significance, as the variance of achievement test scores significantly increased from September to April.

## 9.6   SUMMARY

In this chapter we described testing hypotheses about variances. Several inferential tests and new concepts were discussed. The new concepts introduced were the sampling distributions of the variance, the $F$ distribution, and homogeneity of variance tests. The first inferential test discussed was the test of a single variance, followed by a test of two dependent variances. Next we examined several tests of two or more independent variances. Here we considered the following traditional procedures: the $F$ ratio test, Hartley's $F_{max}$ test, Cochran's $C$ test, Bartlett's $\chi^2$ test, and Levene's test. Unfortunately, these tests are not very robust to violation of the normality assumption. We then discussed two newer procedures that are relatively robust to nonnormality, the Brown-Forsythe procedure and the O'Brien procedure. Examples were presented for each of the recommended tests. At this point you should have met the following objectives: (a) be able to understand the basic concepts underlying tests of variances, (b) be able to select the appropriate test, and (c) be able to compute and interpret the results from the appropriate test. In chapter 10 we discuss correlation coefficients, as well as inferential tests involving correlations.

## PROBLEMS

### Conceptual Problems

1.  Which of the following tests of homogeneity of variance is most robust to assumption violations?

    a.   $F$ ratio test

    b.   Bartlett's chi-square test

    c.   the O'Brien procedure

    d.   Hartley's $F_{max}$ test

2.  Cochran's $C$ test assumes equal sample sizes. True or false?

3.  I assert that if two dependent sample variances are identical, I would not be able to reject the null hypothesis. Am I correct?

4.  Suppose that I wish to test the following hypotheses at the .01 level of significance:

$$H_0: \sigma^2 = 250$$
$$H_1: \sigma^2 > 250$$

A sample variance of 233 is observed. I assert that if I compute the $\chi^2$ test statistic and compare it to the $\chi^2$ table, it is possible that I could reject the null hypothesis. Am I correct?

5.  If the 90% CI for a single variance extends from 25.7 to 33.6, I assert that the null hypothesis would definitely be rejected at the .10 level. Am I correct?

6.  If the mean of the sampling distribution of the difference between two variances equals 0, I assert that both samples probably represent a single population. Am I correct?

7.  Which of the following is an example of two dependent samples?

    a.  pretest scores of males in one course and posttest scores of females in another course

    b.  husbands and their wives in your neighborhood

    c.  softball players at your school and football players at your school

    d.  professors in education and professors in psychology

8.  The mean of the $F$ distribution increases as degrees of freedom denominator ($\nu_2$) increase. True or false?

## Computational Problems

1.  The following random sample of scores on a preschool ability test is obtained from a normally distributed population of 4-year olds:

    | 20 | 22 | 24 | 30 | 18 | 22 | 29 | 27 |
    |----|----|----|----|----|----|----|----|
    | 25 | 21 | 19 | 22 | 38 | 26 | 17 | 25 |

    a.  Test the following hypotheses at the .10 level of significance:

    $$H_0: \sigma^2 = 75$$
    $$H_1: \sigma^2 \neq 75$$

    b.  Construct a 90% CI.

2.  The following two independent random samples of number of CDs owned are obtained from two populations of undergraduate and graduate students, respectively:

    | *Sample 1 data:* | | | | | | *Sample 2 data:* | | | | |
    |----|----|----|----|----|---|----|----|----|----|----|
    | 42 | 36 | 47 | 35 | 46 | | 45 | 50 | 57 | 58 | 43 |
    | 37 | 52 | 44 | 47 | 51 | | 52 | 43 | 60 | 41 | 49 |
    | 56 | 54 | 55 | 50 | 40 | | 44 | 51 | 49 | 55 | 56 |
    | 40 | 46 | 41 | | | | | | | | |

    Test the following hypotheses at the .05 level of significance using the Brown—Forsythe and O'Brien procedures:

    $$H_0: \sigma_1^2 - \sigma_2^2 = 0$$
    $$H_1: \sigma_1^2 - \sigma_2^2 \neq 0$$

3. The following summary statistics are available for two dependent random samples of brothers and sisters, respectively, on their allowance for the past month: $s_1^2 = 49$, $s_2^2 = 25$, $n = 32$, $r_{12} = .60$.

   Test the following hypotheses at the .05 level of significance:

   $$H_0: \sigma_1^2 - \sigma_2^2 = 0$$
   $$H_1: \sigma_1^2 - \sigma_2^2 \neq 0$$

4. A random sample of 21 statistics exam scores is collected with a sample mean of 50 and a sample variance of 10. Test the following hypotheses at the .05 level of significance:

   $$H_0: \sigma^2 = 25$$
   $$H_1: \sigma^2 \neq 25$$

5. A pretest was given at the beginning of a history course and a posttest at the end of the course. The pretest variance is 36, the posttest variance is 64, sample size is 31, and the pretest-posttest correlation is .8. Test the null hypothesis that the two dependent variances are equal against a nondirectional alternative at the .01 level of significance.

## Interpretive Problem

Use the statistics survey dataset from the CD to determine if there are gender differences among the variances for any items of interest. Some example items might include the following:

a. Item #6: amount spent at last hair appointment

b. Item #7: number of compact disks owned

c. Item #10: amount of exercise per week

d. Item #15: number of alcoholic drinks per week

e. Item #21: number of hours studied per week

# 10

# BIVARIATE MEASURES OF ASSOCIATION

## Chapter Outline

1. Scatterplot
2. Covariance
3. Pearson product-moment correlation coefficient
4. Inferences About the Pearson product-moment correlation coefficient
    Inferences for a single sample
    Inferences for two independent samples
5. Some issues regarding correlations
6. Other measures of association
7. SPSS

## Key Concepts

1. Scatterplot
2. Strength and direction
3. Covariance
4. Correlation coefficient
5. Fisher's Z transformation
6. Linearity assumption, causation, and restriction of range issues

We have considered various inferential tests in the last four chapters, specifically those that deal with tests of means, proportions, and variances. In this chapter we examine measures of association as well as inferences involving measures of association. Methods for directly determining the relationship among two variables are known as **bivariate analysis**, rather than **univariate analysis** that is only concerned with a single variable. The indices used to directly describe the relationship among two variables are known as **correlation coefficients** (in the old days known as co-relation) or as **measures of association**.

These measures of association allow us to determine how two variables are related to one another and can be useful in two applications, (a) as a descriptive statistic and (b) as an inferential test. First, a researcher may want to compute a correlation coefficient for its own sake, simply to tell the researcher precisely how two variables are related or associated. For example, we may want to determine whether there is a relationship between the GRE-Quantitative (GRE-Q) subtest and performance on a statistics exam. Do students who score relatively high on the GRE-Q perform better on a statistics exam than do students who score relatively low on the GRE-Q? In other words, as scores increase on the GRE-Q, do they also correspondingly increase their performance on a statistics exam.

Second, we may want to use an inferential test to assess whether (a) a correlation is significantly different from zero or (b) two correlations are significantly different from one another. For example, is the correlation between GRE-Q and statistics exam performance significantly different from zero? As a second example, is the correlation between GRE-Q and statistics exam performance the same for younger students as it is for older students?

The following topics are covered in this chapter: scatterplot; covariance; Pearson product-moment correlation coefficient; inferences about the Pearson product-moment correlation coefficient; some issues regarding correlations; and other measures of association. We utilize some of the basic concepts previously covered in chapters 6 through 9. New concepts to be discussed include the following: scatterplot; strength and direction; covariance; correlation coefficient; Fisher's Z transformation; and linearity assumption, causation, and restriction of range issues. Our objectives are that by the end of this chapter, you will be able to (a) understand the concepts underlying the correlation coefficient and correlation inferential tests, (b) select the appropriate type of correlation, and (c) compute and interpret the appropriate correlation and inferential test.

## 10.1 SCATTERPLOT

This section deals with an important concept underlying the relationship among two variables, the scatterplot. Later sections move us into ways of measuring the relationship among two variables. First, however, we need to set up the situation where we have data on two different variables for each of $N$ individuals in the population. Table 10.1 displays such a situation. The first column is simply an index of the individuals in the population, from $i = 1, ..., N$, where $N$ is the total number of individuals in the population. The second column denotes the values obtained for the first variable $X$. Thus, $X_1 = 10$ means that the first individual had a score of 10 on variable $X$. The third column provides the values for the second variable $Y$. Thus, $Y_1 = 20$ indicates that the first individual had a score of 20 on variable $Y$. In an actual data table, only the scores would be shown, not the $X_i$ and $Y_i$ notation. Thus we have a tabular method for depicting the data of a two variable situation in Table 10.1.

**TABLE 10.1**
Layout for Correlational Data

| Individual | X | Y |
| --- | --- | --- |
| 1 | $X_1 = 10$ | $Y_1 = 20$ |
| 2 | $X_2 = 12$ | $Y_2 = 28$ |
| 3 | $X_3 = 20$ | $Y_3 = 33$ |
| . | . | . |
| . | . | . |
| . | . | . |
| N | $X_N = 44$ | $Y_N = 65$ |

A graphical method for depicting the relationship among two variables is to plot the pair of scores on $X$ and $Y$ for each individual on a two-dimensional figure known as a **scatterplot** (or scattergram). Each individual has two scores in a two-dimensional coordinate system, denoted by $(X, Y)$. For example, individual 1 has the scores of (10, 20). An example scatterplot is shown in Fig. 10.1. The $X$ axis (the horizontal axis or abscissa) represents the values for variable $X$ and the $Y$ axis (the vertical axis or ordinate) represents the values for variable $Y$. Each point on the scatterplot represents a pair of scores $(X, Y)$ for a particular individual. Thus individual 1 has a point at $X = 10$ and $Y = 20$ (the circled point). Points for other individuals are also shown. In essence, the scatterplot is actually a bivariate frequency distribution. The points typically take the shape of an ellipse (i.e., a football shape), as is the case for Fig. 10.1.

The scatterplot allows the researcher to evaluate both the direction and the strength of the relationship among $X$ and $Y$. The **direction** of the relationship has to do with whether the relationship is positive or negative. A positive relationship occurs when as scores on variable $X$

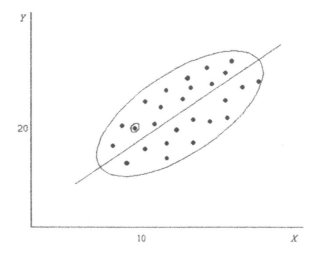

**FIG. 10.1   Scatterplot.**

increase (from left to right), scores on variable $Y$ also increase (from bottom to top). Thus Fig. 10.1 indicates a positive relationship among $X$ and $Y$. Examples of different scatterplots are shown in Fig. 10.2. Fig. 10.2(a) and Fig. 10.2(d) both display positive relationships. A negative relationship, sometimes called an inverse relationship, occurs when as scores on variable $X$ increase (from left to right), scores on variable $Y$ decrease (from top to bottom). Fig. 10.2(b) and Fig. 10.2(e) are examples of negative relationships. There is no relationship between $X$ and $Y$ when for a large value of $X$, a large or a small value of $Y$ can occur, and for a small value of $X$, a large or a small value of $Y$ can also occur. In other words, $X$ and $Y$ are not related, as shown in Fig. 10.2(c).

The **strength** of the relationship among $X$ and $Y$ is determined by the scatter of the points (hence the name scatterplot). First, we draw a straight line through the points which cuts the bivariate distribution in half, as shown in Figs. 10.1 and 10.2. In chapter 17 we note that this line is known as the regression line. If the scatter is such that the points tend to fall close to the line, then this is indicative of a strong relationship among $X$ and $Y$. Both Fig. 10.2(a) and Fig. 10.2(b) denote strong relationships. If the scatter is such that the points are widely scattered around the line, then this is indicative of a weak relationship among $X$ and $Y$. Both Fig. 10.2(d) and Fig. 10.2(e) denote weak relationships. To summarize Fig. 10.2, part (a) represents a strong positive relationship, part (b) a strong negative relationship, part (c) no relationship, part (d) a weak positive relationship, and part (e) a weak negative relationship. The scatterplot, then, is useful for providing a quick indication of the nature of the relationship among variables $X$ and $Y$.

## 10.2   COVARIANCE

The remainder of this chapter deals with statistical methods for measuring the relationship among variables $X$ and $Y$. The first such method is known as the **covariance**. The covariance conceptually is the shared variance (or co-variance) among $X$ and $Y$. The population covariance is denoted by $\sigma_{XY}$ and the conceptual formula is given as

$$\sigma_{XY} = \frac{\sum_{i=1}^{N}(X_i - \mu_X)(Y_i - \mu_Y)}{N}$$

where $X_i$ and $Y_i$ are the scores on variables $X$ and $Y$ for individual $i$, respectively, and $\mu_X$ and $\mu_Y$ are the population means for variables $X$ and $Y$, respectively. This equation looks similar to the computational formula for the variance presented in chapter 3 where deviation scores from the mean are computed for each individual. The conceptual formula for the covariance is essentially an average of the paired deviation score products. If variables $X$ and $Y$ are positively related, then the deviation scores will tend to be of similar signs, their products will tend to be positive, and the covariance will be a positive value (i.e., $\sigma_{XY} > 0$). If variables $X$ and $Y$ are negatively related, then the deviation scores will tend to be of opposite signs, their products will tend to be negative, and the covariance will be a negative value (i.e., $\sigma_{XY} < 0$).

The sample covariance is denoted by $s_{XY}$, and the conceptual formula becomes

$$s_{XY} = \frac{\sum_{i=1}^{n}(X_i - \overline{X})(Y_i - \overline{Y})}{n - 1}$$

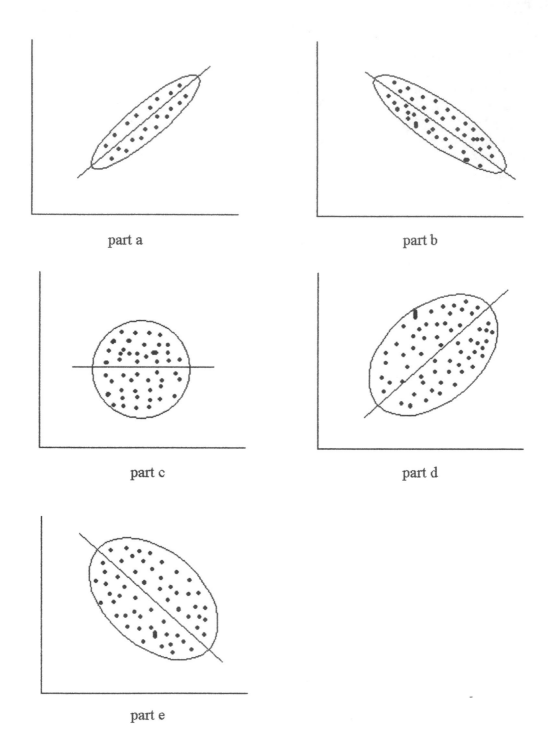

part a

part b

part c

part d

part e

FIG. 10.2    Examples of possible scatterplots.

where $\bar{X}$ and $\bar{Y}$ are the sample means for variables $X$ and $Y$, respectively, and $n$ is sample size. Note that the denominator becomes $n - 1$ so as to yield an unbiased sample estimate of the population covariance (i.e., similar to the sample variance situation).

The conceptual formula is unwieldy and error prone for other than small samples. Thus a computational formula for the population covariance has been developed as

$$\sigma_{XY} = \frac{N\left(\sum_{i=1}^{N} X_i Y_i\right) - \left(\sum_{i=1}^{N} X_i\right)\left(\sum_{i=1}^{N} Y_1\right)}{N^2}$$

where the first summation involves the cross-product of $X$ multiplied by $Y$ for each individual summed across all $N$ individuals, and the other terms should be familiar. The computational formula for the sample covariance is

$$s_{XY} = \frac{n\left(\sum_{i=1}^{n} X_i Y_i\right) - \left(\sum_{i=1}^{n} X_i\right)\left(\sum_{i=1}^{n} Y_i\right)}{n(n-1)}$$

where the denominator is $n(n-1)$ so as to yield an unbiased sample estimate of the population covariance.

Table 10.2 gives an example of a population situation where a strong positive relationship is expected because as $X$ (number of children in a family) increases $Y$ (number of pets in a family) also increases. Here $\sigma_{XY}$ is computed as

$$\sigma_{XY} = \frac{N\left(\sum_{i=1}^{N} X_i Y_i\right) - \left(\sum_{i=1}^{N} X_i\right)\left(\sum_{i=1}^{N} Y_i\right)}{N^2} = \frac{5(108) - (15)(30)}{25} = 3.6000$$

The sign indicates that the relationship between $X$ and $Y$ is indeed positive. That is, the more children a family has, the more pets they tend to have. However, like the variance, the value of

**TABLE 10.2**
Example Correlational Data ($X$ = # children, $Y$ = # pets)

| Individual | X | Y | XY | $X^2$ | $Y^2$ | Rank X | Rank Y | (Rank X − Rank Y)² |
|---|---|---|---|---|---|---|---|---|
| 1 | 1 | 2 | 2 | 1 | 4 | 1 | 1 | 0 |
| 2 | 2 | 6 | 12 | 4 | 36 | 2 | 3 | 1 |
| 3 | 3 | 4 | 12 | 9 | 16 | 3 | 2 | 1 |
| 4 | 4 | 8 | 32 | 16 | 64 | 4 | 4 | 0 |
| 5 | 5 | 10 | 50 | 25 | 100 | 5 | 5 | 0 |
| sums | 15 | 30 | 108 | 55 | 220 | | | 2 |

the covariance depends on the scales of the variables involved. Thus, interpretation of the magnitude of a single covariance is difficult, as it can take on literally any value. We see shortly that the correlation coefficient takes care of this problem. For this reason you are only likely to see the covariance utilized in the analysis of covariance (chap. 14) and structural equation modeling (a multivariate technique beyond the scope of this text).

## 10.3   PEARSON PRODUCT-MOMENT CORRELATION COEFFICIENT

Other methods for measuring the relationship among $X$ and $Y$ have been developed that are easier to interpret than the covariance. We refer to these measures as **correlation coefficients**. The first correlation coefficient we consider is the **Pearson product-moment correlation coefficient**, developed by the famous statistician Karl Pearson and simply referred to as the Pearson here. The Pearson can be considered in several different forms, where the population value is denoted by $\rho_{XY}$ (rho) and the sample value by $r_{XY}$. One conceptual form of the Pearson is a product of standardized $z$ scores (previously described in chap. 4). This formula for the Pearson is given as

$$\rho_{XY} = \frac{\sum_{i=1}^{N}(z_X)(z_Y)}{N}$$

where $z_X$ and $z_Y$ are the $z$ scores for variables $X$ and $Y$ respectively, whose product is taken for each individual and summed across all $N$ individuals.

As $z$ scores are standardized versions of raw scores, so the Pearson is a standardized version of the covariance. The sign of the Pearson denotes the direction of the relationship (e.g., positive or negative), and the value of the Pearson denotes the strength of the relationship. The Pearson falls on a scale from $-1.00$ to $+1.00$, where $-1.00$ indicates a perfect negative relationship, 0 indicates no relationship, and $+1.00$ indicates a perfect positive relationship. Values near .50 or $-.50$ are considered moderate relationships, values near 0 weak relationships, and values near $+1.00$ or $-1.00$ strong relationships (although these are subjective terms).

There are other forms of the Pearson. A second conceptual form of the Pearson is in terms of the covariance and the standard deviations and is given as

$$\rho_{XY} = \frac{\sigma_{XY}}{(\sigma_X)(\sigma_Y)}$$

This form is useful when the covariance and standard deviations are already available. A final form of the Pearson is the computational formula, written as

$$\rho_{XY} = \frac{N\left(\sum_{i=1}^{N} X_i Y_i\right) - \left(\sum_{i=1}^{N} X_i\right)\left(\sum_{i=1}^{N} Y_i\right)}{\sqrt{\left[N\left(\sum_{i=1}^{N} X_i^2\right) - \left(\sum_{i=1}^{N} X_i\right)^2\right]\left[N\left(\sum_{i=1}^{N} Y_i^2\right) - \left(\sum_{i=1}^{N} Y_i\right)^2\right]}}$$

where all terms should be familiar from the computational formulas of the variance and covariance. This is the formula to use for hand computations, as it is more error-free than the other previously given formulas. For the example children–pet data given in Table 10.2, we see that the Pearson correlation is computed as follows:

$$\rho_{XY} = \frac{N\left(\sum_{i=1}^{N} X_i Y_i\right) - \left(\sum_{i=1}^{N} X_i\right)\left(\sum_{i=1}^{N} Y_i\right)}{\sqrt{\left[N\left(\sum_{i=1}^{N} X_i^2\right) - \left(\sum_{i=1}^{N} X_i\right)^2\right]\left[N\left(\sum_{i=1}^{N} Y_i^2\right) - \left(\sum_{i=1}^{N} Y_i\right)^2\right]}} = \frac{5(108) - (15)(30)}{\sqrt{\left[5(55) - (15)^2\right]\left[5(220) - (30)^2\right]}} = .90$$

Thus, there is a very strong positive relationship among variables $X$ (the number of children) and $Y$ (the number of pets). The sample correlation is denoted by $r_{XY}$. The formulas are essentially the same for the sample correlation $r_{XY}$ and the population correlation $\rho_{XY}$, except that $n$ is substituted for $N$. For example, the computational formula for the sample correlation is

$$r_{XY} = \frac{n\left(\sum_{i=1}^{n} X_i Y_i\right) - \left(\sum_{i=1}^{n} X_i\right)\left(\sum_{i=1}^{n} Y_i\right)}{\sqrt{\left[n\left(\sum_{i=1}^{n} X_i^2\right) - \left(\sum_{i=1}^{n} X_i\right)^2\right]\left[n\left(\sum_{i=1}^{n} Y_i^2\right) - \left(\sum_{i=1}^{n} Y_i\right)^2\right]}}$$

Unlike the sample variance and covariance, the sample correlation has no correction for bias.

## 10.4 INFERENCES ABOUT THE PEARSON PRODUCT-MOMENT CORRELATION COEFFICIENT

Once a researcher has computed one or more Pearson correlation coefficients, it is often useful to know whether the sample correlations are significantly different from zero. Thus we need to visit the world of inferential statistics again. In this section we consider two different inferential tests, first for testing whether a single sample correlation is significantly different from zero, and second for testing whether two independent sample correlations are significantly different.

### 10.4.1 Inferences for a Single Sample

This inferential test is appropriate when you are interested in determining whether the correlation among variables $X$ and $Y$ for a single sample is significantly different from zero. For example, is the correlation between the number of years of education and current income significantly different from zero? The null hypothesis is written as

$$H_0: \rho = 0$$

A nondirectional alternative hypothesis, where we are willing to reject the null if the sample correlation is either significantly greater than or less than zero, is nearly always utilized. Unfortunately, the sampling distribution of the sample Pearson $r$ is too complex to be of much value to the applied researcher. For testing whether the correlation is different from zero, a transformation of $r$ can be used to generate a $t$ distributed test statistic. The test statistic is

$$t = r \sqrt{\frac{n-2}{1-r^2}}$$

which is distributed as $t$ with $v = n - 2$ degrees of freedom, assuming that both $X$ and $Y$ are normally distributed (although even if one variable is normal and the other is not, the $t$ distribution may still apply; see Hogg & Craig, 1970). It is also assumed that the scores of individuals are independent of one another.

It should be noted for inferential tests of correlations that sample size plays a role in determining statistical significance. For instance, this particular test is based on $n - 2$ degrees of freedom. If sample size is small (e.g., 10), then it is difficult to reject the null hypothesis except for very strong correlations. If sample size is large (e.g., 200), then it is easy to reject to null hypothesis for all but very weak correlations. Thus the statistical significance of a correlation is definitely a function of sample size, both for tests of a single correlation and for tests of two correlations.

Effect size and power are always important, particularly here where sample size plays such a large role. Cohen (1988) proposed using $r$ as a measure of effect size, using the subjective standard (ignoring the sign of the correlation) of $r = .1$ as a weak effect, $r = .3$ as a moderate effect, and $r = .5$ as a strong effect. These standards were developed in certain areas of inquiry, thus other standards may be applied elsewhere. Cohen also has a nice series of power tables in his chapter 3 for determining power and sample size when planning a correlational study. As for confidence intervals, Wilcox (1996) notes that "many methods have been proposed for computing confidence intervals for $\rho$, but it seems that a satisfactory method for applied work has yet to be derived" (p. 303). Thus a confidence interval procedure is not recommended, even for large samples.

From the example children–pet data, we want to determine whether the sample Pearson correlation is significantly different from zero, with a nondirectional alternative hypothesis and at the .05 level of significance. The test statistic is computed as follows:

$$t = r \sqrt{\frac{n-2}{1-r^2}} = .9000 \sqrt{\frac{5-2}{1-.81}} = 3.5762$$

The critical values from Appendix Table 2 are $\pm_{\alpha_2} t_3 = \pm 3.182$. Thus we would reject the null hypothesis, as the test statistic exceeds the critical value, and conclude the correlation among variables $X$ and $Y$ is significantly different from zero. In summary, there is a strong, positive, statistically significant correlation between the number of children and the number of pets.

## 10.4.2   Inferences for Two Independent Samples

In another situation, the researcher may have collected data from two different independent samples. One can determine whether the correlations among variables $X$ and $Y$ are equal for these two independent samples of observations. For example, is the correlation among height and weight the same for children and adults? Here the null hypothesis is written as

$$H_0: \rho_1 - \rho_2 = 0$$

where $\rho_1$ is the correlation among $X$ and $Y$ for sample 1 and $\rho_2$ is the correlation among $X$ and $Y$ for sample 2. However, because correlations are not normally distributed for every value of $\rho$, a transformation is necessary. This transformation is known as **Fisher's $Z$ transformation**, named after the famous statistician Sir Ronald A. Fisher, which is approximately normally distributed regardless of the value of $\rho$. Appendix Table 5 is used to convert a sample correlation $r$ to a Fisher's $Z$ transformed value. Note that Fisher's $Z$ is a totally different statistic from any $z$ score or statistic previously covered.

The test statistic for this hypothesis is

$$z = \frac{Z_1 - Z_2}{\sqrt{\dfrac{1}{n_1 - 3} + \dfrac{1}{n_2 - 3}}}$$

where $n_1$ and $n_2$ are the sizes of the two samples and $Z_1$ and $Z_2$ are the Fisher's $Z$ transformed values for the two samples. The test statistic is then compared to critical values from the $z$ distribution in Appendix Table 1. For a nondirectional alternative hypothesis where the two correlations may be different in either direction, then the critical values are $\pm_{\alpha_2} z$. Directional alternative hypotheses where the correlations are different in a particular direction can also be tested by looking in the appropriate tail of the $z$ distribution (i.e., either $+_{\alpha_1} z$ or $-_{\alpha_1} z$).

Cohen (1988) proposed a measure of effect size for the difference between two independent correlations as $q = Z_1 - Z_2$. The subjective standards proposed (ignoring the sign) are $q = .1$ as a weak effect, $q = .3$ as a moderate effect, and $q = .5$ as a strong effect (although standards vary across disciplines). A nice set of power tables for planning purposes is contained in chapter 4 of Cohen. Once again, while confidence interval procedures have been developed, none of these have been viewed as acceptable (Marascuilo & Serlin, 1988; Wilcox, 2003).

Consider the following example. Two samples have been independently drawn of 28 children (sample 1) and 28 adults (sample 2). For each sample, the correlations among height and weight were computed to be $r_{children} = .8$ and $r_{adults} = .4$. A nondirectional alternative hypothesis is utilized where the level of significance is set at .05. From Appendix Table 5, we first determine the Fisher's $Z$ transformed values to be $Z_{children} = 1.099$ and $Z_{adults} = .4236$. Then the test statistic $z$ is computed as follows:

$$z = \frac{Z_1 - Z_2}{\sqrt{\dfrac{1}{n_1 - 3} + \dfrac{1}{n_2 - 3}}} = \frac{1.099 - .4236}{\sqrt{\dfrac{1}{25} + \dfrac{1}{25}}} = 2.3879$$

From Appendix Table 1, the critical values are $\pm_{\alpha_2} z = 1.96$. Our decision then is to reject the null hypothesis and conclude that height and weight do not have the same correlation for children and adults. In other words, there is a statistically significant difference of the height—weight correlation between children and adults with a strong effect size. This inferential test assumes both variables are normally distributed for each population and that scores are independent across individuals; however, the procedure is not very robust to nonnormality as the $Z$ transformation assumes normality (Duncan & Layard, 1973; Yu & Dunn, 1982; Wilcox, 2003). Thus caution should be exercised in using the $z$ test when data are nonnormal (e.g., Yu and Dunn recommend the use of Kendall's $\tau$ as discussed later in this chapter).

## 10.5    SOME ISSUES REGARDING CORRELATIONS

There are several issues about the Pearson and other types of correlations that you should be aware of. These issues are concerned with the assumption of linearity, correlation and causation, and restriction of range.

### 10.5.1    Assumption of Linearity

First, each of the correlations in this chapter assumes that the relationship among $X$ and $Y$ is a **linear relationship**. In fact, these measures of relationship are really linear measures of relationship. Recall from earlier in the chapter the scatterplots that we fit a straight line to. The linearity assumption means that a straight line provides a reasonable fit to the data. If the relationship is not a linear one, then the linearity assumption is violated. However, these correlational methods will still go ahead and fit a straight line to the data, albeit inappropriately. The result of such a violation is that the strength of the relationship will be reduced. In other words, the linear correlation will be much closer to zero than the true nonlinear relationship.

For example, there is a perfect curvilinear relationship shown by the data in Fig. 10.3 where all of the points fall precisely on the curved line. Something like this might occur if you correlate age with time in the mile run, as younger and older folks would take longer to run this distance than others. If these data are fit by a straight line, then the correlation will be severely reduced, in this case, to a value of zero (i.e., the horizontal straight line that runs through the curved line). This is another good reason to always examine your data. The computer may determine that the Pearson correlation among variables $X$ and $Y$ is small or around zero. However, on examination of the data, you might find that the relationship is indeed nonlinear; thus, you should get to know your data. We return to the assessment of nonlinear relationships in chapter 17.

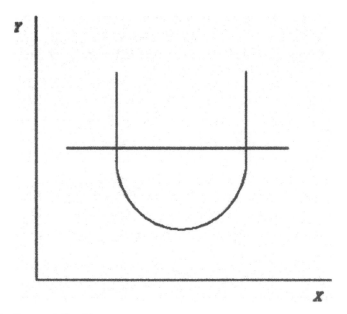

FIG. 10.3    Nonlinear relationship.

### 10.5.2 Correlation and Causality

A second matter to consider is an often-made misinterpretation of a correlation. Many individuals (e.g., researchers, the public, and the media) often infer a causal relationship from a strong correlation. However, a correlation by itself should never be used to infer **causation**. In particular, a high correlation among variables $X$ and $Y$ does not imply that one variable is causing the other; it simply means that these two variables are related in some fashion. There are many reasons why variables $X$ and $Y$ are highly correlated. A high correlation could be the result of (a) $X$ causing $Y$, or (b) $Y$ causing $X$, or (c) a third variable $Z$ causing both $X$ and $Y$, or (d) even many more variables being involved. The only methods that can strictly be used to infer cause are experimental methods where one variable is manipulated by the researcher (the cause), a second variable is subsequently observed (the effect), and all other variables are controlled.

### 10.5.3 Restriction of Range

A final issue to consider is the effect of **restriction of the range** of scores on one or both variables. For example, suppose that we are interested in the relationship among GRE scores and graduate grade point average (GGPA). In the entire population of students, the relationship might be depicted by the scatterplot shown in Fig. 10.4. Say the Pearson correlation is found to be .60 as depicted by the entire sample in the full scatterplot. Now we take a more restricted population of students, those students at highly selective Ivy-Covered University (ICU). ICU only admits students whose GRE scores are above the cutoff score shown in Fig. 10.4. Because of restriction of range in the scores of the GRE variable, the strength of the relationship among GRE and GGPA is reduced to a Pearson correlation of .20, where only the subsample portion of the plot to the right of the cutoff score is involved. Thus when scores on one or both vari-

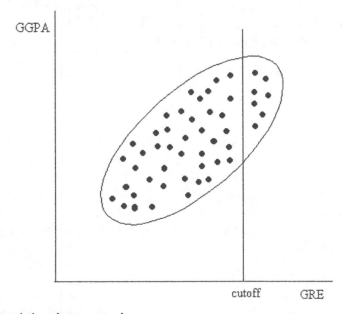

**FIG. 10.4   Restriction of range example.**

ables are restricted due to the nature of the sample or population, then the magnitude of the correlation will usually be reduced (although see an exception in Fig. 6.3 from Wilcox, 2003).

It is difficult for two variables to be highly related when one or both variables have little variability. Recall that one version of the Pearson formula consisted of standard deviations in the denominator. As the size of the standard deviation for a variable is reduced, all else being equal, so too will the size of correlations with other variables. In other words, we need sufficient variation for a relationship to be evident. Otherwise the correlation is likely to be reduced in magnitude and you may miss an important correlation. If you have to use this restrictive subsample, then choose measures of greater variability for correlational purposes.

Outliers, observations that are different from the bulk of the observations, also reduce the magnitude of correlations. If one observation is quite different from the rest such that it fell outside of the ellipse, then the correlation would be smaller in magnitude (e.g., closer to zero) than the correlation without the outlier. We discuss outliers in this context in chapter 17.

## 10.6   OTHER MEASURES OF ASSOCIATION

Thus far we have considered one type of correlation, the Pearson product-moment correlation coefficient. The Pearson is most appropriate when both variables are at least interval level. That is, both variables $X$ and $Y$ are interval or ratio level variables. If both variables are not at least interval level, then other measures of association should be considered. In this section we examine in detail the Spearman and phi types of correlation coefficients and briefly mention several other types.

Spearman's rank correlation coefficient is appropriate when both variables are ordinal level. This type of correlation was developed by Charles Spearman, the famous quantitative psychologist. Recall from chapter 1 that ordinal data are where individuals have been rank ordered, such as class rank. Thus, for both variables, either the data are already available in ranks, or the researcher converts the raw data to ranks prior to the analysis.

The equation for computing Spearman's correlation is

$$\rho_s = 1 - \frac{6\sum_{i=1}^{N}(X_i - Y_i)^2}{N(N^2 - 1)}$$

where $\rho_s$ denotes the population Spearman correlation and $(X_i - Y_i)$ represents the difference between the ranks on variables $X$ and $Y$ for individual $i$. The sample Spearman correlation is denoted by $r_s$ where $n$ replaces $N$, but otherwise the equation remains the same. In case you were wondering where the 6 in the equation comes from, you will find an interesting article by Lamb (1984). Unfortunately, this particular computational formula is only appropriate when there are no ties among the ranks for either variable. With ties, the formula given is only approximate, depending on the number of ties. In the case of ties, particularly when there are more than just a handful, many researchers recommend using Kendall's $\tau$ (tau) as an alternative correlation (e.g., Wilcox, 1996).

As an example, consider the children–pets data again in Table 10.2. To the right of the table, you see the last three columns labeled as rank $X$, rank $Y$, and (rank $X$ − rank $Y$)$^2$. The raw scores were converted to ranks, where the lowest raw score received a rank of 1. The last column lists the squared rank differences. As there were no ties, the computations are as follows:

$$\rho_s = 1 - \frac{6\sum\limits_{i=1}^{N}(X_i - Y_i)^2}{N(N^2 - 1)} = 1 - \frac{6(2)}{5(24)} = .9000$$

Thus again there is a strong positive relationship among variables $X$ and $Y$. It is a coincidence that $\rho = \rho_s$ for this dataset, but not so for computational problem 1 at the end of this chapter.

To test whether a sample Spearman correlation is significantly different from zero, we examine the following null hypothesis:

$$H_0: \rho_s = 0$$

The test statistic is given as

$$t = \frac{r_s \sqrt{n-2}}{\sqrt{1 - r_s^2}}$$

which is approximately distributed as a $t$ distribution with $v = n - 2$ degrees of freedom (Ramsey, 1989). The approximation works best when $n$ is at least 10. A nondirectional alternative hypothesis, where we are willing to reject the null if the sample correlation is either significantly greater than or less than zero, is nearly always utilized. From the example, we want to determine whether the sample Spearman correlation is significantly different from zero at the .05 level of significance. For a nondirectional alternative hypothesis, the test statistic is computed as

$$t = \frac{r_s \sqrt{n-2}}{\sqrt{1 - r_s^2}} = \frac{.9000 \sqrt{5-2}}{\sqrt{1 - .81}} = 3.5762$$

where the critical values from Appendix Table 2 are $\pm_{\alpha_2} t_3 = \pm 3.182$. Thus we would reject the null hypothesis and conclude that the correlation is significantly different from zero, strong, and positive. The exact sampling distribution for when $3 \le n \le 18$ is given by Ramsey.

The phi coefficient $\phi$ is appropriate when both variables are dichotomous in nature (statistically equivalent to the Pearson). Recall from chapter 1 that a dichotomous variable is one consisting of only two categories, such as gender, pass/fail, or enrolled/dropped out. When correlating two dichotomous variables, one can think of a 2×2 contingency table as previously discussed in chapter 8. For instance, to determine if there is a relationship among gender and whether students are still enrolled since freshman year, a contingency table like Table 10.3 can be constructed. Here the columns correspond to the two levels of the status variable, enrolled (coded 1) or dropped out (0), and the rows correspond to the two levels of the gender variable, female (1) or male (0). The cells indicate the frequencies for the particular combinations of the levels of the two variables. If the frequencies in the cells are denoted by letters, then $a$ is females dropped out, $b$ is females enrolled, $c$ is males dropped out, and $d$ is males enrolled.

**TABLE 10.3**

Contingency Table for Phi Correlation

| | Enrollment Status | | |
|---|---|---|---|
| Student Gender | Dropped Out 0 | Enrolled 1 | |
| Female 1 | $a = 5$ | $b = 20$ | 25 |
| Male 0 | $c = 15$ | $d = 10$ | 25 |
| | 20 | 30 | 50 |

The equation for computing the phi coefficient is

$$\rho_\phi = \frac{(bc - ad)}{\sqrt{(a+c)(b+d)(a+b)(c+d)}}$$

where $\rho_\phi$ denotes the population phi coefficient (for consistency's sake, although typically written as $\phi$), and $r_\phi$ denotes the sample phi coefficient using the same equation. Note that the $bc$ product involves the consistent cells, where both values are the same, either both 0 or both 1, and the $ad$ product involves the inconsistent cells, where both values are different.

Using the example data from Table 10.3, we compute the phi coefficient to be

$$\rho_\phi = \frac{(bc - ad)}{\sqrt{(a+c)(b+d)(a+b)(c+d)}} = \frac{(300 - 50)}{\sqrt{(20)(30)(25)(25)}} = .4082$$

Thus there is a moderate, positive relationship between gender and enrollment status. We see from the table that a larger proportion of females than males are still enrolled.

To test whether a sample phi correlation is significantly different from zero, we test the following null hypothesis:

$$H_0: \rho_\phi = 0$$

The test statistic is given as

$$\chi^2 = n\, r_\phi^2$$

which is distributed as a $\chi^2$ distribution with 1 degree of freedom. From the example, we want to determine whether the sample phi correlation is significantly different from zero at the .05 level of significance. The test statistic is computed as

$$\chi^2 = n\, r_\phi^2 = 50(.4082)^2 = 8.3314$$

and the critical value from Appendix Table 3 is $_{.05}\chi_1^2 = 3.84$. Thus we would reject the null hypothesis and conclude that the correlation among gender and enrollment status is significantly different from zero.

Other types of correlations have been developed for different combinations of types of variables, but these are rarely used in practice and are unavailable in most statistical packages (e.g., rank biserial and point biserial). Table 10.4 provides suggestions for when different types of correlations are most appropriate. We mention briefly the two other types of correlations in the table: the rank biserial correlation is appropriate when one variable is dichotomous and the other variable is ordinal, whereas the point biserial correlation is appropriate when one variable is dichotomous and the other variable is interval or ratio (statistically equivalent to the Pearson).

## 10.7   SPSS

Finally let us see what SPSS has to offer in terms of measures of association, including an APA style paragraph detailing the results from an example dataset. There are two programs for obtaining measures of association in SPSS, the Bivariate Correlation program and the Crosstabs program. To use the Bivariate Correlation program, go to the "Analyze" pulldown, into "Correlate," and then into "Bivariate." On the "Bivariate Correlation" screen, click the variables you want to correlate into the "Variables" box on the right-hand side. Below that check which of the following correlations is desired: Pearson, Kendall's $\tau$, and/or Spearman. Then below that are radio buttons for whether you want to conduct one- or two-tailed tests of significance, and at the very bottom check if you want to "Flag significant correlations" (which simply means placing an asterisk next to significant correlations). If you click on the "Options" button, you can also obtain means, standard deviations, and/or covariances. Finally click on "OK" to run the analysis. The output for the child–pet data is given in Table 10.5. We asked for both the Pearson and Spearman correlations, thus the top box gives the Pearson results and the bottom box the Spearman results. In both cases the output presents the correlation, sample size (N in SPSS language, although denoted as $n$ by everyone else), exact level of significance, and asterisks for significant correlations.

The Crosstabs program has already been discussed in chapter 8, but it can also be used for obtaining some measures of association. Go to the "Analyze" pulldown, into "Descriptive Statistics," and then into "Crosstabs." The setup from the main screen has already been described

TABLE 10.4
Different Types of Correlation Coefficients

| Variable Y | Variable X | | |
| | Dichotomous | Ordinal | Interval/Ratio |
|---|---|---|---|
| Dichotomous | Phi | Rank biserial | Point biserial |
| Ordinal | Rank biserial | Spearman or Kendall's $\tau$ | Spearman or Kendall's $\tau$ or Pearson |
| Interval/ratio | Point biserial | Spearman or Kendall's $\tau$ or Pearson | Pearson |

**TABLE 10.5**
SPSS Results for Child–Pet Data

*Correlations*

|  |  | Children | Pets |
|---|---|---|---|
| Children | Pearson Correlation | 1 | .900* |
|  | Sig. (2-tailed) |  | .037 |
|  | N | 5 | 5 |
| Pets | Pearson Correlation | .900* | 1 |
|  | Sig. (2-tailed) | .037 |  |
|  | N | 5 | 5 |

*Correlation is significant at the 0.05 level (2-tailed).

*Correlations*

|  |  |  | Children | Pets |
|---|---|---|---|---|
| Spearman's rho | children | Correlation Coefficient | 1.000 | .900* |
|  |  | Sig. (2-tailed) | . | .037 |
|  |  | N | 5 | 5 |
|  | pets | Correlation Coefficient | .900* | 1.000 |
|  |  | Sig. (2-tailed) | .037 | . |
|  |  | N | 5 | 5 |

*Correlation is significant at the 0.05 level (2-tailed).

in chapter 8. To obtain measures of association, click on the "Statistics" button, where you can obtain phi, Kendall's $\tau$, Spearman, Pearson, as well as other measures of association not described in this chapter.

Here is an example paragraph describing the results of the relationship among the number of children and the number of pets. As these are both ratio variables, the Pearson correlation is the most appropriate measure of association. The Pearson correlation between children and pets is .90, which is positive, has a strong effect size, and is statistically different from zero ($r = .90$, $n = 5$, $p = .037$). Thus the null hypothesis that the correlation would be zero was rejected at the .05 level of significance. The output appears in the top box of Table 10.5. We see also that SPSS does not provide any output in terms of confidence intervals, power, or effect size. Effect size is easily determined utilizing Cohen's (1988) subjective standards and we have not recommended confidence interval procedures anyway. *A priori* and *post hoc* power could again be determined using the specialized software described elsewhere in this text, or you can consult *a priori* power tables (e.g., Cohen).

## 10.8   SUMMARY

In this chapter we described various measures of the association or correlation among two variables. Several new concepts and descriptive and inferential statistics were discussed. The new concepts were as follows: scatterplot; strength and direction; covariance; correlation coefficient; Fisher's $Z$ transformation; and linearity assumption, causation and restriction of range issues. We began by introducing the scatterplot as a graphical method for depicting the association among two variables. Next we examined the covariance as an unstandardized measure of association. Then we considered the Pearson product-moment correlation coefficient, first as a descriptive statistic and then as a method for making inferences when there are either one or two samples of observations. Some important issues about the correlational measures were also discussed. Finally, a few other measures of association were introduced, in particular, the Spearman rank correlation coefficient and the phi coefficient. At this point you should have met the following objectives: (a) be able to understand the concepts underlying the correlation coefficient and correlation inferential tests, (b) be able to select the appropriate type of correlation, and (c) be able to compute and interpret the appropriate correlation and correlation inferential test. In Chapter 11 we discuss the one factor analysis of variance, the logical extension of the independent $t$ test for assessing mean differences among two or more groups.

## PROBLEMS

### Conceptual Problems

1.   The variance of $X$ is 9, the variance of $Y$ is 4, and the covariance between $X$ and $Y$ is 2. What is $r_{XY}$?

    a.   .039

    b.   .056

    c.   .233

    d.   .333

2.   Which of the following correlation coefficients, each obtained from a sample of 1000 children, indicates the weakest relationship?

    a.   $-.90$

    b.   $-.30$

    c.   $+.20$

    d.   $+.80$

3.   If the relationship between two variables is linear,

    a.   the relation can be most accurately represented by a straight line.

    b.   all the points will fall on a curved line.

    c.   the relationship is best represented by a curved line.

    d.   all the points must fall exactly on a straight line.

4.   In testing the null hypothesis that a correlation is equal to zero, the critical value decreases as $\alpha$ decreases. True or false?

5.   If the variances of $X$ and $Y$ are increased, but their covariance remains constant, the value of $r_{XY}$ will be unchanged. True or false?

6.  We compute $r_{XY} = .50$ for a sample of students on variables $X$ and $Y$. I assert that if the low-scoring students on variable $X$ are removed, then the new value of $r_{XY}$ would most likely be less than .50. Am I correct?

7.  Two variables are linearly related such that there is a perfect relationship between $X$ and $Y$. I assert that $r_{XY}$ must be equal to either $+1.00$ or $-1.00$. Am I correct?

8.  If the number of credit cards owned and the number of cars owned are strongly positively correlated, then those with more credit cards tend to own more cars. True or false?

9.  A statistical consultant at a rival university found the correlation between GRE Quantitative scores and statistics grades to be $+2.0$. I assert that the administration should be advised to congratulate the students and faculty on their great work in the classroom. Am I correct?

10. If $X$ correlates significantly with $Y$, then $X$ is necessarily a cause of $Y$. True or false?

11. If both $X$ and $Y$ are ordinal variables, then the most appropriate measure of association is the Pearson. True or false?

## Computational Problems

1.  You are given the following pairs of sample scores on $X$ (number of credit cards in your possession) and $Y$ (number of those credit cards with balances):

    | $X$ | $Y$ |
    |-----|-----|
    | 5 | 4 |
    | 6 | 1 |
    | 4 | 3 |
    | 8 | 7 |
    | 2 | 2 |

    a.  Graph a scatterplot of the data.
    b.  Compute the covariance.
    c.  Compute the Pearson product-moment correlation coefficient.
    d.  Compute the Spearman correlation coefficient.

2.  If $r_{XY} = .17$ for a random sample of size 84, test the hypothesis that the population Pearson is significantly different from 0 (conduct a two-tailed test at the .05 level of significance).

3.  The correlation between vocabulary size and mother's age is .50 for 12 rural children and .85 for 17 inner-city children. Does the correlation for rural children differ from that of the inner-city children at the .05 level of significance?

4. You are given the following pairs of sample scores on $X$ (number of coins in possession) and $Y$ (number of bills in possession):

   | X | Y |
   |---|---|
   | 1 | 1 |
   | 2 | 3 |
   | 3 | 5 |
   | 4 | 5 |
   | 5 | 3 |
   | 6 | 1 |

   a. Graph a scatterplot of the data.

   b. Describe the relationship between $X$ and $Y$.

   c. What do you think the Pearson correlation will be?

5. Six adults were assessed on the number of minutes to read a government report ($X$) and the number of items correct on a test of the content of that report ($Y$). Use the data below to determine the Pearson correlation and the effect size.

   | X | Y |
   |----|----|
   | 10 | 17 |
   | 8  | 17 |
   | 15 | 13 |
   | 12 | 16 |
   | 14 | 15 |
   | 16 | 12 |

## Interpretive Problem

1. Select two interval/ratio variables from the statistics survey dataset on the CD. Use SPSS to generate the appropriate correlation, determine statistical significance, and examine the scatterplot.

2. Select two ordinal variables from the statistics survey dataset on the CD. Use SPSS to generate the appropriate correlation, determine statistical significance, and examine the scatterplot.

# 11

# ONE-FACTOR ANALYSIS OF VARIANCE— FIXED-EFFECTS MODEL

## Chapter Outline

1.    Characteristics of the one-factor ANOVA model
2.    The layout of the data
3.    ANOVA theory
        General theory and logic
        Partitioning the sums of squares
        The ANOVA summary table
4.    The ANOVA model
        The model
        Estimation of the parameters of the model
        Effect size measures, confidence intervals, and power
        An example
5.    Assumptions and violation of assumptions
        Independence
        Homogeneity of variance
        Normality
6.    The unequal $n$'s or unbalanced design
7.    Alternative ANOVA procedures
8.    SPSS

## Key Concepts

1. Between- and within-groups variability
2. Sources of variation
3. Partitioning the sums of squares
4. The ANOVA model

In the last five chapters our discussion has dealt with various inferential statistics, including inferences about means. The next six chapters are concerned with different analysis of variance (ANOVA) models. In this chapter we consider the most basic ANOVA model, known as the one-factor analysis of variance model. Recall the independent $t$ test from chapter 7 where the means from two independent samples were compared. What if you wish to compare more than two means? The answer is to use the **analysis of variance**. At this point you may be wondering why the procedure is called the analysis of variance rather than the analysis of means, because the intent is to study possible mean differences. One way of comparing a set of means is to think in terms of the variability among those means. If the sample means are all the same, then the variability of those means would be zero. If the sample means are not all the same, then the variability of those means would be somewhat greater than zero. In general, the greater the mean differences, the greater is the variability of the means. Thus mean differences are studied by looking at the variability of the means; hence, the term analysis of variance is appropriate rather than analysis of means (further discussed in this chapter).

We use $X$ to denote our single **independent variable**, which we typically refer to as a **factor**, and $Y$ to denote our **dependent** (or **criterion**) **variable**. Thus the one-factor ANOVA is a bivariate or two variable procedure. Our interest here is in determining whether mean differences exist on the dependent variable. Stated another way, the researcher is interested in the influence of the independent variable on the dependent variable. For example, a researcher may want to determine the influence that method of instruction has on statistics achievement. The independent variable or factor would be method of instruction and the dependent variable would be statistics achievement. Three different methods of instruction that might be compared are large lecture hall instruction, small-group instruction, and computer-assisted instruction. Students would be randomly assigned to one of the three methods of instruction and at the end of the semester evaluated as to their level of achievement in statistics. These results would be of interest to a statistics instructor in determining the most effective method of instruction. Thus, the instructor may opt for the method of instruction that yields the highest mean achievement.

There are a number of new concepts introduced in this chapter. These concepts include the following: independent and dependent variables; between- and within-groups variability; fixed-

and random-effects; the linear model; partitioning of the sums of squares; degrees of freedom, mean square terms, and $F$ ratios; the ANOVA summary table; balanced and unbalanced models; and alternative ANOVA procedures. Our objectives are that by the end of this chapter, you will be able to (a) understand the characteristics and concepts underlying the one-factor ANOVA, (b) generate and interpret the results of a one-factor ANOVA, and (c) understand and evaluate the assumptions of the one-factor ANOVA.

## 11.1   CHARACTERISTICS OF THE ONE-FACTOR ANOVA MODEL

This section describes the distinguishing characteristics of the one-factor ANOVA model. Suppose you are interested in comparing the means of two independent samples. Here the independent $t$ test would be the method of choice (or perhaps Welch's $t'$ or the Mann-Whitney-Wilcoxon test). What if your interest is in comparing the means of more than two independent samples? One possibility is to conduct multiple independent $t$ tests on each pair of means. For example, if you wished to determine whether the means from five independent samples are the same, you could do all possible pairwise $t$ tests. In this case the following null hypotheses could be evaluated: $\mu_1 = \mu_2$, $\mu_1 = \mu_3$, $\mu_1 = \mu_4$, $\mu_1 = \mu_5$, $\mu_2 = \mu_3$, $\mu_2 = \mu_4$, $\mu_2 = \mu_5$, $\mu_3 = \mu_4$, $\mu_3 = \mu_5$, and $\mu_4 = \mu_5$. Thus we would have to carry out 10 different independent $t$ tests. The number of possible pairwise $t$ tests that could be done for $J$ means is equal to $\frac{1}{2}[J(J-1)]$.

Is there a problem in conducting so many $t$ tests? Yes, the problem has to do with the probability of making a Type I error (i.e., $\alpha$), where the researcher incorrectly rejects a true null hypothesis. Although the $\alpha$ level for each $t$ test can be controlled at a specified nominal level, say .05, what happens to the overall $\alpha$ level for the entire set of tests? The overall $\alpha$ level for the entire set of tests (i.e., $\alpha_{\text{total}}$), often called the **experiment-wise Type I error rate**, is larger than the $\alpha$ level for each of the individual $t$ tests.

In our example we are interested in comparing the means for 10 pairs of groups. A $t$ test is conducted for each of the 10 pairs of groups at $\alpha = .05$. Although each test controls the $\alpha$ level at .05, the overall $\alpha$ level will be larger because the risk of a Type I error accumulates across the tests. For each test we are taking a risk; the more tests we do, the more risks we are taking. This can be explained by considering the risk you take each day you drive your car to school or work. The risk of an accident is small for any one day; however, over the period of a year the risk of an accident is much larger.

For $C$ independent (or orthogonal) tests the experiment-wise error is as follows.

$$\alpha_{\text{total}} = 1 - (1 - \alpha)^C$$

Assume for the moment that our 10 tests are independent (although they are not). If we go ahead with our 10 $t$ tests at $\alpha = .05$, then the experiment-wise error rate is

$$\alpha_{\text{total}} = 1 - (1 - .05)^{10} = 1 - .60 = .40$$

Although we are seemingly controlling our $\alpha$ level at the .05 level, the probability of making a Type I error across all 10 tests is .40. In other words, in the long run, 4 times out of 10 we will make a Type I error. Thus we do not want to do all possible $t$ tests. Before we move on, the experiment-wise error rate for $C$ dependent tests (which would be the case when doing all possible pairwise $t$ tests, as in our example) is more difficult to determine, so let us just say that

$$\alpha \leq \alpha_{total} \leq C\alpha$$

Are there other options available to us where we can maintain better control over our experiment-wise error rate? The optimal solution, in terms of maintaining control over our overall $\alpha$ level as well as maximizing power, is to conduct one overall test, often called an **omnibus test**. Recall that power has to do with the probability of correctly rejecting a false null hypothesis. The omnibus test could assess the equality of all of the means simultaneously and is the one used in the analysis of variance. The one-factor analysis of variance, then, represents an extension of the independent $t$ test for two or more independent sample means, where the experiment-wise error rate is controlled.

In addition, the one-factor ANOVA has only one independent variable or factor with two or more levels. The independent variable is a discrete or grouping variable, where each subject responds to only one level. The levels represent the different samples or groups or treatments whose means are to be compared. In our example, method of instruction is the independent variable with three levels: large lecture hall, small-group, and computer-assisted. There are two ways of conceptually thinking about the selection of levels. In the fixed-effects model, all levels that the researcher is interested in are included in the design and analysis for the study. As a result, generalizations can only be made about those particular levels of the independent variable that are actually selected. For instance, if a researcher is only interested in three methods of instruction—large lecture hall, small-group and computer-assisted—then only those levels are incorporated into the study. Generalizations about other methods of instruction cannot be made because no other methods were considered for selection. Other examples of fixed-effects independent variables might be SES, gender, specific types of drug treatment, age group, weight, or marital status.

In the random-effects model, the researcher randomly samples some levels of the independent variable from the population of levels. As a result, generalizations can be made about all of the levels in the population, even those not actually sampled. For instance, a researcher interested in teacher effectiveness may have randomly sampled history teachers (i.e., the independent variable) from the population of history teachers in a particular school district. Generalizations can then be made about other history teachers in that school district not actually sampled. The random selection of levels is much the same as the random selection of individuals or objects in the random sampling process. This is the nature of inferential statistics, where inferences are made about a population (of individuals, objects, or levels) from a sample. Other examples of random-effects independent variables might be randomly selected classrooms, types of medication, animals, or time (e.g., hours, days). The remainder of this chapter is concerned with the fixed-effects model. Chapter 15 discusses the random-effects model in more detail.

In the fixed-effects model, once the levels of the independent variable are selected, subjects (i.e., persons or objects) are randomly assigned to the levels of the independent variable. In certain situations, the researcher does not have control over which level a subject is assigned to. The groups already may be in place when the researcher arrives on the scene. For instance, students may be assigned to their classes at the beginning of the year by the school administration. Researchers typically have little input regarding class assignments. In another situation, it may be theoretically impossible to assign subjects to groups. For example, as much as we might like, researchers cannot randomly assign individuals to an age level. Thus, a distinction needs to be made about whether or not the researcher can control the assignment of subjects to groups. Although the analysis will not be altered, the interpretation of the results will be. When researchers have control over group assignments, the extent to which they can generalize their findings is greater than for those researchers who do not have such control. For further information on the differences between true experimental designs (i.e., with random assignment) and quasi-experimental designs (i.e., without random assignment), see Campbell and Stanley (1966) and Cook and Campbell (1979).

Moreover, in the model being considered here, each subject is exposed to only one level of the independent variable. Chapter 15 deals with models where a subject is exposed to multiple levels of an independent variable; these are known as **repeated-measures models**. For example, a researcher may be interested in observing a group of young children repeatedly over a period of several years. Thus, each child might be observed every 6 months from birth to age 5 years. This would require a repeated-measures design because the observations of a particular child over time are obviously not independent observations.

One final characteristic is the measurement scale of the independent and dependent variables. In the analysis of variance, it is assumed that the scale of measurement on the dependent variable is at the interval or ratio level. If the dependent variable is measured at the ordinal level, then the nonparametric equivalent, the Kruskal-Wallis test, should be considered (discussed later in this chapter). If the dependent variable shares properties of both the ordinal and interval levels (e.g., grade point average), then both the ANOVA and Kruskal-Wallis procedures should be considered to cross-reference any potential effects of the measurement scale. As previously mentioned, the independent variable is a grouping or discrete variable, so it can be measured on any scale.

In summary, the characteristics of the one-factor analysis of variance fixed-effects model are as follows: (a) control of the experiment-wise error rate through an omnibus test; (b) one independent variable with two or more levels; (c) the levels of the independent variable are fixed by the researcher; (d) subjects are randomly assigned to these levels; (e) subjects are exposed to only one level of the independent variable; and (f) the dependent variable is measured at least at the interval level, although the Kruskal-Wallis one-factor ANOVA can be considered for an ordinal level dependent variable. In the context of experimental design, the one-factor analysis of variance is often referred to as the **completely randomized design**.

## 11.2 THE LAYOUT OF THE DATA

Before we get into the theory and analysis of the data, let us examine one tabular form of the data, known as the layout of the data. We designate each observation as $Y_{ij}$, where the $j$ subscript tells us what group or level the observation belongs to and the $i$ subscript tells us the observation or identification number within that group. For instance, $Y_{34}$ would mean this is the third observation in the fourth group or level of the independent variable. The first subscript ranges over $i = 1, ..., n$ and the second subscript ranges over $j = 1, ..., J$. Thus there are $J$ levels of the independent variable and $n$ subjects in each group, for a total of $Jn = N$ total observations. For now, presume there are $n$ subjects in each group in order to simplify matters; this is referred to as the **equal $n$'s** or **balanced case**. Later on in this chapter, we consider the **unequal $n$'s** or **unbalanced case**.

The layout of the data is shown in Table 11.1. Here we see that each column represents the observations for a particular group or level of the independent variable. At the bottom of each column are the sample group means ($\overline{Y}_{.j}$), with the overall sample mean ($\overline{Y}_{..}$) to the far right. In conclusion, the layout of the data is one form in which the researcher can think about the data.

## 11.3 ANOVA THEORY

This section examines the underlying theory and logic of the analysis of variance, the sums of squares, and the ANOVA summary table. As noted previously, in the analysis of variance mean differences are tested by looking at the variability of the means. This section shows precisely how this is done.

### 11.3.1 General Theory and Logic

We begin with the hypotheses to be tested in the analysis of variance. In the two-group situation of the independent $t$ test, the null and alternative hypotheses for a two-tailed test are as follows:

$$H_0: \mu_1 = \mu_2$$
$$H_1: \mu_1 \neq \mu_2$$

In the multiple-group situation, we have already seen the problem that occurs when multiple independent $t$ tests are conducted for each pair of population means (i.e., increased likelihood of a Type I error). We concluded that the solution was to use an omnibus test where the equality

**TABLE 11.1**
Layout for the One-Factor ANOVA Model

| | | | | | | |
|---|---|---|---|---|---|---|
| | *Level of the Independent Variable* | | | | | |
| | *1* | *2* | *3* | ... | *J* | |
| | $Y_{11}$ | $Y_{12}$ | $Y_{13}$ | ... | $Y_{1J}$ | |
| | $Y_{21}$ | $Y_{22}$ | $Y_{23}$ | ... | $Y_{2J}$ | |
| | $Y_{31}$ | $Y_{32}$ | $Y_{33}$ | ... | $Y_{3J}$ | |
| | . | . | . | ... | . | |
| | . | . | . | ... | . | |
| | . | . | . | ... | . | |
| | $Y_{n1}$ | $Y_{n2}$ | $Y_{n3}$ | ... | $Y_{nJ}$ | |
| mean: | $\overline{Y}_{.1}$ | $\overline{Y}_{.2}$ | $\overline{Y}_{.3}$ | ... | $\overline{Y}_{.J}$ | $\overline{Y}_{..}$ |

of all of the means could be assessed simultaneously. The hypotheses for the omnibus analysis of variance test are as follows:

$$H_0: \mu_1 = \mu_2 = \mu_3 = \ldots = \mu_J$$

$$H_1: \text{not all the } \mu_j \text{ are equal}$$

Here $H_1$ is purposely written in a general form to cover the multitude of possible mean differences that could arise. These range from only two of the means being different to all of the means being different from one another. Thus, because of the way $H_1$ has been written, only a nondirectional alternative is appropriate. If $H_0$ were to be rejected, then the researcher might want to consider a multiple comparison procedure so as to determine which means or combination of means are significantly different (see chap. 12).

As was mentioned in the introduction to this chapter, the analysis of mean differences is actually carried out by looking at variability of the means. At first this seems strange. If one wants to test for mean differences, then do a test of means. If one wants to test for variance differences, then do a test of variances. These statements should make sense because logic pervades the field of statistics. And they do for the two-group situation. For the multiple-group situation, we already know things get a bit more complicated.

Say a researcher is interested in the influence of amount of daily study time on statistics achievement. Three groups were formed based on the amount of daily study time in statistics, ½ hour, 1 hour, and 2 hours. Is there a differential influence of amount of time studied on subsequent mean statistics achievement (e.g., statistics final exam)? We would expect that the more one studied statistics, the higher the statistics mean achievement would be. One possible outcome in the population is where the amount of study time does not influence statistics achievement; here the population means will be equal. That is, the null hypothesis of equal group means is true. Thus the three groups will actually be three samples from the same population of students, with mean $\mu$. The means are equal; thus there is no variability among the three group means. A second possible outcome in the population is where the amount of study time does influence statistics achievement; here the population means will not be equal. That is, the null hypothesis is false. Thus the three groups will not be three samples from the same population of students, but rather, each group will represent a sample from a distinct population of students receiving that particular amount of study time, with mean $\mu_j$. The means are not equal, so there is variability among the three group means. In summary, the statistical question becomes whether the difference between the sample means is due to the usual sampling variability expected from a single population, or the result of a true difference between the sample means from different populations.

We conceptually define **within-groups variability** as the variability of the observations within a group combined across groups, and **between-groups variability** as the variability between the group means. In Fig. 11.1, the horizontal axis represents low and high variability within the groups. The vertical axis represents low and high variability between the groups. In the upper left-hand plot, there is low variability both within and between the groups. That is, performance is very consistent, both within each group as well as across groups. Here within- and between-group variability are both low, and it is quite unlikely that one would reject $H_0$. In the upper right-hand plot, there is high variability within the groups and low variability between the groups. That is,

**Variability Within-Groups**

Low                                                            High

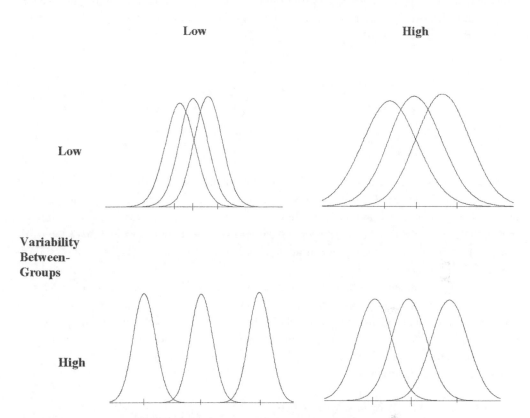

FIG. 11.1    Conceptual look at between- and within-groups variability.

performance is very consistent across groups, but quite variable within each group. Here within-group variability exceeds between-group variability, and again it is quite unlikely that one would reject $H_0$. In the lower left-hand plot, there is low variability within the groups and high variability between groups. That is, performance is very consistent within each group, but quite variable across groups. Here between-group variability exceeds within-group variability, and it is quite likely that one would reject $H_0$. In the lower right-hand plot, there is high variability both within and between the groups. That is, performance is quite variable within each group, as well as across the groups. Here within- and between-group variability are both high, and depending on the relative amounts of between- and within-group variability, one may or may not reject $H_0$. In summary, the optimal situation when seeking to reject $H_0$ is the one represented by high variability between the groups and low variability within the groups.

## 11.3.2    Partitioning the Sums of Squares

The partitioning of the sums of squares is a new concept in this chapter, which is also an important concept in regression analysis (from chaps. 17 & 18). In part this is because both are forms of the general linear model (GLM) (to be further discussed). Let us begin with the total sum of squares in $Y$, denoted as $SS_{total}$. The term $SS_{total}$ represents the amount of total variation in $Y$. The next step is to partition the total variation into variation between the groups, denoted by $SS_{betw}$, and variation within the groups, denoted by $SS_{with}$. In the one-factor analysis of variance we therefore partition $SS_{total}$ as follows:

$$SS_{total} = SS_{betw} + SS_{with}$$

or

$$\sum_{i=1}^{n} \sum_{j=1}^{J} \left( Y_{ij} - \overline{Y}_{..} \right)^2 = \sum_{i=1}^{n} \sum_{j=1}^{J} \left( \overline{Y}_{.j} - \overline{Y}_{..} \right)^2 + \sum_{i=1}^{n} \sum_{j=1}^{J} \left( Y_{ij} - \overline{Y}_{.j} \right)^2$$

where $SS_{total}$ is the total sum of squares due to variation among all of the observations without regard to group membership, $SS_{betw}$ is the between-groups sum of squares due to the variation between the group means, and $SS_{with}$ is the within-groups sum of squares due to the variation within the groups combined across groups. We refer to this particular formulation of the partitioned sums of squares as the **definitional** (or **conceptual**) **formula**, because each term literally defines a form of variation.

Due to computational complexity and computational error, the definitional formula is rarely used with real data. Instead **computational formula** for the partitioned sums of squares are used for hand computations. However, since nearly all data analysis at this level utilize computer software, we defer to the software to actually perform an analysis of variance (SPSS details are provided toward the end of this chapter). A complete example of the analysis of variance is also considered later in this chapter.

### 11.3.3   The ANOVA Summary Table

An important result of the analysis is the **ANOVA summary table**. The purpose of the summary table is to literally summarize the analysis of variance. A general form of the summary table is shown in Table 11.2. The first column lists the sources of variation in the model. As we already know, in the one-factor model the total variation is partitioned into between-groups variation and within-groups variation. The second column notes the sums of squares terms computed for each source (i.e., $SS_{betw}$, $SS_{with}$, and $SS_{total}$).

The third column gives the degrees of freedom for each source. Recall that, in general, degrees of freedom has to do with the number of observations that are free to vary. For example, if a sample mean and all of the sample observations except for one are known, then the final

**TABLE 11.2**
Analysis of Variance Summary Table

| Source | SS | df | MS | F |
|--------|-----|------|-----|-----|
| Between groups | $SS_{betw}$ | $J - 1$ | $MS_{betw}$ | $MS_{betw} / MS_{with}$ |
| Within groups | $SS_{with}$ | $N - J$ | $MS_{with}$ | |
| Total | $SS_{total}$ | $N - 1$ | | |

observation is not free to vary. That is, the final observation is predetermined to be a particular value. For instance, say the mean is 10 and there are three observations, 7, 11, and an unknown observation. First, the sum of the three observations must be 30 for the mean to be 10. Second, the sum of the known observations is 18. Therefore the unknown observation must be 12. Otherwise the sample mean would not be exactly equal to 10.

For the between-groups source, the definitional formula is concerned with the deviation of each group mean from the overall mean. There are $J$ group means, so the $df_{betw}$ must be $J - 1$. Why? If there are $J$ group means and we know the overall mean, then only $J - 1$ of the group means are free to vary. In other words, if we know the overall mean and all but one of the group means, then the final unknown group mean is predetermined. For the within-groups source, the definitional formula is concerned with the deviation of each observation from its respective group mean. There are $n$ observations in each group; consequently, there are $n - 1$ degrees of freedom in each group and $J$ groups. Why are there $n - 1$ degrees of freedom in each group? If there are $n$ observations in each group, then only $n - 1$ of the observations are free to vary. In other words, if we know the group mean and all but one of the observations for that group, then the final unknown observation for that group is predetermined. There are $J$ groups, so the $df_{with}$ is $J(n - 1)$ or $N - J$. For the total source, the definitional formula is concerned with the deviation of each observation from the overall mean. There are $N$ total observations; therefore the $df_{total}$ must be $N - 1$. Why? If there are $N$ total observations and we know the overall mean, then only $N - 1$ of the observations are free to vary. In other words, if we know the overall mean and all but one of the $N$ observations, then the final unknown observation is predetermined.

Why is the number of degrees of freedom important in the analysis of variance? Suppose two researchers have conducted similar studies, except Researcher A uses 20 observations per group and Researcher B uses 10 observations per group. Each researcher obtains a $SS_{with}$ of 15. Would it be fair to say that the result for the two studies is the same? Such a comparison would be unfair because $SS_{with}$ is influenced by the number of observations per group. A fair comparison would be to weight the $SS_{with}$ terms by their respective number of degrees of freedom. Similarly, it would not be fair to compare the $SS_{betw}$ terms from two similar studies based on different numbers of groups. A fair comparision would be to weight the $SS_{betw}$ terms by their respective number of degrees of freedom. The method of weighting a sum of squares term by the number of degrees of freedom on which it is based yields what is called a **mean squares** term. Thus $MS_{betw} = SS_{betw}/df_{betw}$ and $MS_{with} = SS_{with}/df_{with}$, as shown in the fourth column of Table 11.2. They are referred to as mean squares because they represent a summed quantity that is weighted by the number of observations used in the sum itself, like the mean. The mean squares terms are also variance estimates because they represent the sum of the squared deviations from a mean divided by their degrees of freedom, like the sample variance $s^2$.

The last column in the ANOVA summary table, the $F$ value, is the summary test statistic of the summary table. The $F$ value is computed by taking the ratio of the two mean squares or variance terms. Thus for the one-factor ANOVA fixed-effects model, the $F$ value is computed as $F = MS_{betw}/MS_{with}$. When developed by Sir Ronald A. Fisher in the 1920s, this test statistic was originally known as the variance ratio because it represents the ratio of two variance estimates. Later the variance ratio was renamed the $F$ ratio by George W. Snedecor (who worked out the table of $F$ values, discussed momentarily) in honor of Fisher ($F$ for Fisher).

The $F$ ratio tells us whether there is more variation between groups than there is within groups, which is required if we are to reject $H_0$. Thus if there is more variation between groups than there is within groups, then $MS_{betw}$ will be larger than $MS_{with}$. As a result of this, the $F$ ratio of $MS_{betw}/MS_{with}$ will be greater than 1. If, on the other hand, the amount of variation between groups is about the same as there is within groups, then $MS_{betw}$ and $MS_{with}$ will be about the same, and the $F$ ratio will be approximately 1. Thus we want to find large $F$ values in order to reject the null hypothesis. The $F$ test statistic is then compared with the $F$ critical value so as to make a decision about the null hypothesis. The critical value is found in the $F$ table of Appendix Table 4 as ${}_\alpha F_{(J-1, N-J)}$. Thus the degrees of freedom are $df_{betw} = J - 1$ for the numerator of the $F$ ratio and $df_{with} = N - J$ for the denominator of the $F$ ratio. The significance test is a one-tailed test so as to be consistent with the alternative hypothesis. The null hypothesis is rejected if the $F$ test statistic exceeds the $F$ critical value.

If the $F$ test statistic exceeds the $F$ critical value, and there are more than two groups, then it is not clear where the differences among the means lie. In this case, some multiple comparison procedure should be used to determine where the mean differences are in the groups; this is the topic of chapter 12. When there are only two groups, it is obvious where the mean difference lies, between groups 1 and 2. For the two-group situation, it is also interesting to note that the $F$ and $t$ test statistics follow the rule of $F = t^2$, for a nondirectional alternative hypothesis in the independent $t$ test. This result occurs when the numerator degrees of freedom for the $F$ ratio is 1. In an actual ANOVA summary table (shown in the next section), except for the source of variation column, it is the values for each of the other entries that are listed in the table. For example, instead of seeing $SS_{betw}$, we would see the computed value of $SS_{betw}$.

## 11.4    THE ANOVA MODEL

In this section we introduce the analysis of variance linear model, the estimation of parameters of the model, effect size measures, confidence intervals, power, and finish up with an example.

### 11.4.1    The Model

The one-factor ANOVA fixed-effects model can be written in terms of population parameters as

$$Y_{ij} = \mu + \alpha_j + \varepsilon_{ij}$$

where $Y$ is the observed score on the dependent (or criterion) variable for individual $i$ in group $j$, $\mu$ is the overall or grand population mean (i.e., regardless of group designation), $\alpha_j$ is the group effect for group $j$, and $\varepsilon_{ij}$ is the random residual error for individual $i$ in group $j$. The residual error can be due to individual differences, measurement error, and/or other factors not under investigation (i.e., other than $X$). The population group effect and residual error are computed as

$$\alpha_j = \mu_{.j} - \mu$$

and

$$\varepsilon_{ij} = Y_{ij} - \mu_{.j}$$

respectively, and $\mu_{.j}$ is the population mean for group $j$, where the initial dot subscript indicates we have averaged across all $i$ individuals in group $j$. That is, the group effect is equal to the difference between the population mean of group $j$ and the overall population mean, whereas the residual error is equal to the difference between an individual's observed score and the population mean of group $j$. The group effect can also be thought of as the average effect of being a member of a particular group. A positive group effect implies a group mean greater than the overall mean, whereas a negative group effect implies a group mean less than the overall mean. Note that in a fixed-effects one-factor model, the population group effects sum to zero. The residual error in the analysis of variance represents that portion of $Y$ not accounted for by $X$.

## 11.4.2 Estimation of the Parameters of the Model

Next we need to estimate the parameters of the model $\mu$, $\alpha_j$, and $\varepsilon_{ij}$. The sample estimates are represented as $\overline{Y}_{..}$, $a_j$, and $e_{ij}$, respectively, where the latter two are computed as

$$a_j = \overline{Y}_{.j} - \overline{Y}_{..}$$

and

$$e_{ij} = Y_{ij} - \overline{Y}_{.j}$$

respectively. Note that $\overline{Y}_{..}$ represents the overall sample mean, where the double dot subscript indicates we have averaged across both the $i$ and $j$ subscripts, and $\overline{Y}_{.j}$ represents the sample mean for group $j$, where the initial dot subscript indicates we have averaged across all $i$ individuals in group $j$.

## 11.4.3 Effect Size Measures, Confidence Intervals, and Power

There are various effect size measures to indicate the strength of association between $X$ and $Y$, that is, the relative strength of the group effect. Let us briefly examine $\eta^2$, $\omega^2$, and Cohen's (1988) $f$. First $\eta^2$ (eta) is known as the correlation ratio (generalization of $R^2$) and represents the proportion of variation in $Y$ explained by the group mean differences in $X$. We find $\eta^2$ to be

$$\eta^2 = \frac{SS_{betw}}{SS_{total}}$$

It is well known that $\eta^2$ is a positively biased statistic (i.e., overestimates the association). The bias is most evident for $n$'s less than 30. Another effect size measure is $\omega^2$ (omega), which is less biased than $\eta^2$. We determine $\omega^2$ as

$$\omega^2 = \frac{SS_{betw} - (J-1)\, MS_{with}}{SS_{total} + MS_{with}}$$

A final effect size measure is $f$ developed by Cohen (1988). We find $f$ as

$$f = \sqrt{\frac{\eta^2}{1 - \eta^2}}$$

These are the most common measures of effect size used for ANOVA models, both in statistics software and in print. Cohen's (1988) subjective standards can be used as follows to interpret these effect sizes: small effect, $f = .1$, $\eta^2$ or $\omega^2 = .01$; medium effect, $f = .25$, $\eta^2$ or $\omega^2 = .06$; large effect, $f = .40$, $\eta^2$ or $\omega^2 = .14$. Note that these are subjective standards developed for particular areas of inquiry; your discipline may use other standards. For further discussion, see Keppel (1982), O'Grady (1982), Wilcox (1987), Cohen (1988), Keppel and Wickens (2004), and Murphy and Myors (2004; which includes software).

Confidence interval procedures are often useful in providing an interval estimate of a population parameter (i.e., mean or mean difference); these allow us to determine the accuracy of the sample estimate. One can form confidence intervals around any sample group mean from an ANOVA (provided in software such as SPSS), although confidence intervals for means have more utility for multiple comparison procedures, as discussed in chapter 12. Confidence interval procedures have also been developed for several effect size measures (Fidler & Thompson, 2001; Smithson, 2001).

As for power (the probability of correctly rejecting a false null hypothesis), one can consider either planned power (*a priori*) or observed power (*post hoc*), as discussed in previous chapters. In the ANOVA context, we know that power is primarily a function of $\alpha$, sample size, and effect size. For planned power, one inputs each of these components either into a statistical table or power chart (nicely arrayed in texts such as Cohen, 1988, or Murphy & Myors, 2004), or into statistical software (such as Power and Precision, Ex-Sample, Gpower, or the software contained in Murphy & Myors, 2004). Planned power is most often used by researchers to determine adequate sample sizes in ANOVA models, which is highly recommended. Many disciplines recommend a minimum power value, such as .80. Thus these methods are a useful way to determine the sample size that would generate a desired level of power. Observed power is determined by some statistics software, such as SPSS, and indicates what the power actually was in a completed study.

### 11.4.4    An Example

Consider now an example problem used throughout this chapter. Our dependent variable is the number of times a student attends statistics lab during one semester (or quarter), whereas the independent variable is the attractiveness of the lab instructor (assuming each instructor is of the same gender and is equally competent). The researcher is interested in whether the attractiveness of the instructor influences student attendance at the statistics lab. The attractiveness groups are defined as follows: Group 1, unattractive; Group 2, slightly attractive; Group 3, moderately attractive; and Group 4, very attractive. Students were randomly assigned to a group at the beginning of the semester, and attendance was taken by the instructor. There were eight students in each group for a total of 32. Students could attend a maximum of 30 lab sessions. In Table 11.3 we see the raw data and sample statistics (means and variances) for each group and overall (far right).

The results are summarized in the ANOVA summary table as shown in Table 11.4. The test statistic is compared to the critical value $_{.05}F_{3,28} = 2.95$ obtained from Appendix Table 4, using the .05 level of significance. The test statistic exceeds the critical value, so we reject $H_0$ and conclude that level of attractiveness is related to mean differences in statistics lab attendance. The exact probability value (*p* value) given by SPSS is .001.

**TABLE 11.3**
Data and Summary Statistics for the Statistics Lab Example

*Number of Statistics Labs Attended by Group*

|  | Group 1 | Group 2 | Group 3 | Group 4 |  |
|---|---|---|---|---|---|
|  | 15 | 20 | 10 | 30 |  |
|  | 10 | 13 | 24 | 22 |  |
|  | 12 | 9 | 29 | 26 |  |
|  | 8 | 22 | 12 | 20 |  |
|  | 21 | 24 | 27 | 29 |  |
|  | 7 | 25 | 21 | 28 |  |
|  | 13 | 18 | 25 | 25 |  |
|  | 3 | 12 | 14 | 15 |  |
| mean: | 11.1250 | 17.8750 | 20.2500 | 24.3750 | 18.4063 |
| variance: | 30.1250 | 35.2679 | 53.0714 | 25.9821 | 56.4425 |

**TABLE 11.4**
Analysis of Variance Summary Table—Statistics Lab Example

| Source | SS | df | MS | F |
|---|---|---|---|---|
| Between groups | 738.5938 | 3 | 246.1979 | 6.8177* |
| Within groups | 1,011.1250 | 28 | 36.1116 |  |
| Total | 1,749.7188 | 31 |  |  |

$*_{.05}F_{3,28} = 2.95$

Next we examine the group effects and residual errors. The group effects are estimated as

$$a_1 = \overline{Y}_{.1} - \overline{Y}_{..} = 11.125 - 18.4063 = -7.2813$$

$$a_2 = \overline{Y}_{.2} - \overline{Y}_{..} = 17.875 - 18.4063 = -0.5313$$

$$a_3 = \overline{Y}_{.3} - \overline{Y}_{..} = 20.250 - 18.4063 = +1.8437$$

$$a_4 = \overline{Y}_{.4} - \overline{Y}_{..} = 24.375 - 18.4063 = +5.9687$$

Thus group 4 has the largest positive group effect, while group 1 has the largest negative group effect. In chapter 12 we use the same data to determine which group means, or combination of group means, are statistically different. The residual errors for each individual by group are shown in Table 11.5 and discussed later in this chapter.

**TABLE 11.5**
Residuals for the Statistics Lab Example by Group

| Group 1 | Group 2 | Group 3 | Group 4 |
|---------|---------|---------|---------|
| 3.875 | 2.125 | −10.250 | 5.625 |
| −1.125 | −4.875 | 3.750 | −2.375 |
| 0.875 | −8.875 | 8.750 | 1.625 |
| −3.125 | 4.125 | −8.250 | −4.375 |
| 9.875 | 6.125 | 6.750 | 4.625 |
| −4.125 | 7.125 | 0.750 | 3.625 |
| 1.875 | 0.125 | 4.750 | 0.625 |
| −8.125 | −5.875 | −6.250 | −9.375 |

Finally we determine the effect size measures. First the correlation ratio $\eta^2$ is

$$\eta^2 = \frac{SS_{betw}}{SS_{total}} = \frac{738.5938}{1,749.7188} = .4221$$

Next $\omega^2$ is found to be

$$\omega^2 = \frac{SS_{betw} - (J-1)\,MS_{with}}{SS_{total} + MS_{with}} = \frac{738.5938 - (3)\,36.1116}{1,749.7188 + 36.1116} = .3529$$

Lastly $f$ is equal to

$$f = \sqrt{\frac{\eta^2}{1-\eta^2}} - \sqrt{\frac{.4221}{1-.4221}} = .8546$$

Based on these effect size measures, we conclude that there is a large effect size for the influence of instructor attractiveness on lab attendance. In addition, if we rank the instructor group means from unattractive (lowest mean) to very attractive (highest mean), we see that the more attractive the instructor, the more inclined the student is to attend lab. We examine multiple comparison procedures with this example data in chapter 12.

## 11.5   ASSUMPTIONS AND VIOLATION OF ASSUMPTIONS

There are three standard assumptions that are made in analysis of variance models, which we are already familiar with from the independent $t$ test. We see these assumpions often in the remainder of this text. The assumptions are concerned with independence, homogeneity of variance, and normality. We also mention some techniques that are appropriate to use in evaluating each assumption.

## 11.5.1   Independence

The first assumption is that each sample is an independent random sample from their respective population. In other words, each sample is randomly drawn for a population and observations are independent of one another (both within samples and across samples). The use of independent random samples is crucial in the analysis of variance. The $F$ ratio is very sensitive to violation of the independence assumption in terms of increased likelihood of a Type I and/or Type II error (e.g., Glass, et al., 1972). This effect can sometimes even be worse with larger samples (Keppel & Wickens, 2004). A violation of the independence assumption may affect the standard errors of the sample means and thus influence any inferences made about those means. One purpose of random assignment of individuals to groups is to achieve independence. If each individual is only observed once and individuals are randomly assigned to groups, then the independence assumption is usually met. If individuals work together during the experiment (e.g., discussion group, group work), then independence may be compromised. Thus a carefully planned, controlled, and conducted research design is the key to satisfying this assumption.

The simplest procedure for assessing independence is to examine residual plots by group. If the independence assumption is satisfied, then the residuals should fall into a random display of points for each group. If the assumption is violated, then the residuals will fall into some type of cyclical pattern. The Durbin-Watson statistic (1950, 1951, 1971) can be used to test for autocorrelation. Violations of the independence assumption generally occur in three situations: when observations are collected over time; when observations are made within blocks; or when observation involves replication. For severe violations of the independence assumption, there is no simple "fix" (e.g., Scariana and Davenport, 1987). For the example data, a plot of the residuals by group is shown in Figure 11.2, and there does appear to be a random display of points for each group.

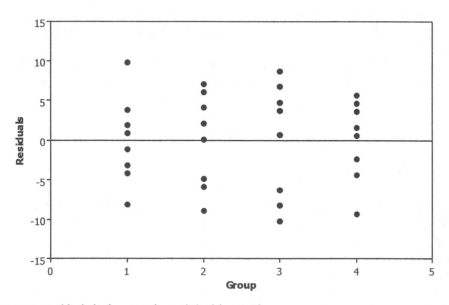

FIG. 11.2   Residual plot by group for statistics lab example.

## 11.5.2    Homogeneity of Variance

The second assumption is that the variances of each population are equal. This is known as the assumption of **homogeneity of variance** or **homoscedasticity**. A violation of the homogeneity assumption can lead to bias in the $SS_{with}$ term, as well as an increase in the Type I error rate and possibly an increase in the Type II error rate. There are two sets of research that have investigated violations of this assumption, classic work and more modern work.

The classic work largely resulted from Box (1954a) and Glass, et al. (1972). Their results indicated that the effect of the violation was small with equal or nearly equal $n$'s across the groups. There is a more serious problem if the larger $n$'s are associated with the smaller variances (actual $\alpha$ > nominal $\alpha$, which is a liberal result), or if the larger $n$'s are associated with the larger variances (actual $\alpha$ < nominal $\alpha$, which is a conservative result) [note that Bradley's (1978) criterion is used in this text, where the actual $\alpha$ should not exceed 1.1 to 1.5 times the nominal $\alpha$]. Thus the suggestion was that heterogeneity was only a concern when there were unequal $n$'s. The classic work only examined minor violations of the assumption (the ratio of largest variance to smallest variance being relatively small), and unfortunately has been largely adapted in textbooks and by users.

The modern work has been conducted by researchers such as Brown and Forsythe (1974), and Wilcox (1986, 1987, 1988, 1989), and nicely summarized by Coombs, et al. (1996). In short, this work indicates that the effect of heterogeneity is more severe than previously thought (poor power; $\alpha$ can be greatly affected), even with equal $n$'s (although having equal $n$'s does reduce the magnitude of the problem). Thus $F$ is not even robust to heterogeneity with equal $n$'s.

Suggestions for dealing with such a violation include (a) using alternative procedures such as the Welch, Brown-Forsythe, and James procedures (e.g., Myers & Well, 1995; Coombs, et al., 1996; Glass & Hopkins, 1996; Wilcox, 1996; Wilcox, 2003; Keppel & Wickens, 2004), (b) reducing $\alpha$ (e.g., Weinberg & Abramowitz, 2002; Keppel & Wickens, 2004), or (c) transforming $Y$ (such as $\sqrt{Y}$, $1/Y$, or log $Y$) (e.g., Weinberg & Abramowitz, 2002; Keppel & Wickens, 2004). The alternative procedures will be more fully described later in this chapter.

In a plot of residuals versus each value of $X$, the consistency of the variance of the conditional residual distributions may be examined. Another method for detecting violation of the homogeneity assumption is the use of formal statistical tests, as discussed in chapter 9. The traditional homogeneity tests (e.g., Levene's test) are commonly available in statistical software, but are not robust to nonnormality. Unfortunately the more robust homogeneity tests are not readily available. For the example data, the residual plot of Fig. 11.2 shows similar variances across the groups, and Levene's test suggests the variances are not different ($p = .451$).

## 11.5.3    Normality

The third assumption is that each of the populations follows the normal distribution. The $F$ test is relatively robust to moderate violations of this assumption (i.e., in terms of Type I and II error rates). Specifically, effects of the violation will be minimal except for small $n$'s, for unequal $n$'s, and/or for extreme nonnormality. Violation of the normality assumption may be a result of outliers. The simplest outlier detection procedure is to look for observations that are more than two or three standard errors from their respective group mean. Formal procedures for the detection of outliers are now available in many statistical packages.

The following graphical techniques can be used to detect violations of the normality assumption: (a) the frequency distributions of the scores or the residuals for each group (through stem-and-leaf plots, box plots, or histograms), (b) the normal probability or quantile plot, or (c) a plot of group means versus group variances (which should be independent of one another). There are also several statistical procedures available for the detection of nonnormality (e.g., the Shapiro-Wilk test, 1965). Transformations can also be used to normalize the data. For instance, a nonlinear relationship between $X$ and $Y$ may result in violations of the normality and/or homoscedasticity assumptions.

In the example data, the residuals shown in Figure 11.2 appear to be somewhat normal in shape, especially considering the groups have fairly small $n$'s. In addition, for the residuals overall, skewness $= -.2389$ and kurtosis $= -1.0191$, indicating a small departure from normality. Thus it appears that all of our assumptions have been satisfied for the example data.

A summary of the assumptions and the effects of their violation for the one-factor analysis of variance design is presented in Table 11.6. Note that in some texts the assumptions are written in terms of the residuals rather than the raw scores, but this makes no difference for our purposes.

## 11.6 THE UNEQUAL *n*'s OR UNBALANCED DESIGN

Up to this point in the chapter, we have only considered the equal $n$'s or balanced case where the number of observations is equal for each group. This was done only to make things simple. However, we need not assume that the $n$'s must be equal (as some textbooks incorrectly do). This section briefly describes the **unequal *n*'s** or **unbalanced case**. For our purposes, the major statistical software handle the analysis of this case for the one-factor model without any special attention. Thus, interpretation of the analysis, the assumptions, and so forth are the same as with the equal $n$'s case. As described in chapter 13, things become a bit more complicated for the unequal $n$'s or unbalanced case with multiple independent variables (or factors).

## 11.7 ALTERNATIVE ANOVA PROCEDURES

There are several alternatives to the parametric one-factor fixed-effects ANOVA. These include the Kruskal-Wallis (1952) one-factor ANOVA, the Welch (1951) test, the Brown-Forsythe

TABLE 11.6
Assumptions and Effects of Violations: One-Factor Design

| Assumption | Effect of Assumption Violation |
| --- | --- |
| Independence | Increased likelihood of a Type I and/or Type II error in the $F$ statistic; influences standard errors of means and thus inferences about those means |
| Homogeneity of variance | Bias in $SS_{with}$; increased likelihood of a Type I and/or Type II error; less effect with equal or nearly equal $n$'s; effect decreases as $n$ increases |
| Normality | Minimal effect with moderate violation; effect less severe with large $n$'s, with equal or nearly equal $n$'s, and/or with homogeneously shaped distributions |

(1974) procedure, and the James (1951) procedures. You may recognize the Welch and Brown–Forsythe procedures as similar alternatives to the independent $t$ test.

The Kruskal-Wallis test makes no normality assumption about the population distributions, although it assumes similar distribution shapes, yet still assumes equal population variances across the groups (although heterogeneity has some effect, it is less than with the parametric ANOVA). When the normality assumption is met, or nearly so (i.e., with mild nonnormality), the parametric ANOVA is slightly more powerful than the Kruskal-Wallis test (i.e., less likelihood of a Type II error). Otherwise the Kruskal-Wallis test is more powerful.

The Kruskal-Wallis procedure works as follows. First, the observations on the dependent measure are ranked, regardless of group assignment (the ranking is done by the computer). That is, the observations are ranked from first through last, disregarding group membership. The procedure essentially tests whether the average of the ranks are different across the groups such that they are unlikely to represent random samples from the same population. Thus, according to the null hypothesis, the mean rank is the same for each group, whereas for the alternative hypothesis the mean rank is not the same across groups. The test statistic is $H$ and is compared to the critical value $_\alpha\chi^2_{J-1}$. The null hypothesis is rejected if the test statistic $H$ exceeds the $\chi^2$ critical value.

There are two situations to consider with this test. First, the $\chi^2$ critical value is really only appropriate when there are at least three groups and at least five observations per group (i.e., the $\chi^2$ is not an exact sampling distribution of $H$). When you are only comparing two groups use the Mann-Whitney-Wilcoxon test (see chap. 7). The second situation is when there are tied ranks, which affect the sampling distribution of $H$. Typically a midranks procedure is used, which results in an overly conservative Kruskal-Wallis test. A correction for ties is commonly used. Unless the number of ties is relatively large, the effect of the correction is minimal.

Using the statistics lab data as an example, we perform the Kruskal-Wallis analysis of variance. The test statistic $H = 13.0610$ is compared with the critical value $_{.05}\chi^2_3 = 7.81$, from Appendix Table 3, and the result is that $H_0$ is rejected ($p = .005$). Thus the Kruskal-Wallis result agrees with the result of the parametric analysis of variance. This should not be surprising because the normality assumption apparently was met. Thus, one would probably not have done the Kruskal-Wallis test for the example data. We merely provide it for purposes of explanation and comparision.

In summary, the Kruskal-Wallis test can be used as an alternative to the parametric one-factor analysis of variance under nonnormality and/or when data are ordinal. Under normality and with interval/ratio data, the parametric ANOVA is more powerful than the Kruskal-Wallis test, and thus is the preferred method of the two.

Next we briefly consider the following procedures for the heteroscedasticity condition: the Welch (1951) test; the Brown-Forsythe (1974) procedure; and the James (1951) first- and second-order procedures (more fully described by Myers & Well, 1995; Coombs, et al., 1996; Wilcox, 1996; and Wilcox, 2003). These procedures do not require homogeneity. Current research suggests that (a) under homogeneity the $F$ test is slightly more powerful than any of these procedures, and (b) under heterogeneity each of these alternative procedures is more powerful than the $F$, although the choice among them depends on several conditions, making a recommendation somewhat complicated (e.g., Clinch & Keselman, 1982; Tomarken & Serlin, 1986; Coombs, et al., 1996). The Kruskal-Wallis test is widely available in the major statistical software, and the Welch and Brown-Forsythe procedures are available in the SPSS one-way ANOVA module. Wilcox (1996, 2003) also provides assistance for these alternative procedures.

## 11.8   SPSS

Finally we consider the use of SPSS for the statistics lab example, including an APA style paragraph of the findings. Note that SPSS needs the data to be in a specific form for any of the analyses below to proceeed, which is different from the layout of the data in Table 11.1. For a one-factor ANOVA, the dataset must consist of two variables or columns. One column or variable is for the level of the independent variable, and the second is for the dependent variable. Each row then represents one individual, indicating the level or group that individual is a member of (1, 2, 3, or 4 in our example), and their score on the dependent variable. Thus we wind up with two long columns of group values and scores.

To conduct a parametric ANOVA through the GLM module, go to the "Analyze" pulldown, into "General Linear Model," and then into the "Univariate" procedure. Click the dependent variable (e.g., labs attended) into the "Dependent Variable" box, and click the fixed-effects factor variable into the "Fixed Factor(s)" box. Click on the "Options" button to obtain such information as "Descriptive Statistics," "Estimates of effect size," "Observed power," and "Homogeneity tests" (i.e., Levene's test) (those are the options that I typically utilize). Click on "Continue" to return to the original dialog box. To obtain a profile plot of means, click on the "Plots" button, move the factor variable name into the "Horizontal axis" box, click on "Add" to generate the plot, and finally click on "Continue" to return to the original dialog box. Then click on "OK" to run the analyses. Selected results are shown in the top three panels of Table 11.7 (ANOVA summary table, information about overall or grand mean, and information about group means, respectively) and the profile plot is shown in Fig. 11.3.

Results from some of the recommended alternative procedures can be obtained from two other SPSS modules. The Kruskal-Wallis procedure is one of the nonparametric tests in SPSS. Beginning with the "Analyze" pulldown, go into "Nonparametric Statistics," then into "K Independent Samples." Click the dependent variable into the "Test Variable List" box and the factor variable into the "Grouping Variable" box. You also have to click on "Define Range" to indicate the values of the grouping variable you wish to use (1 to 4 in the example). In the lower left portion of the screen check "Kruskal-Wallis H" to generate that test, then click on "OK" to find the results as depicted in the fourth panel of Table 11.7.

The Welch and Brown-Forsythe procedures can be found within the One-Way ANOVA program. From the "Analyze" pulldown, go into "Compare Means," then into "One-Way ANOVA." First click the appropriate variables into the "Dependent List" and "Factor" boxes. Click on the "Options" button to find the Welch and Brown-Forsythe procedures, as well as descriptive statistics, Levene's homogeneity of variance test, and a profile plot of means. Then click on "Continue" to return to the original dialog box and click on "OK" to run those procedures. Selected results are given in the bottom panel of Table 11.7. For further details on the use of SPSS for these procedures, be sure to examine books such as Page, Braver, and MacKinnon (2003), or Morgan, Leech, and Barrett (2005).

Finally we come to an example paragraph of the results for the statistics lab example. From Table 11.7 we see that the ANOVA is statistically significant ($F = 6.818$, $df = 3,28$, $p = .001$), effect size is rather large ($\eta^2 = .422$), and observed power is quite strong (.956). The means were 11.125 for the unattractive level, 17.875 for the slightly attractive level, 20.250 for the moderately attractive level, and 24.375 for the very attractive level. The profile plot (Fig. 11.3) depicts that with increasing instructor attractiveness there was a corresponding increase in mean

TABLE 11.7
Selected SPSS Results for the Statistics Lab Example

*Tests of Between-Subjects Effects*

Dependent Variable: dv

| Source | Type III Sum of Squares | df | Mean Square | F | Sig | Partial Eta Squared | Observed Power[a] |
|---|---|---|---|---|---|---|---|
| group | 738.594 | 3 | 246.198 | 6.818 | .001 | .422 | .956 |
| Error | 1011.125 | 28 | 36.112 | | | | |
| Corrected Total | 1749.719 | 31 | | | | | |

a. Computed using alpha = .05

*1. Grand Mean*

Dependent Variable: dv

| | | 95% Confidence Interval | |
|---|---|---|---|
| Mean | Std. Error | Lower Bound | Upper Bound |
| 18.406 | 1.062 | 16.230 | 20.582 |

*2. Group*

Dependent Variable: dv

| | | | 95% Confidence Interval | |
|---|---|---|---|---|
| group | Mean | Std. Error | Lower Bound | Upper Bound |
| 1.00000 | 11.125 | 2.125 | 6.773 | 15.477 |
| 2.00000 | 17.875 | 2.125 | 13.523 | 22.227 |
| 3.00000 | 20.250 | 2.125 | 15.898 | 24.602 |
| 4.00000 | 24.375 | 2.125 | 20.023 | 28.727 |

*Test Statistics[a,b]*

| | dv |
|---|---|
| Chi-Square | 13.061 |
| df | 3 |
| Asymp. Sig. | .005 |

a. Kruskal Wallis Test
b. Grouping Variable: group

*Robust Tests of Equality of Means*

dv

| | Statistic[a] | df1 | df2 | Sig. |
|---|---|---|---|---|
| Welch | 7.862 | 3 | 15.454 | .002 |
| Brown-Forsythe | 6.818 | 3 | 25.882 | .002 |

a. Asymptotically F distributed.

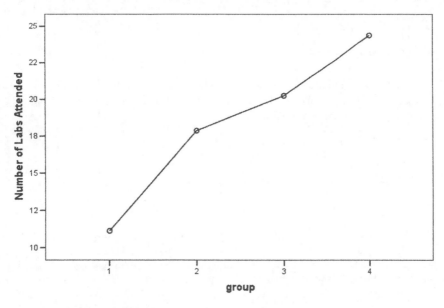

**FIG. 11.3    Profile plot for statistics lab example.**

lab attendance. In examining the residual plot, skewness and kurtosis statistics, and Levene's homogeneity of variance test ($p = .451$), we determined the assumptions were satisfied. For completeness, we also conducted several alternative procedures. The Kruskal-Wallis test ($p = .005$), the Welch procedure ($p = .002$), and the Brown-Forsythe procedure ($p = .002$) also indicated a significant effect, providing further support for the assumptions being satisfied.

## 11.9    SUMMARY

In this chapter, methods involving the comparision of multiple group means for a single independent variable were considered. The chapter began with a look at the characteristics of the analysis of variance including: (a) control of the experiment-wise error rate through an omnibus test; (b) one independent variable with two or more fixed levels; (c) individuals are randomly assigned to groups and then exposed to only one level of the independent variable; and (d) the dependent variable is at least measured at the interval level. Next, a discussion of the theory underlying ANOVA was conducted. Here we examined the concepts of between- and within-groups variability, sources of variation, and partitioning the sums of squares. The ANOVA model was examined. Some discussion was also devoted to the ANOVA assumptions, their assessment, and how to deal with assumption violations. Finally, alternative ANOVA procedures were described. At this point you should have met the following objectives: (a) be able to understand the characteristics and concepts underlying the one-factor ANOVA, (b) be able to compute and interpret the results of a one-factor ANOVA, and (c) be able to understand and evaluate the assumptions of the one-factor ANOVA. Chapter 12 considers a number of multiple comparison procedures for further examination of sets of means. Chapter 13 returns to the analysis of variance and discusses models for which there are more than one independent variable.

## PROBLEMS

### Conceptual Problems

1. Data for three independent random samples each of size four are analyzed by a one-factor analysis of variance fixed-effects model. If the values of the sample means are all equal, what is the value of $MS_{betw}$?

   a.  0

   b.  1

   c.  2

   d.  3

2. For a one-factor analysis of variance fixed-effects model, which of the following is always true?

   a.  $df_{betw} + df_{with} = df_{tot}$

   b.  $SS_{betw} + SS_{with} = SS_{tot}$

   c.  $MS_{betw} + MS_{with} = MS_{tot}$

   d.  all of the above

   e.  both a and b

3. Suppose that $n_1 = 19$, $n_2 = 21$, and $n_3 = 23$. For a one-factor ANOVA, the $df_{with}$ would be

   a.  2

   b.  3

   c.  60

   d.  63

4. In a one-factor ANOVA, $H_0$ asserts that

   a.  all of the population means are equal.

   b.  the between-groups variance estimate and the within-groups variance estimate are both estimates of the same population variance.

   c.  the within-groups sum of squares is equal to the between-groups sum of squares.

   d.  both a and b

5. For a one-factor ANOVA comparing three groups with $n = 10$ in each group, the $F$ ratio would have degrees of freedom equal to

   a.  2, 27

   b.  2, 29

   c.  3, 27

   d.  3, 29

6. Which of the following is not necessary in ANOVA?
    a. Observations are from random and independent samples.
    b. The dependent variable is measured on at least the interval scale.
    c. Populations have equal variances.
    d. Equal sample sizes are necessary.

7. If you find an $F$ ratio of 1.0 in a one-factor ANOVA, it means that
    a. between-group variation exceeds within-group variation.
    b. within-group variation exceeds between-group variation.
    c. between-group variation is equal to within-group variation.
    d. between-group variation exceeds total variation.

8. Suppose students in grades 7, 8, 9, 10, 11, and 12 were compared on absenteeism. If ANOVA were used rather than multiple $t$ tests, the probability of a Type I error would be less. True or False?

9. Mean square is another name for variance or variance estimate. True or False?

10. In ANOVA each independent variable is known as a level. True or False?

11. A negative $F$ ratio is impossible. True or False?

12. Suppose that for a one-factor ANOVA with $J = 4$ and $n = 10$ the four sample means are all equal to 15. I assert that the value of $MS_{with}$ is necessarily equal to zero. Am I correct?

13. With $J = 3$ groups, I assert that if you reject $H_0$ in the one-factor ANOVA you will necessarily conclude that all three group means are different. Am I correct?

14. The homoscedasticity assumption is that the population scores from which each of the samples are drawn are normally distributed. True or False?

15. When analyzing mean differences among more than two samples, doing independent $t$ tests on all possible pairs of means
    a. decreases the probability of a Type I error.
    b. does not change the probability of a Type I error.
    c. increases the probability of a Type I error.
    d. Cannot be determined from the information provided.

16. Suppose for a one-factor fixed-effects ANOVA with $J = 5$ and $n = 15$, the five sample means are all equal to 50. I assert that the $F$ test statistic cannot be significant. Am I correct?

17. The independence assumption in ANOVA is that the observations in the samples do not depend on one another. True or False?

18.   For $J = 2$ and $\alpha = .05$, if the result of the independent $t$ test is significant, then the result of the one-factor fixed-effects ANOVA is uncertain. True or false?

19.   A statistician conducted a one-factor fixed-effects ANOVA and found the $F$ ratio to be less than 0. I assert that this means the between-groups variability is less than the within-groups variability. Am I correct?

## Computational Problems

1.   Complete the following summary table for a one-factor analysis of variance, where there are four groups receiving different headache medications, each with 16 observations, and $\alpha = .05$.

| Source | SS | df | MS | F | Critical Value and Decision |
|--------|-----|-----|-----|---|------------------------------|
| Between | 9.75 | — | — | — | — |
| Within | — | — | — | | |
| Total | 18.75 | — | | | |

2.   A social psychologist wants to determine if type of music has any effect on the number of beers consumed by people in a tavern. Four taverns are selected that have different musical formats. Five people are randomly sampled in each tavern and their beer consumption monitored for three hours. Complete the following one-factor ANOVA summary table using $\alpha = .05$.

| Source | SS | df | MS | F | Critical Value and Decision |
|--------|-----|-----|-----|------|------------------------------|
| Between | — | — | 7.52 | 5.01 | — |
| Within | — | — | — | | |
| Total | — | — | | | |

3.   A psychologist would like to know whether the season (fall, winter, spring, summer) has any consistent effect on people's sexual activity. In the middle of each season a psychologist selects a random sample of $n = 25$ students. Each individual is given a sexual activity questionnaire. A one-factor ANOVA was used to analyze these data. Complete the following ANOVA summary table ($\alpha = .05$).

| Source | SS | df | MS | F | Critical Value and Decision |
|--------|-----|-----|-----|------|------------------------------|
| Between | — | — | — | 5.00 | — |
| Within | 960 | — | — | | |
| Total | — | — | | | |

4.   The following five independent random samples are obtained from five normally distributed populations with equal variances. The dependent variable is number of bank transactions in one month and the groups are five different banks.

| Group 1 | Group 2 | Group 3 | Group 4 | Group 5 |
|---------|---------|---------|---------|---------|
| 16 | 16 | 2 | 5 | 7 |
| 5 | 10 | 9 | 8 | 12 |
| 11 | 7 | 11 | 1 | 14 |
| 23 | 12 | 13 | 5 | 16 |
| 18 | 7 | 10 | 8 | 11 |
| 12 | 4 | 13 | 11 | 9 |
| 12 | 23 | 9 | 9 | 19 |
| 19 | 13 | 9 | 9 | 24 |

Use SPSS to conduct a one-factor analysis of variance to determine if the group means are equal using $\alpha = .05$. Plot the group means and interpret the results.

## Interpretive Problem

Using the statistics survey dataset from the CD, use SPSS to conduct a one-factor fixed-effects ANOVA, where political view is the grouping variable ($J = 5$) and the dependent variable is a variable of interest to you (the following variables look interesting: books; TV; exercise; drinks; GPA; GREQ; CDs; hair appointment). Then write an APA type paragraph describing the results.

# 12

# MULTIPLE COMPARISON PROCEDURES

## Chapter Outline

1.  Concepts of multiple comparison procedures
    Contrasts
    Planned versus post hoc comparisons
    The Type I error rate
    Orthogonal contrasts
2.  Selected multiple comparison procedures
    Planned analysis of trend
    Planned orthogonal contrasts
    Planned contrasts with reference group: Dunnett method
    Other planned contrasts: Dunn (or Bonferroni) and Dunn-Sidak methods
    Complex post hoc contrasts: Scheffe' and Kaiser-Bowden methods
    Simple post hoc contrasts: Tukey HSD, Tukey-Kramer, Fisher LSD, and
        Hayter tests
    Simple post hoc contrasts for unequal variances: Games-Howell, Dunnett T3
        and C tests
    Follow-up tests to Kruskal-Wallis

## Key Concepts

1. Contrast
2. Simple and complex contrasts
3. Planned and post hoc comparisons
4. Contrast- and family-based Type I error rates
5. Orthogonal contrasts

In this chapter our concern is with multiple comparison procedures that involve comparisons among the group means. Recall from chapter 11 the one-factor analysis of variance where the means from two or more samples were compared. What do we do if the omnibus $F$ test leads us to reject $H_0$? First, consider the situation where there are only two samples (e.g., assessing the effectiveness of two types of medication), and $H_0$ has already been rejected in the omnibus test. Why was $H_0$ rejected? The answer should be obvious. Those two sample means must be significantly different, as there is no other way that the omnibus $H_0$ could have been rejected (e.g., one type of medication is more effective than the other).

Second, consider the situation where there are more than two samples (e.g., three types of medication), and $H_0$ has already been rejected in the omnibus test. Why was $H_0$ rejected? The answer is not so obvious. This situation is one where a **multiple comparison procedure** (MCP) would be quite informative. Thus for situations where there are at least three groups and the analysis of variance (ANOVA) $H_0$ has been rejected, some sort of MCP is necessary to determine which means or combination of means are different. Third, consider the situation where the researcher is not even interested in the ANOVA omnibus test, but is only interested in comparisons involving particular means (e.g., certain medications are more effective than a placebo). This is a situation where a MCP is useful for evaluating those specific comparisons.

If the ANOVA omnibus $H_0$ has been rejected, why not do all possible independent $t$ tests? First return to a similar question from Chapter 11. There we asked about doing all possible pairwise independent $t$ tests rather than an ANOVA. The answer there was to do an omnibus $F$ test. The reason was related to the probability of making a Type I error (i.e., $\alpha$), where the researcher incorrectly rejects a true null hypothesis. Although the $\alpha$ level for each $t$ test can be controlled at a specified nominal level, say .05, what would happen to the overall $\alpha$ level for the set of tests? The overall $\alpha$ level for the set of tests, often called the family-wise Type I error rate, would be larger than the $\alpha$ level for each of the individual $t$ tests. The optimal solution, in terms of maintaining control over our overall $\alpha$ level as well as maximizing power, is to conduct one overall omnibus test. The omnibus test assesses the equality of all of the means simultaneously.

The same concept can be applied to the multiple comparison situation. Rather than doing all possible pairwise independent $t$ tests, where the family-wise error could be quite large, one should use a procedure that controls the family-wise error in some way. This can be done with multiple comparison procedures. As pointed out later in the chapter, there are two main methods for taking the Type I error rate into account.

This chapter is concerned with several important new concepts, such as a contrast, planned versus post hoc comparisons, the Type I error rate, and orthogonal contrasts. The remainder of the chapter consists of selected multiple comparison procedures, including when and how to apply them. The terms **comparison** and **contrast** are used here synonymously. Also, MCPs are only applicable for comparing levels of an independent variable that are fixed, in other words, for fixed-effects independent variables, and not for random-effects independent variables. Our objectives are that by the end of this chapter, you will be able to (a) understand the concepts underlying the MCPs, (b) select the appropriate MCP for a given research situation, and (c) determine and interpret the results of MCPs.

## 12.1 CONCEPTS OF MULTIPLE COMPARISON PROCEDURES

This section describes the most important characteristics of the multiple comparison procedures. We begin by defining a contrast, and then move into planned versus post hoc contrasts, the Type I error rates, and orthogonal contrasts.

### 12.1.1 Contrasts

A **contrast** is a weighted combination of the means. For example, one might wish to contrast the following means: (a) Group 1 with Group 2, or (b) the combination of Groups 1 and 2 with Group 3. Statistically a contrast is defined as

$$\psi_i = c_1 \mu_{.1} + c_2 \mu_{.2} + \cdots + c_J \mu_{.J}$$

where the $c_j$ are known as contrast coefficients (or weights), which are positive and negative values and define a particular contrast $\psi_i$, and the $\mu_{.j}$ are population group means. In other words, a contrast is simply a particular combination of the group means, depending on which means the researcher is interested in comparing. It should also be noted that to form a fair or legitimate contrast, $\Sigma_j c_j = 0$ for the equal $n$'s or balanced case, and $\Sigma_j (n_j c_j) = 0$ for the unequal $n$'s or unbalanced case.

For example, suppose you want to compare the means of Groups 1 and 3 for $J = 4$, and call this contrast 1. The contrast would be written as

$$\psi_1 = c_1 \mu_{.1} + c_2 \mu_{.2} + c_3 \mu_{.3} + c_4 \mu_{.4}$$
$$= (+1) \mu_{.1} + (0) \mu_{.2} + (-1) \mu_{.3} + (0) \mu_{.4}$$
$$= \mu_{.1} - \mu_{.3}$$

What hypotheses are we testing when we evaluate a contrast? The null and alternate hypotheses of any specific contrast can be written simply as

$$H_0: \psi_i = 0$$

and

$$H_1: \psi_i \neq 0$$

respectively. Thus we are testing whether a particular combination of means, as defined by the contrast coefficients, are different. How does this relate back to the omnibus $F$ test? The null and alternate hypotheses for the omnibus $F$ test can be written in terms of contrasts as

$$H_0: \text{all } \psi_i = 0$$

and

$$H_1: \text{at least one } \psi_i \neq 0$$

respectively. Here the omnibus test is determining whether any contrast that could be formulated for the set of $J$ means is significant.

Contrasts can be divided into simple or pairwise contrasts, and complex or nonpairwise contrasts. A simple or pairwise contrast is a comparison involving only two means. Let us take as an example the situation where there are $J = 3$ groups. There are three possible distinct pairwise contrasts that could be formed: (a) $\mu_{.1} - \mu_{.2} = 0$, (b) $\mu_{.1} - \mu_{.3} = 0$, and (c) $\mu_{.2} - \mu_{.3} = 0$. It should be obvious that a pairwise contrast involving Groups 1 and 2 is the same contrast whether it is written as $\mu_{.1} - \mu_{.2} = 0$, or as $\mu_{.2} - \mu_{.1} = 0$. In terms of contrast coefficients, these three contrasts could be written in the form of a table as

|  | $c_1$ | $c_2$ | $c_3$ |
|---|---|---|---|
| $\psi_1: \mu_{.1} - \mu_{.2} = 0$ | $+1$ | $-1$ | $0$ |
| $\psi_2: \mu_{.1} - \mu_{.3} = 0$ | $+1$ | $0$ | $-1$ |
| $\psi_3: \mu_{.2} - \mu_{.3} = 0$ | $0$ | $+1$ | $-1$ |

where each contrast is read across the table to determine its contrast coefficients. For example, the first contrast $\psi_1$ does not involve Group 3 because that contrast coefficient is zero, but does involve Groups 1 and 2 because those contrast coefficients are not zero. The coefficients are $+1$ for Group 1 and $-1$ for Group 2; consequently we are interested in examining the difference between Groups 1 and 2. Written in long form so that we can see where the contrast coefficients come from, the three contrasts are as follows:

$$\psi_1 = (+1)\mu_{.1} + (-1)\mu_{.2} + (0)\mu_{.3} = \mu_{.1} - \mu_{.2}$$
$$\psi_2 = (+1)\mu_{.1} + (0)\mu_{.2} + (-1)\mu_{.3} = \mu_{.1} - \mu_{.3}$$
$$\psi_3 = (0)\mu_{.1} + (+1)\mu_{.2} + (-1)\mu_{.3} = \mu_{.2} - \mu_{.3}$$

An easy way to remember the number of possible unique pairwise contrasts that could be written is $\frac{1}{2}[J(J - 1)]$. Thus for $J = 3$ the number of possible unique pairwise contrasts is 3, whereas for $J = 4$ the number of such contrasts is 6.

A complex contrast is a comparison involving more than two means. Continuing with the example of $J = 3$ groups, we might be interested in testing the contrast $\mu_{.1} - \frac{1}{2}(\mu_{.2} + \mu_{.3})$. This contrast is a comparison of the mean for Group 1 with the average of the means for Groups 2 and 3. In terms of contrast coefficients, this contrast would be written as

$$
\begin{array}{cccc}
 & c_1 & c_2 & c_3 \\
\psi_4: \mu_{.1} - \frac{1}{2}\mu_{.2} - \frac{1}{2}\mu_{.3} = 0 & 1 & -\frac{1}{2} & -\frac{1}{2}
\end{array}
$$

Written in long form so that we can see where the contrast coefficients come from, this complex contrast is as follows:

$$\psi_4: = (+1)\mu_{.1} + (-\tfrac{1}{2})\mu_{.2} + (-\tfrac{1}{2})\mu_{.3} = \mu_{.1} - \tfrac{1}{2}\mu_{.2} - \tfrac{1}{2}\mu_{.3}$$

The number of unique complex contrasts is greater than $\frac{1}{2}[J(J - 1)]$ when $J$ is at least 4; in other words, the number of such contrasts that could be formed is quite large when there are more than three groups. Note that the total number of unique pairwise and complex contrasts is $[1 + \frac{1}{2}(3^J - 1) - 2^J]$ (Keppel, 1982). Thus for $J = 4$, one could form 25 total contrasts.

Many of the multiple comparison procedures are based on the same test statistic, which we introduce here as the "standard $t$." The standard $t$ ratio for a contrast is given as

$$t = \frac{\psi'}{s_{\psi'}}$$

where $s_{\psi'}$ represents the standard error of the contrast as

$$s_{\psi'} = \sqrt{MS_{error} \sum_{j=1}^{J} \left( \frac{c_j^2}{n_j} \right)}$$

where the prime (i.e., $'$) indicates that the contrast is based on sample data, and $n_j$ refers to the number of observations in group $j$.

## 12.1.2  Planned Versus Post hoc Comparisons

This section examines specific types of contrasts or comparisons. One way of classifying contrasts is whether the contrasts are formulated prior to the research or following a significant omnibus $F$ test. **Planned contrasts** (also known as specific or a priori contrasts) involve particular comparisons that the researcher is interested in examining prior to data collection. These planned contrasts are generally based on theory, previous research, and/or hypotheses. Here the researcher is interested in certain specific contrasts a priori, where the number of such contrasts is usually small. Planned contrasts are done without regard to the result of the omnibus $F$ test. In other words, the researcher is interested in certain specific contrasts, but not in the omnibus $F$ test that examines all possible contrasts. In this situation the researcher could care less about the multitude of possible contrasts and need not even examine the $F$ test; but rather the concern is only with a few contrasts of substantive interest. In addition, the researcher may not be as concerned with the family-wise error rate for planned comparisons because only a few of them will actually be carried out. Fewer planned comparisons are usually conducted (due to their specificity) than post hoc comparisons (due to their generality), so planned contrasts generally yield narrower confidence intervals, are more powerful, and have a higher likelihood of a Type I error than post hoc comparisons.

**Post hoc contrasts** are formulated such that the researcher provides no advance specification of the actual contrasts to be tested. This type of contrast is done following a significant omnibus *F* test. Post hoc is Latin for "after the fact," referring to contrasts tested after a significant *F* in the ANOVA. Here the researcher may want to take the family-wise error rate into account somehow for purposes of overall protection. Post hoc contrasts are also known as unplanned, a posteriori, or postmortem contrasts. It should be noted that most MCPs are not derived or based on finding a significant *F* in the ANOVA.

### 12.1.3    The Type I Error Rate

How does the researcher deal with the family-wise Type I error rate? Depending on the multiple comparison procedure selected, one may either set $\alpha$ for each contrast or set $\alpha$ for a family of contrasts. In the former category, $\alpha$ is set for each individual contrast. The MCPs in this category are known as **contrast-based**. We designate the $\alpha$ level for contrast-based procedures as $\alpha_{pc}$, as it represents the **per contrast** Type I error rate. Thus $\alpha_{pc}$ represents the probability of making a Type I error for that particular contrast. In the latter category, $\alpha$ is set for a family or set of contrasts. The MCPs in this category are known as **family-wise**. We designate the $\alpha$ level for family-wise procedures as $\alpha_{fw}$, as it represents the family-wise Type I error rate. Thus $\alpha_{fw}$ represents the probability of making at least one Type I error in the family or set of contrasts. For orthogonal (or independent) contrasts, the following property holds:

$$\alpha_{fw} = 1 - (1 - \alpha_{pc})^c$$

where $c = J - 1$ orthogonal contrasts (as defined in the next section). For nonorthogonal contrasts, this property is more complicated in that

$$\alpha_{fw} \leq c\, \alpha_{pc}$$

These properties should be familiar from the discussion in chapter 11, where we were looking at the probability of a Type I error in the use of multiple independent *t* tests.

### 12.1.4    Orthogonal Contrasts

Let us begin this section by defining orthogonal contrasts. A set of contrasts is orthogonal if they represent nonredundant and independent (if the usual ANOVA assumptions are met) sources of variation. For *J* groups, you will only be able to construct $J - 1$ orthogonal contrasts. However, more than one set of orthogonal contrasts may exist; although the contrasts within each set are orthogonal, contrasts across such sets may not be.

For purposes of simplicity, we first consider the equal *n*'s or balanced case. With equal observations per group, two contrasts are defined to be orthogonal if the products of their contrast coefficients sum to zero. That is, two contrasts are orthogonal if

$$\sum_{j=1}^{J} (c_j c_{j'}) = c_1 c_{1'} + c_2 c_{2'} + \ldots + c_j c_{j'} = 0$$

where $j$ and $j'$ represent two distinct contrasts. Thus we see that orthogonality depends on the contrast coefficients, the $c_j$, and not the group means, the $\mu_{.j}$. For example, if $J = 3$, then we can form a set of two orthogonal contrasts. One such set is

$$
\begin{array}{lccc}
 & c_1 & c_2 & c_3 \\
\psi_1: \mu_{.1} - \mu_{.2} = 0 & +1 & -1 & 0 \\
\psi_2: \tfrac{1}{2}\mu_{.1} + \tfrac{1}{2}\mu_{.2} - \mu_{.3} = 0 & +\tfrac{1}{2} & +\tfrac{1}{2} & -1 \\
\hline
 & +\tfrac{1}{2} + & -\tfrac{1}{2} + & 0 = 0
\end{array}
$$

If the sum of the contrast coefficient products for a set of contrasts is equal to zero, then we define this as an orthogonal set of contrasts. A set of two contrasts that are not orthogonal is

$$
\begin{array}{lccc}
 & c_1 & c_2 & c_3 \\
\psi_3: \mu_{.1} - \mu_{.2} = 0 & +1 & -1 & 0 \\
\psi_4: \mu_{.1} - \mu_{.3} = 0 & +1 & 0 & -1 \\
\hline
 & +1 + & 0 + & 0 = +1
\end{array}
$$

Consider a situation where there are three groups and we decide to form three pairwise contrasts, knowing full well that they cannot all be orthogonal. The contrasts we form are

$$
\begin{array}{lccc}
 & c_1 & c_2 & c_3 \\
\psi_1: \mu_{.1} - \mu_{.2} = 0 & +1 & -1 & 0 \\
\psi_2: \mu_{.2} - \mu_{.3} = 0 & 0 & +1 & -1 \\
\psi_3: \mu_{.1} - \mu_{.3} = 0 & +1 & 0 & -1
\end{array}
$$

Say that the group means are $\mu_{.1} = 30$, $\mu_{.2} = 24$, and $\mu_{.3} = 20$. We find $\psi_1 = 6$ for the first contrast, and $\psi_2 = 4$ for the second contrast. Because these three contrasts are not orthogonal and contain totally redundant information about the means, $\psi_3 = 10$ for the third contrast by definition. Thus the third contrast contains no additional information to that contained in the first two contrasts.

Finally, for the unequal $n$'s or unbalanced case, two contrasts are orthogonal if

$$
\sum_{j=1}^{J}\left[\frac{(c_j c_{j'})}{n_j}\right] = 0
$$

The denominator $n_j$ makes it more difficult to find an orthogonal set of contrasts that is of any interest to the researcher (see Pedhazur, 1997, for an example).

## 12.2   SELECTED MULTIPLE COMPARISON PROCEDURES

This section considers a selection of multiple comparison procedures (MCP). These represent the "best" procedures in some sense, in terms of ease of utility, popularity, and control of Type I and II error rates. Other procedures are briefly mentioned. In the interest of consistency, each procedure is discussed in the hypothesis testing situation based on a test statistic. Most, but not all, of the procedures can also be formulated as confidence intervals (sometimes called a **critical difference**), although not discussed here. The first few procedures discussed are for planned comparisons, whereas the remainder of the section is devoted to post hoc comparisons. For each MCP, we describe its major characteristics, and present the test statistic with an example using the example data from chapter 11.

Unless otherwise specified, each MCP makes the standard assumptions of normality, homogeneity of variance, and independence of observations. Some of the procedures do make additional assumptions, such as equal $n$'s per group. Throughout this section we also assume that a two-tailed alternative hypothesis is of interest, although some of the MCPs can also be used with a one-tailed alternative. In general, the MCPs are fairly robust to nonnormality (but not for extreme cases), but are not as robust to departures from homogeneity of variance or from independence (see Pavur, 1988).

## 12.2.1 Planned Analysis of Trend

Trend analysis is a planned MCP useful when the groups represent different quantitative levels of a factor (i.e., an interval or ratio level independent variable). Examples of such a factor might be age, drug dosage, and different amounts of instruction, practice, or trials. Here the researcher is interested in whether the sample means vary with a change in the amount of the independent variable. We define **trend analysis** in the form of orthogonal polynomials, and assume that the levels of the independent variable are equally spaced and the number of observations per group are equal. This is the standard case; other cases are briefly discussed at the end of this section.

Orthogonal polynomial contrasts use the standard $t$ test statistic, which is compared to the critical values of $\pm_{\alpha/2} t_{df(error)}$ obtained from the $t$ table in Appendix Table 2. The form of the contrasts is a bit different and requires a bit of discussion. Orthogonal polynomial contrasts incorporate two concepts, orthogonal contrasts and polynomial regression. For $J$ groups, there can be only $J - 1$ orthogonal contrasts in the set. In polynomial regression, we have terms in the model for a linear trend, a quadratic trend, a cubic trend, and so on. For example, linear trend is represented by a straight line (no bends), quadratic trend by a curve with one bend (U or upside-down U shapes), and cubic trend by a curve with two bends (S shape).

Now put those two ideas together. A set of orthogonal contrasts can be formed where the first contrast evaluates a linear trend, the second a quadratic trend, the third a cubic trend, and so forth. Thus for $J$ groups, the highest order polynomial that could be formed is $J - 1$. With four groups, for example, one could form a set of orthogonal contrasts to assess linear, quadratic, and cubic trend.

You may be wondering just how these contrasts are formed? For $J = 4$ groups, the contrast coefficients for the linear, quadratic, and cubic trends are

|  | $c_1$ | $c_2$ | $c_3$ | $c_4$ |
|---|---|---|---|---|
| $\psi_{linear}$ | $-3$ | $-1$ | $+1$ | $+3$ |
| $\psi_{quadratic}$ | $+1$ | $-1$ | $-1$ | $+1$ |
| $\psi_{cubic}$ | $-1$ | $+3$ | $-3$ | $+1$ |

where the contrasts can be written out as

$$\psi_{linear} = (-3)\mu_{.1} + (-1)\mu_{.2} + (+1)\mu_{.3} + (+3)\mu_{.4}$$

$$\psi_{quadratic} = (+1)\mu_{.1} + (-1)\mu_{.2} + (-1)\mu_{.3} + (+1)\mu_{.4}$$

$$\psi_{cubic} = (-1)\mu_{.1} + (+3)\mu_{.2} + (-3)\mu_{.3} + (+1)\mu_{.4}$$

These contrast coefficients can be found in Appendix Table 6, for a number of different values of $J$. If you look in the table of contrast coefficients for values of $J$ greater than 6, you see that the coefficients for the higher-order polynomials are not included. As an example, for $J = 7$, coefficients only up through a quintic trend are included. Although they could easily be derived and tested, these higher-order polynomials are usually not of interest to the researcher. In fact, it is rare to find anyone interested in polynomials beyond the cubic because they are difficult to understand and interpret (although statistically sophisticated, they say little to the applied researcher). The contrasts are typically tested sequentially beginning with the linear trend and proceeding to higher-order trends.

Using the example data on the attractiveness of the lab instructors from Chapter 11, let us test for linear, quadratic, and cubic trends. Trend analysis may be relevant for this data because the groups do represent different quantitative levels of an attractiveness factor. Because $J = 4$, we can use the contrast coefficients given previously. The following are the computations:

Critical values: $\pm_{\alpha/2} t_{df(error)} = \pm_{.025} t_{28} = \pm 2.048$

Standard error for linear trend:

$$s_{\psi'} = \sqrt{MS_{error} \sum_{j=1}^{J}\left(\frac{c_j^2}{n_j}\right)} = \sqrt{36.1116(9/8+1/8+1/8+9/8)} = 9.5015$$

Standard error for quadratic trend:

$$s_{\psi'} = \sqrt{MS_{error} \sum_{j=1}^{J}\left(\frac{c_j^2}{n_j}\right)} = \sqrt{36.1116(1/8+1/8+1/8+1/8)} = 4.2492$$

Standard error for cubic trend:

$$s_{\psi'} = \sqrt{MS_{error} \sum_{j=1}^{J}\left(\frac{c_j^2}{n_j}\right)} = \sqrt{36.1116(1/8+9/8+9/8+1/8)} = 9.5015$$

Test statistics:

$$t_{linear} = \frac{-3\overline{Y}_{.1} - 1\overline{Y}_{.2} + 1\overline{Y}_{.3} + 3\overline{Y}_{.4}}{s_{\psi'}}$$

$$= \frac{-3(11.1250) - 1(17.8750) + 1(20.2500) + 3(24.3750)}{9.5015} = 4.4335 \, (significant)$$

$$t_{quadratic} = \frac{1\overline{Y}_{.1} - 1\overline{Y}_{.2} - 1\overline{Y}_{.3} + 1\overline{Y}_{.4}}{s_{\psi'}}$$

$$= \frac{1(11.1250) - 1(17.8750) - 1(20.2500) + 1(24.3750)}{4.2492} = -0.6178 \, (nonsignificant)$$

$$t_{cubic} = \frac{-1\overline{Y}_{.1} + 3\overline{Y}_{.2} - 3\overline{Y}_{.3} + 1\overline{Y}_{.4}}{s_{\psi'}}$$

$$= \frac{-1(11.1250) + 3(17.8750) - 3(20.2500) + 1(24.3750)}{9.5015} = 0.6446 \, (nonsignificant)$$

Thus we see that there is a significant linear trend in the means, but no higher-order trend. This should not be surprising when we plot the means, as shown in Fig. 12.1, where there is a very strong linear trend, and that is about it. In other words, there is a steady increase in mean attendance as the level of attractiveness of the instructor increases. Always plot the means so that you can interpret the results of the contrasts.

Let us make some final points about orthogonal polynomial contrasts. First, be particularly careful about extrapolating beyond the range of the levels investigated. The trend may or may not be the same outside of this range; given only those sample means, we have no way of knowing what the trend is outside of the range. Second, in the unequal $n$'s or unbalanced case, it becomes difficult to formulate a set of orthogonal contrasts that make any sense to the researcher. See the discussion in the next section on planned orthogonal contrasts, as well as

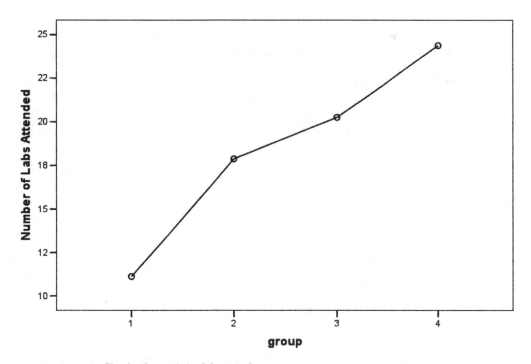

**FIG. 12.1   Profile plot for statistics lab example.**

Kirk (1982). Third, when the levels are not equally spaced, this needs to be taken into account in the contrast coefficients (see Kirk, 1982).

## 12.2.2   Planned Orthogonal Contrasts

Planned orthogonal contrasts (POC) are a MCP where the contrasts are defined ahead of time by the researcher (i.e., planned) and the set of contrasts are orthogonal. The POC method is a contrast-based procedure where the researcher is not concerned with control of the family-wise error rate. The set of contrasts are orthogonal, so the number of contrasts should be small.

Computationally, planned orthogonal contrasts use the standard $t$ test statistic that is compared to the critical values of $\pm_{\alpha/2}\, t_{\text{df(error)}}$ obtained from the $t$ table in Appendix Table 2. Using the example data set from Chapter 11, let us find a set of orthogonal contrasts and complete the computations. Since $J = 4$, we can find at most a set of three (or $J - 1$) orthogonal contrasts. One orthogonal set that seems reasonable for these data is

|            | $c_1$ | $c_2$ | $c_3$ | $c_4$ |
|------------|-------|-------|-------|-------|
| $\psi_1$:  | $+\frac{1}{2}$ | $+\frac{1}{2}$ | $-\frac{1}{2}$ | $-\frac{1}{2}$ |
| $\psi_2$:  | $+1$  | $-1$  | $0$   | $0$   |
| $\psi_3$:  | $0$   | $0$   | $+1$  | $-1$  |

Here we see that the first contrast compares the average of the two least attractive groups with the average of the two most attractive groups, the second contrast compares the two least attractive groups, and the third contrast compares the two most attractive groups. Note that the design is balanced (i.e., the equal $n$'s case). The following are the computations:

Critical values: $\pm_{\alpha/2}\, t_{\text{df(error)}} = \pm_{.025}\, t_{28} = \pm 2.048$

Standard error for contrast 1:

$$s_{\psi'} = \sqrt{MS_{error} \sum_{j=1}^{J}\left(\frac{c_j^2}{n_j}\right)} = \sqrt{36.1116(.25/8 + .25/8 + .25/8 + .25/8)} = 2.1246$$

Standard error for contrasts 2 and 3:

$$s_{\psi'} = \sqrt{MS_{error}\left[\frac{1}{n_j} + \frac{1}{n_{j'}}\right]} = \sqrt{36.1116(1/8 + 1/8)} = 3.0046$$

Test statistics:

$$t_1 = \frac{+\frac{1}{2}\overline{Y}_{.1} + \frac{1}{2}\overline{Y}_{.2} - \frac{1}{2}\overline{Y}_{.3} - \frac{1}{2}\overline{Y}_{.4}}{s_{\psi'}}$$

$$= \frac{+\frac{1}{2}(11.1250) + \frac{1}{2}(17.8750) - \frac{1}{2}(20.2500) - \frac{1}{2}(24.3750)}{2.1246} = -3.6772\ (significant)$$

$$t_2 = \frac{\overline{Y}_1 - \overline{Y}_2}{s_{\psi'}} = \frac{11.1250 - 17.8750}{3.0046} = -2.2466 \; (nonsignific\ldots)$$

$$t_3 = \frac{\overline{Y}_3 - \overline{Y}_4}{s_{\psi'}} = \frac{20.2500 - 24.3750}{3.0046} = -1.3729 \; (nonsignificant)$$

These results indicate that the less attractive groups have significantly lower attendance than the more attractive groups, the two less attractive groups are different, but the two more attractive groups are not different.

There is a practical problem with this procedure because the contrasts of interest may not be orthogonal, or the researcher may not be interested in all of the contrasts of an orthogonal set. Another problem already mentioned occurs when the design is unbalanced, where an orthogonal set of contrasts may be constructed at the expense of meaningful contrasts. My advice is simple. If the contrasts you are interested in are not orthogonal, then use another MCP. If you are not interested in all of the contrasts of an orthogonal set, then use another MCP. If your design is not balanced and the orthogonal contrasts formed are not meaningful, then use another MCP. In each case, if you desire a planned MCP, then we recommend either the Dunnett, Dunn (Bonferroni), or Dunn-Sidak procedure.

We defined the POC as a contrast-based procedure. One could also consider an alternative family-wise method where the $\alpha_{pc}$ level is divided among the contrasts in the set. This procedure is defined by $\alpha_{pc} = \alpha_{fw}/c$, where $c$ is the number of orthogonal contrasts in the set (i.e., $c = J - 1$). As shown later, this borrows a concept from the Dunn (Bonferroni) procedure. If the variances are not equal across the groups, several approximate solutions have been proposed that take the individual group variances into account (see Kirk, 1982).

### 12.2.3 Planned Contrasts with Reference Group: Dunnett Method

A third method of planned comparisons is due to Dunnett (1955). It is designed to test pairwise contrasts where a reference group (e.g., a control or baseline group) is compared to each of the other $J - 1$ groups. Thus a family of prespecified pairwise contrasts is to be evaluated. The Dunnett method is a family-wise MCP and is slightly more powerful than the Dunn procedure (another planned family-wise MCP). The test statistic is the standard $t$ except that the standard error is simplified as follows:

$$s_{\psi'} = \sqrt{MS_{error}\left[\frac{1}{n_j} + \frac{1}{n_c}\right]}$$

where $c$ is the reference group and $j$ is the group to which it is being compared. The test statistic is compared to the critical values $\pm_{\alpha/2} t_{df(error), J-1}$ obtained from the Dunnett table located in Appendix Table 7.

Using the example data set, compare the unattractive group (used as a reference or baseline group) to each of the other three groups. The following are the computations:

Critical values: $\pm_{\alpha/2} t_{df(error), J-1} = \pm_{.025} t_{28,3} \approx \pm 2.48$

Standard error:

$$s_{\psi'} = \sqrt{MS_{error}\left[\frac{1}{n_j} + \frac{1}{n_c}\right]} = \sqrt{36.1116\,[1/8 + 1/8]} = 3.0046$$

Test statistics:

$$t_1 = \frac{\overline{Y}_{.1} - \overline{Y}_{.2}}{s_{\psi'}} = \frac{11.1250 - 17.8750}{3.0046} = -2.2466\ (nonsignificant)$$

$$t_2 = \frac{\overline{Y}_{.1} - \overline{Y}_{.3}}{s_{\psi'}} = \frac{11.1250 - 20.2500}{3.0046} = -3.0370\ (significant)$$

$$t_3 = \frac{\overline{Y}_{.1} - \overline{Y}_{.4}}{s_{\psi'}} = \frac{11.1250 - 24.3750}{3.0046} = -4.4099\ (significant)$$

Here we see that the second group (i.e., slightly attractive) is not significantly different from the baseline group (i.e., unattractive), but the third and fourth more attractive groups do differ from the baseline.

If the variance of the reference group is different from the variances of the other $J - 1$ groups, a modification of this method is described in Dunnett (1964). For related procedures that are less sensitive to unequal group variances, see Wilcox (1987) or Wilcox (1996) (e.g., variation of Dunnett T3 procedure).

## 12.2.4    Other Planned Contrasts: Dunn (or Bonferroni) and Dunn-Sidak Methods

The Dunn (1961) procedure (commonly attributed to Dunn as the developer is unknown), also often called the Bonferroni procedure (because it is based on the Bonferroni inequality), is a planned family-wise MCP. It is designed to test either pairwise or complex contrasts for balanced or unbalanced designs. Thus this MCP is very flexible and may be used to test any planned contrast of interest. Dunn's method uses the standard $t$ test statistic with one important exception. The $\alpha$ level is split up among the set of planned contrasts. Typically the per contrast $\alpha$ level is set at $\alpha/c$, where $c$ is the number of contrasts. That is, $\alpha_{pc} = \alpha_{fw}/c$. According to this rationale, the family-wise Type I error rate will be maintained at $\alpha$. For example, if $\alpha_{fw} = .05$ is desired and there are five contrasts to be tested, then each contrast would be tested at the .01 level of significance. We are reminded that $\alpha$ need not be distributed equally among the set of contrasts, as long as the sum of the individual $\alpha_{pc}$ terms is equal to $\alpha_{fw}$ (Rosenthal & Rosnow, 1985; Keppel & Wickens, 2004).

Computationally, the Dunn method uses the standard $t$ test statistic, which is compared to the critical values of $\pm_{\alpha/c}\,t_{df(error)}$ for a two-tailed test obtained from the table in Appendix Table 8. The table takes the number of contrasts into account without requiring you to split up the $\alpha$. Using the example data set from Chapter 11, for comparison purposes let us test the same set of three orthogonal contrasts that we evaluated with the POC method. These contrasts are

|        | $c_1$  | $c_2$  | $c_3$  | $c_4$  |
|--------|--------|--------|--------|--------|
| $\psi_1$: | $+\frac{1}{2}$ | $+\frac{1}{2}$ | $-\frac{1}{2}$ | $-\frac{1}{2}$ |
| $\psi_2$: | $+1$   | $-1$   | $0$    | $0$    |
| $\psi_3$: | $0$    | $0$    | $+1$   | $-1$   |

The following are the computations:

Critical values: $\pm_{\alpha/c} t_{\text{df(error)}} = \pm_{.05/3} t_{28} \approx \pm 2.539$

Standard error for contrast 1:

$$s_{\psi'} = \sqrt{MS_{error} \sum_{j=1}^{J}\left(\frac{c_j^2}{n_j}\right)} = \sqrt{36.1116(.25/8 + .25/8 + .25/8 + .25/8)} = 2.1246$$

Standard error for contrasts 2 and 3:

$$s_{\psi'} = \sqrt{MS_{error}\left[\frac{1}{n_j} + \frac{1}{n_{j'}}\right]} = \sqrt{36.1116(1/8 + 1/8)} = 3.0046$$

Test statistics:

$$t_1 = \frac{+\frac{1}{2}\overline{Y}_{.1} + \frac{1}{2}\overline{Y}_{.2} - \frac{1}{2}\overline{Y}_{.3} - \frac{1}{2}\overline{Y}_{.4}}{s_{\psi'}}$$

$$= \frac{+\frac{1}{2}(11.1250) + \frac{1}{2}(17.8750) - \frac{1}{2}(20.2500) - \frac{1}{2}(24.3750)}{2.1246} = -3.6772 \ (significant)$$

$$t_2 = \frac{\overline{Y}_{.1} - \overline{Y}_{.2}}{s_{\psi'}} = \frac{11.1250 - 17.8750}{3.0046} = -2.2466 \ (nonsignificant)$$

$$t_3 = \frac{\overline{Y}_{.3} - \overline{Y}_{.4}}{s_{\psi'}} = \frac{20.2500 - 24.3750}{3.0046} = -1.3729 \ (nonsignificant)$$

For this set of contrasts then, we see the same results as were obtained via the POC procedure with the exception of contrast 2, which is now nonsignificant. The reason for this difference lies in the critical values used, which were $\pm 2.048$ for the POC method and $\pm 2.539$ for the Dunn method. Here we see the conservative nature of the Dunn procedure because the critical value is larger than with the POC method, thus making it a bit more difficult to reject $H_0$.

The Dunn procedure is slightly conservative (i.e., not as powerful) in that the true $\alpha_{fw}$ may be less than the specified nominal $\alpha$ level. A less conservative (i.e., more powerful) modification is known as the Dunn—Sidak procedure (Dunn, 1974; Sidak, 1967), and uses slightly different critical values. For more information see Kirk (1982), Wilcox (1987), and Keppel and Wickens (2004). The Bonferroni modification can also be applied to other MCPs.

## 12.2.5   Complex Post Hoc Contrasts: Scheffe' and Kaiser-Bowden Methods

Another early MCP due to Scheffe' (1953) is quite versatile. The Scheffe' procedure can be used for any possible type of comparison, orthogonal or nonorthogonal, pairwise or complex, planned or post hoc, where the family-wise error rate is controlled. The Scheffe' method is so general that the tests are quite conservative (i.e., less powerful), particularly for the pairwise contrasts. This is so because the family of contrasts for the Scheffe' method consists of all possible linear comparisons. To control the Type I error rate for such a large family, the procedure has to be conservative. Thus we recommend the Scheffe' method for complex post hoc comparisons.

The Scheffe' procedure is the only MCP that is necessarily consistent with the results of the $F$ ratio in the analysis of variance. If the $F$ is significant, then at least one contrast from the family of linear contrasts, when tested by the Scheffe' method, will also be significant. Do not forget, however, that this family is infinitely large and you may not even be interested in the significant contrasts. If the $F$ is not significant, then none of the contrasts in the family, when tested by the Scheffe' method, will be significant.

The test statistic for the Scheffe' method is the standard $t$ again. This is compared to the critical value $\sqrt{(J-1)\ _\alpha F_{\ J-1,df(error)}}$ taken from the $F$ table in Appendix Table 4. In other words, the square root of the $F$ critical value is adjusted by $J-1$, which serves to increase the Scheffe' critical value and make the procedure a more conservative one.

Consider a few example contrasts with the Scheffe' method. Using the example data set from chapter 11, for comparison purposes test the same set of three orthogonal contrasts that were evaluated with the POC method. These contrasts are again as follows

|             | $c_1$ | $c_2$ | $c_3$ | $c_4$ |
|-------------|-------|-------|-------|-------|
| $\psi_1$:   | $+\frac{1}{2}$ | $+\frac{1}{2}$ | $-\frac{1}{2}$ | $-\frac{1}{2}$ |
| $\psi_2$:   | $+1$  | $-1$  | $0$   | $0$   |
| $\psi_3$:   | $0$   | $0$   | $+1$  | $-1$  |

The following are the computations:

Critical value:

$$\sqrt{(J-1)\ _\alpha F_{J-1,df(error)}} = \sqrt{(3)\ _{.05}F_{3,28}} = \sqrt{(3)2.95} = 2.97$$

Standard error for contrast 1:

$$s_{\psi'} = \sqrt{MS_{error} \sum_{j=1}^{J} \left( \frac{c_j^2}{n_j} \right)} = \sqrt{36.1116(.25/8 + .25/8 + .25/8 + .25/8)} = 2.1246$$

Standard error for contrasts 2 and 3:

$$s_{\psi'} = \sqrt{MS_{error}\left[\frac{1}{n_j} + \frac{1}{n_{j'}}\right]} = \sqrt{36.1116(1/8 + 1/8)} = 3.0046$$

Test statistics:

$$t_1 = \frac{+\frac{1}{2}\overline{Y}_{.1} + \frac{1}{2}\overline{Y}_{.2} - \frac{1}{2}\overline{Y}_{.3} - \frac{1}{2}\overline{Y}_{.4}}{s_{\psi'}}$$

$$= \frac{+\frac{1}{2}(11.1250) + \frac{1}{2}(17.8750) - \frac{1}{2}(20.2500) - \frac{1}{2}(24.3750)}{2.1246} = -3.6772 \,(significant)$$

$$t_2 = \frac{\overline{Y}_{.1} - \overline{Y}_{.2}}{s_{\psi'}} = \frac{11.1250 - 17.8750}{3.0046} = -2.2466 \,(nonsignificant)$$

$$t_3 = \frac{\overline{Y}_{.3} - \overline{Y}_{.4}}{s_{\psi'}} = \frac{20.2500 - 24.3750}{3.0046} = -1.3729 \,(nonsignificant)$$

Using the Scheffe' method, these results are precisely the same as those obtained via the Dunn procedure. There is somewhat of a difference in the critical values, which were 2.97 for the Scheffe' method, 2.539 for the Dunn method, and 2.048 for the POC method. Here we see that the Scheffe' procedure is even more conservative than the Dunn procedure, thus making it a bit more difficult to reject $H_0$.

For situations where the group variances are unequal, a modification of the Scheffe' method that is less sensitive to unequal variances has been proposed by Brown and Forsythe (1974). Kaiser and Bowden (1983) found that the Brown-Forsythe procedure may cause the actual $\alpha$ level to exceed the nominal $\alpha$ level and thus we recommend the Kaiser-Bowden modification. For more information see Kirk (1982), Wilcox (1987), and Wilcox (1996).

### 12.2.6    Simple Post Hoc Contrasts: Tukey HSD, Tukey-Kramer, Fisher LSD and Hayter Tests

Tukey's (1953) honestly significant difference (HSD) test is one of the most popular post hoc MCPs. The HSD test is a family-wise procedure and is most appropriate for considering all pair-wise contrasts with equal $n$'s per group (i.e., a balanced design). The HSD test is sometimes referred to as the **studentized range test** because it is based on the sampling distribution of the studentized range statistic developed by William Sealy Gossett (forced to use the pseudonym "Student" by his employer, the Guinness brewery). For one approach, the first step in the analysis is to rank order the means from largest $(\overline{Y}_{.1})$ to smallest $(\overline{Y}_{.j})$. The test statistic, or studentized range statistic, is

$$q_i = \frac{\overline{Y}_{.j} - \overline{Y}_{.j'}}{s_{\psi'}}$$

where

$$s_{\psi'} = \sqrt{\frac{MS_{error}}{n}}$$

and $i$ identifies the specific contrast, $j$ and $j'$ designate the two group means to be compared, and $n$ represents the number of observations per group (equal $n$'s per group is required). The test statistic is compared to the critical value $_\alpha q_{df(error),J}$, where $df_{error}$ is equal to $J(n-1)$. A table for these critical values is given in Appendix Table 9.

The first contrast involves a test of the largest pairwise difference in the set of $J$ means ($q_1$). If these means are not significantly different, then the analysis stops because no other pairwise difference would be significant. If these means are different, then we proceed to test the second pairwise difference involving group 1 (i.e., $q_2$). Contrasts involving the largest mean are continued until a nonsignificant difference is found. Then the analysis picks up with the second largest mean and compares it with the smallest mean. Contrasts involving the second largest mean are continued until a nonsignificant difference is detected. The analysis continues with the next largest mean and the smallest mean, and so on, until it is obvious that no other pairwise contrast would be significant.

Finally, consider an example using the HSD procedure with the attractiveness data. The following are the computations:

Critical value: $_\alpha q_{df(error),J} = _{.05}q_{28,4} \approx 3.87$

Standard error:

$$s_{\psi'} = \sqrt{\frac{MS_{error}}{n}} = \sqrt{\frac{36.1116}{8}} = 2.1246$$

Test statistics:

$$q_1 = \frac{\overline{Y}_{.4} - \overline{Y}_{.1}}{s_{\psi'}} = \frac{24.3750 - 11.1250}{2.1246} = 6.2365 \ (significant)$$

$$q_2 = \frac{\overline{Y}_{.4} - \overline{Y}_{.2}}{s_{\psi'}} = \frac{24.3750 - 17.8750}{2.1246} = 3.0594 \ (nonsignificant)$$

$$q_3 = \frac{\overline{Y}_{.3} - \overline{Y}_{.1}}{s_{\psi'}} = \frac{20.2500 - 11.1250}{2.1246} = 4.2949 \ (significant)$$

$$q_4 = \frac{\overline{Y}_{.3} - \overline{Y}_{.2}}{s_{\psi'}} = \frac{20.2500 - 17.8750}{2.1246} = 1.1179 \ (nonsignificant)$$

$$q_5 = \frac{\overline{Y}_{.2} - \overline{Y}_{.1}}{s_{\psi'}} = \frac{17.8750 - 11.1250}{2.1246} = 3.1771 \ (nonsignificant)$$

These results indicate that the group means are significantly different for Groups 1 and 4, and for Groups 1 and 3. Just for completeness, we examine the final possible pairwise contrast involving Groups 3 and 4. However, we already know from the results of previous contrasts that these means cannot possibly be significantly different. The results for this contrast are as follows:

$$q_6 = \frac{\overline{Y}_{.4} - \overline{Y}_{.3}}{s_{\psi'}} = \frac{24.3750 - 20.2500}{2.1246} = 1.9415 \ (nonsignificant)$$

Occasionally researchers need to summarize the results of their pairwise comparisons. Table 12.1 shows the results of Tukey's HSD contrasts for the example data. For ease of interpretation, the means are ordered from lowest to highest. The first row consists of the results for those contrasts that involve Group 1. Thus the mean for Group 1 is different from those of Groups 3 and 4 only. None of the other pairwise contrasts were shown to be significant. Such a table could also be developed for other pairwise MCPs.

The HSD test has exact control of the family-wise error rate assuming normality, homogeneity, and equal $n$'s (better than Dunn or Dunn-Sidak). The HSD procedure is more powerful than the Dunn or Scheffe' procedures for testing all possible pairwise contrasts, although Dunn is more powerful for less than all possible pairwise contrasts. The HSD technique is the recommended MCP as a pairwise method in the equal $n$'s situation. The HSD test is reasonably robust to nonnormality, but not in extreme cases, and not as robust as the Scheffe' MCP.

There are several alternatives to the HSD for the unequal $n$'s case. These include the Tukey-Kramer modification (Tukey, 1953; Kramer, 1956), which assumes normality and homogeneity.

The Tukey-Kramer test statistic is the same as the Tukey HSD except that

$$s_{\psi'} = \sqrt{MS_{error} \left[ \frac{1}{2} \left( \frac{1}{n_1} + \frac{1}{n_2} \right) \right]}$$

The critical value is the same as with the Tukey HSD procedure.

Fisher's (1949) least significant difference (LSD) test, also known as the protected $t$ test, was the first MCP developed and is a pairwise post hoc procedure. It is a sequential procedure where a significant ANOVA $F$ is followed by the LSD test in which all (or perhaps some) pairwise $t$ tests are examined. The standard $t$ test statistic is compared with the critical values of $\pm_{\alpha/2} t_{df(error)}$. The LSD test has precise control of the family-wise error rate for the three group situation, assuming normality and homogeneity, but for more than three groups the protection deteriorates. In that case, a modification due to Hayter (1986) is suggested for more adequate protection. Hayter's test

**TABLE 12.1**
Test Statistics and Results of Tukey HSD Contrasts

|  | Group 1 | Group 2 | Group 3 | Group 4 |
|---|---|---|---|---|
| Group 1 (mean = 11.1250) | — | 3.1771 | 4.2949* | 6.2365* |
| Group 2 (mean = 17.8750) |  | — | 1.1179 | 3.0594 |
| Group 3 (mean = 20.2500) |  |  | — | 1.9415 |
| Group 4 (mean = 24.3750) |  |  |  | — |

*$p < .05$; $_{.05}q_{28,4} = 3.87$

appears to have more power than Tukey HSD and excellent control of family-wise error (Keppel & Wickens, 2004).

### 12.2.7 Simple Post Hoc Contrasts for Unequal Variances: Games-Howell, Dunnett T3 and C Tests

When the group variances are unequal, several alternative procedures are available. These alternatives include the Games-Howell (1976), and Dunnett T3 and C (1980) procedures. According to Wilcox (1996, 2003), T3 is recommended for $n < 50$, Games-Howell for $n > 50$, and C performs about the same as Games-Howell. For further details on these methods, see Kirk (1982), Wilcox (1987, 1996, 2003), Hochberg (1988), and Benjamini and Hochberg (1995).

### 12.2.8 Follow-up Tests to Kruskal-Wallis

Recall from chapter 11 the nonparametric equivalent to the analysis of variance, the Kruskal-Wallis test. Several post hoc procedures are available to follow up a significant Kruskal-Wallis test. The procedures discussed here are the nonparametric equivalents to the Scheffe' and Tukey HSD methods. One may form pairwise or complex contrasts as in the parametric case. The test statistic is $Z$ and given as

$$Z = \frac{\psi_i'}{s_{\psi'}}$$

where

$$s_{\psi'} = \sqrt{\frac{N(N+1)}{12} \sum_{j=1}^{J} \left( \frac{c_j^2}{n_j} \right)}$$

and where $N$ is the total number of observations. For the Scheffe' method, the test statistic $Z$ is compared to the critical value $\sqrt{_\alpha \chi_{J-1}^2}$ obtained from the $\chi^2$ table in Appendix Table 3. For the Tukey procedure, the test statistic $Z$ is compared to the critical value $[_\alpha q_{df(error),J}] / \sqrt{2}$ obtained from the table of critical values for the studentized range statistic in Appendix Table 9.

Let us use the attractiveness data to illustrate. Do not forget that we use the ranked data as described in chapter 11. The rank means for the groups are as follows: Group 1 = 7.7500; Group 2 = 15.2500; Group 3 = 18.7500; Group 4 = 24.2500. Here we only examine two contrasts and then compare the results for both the Scheffe' and Tukey methods. The first contrast compares the two low-attractiveness groups (i.e., Groups 1 and 2), whereas the second contrast compares the two low-attractiveness groups with the two high-attractiveness groups (i.e., Groups 3 and 4). In other words, we examine a pairwise contrast and a complex contrast, respectively. The results are given here.

Critical values:

$$\text{Scheffe'} - \sqrt{_\alpha \chi_{J-1}^2} = \sqrt{_{.05} \chi_3^2} = \sqrt{7.8147} = 2.7955$$

$$\text{Tukey} - [_\alpha q_{df(error),J}] / \sqrt{2} = {_{.05}} q_{28.4} / \sqrt{2} \approx 3.87 / \sqrt{2} \approx 2.7365$$

Standard error for contrast 1:

$$s_{\psi'} = \sqrt{\frac{N(N+1)}{12} \sum_{j=1}^{J} \left(\frac{c_j^2}{n_j}\right)} = \sqrt{\left[\frac{32(33)}{12}\right]\left[\frac{1}{8}+\frac{1}{8}\right]} = 4.6904$$

Standard error for contrast 2:

$$s_{\psi'} = \sqrt{\frac{N(N+1)}{12} \sum_{j=1}^{J} \left(\frac{c_j^2}{n_j}\right)} = \sqrt{\left[\frac{32(33)}{12}\right]\left[\frac{.25}{8}+\frac{.25}{8}+\frac{.25}{8}+\frac{.25}{8}\right]} = 3.3166$$

Test statistics:

$$Z_1 = \frac{\overline{Y}_{.1} - \overline{Y}_{.2}}{s_{\psi'}} = \frac{7.75 - 15.25}{4.6904} = -1.5990 \ (nonsignificant\ for\ both\ procedures)$$

$$Z_2 = \frac{\frac{1}{2}\overline{Y}_{.1} + \frac{1}{2}\overline{Y}_{.2} - \frac{1}{2}\overline{Y}_{.3} - \frac{1}{2}\overline{Y}_{.4}}{s_{\psi'}} = \frac{\frac{1}{2}(7.75) + \frac{1}{2}(15.25) - \frac{1}{2}(18.75) - \frac{1}{2}(24.25)}{3.3166}$$

$$= -3.0151 \ (significant\ for\ both\ procedures)$$

These results agree with most of the other parametric procedures for these particular contrasts. That is, the less attractive groups are not significantly different (only significant with POC), whereas the two less attractive groups are significantly different from the two more attractive groups (significant with all procedures). One could conceivably devise nonparametric equivalent MCPs for methods other than the Scheffe' and Tukey procedures.

## 12.3  SPSS

In our last section we examine what SPSS has to offer in terms of MCPs, including an APA type paragraph of our example findings. Using the GLM module (although the One-Way ANOVA module can also used), go to the "Analyze" pulldown, into "General Linear Model," and then into the "Univariate" procedure. Check the dependent and fixed-effects variables into the appropriate boxes as we did in chapter 11. Click on the "Post Hoc" button, then move the "Factor" variable into the box labelled "Post Hoc Tests for:." There you see numerous MCPs available. Check an appropriate MCP for your situation, click "Continue" to return to the previous screen, then click "OK." Results from the Tukey HSD procedure, just as one example MCP, are shown in Table 12.2. Note that confidence intervals around a mean difference of zero are given to the right for each contrast. To obtain trend analysis contrasts, click the "Contrasts" button. On the resulting screen, click the "Contrasts:" pulldown and scroll down to "Polynomial." Then click "Change," then "Continue" to return to the main screen. Other specific planned contrasts are also available.

The MCP results for the statistics lab example are as follows. After a significant ANOVA $F$, Tukey HSD tests were conducted on all possible pairwise contrasts. The following pairs of groups were found to be significantly different ($p < .05$) (depicted by asterisks next to the mean differences and by significance values less than .05): Groups 1 and 3; Groups 1 and 4. In

**TABLE 12.2**

Tukey HSD SPSS Results for the Statistics Lab Example

*Multiple Comparisons*

*Dependent Variable: dv*
*Tukey HSD*

| (I) group | (J) group | Mean Difference (I–J) | Std. Error | Sig. | 95% Confidence Interval | |
|---|---|---|---|---|---|---|
| | | | | | Lower Bound | Upper Bound |
| 1.00000 | 2.00000 | −6.7500000 | 3.004647 | .135 | −14.9536217 | 1.4536217 |
| | 3.00000 | −9.1250000* | 3.004647 | .025 | −17.3286217 | −.9213783 |
| | 4.00000 | −13.250000* | 3.004647 | .001 | −21.4536217 | −5.0463783 |
| 2.00000 | 1.00000 | 6.7500000 | 3.004647 | .135 | −1.4536217 | 14.9536217 |
| | 3.00000 | −2.3750000 | 3.004647 | .858 | −10.5786217 | 5.8286217 |
| | 4.00000 | −6.5000000 | 3.004647 | .158 | −14.7036217 | 1.7036217 |
| 3.00000 | 1.00000 | 9.1250000* | 3.004647 | .025 | .9213783 | 17.3286217 |
| | 2.00000 | 2.3750000 | 3.004647 | .858 | −5.8286217 | 10.5786217 |
| | 4.00000 | −4.1250000 | 3.004647 | .526 | −12.3286217 | 4.0786217 |
| 4.00000 | 1.00000 | 13.2500000* | 3.004647 | .001 | 5.0463783 | 21.4536217 |
| | 2.00000 | 6.5000000 | 3.004647 | .158 | −1.7036217 | 14.7036217 |
| | 3.00000 | 4.1250000 | 3.004647 | .526 | −4.0786217 | 12.3286217 |

Based on observed means.

*The mean difference is significant at the .05 level.

other words, the least attractive instructor group attended significantly fewer labs than either of the two most attractive instructor groups. Feel free to examine other MCPs for this dataset.

## 12.4   SUMMARY

In this chapter methods involving the comparison of multiple group means for a single independent variable were considered. The chapter began with a look at the characteristics of multiple comparisons including: (a) the definition of a contrast; (b) planned and post hoc comparisons; (c) contrast-based and family-wise Type I error rates; and (d) orthogonal contrasts. Next, we moved into a lengthy discussion of recommended multiple comparison procedures.

Figure 12.2 is a flowchart to assist you in making decisions about which MCP to use. Not every statistician will agree with every decision on the flowchart as there is not a consensus about which MCP is appropriate in every single situation. Nonetheless, this is simply a guide. Whether you use it in its present form, or adapt it for your own needs, we hope you find the figure to be useful in your own research.

At this point you should have met the following objectives: (a) be able to understand the concepts underlying the MCPs, (b) be able to select the appropriate MCP for a given research situation, and (c) be able to determine and interpret the results of MCPs. Chapter 13 returns to the analysis of variance again and discusses models for which there is more than one independent variable.

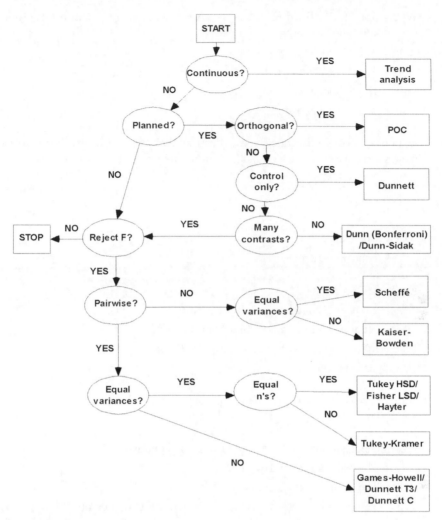

**FIG. 12.2    Flowchart of recommended MCPs.**

## PROBLEMS

### Conceptual Problems

1. The Tukey HSD procedure requires equal $n$'s and equal means. True or false?

2. Which of the following linear combinations of population means is not a legitimate contrast?

    a. $(\mu_{.1} + \mu_{.2} + \mu_{.3})/3 - \mu_{.4}$

    b. $\mu_{.1} - \mu_{.4}$

    c. $(\mu_{.1} + \mu_{.2})/2 - (\mu_{.3} + \mu_{.4})$

    d. $\mu_{.1} - \mu_{.2} + \mu_{.3} - \mu_{.4}$

3.  When a one-factor fixed-effects ANOVA results in a significant $F$ ratio for $J = 2$, one should follow the ANOVA with the

    a.  Tukey HSD method
    b.  Scheffe' method
    c.  Hayter method
    d.  none of the above

4.  If a family-based error rate for $\alpha$ is desired, and hypotheses involving all pairs of means are to be tested, which method of multiple comparisons should be selected?

    a.  Tukey HSD
    b.  Scheffe'
    c.  POC
    d.  Trend analysis
    e.  none of the above

5.  A priori comparisons

    a.  are planned in advance of the research.
    b.  often arise out of theory and prior research.
    c.  may be done without examining the $F$ ratio.
    d.  all of the above

6.  For planned contrasts involving the control group, the Dunn procedure is most appropriate. True or false?

7.  Which is not a property of planned orthogonal contrasts?

    a.  The contrasts are independent.
    b.  The contrasts are post hoc.
    c.  The sum of the cross-products of the contrast coefficients $= 0$.
    d.  If there are $J$ groups, there are $J - 1$ orthogonal contrasts.

8.  Which multiple comparison procedure is most flexible in the contrasts that can be tested?

    a.  planned orthogonal contrasts
    b.  Newman-Keuls
    c.  Dunnett
    d.  Tukey HSD
    e.  Scheffe'

9.  Post hoc tests are necessary after an ANOVA whenever

    a.  $H_0$ is rejected.
    b.  there are more than two groups.
    c.  $H_0$ is rejected and there are more than two groups.
    d.  you should always do post hoc tests after an ANOVA.

10. Post hoc tests are done after ANOVA to determine why $H_0$ was not rejected. True or False?

11. Holding the $\alpha$ level and the number of groups constant, as the $df_{with}$ increases, the critical value of the $q$ decreases. True or False?

12. The Tukey HSD procedure maintains the family Type I error rate at $\alpha$. True or False?

13. The Dunnett procedure assumes equal numbers of observations per group. True or False?

14. For complex post hoc contrasts with unequal group variances, which of the following MCPs is most appropriate?
    a. Kaiser-Bowden
    b. Dunnett
    c. Tukey HSD
    d. Scheffe'

15. A researcher is interested in testing the following contrasts in a $J = 6$ study: Group 1 vs. 2; Group 3 vs. 4; and Group 5 vs. 6. I assert that these contrasts are orthogonal. Am I correct?

16. I assert that rejecting $H_0$ in a one-factor fixed-effects ANOVA with $J = 3$ indicates that all 3 pairs of group means are necessarily significant using the Scheffe' procedure. Am I correct?

17. For complex post hoc contrasts with equal group variances, which of the following MCPs is most appropriate?
    a. planned orthogonal contrasts
    b. Dunnett
    c. Tukey HSD
    d. Scheffe'

18. If the difference between two sample means is 10, I assert that $H_0$ will necessarily be rejected with Tukey's HSD. Am I correct?

19. Suppose all $J = 4$ of the sample means are equal to 100. I assert that it is possible to find a significant contrast with some MCP. Am I correct?

## Computational Problems

1. A one-factor fixed-effects analysis of variance is performed on data for 10 groups of unequal sizes and $H_0$ is rejected at the .01 level of significance. Using the Scheffe' procedure, test the contrast that

$$\bar{Y}_{.2} - \bar{Y}_{.5} = 0$$

at the .01 level of significance given the following information: $df_{with} = 40$, $\overline{Y}_{.2} = 10.8$, $n_2 = 8$, $\overline{Y}_{.5} = 15.8$, $n_5 = 8$, and $MS_{with} = 4$.

2.  A one-factor fixed-effects ANOVA is performed on data from three groups of equal size ($n = 10$) and $H_0$ is rejected at the .01 level. The following values were computed: $MS_{with} = 40$ and the sample means are $\overline{Y}_{.1} = 4.5$, $\overline{Y}_{.2} = 12.5$, and $\overline{Y}_{.3} = 13.0$. Use the Tukey HSD method to test all possible pairwise contrasts.

3.  Using the data from Chapter 11, Computational Problem 4, conduct a trend analysis at the .05 level.

4.  Consider the situation where there are $J = 4$ groups of subjects. Answer the following questions:

    a.  Construct a set of orthogonal contrasts and show that they are orthogonal.

    b.  Is the following contrast legitimate? Why or why not?

$$H_0: \mu_{.1} - (\mu_{.2} + \mu_{.3} + \mu_{.4}).$$

    c.  How might the contrast in part (b) be altered to yield a legitimate contrast?

## Interpretive Problem

For the interpretive problem you selected in chapter 11 (using the statistics survey CD dataset), select an appropriate MCP, apply it using SPSS, and write a paragraph describing the results.

# 13

# FACTORIAL ANALYSIS OF VARIANCE— FIXED-EFFECTS MODEL

## Chapter Outline

1. The two-factor ANOVA model
    Characteristics of the model
    The layout of the data
    The ANOVA model
    Main effects and interaction effects
    Assumptions and violation of assumptions
    Partitioning the sums of squares
    The ANOVA summary table
    Multiple comparison procedures
    Effect size measures, confidence intervals, and power
    An example
2. Three-factor and higher-order ANOVA
    Characteristics of the model
    The ANOVA model
    The ANOVA summary table
    The triple interaction
3. Factorial ANOVA with unequal $n$'s
4. SPSS

## Key Concepts

1.   Main effects
2.   Interaction effects
3.   Partitioning the sums of squares
4.   The ANOVA model
5.   Main effects contrasts, simple and complex interaction contrasts
6.   Nonorthogonal designs

The last two chapters have dealt with the one-factor analysis of variance (ANOVA) model and various multiple comparison procedures (MCPs) for that model. In this chapter we continue our discussion of analysis of variance models by extending the one-factor case to the two- and three-factor models. This chapter seeks an answer to the question, what should we do if we have multiple factors for which we want to make comparisons of the means? In other words, the researcher is interested in the effect of two or more independent variables or factors on the dependent (or criterion) variable. This chapter is most concerned with two- and three-factor models, but the extension to more than three factors, when warranted, is fairly simple.

For example, suppose that a researcher is interested in the effects of textbook choice and time of day on statistics achievement. Thus one independent variable would be the textbook selected for the course, and the second independent variable would be the time of day the course was offered. The researcher hypothesizes that certain texts may be more effective in terms of achievement than others, and that student learning may be greater at certain times of the day. For the time-of-day variable, one might expect that students would not do as well in an early morning section or a late evening section. In the example study, say that the researcher is interested in comparing three textbooks (A, B, and C) and three times of the day (early morning, mid-afternoon, and evening sections). Students would be randomly assigned to sections of statistics based on a combination of textbook and time of day. One group of students might be assigned to the section offered in the evening using textbook A. These results would be of interest to statistics instructors for selecting a textbook and optimal time of the day.

Most of the concepts used in this chapter are the same as those covered in Chapters 11 and 12. In addition, new concepts include main effects, interaction effects, multiple comparison procedures for main and interaction effects, and nonorthogonal designs. Our objectives are that by the end of this chapter, you will be able to (a) understand the characteristics and concepts underlying factorial ANOVA, (b) determine and interpret the results of factorial ANOVA, and (c) understand and evaluate the assumptions of factorial ANOVA.

## 13.1   THE TWO-FACTOR ANOVA MODEL

This section describes the distinguishing characteristics of the two-factor ANOVA model, the layout of the data, the linear model, main effects and interactions, assumptions of the model and their violation, partitioning the sums of squares, the ANOVA summary table, multiple comparison procedures, effect size measures, confidence intervals, and power, and an example.

### 13.1.1   Characteristics of the Model

The first characteristic of the two-factor ANOVA model should be obvious by now, which considers the effect of two factors or independent variables on a dependent variable. Each factor consists of two or more levels. This yields what we call a **factorial design** because more than a single factor is included. We see then that the two-factor ANOVA is an extension of the one-factor ANOVA. Why would a researcher want to complicate things by considering a second factor? Three reasons come to mind. First, the researcher may have a genuine interest in studying the second factor. Rather than studying each factor separately in two analyses, the researcher includes both factors in the same analysis. This allows a test not only of the effect of each individual factor, but of the effect of both factors collectively. This latter effect is known as an **interaction** effect and provides information about whether the two factors are operating independent of one another (i.e., no interaction exists) or whether the two factors are operating together to produce some additional impact (i.e., an interaction exists). If two separate analyses were conducted, one for each independent variable, no information would be obtained about the interaction effect. As becomes evident, the researcher will test three hypotheses, one for each factor individually, and a third for the interaction between the factors. This chapter spends considerable time discussing interactions.

A second reason for including an additional factor is an attempt to reduce the error (or within groups) variation, which is variation that is unexplained by the first factor. The use of a second factor provides a more precise estimate of error variance. For this reason, a two-factor design is generally more powerful than two one-factor designs, as the second factor serves to control for additional extraneous variability. A third reason for considering two factors simultaneously is to provide greater generalizability of results and to provide a more efficient and economical use of observations and resources. Thus the results can be generalized to more situations, and the study will be more cost efficient in terms of time and money.

In addition, for the two-factor ANOVA every level of the first factor (hereafter known as factor A) is paired with every level of the second factor (hereafter known as factor B). In other words, every combination of factors A and B is included in the design of the study, yielding what is referred to as a **fully crossed design**. If some combinations are not included, then the design is not fully crossed and may form some sort of a nested design (see chap. 16). Individuals (or objects or subjects) are randomly assigned to one combination of the two factors. In other words, each individual responds to only one combination of the factors. If individuals respond to more than one combination of the factors, this would be some sort of repeated measures design, which we examine in chapter 15. In this chapter we only consider models where all factors are fixed. Thus the overall design is known as a fixed-effects model. If one or both factors are random, then the design is not a fixed-effects model, which we discuss in chapter 15. It is also assumed that the dependent variable is measured at least at the interval level.

In this section of the chapter, we assume the same number of observations are made for each factor combination. This yields what is known as an orthogonal design, where the effects due to the factors (separately and collectively) are independent. We leave the discussion of the unequal $n$'s factorial ANOVA until later in this chapter. In addition, we assume there are at least two observations per factor combination so as to have within groups variation.

In summary, the characteristics of the two-factor analysis of variance fixed-effects model are as follows: (a) two independent variables each with two or more levels, (b) the levels of both independent variables are fixed by the researcher, (c) subjects are randomly assigned to only one combination of these levels, (d) the two factors are fully crossed, and (e) the dependent variable is measured at least at the interval level. In the context of experimental design, the two-factor analysis of variance is often referred to as the **completely randomized factorial design**.

### 13.1.2    The Layout of the Data

Before we get into the theory and analysis of the data, let us examine one form in which the data can be placed, known as the layout of the data. We designate each observation as $Y_{ijk}$, where the $j$ subscript tells us what level of factor A (e.g., textbook) the observation belongs to, the $k$ subscript tells us what level of factor B (e.g., time of day) the observation belongs to, and the $i$ subscript tells us the observation or identification number within that combination of factor A and factor B. For instance, $Y_{321}$ would mean that this is the third observation in the second level of factor A and the first level of factor B. The first subscript ranges over $i = 1, ..., n$, the second subscript ranges over $j = 1, ..., J$, and the third subscript ranges over $k = 1, ..., K$. Note also that the latter two subscripts denote the cell of an observation. Using the same example, we are referring to the third observation in the 21 cell. Thus there are $J$ levels of factor A, $K$ levels of factor B, and $n$ subjects in each cell, for a total of $JKn = N$ observations. For now we assume there are $n$ subjects in each cell in order to simplify matters; this is referred to as the equal $n$'s case. Later in this chapter, we consider the unequal $n$'s case.

The layout of the sample data is shown in Table 13.1. Here we see that each row represents the observations for a particular level of factor A (textbook), and that each column represents the observations for a particular level of factor B (time). At the bottom of each column are the column means ($\overline{Y}_{.k}$), to the right of each row are the row means ($\overline{Y}_{.j.}$), and in the lower right-hand corner is the overall mean ($\overline{Y}_{...}$). We also need the cell means ($\overline{Y}_{.jk}$), which are shown at the bottom of each cell. Thus the layout is one form in which to think about the data.

### 13.1.3    The ANOVA Model

This section introduces the analysis of variance linear model, as well as estimation of the parameters of the model. The two-factor analysis of variance model is a form of the general linear model like the one-factor ANOVA model of chapter 11. The two-factor ANOVA fixed-effects model can be written in terms of population parameters as

$$Y_{ijk} = \mu + \alpha_j + \beta_k + (\alpha\beta)_{jk} + \varepsilon_{ijk}$$

where $Y_{ijk}$ is the observed score on the criterion variable for individual $i$ in level $j$ of factor A (text) and level $k$ of factor B (time) (or in the $jk$ cell), $\mu$ is the overall or grand population mean

**TABLE 13.1**
Layout for the Two-Factor ANOVA

| Level of Factor A | Level of Factor B | | | | Row Mean |
|---|---|---|---|---|---|
| | *1* | *2* | ... | *K* | |
| 1 | $Y_{111}$ | $Y_{112}$ | ... | $Y_{11K}$ | |
| | . | . | ... | . | |
| | . | . | ... | . | $\bar{Y}_{.1.}$ |
| | . | . | ... | . | |
| | $Y_{n11}$ | $Y_{n12}$ | ... | $Y_{n1K}$ | |
| | $\bar{Y}_{.11}$ | $\bar{Y}_{.12}$ | ... | $\bar{Y}_{.1K}$ | |
| 2 | $Y_{121}$ | $Y_{122}$ | ... | $Y_{12K}$ | |
| | . | . | ... | . | |
| | . | . | ... | . | $\bar{Y}_{.2.}$ |
| | . | . | ... | . | |
| | $Y_{n21}$ | $Y_{n22}$ | ... | $Y_{n2K}$ | |
| | $\bar{Y}_{.21}$ | $\bar{Y}_{.22}$ | ... | $\bar{Y}_{.2K}$ | |
| . | . | . | ... | . | . |
| . | . | . | ... | . | . |
| . | . | . | ... | . | . |
| J | $Y_{1J1}$ | $Y_{1J2}$ | ... | $Y_{1JK}$ | |
| | . | . | ... | . | |
| | . | . | ... | . | $\bar{Y}_{.J.}$ |
| | . | . | ... | . | |
| | $Y_{nJ1}$ | $Y_{nJ2}$ | ... | $Y_{nJK}$ | |
| | $\bar{Y}_{.J1}$ | $\bar{Y}_{.J2}$ | ... | $\bar{Y}_{.JK}$ | |
| Column Mean | $\bar{Y}_{..1}$ | $\bar{Y}_{..2}$ | ... | $\bar{Y}_{..K}$ | $\bar{Y}_{...}$ |

(i.e., regardless of cell designation), $\alpha_j$ is the main effect for level $j$ of factor A (row or text effect), $\beta_k$ is the main effect for level $k$ of factor B (column or time effect), $(\alpha\beta)_{jk}$ is the inter-action effect for the combination of level $j$ of factor A and level $k$ of factor B, and $\varepsilon_{ijk}$ is the random residual error for individual $i$ in cell $jk$. The residual error can be due to individual differences, measurement error, and/or other factors not under investigation.

The population effects and residual error are computed as follows:

$$\alpha_j = \mu_{.j.} - \mu$$
$$\beta_k = \mu_{..k} - \mu$$

$$(\alpha\beta)_{jk} = \mu_{.jk} - (\mu_{.j.} + \mu_{..k} - \mu)$$

$$\varepsilon_{ijk} = Y_{ijk} - \mu_{.jk}$$

That is, the row effect is equal to the difference between the population mean of level $j$ of factor A (a particular text) and the overall population mean, the column effect is equal to the difference between the population mean of level $k$ of factor B (a particular time) and the overall population mean, the interaction effect is the effect of being in a certain combination of the levels of factor A and B (a particular text used at a particular time), whereas the residual error is equal to the difference between an individual's observed score and the population mean of cell $jk$. The row, column, and interaction effects can also be thought of as the average effect of being a member of a particular row, column, or cell, respectively. It should also be noted that the sum of the row effects is equal to zero, the sum of the column effects is equal to zero, and the sum of the interaction effects is equal to zero (both across rows and across columns). This implies, for example, that if there are any nonzero row effects, then the row effects will balance out around zero with some positive and some negative effects.

You may be wondering why the interaction effect looks a little different than the main effects. I have given you the version that is solely a function of population means. A more intuitively convincing conceptual version of this effect is

$$(\alpha\beta)_{jk} = \mu_{.jk} - \alpha_j - \beta_k - \mu$$

which is written in similar fashion to the row and column effects. Here we see that the interaction effect is equal to the population cell mean minus (a) the row effect, (b) the column effect, and (c) the overall population mean. In other words, the interaction is solely a function of cell means without regard to its row effect, column effect, or the overall mean.

To estimate the parameters of the model $\mu$, $\alpha_j$, $\beta_k$, $(\alpha\beta)_{jk}$, and $\varepsilon_{ijk}$, the least squares method of estimation is used as most appropriate for general linear models (e.g., regression, ANOVA). These sample estimates are represented as $\overline{Y}_{...}$, $a_j$, $b_k$, $(ab)_{jk}$, and $e_{ijk}$, respectively, where the latter four are computed as follows, respectively:

$$a_j = \overline{Y}_{.j.} - \overline{Y}_{...}$$

$$b_k = \overline{Y}_{..k} - \overline{Y}_{...}$$

$$(ab)_{jk} = \overline{Y}_{.jk} - (\overline{Y}_{.j.} + \overline{Y}_{..k} - \overline{Y}_{...})$$

$$e_{ijk} = Y_{ijk} - \overline{Y}_{.jk}$$

Note that $\overline{Y}_{...}$ represents the overall sample mean, $\overline{Y}_{.j.}$ represents the sample mean for level $j$ of factor A (a particular text), $\overline{Y}_{..k}$ represents the sample mean for level $k$ of factor B (a particular time), and $\overline{Y}_{.jk}$ represents the sample mean for cell $jk$ (a particular text at a particular time).

For the two-factor ANOVA model there are three sets of hypotheses, one for each of the main effects, and one for the interaction effect. The null and alternative hypotheses, respectively, for testing the main effect of factor A (text) are

$$H_{01}: \mu_{.1.} = \mu_{.2.} = ... = \mu_{.J.}$$

$$H_{11}: \text{not all the } \mu_{.j.} \text{ are equal}$$

The hypotheses for testing the main effect of factor B (time) are

$$H_{02}: \mu_{..1} = \mu_{..2} = ... = \mu_{..K}$$
$$H_{12}: \text{not all the } \mu_{..k} \text{ are equal}$$

Finally, the hypotheses for testing the interaction effect (text with time) are

$$H_{03}: (\mu_{.jk} - \mu_{.j.} - \mu_{..k} + \mu) = 0 \text{ for all } j \text{ and } k$$
$$H_{13}: \text{not all the } (\mu_{.jk} - \mu_{.j.} - \mu_{..k} + \mu) = 0$$

The null hypotheses can also be written in terms of row, column and interaction effects (which may make more intuitive sense) as

$$H_{01}: \alpha_1 = \alpha_2 = ... = \alpha_J = 0$$
$$H_{02}: \beta_1 = \beta_2 = ... = \beta_K = 0$$
$$H_{03}: (\alpha\beta)_{jk} = 0 \text{ for all } j \text{ and } k$$

As in the one-factor model, all of the alternative hypotheses are written in a general form to cover the multitude of possible mean differences that could arise. These range from only two of the means being different to all of the means being different from one another. Also, because of the way the alternative hypotheses have been written, only a nondirectional alternative is appropriate. If one of the null hypotheses is rejected, then consider a multiple comparison procedure so as to determine which means or combination of means are significantly different (discussed later).

### 13.1.4   Main Effects and Interaction Effects

Finally we come to a formal discussion of main effects and interaction effects. A **main effect** of factor A (text) is defined as the effect of factor A, averaged across the levels of factor B (time), on the dependent variable $Y$ (achievement). More precisely, it represents the unique effect of factor A on $Y$, controlling statistically for factor B. A similar statement may be made for the main effect of factor B.

As far as the concept of interaction is concerned, things are a bit more complex. An **interaction** can be defined in any of the following ways: An interaction is said to exist if (a) certain combinations of the two factors produce effects beyond the effects of the two factors when considered separately; (b) the mean differences among the levels of factor A are not constant across (and thus depend on) the levels of factor B; (c) there is a joint effect of factors A and B on $Y$; or (d) there is a unique effect that could not be predicted from knowledge of only the main effects. Let me mention two fairly common examples of interaction effects. The first is known as an aptitude–treatment interaction (ATI). This means that the effectiveness of a particular treatment depends on the aptitude of the individual. In other words, some treatments are more effective for individuals with a high aptitude, and other treatments are more effective for those with a low aptitude. A second example is an interaction between treatment and gender. Here some treatments may be more effective for males and others may be more effective for females. This is often considered in gender studies research.

For some graphical examples of main and interaction effects, take a look at the various plots in Fig. 13.1. Each plot represents the graph of a particular set of cell means, sometimes referred to as a **profile plot**. On the $X$ axis are the levels of factor A (text), the $Y$ axis provides the cell means on the dependent variable $Y$ (achievement), and the lines in the body of the plot represent the levels of factor B (time) (although the specific placement of the two factors here is arbitrary; alternatively factor B could be plotted on the $X$ axis and factor A as the lines). Profile plots provide information about the possible existence of a main effect for A, a main effect for B, and/or an interaction effect. A main effect for factor A, for example, can be examined by taking the means for each level of A and averaging them across the levels of B. If these marginal means for the levels of A are the same or nearly so, this would indicate no main effect for factor A. A main effect for factor B would be assessed by taking the means for each level of B and averaging them across the levels of A. If these marginal means for the levels of B are the same or nearly so, this would imply no main effect for factor B. An interaction effect is determined by whether the cell means for the levels of A are constant across the levels of B (or vice versa). This is easily viewed in a profile plot by checking to see whether or not the lines are parallel. Parallel lines indicate no interaction, whereas nonparallel lines suggest that an interaction may exist. Of course the statistical significance of the main and interaction effects is a matter to be determined by the $F$ statistics. The profile plots only give you a rough idea as to the possible existence of the effects. For instance, lines that are nearly parallel will probably not show up as a significant interaction. It is suggested that the plot can be simplified if the factor with the most levels is shown on the $X$ axis. This cuts down on the number of lines drawn.

The plots shown in Fig. 13.1 represent the eight different sets of results possible for a two-factor design. To simplify matters, only two levels of each factor are used. Figure 13.1 (a) indicates that there is no main effect either for factor A or B, and there is no interaction effect. The lines are horizontal (no A effect), lie nearly on top of one another (no B effect), and are parallel (no interaction effect). Figure 13.1 (b) suggests the presence of an effect due to factor A only (the lines are not horizontal because the mean for $A_1$ is greater than the mean for $A_2$), but are nearly on top of one another (no B effect), and are parallel (no interaction). In Fig. 13.1 (c) we see a separation between the lines for the levels of B ($B_1$ being greater than $B_2$); thus a main effect for B is likely, but the lines are horizontal (no A effect), and are parallel (no interaction).

For Fig. 13.1 (d) there are no main effects (the means for the levels of A are the same, and the means for the levels of B are the same), but an interaction is indicated by the lack of parallel lines. Figure 13.1 (e) suggests a main effect for both factors as shown by mean differences ($A_1$ less than $A_2$, and $B_1$ greater than $B_2$), but no interaction (the lines are parallel). In Fig. 13.1 (f) we see a main effect for A ($A_1$ less than $A_2$) and an interaction are likely, but no main effect for B (little separation between the lines for factor B). For Fig. 13.1 (g) there appears to be a main effect for B ($B_1$ greater than $B_2$) and an interaction, but no main effect for A. Finally, in Fig. 13.1 (h) we see the likelihood of two main effects ($A_1$ less than $A_2$, and $B_1$ greater than $B_2$), and an interaction. Although these are clearly the only possible outcomes from a two-factor design, the precise pattern will differ depending on the obtained cell means. In other words, if your study yields a significant effect only for factor A, your profile plot need not look exactly like Fig. 13.1 (b), but it will retain the same general pattern and interpretation.

In many statistics texts, a big deal is made about the type of interaction shown in the profile plot. A distinction is made between an ordinal interaction and a disordinal interaction. An ordinal

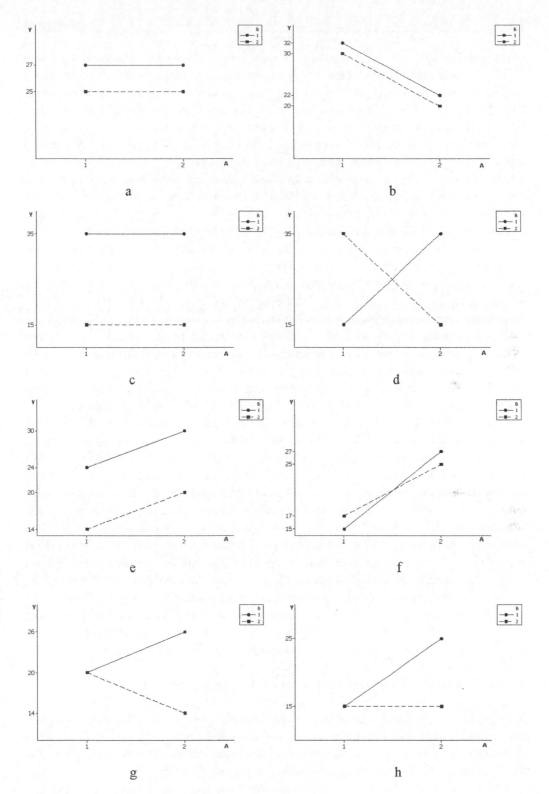

FIG. 13.1    Display of possible two-factor ANOVA effects.

interaction is said to exist when the lines are not parallel and they do not cross; ordinal here means the same relative order of the cell means is maintained across the levels of one of the factors. For example, the means for level 1 of factor B are always greater than the means for level 2 of B, regardless of the level of factor A. A disordinal interaction is said to exist when the lines are not parallel and they do cross. For example, the mean for $B_1$ is greater than the mean for $B_2$ at $A_1$, but the opposite is true at $A_2$. Dwelling on the distinction between the two types of interaction is not recommended as it can depend on which factor is plotted on the $X$ axis. That is, when factor A is plotted on the $X$ axis a disordinal interaction may be shown, and when factor B is plotted on the $X$ axis an ordinal interaction may be shown. The purpose of the profile plot is to simplify interpretation of the results; worrying about the type of interaction may merely serve to confuse that interpretation.

Now for a Lomax commercial about dealing with the interaction effect. Let us consider two possible situations, one where there is a significant interaction effect and one where there is no such effect. If there is no significant interaction effect, then the findings regarding the main effects can be generalized with greater confidence. In this situation, the main effects are known as **additive effects** and an additive linear model with no interaction term could actually be used to describe the data. For example, the results might be that for factor A, the level 1 means always exceed those of level 2 by 10 points, across all levels of factor B. Thus we can make a blanket statement about the constant added benefits of $A_1$ over $A_2$, regardless of the level of factor B. In addition, for the no interaction situation, the main effects are statistically independent of one another; that is, each of the main effects serve as an independent predictor of $Y$.

If there is a significant interaction effect, then the findings regarding the main effects cannot be generalized with such confidence. In this situation, the main effects are not additive and the interaction term must be included in the linear model. For example, the results might be that (a) the mean for $A_1$ is greater than $A_2$ when considering $B_1$, but (b) the mean for $A_1$ is less than $A_2$ when considering $B_2$. Thus we cannot make a blanket statement about the constant added benefits of $A_1$ over $A_2$, because it depends on the level of factor B. In addition, for the interaction situation, the main effects are not statistically independent of one another; that is, each of the main effects does not serve as an independent predictor of $Y$. In order to predict $Y$ well, information is necessary about the levels of factors A and B. Thus in the presence of a significant interaction, generalizations about the main effects must be qualified. A profile plot should be examined so that a proper graphical interpretation of the interaction and main effects can be made. A significant interaction serves as a warning that one cannot generalize statements about a main effect for A over all levels of B. If you obtain a significant interaction, this is an important result. Do not ignore it and go ahead to interpret the main effects.

### 13.1.5   Assumptions and Violation of Assumptions

In chapter 11 we described in detail the assumptions for the one-factor analysis of variance. In the two-factor model, the assumptions are again concerned with independence, homogeneity of variance, and normality. A summary of the effects of their violation is provided in Table 13.2. The same methods for detecting violations described in chapter 11 can be used for this model.

There are only two different wrinkles for the two-factor model as compared to the one-factor model. First, as the effect of heterogeneity is small with balanced designs (equal $n$'s per cell) or nearly balanced designs, and/or with larger $n$'s, this is a reason to strive for such a design.

**TABLE 13.2**
Assumptions and Effects of Violations—Two-Factor Design

| Assumption | Effect of Assumption Violation |
|---|---|
| 1. Independence | Increased likelihood of a Type I and/or Type II error in the $F$ statistic; influences standard errors of means and thus inferences about those means |
| 2. Homogeneity of variance | Bias in $SS_{with}$; increased likelihood of a Type I and/or Type II error; less effect with balanced or nearly balanced design; effect decreases as $n$ increases |
| 3. Normality | Minimal effect with moderate violation; minimal effect with balanced or nearly balanced design; effect decreases as $n$ increases |

Unfortunately, there is very little research on this problem, except the classic Box (1954b) article for a no-interaction model with one observation per cell. There are limited solutions for dealing with a violation of the homogeneity assumption, such as the Welch (1951) test, the Johansen (1980) procedure, and variations described by Wilcox (1996, 2003). Transformations are not usually used, as they may destroy an additive linear model and create interactions that did not previously exist. Nonparametric techniques are not commonly used with the two-factor model, although see the description of the Brunner, Dette, and Munk (1997) procedure in Wilcox (2003). Second, the effect of nonnormality seems to be the same as heterogeneity (Miller, 1997).

## 13.1.6 Partitioning the Sums of Squares

As pointed out in chapter 11, partitioning the sums of squares is an important concept in the analysis of variance. Let us begin with the total sum of squares in $Y$, denoted here as $SS_{total}$. The term $SS_{total}$ represents the amount of total variation among all of the observations without regard to cell membership. The next step is to partition the total variation into variation between the levels of factor A (denoted by $SS_A$), variation between the levels of factor B (denoted by $SS_B$), variation due to the interaction of the levels of factors A and B (denoted by $SS_{AB}$), and variation within the cells combined across cells (denoted by $SS_{with}$). In the two-factor analysis of variance, then, we can partition $SS_{total}$ into

$$SS_{total} = SS_A + SS_B + SS_{AB} + SS_{with}$$

Then computational formulas are used by statistical software to compute these sums of squares.

## 13.1.7 The ANOVA Summary Table

The next step is to assemble the ANOVA summary table. The purpose of the summary table is to simply summarize the analysis of variance. A general form of the summary table for the two-factor case is shown in Table 13.3. The first column lists the sources of variation in the model. We note that the total variation is divided into a within groups source, and a general

**TABLE 13.3**
Two-Factor Analysis of Variance Summary Table

| Source | SS | df | MS | F |
|--------|-----|------|------|------|
| Between: | | | | |
| A | $SS_A$ | $J - 1$ | $MS_A$ | $MS_A / MS_{with}$ |
| B | $SS_B$ | $K - 1$ | $MS_B$ | $MS_B / MS_{with}$ |
| AB | $SS_{AB}$ | $(J - 1)(K - 1)$ | $MS_{AB}$ | $MS_{AB} / MS_{with}$ |
| Within | $SS_{with}$ | $N - JK$ | $MS_{with}$ | |
| Total | $SS_{total}$ | $N - 1$ | | |

between groups source, which is subdivided into sources due to A, B, and the AB interaction. This is in keeping with the spirit of the one-factor model, where total variation was divided into a between groups source (just one because there is only one factor and no interaction term) and a within groups source. The second column provides the computed sums of squares.

The third column gives the degrees of freedom for each source. As always, degrees of freedom have to do with the number of observations that are free to vary in a particular context. Because there are $J$ levels of factor A, then the number of degrees of freedom for the A source is equal to $J - 1$. As there are $J$ means and we know the overall mean, then only $J - 1$ of the means are free to vary. This is the same rationale we have been using throughout this text. As there are $K$ levels of factor B, there are then $K - 1$ degrees of freedom for the B source. For the AB interaction source, we take the product of the degrees of freedom for the main effects. Thus we have as degrees of freedom for AB the product $(J - 1)(K - 1)$. The degrees of freedom within groups is equal to the total number of observations minus the number of cells, $N - JK$. Finally, the degrees of freedom total can be written simply as $N - 1$.

Next, the sum of squares terms are weighted by the appropriate degrees of freedom to generate the mean squares terms. Thus, for instance, $MS_A = SS_A / df_A$. Finally, in the last column of the ANOVA summary table, we have the $F$ values, which represent the summary statistics for the analysis of variance. There are three hypotheses that we are interested in testing, so there will be three $F$ test statistics, for the two main effects and the interaction effect. For the factorial fixed-effects model, each $F$ value is computed by taking the $MS$ for the source that you are interested in testing and dividing it by $MS_{with}$. Thus for each hypothesis, the same error term is used in forming the $F$ ratio (i.e., $MS_{with}$). We return to the two-factor model for cases where the effects are not fixed in chapter 15.

Each of the $F$ test statistics is then compared with the appropriate $F$ critical value so as to make a decision about the relevant null hypothesis. These critical values are found in the $F$ table of Appendix Table 4 as follows: for the test of factor A as $_\alpha F_{J-1,N-JK}$; for the test of factor B as $_\alpha F_{K-1,N-JK}$; and for the test of the interaction as $_\alpha F_{(J-1)(K-1),N-JK}$. Each significance test is a one-tailed test so as to be consistent with the alternative hypothesis. The null hypothesis is rejected if the $F$ test statistic exceeds the $F$ critical value

If the $F$ test statistic does exceed the $F$ critical value, and there is more than one degree of freedom for the source being tested, then it is not clear precisely why the null hypothesis was rejected. For example, if there are three levels of factor A and the null hypothesis for A is rejected, then we are not sure where the mean differences lie among the levels of A. In this case, some multiple comparison procedure should be used to determine where the mean differences are; this is the topic of the next section.

## 13.1.8 Multiple Comparison Procedures

In this section, we extend the concepts related to multiple comparison procedures (MCPs) covered in chapter 12 to the two-factor ANOVA model. This model includes main and interaction effects; consequently you can examine contrasts of both main and interaction effects. In general, the procedures described in chapter 12 can be applied to the two-factor situation. Things become more complicated as we have row and column means (or marginal means), and cell means. Thus we have to be careful about which means are being considered.

Let us begin with contrasts of the main effects. If the effect for factor A is significant, and there are more than two levels of factor A, we can form contrasts that compare the levels of factor A ignoring factor B. Here we would be comparing the means for the levels of factor A, which are marginal means as opposed to cell means. Considering each factor separately is strongly advised; considering the factors simultaneously is to be avoided. Some statistics texts suggest that you consider the design as a one-factor model with $JK$ levels when using MCPs to examine main effects. This is inconsistent with the design and the intent of separating effects, and is not recommended.

For contrasts involving the interaction, my recommendation is to begin with a complex interaction contrast if there are more than four cells in the model. Thus for a $4 \times 4$ design that consists of four levels of A (method of instruction) and four levels of B (instructor), one possibility is to test both $4 \times 2$ complex interaction contrasts. An example of one such contrast is

$$\psi' = \frac{(\overline{Y}_{.11} + \overline{Y}_{.21} + \overline{Y}_{.31} + \overline{Y}_{.41})}{4} - \frac{(\overline{Y}_{.12} + \overline{Y}_{.22} + \overline{Y}_{.32} + \overline{Y}_{.42})}{4}$$

with a standard error of

$$s_{\psi'} = \sqrt{MS_{\text{with}}\left(\sum_{j=1}^{J}\sum_{k=1}^{K}\frac{c_{jk}^2}{n_{jk}}\right)}$$

where $n_{jk}$ is the number of observations in cell $jk$. This contrast would examine the interaction between the four methods of instruction and the first two instructors. A second complex interaction contrast could consider the interaction between the four methods of instruction and the other two instructors.

If the complex interaction contrast is significant, then follow this up with a simple interaction contrast that involves only four cell means. This is a single degree of freedom contrast because it involves only two levels of each factor (known as a **tetrad difference**). An example of such a contrast is

$$\psi' = (\overline{Y}_{.11} - \overline{Y}_{.21}) - (\overline{Y}_{.12} - \overline{Y}_{.22})$$

with a similar standard error term. Using the same example, this contrast would examine the interaction between the first two methods of instruction and the first two instructors.

Most of the MCPs described in chapter 12 can be used for testing main effects and interaction effects (although there is some debate about the appropriate use of interaction contrasts; see Boik, 1979; Marascuilo & Levin, 1970, 1976). Keppel and Wickens (2004) consider interaction contrasts in much detail. Finally, some statistics texts suggest the use of simple main effects in testing a significant interaction. These involve comparing, for example, the levels of factor A at a particular level of factor B, and are generally conducted by further partitioning the sums of squares. However, the simple main effects sums of squares represent a portion of a main effect plus the interaction effect. Thus the simple main effect does not really help us to understand the interaction, and is not recommended here.

### 13.1.9    Effect Size Measures, Confidence Intervals, and Power

Various measures of effect size have been proposed. Let us examine two commonly-used measures, which assume equal variances across the cells. First is partial $\eta^2$, which represents the proportion of variation in $Y$ explained by the effect of interest (i.e., by factor A, or factor B, or the AB interaction). We determine partial $\eta^2$ as follows:

$$\eta_A^2 = SS_A/(SS_A + SS_{with})$$
$$\eta_B^2 = SS_B/(SS_B + SS_{with})$$
$$\eta_{AB}^2 = SS_{AB}/(SS_{AB} + SS_{with})$$

Another effect size measure is the statistic $\omega^2$. We can determine $\omega^2$ as follows:

$$\omega_A^2 = \frac{SS_A - (J-1)\,MS_{with}}{SS_{total} + MS_{with}}$$

$$\omega_B^2 = \frac{SS_B - (K-1)MS_{with}}{SS_{total} + MS_{with}}$$

$$\omega_{AB}^2 = \frac{SS_{AB} - (J-1)(K-1)MS_{with}}{SS_{total} + MS_{with}}$$

Using Cohen's (1988) subjective standards, these effect sizes can be interpreted as follows: small effect, $\eta^2$ or $\omega^2 = .01$; medium effect, $\eta^2$ or $\omega^2 = .06$; large effect, $\eta^2$ or $\omega^2 = .14$. For futher discussion, see Keppel (1982), O'Grady (1982), Wilcox (1987), Cohen (1988), Fidler and Thompson (2001), Keppel and Wickens (2004), and Murphy and Myors (2004; with software).

As mentioned in chapter 11, confidence intervals can be used for providing interval estimates of a population mean or mean difference; this gives us information about the accuracy of a sample estimate. In the case of the two-factor model, we can form confidence intervals for row means, column means, cell means, the overall mean, as well as any possible contrast formed through a multiple comparison procedure. Note also that confidence intervals have been developed for $\eta^2$ and $\omega^2$ (Fidler & Thompson, 2001; Smithson, 2001).

As also mentioned in chapter 11, power can be determined either in the planned or observed (post hoc) power context. For planned power we typically use tables or power charts (e.g., Cohen, 1988 or Murphy & Myors, 2004) or software (e.g., Power and Precision, Ex-Sample, Gpower, or Murphy & Myers software, 2004). These are particularly useful in terms of determining adequate sample sizes when designing a study. Observed power is reported by statistics software, such as SPSS, to indicate the actual power in a given study.

### 13.1.10   An Example

Consider the following illustration of the two-factor design. Here we expand on the example presented in chapter 11 by adding a second factor to the model. Our dependent variable will again be the number of times a student attends statistics lab during one semester (or quarter), factor A is the attractiveness of the lab instructor (assuming each instructor is of the same gender and is equally competent), and factor B is the time of day the lab is offered. Thus the researcher is interested in whether the attractiveness of the instructor, the time of day, or the interaction of attractiveness and time influences student attendance in the statistics lab. The attractiveness levels are defined as (a) unattractive, (b) slightly attractive, (c) moderately attractive, and (d) very attractive. The time of day levels are defined as (a) afternoon lab and (b) evening lab. Students were randomly assigned to a combination of lab instructor and lab time at the beginning of the semester, and attendance was taken by the instructor. There were four students in each cell and eight cells (combinations of instructor and time) for a total of 32 observations. Students could attend a maximum of 30 lab sessions. Table 13.4 depicts the raw data and sample means for each cell (given beneath each cell), column, row, and overall.

The results are summarized in the ANOVA summary table as shown in Table 13.5. The $F$ test statistics are compared to the following critical values obtained from Appendix Table 4 ($\alpha = .05$): $_{.05}F_{3,24} = 3.01$ for the A and AB effects; $_{.05}F_{1,24} = 4.26$ for the B effect. The test statistics exceed the critical values for the A and B effects only, so we reject these $H_0$ and conclude that both the level of attractiveness and the time of day are related to mean differences in statistics lab attendance. The interaction was shown not to be a significant effect. If you would like to see an example of a two-factor design where the interaction is significant, take a look at the end of chapter problems, computational problem 5.

Next we estimate the main and interaction effects. The main effects for the levels of A are estimated to be:

$$a_1 = \bar{Y}_{.1.} - \bar{Y}_{...} = 11.1250 - 18.4063 = -7.2813$$

$$a_2 = \bar{Y}_{.2.} - \bar{Y}_{...} = 17.8750 - 18.4063 = -0.5313$$

$$a_3 = \bar{Y}_{.3.} - \bar{Y}_{...} = 20.2500 - 18.4063 = 1.8437$$

$$a_4 = \bar{Y}_{.4.} - \bar{Y}_{...} = 24.3750 - 18.4063 = 5.9687$$

The main effects for the levels of B are estimated to be:

$$b_1 = \bar{Y}_{..1} - \bar{Y}_{...} = 23.1250 - 18.4063 = 4.7187$$

$$b_2 = \bar{Y}_{..2} - \bar{Y}_{...} = 13.6875 - 18.4063 = -4.7188$$

**TABLE 13.4**

Data for the Statistics Lab Example: Number of Statistics Labs Attended,
by Level of Attractiveness and Time of Day

| Level of Attractiveness | Time of Day Time 1 | Time 2 | Row Mean |
|---|---|---|---|
| Attractiveness 1 | 15 | 10 | 11.1250 |
| | 12 | 8 | |
| | 21 | 7 | |
| | 13 | 3 | |
| | — | — | |
| | 15.2500 | 7.0000 | |
| Attractiveness 2 | 20 | 13 | 17.8750 |
| | 22 | 9 | |
| | 24 | 18 | |
| | 25 | 12 | |
| | — | — | |
| | 22.7500 | 13.0000 | |
| Attractiveness 3 | 24 | 10 | 20.2500 |
| | 29 | 12 | |
| | 27 | 21 | |
| | 25 | 14 | |
| | — | — | |
| | 26.2500 | 14.2500 | |
| Attractiveness 4 | 30 | 22 | 24.3750 |
| | 26 | 20 | |
| | 29 | 25 | |
| | 28 | 15 | |
| | — | — | |
| | 28.2500 | 20.2500 | |
| Column mean | 23.1250 | 13.6875 | 18.4063 |
| | | | (Overall mean) |

**TABLE 13.5**

Two-Factor Analysis of Variance Summary Table—Statistics Lab Example

| Source | SS | df | MS | F |
|---|---|---|---|---|
| Between: | | | | |
| A | 738.5938 | 3 | 246.1979 | 21.3504* |
| B | 712.5313 | 1 | 712.5313 | 61.7911** |
| AB | 21.8438 | 3 | 7.2813 | 0.6314* |
| Within | 276.7500 | 24 | 11.5313 | |
| Total | 1749.7188 | 31 | | |

$*_{.05}F_{3,24} = 3.01$.

$**_{.05}F_{1,24} = 4.26$.

Finally, the interaction effects for the various combinations of the levels of factors A and B are estimated to be:

$$(ab)_{11} = \overline{Y}_{.11} - (\overline{Y}_{.1.} + \overline{Y}_{..1} - \overline{Y}_{...}) = 15.2500 - (11.1250 + 23.1250 - 18.4063) = -0.5937$$

$$(ab)_{12} = \overline{Y}_{.12} - (\overline{Y}_{.1.} + \overline{Y}_{..2} - \overline{Y}_{...}) = 7.0000 - (11.1250 + 13.6875 - 18.4063) = 0.5938$$

$$(ab)_{21} = \overline{Y}_{.21} - (\overline{Y}_{.2.} + \overline{Y}_{..1} - \overline{Y}_{...}) = 22.7500 - (17.875 + 23.1250 - 18.4063) = 0.1563$$

$$(ab)_{22} = \overline{Y}_{.22} - (\overline{Y}_{.2.} + \overline{Y}_{..2} - \overline{Y}_{...}) = 13.000 - (17.8750 + 13.6875 - 18.4063) = -0.1562$$

$$(ab)_{31} = \overline{Y}_{.31} - (\overline{Y}_{.3.} + \overline{Y}_{..1} - \overline{Y}_{...}) = 26.2500 - (20.2500 + 23.1250 - 18.4063) = 1.2813$$

$$(ab)_{32} = \overline{Y}_{.32} - (\overline{Y}_{.3.} + \overline{Y}_{..2} - \overline{Y}_{...}) = 14.2500 - (20.2500 + 13.6875 - 18.4063) = -1.2812$$

$$(ab)_{41} = \overline{Y}_{.41} - (\overline{Y}_{.4.} + \overline{Y}_{..1} - \overline{Y}_{...}) = 28.2500 - (24.3750 + 23.1250 - 18.4063) = -0.8437$$

$$(ab)_{42} = \overline{Y}_{.42} - (\overline{Y}_{.4.} + \overline{Y}_{..2} - \overline{Y}_{...}) = 20.5000 - (24.3750 + 13.6875 - 18.4063) = 0.8438$$

The profile plot shown in Fig. 13.2 graphically depicts these effects. The A effect was significant and has more than two levels, so let us consider one example of a multiple comparison procedure, Tukey's HSD test. Recall from chapter 12 that the HSD test is a family-wise proce-

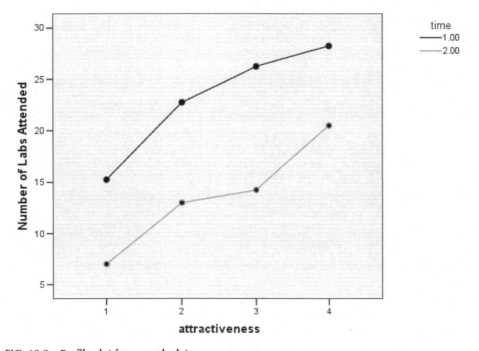

**FIG. 13.2  Profile plot for example data.**

dure most appropriate for considering all pairwise contrasts with a balanced design (which is the case for these data). The following are the computations:

Critical value (obtained from Appendix Table 9):

$$_{\alpha}q_{df\,(\text{with}),J} = {}_{.05}q_{24,4} = 3.901$$

Standard error:

$$s_{\psi'} = \sqrt{\frac{MS_{with}}{n_j}} = \sqrt{\frac{11.5313}{8}} = 1.2006$$

Test statistics:

$$q_1 = \frac{\overline{Y}_{.4.} - \overline{Y}_{.1.}}{s_{\psi'}} = \frac{24.3750 - 11.1250}{1.2006} = 11.0361\,(significant)$$

$$q_2 = \frac{\overline{Y}_{.4.} - \overline{Y}_{.2.}}{s_{\psi'}} = \frac{24.3750 - 17.8750}{1.2006} = 5.4140\,(significant)$$

$$q_3 = \frac{\overline{Y}_{.4.} - \overline{Y}_{.3.}}{s_{\psi'}} = \frac{24.3750 - 20.2500}{1.2006} = 3.4358\,(nonsignificant)$$

$$q_4 = \frac{\overline{Y}_{.3.} - \overline{Y}_{.1.}}{s_{\psi'}} = \frac{20.2500 - 11.1250}{1.2006} = 7.6004\,(significant)$$

$$q_5 = \frac{\overline{Y}_{.3.} - \overline{Y}_{.2.}}{s_{\psi'}} = \frac{20.2500 - 17.8750}{1.2006} = 1.9782\,(nonsignificant)$$

$$q_6 = \frac{\overline{Y}_{.2.} - \overline{Y}_{.1.}}{s_{\psi'}} = \frac{17.8750 - 11.1250}{1.2006} = 5.6222\,(significant)$$

These results indicate that the means for the levels of factor A are significantly different for levels 1 and 4, 2 and 4, 1 and 3, and 1 and 2. Thus level 1 (unattractive) is significantly different from the other three levels of attractiveness, and levels 2 and 4 (slightly unattractive vs. very attractive) are also significantly different.

These results are somewhat different than those found with the one-factor model in chapters 11 and 12 (where levels 1 and 4 as well as 1 and 3 were different). The $MS_{with}$ has been reduced with the introduction of the second factor from 36.1116 to 11.5313 because $SS_{with}$ has been reduced from 1,011.1250 to 276.7500. Although the $SS$ and $MS$ for the attractiveness factor remain unchanged, this resulted in the $F$ test statistic being considerably larger (increased from 6.8177 to 21.3504), although observed power was quite high in both models. Recall that this is one of the benefits we mentioned earlier about the use of additional factors in the model. Also, although the B effect was significant, there are only two levels of the B factor, and thus we need not carry out any multiple comparisons (attendance is better in the afternoon section). Finally, since the interaction was not significant, it is not necessary to consider any related contrasts.

Finally we can estimate the effect size measures. The partial $\eta^2$ are determined to be

$$\eta_A^2 = \frac{SS_A}{SS_A + SS_{with}} = \frac{738.5938}{738.5938 + 276.75} = 0.7274$$

$$\eta_B^2 = \frac{SS_B}{SS_B + SS_{with}} = \frac{712.5313}{712.5313 + 276.75} = 0.7203$$

$$\eta_{AB}^2 = \frac{SS_{AB}}{SS_{AB} + SS_{with}} = \frac{21.8438}{21.8438 + 276.75} = 0.0732$$

We determine the $\omega^2$ to be

$$\omega_A^2 = \frac{SS_A - (J-1)MS_{with}}{SS_{total} + MS_{with}} = \frac{738.5938 - (3)11.5313}{1,749.7188 + 11.5313} = 0.3997$$

$$\omega_B^2 = \frac{SS_B - (K-1)MS_{with}}{SS_{total} + MS_{with}} = \frac{712.5313 - (1)11.5313}{1,749.7188 + 11.5313} = 0.3980$$

$$\omega_{AB}^2 = \frac{SS_{AB} - (J-1)(K-1)MS_{with}}{SS_{total} + MS_{with}} = \frac{21.8438 - (3)11.5313}{1,749.7188 + 11.5313} = 0$$

Based on these effect size measures, one would conclude that there is a large effect for instructor attractiveness and for time of day, but no effect for the time-attractiveness interaction.

## 13.2 THREE-FACTOR AND HIGHER-ORDER ANOVA

### 13.2.1 Characteristics of the Model

All of the characteristics we discussed for the two-factor model apply to the three-factor model, with one obvious exception. There are three factors rather than two. This will result in three main effects (one for each factor, known as A, B, and C), three two-way interactions (known as AB, AC, and BC), and one three-way interaction (known as ABC). Here the only new concept is the three-way interaction, which may be stated as follows: "Is the AB interaction constant across all levels of factor C?" This may also be stated as "AC across the levels of B" or as "BC across the levels of A." These each have the same interpretation as there is only one way of testing the three-way interaction. In short, the three-way interaction can thought of as the two-way interaction is behaving differently across the levels of the third factor.

We do not explicitly consider models with more than three factors (Marascuilo & Serlin, 1988; Myers & Well, 1995; Keppel & Wickens, 2004). However, be warned that such models do exist, and that they will necessitate more main effects, more two-way interactions, more three-way interactions, as well as higher-order interactions. Conceptually, the only change is to add these additional effects to the model.

## 13.2.2  The ANOVA Model

The model for the three factor design is

$$Y_{ijkl} = \mu + \alpha_j + \beta_k + \gamma_l + (\alpha\beta)_{jk} + (\alpha\gamma)_{jl} + (\beta\gamma)_{kl} + (\alpha\beta\gamma)_{jkl} + \varepsilon_{ijkl}$$

where $Y_{ijkl}$ is the observed score on the criterion variable for individual $i$ in level $j$ of factor A, level $k$ of factor B, and level $l$ of factor C (or in the $jkl$ cell), $\mu$ is the overall or grand population mean (i.e., regardless of cell designation), $\alpha_j$ is the effect for level $j$ of factor A, $\beta_k$ is the effect for level $k$ of factor B, $\gamma_l$ is the effect for level $l$ of factor C, $(\alpha\beta)_{jk}$ is the interaction effect for the combination of level $j$ of factor A and level $k$ of factor B, $(\alpha\gamma)_{jl}$ is the interaction effect for the combination of level $j$ of factor A and level $l$ of factor C, $(\beta\gamma)_{kl}$ is the interaction effect for the combination of level $k$ of factor B and level $l$ of factor C, $(\alpha\beta\gamma)_{jkl}$ is the interaction effect for the combination of level $j$ of factor A, level $k$ of factor B, and level $l$ of factor C, and $\varepsilon_{ijkl}$ is the random residual error for individual $i$ in cell $jkl$. Given that there are three main effects, three two-way interactions, and a three-way interaction, there will be an accompanying null and alternative hypothesis for each of these effects. At this point in your statistics career, the hypotheses should be obvious (simply expand on the hypotheses at the beginning of this chapter).

## 13.2.3  The ANOVA Summary Table

The ANOVA summary table for the three-factor model is shown in Table 13.6, with the usual columns for sources of variation, sums of squares, degrees of freedom, mean squares, and $F$.

## 13.2.4  The Triple Interaction

Everything else about the three-factor design follows from the two-factor model. The assumptions are the same, $MS_{\text{with}}$ is the error term used for testing each of the hypotheses in the fixed-

TABLE 13.6
Three-Factor Analysis of Variance Summary Table

| Source | SS | df | MS | F |
|---|---|---|---|---|
| Between: | | | | |
| A | $SS_{\text{A}}$ | $J - 1$ | $MS_{\text{A}}$ | $MS_{\text{A}}/MS_{\text{with}}$ |
| B | $SS_{\text{B}}$ | $K - 1$ | $MS_{\text{B}}$ | $MS_{\text{B}}/MS_{\text{with}}$ |
| C | $SS_{\text{C}}$ | $L - 1$ | $MS_{\text{C}}$ | $MS_{\text{C}}/MS_{\text{with}}$ |
| AB | $SS_{\text{AB}}$ | $(J - 1)(K - 1)$ | $MS_{\text{AB}}$ | $MS_{\text{AB}}/MS_{\text{with}}$ |
| AC | $SS_{\text{AC}}$ | $(J - 1)(L - 1)$ | $MS_{\text{AC}}$ | $MS_{\text{AC}}/MS_{\text{with}}$ |
| BC | $SS_{\text{BC}}$ | $(K - 1)(L - 1)$ | $MS_{\text{BC}}$ | $MS_{\text{BC}}/MS_{\text{with}}$ |
| ABC | $SS_{\text{ABC}}$ | $(J - 1)(K - 1)(L - 1)$ | $MS_{\text{ABC}}$ | $MS_{\text{ABC}}/MS_{\text{with}}$ |
| Within | $SS_{\text{with}}$ | $N - JKL$ | $MS_{\text{with}}$ | |
| Total | $SS_{\text{total}}$ | $N - 1$ | | |

effects model, and the multiple comparison procedures are easily utilized. The main new feature is the three-way interaction. If this interaction is significant, then this means that the two-way interaction is different across the levels of the third factor. This result will need to be taken into account prior to interpreting the two-way interactions and the main effects.

Although the inclusion of additional factors in the design should result in a reduction in $MS_{with}$, there is a price to pay for the study of additional factors. Although the analysis is simple for the computer, you must consider the possibility of significant higher-order interactions. If you find, for example, that the four-way interaction is significant, how do you deal with it? First you have to interpret this interaction, which could be difficult if it is unexpected. Then you may have difficulty in dealing with the interpretation of your other effects. My advice is simple. Do not include additional factors just because they sound interesting. Only include those factors that are theoretically or empirically important. Then if a significant higher-order interaction occurs, you will be in a better position to understand it because you have already thought about its consequences. Reporting that an interaction is significant but not interpretable is not sound research (for additional discussion on this topic, see Keppel & Wickens, 2004).

## 13.3   FACTORIAL ANOVA WITH UNEQUAL *n*'s

Up until this point in the chapter, we have only considered the equal $n$'s or balanced case. That is, the model used was where the number of observations in each cell was equal. This served to make the formulas and equations easier to deal with. However, we need not assume that the $n$'s are equal. In this section we discuss ways to deal with the unequal $n$'s (or unbalanced) case for the two-factor model, although these notions can be transferred to higher-order models as well.

When $n$'s are unequal, things become a bit trickier as the main effects and the interaction effect are not orthogonal. In other words, the sums of squares cannot be partitioned into independent effects. As a result, several computational approaches have been developed. In the old days, prior to the availability of high-speed computers, the standard approach was to use unweighted means analysis. This is essentially an analysis of means, rather than raw scores, which are unweighted by cell size. This approach is only an approximate procedure. Due to the availability of quality statistical software, the unweighted means approach is no longer necessary. Another silly approach is to delete enough data until you have an equal $n$'s model.

There are three more modern approaches. Each of these approaches really test different hypotheses and thus may result in different conclusions: (a) the **sequential approach** (also known as the hierarchical sums of squares approach), (b) the **partially sequential approach** (also known as the partially hierarchical, or experimental design, or method of fitting constants approach), and (c) the **regression approach** (also known as the marginal means or unique approach). There has been considerable debate over the years about the relative merits of each approach (e.g., Applebaum & Cramer, 1974; Carlson & Timm, 1974; Cramer & Applebaum, 1980; Overall, Lee, & Hornick, 1981; Overall & Spiegel, 1969; Timm & Carlson, 1975).

Here is what each approach tests. In the sequential approach, the effects being tested are:

$$\alpha \mid \mu$$
$$\beta \mid \mu, \alpha$$
$$\alpha\beta \mid \mu, \alpha, \beta$$

This indicates, for example, that the effect for factor B is adjusted for (as denoted by the vertical line) the overall mean ($\mu$) and the effect due to factor A ($\alpha$). Thus, each effect is adjusted for prior effects in the sequential order given. Here the $\alpha$ effect is given theoretical or practical priority over the $\beta$ effect. In SAS and SPSS this is the Type I sum of squares method.

In the partially sequential approach, the effects being tested are:

$$\alpha \mid \mu, \beta$$
$$\beta \mid \mu, \alpha$$
$$\alpha\beta \mid \mu, \alpha, \beta$$

There is difference here because each main effect controls for the other main effect, but not for the interaction effect. In SAS and SPSS this is the Type II sum of squares method. This is the only one of the three methods where the sums of squares add up to the total sum of squares. Notice in the sequential and partially sequential approaches that the interaction is not taken into account in estimating the main effects, which is only fine if there is no interaction effect.

In the regression approach, the effects being tested are:

$$\alpha \mid \mu, \beta, \alpha\beta$$
$$\beta \mid \mu, \alpha, \alpha\beta$$
$$\alpha\beta \mid \mu, \alpha, \beta$$

In this approach each effect controls for each of the other effects. In SAS and SPSS this is the Type III sum of squares method. Many statisticians (e.g., Glass & Hopkins, 1996; Keppel & Wickens, 2004; Mickey, Dunn, & Clark, 2004), including myself, recommend exclusive use of the regression approach because each effect is estimated taking the other effects into account. The hypotheses tested in the sequential and partially sequential approaches are seldom of interest and are difficult to interpret (Carlson & Timm, 1974; Kirk, 1982; Overall, Lee, & Hornick, 1981; Timm & Carlson, 1975). The regression approach seems to be conceptually closest to the traditional analysis of variance. When the $n$'s are equal, each of these three approaches tests the same hypotheses and yields the same results.

## 13.4   SPSS

In the last section we look at SPSS for the statistics lab example, as well as an APA paragraph of the results. As already noted in chapter 11, SPSS needs the data to be in a specific form for the analysis to proceeed, which is different from the layout of the data in Table 13.1. For a two-factor ANOVA, the dataset must consist of three variables or columns, one for the level of factor A, one for the level of factor B, and the third for the dependent variable. Each row still represents one individual, indicating the level of factors A and B that individual is a member of, and their score on the dependent variable.

To conduct a parametric ANOVA through the GLM module, go to the "Analyze" pulldown, into "General Linear Model," and then into the "Univariate" procedure. Click the dependent variable (e.g., labs attended) into the "Dependent Variable" box, and click both fixed-effects factor variables into the "Fixed Factor(s)" box. Click on the "Options" button to obtain such information as "Descriptive Statistics," "Estimates of effect size," "Observed power," and "Homogeneity tests" (i.e., Levene's test). Click on "Continue" to return to the original dialog box. To obtain a profile plot of means, click on the "Plots" button, move one factor variable name into the "Horizontal Axis" box, move the other factor variable name into the "Separate Lines" box, click on "Add" to generate the plot, and finally click on "Continue" to return to the original dialog box. To obtain multiple comparison procedures, proceed as you did in chapter 12 by clicking the "Post Hoc" button, then move the "Factor" variables into the "Post Hoc Tests for:" box, check the box for an appropriate procedure, then click "Continue" to return to the previous screen. Then click on "OK" to run the analyses. Selected results are shown in the panels of Table 13.7 (ANOVA summary table, information about different types of means <with confidence intervals>, and Tukey's HSD procedure <with confidence intervals>) and the profile plot is shown in Fig. 13.2. In order to test interaction contrasts in SPSS, syntax is required rather than the use of point-and-click (c.f., Page, Braver, & MacKinnon, 2003). Note also that the SPSS ANOVA summary table will include additional sources of variation that I find not to be useful (i.e., corrected model, intercept, total); thus they are not shown in Table 13.7.

Finally we come to an example paragraph of the results for the statistics lab example. From Table 13.7 we see that the interaction is not significant, there are significant main effects for both attractiveness and time ($F_{\text{attract}} = 21.350$, $df = 3,24$, $p = .001$; $F_{\text{time}} = 61.791$, $df = 1,24$, $p = .001$), with attendance being significantly higher in the afternoon, effect sizes are rather large for attractiveness and time (partial $\eta^2_{\text{attract}} = .727$; partial $\eta^2_{\text{time}} = .720$), and observed power for attractiveness and time is maximal. Tukey HSD post hoc comparisons revealed that the unattractive level had significantly lower attendance than the other levels, and that the slightly attractive level had significantly lower attendence than the very attractive level. The profile plot (Fig. 13.2) summarizes these differences. From the residual plot, skewness and kurtosis statistics, and Levene's homogeneity of variance test ($p = .766$), the assumptions were satisfied.

## 13.5 SUMMARY

This chapter considered methods involving the comparison of means for multiple independent variables. The chapter began with a look at the characteristics of the factorial analysis of variance, including (1) two or more independent variables each with two or more fixed levels; (2) subjects are randomly assigned to cells and then exposed to only one combination of the independent variables; (3) the factors are fully crossed such that all possible combinations of the factors' levels are included in the design; and (4) the dependent variable is at least measured at the interval level. The ANOVA model was examined and followed by a discussion of main effects and, in particular, the interaction effect. Some discussion was also devoted to the ANOVA assumptions. The ANOVA summary table was shown along with partitioning the sums of squares. Multiple comparison procedures were then extended to factorial models. Then effect size measures, confidence intervals, and power were considered. Finally, several approaches were given for the unequal $n$'s case with factorial models. At this point you should have met the following objectives: (a) be able to understand the characteristics and concepts underlying factorial ANOVA, (b) be able to determine and interpret the results of factorial ANOVA, and (c) be able to understand and evaluate the assumptions of factorial ANOVA. In chapter 14 we introduce the analysis of covariance.

**TABLE 13.7**

Selected SPSS Results for the Statistics Lab Example

*Tests of Between-Subjects Effects*

*Dependent Variable: dv*

| Source | Type III Sum of Squares | df | Mean Square | F | Sig. | Partial Eta Squared | Observed Power[a] |
|---|---|---|---|---|---|---|---|
| attract | 738.594 | 3 | 246.198 | 21.350 | .000 | .727 | 1.000 |
| time | 712.531 | 1 | 712.531 | 61.791 | .000 | .720 | 1.000 |
| attract * time | 21.844 | 3 | 7.281 | .631 | .602 | .073 | .162 |
| Error | 276.750 | 24 | 11.531 | | | | |
| Corrected Total | 1749.719 | 31 | | | | | |

[a]Computed using alpha = .05

*1. Grand Mean*

*Dependent Variable: dv*

| | | 95% Confidence Interval | |
|---|---|---|---|
| Mean | Std. Error | Lower Bound | Upper Bound |
| 18.406 | .600 | 17.167 | 19.645 |

*2. attract*

*Dependent Variable: dv*

| | | | 95% Confidence Interval | |
|---|---|---|---|---|
| attract | Mean | Std. Error | Lower Bound | Upper Bound |
| 1.00000 | 11.125 | 1.201 | 8.647 | 13.603 |
| 2.00000 | 17.875 | 1.201 | 15.397 | 20.353 |
| 3.00000 | 20.250 | 1.201 | 17.772 | 22.728 |
| 4.00000 | 24.375 | 1.201 | 21.897 | 26.853 |

*3. time*

*Dependent Variable: dv*

| | | | 95% Confidence Interval | |
|---|---|---|---|---|
| time | Mean | Std. Error | Lower Bound | Upper Bound |
| 1.00 | 23.125 | .849 | 21.373 | 24.877 |
| 2.00 | 13.688 | .849 | 11.935 | 15.440 |

(*continued*)

**TABLE 13.7** (*Continued*)
Selected SPSS Results for the Statistics Lab Example

*4. attract * time*

*Dependent Variable: dv*

| attract | time | Mean | Std. Error | 95% Confidence Interval | |
|---|---|---|---|---|---|
| | | | | Lower Bound | Upper Bound |
| 1.00000 | 1.00 | 15.250 | 1.698 | 11.746 | 18.754 |
| | 2.00 | 7.000 | 1.698 | 3.496 | 10.504 |
| 2.00000 | 1.00 | 22.750 | 1.698 | 19.246 | 26.254 |
| | 2.00 | 13.000 | 1.698 | 9.496 | 16.504 |
| 3.00000 | 1.00 | 26.250 | 1.698 | 22.746 | 29.754 |
| | 2.00 | 14.250 | 1.698 | 10.746 | 17.754 |
| 4.00000 | 1.00 | 28.250 | 1.698 | 24.746 | 31.754 |
| | 2.00 | 20.500 | 1.698 | 16.996 | 24.004 |

*Multiple Comparisons*

*Dependent Variable: dv*
*Tukey HSD*

| (I) attract | (J) attract | Mean Difference (I–J) | Std. Error | Sig. | 95% Confidence Interval | |
|---|---|---|---|---|---|---|
| | | | | | Lower Bound | Upper Bound |
| 1.00000 | 2.00000 | −6.7500000* | 1.697885 | .003 | −11.4338000 | −2.0662000 |
| | 3.00000 | −9.1250000* | 1.697885 | .000 | −13.8088000 | −4.4412000 |
| | 4.00000 | −13.250000* | 1.697885 | .000 | −17.9338000 | −8.5662000 |
| 2.00000 | 1.00000 | 6.7500000* | 1.697885 | .003 | 2.0662000 | 11.4338000 |
| | 3.00000 | −2.3750000 | 1.697885 | .512 | −7.0588000 | 2.3088000 |
| | 4.00000 | −6.5000000* | 1.697885 | .004 | −11.1838000 | −1.8162000 |
| 3.00000 | 1.00000 | 9.1250000* | 1.697885 | .000 | 4.4412000 | 13.8088000 |
| | 2.00000 | 2.3750000 | 1.697885 | .512 | −2.3088000 | 7.0588000 |
| | 4.00000 | −4.1250000 | 1.697885 | .098 | −8.8088000 | .5588000 |
| 4.00000 | 1.00000 | 13.2500000* | 1.697885 | .000 | 8.5662000 | 17.9338000 |
| | 2.00000 | 6.5000000* | 1.697885 | .004 | 1.8162000 | 11.1838000 |
| | 3.00000 | 4.1250000 | 1.697885 | .098 | −.5588000 | 8.8088000 |

Based on observed means.
*The mean difference is significant at the .05 level.

## PROBLEMS

### Conceptual Problems

1. You are given a two-factor design with the following cell means (cell 11 = 25; cell 12 = 75; cell 21 = 50; cell 22 = 50; cell 31 = 75; cell 32 = 25). Assume that the within cell variation is small. Which one of the following conclusions seems most probable?

    a. The row means are significantly different.

    b. The column means are significantly different.

    c. The interaction is significant.

    d. All of the above.

2. In a two-factor ANOVA, one independent variable has five levels and the second has four levels. If each cell has seven observations, what is $df_{with}$?

    a. 20

    b. 120

    c. 139

    d. 140

3. Which of the following conclusions would result in the greatest generalizability of the main effect for factor A across the levels of factor B? The interaction between the independent variables A and B was

    a. not significant at the .25 level.

    b. significant at the .10 level.

    c. significant at the .05 level.

    d. significant at the .01 level.

    e. significant at the .001 level.

4. In a two-factor fixed-effects ANOVA, $F_A = 2$, $df_A = 3$, $df_B = 6$, $df_{AB} = 18$, $df_{with} = 56$. The null hypothesis for factor A can be rejected

    a. at the .01 level.

    b. at the .05 level but not at the .01 level.

    c. at the .10 level but not at the .05 level.

    d. none of the above

5. In ANOVA the interaction of two factors is certainly present when

    a. the two factors are positively correlated.

    b. the two factors are negatively correlated.

    c. row effects are not consistent across columns.

    d. main effects do not account for all of the variation in $Y$.

    e. main effects do account for all of the variation in $Y$.

Questions 6 through 9 are based on the following ANOVA summary table (fixed-effects):

| Source | df | MS | F |
|--------|-----|-----|------|
| A | 2 | 45 | 4.5 |
| B | 1 | 70 | 7.0 |
| AB | 2 | 170 | 17.0 |
| Within | 60 | 10 | |

6. For which source of variation is the null hypothesis rejected at the .01 level of significance?

    a.   A

    b.   B

    c.   AB

    d.   all of the above

7. How many cells are there in the design?

    a.   1

    b.   2

    c.   3

    d.   5

    e.   none of the above

8. The total sample size for the design is

    a.   66

    b.   68

    c.   70

    d.   none of the above

9. $SS_{AB}$ is equal to

    a.   170

    b.   340

    c.   510

    d.   1,020

    e.   none of the above

10. In a design with four factors, how many interactions will there be?

    a.   4

    b.   8

    c.   11

    d.   12

    e.   16

11. Degrees of freedom for the AB interaction are equal to
    a. $df_A - df_B$
    b. $(df_A)(df_B)$
    c. $df_{with} - (df_A + df_B)$
    d. $df_{tot} - df_{with}$

12. A two-factor experiment means that the design includes
    a. two independent variables.
    b. two dependent variables.
    c. an interaction between independent and dependent variables.
    d. exactly two separate groups of subjects.

13. Two independent variables are said to interact when
    a. both variables are equally influenced by a third variable.
    b. the variables are differentially affected by a third variable.
    c. each factor produces a change in the subjects' scores.
    d. the effect of one variable depends on the second variable.

14. If there is an interaction between the independent variables textbook and time of day, this means that the textbook used has the same effect at different times of the day. True or False?

15. If the AB interaction is significant, then at least one of the two main effects must be significant. True or False?

16. I assert that a two-factor experiment (factors A and B) yields no more information than two one-factor experiments (factor A in experiment 1 and factor B in experiment 2). Am I correct?

17. For a two-factor fixed-effects model, if the degrees of freedom for testing factor A = 2,24, then I assert that the degrees of freedom for testing factor B will necessarily be = 2,24. Am I correct?

## Computational Problems

1. Complete the following ANOVA summary table for a two-factor fixed-effects analysis of variance, where there are two levels of factor A (drug) and three levels of factor B (dosage). Each cell includes 26 students. Complete the summary table below where $\alpha = .05$.

| Source | SS | df | MS | F | Critical Value | Decision |
|--------|------|----|----|---|----------------|----------|
| A | 6.15 | — | — | — | — | — |
| B | 10.60 | — | — | — | — | — |
| AB | 9.10 | — | — | — | — | — |
| Within | — | — | — | | | |
| Total | 250.85 | — | | | | |

2. Complete the following ANOVA summary table for a two-factor fixed-effects analysis of variance, where there are three levels of factor A (program) and two levels of factor B (gender). Each cell includes four students. Complete the summary table below where $\alpha = .01$.

| Source | SS | df | MS | F | Critical Value | Decision |
|--------|------|----|----|---|----------------|----------|
| A | 3.64 | — | — | — | — | — |
| B | .57 | — | — | — | — | — |
| AB | 2.07 | — | — | — | — | — |
| Within | — | — | — | | | |
| Total | 8.18 | — | | | | |

3. Conduct a two-factor fixed-effects ANOVA to determine if there are any effects due to A (task type), B (task difficulty), or the AB interaction ($\alpha = .01$). Conduct Tukey HSD post hoc comparisons, if necessary. The following are the scores for the individual cells of the model:

$A_1B_1$: 41, 39, 25, 25, 37, 51, 39, 101

$A_1B_2$: 46, 54, 97, 93, 51, 36, 29, 69

$A_1B_3$: 113, 135, 109, 96, 47, 49, 68, 38

$A_2B_1$: 86, 38, 45, 45, 60, 106, 106, 31

$A_2B_2$: 74, 96, 101, 124, 48, 113, 139, 131

$A_2B_3$: 152, 79, 135, 144, 52, 102, 166, 155

4. An experimenter is interested in the effects of strength of reinforcement (factor A), type of reinforcement (factor B), and sex of the adult administering the reinforcement (factor C) on children's behavior. Each factor consists of two levels. Thirty-two children are randomly assigned to 8 cells (i.e., 4 per cell), one for each of the factor combinations. Using the scores for the individual cells of the model that follow, conduct an three-factor fixed-effects analysis of variance ($\alpha = .05$). If there are any significant interactions, graph and interpret the interactions.

$A_1B_1C_1$: 3, 6, 3, 3

$A_1B_1C_2$: 4, 5, 4, 3

$A_1B_2C_1$: 7, 8, 7, 6

$A_1B_2C_2$: 7, 8, 9, 8

$A_2B_1C_1$: 1, 2, 2, 2

$A_2B_1C_2$: 2, 3, 4, 3

$A_2B_2C_1$: 5, 6, 5, 6

$A_2B_2C_2$: 10, 10, 9, 11

5. A revised version of the example data from this chapter is given below (A = attractiveness, B = time, same levels). Using the scores for the individual cells of the model that follow, conduct a two-factor fixed-effects analysis of variance ($\alpha = .05$). Are the results different?

$A_1B_1$: 10, 8, 7, 3

$A_1B_2$: 15, 12, 21, 13

$A_2B_1$ : 13, 9, 18, 12
$A_2B_2$ : 20, 22, 24, 25
$A_3B_1$ : 24, 29, 27, 25
$A_3B_2$ : 10, 12, 21, 14
$A_4B_1$ : 30, 26, 29, 28
$A_4B_2$ : 22, 20, 25, 15

## Interpretive Problem

Building on the interpretive problem from chapter 11, utilize the statistics survey dataset from the CD. Use SPSS to conduct a two-factor fixed-effects ANOVA, where political view is factor A (as in chapter 11), gender is factor B (a new factor), and the dependent variable is the same one you used previously in chapter 11. Then write an APA style paragraph summarizing the results.

# 14

# INTRODUCTION TO ANALYSIS OF COVARIANCE: THE ONE-FACTOR FIXED-EFFECTS MODEL WITH A SINGLE COVARIATE

## Chapter Outline

1. Characteristics of the model
2. The layout of the data
3. The ANCOVA model
4. The ANCOVA summary table
5. Partitioning the sums of squares
6. Adjusted means and related procedures
7. Assumptions and violation of assumptions
   Independence
   Homogeneity of variance
   Normality
   Linearity
   Fixed independent variable
   Independence of the covariate and the independent variable
   Covariate measured without error
   Homogeneity of regression slopes
8. An example
9. ANCOVA without randomization
10. More complex ANCOVA models
11. Nonparametric ANCOVA procedures
12. SPSS

## Key Concepts

1.  Statistical adjustment
2.  Covariate
3.  Adjusted means
4.  Homogeneity of regression slopes
5.  Independence of the covariate and the independent variable

We have now considered several different analysis of variance (ANOVA) models. As we moved through chapter 13, we saw that the inclusion of additional factors helped to reduce the residual or uncontrolled variation. These additional factors served as "experimental design controls" in that their inclusion in the design helped to reduce the uncontrolled variation. In fact, this could be the reason an additional factor is included in a factorial design.

In this chapter a new type of variable, known as the covariate, is incorporated into the analysis. Rather than serving as an "experimental design control," the covariate serves as a "statistical control" where uncontrolled variation is reduced statistically in the analysis. Thus a model where a covariate is used is known as **analysis of covariance** (ANCOVA). We are most concerned with the one-factor fixed-effects model, although this model can be generalized to any of the other ANOVA designs considered in this text. That is, any of the ANOVA models discussed in the text can also include a covariate, and thus become an ANCOVA model.

Most of the concepts used in this chapter have already been covered in the text. In addition, new concepts include statistical adjustment, covariate, adjusted means, and two new assumptions, homogeneity of regression slopes and independence of the covariate and the independent variable. Our objectives are that by the end of this chapter, you will be able to (a) understand the characteristics and concepts underlying ANCOVA; (b) determine and interpret the results of ANCOVA, including adjusted means and multiple comparison procedures; and (c) understand and evaluate the assumptions of ANCOVA.

## 14.1   CHARACTERISTICS OF THE MODEL

In this section, we describe the distinguishing characteristics of the one-factor fixed-effects ANCOVA model. However, before we begin an extended discussion of these characteristics, consider the following example. Imagine a situation where a statistics professor is scheduled to teach two sections of introductory statistics. The professor, being a cunning researcher, decides to perform a little experiment where Section 1 is taught using the traditional lecture method and Section 2 is taught using extensive graphics, computer simulations, and computer-assisted and calculator-based instruction, using mostly small-group and self-directed instruction. The professor is interested in which section performs better.

Before the study/course begins, the professor thinks about whether there are other variables related to statistics performance that should somehow be taken into account. An obvious one is ability in quantitative methods. From previous research and experience, the professor knows that ability in quantitative methods is highly correlated with performance in statistics and decides to give a measure of quantitative ability in the first class and use that as a covariate in the analysis. A **covariate** (i.e., quantitative ability) is defined as a source of variation not controlled for in the design of the experiment, but that the researcher believes to affect the dependent variable (i.e., course performance). The covariate is used to statistically adjust the dependent variable. For instance, if Section 1 has higher quantitative ability than Section 2, it would be wise to take this into account in the analysis. Otherwise Secction 1 might outperform Section 2 due to their higher quantitative ability rather than due to the method of instruction. This is precisely the point of the analysis of covariance. Some of the more typical examples of covariates in education and the behavioral sciences are pretest (where the dependent variable is the posttest), prior achievement, weight, IQ, aptitude, age, experience, previous training, motivation, and grade point average.

Let us now begin with the characteristics of the ANCOVA model. The first set of characteristics is obvious because they carry over from the one-factor fixed-effects ANOVA model. There is a single independent variable or factor with two or more levels. The levels are fixed by the researcher rather than randomly sampled from a population of levels. Once the levels of the independent variable are selected, subjects or individuals are somehow assigned to these levels or groups. Each subject is then exposed to only one level of the independent variable (although ANCOVA with repeated measures is also possible, but is not discussed here). In our example, method of statistics instruction is the independent variable with two levels or groups, the traditional lecture method and the cutting-edge method.

Situations where the researcher is able to randomly assign subjects to groups are known as **true experimental designs**. Situations where the researcher does not have control over which level a subject is assigned to are known as **quasi-experimental designs**. This lack of control may occur for one of two reasons. First, the groups may be already in place when the researcher arrives on the scene; these groups are referred to as **intact groups** (e.g., based on classroom assignments). Second, it may be theoretically impossible for the researcher to assign subjects to groups (e.g., income level). Thus a distinction is typically made about whether or not the researcher can control the assignment of subjects to groups. The distinction about the use of ANCOVA in true and quasi-experimental situations has been quite controversial over the past few decades; we look at it in more detail later in this chapter. For further information on true experimental designs and quasi-experimental designs, see Campbell and Stanley (1966) and Cook and Campbell (1979). In our example again, if assignment of students to sections is random, then we have a true experimental design. If assignment of students to sections is not random, perhaps already assigned at registration, then we have a quasi-experimental design.

One final item in the first set of characteristics has to do with the measurement scales of the variables. In the analysis of covariance, it is assumed the dependent variable is measured at the interval level or better. If the dependent variable is measured at the ordinal level, then alternative nonparametric procedures described toward the end of this chapter should be considered. It is also assumed the covariate is measured at the interval level or better. No assumption is made about the independent variable as it is a grouping or categorical variable.

The remaining characteristics have to do with the uniqueness of the analysis of covariance. As already mentioned, the analysis of covariance is a form of statistical control developed specifically to reduce unexplained error variation. The covariate (sometimes known as a concomitant variable) is a source of variation not controlled for in the design of the experiment, but believed to affect the dependent variable. In a factorial design, for example, a factor could be included to reduce error variation. However, this represents an experimental design form of control as it is included as a factor in the model.

In ANCOVA, the dependent variable is adjusted statistically to remove the effects of the portion of uncontrolled variation represented by the covariate. The group means on the dependent variable are adjusted so that they represent groups with the same means on the covariate. The analysis of covariance is essentially an analysis of variance on these "adjusted means." This needs further explanation. Consider first the situation of the true experiment involving randomization where there are two groups. Here it is unlikely that the two groups will be statistically different on any variable related to the dependent measure. The two groups should have roughly equivalent means on the covariate, although 5% of the time we would expect a significant difference due to chance at $\alpha = .05$. Thus we typically do not see preexisting differences between the two groups on the covariate in a true experiment. However, the relationship between the covariate and the dependent variable is important. If these variables are linearly related (discussed later), then the use of the covariate in the analysis will serve to reduce the unexplained variation in the model. The greater the magnitude of the correlation, the more uncontrolled variation can be removed, as shown by a reduction in mean square error.

Consider next the situation of the quasi-experiment, that is, without randomization. Here it is more likely that the two groups will be statistically different on the covariate as well as other variables related to the dependent variable. Thus there may indeed be a preexisting difference between the two groups on the covariate. If the groups do differ on the covariate and we ignore it by conducting an ANOVA, our ability to get a precise estimate of the group effects will be reduced as the group effect will be confounded with the effect of the covariate. For instance, if a significant group difference is revealed by the ANOVA, we would not be certain if there was truly a group effect or whether the effect was due to preexisting differences on the covariate, or some combination of group and covariate effects. The analysis of covariance takes the covariate mean difference into account as well as the linear relationship between the covariate and the dependent variable.

Thus, the covariate is used to (a) reduce error variation, (b) take any preexisting group mean difference on the covariate into account, (c) take into account the relationship between the covariate and the dependent variable, and (d) yield a more precise and less biased estimate of the group effects. If error variation is reduced, the analysis of covariance will be more powerful and require smaller sample sizes than the analysis of variance (Keppel & Wickens, 2004; Mickey, Dunn, & Clark, 2004; Myers & Well, 1995). If error variation is not reduced, the analysis of variance is more powerful. A more extensive comparison of ANOVA versus ANCOVA is given in chapter 16. In addition, as shown later, one degree of freedom is lost from the error term for each covariate used. This results in a larger critical value for the $F$ test and makes it a bit more difficult to find a significant $F$ test statistic. This is the major cost of using a covariate. If the covariate is not effective in reducing error variance, then we are worse off than if we had ignored the covariate. Importance references on ANCOVA include Elashoff (1969) and Huitema (1980).

## 14.2 THE LAYOUT OF THE DATA

Before we get into the theory and subsequent analysis of the data, let us examine the layout of the data. We designate each observation on the dependent or criterion variable as $Y_{ij}$, where the $j$ subscript tells us what group or level the observation belongs to and the $i$ subscript tells us the observation or identification number within that group. The first subscript ranges over $i = 1, ..., n_j$ and the second subscript ranges over $j = 1, ..., J$. Thus there are $J$ levels of the independent variable and $n_j$ subjects in group $j$. We designate each observation on the covariate as $X_{ij}$, where the subscripts have the same meaning.

The layout of the data is shown in Table 14.1. Here we see that each pair of columns represents the observations for a particular group or level of the independent variable on the dependent variable and the covariate. At the bottom of the pair of columns for each group $j$ are the group means ($\overline{Y}_j, \overline{X}_j$). Although the table shows there are $n$ observations for each group, we need not make such a restriction, as this was done only for purposes of simplifying the table.

## 14.3 THE ANCOVA MODEL

The analysis of covariance model is a form of the general linear model much like the models shown in the last few chapters of this text. The one-factor ANCOVA fixed-effects model can be written in terms of population parameters as

$$Y_{ij} = \mu_Y + \alpha_j + \beta_w(X_{ij} - \mu_X) + \varepsilon_{ij}$$

where $Y_{ij}$ is the observed score on the dependent variable for individual $i$ in group $j$, $\mu_Y$ is the overall or grand population mean (i.e., regardless of group designation) for the dependent variable $Y$, $\alpha_j$ is the group effect for group $j$, $\beta_w$ is the within groups regression slope from the regression of $Y$ on $X$, $X_{ij}$ is the observed score on the covariate for individual $i$ in group $j$, $\mu_X$ is the overall or grand population mean (i.e., regardless of group designation) for the covariate $X$, and $\varepsilon_{ij}$ is the random residual error for individual $i$ in group $j$. The residual error can be due to individual differences, measurement error, and/or other factors not under investigation. As you would expect, the least squares sample estimators for each of these parameters are as follows: $\overline{Y}$ for $\mu_Y$, $\overline{X}$ for $\mu_X$, $a_j$ for $\alpha_j$, $b_w$ for $\beta_w$, and $e_{ij}$ for $\varepsilon_{ij}$. The sum of the group effects is equal to

**TABLE 14.1**
Layout for the One-Factor ANCOVA

| *Level of the Independent Variable* | | | | | | |
|---|---|---|---|---|---|---|
| *1* | | *2* | | ... | *J* | |
| $Y_{11}$ | $X_{11}$ | $Y_{12}$ | $X_{12}$ | ... | $Y_{1J}$ | $X_{1J}$ |
| $Y_{21}$ | $X_{21}$ | $Y_{22}$ | $X_{22}$ | ... | $Y_{2J}$ | $X_{2J}$ |
| ... | ... | ... | ... | ... | ... | ... |
| $Y_{n1}$ | $X_{n1}$ | $Y_{n2}$ | $X_{n2}$ | ... | $Y_{nJ}$ | $X_{nJ}$ |
| $\overline{Y}_{.1}$ | $\overline{X}_{.1}$ | $\overline{Y}_{.2}$ | $\overline{X}_{.2}$ | ... | $\overline{Y}_{.J}$ | $\overline{X}_{.J}$ |

zero. This implies that if there are any nonzero group effects, then the group effects will balance out around zero with some positive and some negative effects.

The hypotheses consist of testing the equality of the adjusted means (defined by $\mu'_{.j}$ and discussed later) as follows:

$$H_0: \mu'_{.1} = \mu'_{.2} = ... = \mu'_{.J}$$

$$H_1: \text{not all the } \mu'_{.j} \text{ are equal}$$

## 14.4   THE ANCOVA SUMMARY TABLE

We turn our attention to the familiar summary table, this time for the one-factor ANCOVA model. A general form of the summary table is shown in Table 14.2. Under the first column you see the following sources: adjusted between groups variation, adjusted within groups variation, variation due to the covariate, and total variation. The second column notes the sums of squares terms for each source (i.e., $SS_{betw(adj)}$, $SS_{with(adj)}$, $SS_{cov}$, and $SS_{total}$).

The third column gives the degrees of freedom for each source. For the adjusted between groups source, because there are $J$ group means, the $df_{betw(adj)}$ is $J - 1$, the same as in the one-factor ANOVA model. For the adjusted within groups source, because there are $N$ total observations and $J$ groups, we would expect the degrees of freedom within to be $N - J$, because this was the case in the one-factor ANOVA model. However, as we pointed out in the characteristics of the ANCOVA model, a price is paid for the use of a covariate. There is a price here because we lose one degree of freedom from the within term for the covariate, so that $df_{with(adj)}$ is $N - J - 1$. For multiple covariates, we lose one degree of freedom for each covariate used (see later discussion). This degree of freedom has gone to the covariate source such that $df_{cov}$ is equal to 1. Finally, for the total source, because there are $N$ total observations, the $df_{total}$ is the usual $N - 1$.

The fourth column gives the mean squares for each source of variation. As always, the mean squares represent the sum of squares weighted by their respective degrees of freedom. Thus $MS_{betw(adj)} = SS_{betw(adj)}/(J - 1)$, $MS_{with(adj)} = SS_{with(adj)}/(N - J - 1)$, and $MS_{cov} = SS_{cov}/1$. The last column in the ANCOVA summary table is for the $F$ values. Thus for the one-factor fixed-effects ANCOVA model, the $F$ value to test for differences between the adjusted means is computed as $F = MS_{betw(adj)}/MS_{with(adj)}$. A second $F$ value, which is obviously not included in the ANOVA model, is the test of the covariate. To be specific, this $F$ is actually testing the

**TABLE 14.2**
One-Factor Analysis of Covariance Summary Table

| Source | SS | df | MS | F |
|--------|-----|------|------|-----|
| Adjusted between | $SS_{betw(adj)}$ | $J - 1$ | $MS_{betw(adj)}$ | $MS_{betw(adj)}/MS_{with(adj)}$ |
| Adjusted within | $SS_{with(adj)}$ | $N - J - 1$ | $MS_{with(adj)}$ | |
| Covariate | $SS_{cov}$ | 1 | $MS_{cov}$ | $MS_{cov}/MS_{with(adj)}$ |
| Total | $SS_{total}$ | $N - 1$ | | |

hypothesis of $H_0$: $\beta_w = 0$. If the slope is equal to zero, then the covariate and the dependent variable are uncorrelated. This $F$ value is equal to $F = MS_{cov}/MS_{with(adj)}$.

The critical value for the test of difference between the adjusted means is $_\alpha F_{J-1,N-J-1}$. The critical value for the test of the covariate is $_\alpha F_{1,N-J-1}$. The null hypotheses in each case are rejected if the $F$ test statistic exceeds the $F$ critical value. The critical values are found in the $F$ table of Appendix Table 4.

If the $F$ test statistic for the adjusted means exceeds the $F$ critical value, and there are more than two groups, then it is not clear exactly how the means are different. In this case, some multiple comparison procedure may be used to determine where the mean differences are (see later discussion). For the test of the covariate (or within groups regression slope), we hope that the $F$ test statistic does exceed the $F$ critical value. Otherwise the power and precision of the test of the adjusted means in ANCOVA will be lower than the test of the unadjusted means in ANOVA because the covariate is not significantly related to the dependent variable.

## 14.5  PARTITIONING THE SUMS OF SQUARES

As seen already, the partitioning of the sums of squares is the backbone of all general linear models, whether we are dealing with an ANOVA model, a linear regression model, or an ANCOVA model. As always, the first step is to partition the total variation into its relevant sources of variation. As we have learned from the previous section, the sources of variation for the one-factor ANCOVA model are adjusted between groups, adjusted within groups, and the covariate. This is written as

$$SS_{total} = SS_{betw(adj)} + SS_{with(adj)} + SS_{cov}$$

From this point the statistical software is used to handle the remaining computations.

## 14.6  ADJUSTED MEANS AND RELATED PROCEDURES

In this section we formally define the adjusted mean, briefly examine several multiple comparison procedures, and consider power, confidence intervals, and effect size measures.

We have spent considerable time already discussing the analysis of the adjusted means. Now it is time to define them. The adjusted mean is denoted by $\overline{Y}'_{.j}$ and estimated by

$$\overline{Y}'_{.j} = \overline{Y}_{.j} - b_w (\overline{X}_{.j} - \overline{X}_{..})$$

Here it should be noted that the adjusted mean is equal to the unadjusted mean minus the adjustment. The adjustment is a function of the within groups regression slope and the difference between the group mean and the overall mean for the covariate. No adjustment will be made if (a) $b_w = 0$ (i.e., $X$ and $Y$ are unrelated), or (b) the group means on the covariate are all the same. Thus, in both of these cases $\overline{Y}_{.j} = \overline{Y}'_{.j}$. In all other cases, at least some adjustment will be made for some of the group means (although not necessarily for all of the group means).

You may be wondering how this adjustment actually works. Let us assume the covariate and the dependent variable are positively correlated such that $b_w$ is also positive, and there are two treatment groups with equal $n$'s that differ on the covariate. If Group 1 has a higher mean on both the covariate and the dependent variable than Group 2, then the adjusted means will be closer together than the unadjusted means. For our first example, if $b_w = 1$, $\overline{Y}_{.1} = 50$, $\overline{Y}_{.2} = 30$, $\overline{X}_{.1} = 20$, $\overline{X}_{.2} = 10$, $\overline{X}_{..} = 15$, then the adjusted means are equal to the following:

$$\overline{Y}'_{.1} = \overline{Y}_{.1} - b_w(\overline{X}_{.1} - \overline{X}_{..}) = 50 - 1(20 - 15) = 45$$

$$\overline{Y}'_{.2} = \overline{Y}_{.2} - b_w(\overline{X}_{.2} - \overline{X}_{..}) = 30 - 1(10 - 15) = 35$$

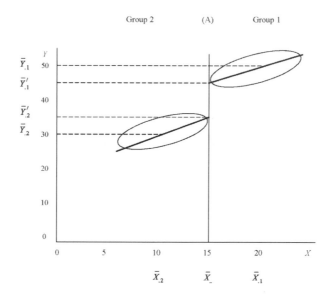

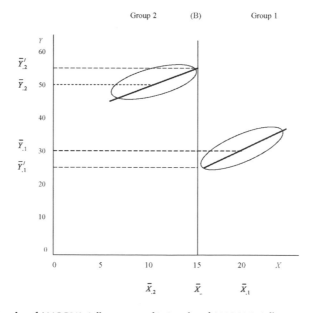

**FIG. 14.1**    **(a) Graphs of ANCOVA Adjustments. (b) Graphs of ANCOVA Adjustments.**

This is shown graphically in Fig. 14.1(a). In looking at the covariate $X$, we see that Group 1 has a higher mean ($\overline{X}_{.1} = 20$) than Group 2 ($\overline{X}_{.2} = 10$) by 10 points. The vertical line represents the overall mean on the covariate ($\overline{X}_{..} = 15$). In looking at the dependent variable $Y$, we see that Group 1 has a higher mean ($\overline{Y}_{.1} = 50$) than Group 2 ($\overline{Y}_{.2} = 30$) by 20 points. The diagonal lines represent the regression lines for each group with $b_w = 1.0$. The points at which the regression lines intersect (or cross) the vertical line ($\overline{X}_{..} = 15$) represent on the $Y$ scale the values of the adjusted means. Here we see that the adjusted mean for Group 1 ($\overline{Y}'_1 = 45$) is larger than the adjusted mean for Group 2 ($\overline{Y}'_2 = 35$) by 10 points. Thus, because of the preexisting difference on the covariate, the adjusted means here are somewhat closer together than the unadjusted means (10 points vs. 20 points, respectively).

If Group 1 has a higher mean on the covariate and a lower mean on the dependent variable than Group 2, then the adjusted means will be further apart than the unadjusted means. As a second example, if $b_w = 1$, $\overline{Y}_{.1} = 30$, $\overline{Y}_{.2} = 50$, $\overline{X}_{.1} = 20$, $\overline{X}_{.2} = 10$, $\overline{X}_{..} = 15$, then the adjusted means are

$$\overline{Y}'_1 = \overline{Y}_{.1} - b_w(\overline{X}_{.1} - \overline{X}_{..}) = 30 - 1(20 - 15) = 25$$
$$\overline{Y}'_2 = \overline{Y}_{.2} - b_w(\overline{X}_{.2} - \overline{X}_{..}) = 50 - 1(10 - 15) = 55$$

This is shown graphically in Fig. 14.1(b) where the unadjusted means differ by 20 points and the adjusted means differ by 30 points. There are obviously other possible situations.

Let us briefly examine multiple comparison procedures (MCPs) for use in the analysis of covariance situation. Most of the procedures described in chapter 12 can be adapted for use with a covariate, although a few procedures are not mentioned here as critical values do not currently exist. The adapted procedures involve a different form of the standard error of a contrast. The contrasts are formed based on adjusted means, of course. Let me briefly outline just a few procedures. Each of the test statistics has as its numerator the contrast $\psi'$, such as $\psi' = \overline{Y}'_1 - \overline{Y}'_2$. The standard errors do differ somewhat depending on the specific MCP.

The example procedures briefly described here are easily translated from the ANOVA into the ANCOVA context. Dunn's (or Bonferroni) method is appropriate to use for a small number of planned contrasts (still utilizing the critical values from Appendix Table 8). Scheffe's procedure can be used for unplanned complex contrasts with equal group variances (again based on the $F$ table in Appendix Table 4). Tukey's HSD test is most desirous for unplanned pairwise contrasts with equal $n$'s per group. There has been some discussion in the literature about the appropriateness of this test in ANCOVA. Most statisticians currently argue that the procedure is only appropriate when the covariate is fixed, when in fact it is almost always random. As a result the Bryant-Paulson (1976) generalization of the Tukey procedure has been developed for the random covariate case. The test statistic is compared to the critical value $_\alpha q_{X, df(\text{error}), J}$ taken from Appendix Table 11, where $X$ is the number of covariates. If the group sizes are unequal, the harmonic mean can be used in ANCOVA (Huitema, 1980). A generalization of the Tukey-Bryant procedure for unequal $n$'s ANCOVA was developed by Hochberg and Varon-Salomon (1984) (also see Hochberg & Tamhane, 1987; Miller, 1997).

Finally a comment about power, confidence intervals, and effect size measures for the one-factor ANCOVA model. In short, these procedures work the same as in the one factor-ANOVA model, except that they are based on adjusted means (Cohen, 1988). Nothing more than that.

## 14.7    ASSUMPTIONS AND VIOLATION OF ASSUMPTIONS

The introduction of a covariate requires several assumptions beyond the traditional ANOVA assumptions. For the familiar assumptions, the discussion is kept to a minimum as these have already been described in chapters 11 and 13. The new assumptions are as follows: (a) linearity, (b) independence of the covariate and the independent variable, (c) the covariate is measured without error, and (d) homogeneity of the regression slopes. In this section, we describe each assumption, how each assumption can be evaluated, the effects that a violation of the assumption might have, and how one might deal with a serious violation.

### 14.7.1    Independence

As in previous ANOVA models, in ANCOVA it is assumed that each sample is randomly drawn from their respective populations and observations are independent of one another (both within and across samples). The use of independent random samples is also crucial in the analysis of covariance. The $F$ ratio is very sensitive to violation of the independence assumption in terms of increased likelihood of a Type I and/or Type II error. A violation of the independence assumption may affect the standard errors of the sample adjusted means and thus influence any inferences made about those means. One purpose of random assignment of individuals to groups is to achieve independence. If each individual is only observed once and individuals are randomly assigned to groups, then the independence assumption is usually met. Random assignment is important for valid interpretation of the $F$ test and of multiple comparison procedures. Otherwise, the $F$ test and adjusted means may be biased.

The simplest procedure for assessing independence is to examine residual plots by group. If the independence assumption is satisfied, then the residuals should fall into a random display of points. If the assumption is violated, then the residuals will fall into some type of cyclical pattern. As discussed in chapter 11, the Durbin-Watson statistic (1950, 1951, 1971) can be used to test for autocorrelation. Violations of the independence assumption generally occur in the three situations we mentioned in chapter 11: time series data, observations within blocks, or replication. For severe violations of the independence assumption, there is no simple "fix" such as the use of transformations or nonparametric tests (see Scariana & Davenport, 1987).

### 14.7.2    Homogeneity of Variance

The second assumption is that the variances of each population are the same, the homogeneity of variance assumption. A violation of the homogeneity assumption may lead to bias in the $SS_{with}$ term, as well as an increase in the Type I error rate and possibly an increase in the Type II error rate. A summary of Monte Carlo research on ANCOVA assumption violations by Harwell (2003) indicates that the effect of the violation is negligible with equal or nearly equal $n$'s across the groups. There is a more serious problem if the larger $n$'s are associated with the smaller variances (actual $\alpha$ > nominal $\alpha$, which is a liberal result), or if the larger $n$'s are associated with the larger variances (actual $\alpha$ < nominal $\alpha$, which is a conservative result).

In a plot of $Y$ versus the covariate $X$ for each group, the variability of the distributions may be examined. Another method for detecting violation of the homogeneity assumption is the use of formal statistical tests, as discussed in chapter 11. Several solutions are available for dealing with a violation of the homogeneity assumption. These include the use of variance stabilizing transformations, or other ANCOVA models that are less sensitive to unequal variances, such as nonparametric ANCOVA procedures (described at the end of this chapter).

### 14.7.3 Normality

The third assumption is that each of the populations follows the normal distribution. Based on the classic work by Box and Anderson (1962) and Atiqullah (1964), as well as the summarization of modern Monte Carlo work by Harwell (2003), the $F$ test is relatively robust to nonnormal $Y$ distributions, "minimizing the role of a normally distributed $X$" (Harwell, 2003, p. 62). Thus we need only really be concerned with serious nonnormality.

The following graphical techniques can be used to detect violation of the normality assumption: (a) frequency distributions (such as stem-and-leaf plots, box plots, or histograms), or (b) normal probability plots. There are also several statistical procedures available for the detection of nonnormality (such as the Shapiro-Wilk test, 1965). Transformations can also be used to normalize the data, as previously discussed in chapter 11. In addition, one can use one of the rank ANCOVA procedures previously mentioned.

### 14.7.4 Linearity

The next assumption holds that the regression of $Y$ on $X$ is linear. If the relationship between $X$ and $Y$ is not linear, the use of the usual ANCOVA procedure is not appropriate, just as linear regression (see chapter 17) would not be appropriate. In ANCOVA (and correlation and linear regression), we fit a straight line to the data points. When the relationship is nonlinear, a straight line will not fit the data particularly well. In addition, the magnitude of the linear correlation will be smaller. If the relationship is not linear, the estimate of the group effects will be biased, and the adjustments made in $SS_{with}$ and $SS_{betw}$ will be smaller.

Violations of the linearity assumption can generally be detected by looking at plots of $Y$ versus $X$, overall and for each group. Once a serious violation of the linearity assumption has been detected, there are two alternatives that one can use, transformations and nonlinear ANCOVA. Transformations on one or both variables can be used to achieve linearity (Keppel & Wickens, 2004). The second option is to use nonlinear ANCOVA methods as described by Huitema (1980) and Keppel and Wickens (2004).

### 14.7.5 Fixed Independent Variable

The fifth assumption states that the levels of the independent variable are fixed by the researcher. This results in a fixed-effects model rather than a random-effects model. As in the one-factor ANOVA model, the one-factor ANCOVA model is the same computationally in the fixed- and random-effects cases. The summary of Monte Carlo research by Harwell (2003) indicates that the impact of a random-effect on the $F$ test is minimal.

### 14.7.6    Independence of the Covariate and the Independent Variable

A condition of the ANCOVA model (although not an assumption) requires that the covariate and the independent variable be independent. That is, the covariate is not influenced by the independent or treatment variable. If the covariate is affected by the treatment itself, then the use of the covariate in the analysis either (a) may remove part of the treatment effect or produce a spurious (inflated) treatment effect, or (b) may alter the covariate scores as a result of the treatment being administered prior to obtaining the covariate data. The obvious solution to this potential problem is to obtain the covariate scores prior to the administration of the treatment. In other words, be alert prior to the study for possible covariate candidates.

Let us consider an example where this condition is obviously violated. A psychologist is interested in which of several hypnosis treatments is most successful in reducing or eliminating cigarette smoking. A group of heavy smokers is randomly assigned to the hypnosis treatments. After the treatments have been completed, the researcher suspects that some patients are more susceptible to hypnosis (i.e., more suggestible) than others. By using suggestibility as a covariate, the researcher would not be able to determine whether group differences were a result of hypnosis treatment, suggestibility, or some combination. Thus, the measurement of suggestibility after the hypnosis treatments have been administered would be ill-advised. An extended discussion of this condition is given in Maxwell and Delaney (1990).

### 14.7.7    Covariate Measured Without Error

An assumption that we have not yet encountered in this text purports that the covariate is measured without error. This is of special concern in education and the behavioral sciences where variables are often measured with considerable measurement error. In randomized experiments, $b_w$ will be underestimated so that less of the covariate effect is removed from the dependent variable (i.e., the adjustments will be smaller). In addition, the reduction in the unexplained variation will not be as great and the $F$ test will not be as powerful. The $F$ test is generally conservative in terms of Type I error (the actual $\alpha$ will be less than the nominal $\alpha$). However, the treatment effects will not be biased. In quasi-experimental designs, $b_w$ will also be underestimated with similar effects. However, the treatment effects may be seriously biased. A method by Porter (1967) is suggested for this situation.

There is considerable discussion about the effects of measurement error (e.g., Cohen & Cohen, 1983; Huitema, 1980; Keppel & Wickens, 2004; Lord, 1960, 1967, 1969; Mickey, Dunn, & Clark, 2004; Pedhazur, 1997; Porter, 1967; Reichardt, 1979; Weisberg, 1979). Obvious violations of this assumption can be detected by computing the reliability of the covariate prior to the study or from previous research. This is the minimum that should be done. One may also want to consider the validity of the covariate as well, where validity may be defined as the extent to which an instrument measures what it was intended to measure.

### 14.7.8    Homogeneity of Regression Slopes

The final assumption puts forth that the slopes of the regression lines are the same for each group. Here we assume that $\beta_1 = \beta_2 = \ldots = \beta_J$. This is an important assumption because it allows us to use $b_w$, the sample estimator of $\beta_w$, as the within groups regression slope. Assuming that the group slopes are parallel allows us to test for group intercept differences, which is all we are really doing when we test for differences among the adjusted means. Without this assumption, groups can differ on both the regression slope and intercept, and $\beta_w$ cannot legitimately be used. If the slopes differ, then the regression lines interact in some way. As a result the size of the group differences in $Y$ will depend on the value of $X$. For example, Treatment 1 may be most effective for low values of the covariate, Treatment 2 may be most effective for middle values of the covariate, and Treatment 3 may be most effective for high values of the covariate. Thus, we do not have constant differences between the groups across the values of the covariate. A straightforward interpretation is not possible, which is the same situation in factorial ANOVA when the interaction between factor A and factor B is found to be significant. Thus unequal slopes in ANCOVA represent a type of interaction.

There are other potential outcomes if this assumption is violated. Without homogeneous regression slopes, the use of $\beta_w$ can yield biased adjusted means and can affect the $F$ test. Earlier simulation studies by Peckham (1968) and Glass, Peckham and Sanders (1972) suggests that for the one-factor fixed-effects model the effects will be minimal. Later analytical research by Rogosa (1980) suggests that there is little effect on the $F$ test for balanced designs with equal variances, but is less robust for mild heterogeneity. However, a summary of modern Monte Carlo work by Harwell (2003) indicates that the effect of slope heterogeneity on the $F$ test is (a) negligible with equal $n$'s and equal covariate means (randomized studies), (b) modest with equal $n$'s and unequal covariate means (non-randomized studies), and (c) modest with unequal $n$'s.

A formal statistical procedure is often conducted to test for homogeneity of slopes using statistical software such as SPSS (discussed later in this chapter), although the eyeball method (i.e., see if the slopes look about the same) can be a good starting point. Some alternative tests for equality of slopes when the variances are unequal is provided by Tabatabai and Tan (1985).

Several alternatives are available if the homogeneity of slopes assumption is violated. The first is to use the concomitant variable, not as a covariate, but as a blocking variable. This will work because this assumption is not made for the randomized block design (see chap. 16). A second option, and not a very desirable one, is to analyze each group separately with its own slope or subsets of the groups having equal slopes. A third possibility is to use interaction terms between the covariate and the independent variable and conduct a regression analysis (see Agresti & Finlay, 1986). A fourth option is to use the Johnson-Neyman (1936) technique, whose purpose is to determine the values of $X$ that are related to significant group differences on $Y$. This procedure is beyond the scope of this text, and the interested reader is referred to Huitema (1980) or Wilcox (1987). A fifth option is use more modern robust methods (e.g., Maxwell & Delaney, 1990; Wilcox, 2003).

A summary of the ANCOVA assumptions is presented in Table 14.3.

## 14.8   AN EXAMPLE

Consider the following illustration of what we have covered in this chapter. Our dependent variable is the score on a statistics quiz (with a maximum possible score of 6), the covariate is the score on an aptitude test for statistics taken at the beginning of the course (with a maximum possible score of 10), and the independent variable is the section of statistics taken (where Group

**TABLE 14.3**

Assumptions and Effects of Violations—One-Factor ANCOVA

| Assumption | Effect of Assumption Violation |
|---|---|
| 1. Independence | Increased likelihood of a Type I and/or Type II error in $F$; affects standard errors of means and inferences about those means. |
| 2. Homogeneity of variance | Bias in $SS_{with}$; increased likelihood of a Type I and/or Type II error; negligible effect with equal or nearly equal $n$'s; otherwise more serious problem if the larger $n$'s are associated with the smaller variances (increased $\alpha$) or larger variances (decreased $\alpha$). |
| 3. Normality | $F$ test relatively robust to nonnormal $Y$, minimizing the role of nonnormal $X$. |
| 4. Linearity | Reduced magnitude of $r_{XY}$; straight line will not fit data well; estimate of group effects biased; adjustments made in $SS$ smaller. |
| 5. Fixed-effect | Minimal impact. |
| 6. Independence of covariate and independent variable | May reduce or increase group effects; may alter covariate scores. |
| 7. Covariate measured without error | True experiment: $b_w$ underestimated; adjustments smaller; reduction in unexplained variation smaller; $F$ less powerful; reduced likelihood of Type I error. |
|  | Quasi-experiment: $b_w$ underestimated; adjustments smaller; group effects seriously biased. |
| 8. Homogeneity of slopes | Negligible effect with equal $n$'s in true experiment; modest effect with equal $n$'s in quasi-experiment; modest effect with unequal $n$'s. |

1 receives the traditional lecture method and Group 2 receives the modern innovative method). Thus the researcher is interested in whether the method of instruction influences student performance in statistics, controlling for statistics aptitude (assume we have developed a measure that is relatively error-free). Students are randomly assigned to one of the two groups at the beginning of the semester when the measure of statistics aptitude is administered. There are 6 students in each group for a total of 12. The layout of the data is shown in Table 14.4, where we see the data and sample statistics (means, variances, slopes, and correlations).

The results are summarized in the ANCOVA summary table as shown in the top panel of Table 14.5. The ANCOVA test statistics are compared to the critical value $_{.05}F_{1,9} = 5.12$ obtained from Appendix Table 4, using the .05 level of significance. Both test statistics exceed the critical value, so we reject $H_0$ in each case. We conclude that the quiz score means do differ for the two statistics groups when adjusted for aptitude in statistics, and the slope of the regression of $Y$ on $X$ is significantly different from zero (i.e., the test of the covariate). Just to be complete, the results for the analysis of variance on $Y$ are shown in the bottom panel of Table 14.5. We see that in the analysis of the unadjusted means (i.e., the ANOVA), there is no significant group difference. Thus the adjustment yielded a different statistical result. The covariate also "did its thing" in that a reduction in $MS_{with}$ resulted due to the strong relationship between the covariate and the dependent variable (i.e., $r_{XY} = 0.7203$ overall).

**TABLE 14.4**
Data and Summary Statistics for the Statistics Instruction Example

| Statistic | Group 1 | | Group 2 | | Overall | |
|---|---|---|---|---|---|---|
| | Quiz (Y) | Aptitude (X) | Quiz (Y) | Aptitude (X) | Quiz (Y) | Aptitude (X) |
| | 1 | 4 | 1 | 1 | | |
| | 2 | 3 | 2 | 3 | | |
| | 3 | 5 | 4 | 2 | | |
| | 4 | 6 | 5 | 4 | | |
| | 5 | 7 | 6 | 5 | | |
| | 6 | 9 | 6 | 7 | | |
| Means | 3.5000 | 5.6667 | 4.0000 | 3.6667 | 3.7500 | 4.6667 |
| Variances | 3.5000 | 4.6667 | 4.4000 | 4.6667 | 3.6591 | 5.3333 |
| $b_{YX}$ | 0.8143 | | 0.8143 | | 0.5966 | |
| $r_{XY}$ | 0.9403 | | 0.8386 | | 0.7203 | |
| Adjusted means | 2.6857 | | 4.8143 | | | |

**TABLE 14.5**
One-Factor ANCOVA and ANOVA Summary Tables—Statistics Instruction Example

| Source | SS | df | MS | F |
|---|---|---|---|---|
| ANCOVA | | | | |
|   Adjusted between | 10.8127 | 1 | 10.8127 | 11.3734* |
|   Adjusted within | 8.5560 | 9 | 0.9507 | |
|   Covariate | 20.8813 | 1 | 20.8813 | 21.9641* |
|   Total | 40.2500 | 11 | | |
| ANOVA | | | | |
|   Between | 0.7500 | 1 | 0.7500 | 0.1899** |
|   Within | 39.5000 | 10 | 3.9500 | |
|   Total | 40.2500 | 11 | | |

* $_{.05}F_{1,9} = 5.12$
** $_{.05}F_{1,10} = 4.96$

Let us next examine the adjusted means, as shown in Table 14.4. Here we see that with the unadjusted means, there is a 0.5000 point difference in favor of Group 2, whereas for the adjusted means there is a 2.1286 point difference in favor of Group 2. In other words, the adjustment in this case resulted in a greater difference between the adjusted means than between the unadjusted means. Since there are only two groups, a multiple comparison procedure is unnecessary (although we consider this in the SPSS section).

## 14.9   ANCOVA WITHOUT RANDOMIZATION

There is a great deal of discussion and controversy, particularly in education and the behavioral sciences, about the use of the analysis of covariance in situations where randomization is not conducted. **Randomization** is defined as an experiment where individuals are randomly assigned to groups (or cells in a factorial design). In the Campbell and Stanley (1966) system of experimental design, these designs are known as **true experiments**.

In certain situations, randomization either has not occurred or is not possible due to the circumstances. The best example is the situation where there are **intact groups**, which are groups that have been formed prior to the researcher arriving on the scene. Either the researcher chooses not to randomly assign these individuals to groups through a reassignment (e.g., it is just easier to keep the groups in their current form) or the researcher cannot randomly assign them (legally, ethically, or otherwise). When randomization does not occur, the resulting designs are known as **quasi-experimental**. For instance, in classroom research the researcher is almost never able to come into a school district and randomly assign students to groups. Once students are given their classroom assignments at the beginning of the year, that is that. On occasion, the researcher might be able to pull a few students out of several classrooms, randomly assign them to groups, and conduct a true experiment. In general, this is possible only on a very small scale and for short periods of time.

Let me briefly consider the issues here as not all statisticians agree. In true experiments (i.e., with randomization), there is no cause for concern (except for dealing with the statistical assumptions). The analysis of covariance is more powerful and has greater precision for true experiments than for quasi-experiments. So if you have a choice, go with a true experimental situation (which is a big if). In a true experiment, the probability that the groups differ on the covariate or any other concomitant variable is equal to $\alpha$. That is, the likelihood that the group means will be different on the covariate is small, and thus the adjustment in the group means may be small. The payoff is in the possibility that the error term will be greatly reduced.

In quasi-experiments, there are several possible causes for concern. Although this is the situation where the researcher needs the most help, this is also the situation where less help is available. Here it is more likely that there will be significant differences among the group means on the covariate. Thus the adjustment in the group means can be substantial (assuming that $b_w$ is different from zero). Because there are significant mean differences on the covariate, any of the following may occur: (a) it is likely that the groups may be different on other important characteristics as well, which have not been controlled for either statistically or experimentally; (b) the homogeneity of regression slopes assumption is less likely to be met; (c) adjusting for the covariate may remove part of the treatment effect; (d) equating groups on the covariate may be an extrapolation beyond the range of possible values that occur for a particular group (e.g., see the examples by Lord, 1967, 1969, on trying to equate men and women, or by Ferguson & Takane, 1989, on trying to equate mice and elephants; these groups should not be equated on the covariate because their distributions on the covariate do not overlap); (e) although the slopes may be equal for the range of $X$'s obtained, when extrapolating beyond the range of scores the slopes may not be equal; (f) the standard errors of the adjusted means may increase, making tests of the adjusted means not significant; and (g) there may be differential growth in the groups confounding the results (e.g., adult vs. child groups). Although one should be cautious about the use of ANCOVA in quasi-experiments, this is not to suggest that ANCOVA should never be used in such situations. Just be extra careful and do not go too far in terms of interpreting your results. If at all possible, replicate your study. For further discussion see Huitema (1980), or Porter and Raudenbush (1987).

## 14.10   MORE COMPLEX ANCOVA MODELS

The one-factor ANCOVA model can be extended to more complex models in much the same way as we expanded the one-factor ANOVA model. Thus one can evaluate ANCOVA designs that involve any of the following characteristics: (a) factorial designs (i.e., having more than one factor); (b) fixed-, random- and mixed-effects designs; (c) repeated measures and split-plot (mixed) designs; (d) hierarchical designs; and (e) randomized block designs. Conceptually there is nothing new for these types of ANCOVA designs, and you should have no trouble getting a statistical package to do such analyses. For further information on these designs see Huitema (1980), Keppel (1982), Kirk (1982), Myers and Well (1995), Page, Braver and MacKinnon (2003), or Keppel and Wickens (2004). One can also utilize multiple covariates in an analysis of covariance design; for further information see Huitema (1980), Kirk (1982), Myers and Well (1995), Page, Braver and MacKinnon (2003), or Keppel and Wickens (2004).

## 14.11   NONPARAMETRIC ANCOVA PROCEDURES

In situations where the assumptions of normality, homogeneity of variance, and/or linearity have been seriously violated, one alternative is to consider nonparametric ANCOVA procedures. Some rank ANCOVA procedures have been proposed by Quade (1967), Puri and Sen (1969), Conover and Iman (1982), and Rutherford (1992). For a description of such procedures, see these references as well as Huitema (1980), Harwell (2003), or Wilcox (2003).

## 14.12   SPSS

Finally we consider SPSS for the statistics instruction example, including an APA paragraph of the results. As noted in previous chapters, SPSS needs the data to be in a specific form for the analysis to proceed, which is different from the layout of the data in Table 14.1. For a one-factor ANCOVA with a single covariate, the dataset must contain three variables or columns, one for the level of the factor or independent variable, one for the covariate, and a third for the dependent variable. Each row still represents one individual, displaying the level of the factor they are a member of, as well as their scores on the covariate and dependent variables.

   To conduct an ANCOVA through the GLM module, go to the "Analyze" pulldown, into "General Linear Model," and then into the "Univariate" procedure. Click the dependent variable (e.g., quiz) into the "Dependent Variable" box, click the fixed-effects factor variable (e.g., group) into the "Fixed Factor(s)" box, and click the covariate (e.g., aptitude) into the "Covariate(s)" box. Click on the "Options" button to obtain such information as "Descriptive Statistics" (unadjusted means), "Estimates of effect size," "Observed power," and "Homogeneity tests." While there, move the listings in the "Factor(s) and Factor Interactions:" box into the "Display Means for:" box to generate adjusted means. Also check the box called "Compare Main Effects," then open the pulldown for "Confidence interval adjustment" to chose among the LSD, Bonferroni, or Sidak multiple comparison procedures of the adjusted means. Click on "Continue" to return to the original dialog box. Notice that the "Post Hoc" option button is not active, thus you are restricted to the three MCPs just mentioned. To obtain a profile plot of adjusted means, click on the "Plots" button, move the factor variable name into the "Horizontal Axis" box, click on "Add" to generate the plot, and finally click on "Continue" to return to the original dialog box. Finally, in order to generate the appropriate sources of variation and results as recommended in this chapter, you need to click on the "Model" button, then select "Type I" from the "Sum of squares" pulldown, and click on "Continue" to go back to the main dialog box. Then click on "OK" to run the analysis.

In order the test the homogeneity of slopes assumption, you will need to rerun the analysis. Keep every screen the same as before, with one exception. Return to the "Model" screen. Click on the "Custom" button to build a custom model to include the interaction between the independent and covariate variables. To do this, under the "Build Terms" pulldown, make sure that "Main effects" is showing. Click first the independent variable, then the covariate into the right-hand "Model" box using the arrow. Then change the "Build Terms" pulldown to "Interaction" and click both variables at the same time (e.g., using the shift key) into the righthand "Model" box. There should be three terms in that box, the interaction and two main effects. Then click "Continue" to return to the main screen and "OK" to generate the analysis.

Selected results are shown in the panels of Table 14.6. The top panel shows the ANCOVA summary table for the homogeneity of slopes test. Here the only thing that we care about is the test of the interaction, which we want to be nonsignificant. The middle panel shows the ANCOVA summary table for the main analysis, while the bottom panel displays the unadjusted means, the adjusted means (with confidence intervals), and the results of the Bonferroni test (with confidence intervals). From the summary tables I have again deleted additional sources of variation that I find not to be useful.

Finally we come to an example paragraph of the results for the statistics lab example. From the top panel of Table 14.6, we see that the interaction between the covariate and the independent variable is not significant, thus the homogeneity of slopes assumption has been satisfied. In the middel panel of the table, the slope is significantly different from zero ($F_{aptitude} = 21.961$, $df = 1,9$, $p = .001$), while the adjusted group effect is significant ($F_{group} = 11.372$, $df = 1,9$, $p = .008$) with a strong effect size and power (partial $\eta^2_{group} = .558$, observed power = .850). The bottom panel shows that while the unadjusted group mean was larger for the innovative instruction group by only .50, the adjusted mean for that group was larger by 2.128. Thus the use of the covariate resulted in a large significant difference between the instructional groups.

## 14.13  SUMMARY

In this chapter methods involving the comparison of adjusted group means for a single independent variable were considered. The chapter began with a look at the unique characteristics of the analysis of covariance, including: (a) statistical control through the use of a covariate; (b) the dependent variable means adjusted by the covariate; (c) the covariate used to reduce error variation; (d) the relationship between the covariate and the dependent variable taken into account in the adjustment; and (e) the covariate measured at least at the interval level. The layout of the data was shown, followed by an examination of the ANCOVA model, and the ANCOVA summary table. Next the estimation of the adjusted means was considered along with several different multiple comparison procedures. Some discussion was also devoted to the ANCOVA assumptions, their assessment, and how to deal with assumption violations. We illustrated the

TABLE 14.6
Selected SPSS Results for the Statistics Instruction Example

*Homogeneity of Slopes Test*

*Dependent Variable: quiz*

| Source | Type I Sum of Squares | df | Mean Square | F | Sig. | Partial Eta Squared | Observed Power[a] |
|---|---|---|---|---|---|---|---|
| group | .750 | 1 | .750 | .701 | .427 | .081 | .115 |
| aptitude | 30.943 | 1 | 30.943 | 28.928 | .001 | .783 | .997 |
| group* aptitude | .000 | 1 | .000 | .000 | 1.000 | .000 | .050 |
| Error | 8.557 | 8 | 1.070 | | | | |
| Corrected Total | 40.250 | 11 | | | | | |

[a]Computed using alpha = .05

*ANCOVA Summary Table*

*Dependent Variable: quiz*

| Source | Type I Sum of Squares | df | Mean Square | F | Sig. | Partial Eta Squared | Observed Power[a] |
|---|---|---|---|---|---|---|---|
| aptitude | 20.881 | 1 | 20.881 | 21.961 | .001 | .709 | .986 |
| group | 10.812 | 1 | 10.812 | 11.372 | .008 | .558 | .850 |
| Error | 8.557 | 9 | .951 | | | | |
| Corrected Total | 40.250 | 11 | | | | | |

[a]Computed using alpha = .05

*Descriptive Statistics (unadjusted means)*

*Dependent Variable: quiz*

| group | Mean | Std. Deviation | N |
|---|---|---|---|
| 1.00 | 3.5000 | 1.87083 | 6 |
| 2.00 | 4.0000 | 2.09762 | 6 |
| Total | 3.7500 | 1.91288 | 12 |

*Estimates (adjusted means)*

*Dependent Variable: quiz*

| | | | 95% Confidence Interval | |
|---|---|---|---|---|
| group | Mean | Std. Error | Lower Bound | Upper Bound |
| 1.00 | 2.686[a] | .423 | 1.729 | 3.642 |
| 2.00 | 4.814[a] | .423 | 3.858 | 5.771 |

[a]Covariates appearing in the model are evaluated at the following values: aptitude = 4.6667.

*(continued)*

TABLE 14.6 *(continued)*
Selected SPSS Results for the Statistics Instruction Example

*Pairwise Comparisons*

*Dependent Variable: quiz*

| | | Mean Difference | | | 95% Confidence Interval for Difference[a] | |
|---|---|---|---|---|---|---|
| *(I) group* | *(J) group* | *(I–J)* | *Std. Error* | *Sig.*[a] | *Lower Bound* | *Upper Bound* |
| 1.00 | 2.00 | −2.129* | .631 | .008 | −3.556 | −.701 |
| 2.00 | 1.00 | 2.129* | .631 | .008 | .701 | 3.556 |

Based on estimated marginal means

*The mean difference is significant at the .05 level.

[a]Adjustment for multiple comparisons: Bonferroni.

use of the analysis of covariance by looking at an example. Finally, we finished off the chapter by briefly examining (a) some cautions about the use of ANCOVA in situations without randomization; (b) ANCOVA for models having multiple factors and/or multiple covariates; (c) nonparametric ANCOVA procedures; and (d) SPSS. At this point you should have met the following objectives: (a) be able to understand the characteristics and concepts underlying ANCOVA, (b) be able to determine and interpret the results of ANCOVA, including adjusted means and multiple comparison procedures, and (c) be able to understand and evaluate the assumptions of ANCOVA. Chapter 15 goes beyond the fixed-effects models we have discussed thus far and considers random- and mixed-effects models.

## PROBLEMS

### Conceptual Problems

1. If the correlation between the covariate $X$ and the dependent variable $Y$ differs markedly in the two treatment groups, it seems likely that
   a. the assumption of normality is suspect.
   b. the assumption of parallel regression lines is suspect.
   c. a nonlinear relation exists between $X$ and $Y$.
   d. the adjusted means for $Y$ differ significantly.

2. If for both the treatment and control groups the correlation between the covariate $X$ and the dependent variable $Y$ is substantial but negative, the error variation for ANCOVA as compared to that for ANOVA is
   a. less.
   b. about the same.

    c.   greater.

    d.   unpredictably different.

3.    An experiment was conducted to compare three different instructional strategies. Fifteen subjects were included in each group. The same test was administered prior to and after the treatments. If both pretest and IQ are used as covariates, what is the degrees of freedom for the error term?

    a.   2

    b.   40

    c.   41

    d.   42

4.    The effects of a training program concerned with educating heart attack patients to the benefits of moderate exercise was examined. A group of recent heart attack patients was randomly divided into two groups; one group received the training program and the other did not. The dependent variable was the amount of time taken to jog three laps, with the weight of the patient after the program used as a covariate. Examination of the data after the study revealed that the covariate means of the two groups differed. Which of the following assumptions is most clearly violated?

    a.   linearity

    b.   homogeneity of regression coefficients

    c.   independence of the treatment and the covariate

    d.   normality

5.    In ANCOVA, the covariate is a variable which should have a

    a.   low positive correlation with the dependent variable.

    b.   high positive correlation with the independent variable.

    c.   high positive correlation with the dependent variable.

    d.   zero correlation with the dependent variable.

6.    In ANCOVA how will the correlation of zero between the covariate and the dependent variable appear?

    a.   unequal group means on the dependent variable.

    b.   unequal group means on the covariate.

    c.   regression of the dependent variable on the covariate with $b = 0$.

    d.   regression of the dependent variable on the covariate with $b = 1$.

7.    Which of the following is not a necessary requirement for using ANCOVA?

    a.   Covariate scores are not affected by the treatment.

    b.   There is a linear relationship between the covariate and the dependent variable.

    c.   The covariate variable is the same measure as the dependent variable.

    d.   Regression slopes for the groups are similar.

8.  Which of the following is the most desirable situation to use ANCOVA?

    a.  The slope of the regression line equals zero.

    b.  The variance of the dependent variable for a specific covariate score is relatively large.

    c.  The correlation between the covariate and the dependent variable is $-.95$.

    d.  The correlation between the covariate and the dependent variable is .60.

9.  A group of students was randomly assigned to one of three instructional strategies. Data from the study indicated an interaction between slope and treatment group. It seems likely that

    a.  the assumption of normality is suspect.

    b.  the assumption of homogeneity of regression lines is suspect.

    c.  a nonlinear relation exists between $X$ and $Y$.

    d.  the covariate is not independent of the treatment.

10. If the mean on the dependent variable GPA ($Y$) for persons of middle social class ($X$) is higher than for persons of lower and higher social classes, one would expect that

    a.  the relationship between $X$ and $Y$ is curvilinear.

    b.  the covariate $X$ contains substantial measurement error.

    c.  GPA is not normally distributed.

    d.  social class is not related to GPA.

11. If both the covariate and the dependent variable are assessed after the treatment has been concluded, and if both are affected by the treatment, the use of ANCOVA for these data would likely result in

    a.  an inflated $F$ ratio for the treatment effect.

    b.  an exaggerated difference in the adjusted means.

    c.  an underestimate of the treatment effect.

    d.  an inflated value of the correlation $r_w$.

12. When the covariate correlates $+.5$ with the dependent variable, I assert that the adjusted $MS_{with}$ from the ANCOVA will be less than the $MS_{with}$ from the ANOVA. Am I correct?

13. For each of two groups, the correlation between the covariate and the dependent variable is substantial, but negative in direction. I assert that the error variance for ANCOVA, as compared to that for ANOVA, is greater. Am I correct?

14. In ANCOVA, $X$ is known as a factor. True or false?

15. A study was conducted to compare 6 types of diets. Twelve subjects were included in each group. Their weights were taken prior to and after treatment. If pre-weight is used as a covariate, what is the degrees of freedom for the error term?

    a.   5

    b.   65

    c.   66

    d.   71

16.    A researcher conducts both a one-factor ANOVA and a one-factor ANCOVA on the same data. In comparing the adjusted group means to the unadjusted group means, they find that for each group, the adjusted mean is equal to the unadjusted mean. I assert that the researcher must have made a computational error. Am I correct?

17.    The correlation between the covariate and the dependent variable is zero. I assert that ANCOVA is still preferred over ANOVA. Am I correct?

18.    If there is a nonlinear relationship between the covariate $X$ and the dependent variable $Y$, then it is very likely that

    a.   there will be less reduction in $SS_{with}$.

    b.   the group effects will be biased.

    c.   the correlation between $X$ and $Y$ will be smaller in magnitude.

    d.   all of the above

## Computational Problems

1.    Consider the analysis of covariance situation where the dependent variable $Y$ is the posttest of an achievement test and the covariate $X$ is the pretest of the same test. Given the data that follow, where there are three groups, (a) calculate the adjusted $Y$ values assuming that $b_w = 1.00$, and (b) determine what effects the adjustment had on the posttest results.

| Group | $X$ | $\bar{X}$ | $Y$ | $\bar{Y}$ |
|-------|-----|-----------|-----|-----------|
| 1 | 40 | | 120 | |
| | 50 | 50 | 125 | 125 |
| | 60 | | 130 | |
| 2 | 70 | | 140 | |
| | 75 | 75 | 150 | 150 |
| | 80 | | 160 | |
| 3 | 90 | | 160 | |
| | 100 | 100 | 175 | 175 |
| | 110 | | 190 | |

2.    Below are four independent random samples (different methods of instruction) of paired values of the covariate IQ $(X)$ and the dependent variable essay score $(Y)$. Conduct an analysis of variance on $Y$, an analysis of covariance on $Y$ using $X$ as a covariate, and compare the results ($\alpha = .05$). Determine the unadjusted and adjusted means.

| Group 1 | | Group 2 | | Group 3 | | Group 4 | |
|---|---|---|---|---|---|---|---|
| X | Y | X | Y | X | Y | X | Y |
| 94 | 14 | 80 | 38 | 92 | 55 | 94 | 24 |
| 96 | 19 | 84 | 34 | 96 | 53 | 94 | 37 |
| 98 | 17 | 90 | 43 | 99 | 55 | 98 | 22 |
| 100 | 38 | 97 | 43 | 101 | 52 | 100 | 43 |
| 102 | 40 | 97 | 61 | 102 | 35 | 103 | 49 |
| 105 | 26 | 112 | 63 | 104 | 46 | 104 | 24 |
| 109 | 41 | 115 | 93 | 107 | 57 | 104 | 41 |
| 110 | 28 | 118 | 74 | 110 | 55 | 108 | 26 |
| 111 | 36 | 120 | 76 | 111 | 42 | 113 | 70 |
| 130 | 66 | 120 | 79 | 118 | 81 | 115 | 63 |

3.  A communication researcher wants to know which of five versions of commercials for a new television show is most effective in terms of viewing likelihood. Each commercial is viewed by 6 students. A one-factor ANCOVA was used to analyze these data where the covariate was amount of television viewed per week. Complete the ANCOVA summary table below ($\alpha = .05$).

| Source | SS | df | MS | F | Critical Value and Decision |
|---|---|---|---|---|---|
| Between adjusted | 96 | — | — | — | — |
| Within adjusted | 192 | — | — | | |
| Covariate | — | — | — | — | — |
| Total | 328 | — | | | |

## Interpretive Problem

For the interpretive problem you selected in chapter 11 (using the statistics survey CD dataset), select an appropriate covariate. Use SPSS to run a one-factor ANOVA, a one-factor ANCOVA, and then compare and contrast the results. Which method would you select and why?

# 15

# RANDOM- AND MIXED-EFFECTS ANALYSIS OF VARIANCE MODELS

## Chapter Outline

1. The one-factor random-effects model
   Characteristics of the model
   The ANOVA model
   ANOVA summary table
   Assumptions and violation of assumptions
   Multiple comparison procedures
2. The two-factor random-effects model
   Characteristics of the model
   The ANOVA model
   ANOVA summary table
   Assumptions and violation of assumptions
   Multiple comparison procedures
3. The two-factor mixed-effects model
   Characteristics of the model
   The ANOVA model
   ANOVA summary table
   Assumptions and violation of assumptions
   Multiple comparison procedures
4. The one-factor repeated measures design
   Characteristics of the model
   The layout of the data

The ANOVA model
Assumptions and violation of assumptions
ANOVA summary table
Multiple comparison procedures
Alternative ANOVA procedures
An example
5.    The two-factor split-plot or mixed design
Characteristics of the model
The layout of the data
The ANOVA model
Assumptions and violation of assumptions
ANOVA summary table
Multiple comparison procedures
An example
6.    SPSS

## Key Concepts

1.    Fixed-, random-, and mixed-effects models
2.    Repeated measures models
3.    Compound symmetry/sphericity assumption
4.    Friedman repeated measures test based on ranks
5.    Split-plot or mixed designs (i.e., both between and within subjects factors)

In this chapter we continue our discussion of the analysis of variance (ANOVA) by considering models in which there is a random-effects factor, previously discussed in chapter 11. These models include the one-factor and factorial designs, as well as repeated measures designs. As becomes evident, repeated measures designs are used when there is at least one factor where each individual is exposed to all levels of that factor. This factor is referred to as a **repeated factor**, for obvious reasons. This chapter is most concerned with one- and two-factor random-effects models, the two-factor mixed-effects model, and one- and two-factor repeated measures designs.

It should be noted that effect size measures, power, and confidence intervals can be determined in the same fashion for the models in this chapter as for previously described ANOVA models. The standard effect size measures already described are applicable (i.e., $\omega^2$ and $\eta^2$), although the intraclass correlation coefficient, $\rho_I$, can be utilized for random effects (similarly interpreted). For additional discussion of these issues in the context of this chapter, see Cohen (1988), Fidler and Thompson (2001), Keppel and Wickens (2004), Murphy and Myors (2004), and Wilcox (1996, 2003).

Many of the concepts used in this chapter are the same as those covered in chapters 11 through 14. In addition, the following new concepts are addressed: random- and mixed-effects factors, repeated measures factors, the compound symmetry/sphericity assumption, and mixed designs. Our objectives are that by the end of this chapter, you will be able to (a) understand the characteristics and concepts underlying random- and mixed-effects ANOVA models, (b) determine and interpret the results of random- and mixed-effects ANOVA models, and (c) understand and evaluate the assumptions of random- and mixed-effects ANOVA models.

## 15.1 THE ONE-FACTOR RANDOM-EFFECTS MODEL

This section describes the distinguishing characteristics of the one-factor random-effects ANOVA model, the linear model, the ANOVA summary table, assumptions and their violation, and multiple comparison procedures.

### 15.1.1 Characteristics of the Model

The characteristics of the one-factor fixed-effects ANOVA model have already been covered in chapter 11. These characteristics include (a) one factor (or independent variable) with two or more levels, (b) all levels of the factor of interest are included in the design (i.e., a fixed-effects factor), (c) subjects are randomly assigned to one level of the factor, and (d) the dependent variable is measured at least at the interval level. Thus the overall design is a fixed-effects model, where there is one factor and the individuals respond to only one level of the factor. If individuals respond to more than one level of the factor, then this is a repeated measures design, as shown later in this chapter.

The characteristics of the one-factor random-effects ANOVA model are the same with one obvious exception. This has to do with the selection of the levels of the factor. In the fixed-effects case, researchers select all of the levels of interest, because they are only interested in making generalizations (or inferences) about those particular levels. Thus in replications of the design, each replicate would use precisely the same levels. Examples of factors that are typically fixed include SES, gender, specific types of drug treatment, age group, weight, or marital status.

In the random-effects case, researchers randomly select levels from the population of levels, because they are interested in making generalizations (or inferences) about the entire population of levels, not merely those that have been sampled. Thus in replications of the design, each replicate need not have the same levels included. The concept of random selection of factor levels from the population of levels is the same as the random selection of subjects from the population. Here the researcher is making an inference from the sampled levels to the population of levels, instead of making an inference from the sample of individuals to the population of individuals. In a random-effects design then, a random sample of factor levels is selected in the same way as a random sample of individuals is selected.

For instance, a researcher interested in teacher effectiveness may have randomly sampled history teachers (i.e., the independent variable) from the population of history teachers in a particular school district. Generalizations can then be made about other history teachers in that school district not actually sampled. Other examples of factors that are typically random include randomly selected classrooms, types of medication, observers or raters, time (seconds, minutes, hours, days, weeks, etc.), animals, students, or schools. It should be noted that in educational settings, the random selection of schools, classes, teachers, and/or students is not often possible. Here we would need to consider such factors as fixed rather than random effects.

### 15.1.2  The ANOVA Model

The one-factor ANOVA random-effects model is written in terms of population parameters as

$$Y_{ij} = \mu + a_j + \varepsilon_{ij}$$

where $Y_{ij}$ is the observed score on the dependent variable for individual $i$ in level $j$ of factor A, $\mu$ is the overall or grand population mean, $a_j$ is the random effect for level $j$ of factor A, and $\varepsilon_{ij}$ is the random residual error for individual $i$ for level $j$. The residual error can be due to individual differences, measurement error, and/or other factors not under investigation. Note that we use $a_j$ to designate the random effects to differentiate them from $\alpha_j$ in the fixed-effects model.

Because the random-effects model consists of only a sample of the effects from the population, the sum of the sampled effects is not necessarily zero. For instance, we may select a sample having only positive effects (e.g., all very effective teachers). If the entire population of effects were examined, then the sum of these effects would indeed be zero.

For the one-factor random-effects ANOVA model, the hypotheses for testing the effect of factor A are

$$H_0: \sigma_a^2 = 0$$
$$H_1: \sigma_a^2 > 0$$

Recall for the one-factor fixed-effects ANOVA model that the hypotheses for testing the effect of factor A are

$$H_0: \mu_{.1} = \mu_{.2} = ... = \mu_{.J}$$
$$H_1: \text{not all the } \mu_{.j} \text{ are equal}$$

This reflects the difference in the inferences made in the random- and fixed-effects models. In the fixed-effects case the null hypothesis is about specific means, whereas in the random-effects case the null hypothesis is about variation among the population of means. As becomes evident, the difference in the models is also reflected in the multiple comparison procedures.

### 15.1.3  ANOVA Summary Table

Here there are very few differences between the one-factor random-effects and one-factor fixed-effects models. The sources of variation are still A (or between), within, and total. The sums of squares, degrees of freedom, mean squares, $F$ test statistic, and critical value are determined in the same way as in the fixed-effects case. Obviously then, the ANOVA summary table looks the same as well. Using the example from chapter 11, assuming the model is now a random-effects model, we again obtain a test statistic $F = 6.8177$, which is significant at the .05 level.

### 15.1.4 Assumptions and Violation of Assumptions

In chapter 11 we described the assumptions for the one-factor fixed-effects model. The assumptions are nearly the same for the one-factor random-effects model and we need not devote much attention to them here. In short, the assumptions are again concerned with the distribution of the dependent variable scores, specifically that scores are random and independent, coming from normally distributed populations with equal population variances. The effect of assumption violations and how to deal with them have been thoroughly discussed in chapter 11 (although see Wilcox, 1996, 2003, for alternative procedures when variances are unequal).

Additional assumptions must be made for the random-effects model. These assumptions deal with the effects for the levels of the independent variable, the $a_j$. First, here are a few words about the $a_j$. The random group effects $a_j$ are computed, in the population, by the following:

$$a_j = \mu_{.j} - \mu_{..}$$

For example, $a_3$ represents the effect for being a member of Group 3. If the overall mean $\mu_{..}$ is 60 and $\mu_{.3}$ is 100, then the group effect would be

$$a_3 = \mu_{.3} - \mu_{..} = 100 - 60 = 40$$

Thus, the effect for being a member of Group 3 is an increase of 40 points.

The assumptions are that the $a_j$ group effects are randomly and independently sampled from the normally distributed population of group effects, with a population mean of zero and a population variance of $\sigma_a^2$. Stated another way, there is a population of group effects out there from which we are taking a random sample. For example, with teacher as the factor of interest, we are interested in examining the effectiveness of teachers. We take a random sample from the population of second-grade teachers. For these teachers we measure their effectiveness in the classroom and generate an effect for each teacher (i.e., the $a_j$). These effects indicate the extent to which a particular teacher is more or less effective than the population of teachers. Their effects are known as random effects because the teachers are randomly selected. In selecting teachers, each teacher is selected independently of all other teachers to prevent a biased sample.

The effects of the violation of the assumptions about the $a_j$ are the same as with the dependent variable scores. The $F$ test is quite robust to nonnormality of the $a_j$ terms, and unequal variances of the $a_j$ terms. However, the $F$ test is quite sensitive to nonindependence among the $a_j$ terms, with no known solutions. A summary of the assumptions and the effects of their violation for the one-factor random-effects model is presented in Table 15.1.

### 15.1.5 Multiple Comparison Procedures

Let us think for a moment about the use of multiple comparison procedures for the random-effects model. In general, the researcher is not usually interested in making inferences about just the levels of A that were sampled. Thus, estimation of the $a_j$ terms does not provide us with

**TABLE 15.1**

Assumptions and Effects of Violations—One-Factor Random-Effects Model

| *Assumption* | *Effect of Assumption Violation* |
| --- | --- |
| 1. Independence | Increased likelihood of a Type I and/or Type II error in $F$; affects standard errors of means and inferences about those means. |
| 2. Homogeneity of variance | Bias in $SS_{with}$; increased likelihood of a Type I and/or Type II error; small effect with equal or nearly equal $n$'s; otherwise effect decreases as $n$ increases. |
| 3. Normality | Minimal effect with equal or nearly equal $n$'s. |

any information about the $a_j$ terms that were not sampled. Also, the $a_j$ terms cannot be summarized by their mean, as they do not necessarily sum to zero for the levels sampled, only for the population of levels.

## 15.2   THE TWO-FACTOR RANDOM-EFFECTS MODEL

In this section, we describe the distinguishing characteristics of the two-factor random-effects ANOVA model, the linear model, the ANOVA summary table, assumptions of the model and their violation, and multiple comparison procedures.

### 15.2.1   Characteristics of the Model

The characteristics of the one-factor random-effects ANOVA model have already been covered in this chapter, and of the two-factor fixed-effects model in chapter 13. Here we extend and combine these characteristics to form the two-factor random-effects model. These characteristics include (a) two factors (or independent variables) each with two or more levels, (b) the levels of each of the factors are randomly sampled from the population of levels (i.e., two random-effects factors), (c) subjects are randomly assigned to one combination of the levels of the two factors, and (d) the dependent variable is measured at least at the interval level. Thus the overall design is a random-effects model, with two factors, and the individuals respond to only one combination of the levels of the two factors (not a popular model in education and the behavioral sciences). If individuals respond to more than one combination of the levels of the two factors, then this is a repeated measures design (discussed later in this chapter).

### 15.2.2   The ANOVA Model

The two-factor ANOVA random-effects model is written in terms of population parameters as

$$Y_{ijk} = \mu + a_j + b_k + (ab)_{jk} + \varepsilon_{ijk}$$

where $Y_{ijk}$ is the observed score on the dependent variable for individual $i$ in level $j$ of factor A and level $k$ of factor B (or in the $jk$ cell), $\mu$ is the overall or grand population mean (i.e., regardless of cell designation), $a_j$ is the random effect for level $j$ of factor A (row effect), $b_k$ is the random effect for level $k$ of factor B (column effect), $(ab)_{jk}$ is the interaction random effect for the combination of level $j$ of factor A and level $k$ of factor B, and $\varepsilon_{ijk}$ is the random residual error for individual $i$ in cell $jk$. The residual error can be due to individual differences, measurement error, and/or other factors not under investigation. Note that we use $a_j$, $b_k$, and $(ab)_{jk}$ to designate the random effects to differentiate them from the $\alpha_j$, $\beta_k$, and $(\alpha\beta)_{jk}$ in the fixed-effects model. Finally, there is no requirement that the sum of the main or interaction effects is equal to zero as only a sample of these effects are taken from the population of effects.

There are three sets of hypotheses, one for each main effect and one for the interaction effect. The null and alternative hypotheses, respectively, for testing the effect of factor A are

$$H_{01}: \sigma_a^2 = 0$$
$$H_{11}: \sigma_a^2 > 0$$

The hypotheses for testing the effect of factor B are

$$H_{02}: \sigma_b^2 = 0$$
$$H_{12}: \sigma_b^2 > 0$$

Finally, the hypotheses for testing the interaction effect are

$$H_{03}: \sigma_{ab}^2 = 0$$
$$H_{13}: \sigma_{ab}^2 > 0$$

These hypotheses again reflect the difference in the inferences made in the random- and fixed-effects models. In the fixed-effects case the null hypotheses are about means, whereas in the random-effects case the null hypotheses are about variation among the means.

### 15.2.3 ANOVA Summary Table

Here there are very few differences between the two-factor fixed-effects and random-effects models. The sources of variation are still A, B, AB, within, and total. The sums of squares, degrees of freedom, and mean squares are determined the same as in the fixed-effects case. However, the $F$ test statistics are different, as well as the critical values used. The $F$ test statistics are formed for the test of factor A as

$$F_A = \frac{MS_A}{MS_{AB}}$$

for the test of factor B as

$$F_B = \frac{MS_B}{MS_{AB}}$$

and for the test of the AB interaction as

$$F_{AB} = \frac{MS_{AB}}{MS_{with}}$$

Recall that in the fixed-effects model, the $MS_{with}$ was used as the error term for all three hypotheses. However, in the random-effects model, the $MS_{with}$ is used as the error term only for the test of the interaction. The $MS_{AB}$ is used as the error term for the tests of the main effects. The critical values used are those based on the degrees of freedom for the numerator and denominator of each hypothesis tested. Thus using the example from chapter 13, assuming that the model is now a random-effects model, we obtain as our test statistic for the test of factor A

$$F_A = \frac{MS_A}{MS_{AB}} = \frac{246.1979}{7.2813} = 33.8124$$

for the test of factor B

$$F_B = \frac{MS_B}{MS_{AB}} = \frac{712.5313}{7.2813} = 97.8577$$

and for the test of the AB interaction

$$F_{AB} = \frac{MS_{AB}}{MS_{with}} = \frac{7.2813}{11.5313} = 0.6314$$

The critical value for the test of factor A is found in the $F$ table of Appendix Table 4 as $_{\alpha}F_{J-1,(J-1)(K-1)}$, which for the example is $_{.05}F_{3,3} = 9.28$, and is significant at the .05 level. The critical value for the test of factor B is found in the $F$ table as $_{\alpha}F_{K-1,(J-1)(K-1)}$, which for the example is $_{.05}F_{1,3} = 10.13$, and is significant at the .05 level. The critical value for the test of the interaction is found in the $F$ table as $_{\alpha}F_{(J-1)(K-1),N-JK}$, which for the example is $_{.05}F_{3,24} = 3.01$, and is not significant at the .05 level. It just so happens for the example data that the results for the random- and fixed-effects models are the same. This will not always be the case.

### 15.2.4 Assumptions and Violation of Assumptions

Previously we described the assumptions for the one-factor random-effects model. The assumptions are nearly the same for the two-factor random-effects model and we need not devote much attention to them here. As before, the assumptions are concerned with the distribution of the dependent variable scores, and of the random-effects (sampled levels of the independent variables, the $a_j$, $b_k$, and their interaction $(ab)_{jk}$). However, there are a few new wrinkles. Little is known about the effect of unequal variances (i.e., heteroscedasticity) or dependence for the random-effects model. For violation of the normality assumption, effects are known to be substantial. A summary of the assumptions and the effects of their violation for the two-factor random-effects model is presented in Table 15.2.

### 15.2.5 Multiple Comparison Procedures

The story of multiple comparisons for the two-factor random-effects model is the same as that for the one-factor random-effects model. In general, the researcher is not usually interested in making inferences about just the levels of A, B, or AB that were sampled. Thus, estimation of the $a_j$, $b_k$, or $(ab)_{jk}$ terms do not provide us with any information about the $a_j$, $b_k$, or $(ab)_{jk}$ terms that were not sampled. Also, the $a_j$, $b_k$, or $(ab)_{jk}$ terms cannot be summarized by their

**TABLE 15.2**
Assumptions and Effects of Violations—Two-Factor Random-Effects Model

| Assumption | Effect of Assumption Violation |
|---|---|
| 1. Independence | Little is known about the effects of dependence; however, based on the fixed-effects model, we might expect the following: increased likelihood of a Type I and/or Type II error in $F$; affects standard errors of means and inferences about those means. |
| 2. Homogeneity of variance | Little is known about the effects of heteroscedasticity; however, based on the fixed-effects model, we might expect the following: bias in $SS_{with}$; increased likelihood of a Type I and/or Type II error; small effect with equal or nearly equal $n$'s; otherwise effect decreases as $n$ increases. |
| 3. Normality | Minimal effect with equal or nearly equal $n$'s; otherwise substantial effects. |

means, as they will not necessarily sum to zero for the levels sampled, only for the population of levels.

## 15.3 THE TWO-FACTOR MIXED-EFFECTS MODEL

This section describes the distinguishing characteristics of the two-factor mixed-effects ANOVA model, the linear model, the ANOVA summary table, assumptions of the model and their violation, and multiple comparison procedures.

### 15.3.1 Characteristics of the Model

The characteristics of the two-factor random-effects ANOVA model have already been covered in the preceding section, and of the two-factor fixed-effects model in chapter 13. Here we combine these characteristics to form the two-factor mixed-effects model. These characteristics include (a) two factors (or independent variables) each with two or more levels, (b) the levels for one of the factors are randomly sampled from the population of levels (i.e., the random-effects factor) and all of the levels of interest for the second factor are included in the design (i.e., the fixed-effects factor), (c) subjects are randomly selected and assigned to one combination of the levels of the two factors, and (d) the dependent variable is measured at least at the interval level. Thus the overall design is a mixed-effects model, with one fixed-effects factor and one random-effects factor, and individuals respond to only one combination of the levels of the two factors. If individuals respond to more than one combination, then this is a repeated measures design.

### 15.3.2 The ANOVA Model

There are actually two variations of the two-factor mixed-effects model, one where factor A is fixed and factor B is random, and the other where factor A is random and factor B is fixed. The labeling of a factor as A or B is arbitrary, so we only consider the former variation where A is fixed and B is random. For the latter variation merely switch the labels of the factors. The two-factor ANOVA mixed-effects model is written in terms of population parameters as

$$Y_{ijk} = \mu + \alpha_j + b_k + (\alpha b)_{jk} + \varepsilon_{ijk}$$

where $Y_{ijk}$ is the observed score on the dependent variable for individual $i$ in level $j$ of factor A and level $k$ of factor B (or in the $jk$ cell), $\mu$ is the overall or grand population mean (i.e., regardless of cell designation), $\alpha_j$ is the fixed effect for level $j$ of factor A (row effect), $b_k$ is the random effect for level $k$ of factor B (column effect), $(\alpha b)_{jk}$ is the interaction mixed effect for the combination of level $j$ of factor A and level $k$ of factor B, and $\varepsilon_{ijk}$ is the random residual error for individual $i$ in cell $jk$. The residual error can be due to individual differences, measurement error, and/or other factors not under investigation. Note that we use $b_k$ and $(\alpha b)_{jk}$ to designate the random and mixed effects to differentiate them from $\beta_k$ and $(\alpha\beta)_{jk}$ in the fixed-effects model.

As shown in Fig. 15.1, due to the nature of the mixed-effects model, only some of the columns are randomly selected for inclusion in the design. Each cell of the design will include row ($\alpha$), column ($b$), and interaction ($\alpha b$) effects. With an equal $n$'s model, if we sum these effects for a given column, then the effects will sum to zero. However, if we sum these effects for a given row, then the effects will not sum to zero, as some columns were not sampled.

The null and alternative hypotheses, respectively, for testing the effect of factor A are

$$H_{01}: \mu_{.1.} = \mu_{.2.} = ... = \mu_{.J.}$$

$$H_{11}: \text{not all the } \mu_{.j.} \text{ are equal}$$

The hypotheses for testing the effect of factor B are

$$H_{02}: \sigma_b^2 = 0$$

$$H_{12}: \sigma_b^2 > 0$$

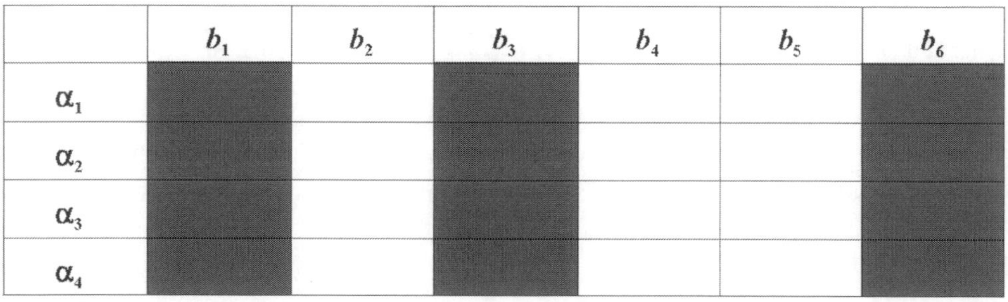

|  | $b_1$ | $b_2$ | $b_3$ | $b_4$ | $b_5$ | $b_6$ |
|---|---|---|---|---|---|---|
| $\alpha_1$ | | | | | | |
| $\alpha_2$ | | | | | | |
| $\alpha_3$ | | | | | | |
| $\alpha_4$ | | | | | | |

FIG. 15.1. Conditions for the two-factor mixed-effects model. Although all four levels of factor A are selected by the researcher (A is fixed), only three of the six levels of factor B are selected (B is random). If the levels of B selected are 1, 3, and 6, then the design will only consist of the shaded cells. In each cell of the design are row, column, and cell effects. If we sum these effects for a given column, then the effects will sum to zero. If we sum these effects for a given row, then the effects will not sum to zero (due to missing cells).

Finally, the hypotheses for testing the interaction effect are

$$H_{03}: \sigma_{\alpha b}^2 = 0$$

$$H_{13}: \sigma_{\alpha b}^2 > 0$$

These hypotheses reflect the difference in the inferences made in the mixed-effects model. Here we see that the hypotheses about the fixed-effect A (the main effect of A) are about means, whereas the hypotheses involving the random-effect B (the main effect of B and the interaction effect AB) are about variation among the means.

### 15.3.3    ANOVA Summary Table

Here there are very few differences between the two-factor fixed-effects, random-effects, and mixed-effects models. The sources of variation are again A, B, AB, within, and total. The sums of squares, degrees of freedom, and mean squares are determined the same as in the fixed-effects case. However, the $F$ test statistics are different, as well as the critical values used. The $F$ test statistics are formed for the test of factor A, the fixed effect, as

$$F_A = \frac{MS_A}{MS_{AB}}$$

for the test of factor B, the random effect, as

$$F_B = \frac{MS_B}{MS_{with}}$$

and for the test of the AB interaction, the mixed effect, as

$$F_{AB} = \frac{MS_{AB}}{MS_{with}}$$

Recall that in the fixed-effects model, the $MS_{with}$ is used as the error term for all three hypotheses. However, in the random-effects model, the $MS_{with}$ is used as the error term only for the test of the interaction, and the $MS_{AB}$ is used as the error term for the tests of the main effects. Finally, in the mixed-effects model, the $MS_{with}$ is used as the error term for the test of B and the interaction, whereas the $MS_{AB}$ is used as the error term for the test of A. The critical values used are those based on the degrees of freedom for the numerator and denominator of each hypothesis tested.

Thus using the example from chapter 13, assuming the model is now a mixed-effects model, we obtain as our test statistic for the test of factor A

$$F_A = \frac{MS_A}{MS_{AB}} = \frac{246.1979}{7.2813} = 33.8124$$

for the test of factor B

$$F_B = \frac{MS_B}{MS_{with}} = \frac{712.5313}{11.5313} = 61.7911$$

and for the test of the AB interaction

$$F_{AB} = \frac{MS_{AB}}{MS_{with}} = \frac{7.2813}{11.5313} = 0.6314$$

The critical value for the test of factor A is found in the $F$ table as $_{\alpha}F_{J-1,(J-1)(K-1)}$, which for the example is $_{.05}F_{3,3} = 9.28$, and is significant at the .05 level. The critical value for the test of factor B is found in the $F$ table as $_{\alpha}F_{K-1,N-JK}$, which for the example is $_{.05}F_{1,24} = 4.26$, and is significant at the .05 level. The critical value for the test of the interaction is found in the $F$ table as $_{\alpha}F_{(J-1)(K-1),N-JK}$, which for the example is $_{.05}F_{3,24} = 3.01$, and is not significant at the .05 level. It just so happens for the example data that the results for the mixed-, random-, and fixed-effects models are the same. This is not always the case.

### 15.3.4    Assumptions and Violation of Assumptions

Previously we described the assumptions for the two-factor random-effects model. The assumptions are nearly the same for the two-factor mixed-effects model and we need not devote much attention to them here. As before, the assumptions are concerned with the distribution of the dependent variable scores and of the random effects. However, note that not much is known about the effects of dependence or heteroscedasticity for random effects, although we expect the effects are the same as for the fixed-effects case. A summary of the assumptions and the effects of their violation for the two-factor mixed-effects model are presented in Table 15.3.

### 15.3.5    Multiple Comparison Procedures

For multiple comparisons of the two-factor mixed-effects model, the researcher is not usually interested in making inferences about just the levels of B or AB that were randomly sampled. Thus, estimation of the $b_k$ or $(\alpha b)_{jk}$ terms does not provide us with any information about the

**TABLE 15.3**
Assumptions and Effects of Violations—Two-Factor Mixed-Effects Model

| *Assumption* | *Effect of Assumption Violation* |
|---|---|
| 1. Independence | Little is known about the effects of dependence; however, based on the fixed-effects model, we might expect the following: increased likelihood of a Type I and/or Type II error in $F$; affects standard errors of means and inferences about those means. |
| 2. Homogeneity of variance | Little is known about the effects of heteroscedasticity; however, based on the fixed-effects model, we might expect the following: bias in $SS_{with}$; increased likelihood of a Type I and/or Type II error; small effect with equal or nearly equal $n$'s; otherwise effect decreases as $n$ increases. |
| 3. Normality | Minimal effect with equal or nearly equal $n$'s; otherwise substantial effects. |

$b_k$ or $(\alpha b)_{jk}$ terms not sampled. Also, the $b_k$ or $(\alpha b)_{jk}$ terms cannot be summarized by their means as they will not necessarily sum to zero for the levels sampled, only for the population of levels. However, inferences about the fixed-factor A can be made in the same way they were made for the two-factor fixed-effects model. We have already used the example data to look at some multiple comparison procedures in chapter 13.

This concludes our discussion of random- and mixed-effects models for the one- and two-factor designs. For three-factor designs see Keppel (1982) or Keppel and Wickens (2004). In the major statistical software, the analysis of random effects can be treated as follows: in SAS PROC GLM, use the RANDOM statement to designate random effects; in SPSS GLM, random effects can also be designated.

## 15.4 THE ONE-FACTOR REPEATED MEASURES DESIGN

In this section, we describe the distinguishing characteristics of the one-factor repeated measures ANOVA model, the layout of the data, the linear model, assumptions of the model and their violation, the ANOVA summary table, multiple comparison procedures, alternative ANOVA procedures, and an example.

### 15.4.1  Characteristics of the Model

The characteristics of the one-factor repeated measures ANOVA model are somewhat similar to the one-factor fixed-effects model, yet there are a number of obvious exceptions. The first unique characteristic has to do with the fact that each subject responds to each level of factor A. This is in contrast to the nonrepeated case where each subject is exposed to only one level of factor A. The one-factor repeated measures model is the logical extension to the dependent $t$ test. Although in the dependent $t$ test there are only two levels of the independent variable, in the one-factor repeated measures model two or more levels of the independent variable are utilized.

This design is often referred to as a **within subjects design**, as each subject responds to each level of factor A. Thus subjects serve as their own controls such that individual differences are taken into account. This was not the case in any of the previously discussed models. As a result subjects' scores are not independent across the levels of factor A. Compare this design to the one-factor fixed-effects model where total variation was decomposed into variation due to A and due to the residual. In the one-factor repeated measures design, residual variation is further decomposed into variation due to subjects and variation due to the interaction between A and subjects. The reduction in the residual sum of squares yields a more powerful design and more precision in terms of estimating the effects of A, and thus is more economical in that less subjects are necessary than in previously discussed models (Murphy & Myors, 2004).

The one-factor repeated measures design is also a mixed model. The subjects factor is a random effect, whereas the A factor is almost always a fixed effect. If time is the fixed effect, then the researcher can examine phenomena over time. Finally, the one-factor repeated measures design is similar in some ways to the two-factor mixed-effects design except with one subject per cell. In other words, the one-factor repeated measures design is really a special case of the two-factor mixed-effects design with $n = 1$ per cell. Unequal $n$'s can only happen when subjects miss the administration of one or more levels of factor A.

On the down side, the repeated measures design includes some risk of carry-over effects from one level of A to another because each subject responds to all levels of A. As examples of the carry-over effect, subjects' performance may be altered due to fatigue (decreased performance), practice (increased performance), and sensitization (increased performance) effects. These effects may be minimized by (a) counterbalancing the order of administration of the levels of A so that each subject does not receive the same order of the levels of A (this can also minimize problems with the compound symmetry assumption; see later discussion), (b) allowing some time to pass between the administration of the levels of A, or (c) matching or blocking similar subjects with the assumption of subjects within a block being randomly assigned to a level of A. This last method is a type of randomized block design (see chap. 16).

### 15.4.2    The Layout of the Data

The layout of the data for the one-factor repeated measures model is shown in Table 15.4. Here we see the columns designated as the levels of factor A and the rows as the subjects. Row, column and overall means are also shown, although the subject means are seldom of any utility (and thus are not reported in research studies). Here you see that the layout of the data looks the same as the two-factor model, although there is only one observation per cell.

### 15.4.3    The ANOVA Model

The one-factor repeated measures ANOVA model is written in terms of population parameters as

$$Y_{ij} = \mu + \alpha_j + s_i + (s\alpha)_{ij} + \varepsilon_{ij}$$

where $Y_{ij}$ is the observed score on the dependent variable for individual $i$ responding to level $j$ of factor A, $\mu$ is the overall or grand population mean, $\alpha_j$ is the fixed effect for level $j$ of factor A, $s_i$ is the random effect for subject $i$ of the subject factor, $(s\alpha)_{ij}$ is the interaction between subject $i$ and level $j$, and $\varepsilon_{ij}$ is the random residual error for individual $i$ in level $j$. The residual

TABLE 15.4
Layout for the One-Factor Repeated Measures ANOVA

| Level of Factor S | Level of Factor A (Repeated Factor) | | | | |
| | 1 | 2 | ... | J | Row Mean |
| --- | --- | --- | --- | --- | --- |
| 1 | $Y_{11}$ | $Y_{12}$ | ... | $Y_{1J}$ | $\bar{Y}_{1.}$ |
| 2 | $Y_{21}$ | $Y_{22}$ | ... | $Y_{2J}$ | $\bar{Y}_{2.}$ |
| ... | ... | ... | ... | ... | ... |
| $n$ | $Y_{n1}$ | $Y_{n2}$ | ... | $Y_{nJ}$ | $\bar{Y}_{n.}$ |
| Column mean | $\bar{Y}_{.1}$ | $\bar{Y}_{.2}$ | ... | $\bar{Y}_{.J}$ | $\bar{Y}_{..}$ |

error can be due to measurement error, and/or other factors not under investigation. From the model you can see this is similar to the two-factor model with one observation per cell. Also, the fixed effect is denoted by $\alpha$ and the random effect by $s$; thus we have a mixed-effects model. Finally, for the equal $n$'s model, the effects for $\alpha$ and $s\alpha$ sum to zero for each subject (or row).

The hypotheses for testing the effect of factor A are

$$H_{01}: \mu_{.1} = \mu_{.2} = ... = \mu_{.J}$$

$$H_{11}: \text{not all the } \mu_{.j} \text{ are equal}$$

The hypotheses are written in terms of means because factor A is a fixed effect.

## 15.4.4   Assumptions and Violation of Assumptions

Previously we described the assumptions for the two-factor mixed-effects model. The assumptions are nearly the same for the one-factor repeated measures model and are again mainly concerned with the distribution of the dependent variable scores and of the random effects.

A new assumption is known as **compound symmetry** and states that the covariances between the scores of the subjects across the levels of the repeated factor A are constant. In other words, the covariances for all pairs of levels of the fixed factor are the same across the population of random effects (i.e., the subjects). The analysis of variance is not particularly robust to a violation of this assumption. In particular, the assumption is often violated when factor A is time, as the relationship between adjacent levels of A is strongest. If the assumption is violated, three alternative procedures are available. The first is to limit the levels of factor A either to those that meet the assumption, or to two (in which case there would be only one covariance). The second, and more plausible, alternative is to use adjusted $F$ tests. These are reported shortly. The third is to use multivariate analysis of variance, which has no compound symmetry assumption, but is slightly less powerful.

Huynh and Feldt (1970) showed that the compound symmetry assumption is a sufficient but not necessary condition for the validity of the $F$ test. Thus the $F$ test may also be valid under less stringent conditions. The necessary and sufficient condition for the validity of the $F$ test is known as **sphericity**. This assumes that the variance of the difference scores for each pair of factor levels is the same. Further discussion of sphericity is beyond the scope of this text (see Keppel, 1982, Kirk, 1982, or Myers & Well, 1995). A summary of the assumptions and the effects of their violation for the one-factor repeated measures design is presented in Table 15.5.

## 15.4.5   ANOVA Summary Table

The sources of variation for this model are similar to those for the two-factor model, except that there is no within cell variation. The ANOVA summary table is shown in Table 15.6, where we see the following sources of variation: A, subjects (denoted by S), the SA interaction, and total. The test of subject differences is of no real interest. Quite naturally, we expect there to be variation among the subjects. From the table we see that although three mean square terms can be computed, only one $F$ ratio results for the test of factor A; thus the subjects effect cannot be tested anyway as there is no appropriate error term.

**TABLE 15.5**

Assumptions and Effects of Violations—One-Factor Repeated Measures Model

| Assumption | Effect of Assumption Violation |
|---|---|
| 1. Independence | Little is known about the effects of dependence; however, based on the fixed-effects model, we might expect the following: increased likelihood of a Type I and/or Type II error in $F$; affects standard errors of means and inferences about those means. |
| 2. Homogeneity of variance | Little is known about the effects of heteroscedasticity; however, based on the fixed-effects model, we might expect the following: bias in $SS_{SA}$; increased likelihood of a Type I and/or Type II error; small effect with equal or nearly equal $n$'s; otherwise effect decreases as $n$ increases. |
| 3. Normality | Minimal effect with equal or nearly equal $n$'s; otherwise substantial effects. |
| 4. Sphericity | $F$ not particularly robust; consider usual $F$ test, Geisser-Greenhouse conservative $F$ test, and adjusted (Box) $F$ test, if necessary. |

**TABLE 15.6**

One-Factor Repeated Measures ANOVA Summary Table

| Source | SS | df | MS | F |
|---|---|---|---|---|
| A | $SS_A$ | $J - 1$ | $MS_A$ | $MS_A/MS_{SA}$ |
| S | $SS_S$ | $n - 1$ | $MS_S$ | |
| SA | $SS_{SA}$ | $(J - 1)(n - 1)$ | $MS_{SA}$ | |
| Total | $SS_{total}$ | $N - 1$ | | |

Next we need to consider the sums of squares for the one-factor repeated measures model. If we take the total sum of squares and decompose it, we have

$$SS_{total} = SS_A + SS_S + SS_{SA}$$

These three terms can then be computed by statistical software. The degrees of freedom, mean squares, and $F$ ratio are determined as shown in Table 15.6.

As noted earlier in the discussion of assumptions for this model, the $F$ test is not very robust to violation of the compound symmetry assumption. This assumption is often violated in education and the behavioral sciences; consequently, statisticians have spent considerable time studying this problem. Research suggests that the following sequential procedure be used in the test of factor A. First, do the usual $F$ test that is quite liberal in terms of rejecting $H_0$ too often. If $H_0$ is not rejected, then stop. If $H_0$ is rejected, then continue with step 2, which is to use the Geisser-Greenhouse (1958) conservative $F$ test. For the model being considered here, the degrees of freedom for the $F$ critical value are adjusted to be 1 and $n - 1$. If $H_0$ is rejected, then stop. This would indicate that both the liberal and conservative tests reached the same conclusion to reject $H_0$. If $H_0$ is not rejected, then the two tests did not reach the same conclusion, and a further test (a tie-breaker) should be undertaken. Thus in step 3 an adjusted $F$ test is conducted. The adjustment is known as Box's (1954b) correction (usually referred to as the Huynh & Feldt [1970] procedure). Here the numerator degrees of freedom are $(J - 1)\varepsilon$, and the denominator degrees of freedom are $(J - 1)(n - 1)\varepsilon$, where $\varepsilon$ is the correction factor (not to be confused with the residual term $\varepsilon$). The correction factor is quite complex and is not shown here (see Keppel & Wickens, 2004, Myers, 1979, Myers & Well, 1995, or Wilcox, 1987). Most major statistical software conducts the Geisser-Greenhouse and Huynh and Feldt tests. The Huynh and Feldt test is recommended due to greater power (Keppel & Wickens, 2004; Myers & Well, 1995); thus when available, you can simply use the Huynh and Feldt procedure rather than the previously recommended sequence.

### 15.4.6   Multiple Comparison Procedures

If the null hypothesis for the A factor is rejected and there are more than two levels of the factor, then the researcher may be interested in which means or combinations of means are different. This could be assessed, as we have seen in previous chapters, by the use of some multiple comparison procedure (MCP). In general, most of the MCPs outlined in chapter 12 can be used in the one-factor repeated measures model (additional discussion in Keppel & Wickens, 2004, and Mickey, Dunn, & Clark, 2004).

It has been shown that these MCPs are seriously affected by a violation of the compound symmetry assumption. In this situation two alternatives are recommended. The first alternative is, rather than using the same error term for each contrast (i.e., $MS_{SA}$), to use a separate error term for each contrast tested. Then many of the MCPs previously covered in chapter 12 can be used. This complicates matters considerably (see Keppel, 1982, Keppel & Wickens, 2004, or Kirk, 1982). A second alternative, recommended by Maxwell (1980) and Wilcox (1987), involves the use of multiple dependent $t$ tests where the $\alpha$ level is adjusted much like the Bonferroni procedure. Maxwell concluded that this procedure is better than many of the other MCPs. For other similar procedures, see Hochberg and Tamhane (1987).

### 15.4.7   Alternative ANOVA Procedures

There are several alternative procedures to the one-factor repeated measures ANOVA model. These include the Friedman (1937) test, as well as others, such as the Agresti and Pendergast (1986) test. The Friedman test, like the Kruskal-Wallis test, is a nonparametric procedure based on ranks. However, the Kruskal-Wallis test cannot be used in a repeated measures model as it assumes that the individual scores are independent. This is obviously not the case in the one-factor repeated measures model where each individual is exposed to all levels of factor A.

Let me outline how the Friedman test is conducted. First, scores are ranked within subject. For instance, if there are $J = 4$ levels of factor A, then each subjects' scores would be ranked from 1 to 4. From this, one can compute a mean ranking for each level of factor A. The null hypothesis essentially becomes a test of whether the mean rankings for each of the levels of A are equal. The test statistic is a $\chi^2$ statistic. In the case of tied ranks, either the available ranks can be averaged, or a correction factor can be used as done with the Kruskal-Wallis test (see chap.

11). The test statistic is compared to the critical value of $_\alpha\chi^2_{J-1}$ (see Appendix Table 3). The null hypothesis that the mean rankings are the same for the levels of factor A is rejected if the test statistic exceeds the critical value.

You may also recall from the Kruskal-Wallis test the problem with small $n$'s in terms of the test statistic not being precisely a $\chi^2$. The same problem exists with the Friedman test when $J < 6$ and $n < 6$, so I suggest you consult the table of critical values in Marascuilo and McSweeney (1977, Table A-22, p. 521). The Friedman test, like the Kruskal-Wallis test, assumes that the population distributions have the same shape (although not necessarily normal) and variability, and that the dependent measure is continuous. For a discussion of other alternative nonparametric procedures, see Agresti and Pendergast (1986), Myers and Well (1995), and Wilcox (1987, 1996, 2003). For information on more advanced within subjects ANOVA models, see Cotton (1998), Keppel and Wickens (2004), and Myers and Well (1995).

Various multiple comparison procedures (MCPs) can be used for the Friedman test. For the most part these MCPs are analogs to their parametric equivalents. In the case of planned (or a priori) pairwise comparisons, one may use multiple matched-pair Wilcoxon tests (i.e., a form of the Kruskal-Wallis test for two groups) in a Bonferroni form (i.e., taking the number of contrasts into account through an adjustment of the $\alpha$ level). For post hoc comparisons, numerous parametric analogs are available. For additional discussion on MCPs for this model, see Marascuilo and McSweeney (1977).

## 15.4.8   An Example

Let us consider an example to illustrate the procedures used in this section. The data are shown in Table 15.7 where there are eight subjects, each of whom has been evaluated by four raters on a task of writing assessment. First, let us take a look at the results for the parametric ANOVA model, as shown in Table 15.8. The $F$ test statistic is compared to the usual $F$ test critical value

**TABLE 15.7**
Data for the Writing Assessment Example—One-Factor Design: Raw Scores
and Rank Scores on the Writing Assessment Task by Subject and Rater

| Subject | Rater 1 Raw | Rater 1 Rank | Rater 2 Raw | Rater 2 Rank | Rater 3 Raw | Rater 3 Rank | Rater 4 Raw | Rater 4 Rank |
|---------|-----|------|-----|------|-----|------|-----|------|
| 1 | 3 | 1 | 4 | 2 | 7 | 3 | 8 | 4 |
| 2 | 6 | 2 | 5 | 1 | 8 | 3 | 9 | 4 |
| 3 | 3 | 1 | 4 | 2 | 7 | 3 | 9 | 4 |
| 4 | 3 | 1 | 4 | 2 | 6 | 3 | 8 | 4 |
| 5 | 1 | 1 | 2 | 2 | 5 | 3 | 10 | 4 |
| 6 | 2 | 1 | 3 | 2 | 6 | 3 | 10 | 4 |
| 7 | 2 | 1 | 4 | 2 | 5 | 3 | 9 | 4 |
| 8 | 2 | 1 | 3 | 2 | 6 | 3 | 10 | 4 |

**TABLE 15.8**
One-Factor Repeated Measures ANOVA Summary Table for the Writing Assessment Example

| Source | SS | df | MS | F |
|---|---|---|---|---|
| Within subjects: | | | | |
| Rater (A) | 198.125 | 3 | 66.042 | 73.477* |
| Error (SA) | 18.875 | 21 | 0.899 | |
| Between subjects: | | | | |
| Error (S) | 14.875 | 7 | 2.125 | |
| Total | 231.875 | 31 | | |

$*_{.05}F_{3,21} = 3.07$

of $_{.05}F_{3,21} = 3.07$, which is significant. For the Geisser-Greenhouse conservative procedure, the test statistic is compared to the critical value of $_{.05}F_{1,7} = 5.59$, which is also significant. The two procedures both yield a statistically significant result; thus we need not be concerned with a violation of the compound symmetry assumption. As an example MCP, the Bonferroni procedure determined that all pairs of raters are significantly different from one another except for Rater 1 versus Rater 2.

Finally, let us take a look at the Friedman test. The test statistic is $\chi^2 = 22.9500$. This test statistic is compared to the critical value $_{.05}\chi_3^2 = 7.8147$, which is significant. Thus the conclusions for the parametric ANOVA and nonparametric Friedman tests are the same here. This will not always be the case, particularly when ANOVA assumptions are violated.

## 15.5   THE TWO-FACTOR SPLIT-PLOT OR MIXED DESIGN

In this section, we describe the distinguishing characteristics of the two-factor split-plot or mixed ANOVA design, the layout of the data, the linear model, assumptions and their violation, the ANOVA summary table, multiple comparison procedures, and an example.

### 15.5.1   Characteristics of the Model

The characteristics of the two-factor split-plot or mixed ANOVA design are a combination of the characteristics of the one-factor repeated measures and the two-factor fixed-effects models. It is unique because there are two factors, only one of which is repeated. For this reason the design is often called a **mixed design**. Thus, one of the factors is a between subjects factor, the other is a within subjects factor, and the result is known as a **split-plot design** (from agricultural research). Each subject then responds to every level of the repeated factor, but to only one level of the nonrepeated factor. Subjects then serve as their own controls for the repeated factor, but not for the nonrepeated factor. The other characteristics carry over from the one-factor repeated measures model and the two-factor model.

## 15.5.2   The Layout of the Data

The layout of the data for the two-factor split-plot or mixed design is shown in Table 15.9. Here we see the rows designated as the levels of factor A, the between subjects or nonrepeated factor, and the columns as the levels of factor B, the within subjects or repeated factor. Within

**TABLE 15.9**
Layout for the Two-Factor Split-Plot or Mixed ANOVA

| Level of Factor A (Nonrepeated Factor) | Level of Factor B (Repeated Factor) | | | | Row Mean |
|:---:|:---:|:---:|:---:|:---:|:---:|
| | 1 | 2 | ... | K | |
| 1 | $Y_{111}$ | $Y_{112}$ | ... | $Y_{11K}$ | |
| | . | . | ... | . | |
| | . | . | ... | . | $\overline{Y}_{.1.}$ |
| | . | . | ... | . | |
| | $Y_{n11}$ | $Y_{n12}$ | ... | $Y_{n1K}$ | |
| | $\overline{Y}_{.11}$ | $\overline{Y}_{.12}$ | ... | $\overline{Y}_{.1K}$ | |
| 2 | $Y_{121}$ | $Y_{122}$ | ... | $Y_{12K}$ | |
| | . | . | ... | . | |
| | . | . | ... | . | $\overline{Y}_{.2.}$ |
| | . | . | ... | . | |
| | $Y_{n21}$ | $Y_{n22}$ | ... | $Y_{n2K}$ | |
| | $\overline{Y}_{.21}$ | $\overline{Y}_{.22}$ | ... | $\overline{Y}_{.2K}$ | |
| . | . | . | ... | . | . |
| . | . | . | ... | . | . |
| . | . | . | ... | . | . |
| J | $Y_{1J1}$ | $Y_{1J2}$ | ... | $Y_{1JK}$ | |
| | . | . | ... | . | |
| | . | . | ... | . | $\overline{Y}_{.J.}$ |
| | . | . | ... | . | |
| | $Y_{nJ1}$ | $Y_{nJ2}$ | ... | $Y_{nJK}$ | |
| | $\overline{Y}_{.J1}$ | $\overline{Y}_{.J2}$ | ... | $\overline{Y}_{.JK}$ | |
| Column Mean | $\overline{Y}_{..1}$ | $\overline{Y}_{..2}$ | ... | $\overline{Y}_{..K}$ | $\overline{Y}_{...}$ |

*Note:* Each subject is measured at all levels of factor B, but at only one level of factor A.

each factor level combination or cell are the subjects. Notice that the same subjects appear at all levels of factor B, but only at one level of factor A. Row, column, cell, and overall means are also shown. Here you see that the layout of the data looks the same as the two-factor model.

### 15.5.3 The ANOVA Model

The two factor split-plot model can be written in terms of population parameters as

$$Y_{ijk} = \mu + \alpha_j + s_{i(j)} + \beta_k + (\alpha\beta)_{jk} + (\beta s)_{ki(j)} + \varepsilon_{ijk}$$

where $Y_{ijk}$ is the observed score on the dependent variable for individual $i$ in level $j$ of factor A and level $k$ of factor B (i.e., the $jk$ cell), $\mu$ is the overall or grand population mean (i.e., regardless of cell designation), $\alpha_j$ is the effect for level $j$ of factor A (row effect for the nonrepeated factor), $s_{i(j)}$ is the effect of subject $i$ that is nested within level $j$ of factor A (i.e., $i(j)$ denotes that $i$ is nested within $j$), $\beta_k$ is the effect for level $k$ of factor B (column effect for the repeated factor), $(\alpha\beta)_{jk}$ is the interaction effect for the combination of level $j$ of factor A and level $k$ of factor B, $(\beta s)_{ki(j)}$ is the interaction effect for the combination of level $k$ of factor B and subject $i$ that is nested within level $j$ of factor A, and $\varepsilon_{ijk}$ is the random residual error for individual $i$ in cell $jk$.

We use the terminology "subjects are nested within factor A" to indicate that a particular subject $s_i$ is only exposed to one level of factor A, level $j$. This observation is then denoted in the subjects effect by $s_{i(j)}$ and in the interaction effect by $(\beta s)_{ki(j)}$. This is due to the fact that not all possible combinations of subject with the levels of factor A are included in the model. A more extended discussion of designs with nested factors is given in chapter 16. The residual error can be due to individual differences, measurement error, and/or other factors not under investigation. We assume for now that A and B are fixed-effects factors and that S is a random-effects factor.

It should be mentioned that for the equal $n$'s model, the sum of the row effects, the sum of the column effects, and the sum of the interaction effects are all equal to zero, both across rows and across columns. This implies, for example, that if there are any nonzero row effects, then the row effects will balance out around zero with some positive and some negative effects.

The hypotheses to be tested here are exactly the same as in the nonrepeated two-factor ANOVA model (see chap. 13). If one of the null hypotheses is rejected, then the researcher may want to consider a multiple comparison procedure so as to determine which means or combination of means are significantly different (discussed later in this chapter).

### 15.5.4 Assumptions and Violation of Assumptions

Previously we described the assumptions for the two-factor models and the one-factor repeated measures model. The assumptions for the two-factor split-plot or mixed design are actually a combination of these two sets of assumptions.

The assumptions can be divided into two sets of assumptions, one for the between subjects factor, and one for the within subjects factor. For the between subjects factor, we have the usual assumptions of population scores being random, independent, and normally distributed with equal variances. For the within subjects factor, the assumption is the already familiar compound symmetry assumption. For this design, the assumption involves the population covariances for all pairs of the levels of the within subjects factor (i.e., $k$ and $k'$) being equal, at each level of the between subjects factor (for all levels $j$). To deal with this assumption, we look at alternative $F$ tests in the next section. A summary of the assumptions and the effects of their violation for the two-factor split-plot or mixed design are presented in Table 15.10.

### 15.5.5   ANOVA Summary Table

The ANOVA summary table is shown in Table 15.11, where we see the following sources of variation: A, S, B, AB, BS, and total. The table is divided into within subjects sources and between subjects sources. The between subjects sources are A and S, where S will be used as the error term for the test of factor A. The within subjects sources are B, AB, and BS, where BS will be used as the error term for the test of factor B and of the AB interaction.

TABLE 15.10
Assumptions and Effects of Violations—Two-Factor Split-Plot or Mixed Model

| *Assumption* | *Effect of Assumption Violation* |
|---|---|
| 1. Independence | Increased likelihood of a Type I and/or Type II error in $F$; affects standard errors of means and inferences about those means. |
| 2. Homogeneity of variance | Bias in error terms; increased likelihood of a Type I and/or Type II error; small effect with equal or nearly equal $n$'s; otherwise effect decreases as $n$ increases. |
| 3. Normality | Minimal effect with equal or nearly equal $n$'s; otherwise substantial effects. |
| 4. Sphericity | $F$ not particularly robust; consider usual $F$ test, Geisser-Greenhouse conservative $F$ test, and adjusted (Box) $F$ test, if necessary. |

TABLE 15.11
Two-Factor Split-Plot or Mixed Model ANOVA Summary Table

| *Source* | *SS* | *df* | *MS* | *F* |
|---|---|---|---|---|
| Between subjects: | | | | |
| A | $SS_A$ | $J - 1$ | $MS_A$ | $MS_A/MS_S$ |
| S | $SS_S$ | $J(n - 1)$ | $MS_S$ | |
| Within subjects: | | | | |
| B | $SS_B$ | $K - 1$ | $MS_B$ | $MS_B/MS_{BS}$ |
| AB | $SS_{AB}$ | $(J - 1)(K - 1)$ | $MS_{AB}$ | $MS_{AB}/MS_{BS}$ |
| BS | $SS_{BS}$ | $(K - 1)J(n - 1)$ | $MS_{BS}$ | |
| Total | $SS_{total}$ | $N - 1$ | | |

Next we need to consider the sums of squares for the two-factor mixed design. Taking the total sum of squares and decomposing it yields

$$SS_{total} = SS_A + SS_S + SS_B + SS_{AB} + SS_{BS}$$

We leave the computation of these five terms for statistical software. The degrees of freedom, mean squares, and $F$ ratios are computed as shown in Table 15.11.

As the compound symmetry assumption is often violated, we again suggest the following sequential procedure to test for B and for AB. First, do the usual $F$ test, which is quite liberal in terms of rejecting $H_0$ too often. If $H_0$ is not rejected, then stop. If $H_0$ is rejected, then continue with step 2, which is to use the Geisser-Greenhouse (1958) conservative $F$ test. For the model under consideration here, the degrees of freedom for the $F$ critical values are adjusted to be 1 and $J (n - 1)$ for the test of B, and $J - 1$ and $J (n - 1)$ for the test of the AB interaction. There is no conservative test necessary for factor A, the nonrepeated factor. If $H_0$ is rejected, then stop. This would indicate that both the liberal and conservative tests reached the same conclusion to reject $H_0$. If $H_0$ is not rejected, then the two tests did not yield the same conclusion, and an adjusted $F$ test is conducted. The adjustment is known as Box's (1954b) correction (or the Huynh & Feldt [1970] procedure). Most major statistical software conducts the Geisser-Greenhouse and Huynh and Feldt tests.

### 15.5.6 Multiple Comparison Procedures

Consider the situation where the null hypothesis for any of the three hypotheses is rejected (i.e., for A, B, and/or AB). If there is more than one degree of freedom for any of these hypotheses, then the researcher may be interested in which means or combinations of means are different. This could be assessed again by the use of some multiple comparison procedure (MCP). Thus the procedures outlined in chapter 13 (i.e., main effects, simple and complex interaction contrasts) for the regular two-factor ANOVA model can be adapted to this model.

However, it has been shown that the MCPs involving the repeated factor are seriously affected by a violation of the compound symmetry assumption. In this situation, two alternatives are recommended. The first alternative is, rather than using the same error term for each contrast involving the repeated factor (i.e., $MS_B$ or $MS_{AB}$), to use a separate error term for each contrast tested. Then many of the MCPs previously covered in chapter 12 can be used. This complicates matters considerably (see Keppel, 1982, Keppel & Wickens, 2004, or Kirk, 1982). The second and simpler alternative is suggested by Shavelson (1988). He recommended that the appropriate error terms be used in MCPs involving the main effects, but for interaction contrasts both error terms be pooled together (this procedure is conservative, yet simpler than the first alternative).

### 15.5.7 An Example

Consider now an example problem to illustrate the two-factor mixed design. Here we expand on the example presented earlier in this chapter by adding a second factor to the model. The data are shown in Table 15.12 where there are eight subjects, each of whom has been evaluated by four raters on a task of writing assessment. The possible ratings range from 1 (lowest rating) to

**TABLE 15.12**

Data for the Writing Assessment Example—Two-Factor Design: Raw Scores
on the Writing Assessment Task by Instructor and Rater

| Factor A (Non-(repeated factor): | | Factor B (Repeated factor) | | | |
|---|---|---|---|---|---|
| Instructor | Subject | Rater 1 | Rater 2 | Rater 3 | Rater 4 |
| 1 | 1 | 3 | 4 | 7 | 8 |
|  | 2 | 6 | 5 | 8 | 9 |
|  | 3 | 3 | 4 | 7 | 9 |
|  | 4 | 3 | 4 | 6 | 8 |
| 2 | 5 | 1 | 2 | 5 | 10 |
|  | 6 | 2 | 3 | 6 | 10 |
|  | 7 | 2 | 4 | 5 | 9 |
|  | 8 | 2 | 3 | 6 | 10 |

10 (highest rating). Factor A represents the instructors of English composition, where the first four subjects are randomly assigned to level 1 of factor A (i.e., instructor 1) and the last four to level 2 of factor A (i.e., instructor 2). Thus factor B (i.e., rater) is repeated and factor A (i.e., instructor) is not repeated. The ANOVA summary table is shown in Table 15.13.

The test statistics are compared to the following usual $F$ test critical values: for A, $_{.05}F_{1,6} = 5.99$, which is not significant; for B, $_{.05}F_{3,18} = 3.16$, which is significant; and for AB, $_{.05}F_{3,18} = 3.16$, which is significant. For the Geisser-Greenhouse conservative procedure, the test statistics are compared to the following critical values: for A no conservative procedure is necessary; for B, $_{.05}F_{1,6} = 5.99$, which is also significant; and for AB, $_{.05}F_{1,6} = 5.99$, which is also significant. The two procedures both yield a statistically significant result for B and for AB; thus we need not be concerned with a violation of the compound symmetry assumption. A profile plot of the interaction is shown in Figure 15.2.

There is a significant AB interaction, so we should follow this up with simple interaction contrasts, each involving only four cell means. As an example of a MCP, consider the contrast

$$\psi' = \frac{(\overline{Y}_{.11} - \overline{Y}_{.21}) - (\overline{Y}_{.14} - \overline{Y}_{.24})}{4} = \frac{(3.7500 - 1.7500) - (8.5000 - 9.7500)}{4} = 0.8125$$

with a standard error of

$$se_{\psi'} = \sqrt{MS_{BS}\left(\frac{\displaystyle\sum_{j=1}^{J}\sum_{k=1}^{K} c_{jk}^2}{n_{jk}}\right)} = \sqrt{0.3472\,\frac{(1/16 + 1/16 + 1/16 + 1/16)}{4}} = 0.1473$$

**TABLE 15.13**
Two-Factor Split-plot ANOVA Summary Table for the Writing Assessment Example

| Source | SS | df | MS | F |
|---|---|---|---|---|
| Within subjects: | | | | |
| Rater (B) | 198.125 | 3 | 66.042 | 190.200* |
| Instructor x Rater | 12.625 | 3 | 4.208 | 12.120* |
| Error (BS) | 6.250 | 18 | 0.347 | |
| Between subjects: | | | | |
| Instructor (A) | 6.125 | 1 | 6.125 | 4.200** |
| Error (S) | 8.750 | 6 | 1.458 | |
| Total | 231.875 | 31 | | |

$*_{.05}F_{3,18} = 3.16$
$**_{.05}F_{1,6} = 5.99$

Using the Scheffe' procedure we formulate as the test statistic

$$t = \frac{\psi'}{se_{\psi'}} = \frac{0.8125}{0.1473} = 5.5160$$

This is compared with the critical value of

$$\sqrt{(J-1)(K-1)} \, _{\alpha}F_{(J-1)(K-1),(K-1)J(n-1)} = \sqrt{3(_{.05}F_{3,18})} = \sqrt{3(3.16)} = 3.0790$$

Thus we may conclude that the tetrad difference between the first and second levels of factor A (instructor) and the first and fourth levels of factor B (rater) is significant. In other words, Rater 1 finds better writing among the students of Instructor 1 than Instructor 2, whereas Rater 4 finds better writing among the students of Instructor 2 than Instructor 1.

Although we have only considered the basic repeated measures designs here, more complex repeated measures designs also exist. For further information see Myers (1979), Keppel (1982), Kirk (1982), Myers and Well (1995), Glass and Hopkins (1996), Cotton (1998), Keppel and Wickens (2004), as well as alternative ANOVA procedures described by Wilcox (2003) and McCulloch (2005). To analyze repeated measures designs in SAS, use the GLM procedure with the REPEATED statement. In SPSS GLM use the repeated measures program.

## 15.6  SPSS

Finally we consider SPSS for the models presented in this chapter, as well as an APA paragraph of selected results. Note that all of the designs in this chapter are discussed in the SPSS context by Page, Braver, and MacKinnon (2003). To conduct a one-factor random-effects ANOVA, there are only two differences from the one-factor fixed-effects ANOVA. Otherwise, the form of the data and the conduct of the analyses are exactly the same. First, on the GLM main screen click the factor name into the "Random Factor(s)" box rather than the "Fixed Factor(s)" box. Second, on the same screen notice that the "Post hoc" option button is not active.

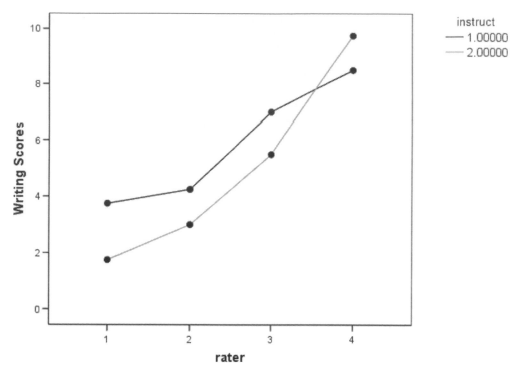

FIG. 15.2. Profile plot for example writing data.

Posthoc MCPs are only available from the "Options" screen, where you go to the "Compare main effects" pulldown to reveal the Tukey LSD, Bonferroni, and Sidak procedures. However, we have already mentioned that MCPs are not generally of interest for this model.

To run a two-factor random-effects ANOVA, there are the same two differences from the two-factor fixed-effects ANOVA. First, on the GLM screen, click both factor names into the "Random Factor(s)" box rather than the "Fixed Factor(s)" box. Second, the same situation exists with MCPs.

To conduct a two-factor mixed-effects ANOVA, there are three differences from the two-factor fixed-effects ANOVA. First, on the GLM screen, click the appropriate factors into the "Random Factor(s)" and "Fixed Factor(s)" boxes. Second, posthoc MCPs for the fixed-effects factor are available from either the "Post Hoc" or "Options" screens, while for the random-effects factor they are only available from the "Options" screen. Third, the $F$ statistics for the main effects of mixed-effects models are incorrect in SPSS as the wrong error terms are used (when using the point-and-click features). As described in Lomax and Surman (2007), you either need to (a) compute the $F$ statistics by hand from the $MS$ values (which are correct), (b) use SPSS syntax to indicate the correct error terms, or (c) use a different software package.

In order to run a one-factor repeated measures ANOVA, the data have to be in the following form. All of the scores for each subject must be in one row of the dataset. For example, if there are four raters who assess each student's essay, there will be variables for each rater (e.g., Rater1 through Rater4; example dataset on the CD).

To conduct a parametric one-factor repeated measures ANOVA through the GLM module, go into the "Repeated Measures" procedure rather than the "Univariate" procedure. A screen will come up called "Repeated Measures Define Factor(s)." First input into the "Within-Subject Factor Name:" box the name you wish to give the repeated factor. This is necessary as there is no single variable representing this factor, only variables representing each level of the factor. In our example there are four levels of rater and thus four variables. Let us call the within subjects factor "rater." Then type in the number of levels of the factor (e.g., 4), click "Add," then click on "Define" to move to the main screen called "Repeated Measures." Here you see a heading called "Within-Subject Variables:" with the newly defined factor rater in parentheses. Inside the box are spaces for each of the levels of that factor with question marks. Move the appropriate variables from the dataset into that box, which then attaches a particular variable with a particular level. The "Plots" box can be used as always, the "Post Hoc" box is not active, and the "Options" box can also be used as before (this is the proper place to obtain posthoc MCPs of Tukey LSD, Bonferroni, and Sidak). These results are shown in the top panel of Table 15.14. To perform Friedman's test, go to the "Analyze" pulldown, into "Nonparametric Tests," and then into "K Related Samples." Click the variables representing the levels of the repeated factor

**TABLE 15.14**

Selected SPSS Results for the Writing Assessment Example

*One-Factor Repeated Measures ANOVA.*

*Descriptive Statistics*

|  | Mean | Std. Deviation | N |
|---|---|---|---|
| rater1 | 2.7500000 | 1.48804762 | 8 |
| rater2 | 3.6250000 | .91612538 | 8 |
| rater3 | 6.2500000 | 1.03509834 | 8 |
| rater4 | 9.1250000 | .83452296 | 8 |

*Tests of Within-Subjects Effects*

*Measure: MEASURE 1*

| Source | | Type III Sum of Squares | df | Mean Square | F | Sig. | Partial Eta Squared | Observed Power[a] |
|---|---|---|---|---|---|---|---|---|
| rater | Sphericity Assumed | 198.125 | 3 | 66.042 | 73.477 | .000 | .913 | 1.000 |
|  | Greenhouse-Geisser | 198.125 | 1.428 | 138.760 | 73.477 | .000 | .913 | 1.000 |
|  | Huynh-Feldt | 198.125 | 1.691 | 117.163 | 73.477 | .000 | .913 | 1.000 |
| Error(rater) | Sphericity Assumed | 18.875 | 21 | .899 |  |  |  |  |
|  | Greenhouse-Geisser | 18.875 | 9.995 | 1.888 |  |  |  |  |
|  | Huynh-Feldt | 18.875 | 11.837 | 1.595 |  |  |  |  |

[a]Computed using alpha = .05

*(continued)*

TABLE 15.14 (*continued*)
Selected SPSS Results for the Writing Assessment Example

*Tests of Between-Subjects Effects*

*Measure: MEASURE 1*
*Transformed Variable: Average*

| Source | Type III Sum of Squares | df | Mean Square |
|--------|------------------------|-----|-------------|
| Error | 14.875 | 7 | 2.125 |

[a]Computed using alpha = .05

*Pairwise Comparisons*

*Measure: MEASURE 1*

| (I)rater | (J)rater | Mean Difference (I–J) | Std. Error | Sig.[a] | 95% Confidence Interval for Difference[a] Lower Bound | 95% Confidence Interval for Difference[a] Upper Bound |
|----------|----------|------------------------|------------|---------|-------------|-------------|
| 1 | 2 | −.875 | .295 | .126 | −1.948 | .198 |
|   | 3 | −3.500* | .267 | .000 | −4.472 | −2.528 |
|   | 4 | −6.375* | .706 | .000 | −8.940 | −3.810 |
| 2 | 1 | .875 | .295 | .126 | −.198 | 1.948 |
|   | 3 | −2.625* | .263 | .000 | −3.581 | −1.669 |
|   | 4 | −5.500* | .567 | .000 | −7.561 | −3.439 |
| 3 | 1 | 3.500* | .267 | .000 | 2.528 | 4.472 |
|   | 2 | 2.625* | .263 | .000 | 1.669 | 3.581 |
|   | 4 | −2.875* | .549 | .007 | −4.871 | −.879 |
| 4 | 1 | 6.375* | .706 | .000 | 3.810 | 8.940 |
|   | 2 | 5.500* | .567 | .000 | 3.439 | 7.561 |
|   | 3 | 2.875* | .549 | .007 | .879 | 4.871 |

Based on estimated marginal means

*The mean difference is significant at the .05 level.

[a]Adjustment for multiple comparisons: Bonferroni.

*Friedman Test:*

*Ranks*

| | Mean Rank |
|--------|-----------|
| rater1 | 1.13 |
| rater2 | 1.88 |
| rater3 | 3.00 |
| rater4 | 4.00 |

*Test Statistics*$_a$

| N | 8 |
|------------|--------|
| Chi-Square | 22.950 |
| Df | 3 |
| Asymp. Sig. | .000 |

[a]Friedman Test

**TABLE 15.14** (*continued*)
Selected SPSS Results for the Writing Assessment Example

*Two-factor Split-plot ANOVA:*

*Descriptive Statistics*

|  | Instruct | Mean | Std. Deviation | N |
|---|---|---|---|---|
| rater1 | 1.00000 | 3.7500000 | 1.50000000 | 4 |
|  | 2.00000 | 1.7500000 | .50000000 | 4 |
|  | Total | 2.7500000 | 1.48804762 | 8 |
| rater2 | 1.00000 | 4.2500000 | .50000000 | 4 |
|  | 2.00000 | 3.0000000 | .81649658 | 4 |
|  | Total | 3.6250000 | .91612538 | 8 |
| rater3 | 1.00000 | 7.0000000 | .81649658 | 4 |
|  | 2.00000 | 5.5000000 | .57735027 | 4 |
|  | Total | 6.2500000 | 1.03509834 | 8 |
| rater4 | 1.0000 | 8.5000000 | .57735027 | 4 |
|  | 2.00000 | 9.7500000 | .50000000 | 4 |
|  | Total | 9.1250000 | .83452296 | 8 |

*Tests of Within-Subjects Effects*

*Measure: MEASURE 1*

| Source | | Type III Sum of Squares | df | Mean Square | F | Sig. | Partial Eta Squared | Observed Power[a] |
|---|---|---|---|---|---|---|---|---|
| rater | Sphericity Assumed | 198.125 | 3 | 66.042 | 190.200 | .000 | .969 | 1.000 |
|  | Greenhouse-Geisser | 198.125 | 2.119 | 93.515 | 190.200 | .000 | .969 | 1.000 |
|  | Huynh-Feldt | 198.125 | 3.000 | 66.042 | 190.200 | .000 | .969 | 1.000 |
| rater* instruct | Sphericity Assumed | 12.625 | 3 | 4.208 | 12.120 | .000 | .669 | .998 |
|  | Greenhouse-Geisser | 12.625 | 2.119 | 5.959 | 12.120 | .001 | .669 | .983 |
|  | Huynh-Feldt | 12.625 | 3.000 | 4.208 | 12.120 | .000 | .669 | .998 |
| Error(rater) | Sphericity Assumed | 6.250 | 18 | .347 |  |  |  |  |
|  | Greenhouse-Geisser | 6.250 | 12.712 | .492 |  |  |  |  |
|  | Huynh-Feldt | 6.250 | 18.000 | .347 |  |  |  |  |

[a]Computed using alpha =.05

**TABLE 15.14**

(*Continued*)

---

*Tests of Between-Subjects Effects*

*Measure: MEASURE 1*
*Transformed Variable: Average*

| Source | Type III Sum of Squares | df | Mean Square | F | Sig. | Partial Eta Squared | Observed Power[a] |
|---|---|---|---|---|---|---|---|
| Instruct | 6.125 | 1 | 6.125 | 4.200 | .086 | .412 | .407 |
| Error | 8.750 | 6 | 1.458 | | | | |

[a]Computed using alpha = .05

---

*Pairwise Comparisons*

*Measure: MEASURE 1*

| (I)rater | (J)rater | Mean Difference (I–J) | Std. Error | Sig.[a] | 95% Confidence Interval for Difference[a] | |
|---|---|---|---|---|---|---|
| | | | | | Lower Bound | Upper Bound |
| 1 | 2 | −.875 | .280 | .122 | −1.955 | .205 |
| | 3 | −3.500* | .270 | .000 | −4.543 | −2.457 |
| | 4 | −6.375* | .375 | .000 | −7.824 | −4.926 |
| 2 | 1 | .875 | .280 | .122 | −.205 | 1.955 |
| | 3 | −2.625* | .280 | .000 | −3.705 | −1.545 |
| | 4 | −5.500* | .339 | .000 | −6.808 | −4.192 |
| 3 | 1 | 3.500* | .270 | .000 | 2.457 | 4.543 |
| | 2 | 2.625* | .280 | .000 | 1.545 | 3.705 |
| | 4 | −2.875* | .191 | .000 | −3.613 | −2.137 |
| 4 | 1 | 6.375* | .375 | .000 | 4.926 | 7.824 |
| | 2 | 5.500* | .339 | .000 | 4.192 | 6.808 |
| | 3 | 2.875* | .191 | .000 | 2.137 | 3.613 |

Based on estimated marginal means

*The mean difference is significant at the .05 level.

[a]Adjustment for multiple comparisons: Bonferroni.

into the "Test Variables:" box, check Friedman as "Test Type," and click on "OK" to generate the output. These results are shown in the middle panel of Table 15.14.

To conduct the two-factor split-plot ANOVA, the dataset must include variables for each level of the repeated factor (as in the one-factor repeated measures ANOVA), and an additional variable for the nonrepeated factor (example dataset on CD). Return to the "Repeated Measures" program and generate the repeated factor. From the main screen, the one addition is to click the nonrepeated factor variable name into the "Between-Subjects Factor(s):" box. Otherwise, the options work as before. These results are shown in the bottom panel of Table 15.14.

Finally, here is an example paragraph of the results for the two-factor split-plot design (feel free to write similar paragraphs for the other models in this chapter). From Table 15.14 we see that there is a significant main effect for rater ($F_{rater} = 190.200$, $df = 3,18$, $p = .001$), a significant interaction between rater and instructor ($F_{rater \times instructor} = 12.120$, $df = 3,18$, $p = .001$), but the main effect for instructor is not significant. The sphericity assumption was upheld in that the same results were obtained for the usual, Geisser-Greenhouse, and Huynh and Feldt $F$ tests. Effect sizes were rather large for the significant effects (partial $\eta^2_{rater} = .969$; partial $\eta^2_{rater \times instructor} = .669$) with maximum observed power, but less so for the nonsignificant effect (partial $\eta^2_{instructor} = .412$, power = .407). The raters were quite inconsistent in that Bonferroni MCPs revealed significant differences among all pairs of raters except for rater 1 versus rater 2. From the profile plot in Figure 15.2, we see that while rater 4 found the students of instructor 2 to have better essays, the other raters liked the essays written by the students of instructor 1. It is suggested that a more detailed plan for evaluating essays, including rater training, be implemented in the future.

## 15.7  SUMMARY

In this chapter methods involving the comparision of means for random- and mixed-effects models were considered. Five different models were examined; these included the one-factor random-effects model, the two-factor random- and mixed-effects models, the one-factor repeated measures model, and the two-factor split-plot or mixed design. Included for each design were the usual topics of model characteristics, the linear model, assumptions of the model and the effects of their violation, the ANOVA summary table, and multiple comparison procedures. Also included for particular designs was a discussion of the compound symmetry assumption, and alternative ANOVA procedures. At this point you should have met the following objectives: (a) be able to understand the characteristics and concepts underlying random- and mixed-effects ANOVA models, (b) be able to determine and interpret the results of random- and mixed-effects ANOVA models, and (c) be able to understand and evaluate the assumptions of random- and mixed-effects ANOVA models. In chapter 16, we continue our extended tour of the analysis of variance by looking at hierarchical designs that involve a factor nested within another factor, and randomized block designs, which we have very briefly introduced in this chapter.

## PROBLEMS

### Conceptual Problems

1. When an ANOVA design includes a random factor that is crossed with a fixed factor, the design illustrates which type of model?

   a. fixed

   b. mixed

   c. random

   d. crossed

2. The denominator of the $F$ ratio used to test the interaction in a two-factor ANOVA is $MS_{with}$ in

   a. the fixed-effects model.

   b. the random-effects model.

   c. the mixed-effects model.

   d. All of the above.

3. A course consists of five units, the order of presentation of which is varied. A researcher used a $5 \times 2$ ANOVA design with order (five different randomly selected orders) and gender serving as factors. Which ANOVA model is illustrated by this design?

   a. the fixed-effects model

   b. the random-effects model

   c. the mixed-effects model

   d. the nested model

4. If a given set of data were analyzed with both a one-factor fixed-effects ANOVA and a one-factor random-effects ANOVA, the $F$ ratio for the random-effects model will be greater than the $F$ ratio for the fixed-effects model. True or False?

5. A repeated measures design is necessarily an example of the random-effects model. True or False?

6. Suppose researchers A and B perform a two-factor ANOVA on the same data, but that A assumes a fixed-effects model and B assumes a random-effects model. I assert that if A finds the interaction significant at the .05 level, B will also find the interaction significant at the .05 level. Am I correct?

7. I assert that $MS_{with}$ should always be used as the denominator for all $F$ ratios in any two-factor analysis of variance. Am I correct?

8. I assert that in a one-factor repeated measures ANOVA and a two-factor split-plot ANOVA, the $SS_{total}$ will be exactly the same when using the same data. Am I correct?

9. Football players are each exposed to all three different counterbalanced coaching strategies, one per month. This is an example of which type of model?

    a. one-factor fixed-effects ANOVA model

    b. one-factor repeated-measures ANOVA model

    c. one-factor random-effects ANOVA model

    d. one-factor fixed-effects ANCOVA model

10. A two-factor split-plot design involves which of the following?

    a. two repeated factors

    b. two nonrepeated factors

    c. one repeated factor and one nonrepeated factor

    d. farmers splitting up their land

11. The interaction between factors L and M can be assessed only if

    a. both factors are crossed.

    b. both factors are random.

    c. both factors are fixed.

    d. factor L is a repeated factor.

12. A student factor is almost always random. True or false?

13. In a two-factor split-plot design, there are two interaction terms. Hypotheses can actually be tested for how many interactions?

    a. 0

    b. 1

    c. 2

    d. cannot be determined

14. In a one-factor repeated measures ANOVA, the $F$ test is quite robust to violation of the sphericity assumption, and thus we never need to worry about it. True or false?

## Computational Problems

1. Complete the following summary table for a two-factor analysis of variance, where there are three levels of factor A (fixed method effect) and two levels of factor B (random teacher effect). Each cell of the design includes 4 students. Complete the following summary table ($\alpha = .01$).

| Source | SS | df | MS | F | Critical Value and Decision | |
|--------|------|----|----|---|---|---|
| A | 3.64 | — | — | — | — | — |
| B | 0.57 | — | — | — | — | — |
| AB | 2.07 | — | — | — | — | — |
| Within | — | — | — | | | |
| Total | 8.18 | — | | | | |

2.  A researcher tested whether aerobics increased the fitness level of eight undergraduate students participating over a four-month period. Students were measured at the end of each month using a ten-point fitness measure (10 being most fit). The data are shown here. Conduct an ANOVA to determine the effectiveness of the program, using $\alpha = .05$. Use the Bonferroni method to detect exactly where the differences are among the time points (if they are different).

| Subject | Time 1 | Time 2 | Time 3 | Time 4 |
|---------|--------|--------|--------|--------|
| 1 | 3 | 4 | 6 | 9 |
| 2 | 4 | 7 | 5 | 10 |
| 3 | 5 | 7 | 7 | 8 |
| 4 | 1 | 3 | 5 | 7 |
| 5 | 3 | 4 | 7 | 9 |
| 6 | 2 | 5 | 6 | 7 |
| 7 | 1 | 4 | 6 | 9 |
| 8 | 2 | 4 | 5 | 6 |

3.  Using the same data as in Computational Problem #2, conduct a two-factor split-plot ANOVA, where the first four subjects participate in a step aerobics problem and the last four subjects participate in a spinning program ($\alpha = 05$).

4.  As a statistical consultant, a researcher comes to you with the following partial SPSS output (sphericity assumed). In a two-factor split-plot ANOVA design, rater is the repeated factor, gender of the rater is the nonrepeated factor, and the dependent variable is history exam scores. (a) Are the effects significant (which you must determine, as significance is missing, using $\alpha = .05$)? (b) What are the implications of these results in terms of rating the history exam?

Tests of Within-Subjects Effects

| Source | Type III SS | df | MS | F |
|--------|-------------|-----|------|------|
| RATER | 298.38 | 3 | 99.46 | 30.47 |
| RATER * GENDER | 184.38 | 3 | 61.46 | 18.83 |
| ERROR(RATER) | 58.75 | 18 | 3.26 | |

Tests of Between-Subjects Effects

| Source | Type III SS | df | MS | F |
|--------|-------------|-----|------|------|
| GENDER | 153.13 | 1 | 153.13 | 20.76 |
| Error | 44.25 | 6 | 7.38 | |

**Interpretive Problem**

Using the same interpretive problem you developed in Chapter 13, conduct two-factor ANOVAs using the fixed-effects, random-effects, and mixed-effects designs. Determine whether the nature of the factors makes any difference in the results

# 16

# HIERARCHICAL AND RANDOMIZED BLOCK ANALYSIS OF VARIANCE MODELS

## Chapter Outline

1. The two-factor hierarchical model
    Characteristics of the model
    The layout of the data
    The ANOVA model
    ANOVA summary table
    Multiple comparison procedures
    An example
2. The two-factor randomized block design for $n = 1$
    Characteristics of the model
    The layout of the data
    The ANOVA model
    Assumptions and violation of assumptions
    ANOVA summary table
    Multiple comparison procedures
    Methods of block formation
    An example
3. The two-factor randomized block design for $n > 1$
4. The Friedman test
5. Comparison of various ANOVA models
6. SPSS

## Key Concepts

1.   Crossed designs and nested designs
2.   Confounding
3.   Randomized block designs
4.   Methods of blocking

In the last several chapters our discussion has dealt with different analysis of variance (ANOVA) models. In this chapter we complete our discussion of the analysis of variance by considering models in which there are multiple factors, but where at least one of the factors is either a nested factor or a blocking factor. As becomes evident when we define these models, this results in a nested or hierarchical design and a blocking design, respectively. In this chapter we are most concerned with the two-factor nested model and the two-factor randomized block model, although these models can be generalized to designs with more than two factors. Most of the concepts used in this chapter are the same as those covered in previous chapters. In addition, new concepts include crossed and nested factors, confounding, blocking factors, and methods of blocking. Our objectives are that by the end of this chapter, you will be able to (a) understand the characteristics and concepts underlying hierarchical and randomized block ANOVA models, (b) determine and interpret the results of hierarchical and randomized block ANOVA models, (c) understand and evaluate the assumptions of hierarchical and randomized block ANOVA models, and (d) compare different ANOVA models and select an appropriate model.

## 16.1   THE TWO-FACTOR HIERARCHICAL MODEL

In this section, we describe the distinguishing characteristics of the two-factor hierarchical ANOVA model, the layout of the data, the linear model, the ANOVA summary table, and multiple comparison procedures.

### 16.1.1   Characteristics of the Model

The characteristics of the two-factor fixed-, random-, and mixed-effects models have already been covered in chapters 13 and 15. Here we consider a special form of the two-factor model where one factor is nested within another factor. An example is the best introduction to this model. Suppose you are interested in which of several different major teaching pedagogies (e.g., worksheet, math manipulative, and computer-based approaches) results in the highest level of achievement in mathematics among second-grade students. Thus math achievement is the dependent variable and teaching pedagogy is one factor. A second factor is teacher. That is, you may also believe that some teachers are more effective than others, which results in different levels of student achievement. However, each teacher has only one class of students and thus only one major teaching pedagogy. In other words, all combinations of the pedagogy and teacher factors are not possible. This design is known as a **nested** or **hierarchical design** because the teacher factor is nested within the pedagogy factor. This is in contrast to a two-factor **crossed design** where all possible combinations of the two factors are included. The two-factor designs described in chapters 13 and 15 were all crossed designs.

Let me give a more precise definition of crossed and nested designs. A two-factor completely crossed design (or **complete factorial design**) is one where every level of factor A occurs in combination with every level of factor B. A two-factor nested design (or **incomplete factorial design**) of factor B being nested within factor A is one where the levels of factor B occur for only one level of factor A. We denote this particular nested design as B(A), which is read as factor B being nested within factor A (in other references you may see this written as B : A or as B|A). To return to our example, the teacher factor (factor B) is nested within the method factor (factor A) because each teacher utilizes only one major teaching pedagogy.

These models are shown graphically in Fig. 16.1. In Fig. 16.1(a) a completely crossed or complete factorial design is shown where there are 2 levels of factor A and 6 levels of factor B. Thus, there are 12 possible factor combinations that would all be included in a completely crossed design. The shaded region indicates the combinations that might be included in a nested or incomplete factorial design where factor B is nested within factor A. Although the number

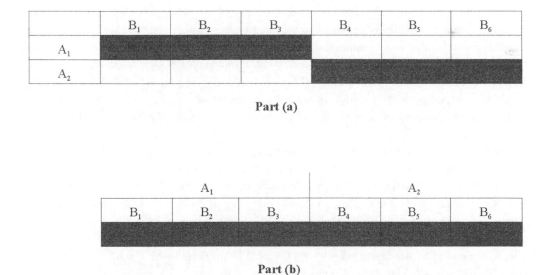

Part (a)

Part (b)

**FIG. 16.1    Two-factor completely crossed versus nested designs. (a) The completely crossed design. The shaded region indicates the cells that would be included in a nested design where factor B is nested within factor A. In the nested design, factor A has two levels and factor B has three levels within each level of factor A. You see that only 6 of the 12 possible cells are filled in the nested design. (b) The same nested design in traditional form. The shaded region indicates the cells included in the nested design (i.e., the same 6 as shown in the first part).**

of levels of each factor remains the same, factor B now has only three levels within each level of factor A. For $A_1$ we see only $B_1$, $B_2$, and $B_3$, whereas for $A_2$ we see only $B_4$, $B_5$, and $B_6$. Thus, only 6 of the possible 12 factor combinations are included in the nested design. For example, level 1 of factor B occurs only with level 1 of factor A. In summary, Fig. 16.1(a) shows that the nested or incomplete factorial design consists of only a portion of the completely crossed design (the shaded regions). In Fig. 16.1(b) we see the nested design depicted in its more traditional form. Here you see that the 6 factor combinations not included are not even shown (e.g., $A_1$ with $B_4$). Other examples of the two-factor nested design are where (a) school is nested within school district, (b) faculty member is nested within department, (c) individual is nested within gender, and (d) county is nested within state.

Thus with this design, one factor is nested within another factor, rather than the two factors being crossed. As is shown in more detail later in this chapter, the nesting characteristic has some interesting and distinct outcomes. For now some mention should be made of these outcomes. **Nesting** is a particular type of confounding among the factors being investigated, where the AB interaction is part of the B effect (or is **confounded** with B) and therefore cannot be investigated. In the ANOVA model and the ANOVA summary table, there will not be an interaction term or source of variation. This is due to the fact that each level of factor B occurs in combination with only one level of factor A. We cannot compare for a particular level of B all levels of factor A, as a level of B only occurs with one level of A.

Confounding may occur for two reasons. First, the confounding may be intentional due to practical reasons, such as a reduction in the number of individuals to be observed. Fewer individuals would be necessary in a nested design, as compared to a crossed design, due to the fact that there are fewer cells in the model. Second, the confounding may be absolutely necessary because crossing may not be possible. For example, school is nested within school district because a particular school can only be a member of one school district. The nested factor (here factor B) may be a nuisance variable that the researcher wants to take into account in terms of explaining or predicting the dependent variable $Y$. An error commonly made is to ignore the nuisance variable B and go ahead with a one-factor design using only factor A. This design may result in a biased test of factor A such that the $F$ ratio is inflated. Thus $H_0$ would be rejected more often that it should be, serving to increase the actual $\alpha$ level over that specified by the researcher and thereby increase the likelihood of a Type I error. The $F$ test is then too liberal.

Let me make two further points about this first characteristic. First, in the one-factor design discussed in chapter 11, we have already seen nesting going on in a different way. Here subjects were nested within factor A because each subject only responded to one level of factor A. It was only when we got to repeated measures designs in chapter 15 that individuals were allowed to respond to more than one level of a factor. For the repeated measures design we actually had a completely crossed design of subjects by factor A. Second, Glass and Hopkins (1996) give a nice example of a nested design with teachers being nested within schools, where each school is like a nest having multiple eggs or teachers.

The remaining characteristics should be familiar. These include the following: (a) two factors (or independent variables), each with two or more levels; (b) the levels of each of the factors may be either randomly sampled from the population of levels or fixed by the researcher (i.e., the model may be fixed, mixed, or random); (c) subjects are randomly assigned to one combination of the levels of the two factors; and (d) the dependent variable is measured at least at the interval level. If individuals respond to more than one combination of the levels of the two factors, then this is a repeated measures design (see chap. 15).

For simplicity we again assume the design is balanced. For the two-factor nested design, a design is balanced if (a) the number of observations within each factor combination are equal, and (b) the number of levels of the nested factor within each level of the other factor are equal. The first portion of this statement should be quite familiar from factorial designs, so no further explanation is necessary. The second portion of this statement is unique to this design and requires a brief explanation. As an example, say factor B is nested within factor A and factor A has two levels. On the one hand, factor B may have the same number of levels for each level of factor A. This occurs if there are three levels of factor B under level 1 of factor A (i.e., $A_1$) and also three levels of factor B under level 2 of factor A (i.e., $A_2$). On the other hand, factor B may not have the same number of levels for each level of factor A. This occurs if there are three levels of factor B under $A_1$ and only two levels of factor B under $A_2$. If the design is unbalanced, see the discussion in Kirk (1982) and Dunn and Clark (1987), although most statistical software can deal with this type of unbalanced design.

### 16.1.2 The Layout of the Data

The layout of the data for the two-factor nested design is shown in Table 16.1. To simplify matters, I have limited the number of levels of the factors to two levels of factor A and three levels of factor B. This only serves as an example layout because many other possibilities obviously exist. Here we see the major set of columns designated as the levels of factor A, the nonnested factor, and for each level of A the minor set of columns are the levels of factor B, the nested factor. Within each factor level combination or cell are the subjects. Means are shown for each cell, for the levels of factor A, and overall. Note that the means for the levels of factor B need not be shown, as they are the same as the cell means. For instance $\overline{Y}_{.11}$ is the same as $\overline{Y}_{..1}$ (not shown) as $B_1$ only occurs once. This is another result of the nesting.

**TABLE 16.1**
Layout for the Two-Factor Nested Design

|  | $A_1$ | | | $A_2$ | | |
|---|---|---|---|---|---|---|
|  | $B_1$ | $B_2$ | $B_3$ | $B_4$ | $B_5$ | $B_6$ |
|  | $Y_{111}$ | $Y_{112}$ | $Y_{113}$ | $Y_{124}$ | $Y_{125}$ | $Y_{126}$ |
|  | . | . | . | . | . | . |
|  | . | . | . | . | . | . |
|  | . | . | . | . | . | . |
|  | $Y_{n11}$ | $Y_{n12}$ | $Y_{n13}$ | $Y_{n24}$ | $Y_{n25}$ | $Y_{n26}$ |
| Cell means | $\overline{Y}_{.11}$ | $\overline{Y}_{.12}$ | $\overline{Y}_{.13}$ | $\overline{Y}_{.24}$ | $\overline{Y}_{.25}$ | $\overline{Y}_{.26}$ |
| A means |  | $\overline{Y}_{.1.}$ |  |  | $\overline{Y}_{.2.}$ |  |
| Overall mean |  |  |  | $\overline{Y}_{...}$ |  |  |

### 16.1.3 The ANOVA Model

The nested factor is almost always random (Glass & Hopkins, 1996; Keppel & Wickens, 2004; Mickey, Dunn, & Clark, 2004; Page, Braver, & MacKinnon, 2003). As a result, the two-factor nested ANOVA is usually a mixed-effects model where the nonnested factor is fixed and the nested factor is random. Thus the two-factor mixed-effects nested ANOVA model is written in terms of population parameters as

$$Y_{ijk} = \mu + \alpha_j + b_{k(j)} + \varepsilon_{ijk}$$

where $Y_{ijk}$ is the observed score on the dependent variable for individual $i$ in level $j$ of factor A and level $k$ of factor B (or in the $jk$ cell), $\mu$ is the overall or grand population mean (i.e., regardless of cell designation), $\alpha_j$ is the fixed effect for level $j$ of factor A, $b_{k(j)}$ is the random effect for level $k$ of factor B, and $\varepsilon_{ijk}$ is the random residual error for individual $i$ in cell $jk$. Notice that there is no interaction term in the model, and also that the effect for factor B is denoted by $b_{k(j)}$. This tells us that factor B is nested within factor A. The residual error can be due to individual differences, measurement error, and/or other factors not under investigation. We consider the fixed-, mixed-, and random-effects cases later in this chapter.

For the two-factor mixed-effects nested ANOVA model, there are only two sets of hypotheses, one for each of the main effects, because there is no interaction effect. The null and alternative hypotheses, respectively, for testing the effect of factor A are

$$H_{01}: \mu_{.1.} = \mu_{.2.} = ... = \mu_{.J.}$$
$$H_{11}: \text{not all the } \mu_{.j.} \text{ are equal}$$

The hypotheses for testing the effect of factor B are

$$H_{02}: \sigma_b^2 = 0$$
$$H_{12}: \sigma_b^2 > 0$$

These hypotheses reflect the inferences made in the fixed-, mixed-, and random-effects models (as fully described in chap. 15). For fixed main effects the null hypotheses are about means, whereas for random main effects the null hypotheses are about variation among the means. As we already know, the difference in the models is also reflected in the multiple comparison procedures. As before, we do need to pay particular attention to whether the model is fixed, mixed, or random. The assumptions about the two-factor nested model are exactly the same as with the two-factor crossed model, and thus we need not provide any additional discussion. In addition, procedures for determining power, confidence intervals, and effect size are the same as with the two-factor crossed model.

### 16.1.4 ANOVA Summary Table

The computations of the two-factor mixed-effects nested model are somewhat similar to those of the two-factor mixed-effects crossed model. The main difference lies in the fact that there is no interaction term. The ANOVA summary table is shown in Table 16.2, where we see the following

TABLE 16.2
Two-Factor Nested Design ANOVA Summary Table—Mixed Effects Model

| Source | SS | df | MS | F |
|--------|----|----|----|---|
| A | $SS_A$ | $J - 1$ | $MS_A$ | $MS_A/MS_{B(A)}$ |
| B(A) | $SS_{B(A)}$ | $J(K_{(j)} - 1)$ | $MS_{B(A)}$ | $MS_{B(A)}/MS_{with}$ |
| Within | $SS_{with}$ | $JK_{(j)}(n - 1)$ | $MS_{with}$ | |
| Total | $SS_{total}$ | $N - 1$ | | |

sources of variation: A, B(A), within cells, and total. There we see that only two $F$ ratios can be formed, one for each of the two main effects, because no interaction term is estimated.

If we take the total sum of squares and decompose it, we have

$$SS_{total} = SS_A + SS_{B(A)} + SS_{with}$$

We leave the computations involving these terms to the statistical software. The degrees of freedom, mean squares, and $F$ ratios are determined as shown in Table 16.2, assuming a mixed-effects model. The critical value for the test of factor A is $_\alpha F_{J-1, J(K(j)-1)}$ and for the test of factor B is $_\alpha F_{J(K(j)-1), JK(j)(n-1)}$. Let me explain something about the degrees of freedom. The degrees of freedom for B(A) are equal to $J(K_{(j)} - 1)$. This means that for a design with two levels of factor A and three levels of factor B within each level of A (for a total of six levels of B), the degrees of freedom are equal to $2(3 - 1) = 4$. This is not the same as the degrees of freedom for a completely crossed design where $df_B$ would be 5. The degrees of freedom for within are equal to $JK_{(j)}(n - 1)$. For this same design with $n = 10$, then the degrees of freedom within are equal to $(2)(3)(10 - 1) = 54$ (i.e., 6 cells with 9 degrees of freedom per cell).

The appropriate error terms for each of the fixed-, random-, and mixed-effects models are as follows. For the fixed-effects model, both $F$ ratios use the within source as the error term. For the random-effects model, the appropriate error term for the test of A is $MS_{B(A)}$ and for the test of B is $MS_{with}$. For the mixed-effects model where A is fixed and B is random, the appropriate error term for the test of A is $MS_{B(A)}$ and for the test of B is $MS_{with}$. As already mentioned, this is the predominant model in education and the behavioral sciences. Finally, for the mixed-effects model where A is random and B is fixed, both $F$ ratios use the within source as the error term.

### 16.1.5 Multiple Comparison Procedures

This section considers multiple comparison procedures (MCPs) for the two-factor nested design. First of all, the researcher is usually not interested in making inferences about random effects. Second, for MCPs based on the levels of factor A (the nonnested factor), there is nothing new to report. Third, for MCPs based on the levels of factor B (the nested factor), this is a different situation. The researcher is not usually as interested in MCPs about the nested factor as compared to the nonnested factor because inferences about the levels of factor B are not even generalizable across the levels of factor A, due to the nesting. If you are nonetheless interested in MCPs for factor B, by necessity you have to look within a level of A to formulate a contrast. Otherwise MCPs are conducted as before. For more complex nested designs, see Myers (1979), Kirk (1982), Dunn and Clark (1987), Myers and Well (1995), or Keppel and Wickens (2004).

## 16.1.6   An Example

Let us consider an example to illustrate the procedures in this section. The data are shown in Table 16.3. Factor A is approach to the teaching of reading (basal vs. whole language approaches), and factor B is teacher. Thus there are two teachers using the basal approach and two different teachers using the whole language approach. The researcher is interested in the effects these factors have on student's reading comprehension in the first grade. Thus the dependent variable is a measure of reading comprehension. Six students are randomly assigned to each approach-teacher combination for small-group instruction. This particular example is a mixed model, where factor A (teaching method) is a fixed effect and factor B (teacher) is a random effect. The results are shown in the ANOVA summary table of Table 16.4.

From Appendix Table 4, the critical value for the test of factor A is $_{\alpha}F_{J-1,J(K(j)-1)} = {_{.05}}F_{1,2}$ = 18.51, and the critical value for the test of factor B is $_{\alpha}F_{J(K(j)-1),JK(j)(n-1)} = {_{.05}}F_{2,20} =$ 3.49. Thus there is a significant difference between the two approaches to reading instruction at the .05 level of significance, and there is no significant difference between the teachers. When we look at the means for the levels of factor A, we see that the mean comprehension score for the whole language approach ($\overline{Y}_{.2.} = 10.8333$) is greater than the mean for the basal approach ($\overline{Y}_{.1.} = 3.3333$). No post hoc multiple comparisons are really necessary here given the results obtained.

**TABLE 16.3**
Data for the Teaching Reading Example—Two-Factor Nested Design

| | *Reading Approaches:* | | | |
| --- | --- | --- | --- | --- |
| | *A₁ (Basal)* | | *A₂ (Whole Language)* | |
| | *Teacher B₁* | *Teacher B₂* | *Teacher B₃* | *Teacher B₄* |
| | 1 | 1 | 7 | 8 |
| | 1 | 3 | 8 | 9 |
| | 2 | 3 | 8 | 11 |
| | 4 | 4 | 10 | 13 |
| | 4 | 6 | 12 | 14 |
| | 5 | 6 | 15 | 15 |
| Cell means | 2.8333 | 3.8333 | 10.0000 | 11.6667 |
| A means | 3.3333 | | 10.8333 | |
| Overall mean | | 7.0833 | | |

**TABLE 16.4**
Two-Factor Nested Design ANOVA Summary Table—Teaching Reading Example

| Source | SS | df | MS | F |
|--------|-----|-----|-----|-----|
| A | 337.5000 | 1 | 337.5000 | 59.5585* |
| B(A) | 11.3333 | 2 | 5.6667 | 0.9524** |
| Within | 119.0000 | 20 | 5.9500 | |
| Total | 467.8333 | 23 | | |

\* $_{.05}F_{1,2} = 18.51$

\*\* $_{.05}F_{2,20} = 3.49$

## 16.2    THE TWO-FACTOR RANDOMIZED BLOCK DESIGN FOR $n = 1$

In this section, we describe the distinguishing characteristics of the two-factor randomized block ANOVA model for one observation per cell, the layout of the data, the linear model, assumptions and their violation, the ANOVA summary table, multiple comparison procedures, and methods of block formation.

### 16.2.1    Characteristics of the Model

The characteristics of the two-factor randomized block ANOVA model are quite similar to those of the regular two-factor model, as well as sharing a few characteristics with the one-factor repeated measures design. There is one obvious exception, which has to do with the nature of the factors being used. Here there will be two factors, each with at least two levels. One factor is known as the **treatment factor** and is referred to as factor A (a treatment factor is what we have been considering in the last five chapters). The second factor is known as the **blocking factor** and is referred to as factor B. A blocking factor is a new concept and requires some discussion.

Take an ordinary one-factor design, where the single factor is a treatment factor (e.g., method of exercising) and the researcher is interested in its effect on some dependent variable (e.g., % body fat). Despite individuals being randomly assigned to a treatment group, the groups may be different due to a nuisance variable operating in a nonrandom way. For instance, Group 1 may have mostly older adults and Group 2 may have mostly younger adults. Thus, it is likely that Group 2 will be favored over Group 1 because age, the nuisance variable, has not been properly balanced out across the groups by randomization.

One way to deal with this problem is to control the effect of the nuisance variable by incorporating it into the design of the study. Including the blocking or nuisance variable as a factor in the design will result in a reduction in residual variation (due to some portion of individual differences being explained) and an increase in power (Glass & Hopkins, 1996; Keppel & Wickens, 2004). The blocking factor is selected based on the strength of its relationship to the dependent variable, where an unrelated blocking variable would not reduce residual variation. It would be reasonable to expect, then, that variability among individuals within a block (e.g., within younger adults) should be less than variability among individuals between blocks (e.g., between younger and older adults). Thus each block represents the formation of a matched set of individuals, that is, matched on the blocking variable, but not necessarily matched on any other nuisance variable. Using our example, we expect that in general, adults within a particular age block (i.e., older or younger blocks) will be more similar in terms of variables related to body fat than adults across blocks.

Let us consider several examples of blocking factors. Some blocking factors are naturally occurring blocks such as siblings, friends, neighbors, plots of land, and time. Other blocking factors are not naturally occurring, but can be formed by the researcher. Examples of this type include grade point average, age, weight, aptitude test scores, intelligence test scores, socio-economic status, and school or district size.

Let me make some summary statements about characteristics of blocking designs. First, designs that include one or more blocking factors are known as **randomized block designs**, also known as matching designs or treatment by block designs. The researcher's main interest is in the treatment factor. The purpose of the blocking factor is to reduce residual variation. Thus the researcher is not as much interested in the test of the blocking factor (possibly not at all) as compared to the treatment factor. Thus there is at least one blocking factor and one treatment factor, each with two or more levels. Second, each subject falls into only one block in the design and is subsequently randomly assigned to one level of the treatment factor within that block. Thus subjects within a block serve as their own controls such that some portion of their individual differences is taken into account. As a result, subjects' scores are not independent within a particular block. Third, for purposes of this section, we assume there is only one subject for each treatment-block level combination. As a result, the model does not include an interaction term. Later we consider the multiple observations case, where there is an interaction term in the model. Finally, the dependent variable is measured at least at the interval level.

## 16.2.2 The Layout of the Data

The layout of the data for the two-factor randomized block model is shown in Table 16.5. Here we see the columns designated as the levels of blocking factor B and the rows as the levels of treatment factor A. Row, block, and overall means are also shown. Here you see that the layout of the data looks the same as the two-factor model, but with a single observation per cell.

## 16.2.3 The ANOVA Model

The two-factor fixed-effects randomized block ANOVA model is written in terms of population parameters as

$$Y_{jk} = \mu + \alpha_j + \beta_k + \varepsilon_{jk}$$

where $Y_{jk}$ is the observed score on the dependent variable for the individual responding to level $j$ of factor A and level $k$ of block B, $\mu$ is the overall or grand population mean, $\alpha_j$ is the fixed effect for level $j$ of factor A, $\beta_k$ is the fixed effect for level $k$ of the block B, and $\varepsilon_{jk}$ is the random residual error for the individual in cell $jk$. The residual error can be due to measurement error, individual differences, and/or other factors not under investigation. You can see this is

**TABLE 16.5**
Layout for the Two-Factor Randomized Block Design

| Level of Factor A | Level of Factor B | | | | Row mean |
|---|---|---|---|---|---|
| | *1* | *2* | ... | *K* | |
| 1 | $Y_{11}$ | $Y_{12}$ | ... | $Y_{1K}$ | $\bar{Y}_{1.}$ |
| 2 | $Y_{21}$ | $Y_{22}$ | ... | $Y_{2K}$ | $\bar{Y}_{2.}$ |
| . | . | . | ... | . | . |
| . | . | . | ... | . | . |
| . | . | . | ... | . | . |
| *J* | $Y_{J1}$ | $Y_{J2}$ | ... | $Y_{JK}$ | $\bar{Y}_{J.}$ |
| Block mean | $\bar{Y}_{.1}$ | $\bar{Y}_{.2}$ | ... | $\bar{Y}_{.K}$ | $\bar{Y}_{..}$ |

similar to the two-factor fully-crossed model with one observation per cell (i.e., $i = 1$ making the $i$ subscript unnecessary), and with no interaction term included. Also, the effects are denoted by $\alpha$ and $\beta$ given we have a fixed-effects model. Note that the row and column effects both sum to zero in the fixed-effects model.

The hypotheses for testing the effect of factor A are

$$H_{01}: \mu_{1.} = \mu_{2.} = ... = \mu_{J.}$$
$$H_{11}: \text{not all the } \mu_{j.} \text{ are equal}$$

and for testing the effect of factor B are

$$H_{02}: \mu_{.1} = \mu_{.2} = ... = \mu_{.K}$$
$$H_{12}: \text{not all the } \mu_{.k} \text{ are equal}$$

The factors are both fixed, so the hypotheses are written in terms of means.

### 16.2.4    Assumptions and Violation of Assumptions

In chapter 15 we described the assumptions for the one-factor repeated measures model. The assumptions are nearly the same for the two-factor randomized block model and we need not devote much attention to them here. As before, the assumptions are mainly concerned with independence, normality, and homogeneity of variance of the population scores on the dependent variable.

Another assumption is **compound symmetry** and is necessary because the observations within a block are not independent. The assumption states that the population covariances for all pairs of the levels of the treatment factor A (i.e., $j$ and $j'$) are equal. The analysis of variance is not particularly robust to a violation of this assumption. If the assumption is violated, three alternative procedures are available. The first is to limit the levels of factor A either to those that meet the assumption or to two levels (in which case there is only one covariance). The second, and more plausible, alternative is to use adjusted $F$ tests. These are reported shortly. The third is to use multivariate analysis of variance, which has no compound symmetry assumption, but is slightly less powerful.

Huynh and Feldt (1970) showed that the compound symmetry assumption is a sufficient but unnecessary condition for the test of treatment factor A to be $F$ distributed. Thus the $F$ test may also be valid under less stringent conditions. The necessary and sufficient condition for the validity of the $F$ test of A is known as **sphericity**. This assumes that the variance of the difference scores for each pair of factor levels is the same. Further discussion of sphericity is beyond the scope of this text (see Keppel, 1982, or Kirk, 1982).

A final assumption purports that there is no interaction between the treatment and blocking factors. This is obviously an assumption of the model because no interaction term is included. Such a model is often referred to as an **additive model**. As was mentioned previously, in this model the interaction is confounded with the error term. Violation of the additivity assumption allows the test of factor A to be negatively biased; this means an increased probability of committing a Type II error. In other words, if $H_0$ is rejected, then we are confident that $H_0$ is really false. If $H_0$ is not rejected, then our interpretation is ambiguous as $H_0$ may or may not be really true. Here you would not know whether $H_0$ was true or not, as there might really be a difference, but the test may not be powerful enough to detect it. Also, the power of the test of factor A is reduced by a violation of the additivity assumption. The assumption may be tested by Tukey's (1949) test of additivity (see Hays, 1988; Kirk, 1982; Timm, 2002), which generates an $F$ test statistic that is compared to the critical value of $_\alpha F_{1,[(J-1)(K-1)-1]}$. If the test is nonsignificant, then the model is additive and the assumption has been met. If the test is significant, then the model is not additive and the assumption has not been met. A summary of the assumptions and the effects of their violation for this model are presented in Table 16.6.

## 16.2.5    ANOVA Summary Table

The sources of variation for this model are similar to those of the regular two-factor model, except there is no interaction term. The ANOVA summary table is shown in Table 16.7, where

**TABLE 16.6**
Assumptions and Effects of Violations—Two-Factor Randomized Block ANOVA

| Assumption | Effect of Assumption Violation |
| --- | --- |
| 1. Independence | Increased likelihood of a Type I and/or Type II error in $F$; affects standard errors of means and inferences about those means. |
| 2. Homogeneity of variance | Small effect with equal or nearly equal $n$'s; otherwise effect decreases as $n$ increases. |
| 3. Normality | Minimal effect with equal or nearly equal $n$'s. |
| 4. Sphericity | Fairly serious effect. |
| 5. No interaction between treatment and blocks | Increased likelihood of a Type II error for the test of factor A and thus reduced power. |

**TABLE 16.7**
Two-Factor Randomized Block Design ANOVA Summary Table

| Source | SS | df | MS | F |
|--------|-----|------|------|-----|
| A | $SS_A$ | $J - 1$ | $MS_A$ | $MS_A/MS_{res}$ |
| B | $SS_B$ | $K - 1$ | $MS_B$ | $MS_B/MS_{res}$ |
| Residual | $SS_{res}$ | $(J - 1)(K - 1)$ | $MS_{res}$ | |
| Total | $SS_{total}$ | $N - 1$ | | |

we see the following sources of variation: A (treatments), B (blocks), residual, and total. The test of block differences is usually of no real interest. In general, we expect there to be differences between the blocks. From the table we see that two $F$ ratios can be formed.

If we take the total sum of squares and decompose it, we have

$$SS_{total} = SS_A + SS_B + SS_{res}$$

The remaining computations are determined by statistical software. The degrees of freedom, mean squares, and $F$ ratios are also shown in Table 16.7.

Earlier in the discussion on the two-factor randomized block design, I mentioned that the $F$ test is not very robust to a violation of the sphericity assumption. We again recommend the following sequential procedure be used in the test of factor A. First, do the usual $F$ test, which is quite liberal in terms of rejecting $H_0$ too often, where the degrees of freedom are $J - 1$ and $(J - 1)(K - 1)$. If $H_0$ is not rejected, then stop. If $H_0$ is rejected, then continue with step 2, which is to use the Geisser-Greenhouse (1958) conservative $F$ test. For the model we are considering, the degrees of freedom for the $F$ critical value are adjusted to be 1 and $K - 1$. If $H_0$ is rejected, then stop. This would indicate that both the liberal and conservative tests reached the same conclusion, that is, to reject $H_0$. If $H_0$ is not rejected, then the two tests did not reach the same conclusion, and a further test should be undertaken. Thus in step 3 an adjusted $F$ test is conducted. The adjustment is known as Box's (1954b) correction (the Huynh & Feldt [1970] procedure). Here the degrees of freedom are equal to $(J - 1) \varepsilon$ and $(J - 1) (K - 1)\varepsilon$, where $\varepsilon$ is the correction factor (see Kirk, 1982). It is now fairly routine for the major statistical software to conduct the Geisser—Greenhouse and Huynh and Feldt tests.

Note that the residual is the proper error term for the fixed-, random-, and mixed-effects models. One may also be interested in an assessment of the effect size for the treatment factor A (the effect size of the blocking factor B is usually not of interest). As in previously presented ANOVA models, effect size measures such as $\omega^2$ and $\eta^2$ should be considered. Finally, the procedures for determing confidence intervals and power are the same as in previous models.

## 16.2.6  Multiple Comparison Procedures

If the null hypothesis for either the A or B factor is rejected and there are more than two levels of the factor, then the researcher may be interested in which means or combinations of means are different. This could be assessed, as put forth in previous chapters, by the use of some multiple comparison procedure (MCP). In general, the use of MCPs outlined in chapter 12 is unchanged if the sphericity assumption is met. If the assumption is not met, then $MS_{res}$ is not the appropriate error term, and the alternatives recommended in chapter 15 should be considered (see Boik, 1981; Kirk, 1982; or Maxwell, 1980).

### 16.2.7 Methods of Block Formation

There are different methods available for the formation of blocks. This discussion borrows heavily from the work of Pingel (1969) in defining five such methods. The first method is the **predefined value blocking method**, where the blocking factor is an ordinal variable. Here the researcher specifies $K$ different population values of the blocking variable. For each of these values (i.e., a fixed effect), individuals are randomly assigned to the levels of the treatment factor. Thus individuals within a block have the same value on the blocking variable. For example, if class rank is the blocking variable, the levels might be the top third, middle third, and bottom third of the class.

The second method is the **predefined range blocking method**, where the blocking factor is an interval variable. Here the researcher specifies $K$ mutually exclusive ranges in the population distribution of the blocking variable, where the probability of obtaining a value of the blocking variable in each range may be specified as $\dfrac{1}{K}$. For each of these ranges (i.e., a fixed effect), individuals are randomly assigned to the levels of the treatment factor. Thus individuals within a block are in the same range on the blocking variable. For example, if the Graduate Record Exam-Verbal score is the blocking variable, the levels might be 200–400, 401–600, and 601–800.

The third method is the **sampled value blocking method**, where the blocking variable is an ordinal variable. Here the researcher randomly samples $K$ population values of the blocking variable (i.e., a random effect). For each of these values, individuals are randomly assigned to the levels of the treatment factor. Thus individuals within a block have the same value on the blocking variable. For example, if class rank is again the blocking variable, only this time measured in tenths, the researcher might randomly select 3 levels from the population of 10.

The fourth method is the **sampled range blocking method**, where the blocking variable is an interval variable. Here the researcher randomly samples $N$ individuals from the population, such that $N = JK$, where $K$ is the number of blocks desired (i.e., a fixed effect) and $J$ is the number of treatment groups. These individuals are ranked according to their values on the blocking variable from 1 to $N$. The first block consists of those individuals ranked from 1 to $J$, the second block of those ranked from $J + 1$ to $2J$, and so on. Finally individuals within a block are randomly assigned to the $J$ treatment groups. For example, consider the GRE–Verbal again as the blocking variable, where there are $J = 4$ treatment groups, $K = 10$ blocks, and thus $N = JK = 40$ individuals. The top 4 ranked individuals on the GRE–Verbal would constitute the first block and they would be randomly assigned to the four groups. The next 4 ranked individuals would constitute the second block, and so on.

The fifth method is the **post hoc blocking method**. Here the researcher has already designed the study and collected the data, without the benefit of a blocking variable. After the fact, a blocking variable is identified and incorporated into the analysis. It is possible to implement any of the four preceding procedures on a post hoc basis.

Based on the research of Pingel (1969), some statements can be made about the precision of these methods in terms of a reduction in residual variability and better estimation of the treatment effect. In general, for an ordinal blocking variable, the predefined value blocking method is more precise than the sampled value blocking method. Likewise, for an interval blocking variable, the predefined range blocking method is more precise than the sampled range blocking method. Finally, the post hoc blocking method is the least precise of the methods discussed. For a discussion of selecting the optimal number of blocks, see Feldt (1958) (highly recommended), as well as Myers (1979), Myers and Well (1995), or Keppel and Wickens (2004). They make the following recommendations about the optimal number of blocks: if $r_{xy} = .2$, then use five blocks; if $r_{xy} = .4$, then use four blocks, if $r_{xy} = .6$, then use three blocks, and if $r_{xy} = .8$, then use two blocks.

## 16.2.8  An Example

Let us consider an example to illustrate the procedures in this section. The data are shown in Table 16.8. The blocking factor is age (i.e., 20, 30, 40, and 50 years of age), the treatment factor is number of workouts per week (i.e., 1, 2, 3, and 4), and the dependent variable is amount of weight lost during the first month. Assume we have a fixed-effects model. Table 16.9 contains the resultant ANOVA summary table.

**TABLE 16.8**
Data for the Exercise Example—Two-Factor Randomized Block Design

| Exercise Program | Age | | | | Row Means |
|---|---|---|---|---|---|
| | 20 | 30 | 40 | 50 | |
| 1/week | 3 | 2 | 1 | 0 | 1.5000 |
| 2/week | 6 | 5 | 4 | 2 | 4.2500 |
| 3/week | 10 | 8 | 7 | 6 | 7.7500 |
| 4/week | 9 | 7 | 8 | 7 | 7.7500 |
| Block means | 7.0000 | 5.5000 | 5.0000 | 3.7500 | 5.3125 (Overall mean) |

**TABLE 16.9**
Two-Factor Randomized Block Design ANOVA Summary Table—Exercise Example

| Source | SS | df | MS | F |
|---|---|---|---|---|
| A | 21.6875 | 3 | 7.2292 | 18.2648* |
| B | 110.1875 | 3 | 36.7292 | 92.7974* |
| Residual | 3.5625 | 9 | 0.3958 | |
| Total | 135.4375 | 15 | | |

$*_{.05}F_{3,9} = 3.86$.

The test statistics are both compared to the usual $F$ test critical value of $_{.05}F_{3,9} = 3.86$ (from Appendix Table 4), so that both tests are significant. The Geisser-Greenhouse conservative procedure is necessary for the test of factor A; here the test statistic is compared to the critical value of $_{.05}F_{1,3} = 10.13$, which is also significant. The two procedures both yield a statistically significant result, so we need not be concerned with a violation of the sphericity assumption for the test of A. In summary, the effects of amount of exercise undertaken and age on amount of weight lost are both statistically significant beyond the .05 level of significance.

Next we need to test the additivity assumption using Tukey's (1949) test of additivity. The $F$ test statistic is equal to 0.1010, which is compared to the critical value of $_{.05}F_{1,8} = 5.32$ from Appendix Table 4. The test is nonsignificant, so the model is additive and the assumption has been met.

As an example of a MCP, the Tukey HSD procedure is used to test for the equivalence of exercising once a week ($j = 1$) and four times a week ($j = 4$), where the contrast is written as $\overline{Y}_{4.} - \overline{Y}_{1.}$. The means for these groups are 1.5000 for the once a week program and 7.7500 for the four times a week program. The standard error is

$$s_{\psi'} = \sqrt{\frac{MS_{res}}{J}} = \sqrt{\frac{0.3958}{4}} = 0.3146$$

and the studentized range statistic is

$$q = \frac{\overline{Y}_{4.} - \overline{Y}_{1.}}{s_{\psi'}} = \frac{7.7500 - 1.5000}{0.3146} = 19.8665$$

The critical value is $_{.05}q_{9,4} = 4.415$ (from Appendix Table 9). The test statistic exceeds the critical value; thus we conclude that the means for groups 1 and 4 are significantly different at the .05 level (i.e., more frequent exercise helps one to lose more weight).

## 16.3    THE TWO-FACTOR RANDOMIZED BLOCK DESIGN FOR $n > 1$

For two-factor randomized block designs with more than one observation per cell, there is little that we have not already covered. First, the characteristics are exactly the same as with the $n = 1$ model, with the obvious exception that when $n > 1$, an interaction term exists. Second, the layout of the data, the model, the ANOVA summary table, and the multiple comparison procedures are the same as in the regular two-factor model. The assumptions are the same as with the $n = 1$ model, except the assumption of additivity is not necessary, because an interaction term exists. The sphericity assumption is required for those tests that use $MS_{AB}$ as the error term. We do not mean to minimize the importance of this popular model; however, there really is no additional information to provide. For a discussion of other randomized block designs, see Kirk (1982).

## 16.4    THE FRIEDMAN TEST

There is a nonparametric equivalent to the two-factor randomized block ANOVA model. The test was developed by Friedman (1937) and is based on ranks. For the case of $n = 1$, the procedure is precisely the same as the Friedman test in the one-factor repeated measures model (see chap. 15). For the case of $n > 1$, the procedure is slightly different. First, all of the scores within each block are ranked for that block. For instance, if there are $J = 4$ levels of factor A and $n = 10$ individuals per cell, then each block's scores would be ranked from 1 to 40. From this, a mean ranking can be determined for each level of factor A. The null hypothesis tests whether the mean rankings for each of the levels of A are equal. The test statistic is a $\chi^2$, which is compared to the critical value of $_{\alpha}\chi^2_{J-1}$ (see Appendix Table 3), where the null hypothesis is rejected if the test statistic exceeds the critical value.

In the case of tied ranks, either the available ranks can be averaged, or a correction factor can be used (see chap. 15). You may also recall the problem with small $n$'s in terms of the test statistic not being precisely a $\chi^2$. For situations where $J < 6$ and $n < 6$, consult the table of critical values in Marascuilo and McSweeney (1977, Table A-22, p. 521). The Friedman test assumes that the population distributions have the same shape (although not necessarily normal) and the same variability, and the dependent measure is continuous. For alternative nonparametric procedures, see the discussion in chapter 15.

Various multiple comparison procedures (MCPs) can be used for the nonparametric two-factor randomized block model. For the most part these MCPs are analogs to their parametric equivalents. In the case of planned pairwise comparisons, one may use multiple matched-pair Wilcoxon tests in a Bonferroni form (i.e., taking the number of contrasts into account by splitting up the $\alpha$ level). Due to the nature of planned comparisons, these are more powerful than the Friedman test. For post hoc comparisons, two example MCPs are the Tukey HSD analog for pairwise contrasts, and the Scheffe' analog for complex contrasts. For additional discussion about the use of MCPs for this model, see Marascuilo and McSweeney (1977). For an example of the Friedman test, return to chapter 15. Finally, note that MCPs are not usually conducted on the blocking factor as they are rarely of interest to the applied researcher.

## 16.5   COMPARISON OF VARIOUS ANOVA MODELS

How do various ANOVA models we have considered compare in terms of power and precision? Recall again that **power** is defined as the probability of rejecting $H_0$ when $H_0$ is false, and **precision** is defined as a measure of our ability to obtain good estimates of the treatment effects. The classic literature on this topic revolves around the correlation between the dependent variable $Y$ and the covariate or concomitant variable $X$ (i.e., $r_{xy}$). First let us compare the one-factor ANOVA and one-factor ANCOVA models. If $r_{xy}$ is not significantly different from zero, then the amount of unexplained variation will be the same in the two models, and no statistical adjustment will be made on the group means. In this situation, the ANOVA model is more powerful, as we lose one degree of freedom for each covariate used in the ANCOVA model. If $r_{xy}$ is significantly different from zero, then the amount of unexplained variation will be smaller in the ANCOVA model as compared to the ANOVA model. Here the ANCOVA model is more powerful and is more precise as compared to the ANOVA model. According to one rule of thumb, if $r_{xy} < .2$, then ignore the covariate or concomitant variable and use the one-factor analysis of variance. Otherwise, take the concomitant variable into account somehow.

How should we take the concomitant variable into account if $r_{xy} > .2$? The two best possibilities are the analysis of covariance design (chap. 14) and the randomized block design. That is, the concomitant variable can be used either as a covariate through a statistical form of control, or as a blocking factor through an experimental form of control. As suggested by the classic work of Feldt (1958), if $.2 < r_{xy} < .4$, then use the concomitant variable as a blocking factor in a randomized block design as it is the most powerful and precise design. If $r_{xy} > .6$, then use the concomitant variable as a covariate in an ANCOVA design as it is the most powerful and precise design. If $.4 < r_{xy} < .6$, then the randomized block and ANCOVA designs are about equal in terms of power and precision.

However, Maxwell, Delaney, and Dill (1984) showed that the correlation between the covariate and dependent variable should not be the ultimate criterion in deciding whether to use an ANCOVA or randomized block design. These designs differ in two ways: (a) whether the concomitant variable is treated as continuous (ANCOVA) or categorical (randomized block), and (b) whether individuals are assigned to groups based on the concomitant variable (randomized blocks) or without regard to the concomitant variable (ANCOVA). Thus the Feldt (1958) comparison of these particular models is not a fair one in that the models differ in these two ways. The ANCOVA model makes full use of the information contained in the concomitant variable, whereas in the randomized block model some information is lost due to the categorization. In examining nine different models, Maxwell and colleagues suggest that $r_{xy}$ should not be the sole factor in the choice of a design (given that $r_{xy}$ is at least .3), but that two other factors be considered. The first factor is whether scores on the concomitant variable are available prior to the assignment of individuals to groups. If so, power will be increased by assigning individuals to groups based on the concomitant variable (i.e., blocking). The second factor is whether $X$ and $Y$ are linearly related. If so, the use of ANCOVA with a continuous concomitant variable is more powerful because linearity is an assumption of the model (Keppel & Wickens, 2004; Myers & Well, 1995). If not, either the concomitant variable should be used as a blocking variable, or some sort of nonlinear ANCOVA model should be used.

There are a few other decision criteria you may want to consider in choosing between the randomized block and ANCOVA designs. First, in some situations, blocking may be difficult to carry out. For instance, we may not be able to find enough homogeneous individuals to constitute a block. If the blocks formed are not very homogeneous, this defeats the whole purpose of blocking. Second, the interaction of the independent variable and the concomitant variable may be an important effect to study. In this case, use the randomized block design with multiple individuals per cell. If the interaction is significant, this violates the assumption of homogeneity of regression slopes in the analysis of covariance design, but does not violate any assumption in the randomized block design. Third, it should be obvious by now that the assumptions of the ANCOVA design are much more restrictive than in the randomized block design. Thus when important assumptions are likely to be seriously violated, the randomized block design is preferable.

There are other alternative designs for incorporating the concomitant variable as a pretest, such as an analysis of variance on gain (the difference between posttest and pretest), or a mixed (split-plot) design where the pretest and posttest measures are treated as the levels of a repeated factor. Based on the research of Huck and McLean (1975) and Jennings (1988), the ANCOVA model is generally preferred over these other two models. For further discussion see Reichardt (1979), Huitema (1980), or Kirk (1982).

## 16.6  SPSS

In this last section we examine SPSS for the models presented in this chapter, including an APA paragraph of selected results. As we see, SPSS is rather limited in terms of what it can do for hierarchical and randomized block designs. To conduct a two-factor mixed-effects hierarchical ANOVA, there are a few differences from other ANOVA models we have considered in this text. To begin, on the GLM Univariate main screen click the nested "teacher" factor name into the "Random Factor(s)" box, the nonnested "method" factor into the "Fixed Factor(s)" box, and the dependent variable "score" into the "Dependent variable" box. Second, move into the "Model" option, click the "Custom" radio button, and use the "Build Terms" arrow and pulldown to build a model on the righthand side with terms for the main effect "method" and the interaction effect "method*teacher." Thus the model should not include a main effect term for "teacher." The interaction term is necessary to trick SPSS into computing the main effect B(A) for the nested factor (which SPSS calls "method*teacher," but is actually "teacher"), and thus generate the proper ANOVA summary table. Finally, the "Posthoc" option will only allow you to obtain post hoc MCPs for the nonnested factor. For post hoc MCPs on the nested factor (although generally not of interest), go to the "Options" screen, then to the "Compare main effects" pulldown to find the Tukey LSD, Bonferroni, and Sidak procedures. Otherwise everything is the same as in other ANOVA models. Selected results are shown in the top panel of Table 16.10.

To run a two-factor fixed-effects randomized block ANOVA for $n = 1$, there a few differences from the regular two-factor fixed-effects ANOVA. First, a custom model must again be built. Here you go into the "Model" option, click the "Custom" radio button, and use the "Build Terms" arrow and pulldown to build a model on the righthand side with main effect terms for "age" and "exercise." Thus the model should not include an interaction term. This will then generate the proper ANOVA summary table. Second, the test of additivity is not available in this module of SPSS. Third, the adjusted $F$ tests (i.e., the Geisser-Greenhouse and Huynh & Feldt procedures) are not available in this module. All other ANOVA procedures that you are familiar with will operate as before. Selected results are shown in the bottom panel of Table 16.10.

To run a two-factor randomized block ANOVA for $n > 1$, the procedures are exactly the same as with the regular two-factor ANOVA. However, the adjusted $F$ tests are not available. Lastly, the Friedman test can be run as previously described in chapter 15.

Finally, here is an example paragraph of the results for the two-factor hierarchical example (feel free to write a similar paragraph for the two-factor randomized block example). From Table 16.10, we see that there is a significant main effect for method ($F_{method} = 59.559$, $df = 1,2$, $p = .016$), but the main effect for teacher is not significant (shown as "method*teacher" in the SPSS ANOVA summary table). Effect size is rather large for the method effect (partial $\eta^2_{method} = .968$), with high observed power (.948), but expectedly less so for the nonsignificant teacher effect (partial $\eta^2_{teacher} = .087$, power = .192). Reading comprehension scores were significantly higher for students taught by the whole language method than by the basal method.

**TABLE 16.10**
Selected SPSS Results for the Teaching Reading and Exercise Examples

Nested teaching reading example:

*Descriptive Statistics*

*Dependent Variable: score*

| method | teacher | Mean | Std. Deviation | N |
|--------|---------|------|----------------|---|
| basal | 1.00 | 2.8333 | 1.72240 | 6 |
| | 2.00 | 3.8333 | 1.94079 | 6 |
| | Total | 3.3333 | 1.82574 | 12 |
| whole | 3.00 | 10.0000 | 3.03315 | 6 |
| | 4.00 | 11.6667 | 2.80476 | 6 |
| | Total | 10.8333 | 2.91807 | 12 |
| Total | 1.00 | 2.8333 | 1.72240 | 6 |
| | 2.00 | 3.8333 | 1.94079 | 6 |
| | 3.00 | 10.0000 | 3.03315 | 6 |
| | 4.00 | 11.6667 | 2.80476 | 6 |
| | Total | 7.0833 | 4.51005 | 24 |

*Tests of Between-Subjects Effects*

*Dependent Variable: score*

| Source | | Type III Sum of Squares | df | Mean Square | F | Sig. | Partial Eta Squared | Observed Power[a] |
|--------|------------|------|----|--------|--------|------|------|------|
| method | Hypothesis | 337.500 | 1 | 337.500 | 59.559 | .016 | .968 | .948 |
| | Error | 11.333 | 2 | 5.667 | | | | |
| method* | Hypothesis | 11.333 | 2 | 5.667 | .952 | .403 | .087 | 192 |
| teacher | Error | 119.000 | 20 | 5.950 | | | | |

[a]Computed using alpha = .05

Randomized block exercise example:

*Tests of Between-Subjects Effects*

*Dependent Variable: wghtlost*

| Source | Type III Sum of Squares | df | Mean Square | F | Sig. | Partial Eta Squared | Observed Power[a] |
|--------|------|----|------|--------|------|------|------|
| age | 21.688 | 3 | 7.229 | 18.263 | .000 | .859 | .999 |
| exercise | 110.188 | 3 | 36.729 | 92.789 | .000 | .969 | 1.000 |
| Error | 3.563 | 9 | .396 | | | | |
| Corrected Total | 135.438 | 15 | | | | | |

[a]Computed using alpha = .05

(*continued*)

*Estimates*

*Dependent Variable: wghtlost*

| age | Mean | Std. Error | 95% Confidence Interval | |
|---|---|---|---|---|
| | | | Lower Bound | Upper Bound |
| 20.00 | 7.000 | .315 | 6.288 | 7.712 |
| 30.00 | 5.500 | .315 | 4.788 | 6.212 |
| 40.00 | 5.000 | .315 | 4.288 | 5.712 |
| 50.00 | 3.750 | .315 | 3.038 | 4.462 |

*Pairwise Comparisons*

*Dependent Variable: wghtlost*

| (I) age | (J) age | Mean Difference (I–J) | Std. Error | Sig.[a] | 95% Confidence Interval for Difference[a] | |
|---|---|---|---|---|---|---|
| | | | | | Lower Bound | Upper Bound |
| 20.00 | 30.00 | 1.500* | .445 | .049 | .003 | 2.997 |
| | 40.00 | 2.000* | .445 | .009 | .503 | 3.497 |
| | 50.00 | 3.250* | .445 | .000 | 1.753 | 4.747 |
| 30.00 | 20.00 | −1.500* | .445 | .049 | −2.997 | −.003 |
| | 40.00 | .500 | .445 | 1.000 | −.997 | 1.997 |
| | 50.00 | 1.750* | .445 | .021 | .253 | 3.247 |
| 40.00 | 20.00 | −2.000* | .445 | .009 | −3.497 | −.503 |
| | 30.00 | −.500 | .445 | 1.000 | −1.997 | .997 |
| | 50.00 | 1.250 | .445 | .122 | −.247 | 2.747 |
| 50.00 | 20.00 | −3.250* | .445 | .000 | −4.747 | −1.753 |
| | 30.00 | −1.750* | .445 | .021 | −3.247 | −.253 |
| | 40.00 | −1.250 | .445 | .122 | −2.747 | .247 |

Based on estimated marginal means

*The mean difference is significant at the .05 level.

[a]Adjustment for multiple comparisons: Bonferroni.

(*continued*)

TABLE 16.10 (*continued*)
Selected SPSS Results for the Teaching Reading and Exercise Examples

*Estimates*

*Dependent Variable: wghtlost*

| | | | 95% Confidence Interval | |
| | | | --- | --- |
| exercise | Mean | Std. Error | Lower Bound | Upper Bound |
| 1.00 | 1.500 | .315 | .788 | 2.212 |
| 2.00 | 4.250 | .315 | 3.538 | 4.962 |
| 3.00 | 7.750 | .315 | 7.038 | 8.462 |
| 4.00 | 7.750 | .315 | 7.038 | 8.462 |

*Pairwise Comparisons*

*Dependent Variable: wghtlost*

| (I) exercise | (J) exercise | Mean Difference (I–J) | Std. Error | Sig.[a] | 95% Confidence Interval for Difference[a] | |
| --- | --- | --- | --- | --- | --- | --- |
| | | | | | Lower Bound | Upper Bound |
| 1.00 | 2.00 | −2.750* | .445 | .001 | −4.247 | −1.253 |
| | 3.00 | −6.250* | .445 | .000 | −7.747 | −4.753 |
| | 4.00 | −6.250* | .445 | .000 | −7.747 | −4.753 |
| 2.00 | 1.00 | 2.750* | .445 | .001 | 1.253 | 4.247 |
| | 3.00 | −3.500* | .445 | .000 | −4.997 | −2.003 |
| | 4.00 | −3.500* | .445 | .000 | −4.997 | −2.003 |
| 3.00 | 1.00 | 6.250* | .445 | .000 | 4.753 | 7.747 |
| | 2.00 | 3.500* | .445 | .000 | 2.003 | 4.997 |
| | 4.00 | .000 | .445 | 1.000 | −1.497 | 1.497 |
| 4.00 | 1.00 | 6.250* | .445 | .000 | 4.753 | 7.747 |
| | 2.00 | 3.500* | .445 | .000 | 2.003 | 4.997 |
| | 3.00 | .000 | .445 | 1.000 | −1.497 | 1.497 |

Based on estimated marginal means

*The mean difference is significant at the .05 level.

[a]Adjustment for multiple comparisons: Bonferroni.

## 16.7 SUMMARY

In this chapter models involving nested and blocking factors for the two-factor case were considered. Three different models were examined; these included the two-factor hierarchical design, the two-factor randomized block design with one observation per cell, and the two-factor randomized block design with multiple observations per cell. Included for each design were the usual topics of model characteristics, the layout of the data, the linear model, assumptions of the model and dealing with their violation, the ANOVA summary table, and multiple comparison procedures. Also included for particular designs was a discussion of the compound symmetry/sphericity assumption, and the Friedman test based on ranks. We concluded with a comparison of various ANOVA models on precision and power. At this point you should have met the following objectives: (a) be able to understand the characteristics and concepts underlying hierarchical and randomized block ANOVA models, (b) be able to determine and interpret the results of hierarchical and randomized block ANOVA models, (c) be able to understand and evaluate the assumptions of hierarchical and randomized block ANOVA models, and (d) be able to compare different ANOVA models and select an appropriate model. This chapter concludes our extended discussion of ANOVA models. In the remaining two chapters of the text, we discuss regression models where the dependent variable is predicted by one or more independent variables or predictors (chaps. 17 and 18, respectively).

## PROBLEMS

### Conceptual Problems

1. To study the effectiveness of three spelling methods, 45 subjects are randomly selected from the 4th graders in a particular elementary school. Based on the order of their IQ scores, subjects are grouped into high, middle, and low IQ groups, 15 in each. Subjects in each group are randomly assigned to one of the three methods of spelling, 5 each. Which of the following methods of blocking is employed here?
   a. predefined value blocking
   b. predefined range blocking
   c. sampled value blocking
   d. sampled range blocking

2. If three teachers employ method A and three other teachers employ method B, then
   a. teachers are nested within method.
   b. teachers are crossed with methods.
   c. methods are nested within teacher.
   d. cannot be determined.

3. The interaction of factors A and B can be assessed only if
   a. both factors are fixed.
   b. both factors are random.
   c. factor A is nested within factor B.
   d. factors A and B are crossed.

4. In a two-factor design, factor A is nested within factor B if

    a. at each level of A each level of B appears.

    b. at each level of A unique levels of B appear.

    c. at each level of B unique levels of A appear.

    d. cannot be determined

5. Five teachers use an experimental method of teaching statistics, and five other teachers use the traditional method. If factor M is method of teaching, and factor T is teacher, this design can be denoted by

    a. T(M)

    b. T × M

    c. M × T

    d. M(T)

6. If factor C is nested within factors A and B, this is denoted as AB(C). True or False?

7. A design in which all levels of each factor are found in combination with each level of every other factor is necessarily a nested design. True or False?

8. To determine if counseling method E is uniformly superior to method C for the population of counselors, of which those in the study can be considered to be a random sample, one needs a nested design with a mixed model. True or False?

9. I assert that the predefined value method of block formation is more effective than the sampled value method in reducing unexplained variability. Am I correct?

10. For the interaction to be tested in a two-factor randomized block design, it is required that

    a. both factors be fixed.

    b. both factors be random.

    c. $n = 1$.

    d. $n > 1$.

11. Five medical professors use a computer-based method of teaching and five other medical professors use a lecture-based method of teaching. This is an example of which type of design?

    a. completely crossed design

    b. repeated measures design

    c. hierarchical design

    d. randomized block design

12. In a randomized block study, the correlation between the blocking factor and the dependent variable is .35. I assert that the residual variation will be smaller when using the blocking variable than without. Am I correct?

13. In a two-factor hierarchical design with 2 levels of factor A and 3 levels of factor B nested within each level of A, how many $F$ ratios can be tested?

    a.  1

    b.  2

    c.  3

    d.  cannot be determined

14. If the correlation between the concomitant variable and dependent variable is $-.80$, which of the following designs is recommended?

    a.  ANCOVA

    b.  one-factor ANOVA

    c.  randomized block ANOVA

    d.  all of the above

15. IQ must be used as a treatment factor. True or false?

16. Which of the following blocking methods best estimates the treatment effects?

    a.  predefined value blocking

    b.  post hoc predefined value blocking

    c.  sampled value blocking

    d.  sampled range blocking

## Computational Problems

1. An experiment was conducted to compare three types of behavior modification in classrooms (1, 2, and 3) using age as a blocking variable (4-, 6-, and 8-year old children). The mean scores on the dependent variable, number of instances of disruptive behavior, are listed here for each cell. The intention of the treatments is to minimize the number of disruptions.

| Types of behavior | Age | | |
| modification | 4-years | 6-years | 8-years |
| --- | --- | --- | --- |
| 1 | 20 | 40 | 40 |
| 2 | 50 | 30 | 20 |
| 3 | 50 | 40 | 30 |

Use these cell means to graph the interaction between type of behavior modification and age.

    a)  Is there an interaction between type of behavior modification and age?

    b)  What kind of recommendation would you make to teachers?

2.  An experiment tested three types of perfume (or after shave)(tame, sexy, and musk) when worn by light-haired and dark-haired women (or men). Thus hair color is a blocking variable. The dependent measure was attractiveness defined as the number of times during a 2-week period that other persons complimented a subject on their perfume (or after shave). There were five subjects in each cell. Complete the summary table below, assuming a fixed-effects model, where $\alpha = .05$.

| Source | SS | df | MS | F | Critical Value and Decision |
|--------|-----|-----|-----|-----|-----|
| Perfume (A) | 200 | — | — | — | — — |
| Hair color (B) | 100 | — | — | — | — — |
| Interaction (AB) | 20 | — | — | — | — — |
| Within | 240 | — | — | | |
| Total | — | — | | | |

3.  A mathematics professor wants to know which of three approches to teaching calculus resulted in the best test performance (section 1, 2, or 3). Scores on the GRE-Quantitative portion were used as a blocking variable (block 1: 200–400; block 2: 401–600; block 3: 601–800). The data are shown here. Conduct a two-factor randomized block ANOVA ($\alpha = .05$) and Bonferroni MCPs using SPSS to determine the results of the study.

| Subject | Section | GRE-Q | Test Score |
|---------|---------|-------|------------|
| 1 | 1 | 1 | 90 |
| 2 | 1 | 2 | 93 |
| 3 | 1 | 3 | 100 |
| 4 | 2 | 1 | 88 |
| 5 | 2 | 2 | 90 |
| 6 | 2 | 3 | 97 |
| 7 | 3 | 1 | 79 |
| 8 | 3 | 2 | 85 |
| 9 | 3 | 3 | 92 |

## Interpretive Problem

Take the one-factor ANOVA interpretive problem you developed in chapter 11. What are some reasonable blocking variables to consider? Which type of blocking would be best in your situation? Select a blocking variable from the same dataset and conduct a two-factor ANOVA. Compare these results with the one-factor ANOVA results (without the blocking factor) to determine how useful the blocking variable was in terms of reducing residual variability.

# 17

## SIMPLE LINEAR REGRESSION

### Chapter Outline

1. The concepts of simple linear regression
2. The population simple linear regression model
3. The sample simple linear regression model
   Unstandardized regression model
   Standardized regression model
   Prediction errors
   Least squares criterion
   Proportion of predictable variation (coefficient of determination)
   Significance tests and confidence intervals
   Assumptions and violation of assumptions
4. SPSS

### Key Concepts

1. Slope and intercept of a straight line
2. Regression model
3. Prediction errors/residuals
4. Standardized and unstandardized regression coefficients
5. Proportion of variation accounted for; coefficient of determination

In chapter 10 we considered various bivariate measures of association. Specifically, the chapter dealt with the topics of scatterplot, covariance, types of correlation coefficients, and their resulting inferential tests. Thus the chapter was concerned with addressing the question of the extent to which two variables are associated or related. In this chapter we extend our discussion of two variables to address the question of the extent to which one variable can be used to predict or explain another variable.

Beginning in chapter 11 we examined various analysis of variance (ANOVA) models. It should be mentioned again that ANOVA and regression are both forms of the same general linear model (GLM), where the relationship between one or more independent variables and one dependent variable is evaluated. The major difference between the two procedures is that in ANOVA the independent variables are discrete variables while in regression the independent variables are continuous variables. Otherwise there is considerable overlap of these two procedures in terms of concepts and their implementation.

When considering the relationship between two variables (say $X$ and $Y$), the researcher usually determines some measure of relationship between those variables, such as a correlation coefficient (e.g., $r_{XY}$, the Pearson product moment correlation coefficient), as we did in chapter 10. Another way of looking at how two variables may be related is through regression analysis, in terms of prediction. That is, we evaluate the ability of one variable to predict a second. Here we adopt the usual notation where $X$ is defined as the **independent** or **predictor variable**, and $Y$ as the **dependent** or **criterion variable**.

For example, an admissions officer might want to use Graduate Record Exam (GRE) scores to predict graduate-level grade point averages (GPA) to make admissions decisions for a sample of applicants to a university or college (the GRE assesses general aptitude for graduate study). The research question of interest is how well does the GRE (the independent or predictor variable) predict performance in graduate school (the dependent or criterion variable)? This is an example of simple linear regression where only a single predictor variable is included in the analysis. The use of the GRE in predicting GPA requires that these variables have a correlation different from zero. Otherwise the GRE will have little utility in predicting GPA. For education and the behavioral sciences, the use of a single predictor does not usually result in reasonable prediction. Thus chapter 18 considers the case of multiple predictor variables through multiple linear regression.

In this chapter we consider the concepts of slope, intercept, regression model, unstandardized and standardized regression coefficients, residuals, proportion of variation accounted for, tests of significance, and statistical assumptions. Our objectives are that by the end of this chapter, you will be able to (a) understand the concepts underlying simple linear regression, (b) determine and interpret the results of simple linear regression, and (c) understand and evaluate the assumptions of simple linear regression.

## 17.1   THE CONCEPTS OF SIMPLE LINEAR REGRESSION

Let us consider the basic concepts involved in simple linear regression. Many years ago when you had algebra, you learned about an equation used to describe a straight line,

$$Y = bX + a$$

Here the predictor variable $X$ is used to predict the criterion variable $Y$. The **slope** of the line is denoted by $b$ and indicates the number of $Y$ units the line changes for a one-unit change in $X$. You may find it easier to think about the slope as measuring tilt or steepness. The $Y$-intercept is denoted by $a$ and is the point at which the line intersects or crosses the $Y$ axis. To be more specific, $a$ is the value of $Y$ when $X$ is equal to zero. Hereafter we use the term **intercept** rather than $Y$-intercept to keep it simple.

Consider the plot of the straight line $Y = 0.5X + 1.0$ as shown in Fig. 17.1. Here we see that the line clearly intersects the $Y$ axis at $Y = 1.0$; thus the intercept is equal to one. The slope of a line is defined, more specifically, as the change in $Y$ divided by the change in $X$.

$$b = \frac{\Delta Y}{\Delta X} \text{ or } \frac{Y_2 - Y_1}{X_2 - X_1}$$

For instance, take two points shown in Fig. 17.1, $(X_1, Y_1)$ and $(X_2, Y_2)$, that fall on the straight line with coordinates $(0,1)$ and $(4,3)$, respectively. We compute the slope for those two points to be $(3 - 1) / (4 - 0) = 0.5$. If we were to select any other two points that fall on the straight line, then the slope for those two points would also be equal to 0.5. That is, regardless of the two points on the line that we select, the slope will always be the same, constant value of 0.5. This is true because we only need two points to define a particular straight line. That is, with the points $(0,1)$ and $(4,3)$ we can draw only one straight line that passes through both of those points, and that line has a slope of 0.5 and an intercept of 1.0.

Let us take the concepts of slope, intercept, and straight line and apply them in the context of correlation so that we can study the relationship between the variables $X$ and $Y$. If the slope of the line is a positive value (e.g., Fig. 17.1), where as $X$ increases $Y$ increases, then the correlation

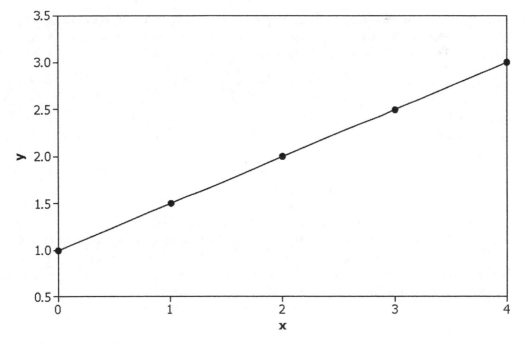

**FIG. 17.1   Plot of line:** $Y = 0.5X + 1.0$.

will be positive. If the slope of the line is zero, where the line is parallel or horizontal to the $X$ axis such that as $X$ increases $Y$ remains constant, then the correlation will be zero. If the slope of the line is a negative value, where as $X$ increases $Y$ decreases (i.e., the line decreases from left to right), then the correlation will be negative. Thus the sign of the slope corresponds to the sign of the correlation.

## 17.2  THE POPULATION SIMPLE LINEAR REGRESSION MODEL

Let us take these concepts and apply them to simple linear regression. Consider the situation where we have the entire population of individuals' scores on both variables $X$ (GRE) and $Y$ (GPA). We define the linear regression model as the equation for a straight line. This yields an equation for the regression of $Y$ the criterion, given $X$ the predictor, often stated as the regression of $Y$ on $X$, although more easily understood as $Y$ being predicted by $X$.

The **population regression model** for $Y$ being predicted by $X$ is

$$Y_i = \beta_{YX} X_i + \alpha_{YX} + \varepsilon_i$$

where $Y$ is the criterion variable, $X$ is the predictor variable, $\beta_{YX}$ is the population slope for $Y$ predicted by $X$, $\alpha_{YX}$ is the population intercept for $Y$ predicted by $X$, $\varepsilon_i$ are the population residuals or errors of prediction (the part of $Y_i$ not predicted from $X_i$), and $i$ represents an index for a particular individual (or object). The index $i$ can take on values from 1 to $N$, where $N$ is the size of the population, written as $i = 1, ..., N$.

The **population prediction model** is

$$Y_i' = \beta_{YX} X_i + \alpha_{YX}$$

where $Y_i'$ is the predicted value of $Y$ given a specific value of $X$. That is, $Y_i$ is the actual score obtained by individual $i$, while $Y_i'$ is the predicted score based on their $X$ score for that same individual. Thus, we see that the population prediction error is defined as

$$\varepsilon_i = Y_i - Y_i'$$

There is only one difference between the regression and prediction models. The regression model explicitly includes prediction error as $\varepsilon_i$ whereas the prediction model includes prediction error implicitly as part of $Y_i'$.

Consider for a moment a practical application of the difference between the regression and prediction models. Frequently a researcher will develop a regression model for a population where $X$ and $Y$ are both known, and then use the prediction model to actually predict $Y$ when only $X$ is known (i.e., $Y$ will not be known until later). Using the GRE example, the admissions officer first develops a regression model for a population of students currently attending the university so as to have a current measure of GPA. This yields the slope and intercept. Then the prediction model is used to predict future GPA and make admission decisions for next year's population of applicants based on their GRE scores.

A simple method for determining the population slope and intercept is as

$$\beta_{YX} = \rho_{XY} \frac{\sigma_Y}{\sigma_X}$$

and

$$\alpha_{YX} = \mu_Y - \beta_{YX}\, \mu_X$$

where $\sigma_Y$ and $\sigma_X$ are the population standard deviations for $Y$ and $X$ respectively, $\rho_{XY}$ is the population correlation between $X$ and $Y$, and $\mu_Y$ and $\mu_X$ are the population means for $Y$ and $X$ respectively. Note that the previously used method for determining the slope and intercept of a straight line is not appropriate in regression analysis.

## 17.3 THE SAMPLE SIMPLE LINEAR REGRESSION MODEL

### 17.3.1 Unstandardized Regression Model

Let us return to the real world of sample statistics and consider the sample simple linear regression model. As usual, Greek letters refer to population parameters and English letters refer to sample statistics. The sample regression model for predicting $Y$ from $X$ is

$$Y_i = b_{YX}\, X_i + a_{YX} + e_i$$

where $Y$ and $X$ are as before, $b_{YX}$ is the sample slope for $Y$ predicted by $X$, $a_{YX}$ is the sample intercept for $Y$ predicted by $X$, $e_i$ are sample residuals or errors of prediction (the part of $Y_i$ not predictable from $X_i$), and $i$ represents an index for an individual (or object). The index $i$ can take on values from 1 to $n$, where $n$ is the size of the sample, and is written as $i = 1, ..., n$.

The sample prediction model is

$$Y_i' = b_{YX}\, X_i + a_{YX}$$

where $Y_i'$ is the predicted value of $Y$ given a specific value of $X$. Thus, we see that the sample prediction error is defined as

$$e_i = Y_i - Y_i'$$

The difference between the regression and prediction models is the same as previously discussed except now we are dealing with a sample rather than a population.

The sample slope and intercept can be determined by

$$b_{YX} = r_{XY}\, \frac{s_Y}{s_X}$$

and

$$a_{YX} = \overline{Y} - b_{YX}\, \overline{X}$$

where $s_Y$ and $s_X$ are the sample standard deviations for $Y$ and $X$ respectively, $r_{XY}$ is the sample correlation between $X$ and $Y$, and $\overline{Y}$ and $\overline{X}$ are the sample means for $Y$ and $X$ respectively. The sample slope is referred to alternately as (a) the expected or predicted change in $Y$ for a one-unit change in $X$ and (b) the unstandardized or raw regression coefficient. The sample intercept is referred to alternately as (a) the point at which the regression line intersects (or crosses) the $Y$ axis and (b) the value of $Y$ when $X$ is zero.

Consider now the analysis of a realistic example to be followed throughout this chapter. Let us use the GRE-Quantitative (GRE-Q) subtest to predict midterm scores of an introductory statistics course. The GRE-Q has a possible range of 20 to 80 points (if we remove the unnecessary last digit of zero), and the statistics midterm has a possible range of 0 to 50 points. Given the sample of 10 statistics students shown in Table 17.1, let us work through a simple linear regression analysis. The observation numbers ($i = 1, ..., 10$), and values for the GRE-Q ($X$) and midterm ($Y$) variables are given in the first three columns of the table, respectively. The other columns are discussed as we go along.

The sample statistics for the GRE-Q are $\bar{X} = 55.5$ and $s_X = 13.1339$, for the statistics midterm are $\bar{Y} = 38$ and $s_Y = 7.5130$, and the correlation $r_{XY}$ is 0.9177. The sample slope and intercept are computed as follows:

$$b_{YX} = r_{XY}\frac{s_Y}{s_X} = 0.9177\frac{7.5130}{13.1339} = 0.5250$$

and

$$a_{YX} = \bar{Y} - b_{YX}\bar{X} = 38 - 0.5250\,(55.5) = 8.8625$$

Let us interpret the slope and intercept values. A slope of 0.5250 means that if your score on the GRE-Q is increased by one point, then your predicted score on the statistics midterm will be increased by 0.5250 points. An intercept of 8.8625 means that if your score on the GRE-Q is zero (although not possible as you receive 200 points for showing up), then your score on the statistics midterm is 8.8625. The sample simple linear regression model becomes

$$Y_i = b_{YX}X_i + a_{YX} + e_i = .5250X_i + 8.8625 + e_i$$

If your score on the GRE-Q is 63, then your predicted score on the statistics midterm is

$$Y_i' = .5250\,(63) + 8.8625 = 41.9375$$

**TABLE 17.1**
Statistics Midterm Example Regression Data

| Student | GRE-Q (X) | Midterm (Y) | Residual (e) | Predicted Midterm (Y') |
|---------|-----------|-------------|--------------|------------------------|
| 1 | 37 | 32 | 3.7125 | 28.2875 |
| 2 | 45 | 36 | 3.5125 | 32.4875 |
| 3 | 43 | 27 | −4.4375 | 31.4375 |
| 4 | 50 | 34 | −1.1125 | 35.1125 |
| 5 | 65 | 45 | 2.0125 | 42.9875 |
| 6 | 72 | 49 | 2.3375 | 46.6625 |
| 7 | 61 | 42 | 1.1125 | 40.8875 |
| 8 | 57 | 38 | −0.7875 | 38.7875 |
| 9 | 48 | 30 | −4.0625 | 34.0625 |
| 10 | 77 | 47 | −2.2875 | 49.2875 |

Thus based on the prediction model developed, your predicted score on the midterm is approximately 42; however, as becomes evident, predictions are generally not perfect.

## 17.3.2   Standardized Regression Model

Up until now the computations in simple linear regression have involved the use of raw scores. For this reason we call this the unstandardized regression model. The slope estimate is an unstandardized or raw regression slope because it is the predicted change in $Y$ raw score units for a one raw score unit change in $X$. We can also express regression in standard $z$ score units as

$$z(X_i) = \frac{X_i - \overline{X}}{s_X} \text{ and } z(Y_i) = \frac{Y_i - \overline{Y}}{s_Y}$$

The means and variances of both standardized variables (i.e., $z_X$ and $z_Y$) are 0 and 1, respectively. The sample standardized linear prediction model becomes

$$z(Y_i') = b_{YX}^* \, z(X_i) = r_{XY} z(X_i)$$

Thus the standardized regression slope $b_{YX}^*$, sometimes referred to as a **beta weight**, is equal to $r_{XY}$. No intercept term is necessary in the prediction model as the mean of the $z$ scores for both $X$ and $Y$ is zero (i.e., $a_{YX}^* = \overline{z}_Y - b_{YX}^* \overline{z}_X = 0$). In summary, the standardized slope is equal to the correlation coefficient and the standardized intercept is equal to zero.

For our statistics midterm example, the sample standardized linear prediction model is

$$z(Y_i') = .9177 \, z(X_i)$$

The slope of .9177 would be interpreted as the expected increase in the statistics midterm in $z$ score units for a one $z$ score unit increase in the GRE-Q. A one $z$ score unit increase is also the same as a one standard deviation increase because the standard deviation of $z$ is equal to one.

When should you consider use of the standardized versus unstandardized regression analyses? According to Pedhazur (1997), $b^*$ is not very stable from sample to sample. For example, at Ivy-Covered University, $b^*$ would vary across different graduating classes (or samples) whereas $b$ would be much more consistent across classes. Thus, in simple regression most researchers prefer the use of $b$. We see later that $b^*$ has some utility in multiple regression.

## 17.3.3   Prediction Errors

Previously we mentioned that perfect prediction of $Y$ from $X$ is extremely unlikely, only occurring with a perfect correlation between $X$ and $Y$ (i.e., $r_{XY} = \pm 1.0$). When developing the regression model, the values of $Y$ are known. Once the slope and intercept have been estimated, we then use the prediction model to predict $Y$ from $X$ when the values of $Y$ are unknown. We have already defined the predicted values of $Y$ as $Y'$. In other words, a predicted value $Y'$ can be computed by plugging the obtained value for $X$ into the prediction model. It can be shown that $Y_i' = Y_i$ for all $i$ only when there is perfect prediction. However, this is extremely unlikely in reality, particularly in simple linear regression using a single predictor.

We can determine a value of $Y'$ for each of the $i$ individuals (objects) from the prediction model. In comparing the actual $Y$ values to the predicted $Y$ values, we obtain the residuals as

$$e_i = Y_i - Y_i'$$

for all $i = 1, ..., n$ individuals or objects in the sample. The $e_i$ are also known as **errors of estimate**, or **prediction errors**, and are that portion of $Y_i$ that is not predictable from $X_i$. The residual terms are random values that are unique to each individual or object.

The residuals and predicted values for the statistics midterm example are shown in the last two columns of Table 17.1, respectively. Consider observation 2, where the observed GRE-Q score is 45 and the observed midterm score is 36. The predicted midterm score is 32.4875 and the residual is $+3.5125$. This indicates that person 2 had a higher observed midterm score than was predicted using the GRE-Q as a predictor. We see that a positive residual indicates the observed criterion score is larger than the predicted criterion score, whereas a negative residual (such as in observation 3) indicates the observed criterion score is smaller than the predicted criterion score. For observation 3, the observed GRE-Q score is 43, the observed midterm score is 27, the predicted midterm score is 31.4375, and thus the residual is $-4.4375$. Person 2 scored higher on the midterm than we predicted, and person 3 scored lower on the midterm than we predicted.

The regression example is shown graphically in the **scatterplot** of Fig. 17.2, where the straight diagonal line represents the regression line. Individuals falling above the regression line have positive residuals (e.g., observation 2) and individuals falling below the regression line have negative residuals (e.g., observation 3). In the residual column of Table 17.1 we see that half of the residuals are positive and half negative, and in Fig. 17.2 that half of the points fall above the regression line and half below the regression line. It can be shown that the mean of the residuals is always zero (i.e., $\bar{e} = 0$) as the sum of the residuals is always zero. This results

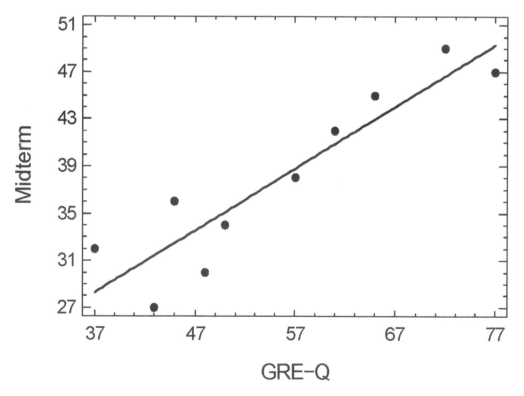

FIG. 17.2   Scatterplot for midterm example.

from the fact that the mean of the observed criterion scores is equal to the mean of the predicted criterion scores (i.e., $\bar{Y} = \bar{Y}'$; 38 for the example).

## 17.3.4    Least Squares Criterion

How was one particular method selected for determining the slope and intercept? Obviously, some standard procedure has to be used. Thus there are statistical criteria that help us decide which method to use in calculating the slope and intercept. The criterion usually used in linear regression analysis (and in all general linear models for that matter) is the **least squares criterion**. According to the least squares criterion, the sum of the squared prediction errors or residuals is smallest. That is, we want to find that regression line, defined by a particular slope and intercept, that results in the smallest sum of the squared residuals. Given the value that we place on the accuracy of prediction, this is the most logical choice of a method for estimating the slope and intercept.

In summary then, the least squares criterion gives us a particular slope and intercept, and thus a particular regression line, such that the sum of the squared residuals is smallest. We often refer to this particular method for calculating the slope and intercept as **least squares estimation**, because $b$ and $a$ represent sample estimates of the population parameters $\beta$ and $\alpha$ obtained using the least squares criterion.

## 17.3.5    Proportion of Predictable Variation (Coefficient of Determination)

How well is the criterion variable $Y$ predicted by the predictor variable $X$? For our example, we want to know how well the statistics midterm scores are predicted by the GRE-Q. Let us consider two possible situations with respect to this example. First, if the GRE-Q is found to be a really good predictor of statistics midterm scores, then instructors could use the GRE-Q information to individualize their instruction to the skill level of each student or class. They could, for example, provide special instruction to those students with low GRE-Q scores, or in general, adjust the level of instruction to fit the quantitative skills of their students. Second, if the GRE-Q is not found to be a very good predictor of statistics midterm scores, then instructors would not find very much use for the GRE-Q in terms of their preparation for the statistics course. They could search for some other more useful predictor, such as prior grades in quantitatively oriented courses or the number of years since the student had algebra. In other words, if a predictor is not found to be particularly useful in predicting the criterion variable, then other relevant predictors should be considered.

How do we determine the utility of a predictor variable? The simplest method involves partitioning the total sum of squares in $Y$, which we denote as $SS_{total}$ (sometimes written as $SS_Y$). This process is much like partitioning the sum of squares in the analysis of variance.

In simple linear regression, we can partition $SS_{total}$ into

$$SS_{total} = SS_{reg} + SS_{res}$$

$$\sum_{i=1}^{n}(Y - \bar{Y})^2 = \sum_{i=1}^{n}(Y' - \bar{Y})^2 + \sum_{i=1}^{n}(Y - Y')^2$$

where $SS_{total}$ is the total sum of squares in $Y$, $SS_{reg}$ is the sum of squares of the regression of $Y$ predicted by $X$ (sometimes written as $SS_{Y'}$), $SS_{res}$ is the sum of squares of the residuals, and the sums are taken over all observations from $i = 1, ..., n$. Thus $SS_{total}$ represents the total variation in the observed $Y$ scores, $SS_{reg}$ the variation in $Y$ predicted by $X$, and $SS_{res}$ the variation in $Y$ not predicted by $X$. Let us write $SS_{total}$, $SS_{reg}$, and $SS_{res}$ as follows:

$$SS_{total} = \frac{n \sum_{i=1}^{n} Y^2 - \left( \sum_{i=1}^{n} Y \right)^2}{n}$$

$$SS_{reg} = r_{XY}^2 SS_{total}$$

$$SS_{res} = (1 - r_{XY}^2) SS_{total}$$

where $r_{XY}^2$ is the squared sample correlation between $X$ and $Y$, commonly referred to as the **coefficient of determination**.

There is no objective gold standard as to how large the coefficient of determination needs to be in order to say a meaningful proportion of variation has been predicted. The coefficient is determined, not just by the quality of the one predictor variable included in the model, but also by the quality of relevant predictor variables not included in the model and by the amount of total variation in $Y$. However, the coefficient of determination can be used both as a measure of effect size and as a test of significance (described in the next section). According to the subjective standards of Cohen (1988), a small effect size is defined as $r^2 = .02$, a medium effect size as $r^2 = .13$, and a large effect size as $r^2 = .51$. For additional information on effect size measures in regression, see Steiger and Fouladi (1992), Mendoza and Stafford (2001), and Smithson (2001; which also includes some discussion of power).

With the sample data of predicting midterm statistics scores from the GRE-Q, let us determine the sums of squares. We can write $SS_{total}$ as follows:

$$SS_{total} = \frac{n \sum_{i=1}^{n} Y^2 - \left( \sum_{i=1}^{n} Y \right)^2}{n} = \frac{10(14,948) - (380)^2}{10} = 508.0000$$

We already know that $r_{XY} = .9177$, so squaring it we obtain $r_{XY}^2 = .8422$. Next we can determine $SS_{reg}$ and $SS_{res}$ as follows:

$$SS_{reg} = r_{XY}^2 SS_{total} = .8422 \,(508.0000) = 427.8376$$

$$SS_{res} = (1 - r_{XY}^2) SS_{total} = (1 - .8422)\,(508.0000) = 80.1624$$

Thus the GRE-Q predicts approximately 84% of the variation in the midterm statistics exam, which is clearly a large effect size. Significance tests are discussed in the next section.

## 17.3.6   Significance Tests and Confidence Intervals

This section describes four procedures used in the simple linear regression context. The first two are tests of statistical significance that generally involve testing whether or not $X$ is a significant predictor of $Y$. Then we consider two confidence interval techniques.

***Test of Significance of*** $r_{XY}^2$.   The first test is the test of the significance of $r_{XY}^2$ (alternatively known as the test of the proportion of variation in $Y$ predicted by $X$). It is important that $r_{XY}^2$ be different from zero in order to have reasonable prediction. The null and alternative hypotheses, respectively, are as follows:

$$H_0: \rho_{XY}^2 = 0$$

$$H_1: \rho_{XY}^2 > 0$$

This test is based on the following test statistic:

$$F = \frac{r^2/m}{(1-r^2)/(n-m-1)}$$

where $F$ indicates that this is an $F$ statistic, $r^2$ is the coefficient of determination, $1 - r^2$ is the proportion of variation in $Y$ that is not predicted by $X$, $m$ is the number of predictors (which in the case of simple linear regression is always 1), and $n$ is the sample size. The $F$ test statistic is compared to the $F$ critical value, always a one-tailed test and at the designated level of significance, with degrees of freedom $m$ and $(n - m - 1)$, as taken from the $F$ table in Appendix Table 4. That is, the tabled critical value is $_\alpha F_{m,(n-m-1)}$.

For the statistics midterm example, we determine the the test statistic to be

$$F = \frac{r^2/m}{(1-r^2)/(n-m-1)} = \frac{.8422/1}{(1-.8422)/(10-1-1)} = 42.6971$$

From Appendix Table 4, the critical value, at the .05 level of significance, is $_{.05}F_{1,8} = 5.32$. The test statistic exceeds the critical value; thus we reject $H_0$ and conclude that $\rho_{XY}^2$ is not equal to zero at the .05 level of significance (i.e., GRE-Q does predict a significant proportion of the variation on the midterm exam).

***Test of Significance of*** $b_{YX}$.   The second test is the test of the significance of the slope or regression coefficient, $b_{YX}$. In other words, is the unstandardized regression coefficient statistically significantly different from zero? This is actually the same as the test of $b^*$, the standardized regression coefficient, so we need not develop a separate test for $b^*$. The null and alternative hypotheses, respectively, are as follows:

$$H_0: \beta_{YX} = 0$$

$$H_1: \beta_{YX} \neq 0$$

To test whether the regression coefficient is equal to zero, we need a standard error for $b$. However, first we need to develop some new concepts. The first new concept is the **variance error of estimate**. Although this is the correct term, it is easier to consider this as the **variance of the residuals**. The variance error of estimate, or variance of the residuals, is defined as

$$s_{res}^2 = \Sigma\, e_i^2/df_{res} = SS_{res}/df_{res} = MS_{res}$$

where the summation is taken from $i = 1, ..., n$ and $df_{res} = (n - m - 1)$ (or $n - 2$ with a single predictor). Two degrees of freedom are lost because we have to estimate the population slope and intercept, $\beta$ and $\alpha$, from the sample data. The variance error of estimate indicates the amount of variation among the residuals. If there are some extremely large residuals, this will result in a relatively large value of $s_{res}^2$, indicating poor prediction overall. If the residuals are generally small, this will result in a comparatively small value of $s_{res}^2$, indicating good prediction overall.

The next new concept is the **standard error of estimate** (sometimes known as the root mean square error). The standard error of estimate is simply the positive square root of the variance error of estimate, and thus is the standard deviation of the residuals or errors of estimate. We denote the standard error of estimate as $s_{res}$. The final new concept is the **standard error of $b$**. We denote the standard error of $b$ as $s_b$ and define it as

$$s_b = \frac{s_{res}}{\sqrt{\left[ n \sum X^2 - (\sum X)^2 \right]/n}} = \frac{s_{res}}{\sqrt{SS_X}}$$

where the summation is taken over $i = 1, ..., n$. We want $s_b$ to be small to reject $H_0$, so we need $s_{res}$ to be small and $SS_X$ to be large. In other words, we want there to be a large spread of scores in $X$. If the variability in $X$ is small, it is difficult for $X$ to be a significant predictor of $Y$.

Now we can put these concepts together into a test statistic to test the significance of $b$. As in many significance tests, the test statistic is formed by the ratio of a parameter estimate divided by its respective standard error. A ratio of the parameter estimate of the slope $b$ to its standard error $s_b$ is formed as

$$t = \frac{b}{s_b}$$

The test statistic $t$ is compared to the critical values of $t$ (in Appendix Table 2), a two-tailed test for a non-directional $H_1$, at the designated level of significance $\alpha$, and with degrees of freedom of $(n - m - 1)$. That is, the tabled critical values are $\pm_{(\alpha/2)} t_{(n-m-1)}$ for a two-tailed test.

In addition, all other things being equal (i.e., same data, same degrees of freedom, same level of significance), both of these significance tests will yield the exact same result. That is, if $X$ is a significant predictor of $Y$, then $H_0$ will be rejected in both tests. If $X$ is not a significant predictor of $Y$, then $H_0$ will not be rejected for either test. In simple linear regression, each of these tests is a method for testing the same general hypothesis and logically should lead the researcher to the exact same conclusion. Thus, there is no need to implement both tests.

We can also form a confidence interval around $b$. As in most confidence interval procedures, it follows the form of the sample estimate plus or minus the tabled critical value multiplied by the standard error. The confidence interval (CI) around $b$ is formed as follows:

$$CI(b) = b \pm {}_{(\alpha/2)} t_{(n-m-1)} s_b$$

Recall that the null hypothesis was written as $H_0$: $\beta = 0$. Therefore, if the confidence interval contains zero, then $\beta$ is not significantly different from zero at the specified $\alpha$ level. This is interpreted to mean that in $(1 - \alpha)\%$ of the sample confidence intervals that would be formed from multiple samples, $\beta$ will be included. This procedure assumes homogeneity of variance (discussed later in this chapter); for alternative procedures see Wilcox (1996, 2003).

Now we can determine the second test statistic for the midterm statistics example. We specify $H_0$: $\beta = 0$ and conduct a two-tailed test. First the variance error of estimate is

$$s_{res}^2 = \sum e_i^2 / df_{res} = SS_{res} / df_{res} = MS_{res} = 80.1578 / 8 = 10.0197$$

The standard error of estimate, $s_{res}$, is $+\sqrt{10.0197} = 3.1654$. Next the standard error of $b$ is

$$s_b = \frac{s_{res}}{\sqrt{[n \sum X^2 - (\sum X)^2]/n}} = \frac{s_{res}}{\sqrt{SS_X}} = \frac{3.1654}{\sqrt{1,552.5000}} = .0803$$

Finally, we determine the test statistic to be

$$t = \frac{b}{s_b} = \frac{.5250}{.0803} = 6.5380$$

To evaluate the null hypothesis, we compare this test statistic to its critical values $\pm_{.025}t_8 = \pm 2.306$. The test statistic exceeds the critical value, so $H_0$ is rejected in favor of $H_1$. We conclude that the slope is indeed significantly different from zero, at the .05 level of significance.

Finally let us determine the confidence interval for $b$ as follows:

$$\text{CI}(b) = b \pm {}_{(\alpha/2)}t_{(n-m-1)}\, s_b = b \pm {}_{.025}t_8\, (s_b)$$
$$= 0.5250 \pm 2.306\, (0.0803) = (0.3398, 0.7102)$$

The interval does not contain zero, the value specified in $H_0$; thus we conclude that $\beta$ is significantly different from zero, at the .05 level of significance.

***Confidence Interval for the Predicted Mean Value of Y.*** The third procedure is to develop a confidence interval for the predicted mean value of $Y$, denoted by $\overline{Y}_0'$, for a specific value of $X_0$. Alternatively, $\overline{Y}_0'$ is referred to as the conditional mean of $Y$ given $X_0$ (more about conditional distributions in the next section). In other words, for a particular predictor score $X_0$, how confident we can be in the predicted mean for $Y$?

The standard error of $\overline{Y}_0'$ is

$$s(\overline{Y}_0') = s_{res}\sqrt{(1/n) + [(X_0 - \overline{X})^2 / SS_X]}$$

In looking at this equation, the further $X_0$ is from $\overline{X}$, the larger the standard error. Thus, the standard error depends on the particular value of $X_0$ selected. In other words, we expect to make our best predictions at the center of the distribution of $X$ scores, and to make our poorest predictions for extreme values of $X$. Thus, the closer the value of the predictor is to the center of the distribution of the $X$ scores, the better the prediction will be.

A confidence interval around $\overline{Y}_0'$ is formed as follows:

$$\text{CI}(\overline{Y}_0') = \overline{Y}_0' \pm {}_{(\alpha/2)}t_{(n-2)}\, s(\overline{Y}_0')$$

Our interpretation is that in $(1 - \alpha)\%$ of the sample confidence intervals that would be formed from multiple samples, the population mean value of $Y$ for a given value of $X$ will be included.

Let us consider an example of this confidence interval procedure with the midterm statistics data. If we take a GRE-Q score of 50, the predicted score on the statistics midterm is 35.1125. A confidence interval for the predicted mean value of 35.1125 is as follows:

$$s(\overline{Y}_0') = s_{res}\sqrt{(1/n) + [(X_0 - \overline{X})^2 / SS_X]} = 3.1654\sqrt{(1/10) + [(50 - 55)^2 / 1,552.5000]} = 1.0786$$

$$\mathrm{CI}(\overline{Y}_0') = \overline{Y}_0' \pm {}_{(\alpha/2)} t {}_{(n-2)} s(\overline{Y}_0') = \overline{Y}_0' \pm {}_{.025} t_8 \, s(\overline{Y}_0')$$

$$= 35.1125 \pm (2.306)(1.0786) = (32.6252, 37.5998)$$

In Fig. 17.3 the confidence interval around $\overline{Y}_0'$ given $X_0$ is plotted as the pair of curved lines closest to the regression line. Here we see graphically that the width of the confidence interval increases the further we move from $\overline{X}$ (where $\overline{X} = 55.5000$).

*Prediction Interval for Individual Values of Y.*    The fourth and final procedure is to develop a prediction interval for an individual predicted value of $Y_0'$ at a specific individual value of $X_0$. That is, the predictor score for a particular individual is known, but the criterion score for that individual has not yet been observed. This is in contrast to the confidence interval just discussed where the individual $Y$ scores have already been observed. Thus the confidence interval deals with the mean of the predicted values, while the prediction interval deals with an individual predicted value not yet observed.

The standard error of $Y_0'$ is

$$s(Y_0') = s_{res} \sqrt{1 + (1/n) + [(X_0 - \overline{X})^2 / SS_X]}$$

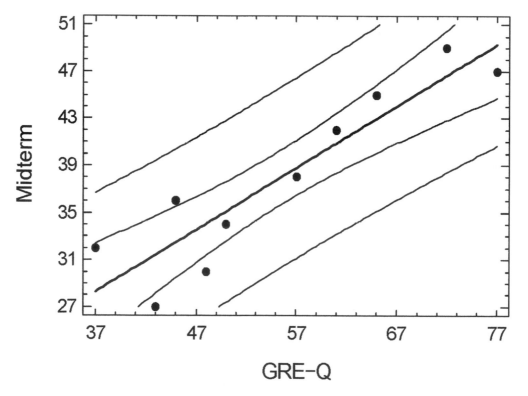

**FIG. 17.3   Confidence intervals for midterm example. The curved lines closest to the regression line are for the 95% CI and the curved lines furthest from the regression line are for the 95% PI.**

The standard error of $Y_0'$ is similar to the standard error of $\overline{Y_0'}$ with the addition of 1 to the equation. Thus the standard error of $Y_0'$ will always be greater than the standard error of $\overline{Y_0'}$ as there is more uncertainty about individual values than about the mean. The further $X_0$ is from $\overline{X}$, the larger the standard error. Thus the standard error again depends on the particular value of $X$, where we have more confidence in predictions for values of $X$ close to $\overline{X}$.

The prediction interval (PI) around $Y'_0$ is formed as follows:

$$PI(Y_0') = Y_0' \pm {}_{(\alpha/2)}t_{(n-2)} \, s(Y_0')$$

Our interpretation is that in $(1 - \alpha)\%$ of the sample prediction intervals that would be formed from multiple samples, the new observation $Y_0$ for a given value of $X$ will be included.

Consider an example of this prediction interval procedure with the midterm statistics data. If we take a GRE-Q score of 50, the predicted score on the statistics midterm is 35.1125. A prediction interval for the predicted individual value of 35.1125 is as follows:

$$s(Y_0') = s_{res}\sqrt{1 + (1/n) + \left[(X_0 - \overline{X})^2 / SS_X\right]} = 3.1654\sqrt{1 + (1/10) + [(50-55)^2/1,552.5000]} = 3.3441$$

$$PI\,(Y_0') = Y_0' \pm {}_{(\alpha/2)}t_{(n-2)} \, s(Y_0') = Y_0' \pm {}_{.025}t_8 \, s(Y_0')$$

$$= 35.1125 \pm (2.306)\,(3.3441) = (27.4010, 42.8240)$$

In Fig. 17.3 the prediction interval around $Y_0'$ given $X_0$ is plotted as the pair of curved lines furthest from the regression line. Here we see graphically that the prediction interval is always wider than its corresponding confidence interval.

## 17.3.7 Assumptions and Violation of Assumptions

In this section we consider the following assumptions involved in simple linear regression: (a) independence; (b) homogeneity; (c) normality; (d) linearity; and (e) fixed $X$. Some discussion is also devoted to the effects of assumption violations and how to detect them.

*Independence.* The first assumption is concerned with independence of the observations. We should be familiar with this assumption from previous chapters (e.g., ANOVA). In regression analysis another way to think about this assumption is that the errors in prediction or residuals (i.e., $e_i$) are assumed to be random and independent. That is, there is no systematic pattern about the errors and each error is independent of the other errors. An example of a systematic pattern would be where for small values of $X$ the residuals tended to be small, whereas for large values of $X$ the residuals tended to be large. Thus there would be a relationship between $X$ and $e$. Dependent errors occur when the error for one individual depends on or is related to the error for another individual as a result of some predictor not being included in the model. For our midterm statistics example, students similar in age might have similar residuals because age was not included as a predictor in the model.

Note that there are several different types of residuals. The $e_i$ are known as **raw residuals** for the same reason that $X_i$ and $Y_i$ are called raw scores, all being in their original scale. The raw residuals are on the same raw score scale as $Y$ with a mean of zero and a variance of $s_{res}^2$. Some researchers dislike raw residuals as their scale depends on the scale of $Y$, and therefore they must temper their interpretation of the residual values. Several different types of **standardized residuals** have been developed, including the original form of standardized residual $e_i/s_{res}$. These values are measured along the $z$ score scale with a mean of 0, a variance of 1, and approximately 95% of the values are within $\pm 2$ units of zero. Some researchers prefer these over raw residuals because they find it easier to detect large residuals. However, if you really think about it, one can easily look at the middle 95% of the raw residuals by just considering the range of $\pm 2$ standard errors (i.e., $\pm 2\, s_{res}$) around zero. Other types of standardized residuals will not be considered here (see Atkinson, 1985; Cook & Weisberg, 1982; Dunn & Clark, 1987; Kleinbaum, Kupper, Muller & Nizam, 1998; Weisberg, 1985).

The simplest procedure for assessing this assumption is to examine a scatterplot ($Y$ versus $X$) or a residual plot (e.g., $e$ versus $X$). If the independence assumption is satisfied, there should be a random display of points. If the assumption is violated, the plot will display some type of pattern; for example, the negative residuals tend to cluster together and positive residuals tend to cluster together. As we know from ANOVA, violation of the independence assumption generally occurs in the following three situations: (a) when the observations are collected over time (the independent variable is a measure of time; consider using the Durban-Watson test [1950, 1951, 1971]); (b) observations are made within blocks, such that the observations within a particular block are more similar than observations in different blocks; or (c) when observation involves replication. Lack of independence affects the estimated standard errors, being under- or overestimated. For serious violations one could consider using generalized or weighted least squares as the method of estimation.

*Homogeneity.*    The second assumption is **homogeneity of variance**, which should also be a familiar assumption (e.g., ANOVA). This assumption must be reframed a bit in the regression context by examining the concept of a **conditional distribution**. In regression analysis, a conditional distribution is defined as the distribution of $Y$ for a particular value of $X$. For instance, in the midterm statistics example, we could consider the conditional distribution of midterm scores for GRE-Q $= 50$; in other words, what the distribution of $Y$ looks like for $X = 50$. We call this a conditional distribution because it represents the distribution of $Y$ conditional on a particular value of $X$ (sometimes denoted as $Y\,|\,X$, read as $Y$ given $X$). We could alternatively examine the conditional distribution of the prediction errors, that is, the distribution of the prediction errors conditional on a particular value of $X$ (i.e., $e\,|\,X$, read as $e$ given $X$). Thus the homogeneity assumption is that the conditional distributions have a constant variance for all values of $X$.

In a plot of the $Y$ scores or the residuals versus $X$, the consistency of the variance of the conditional distributions can be examined. A common violation of this assumption occurs when the conditional residual variance increases as $X$ increases. Here the residual plot is cone- or fan-shaped where the cone opens toward the right. An example of this violation would be where weight is predicted by age, as weight is more easily predicted for young children than it is for adults. Thus residuals would tend to be larger for adults than for children.

If the homogeneity assumption is violated, estimates of the standard errors are larger, and although the regression coefficients remain unbiased, the validity of the significance tests is affected. In fact with larger standard errors, it is more difficult to reject $H_0$, therefore resulting in a larger number of Type II errors. Minor violations of this assumption will have a small net effect; more serious violations occur when the variances are greatly different. In addition, nonconstant variances may also result in the conditional distributions being nonnormal in shape.

If the homogeneity assumption is seriously violated, the simplest solution is to use some sort of transformation, known as **variance stabilizing transformations** (e.g., Weisberg, 1985). Commonly used transformations are the log or square root of $Y$ (e.g., Kleinbaum, Kupper, Muller & Nizam, 1998). These transformations can also often improve on the nonnormality of the conditional distributions. However, this complicates things in terms of dealing with transformed variables rather than the original variables. A better solution is to use generalized or weighted least squares (e.g., Weisberg, 1985). A third solution is to use a form of robust estimation (e.g., Carroll & Ruppert, 1982; Kleinbaum, Kupper, Muller & Nizam, 1998; Wilcox, 1996, 2003).

*Normality.* The third assumption of **normality** should also be familar. In regression the assumption is that the conditional distributions of either $Y$ or the prediction errors are normal in shape. That is, for all values of $X$, the scores on $Y$ or the prediction errors are normally distributed. Oftentimes nonnormal distributions are largely a function of one or a few extreme observations, known as **outliers**. Extreme values may cause nonnormality and seriously affect the regression results. The regression estimates are quite sensitive to outlying observations such that the precision of the estimates is affected, particularly the slope. Also the coefficient of determination can be affected. In general, the regression line will be pulled toward the outlier, because the least squares principle always attempts to find the line that best fits all of the points.

Various rules of thumb are used to crudely detect outliers from a residual plot or scatterplot. A commonly used rule is to define an outlier as an observation more than two standard errors from the mean (i.e., a large distance from the mean). The outlier observation may be a result of (a) a simple recording or data entry error, (b) an error in observation, (c) an improperly functioning instrument, (d) inappropriate use of administration instructions, or (e) a true outlier. If the outlier is the result of an error, correct the error if possible and redo the regression analysis. If the error cannot be corrected, then the observation could be deleted. If the outlier represents an accurate observation, then this observation may contain important theoretical information, and one would be more hesitant to delete it.

A simple procedure to use for single case outliers (i.e., just one outlier) is to perform two regression analyses, both with and without the outlier being included. A comparison of the regression results will provide some indication of the effects of the outlier. Other methods for detecting and dealing with outliers are available, but are not described here (e.g., Andrews & Pregibon, 1978; Barnett & Lewis, 1978; Beckman & Cook, 1983; Cook, 1977; Hawkins, 1980; Kleinbaum, Kupper, Muller & Nizam, 1998; Mickey, Dunn & Clark, 2004; Pedazur, 1997; Rousseeuw & Leroy, 1987; Wilcox, 1996, 2003).

How does one go about detecting violation of the normality assumption? There are two commonly used procedures. The simplest procedure involves checking for symmetry in a histogram, frequency distribution, boxplot, or skewness and kurtosis statistics. Although **non-zero kurtosis** (i.e., a distribution that is either flat or has a sharp peak) will have minimal effect on the regression estimates, **non-zero skewness** (i.e., a distribution that is not symmetric) will have much more impact on these estimates. Thus, finding asymmetrical distributions is a must. For the midterm statistics example, the skewness value for the raw residuals is $-0.2692$. One rule of thumb is to be concerned if the skewness value is larger than 1.5 or 2.0 in magnitude.

Another useful graphical technique is the normal probability plot. With normally distributed data or residuals, the points on the normal probability plot will fall along a straight diagonal line, whereas nonnormal data will not. There is a difficulty with this plot because there is no criterion with which to judge deviation from linearity. A normal probability plot of the raw residuals for the midterm statistics example is shown in Fig. 17.4. Together the skewness and normal probability plot results indicate that the normality assumption is satisfied. It is recommended that skewness and/or the normal probability plot be considered at a minimum.

There are also several statistical procedures available for the detection of nonnormality (e.g., Andrews, 1971; Belsley, Kuh & Welsch, 1980; Ruppert & Carroll, 1980; Wu, 1985). In addition, various transformations are available to transform a nonnormal distribution into a normal distribution. The most commonly used transformations in regression analysis are the log and the square root. However, again there is the problem of dealing with transformed variables measured along some other scale than that of the original variables.

*Linearity.*    The fourth assumption is **linearity**, that there is a linear relationship between $X$ and $Y$, which is also assumed for most correlations. Consider the scatterplot and regression line in Fig. 17.5 where $X$ and $Y$ are not linearly related. Here $X$ and $Y$ form a perfect curvilinear relationship as all of the points fall precisely on a curve. However, fitting a straight line to these points results in a slope of zero as indicated by the solid horizontal line, not useful at all for predicting $Y$ from $X$. For example, age and performance are not linearly related.

If the relationship between $X$ and $Y$ is linear, then the sample slope and intercept will be unbiased estimators of the population slope and intercept, respectively. The linearity assumption is important because, regardless of the value of $X_i$, we always expect $Y_i$ to increase by $b_{YX}$ units for a one-unit increase in $X_i$. If a nonlinear relationship exists, this means that the expected increase

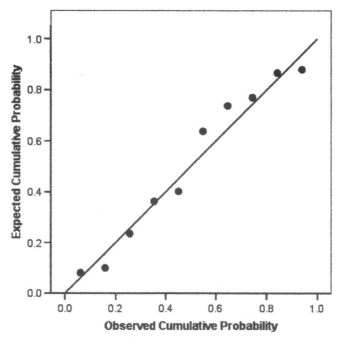

FIG. 17.4    Normal probability plot for midterm example.

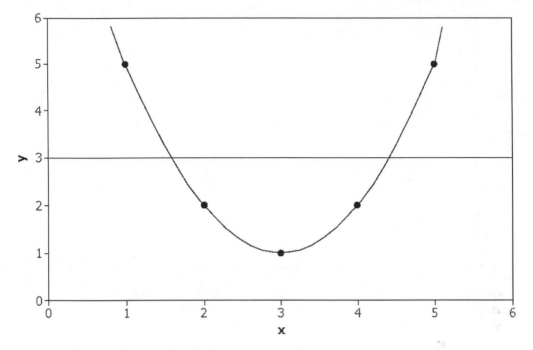

**FIG. 17.5 Nonlinear regression example.**

in $Y_i$ depends on the value of $X_i$. Strictly speaking, linearity in a model refers to there being linearity in the parameters of the model (i.e., $\beta$ and $\alpha$).

Detecting violation of the linearity assumption can often be done by looking at the scatterplot of $Y$ versus $X$. If the linearity assumption is met, we expect to see no systematic pattern of points. While this plot is often satisfactory in simple linear regression, less obvious violations are more easily detected in a residual plot. If the linearity assumption is met, we expect to see a horizontal band of residuals mainly contained within $\pm 2 \, s_{res}$ (or standard errors) across the values of $X$. If the assumption is violated, we expect to see a systematic pattern between $e$ and $X$. Therefore I recommend you examine both the scatterplot and the residual plot. A residual plot for the midterm statistics example is shown in Fig. 17.6. Even with a very small sample, we see a fairly random pattern of residuals, and therefore feel fairly confident that the linearity assumption has been satisfied.

If a serious violation of the linearity assumption has been detected, how should we deal with it? There are two alternative procedures that the researcher can utilize, **transformations** or **nonlinear models**. The first option is to transform either one or both of the variables to achieve linearity. That is, the researcher selects a transformation that subsequently results in a linear relationship between the transformed variables. Then the method of least squares can be used to perform a linear regression analysis on the transformed variables. However, when dealing with transformed variables measured along a different scale, results need to be described in terms of the transformed rather than the original variables. A better option is to use a nonlinear model to examine the relationship between the variables in their original scale (see Wilcox, 1996; 2003; also discussed in chapter 18).

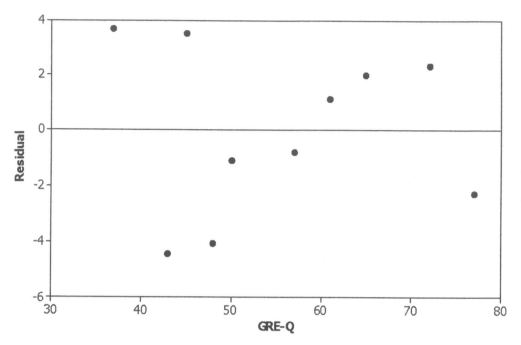

**FIG. 17.6    Residual plot for midterm example.**

***Fixed X.***    The fifth and final assumption is that the values of *X* are **fixed**. That is, *X* is a fixed variable rather than a random variable. This results in the regression model being valid only for those particular values of *X* that were actually observed and used in the analysis. Thus the same values of *X* would be used in replications or repeated samples. You may recall a similar concept in the fixed-effects analysis of variance models previously considered.

Strictly speaking, the regression model and its parameter estimates are only valid for those values of *X* actually sampled. The use of a prediction model, based on one sample of individuals, to predict *Y* for another sample of individuals may be suspect. Depending on the circumstances, the new sample of individuals may actually call for a different set of parameter estimates. Two obvious situations that come to mind are the **extrapolation** and **interpolation** of values of *X*. In general we may not want to make predictions about individuals having *X* scores outside of the range of values used in developing the prediction model; this is defined as extrapolating beyond the sample predictor data. We cannot assume that the function defined by the prediction model is the same outside of the values of *X* that were initially sampled. The prediction errors for the new nonsampled *X* values would be expected to be larger than those for the sampled *X* values because there is no supportive prediction data for the former.

On the other hand, we are not quite as concerned in making predictions about individuals having *X* scores within the range of values used in developing the prediction model; this is defined as interpolating within the range of the sample predictor data. We would feel somewhat more comfortable in assuming that the function defined by the prediction model is the same for other new values of *X* within the range of those initially sampled. For the most part, the fixed *X* assumption is satisfied if the new observations behave like those in the prediction sample. In the interpolation situation, we expect the prediction errors to be somewhat smaller as compared to the extrapolation situation because there is at least some similar supportive prediction data for the former. It has been shown that when other assumptions are met, regression analysis performs just as well when $X$ is a random variable (e.g., Glass & Hopkins, 1996; Myers & Well, 1995; Pedhazur, 1997). There is no corresponding assumption about the nature of $Y$.

In our midterm statistics example, we have more confidence in our prediction for a GRE-Q value of 52 (which did not occur in the sample, but falls within the range of sampled values), than in a value of 20 (which also did not occur, but is much smaller than the smallest value sampled, 37). In fact, this is precisely the rationale underlying the prediction interval previously developed, where the width of the interval increased as an individual's score on the predictor ($X_i$) moved away from the predictor mean ($\overline{X}$).

A summary of the assumptions and the effects of their violation for simple linear regression is presented in Table 17.2.

***Summary.*** The simplest procedure for assessing assumptions is to plot the residuals and see what the plot tells you. Take the midterm statistics problem as an example. Although sample size is quite small in terms of looking at conditional distributions, it would appear that all of our assumptions have been satisfied. All of the residuals are within two standard errors of zero, and there does not seem to be any systematic pattern in the residuals. The distribution of the residuals is nearly symmetric and the normal probability plot looks good. The scatterplot also strongly suggests a linear relationship.

## 17.4 SPSS

Finally we consider SPSS for the simple linear regression model, including an APA paragraph of selected results. To conduct a simple linear regression analysis, go from the "Analyze" pull-down, into "Regression," and then into the "Linear" procedure. Click your dependent variable "midterm" into the "Dependent:" box and the independent variable "GRE-Q" into the "Independent(s):" box. Second, click on the "Statistics" button, where various types of statistics can be requested. At a minimum I suggest you ask for the following: estimates, confidence intervals,

**TABLE 17.2**
Assumptions and Violation of Assumptions—Simple Linear Regression

| Assumption | Effect of Assumption Violation |
|---|---|
| 1. Independence | Influences standard errors of the model |
| 2. Homogeneity | Bias in $s_{res}^2$; may inflate standard errors and thus increase likelihood of a Type II error; may result in nonnormal conditional distributions |
| 3. Normality | Less precise slope, intercept, and $R^2$ |
| 4. Linearity | Bias in slope and intercept; expected change in $Y$ is not a constant and depends on value of $X$; reduced magnitude of coefficient of determination |
| 5. Values of $X$ are fixed | (a) Extrapolating beyond the range of $X$: prediction errors larger, may also bias slope and intercept |
| | (b) Interpolating within the range of $X$: smaller effects than in (a); if other assumptions met, negligible effect |

model fit, and descriptives. If you click on the "Plots" button, you can generate residual plots and the normal probability plot. Finally, click on the "Save" button if you want to save various results (e.g., you can save different types of residuals as well as values from the confidence intervals into your dataset). In Chapter 18 we see other regression modules in SPSS which allow you to consider, for example, generalized or weighted least squares regression, nonlinear regression, and logistic regression. Additional information on regression analysis in SPSS is provided in texts such as Morgan and Griego (1998) and Meyers, Gamst, and Guarino (2006). Selected results for the example are shown in Table 17.3.

Lastly, here is an example paragraph of the results for the midterm statistics example. From the top panel of Table 17.3, we see that $r_{XY}^2 = .842$, indicating that 84% of the variation in midterm scores was predicted by GRE-Q scores. In the middle panel of Table 17.3, the ANOVA summary table indicates that a significant proportion of the total variation in midterm scores was predicted by GRE-Q ($F = 42.700$, $df = 1,8$, $p < .001$). In the bottom panel of Table 17.3 we see the following results: (a) the unstandardized slope (.525) and standardized slope (.918) are sig-

**TABLE 17.3**
Selected SPSS Results for the Midterm Example

*Model Summary*[b]

| Model | R | R Square | Std. Error of the Estimate |
|-------|---|----------|----------------------------|
| 1 | .918[a] | .842 | 3.165 |

[a]Predictors: (Constant), GRE-Q
[b]Dependent Variable: Midterm

*ANOVA*[b]

| Model | | Sum of Squares | df | Mean Square | F | Sig. |
|-------|--|----------------|----|-----|---|------|
| 1 | Regression | 427.842 | 1 | 427.842 | 42.700 | .000[a] |
|   | Residual | 80.158 | 8 | 10.020 | | |
|   | Total | 508.000 | 9 | | | |

[a]Predictors: (Constant), GRE-Q
[b]Dependent Variable: Midterm

*Coefficients*[a]

| Model | | Unstandardized Coefficients | | Standardized Coefficients | | | 95% Confidence Interval for B | |
|-------|--|------|------------|-------|------|------|-------|-------|
| | | B | Std. Error | Beta | t | Sig. | Lower Bound | Upper Bound |
| 1 | (Constant) | 8.865 | 4.570 | | 1.940 | .088 | −1.673 | 19.402 |
|   | GRE-Q | .525 | .080 | .918 | 6.535 | .000 | .340 | .710 |

[a]Dependent Variable: Midterm

nificantly different from zero ($t = 6.535$, $df = 8$, $p < .001$); (b) the confidence interval around the unstandardized slope does not include zero (.340, .710); and (c) the intercept was 8.865. Thus GRE-Q was shown to be a statisticially significant predictor of midterm exam scores.

## 17.5   SUMMARY

In this chapter the method of simple linear regression was described. First we discussed the basic concepts of regression such as the slope and intercept. Next, a formal introduction to the population simple linear regression model was given. These concepts were then extended to the sample situation where a more detailed discussion was given. In the sample context we considered unstandardized and standardized regression coefficients, errors in prediction, the least squares criterion, the coefficient of determination, tests of significance, and a discussion of statistical assumptions. At this point you should have met the following objectives: (a) be able to understand the concepts underlying simple linear regression, (b) be able to determine and interpret the results of simple linear regression, and (c) be able to understand and evaluate the assumptions of simple linear regression. Chapter 18 follows up with a description of multiple regression, where regression models are developed based on two or more predictors.

## PROBLEMS

### Conceptual Problems

1.  A regression intercept represents
    a.   the slope of the line.
    b.   the amount of change in $Y$ given a one unit change in $X$.
    c.   the value of $Y$ when $X$ is equal to zero.
    d.   the strength of the relationship between $X$ and $Y$.

2.  The regression line for predicting final exam grades in history from midterm scores in the same course is found to be $Y' = .61 X + 3.12$. If the value of $X$ increases from 74 to 75, the value of $Y$ will
    a.   increase .61 points.
    b.   increase 1.00 points.
    c.   increase 3.12 points.
    d.   decrease .61 points.

3.  Given that $\mu_X = 14$, $\sigma_X^2 = 36$, $\mu_Y = 14$, $\sigma_Y^2 = 49$, and $Y' = 14$ is the prediction equation for predicting $Y$ from $X$, the variance of the predicted values of $Y'$ is
    a.   0.
    b.   14.
    c.   36.
    d.   49.

4.  In regression analysis, the prediction of $Y$ is *most* accurate for which of the following correlations between $X$ and $Y$?

    a.   $-.90$

    b.   $-.30$

    c.   $+.20$

    d.   $+.80$

5.  If the relationship between two variables is linear,

    a.   all the points fall on a curved line.

    b.   the relationship is best represented by a curved line.

    c.   all the points must fall on a straight line.

    d.   the relationship is best represented by a straight line.

6.  If both $X$ and $Y$ are measured on a $z$ score scale, the regression line will have a slope of

    a.   0.00.

    b.   $+1$ or $-1$.

    c.   $r_{XY}$.

    d.   $s_Y/s_X$.

7.  If the simple linear regression equation for predicting $Y$ from $X$ is $Y' = 25$, then the correlation between $X$ and $Y$ is

    a.   0.00.

    b.   0.25.

    c.   0.50.

    d.   1.00.

8.  The unstandardized regression slope

    a.   may never be negative.

    b.   may never be greater than $+1.00$.

    c.   may never be greater than the correlation coefficient $r_{XY}$.

    d.   none of the above.

9.  If two individuals have the same score on the predictor, their residual scores will

    a.   be necessarily equal.

    b.   depend *only* on their observed scores on $Y$.

    c.   depend *only* on their predicted scores on $Y$.

    d.   depend *only* on the number of individuals that have the same predicted score.

10. If $r_{XY} = .6$, the proportion of variation in $Y$ that is *not* predictable from $X$ is

    a.   .36.

    b.   .40.

    c.   .60.

    d.   .64.

11. Homogeneity assumes that
   a. the range of $Y$ is the same as the range of $X$.
   b. the $X$ and $Y$ distributions have the same mean values.
   c. the variability of the $X$ and the $Y$ distributions is the same.
   d. the conditional variability of $Y$ is the same for all values of $X$.

12. The linear regression slope $b_{YX}$ represents the
   a. amount of change in $X$ expected from a one unit change in $Y$.
   b. amount of change in $Y$ expected from a one unit change in $X$.
   c. correlation between $X$ and $Y$.
   d. error of estimate of $Y$ from $X$.

13. If the correlation between $X$ and $Y$ is zero, then the best prediction of $Y$ that can be made is the mean of $Y$. True or False?

14. If $X$ and $Y$ are highly nonlinear, linear regression is more useful than the situation where $X$ and $Y$ are highly linear. True or False?

15. If the pretest $(X)$ and the posttest $(Y)$ are positively correlated, and your friend receives a pretest score below the mean, then the regression equation would predict that your friend would have a posttest score that is above the mean. True or False?

16. Two variables are linearly related so that given $X$, $Y$ can be predicted without error. I assert that $r_{XY}$ must be equal to either $+1.0$ or $-1.0$. Am I correct?

17. I assert that the simple regression model is structured so that at least two of the actual data points will fall on the regression line. Am I correct?

## Computational Problems

1. You are given the following pairs of scores on $X$ (number of hours studied) and $Y$ (quiz score).

   | $X$ | $Y$ |
   |-----|-----|
   | 4   | 5   |
   | 4   | 6   |
   | 3   | 4   |
   | 7   | 8   |
   | 2   | 4   |

   a) Find the linear regression model for predicting $Y$ from $X$.
   b) Use the prediction model obtained to predict the value of $Y$ for a person who has an $X$ value of 6.

2. The prediction equation for predicting $Y$ (pain indicator) from $X$ (drug dosage) is $Y' = 2.5X + 18$. What is the observed mean for $Y$ if $\mu_X = 40$ and $\sigma_X^2 = 81$?

3.  You are given the following pairs of scores on $X$ (# of years working) and $Y$ (# of raises).

| $X$ | $Y$ |
|-----|-----|
| 2 | 2 |
| 2 | 1 |
| 1 | 1 |
| 1 | 1 |
| 3 | 5 |
| 4 | 4 |
| 5 | 7 |
| 5 | 6 |
| 7 | 7 |
| 6 | 8 |
| 4 | 3 |
| 3 | 3 |
| 6 | 6 |
| 6 | 6 |
| 8 | 10 |
| 9 | 9 |
| 10 | 6 |
| 9 | 6 |
| 4 | 9 |
| 4 | 10 |

Perform the following computations using $\alpha = .05$.

a)  the regression equation of $Y$ predicted by $X$

b)  test of the significance of $X$ as a predictor

c)  plot $Y$ versus $X$

d)  compute the residuals

e)  plot residuals versus $X$

## Interpretive Problem

With the class survey data on the CD, your task is to use SPSS to find a suitable single predictor of current GPA. In other words, select several potential predictors that seem reasonable, and conduct a simple linear regression analysis for each of those predictors individually. Which of those is the best predictor of current GPA?

# 18

# MULTIPLE REGRESSION

## Chapter Outline

1.  Partial and semipartial correlations
      Partial correlation
      Semipartial (part) correlation
2.  Multiple linear regression
      Unstandardized regression model
      Standardized regression model
      Coefficient of multiple determination and multiple correlation
      Significance tests
      Assumptions
3.  Other regression models
4.  SPSS
5.  What's next?

## Key Concepts

1.  Partial and semipartial (part) correlations
2.  Standardized and unstandardized regression coefficients
3.  Coefficient of multiple determination and multiple correlation

In Chapter 17 our concern was with the prediction of a dependent or criterion variable ($Y$) by a single independent or predictor variable ($X$). However, given the types of phenomena we typically deal with in education and the behavioral sciences, the use of a single predictor variable is quite restrictive. In other words, given the complexity of most human, organizational, and animal behaviors, one predictor is usually not sufficient in terms of understanding the criterion. In order to account for a sufficient proportion of variability in the criterion, more than one predictor is necessary. This leads us to analyze the data via multiple regression where two or more predictors are used to predict the criterion variable. Here we adopt the usual notation where the $X$'s are defined as the independent or predictor variables, and $Y$ as the dependent or criterion variable.

For example, our admissions officer might want to use more than just Graduate Record Exam (GRE) scores to predict graduate-level grade point averages (GPA) to make admissions decisions for a sample of applicants to your favorite local university or college. Other potentially useful predictors might be undergraduate grade point average, recommendation letters, writing samples, and/or an evaluation from a personal interview. The research question of interest would now be, how well do the GRE, undergraduate GPA, recommendations, writing samples, and/or interview scores (the independent or predictor variables) predict performance in graduate school (the dependent or criterion variable)? This is an example of a situation where multiple regression using multiple predictor variables might be the method of choice.

Most of the concepts used in simple linear regression from Chapter 17 carry over to multiple regression. This chapter considers the concepts of partial, semipartial, and multiple correlations, standardized and unstandardized regression coefficients, and the coefficient of multiple determination, as well as introduces a number of other types of regression models. Our objectives are that by the end of this chapter, you will be able to (a) determine and interpret the results of partial and semipartial correlations, (b) understand the concepts underlying multiple linear regression, (c) determine and interpret the results of multiple linear regression, (d) understand and evaluate the assumptions of multiple linear regression, and (e) have a basic understanding of other types of regression models.

## 18.1   PARTIAL AND SEMIPARTIAL CORRELATIONS

Prior to a discussion of regression analysis, we need to consider two related concepts in correlational analysis, partial and semipartial correlations. Multiple regression involves the use of two or more predictor variables and one criterion variable; thus there are at a minimum three variables involved in the analysis. If we think about these variables in the context of the Pearson correlation, we have a problem because this correlation can only be used to relate two variables at a time. How do we incorporate additional variables into a correlational analysis? The answer is through partial and semipartial correlations, and later in this chapter, multiple correlations.

### 18.1.1   Partial Correlation

First we discuss the concept of **partial correlation**. The simplest situation consists of three variables, which we label $X_1$, $X_2$, and $X_3$. Here an example of a partial correlation would be the correlation between $X_1$ and $X_2$ where $X_3$ is held constant (i.e., controlled or partialled out). That is, the influence of $X_3$ is removed from both $X_1$ and $X_2$ (both have been adjusted for $X_3$).

Thus the partial correlation here represents the linear relationship between $X_1$ and $X_2$ independent of the linear influence of $X_3$. This particular partial correlation is denoted by $r_{12.3}$, where the $X$'s are not shown for simplicity and the dot indicates that the variables preceding it are to be correlated and the variable(s) following it are to be partialled out. A method for computing $r_{12.3}$ is as follows:

$$r_{12.3} = \frac{r_{12} - r_{13}r_{23}}{\sqrt{\left(1 - r_{13}^2\right)\left(1 - r_{23}^2\right)}}$$

Let us take an example of a situation where a partial correlation might be computed. Say a researcher is interested in the relationship between height ($X_1$) and weight ($X_2$). The sample consists of individuals ranging in age ($X_3$) from 6 months to 65 years. The sample correlations are $r_{12} = .7$, $r_{13} = .1$, and $r_{23} = .6$. We compute $r_{12.3}$ as

$$r_{12.3} = \frac{r_{12} - r_{13}r_{23}}{\sqrt{\left(1 - r_{13}^2\right)\left(1 - r_{23}^2\right)}} = \frac{.7 - (.1).6}{\sqrt{(1 - .01)(1 - .36)}} = .8040$$

We see here that the bivariate correlation between height and weight, ignoring age ($r_{12} = .7$), is smaller than the partial correlation between height and weight controlling for age ($r_{12.3} = .8040$). That is, the relationship between height and weight is stronger when age is held constant (i.e., for a particular age) than it is across all ages. Although we often talk about holding a particular variable constant, in reality variables such as age cannot be held constant artificially.

Some rather interesting partial correlation results can occur in particular situations. At one extreme, if both $r_{13}$ and $r_{23}$ equal zero, then $r_{12} = r_{12.3}$. That is, if the variable being partialled out is uncorrelated with each of the other two variables, then the partialling process will logically not have any effect. At the other extreme, if either $r_{13}$ or $r_{23}$ equals 1, then $r_{12.3}$ cannot be calculated as the denominator is equal to zero (you cannot divide by zero). Thus $r_{12.3}$ is undefined. Later in this chapter we refer to this as perfect collinearity, which is a serious problem. In between these extremes, it is possible for the partial correlation to be greater than or less than its corresponding bivariate correlation (including a change in sign), and even for the partial correlation to be equal to zero when its bivariate correlation is not. For significance tests of partial and semipartial correlations, refer to your favorite statistical software.

### 18.1.2    Semipartial (Part) Correlation

Next the concept of **semipartial correlation** (also called a part correlation) is discussed. The simplest situation consists again of three variables, which we label $X_1$, $X_2$, and $X_3$. Here an example of a semipartial correlation would be the correlation between $X_1$ and $X_2$ where $X_3$ is removed from $X_2$ only. That is, the influence of $X_3$ is removed from $X_2$ only. Thus the semipartial correlation here represents the linear relationship between $X_1$ and $X_2$ after that portion of $X_2$ that can be linearly predicted from $X_3$ has been removed from $X_2$. This particular semipartial correlation is denoted by $r_{1(2.3)}$, where the $X$'s are not shown for simplicity and within the parentheses the dot indicates that the variable(s) following it are to be removed from the variable preceding it. Another use of the semipartial correlation is when we want to examine the predictive power in the prediction of $Y$ from $X_1$ after removing $X_2$ from the prediction. A method for computing $r_{1(2.3)}$ is as follows:

$$r_{1(2.3)} = \frac{r_{12} - r_{13}r_{23}}{\sqrt{1 - r_{23}^2}}$$

Let us take an example of a situation where a semipartial correlation might be computed. Say a researcher is interested in the relationship between GPA ($X_1$) and GRE scores ($X_2$). The researcher would like to remove the influence of intelligence (IQ: $X_3$) from GRE scores, but not from GPA. The sample correlations are $r_{12} = .5$, $r_{13} = .3$, and $r_{23} = .7$. We compute $r_{1(2.3)}$ as

$$r_{1(2.3)} = \frac{r_{12} - r_{13}r_{23}}{\sqrt{1 - r_{23}^2}} = \frac{.5 - (.3).7}{\sqrt{1 - .49}} = .4061$$

Thus the bivariate correlation between GPA and GRE ignoring IQ ($r_{12} = .50$) is larger than the semipartial correlation between GPA and GRE controlling for IQ in GRE ($r_{1(2.3)} = .4061$). As was the case with partial correlations, various values of a semipartial correlation can be obtained depending on the combination of the bivariate correlations. For more information on partial and semipartial correlations, see Hays (1988), Glass and Hopkins (1996), or Pedhazur (1997).

Now that we have considered the correlational relationships among two or more variables (i.e., partial and semipartial correlations), let us move on to an examination of the multiple regression model where there are two or more predictor variables.

## 18.2    MULTIPLE LINEAR REGRESSION

Let us take the concepts we have learned in this and the previous chapter and place them into the context of multiple linear regression. For purposes of brevity, we do not consider the population situation because the sample situation is invoked 99.44% of the time. In this section we discuss the unstandardized and standardized multiple regression models, the coefficient of multiple determination, multiple correlation, tests of significance, and statistical assumptions.

### 18.2.1    Unstandardized Regression Model

The sample multiple linear regression model for predicting $Y$ from $m$ predictors $X_{1,2,...,m}$ is

$$Y_i = b_1 X_{1i} + b_2 X_{2i} + ... + b_m X_{mi} + a + e_i$$

where $Y$ is the criterion variable, the $X_k$'s are the predictor variables where $k = 1, ..., m$, $b_k$ is the sample partial slope of the regression line for $Y$ as predicted by $X_k$, $a$ is the sample intercept of the regression line for $Y$ as predicted by the set of $X_k$'s, $e_i$ are the residuals or errors of prediction (the part of $Y$ not predictable from the $X_k$'s), and $i$ represents an index for an individual or object. The index $i$ can take on values from 1 to $n$ where $n$ is the size of the sample (i.e., $i = 1, ..., n$). The term **partial slope** is used because it represents the slope of $Y$ for a particular $X_k$ in which we have partialled out the influence of the other $X_k$'s, much as we did with the partial correlation.

The sample prediction model is

$$Y'_i = b_1 X_{1i} + b_2 X_{2i} + \ldots + b_m X_{mi} + a$$

where $Y'_i$ is the predicted value of $Y$ for specific values of the $X_k$'s, and the other terms are as before. The difference between the regression and prediction models is the same as in chapter 17. We can compute residuals, the $e_i$, for each of the $i$ individuals or objects by comparing the actual $Y$ values with the predicted $Y$ values as

$$e_i = Y_i - Y'_i$$

for all $i = 1,\ldots, n$ individuals or objects in the sample.

Determining the sample partial slopes and the intercept in the multiple predictor case is rather complicated. To keep it simple, we use a two-predictor model for illustrative purposes. Generally we rely on statistical software for implementing multiple regression. For the two-predictor case the sample partial slopes and the intercept can be determined as

$$b_1 = \frac{(r_{Y1} - r_{Y2}r_{12})s_Y}{\left(1 - r_{12}^2\right)s_1}$$

$$b_2 = \frac{(r_{Y2} - r_{Y1}r_{12})s_Y}{\left(1 - r_{12}^2\right)s_2}$$

$$a = \overline{Y} - b_1 \overline{X}_1 - b_2 \overline{X}_2$$

The sample partial slope $b_1$ is referred to alternately as (a) the expected or predicted change in $Y$ for a one unit change in $X_1$ with $X_2$ held constant (or for individuals with the same score on $X_2$), and (b) the unstandardized or raw regression coefficient. Similar statements may be made for $b_2$. Note the similarity of the partial slope equation to the semipartial correlation. The sample intercept is referred to as the value of $Y$ when $X_1$ and $X_2$ are both zero.

An alternative method for computing the sample partial slopes that involves the use of a partial correlation is as follows:

$$b_1 = r_{Y1.2} \frac{s_Y \sqrt{1 - r_{Y2}^2}}{s_1 \sqrt{1 - r_{12}^2}}$$

$$b_2 = r_{Y2.1} \frac{s_Y \sqrt{1 - r_{Y1}^2}}{s_2 \sqrt{1 - r_{12}^2}}$$

What statistical criterion is used to arrive at the particular values for the partial slopes and intercept? The criterion usually used in multiple linear regression analysis (and in all general linear models [GLM] for that matter) is the least squares criterion. The least squares criterion arrives at those values for the partial slopes and intercept such that the sum of the squared prediction errors or residuals is smallest. That is, we want to find that regression model, defined by a particular set of partial slopes and an intercept, that has the smallest sum of the squared residuals. We often refer to this particular method for calculating the slope and intercept as least squares estimation, because $a$ and the $b_k$'s represent sample estimates of the population parameters $\alpha$ and the $\beta_k$s obtained using the least squares criterion.

Consider now the analysis of a realistic example we will follow in this chapter. We use the GRE—Quantitative + Verbal Total (GRETOT) and undergraduate grade point average (UGPA) to predict graduate grade point average (GGPA). GRETOT has a possible range of 40 to 160 points (if we remove the unnecessary last digit of zero), and GPA is defined as having a possible range of 0.00 to 4.00 points. Given the sample of 11 statistics students as shown in Table 18.1, let us work through a multiple linear regression analysis.

As sample statistics, we compute for GRETOT ($X_1$ or subscript 1) that $\bar{X}_1 = 112.7273$ and $s_1^2 = 266.8182$, for UGPA ($X_2$ or subscript 2) that $\bar{X}_2 = 3.1091$ and $s_2^2 = 0.1609$, and for GGPA ($Y$) that $\bar{Y} = 3.5000$ and $s_Y^2 = 0.1100$. In addition we compute $r_{Y1} = .7845$, $r_{Y2} = .7516$, and $r_{12} = .3011$. The sample partial slopes and intercept are determined as follows:

$$b_1 = \frac{(r_{Y1} - r_{Y2}r_{12})s_Y}{(1 - r_{12}^2)s_1} = \frac{[.7845 - .7516(.3011)].3317}{(1 - .3011^2)16.3346} = .0125$$

$$b_2 = \frac{(r_{Y2} - r_{Y1}r_{12})s_Y}{(1 - r_{12}^2)s_2} = \frac{[.7516 - .7845(.3011)].3317}{(1 - .3011^2).4011} = .4687$$

$$a = \bar{Y} - b_1\bar{X}_1 - b_2\bar{X}_2 = 3.5000 - (.0125)(112.7273) - (.4687)(3.1091) = .63?$$

Let us interpret the partial slope and intercept values. A partial slope of .0125 for GRETOT would mean that if your score on the GRETOT was increased by 1 point, then your graduate grade point average would be increased by .0125 points, controlling for undergraduate grade

**TABLE 18.1**
GRE—GPA Example Data

| Student | GRE-TOT ($X_1$) | UGPA ($X_2$) | GGPA ($Y$) |
|---------|-----------------|--------------|------------|
| 1       | 145             | 3.2          | 4.0        |
| 2       | 120             | 3.7          | 3.9        |
| 3       | 125             | 3.6          | 3.8        |
| 4       | 130             | 2.9          | 3.7        |
| 5       | 110             | 3.5          | 3.6        |
| 6       | 100             | 3.3          | 3.5        |
| 7       | 95              | 3.0          | 3.4        |
| 8       | 115             | 2.7          | 3.3        |
| 9       | 105             | 3.1          | 3.2        |
| 10      | 90              | 2.8          | 3.1        |
| 11      | 105             | 2.4          | 3.0        |

point average. Likewise, a partial slope of .4687 for UGPA would mean that if your undergraduate grade point average was increased by 1 point, then your graduate grade point average would be increased by .4687 points, controlling for GRETOT. An intercept of .6337 would mean that if your scores on the GRETOT and UGPA were both 0, then your graduate grade point average would be .6337. However, it is impossible to obtain a GRETOT score of 0 because you receive 40 points for putting your name on the answer sheet. In a similar way, an undergraduate student could not obtain a UGPA of 0 and be admitted to graduate school.

To put all of this together then, the sample multiple linear regression model is

$$Y_i = b_1 X_{1i} + b_2 X_{2i} + a + e_i = .0125\, X_{1i} + .4687\, X_{2i} + .6337 + e_i$$

If your score on the GRETOT was 130 and your UGPA was 3.5, then your predicted score on the GGPA would be

$$Y_i' = .0125(130) + .4687(3.5000) + .6337 = 3.8992$$

Based on the prediction equation, we predict your GGPA to be around 3.9; however, as we saw in chapter 17, predictions are usually somewhat less than perfect, even with 2 predictors.

## 18.2.2 Standardized Regression Model

Up until this point in the chapter, everything in multiple linear regression has involved the use of raw scores. For this reason we referred to the model as the unstandardized regression model. Often we may want to express the regression in terms of standard $z$ score units rather than in raw score units (as in chap. 17). The means and variances of the standardized variables (e.g., $z_1$, $z_2$, $z_Y$) are 0 and 1, respectively. The sample standardized linear prediction model becomes

$$z(Y_i') = b_1^* z_{1i} + b_2^* z_{2i} + \ldots + b_m^* z_{mi}$$

where $b_k^*$ represents a sample standardized partial slope (sometimes called beta weights) and the other terms are as before. As was the case in simple linear regression, no intercept term is necessary in the standardized prediction model, as the mean of the $z$ scores for all variables is 0. The sample standardized partial slopes are, in general, computed by

$$b_k^* = b_k(s_k/s_Y)$$

For the two predictor case, the standardized partial slopes can be calculated by

$$b_1^* = b_1(s_1/s_Y)$$
$$\text{or} = (r_{Y1} - r_{Y2}r_{12})/(1 - r_{12}^2)$$

and

$$b_2^* = b_2(s_2/s_Y)$$
$$\text{or} = (r_{Y2} - r_{Y1}r_{12})/(1 - r_{12}^2)$$

If $r_{12} = 0$, where the two predictors are uncorrelated, then $b_1^* = r_{Y1}$ and $b_2^* = r_{Y2}$ because the rest of the equation goes away.

For our graduate grade point average example, the standardized partial slopes are equal to

$$b_1^* = b_1(s_1/s_Y) = .0125(16.3346/.3317) = .6156$$
$$b_2^* = b_2(s_2/s_Y) = .4687(.4011/.3317) = .5668$$

The prediction model is then

$$z(Y_i') = .6156\, z_{1i} + .5668\, z_{2i}$$

The standardized partial slope of .6156 for GRETOT would be interpreted as the expected increase in GGPA in $z$ score units for a 1 $z$ score unit increase in the GRETOT, controlling for UGPA. A similar statement may be made for the standardized partial slope of UGPA. The $b_k^*$ can also be interpreted as the expected standard deviation change in $Y$ associated with a 1 standard deviation change in $X_k$ when the other $X_k$'s are held constant.

When would you want to use the standardized versus unstandardized regression analyses? According to Pedhazur (1997), $b_k^*$ is sample specific and is not very stable across different samples due to the variance of $X_k$ changing (as the variance of $X_k$ increases, the value of $b_k^*$ also increases, all else being equal). For example, at Ivy-Covered University, $b_k^*$ would vary across different graduating classes (or samples) while $b_k$ would be much more consistent across classes. Thus most researchers prefer the use of $b_k$ to compare the influence of a particular predictor variable across different samples and/or populations. Pedhazur also states that the $b_k^*$ are of "limited value" (p. 321), but could be reported along with the $b_k$. As Pedhazur and others have reported, the $b_k^*$ can be deceptive in determining the relative importance of the predictors as they are affected by the variances and covariances of both the included predictors and the predictors not included in the model. Thus we recommend the $b_k$ for general purpose use.

### 18.2.3 Coefficient of Multiple Determination and Multiple Correlation

An obvious question now is, How well is the criterion variable predicted by the set of predictor variables? For our example, we are interested in how well the graduate grade point averages are predicted by the GRE total scores and the undergraduate grade point averages. In other words, what is the utility of the set of predictor variables?

The simplest method involves the partitioning of the familiar total sum of squares in $Y$, which we denote as $SS_{total}$. In multiple linear regression, we can write $SS_{total}$ as follows:

$$SS_{total} = [n \Sigma Y_i^2 - (\Sigma Y_i)^2]/n$$
$$\text{or} = (n - 1)\, s_Y^2$$

where we sum over $Y$ from $i = 1, ..., n$. Next we can conceptually partition $SS_{total}$ as

$$SS_{total} = SS_{reg} + SS_{res}$$
$$\Sigma(Y_i - \overline{Y})^2 = \Sigma(Y_i' - \overline{Y})^2 + \Sigma(Y_i - Y_i')^2$$

where $SS_{reg}$ is the regression sum of squares due to the prediction of $Y$ from the $X_k$'s (often written as $SS_{Y'}$), and $SS_{res}$ is the sum of squares due to the residuals.

Before we consider computation of $SS_{reg}$ and $SS_{res}$, let us look at the coefficient of multiple determination. Recall from chapter 17 the coefficient of determination, $r^2_{XY}$. Now consider the multiple predictor version of $r^2_{XY}$, here denoted as $R^2_{Y.1,...,m}$. The subscript tells us that $Y$ is the criterion variable and that $X_{1,...,m}$ are the predictor variables. The simplest procedure for computing $R^2$ is as follows:

$$R^2_{Y.1,...,m} = b^*_1 r_{Y1} + b^*_2 r_{Y2} + ... + b^*_m r_{Ym}$$

The coefficient of multiple determination tells us the proportion of total variation in $Y$ that is predicted from the set of predictor variables. Often we see the coefficient in terms of $SS$ as

$$R^2_{Y.1,...,m} = SS_{reg}/SS_{total}$$

Thus one method for computing $SS_{reg}$ and $SS_{res}$ is from $R^2$ as follows:

$$SS_{reg} = R^2 SS_{total}$$
$$SS_{res} = (1 - R^2)SS_{total} = SS_{total} - SS_{reg}$$

As discussed in chapter 17, there is no objective gold standard as to how large the coefficient of determination needs to be in order to say a meaningful proportion of variation has been predicted. The coefficient is determined, not just by the quality of the predictor variables included in the model, but also by the quality of relevant predictor variables not included in the model and by the amount of total variation in $Y$. However, the coefficient of determination can be used as a measure of effect size. According to the subjective standards of Cohen (1988), a small effect size is defined as $R^2 = .02$, a medium effect size as $R^2 = .13$, and a large effect size as $R^2 = .51$. For additional information on effect size measures in regression, see Steiger and Fouladi (1992), Mendoza and Stafford (2001), and Smithson (2001; which also includes some discussion of power). Note also that $R_{Y.1,...,m}$ is referred to as the multiple correlation coefficient.

With the example of predicting GGPA from GRETOT and UGPA, let us examine the partitioning of the $SS_{total}$, as follows:

$$SS_{total} = (n - 1)s^2_Y = (10).1100 = 1.1000$$

Next we can determine $R^2$ as

$$R^2_{Y.12} = b^*_1 r_{Y1} + b^*_2 r_{Y2} = .6156(.7845) + .5668(.7516) = .9089$$

We can also partition $SS_{total}$ into $SS_{reg}$ and $SS_{res}$, where

$$SS_{reg} = R^2 SS_{total} = .9089(1.1000) = 0.9998$$
$$SS_{res} = (1 - R^2)SS_{total} = (1 - .9089)1.1000 = .1002$$

Finally, let us summarize these results for the example data. We found that the coefficient of multiple determination was equal to .9089. Thus the GRE total score and the undergraduate grade point average predicts around 91% of the variation in the graduate grade point average. This would be quite satisfactory for the college admissions officer in that there is little variation left to be explained, although this result is quite unlikely in actual research in education and the behavioral sciences. Obviously there is a large effect size here.

It should be noted that $R^2$ is sensitive to sample size and to the number of predictor variables. $R$ is a biased estimate of the population multiple correlation due to sampling error in the bivariate correlations and in the standard deviations of $X$ and $Y$. Because $R$ systematically overestimates the population multiple correlation, an adjusted coefficient of multiple determination has been devised. The adjusted $R^2$ ($R^2_{adj}$) is calculated as follows:

$$R^2_{adj} = 1 - (1 - R^2)\left(\frac{n-1}{n-m-1}\right)$$

Thus, $R^2_{adj}$ adjusts for sample size and for the number of predictors in the model; this allows us to compare models fitted to the same set of data with different numbers of predictors or with different samples of data. The difference between $R^2$ and $R^2_{adj}$ is called **shrinkage**.

When $n$ is small relative to $m$, the amount of bias can be large as $R^2$ can be expected to be large by chance alone. In this case the adjustment will be quite large, as it should be. In addition, with small samples, the regression coefficients (i.e., the $b_k$'s) may not be very good estimates of the population values. When $n$ is large relative to $m$, bias will be minimized and generalizations are likely to be better about the population values.

With a large number of predictors, power is reduced, and there is an increased likelihood of a Type I error across the total number of significance tests (i.e., one for each predictor and overall, as we show in the next section). In multiple regression power is a function of sample size, the number of predictors, the level of significance, and the size of the population effect (i.e., for a given predictor, or overall). To determine how large a sample you need relative to the number of predictors, consult power tables (e.g., Cohen, 1988) or power software (e.g., Murphy & Myors, 2004; Power and Precision). Simple advice is to design your research such that the ratio of $n$ to $m$ is large.

For the example data, we determine $R^2_{adj}$ to be

$$R^2_{adj} = 1 - (1 - R^2)\left(\frac{n-1}{n-m-1}\right) = 1 - (1 - .9089)\left(\frac{11-1}{11-2-1}\right) = .8861$$

which in this case indicates a very small adjustment in comparison to $R^2$.

### 18.2.4    Significance Tests

Here we describe two procedures used in multiple linear regression. These involve testing the significance of the overall regression model, and of each individual partial slope (or regression coefficient).

***Test of Significance of the Overall Regression Model.***    The first test is the test of significance of the overall regression model, or alternatively the test of significance of the coefficient of multiple determination. This is a test of all of the $b_k$'s simultaneously. The null and alternative hypotheses, respectively, are as follows:

$$H_0: \beta_1 = \beta_2 = ... = \beta_k = 0$$

$$H_1: \text{not all the } \beta_k = 0$$

If $H_0$ is rejected, then one or more of the individual regression coefficients (i.e., the $b_k$) is statistically significantly different from zero (if assumptions are satisfied, as discussed later). If $H_0$ is not rejected, then none of the individual regression coefficients will be significantly different from zero.

The test is based on the following test statistic:

$$F = \frac{R^2 / m}{(1 - R^2)/(n - m - 1)}$$

where $F$ indicates that this is an $F$ statistic, $m$ is the number of predictors, and $n$ is the sample size. The $F$ test statistic is compared to the $F$ critical value, always a one-tailed test and at the designated level of significance, with degrees of freedom being $m$ and $(n - m - 1)$, as taken from the $F$ table in Appendix Table 4. That is, the tabled critical value is $_\alpha F_{m,(n-m-1)}$. The test statistic can also be written in equivalent form as

$$F = \frac{SS_{reg}/df_{reg}}{SS_{res}/df_{res}} = \frac{MS_{reg}}{MS_{res}}$$

where $df_{reg} = m$ and $df_{res} = (n - m - 1)$.

For the GGPA example, we compute the test statistic as

$$F = \frac{R^2 / m}{(1 - R^2)/(n - m - 1)} = \frac{.9089/2}{(1 - .9089)/(11 - 2 - 1)} = 39.9078$$

or as

$$F = \frac{SS_{reg} / df_{reg}}{SS_{res} / df_{res}} = \frac{0.9998/2}{.1002/8} = 39.9122$$

The critical value, at the .05 level of significance, is $_{.05}F_{2,8} = 4.46$. The test statistic exceeds the critical value, so we reject $H_0$ and conclude that all of the partial slopes are not equal to zero at the .05 level of significance (the two $F$ test statistics differ slightly due to rounding error).

***Test of Significance of $b_k$.***    The second test is the test of the statistical significance of each individual partial slope or regression coefficient, $b_k$. That is, are the individual unstandardized regression coefficients statistically significantly different from zero? This is actually the same as the test of $b_k^*$, so we need not develop a separate test for $b_k^*$. The null and alternative hypotheses, respectively, are as follows:

$$H_0: \beta_k = 0$$

$$H_1: \beta_k \neq 0$$

where $\beta_k$ is the population partial slope for $X_k$.

In multiple regression it is necessary to compute a standard error for each $b_k$. Recall from chapter 17 the variance error of estimate concept. The variance error of estimate is similarly defined for multiple linear regression as

$$s_{res}^2 = SS_{res}/df_{res} = MS_{res}$$

where $df_{res} = (n - m - 1)$. Degrees of freedom are lost as we have to estimate the population partial slopes and intercept, the $\beta_k$'s and $\alpha$, respectively, from the sample data. The variance error of estimate indicates the amount of variation among the residuals. The standard error of estimate is simply the positive square root of the variance error of estimate, and is the standard deviation of the residuals or errors of estimate. We call it the **standard error of estimate**, denoted as $s_{res}$.

Finally, we need to compute a standard error for each $b_k$. Denote the standard error of $b_k$ as $s(b_k)$ and define it as

$$s(b_k) = \frac{s_{res}}{\sqrt{(n-1) s_k^2 (1 - R_k^2)}}$$

where $s_k^2$ is the sample variance for predictor $X_k$, and $R_k^2$ is the squared multiple correlation between $X_k$ and the remaining $X_k$'s. The $R_k^2$ represent the overlap between that predictor ($X_k$) and the remaining predictors. In the case of two predictors, $R_k^2$ is equal to $r_{12}^2$.

The test statistic for testing the significance of the $b_k$'s is as follows:

$$t = \frac{b_k}{s(b_k)}$$

The test statistic $t$ is compared to the critical values of $t$, a two-tailed test for a nondirectional $H_1$, at the designated level of significance, and with degrees of freedom $(n - m - 1)$, as taken from the $t$ table in Appendix Table 2. Thus the tabled critical values are $\pm_{(\alpha/2)} t_{(n-m-1)}$ for a two-tailed test.

We can also form a confidence interval around $b_k$ as follows:

$$\text{CI}\ (b_k) = b_k \pm {}_{(\alpha/2)} t_{(n-m-1)}\ s(b_k)$$

Recall that the null hypothesis tested is $H_0$: $\beta_k = 0$. Therefore, if the confidence interval contains zero, then $b_k$ is not significantly different from zero at the specified $\alpha$ level. This is interpreted to mean that in $(1 - \alpha)\%$ of the sample confidence intervals that would be formed from multiple samples, $\beta_k$ will be included.

Let us compute the second test statistic for the GGPA example. We specify the null hypothesis to be $\beta_k = 0$ and conduct two-tailed tests. First the variance error of estimate is

$$s_{res}^2 = SS_{res}/df_{res} = MS_{res} = .1002/8 = .0125$$

The standard error of estimate, $s_{res}$, is .1118. Next the standard errors of the $b_k$ are found to be

$$s(b_1) = \frac{s_{res}}{\sqrt{(n-1) s_1^2 \left(1 - r_{12}^2\right)}} = \frac{.1118}{\sqrt{(10)\ 266.8182\ (1 - .3011^2)}} = .0023$$

$$s(b_2) = \frac{s_{res}}{\sqrt{(n-1)\,s_2^2\,\left(1 - r_{12}^2\right)}} = \frac{.1118}{\sqrt{(10)\,0.1609\,(1 - .3011^2)}} = .0924$$

Finally we find the $t$ test statistics to be

$$t_1 = b_1/s(b_1) = .0125/.0023 = 5.4348$$

$$t_2 = b_2/s(b_2) = .4687/.0924 = 5.0725$$

To evaluate the null hypotheses, we compare these test statistics to the critical values of $\pm\,_{.025}t_8 = \pm2.306$. Both test statistics exceed the critical value; consequently $H_0$ is rejected in favor of $H_1$ for both predictors. We conclude that the partial slopes are indeed significantly different from zero, at the .05 level of significance.

Finally, let us compute the confidence intervals for the $b_k$'s as follows:

$$\text{CI}\,(b_1) = b_1 \pm\,_{(\alpha/2)}t_{(n-m-1)}\,s(b_1) = b_1 \pm\,_{.025}t_8\,s(b_1) = .0125 \pm 2.306(.0023) = (.0072, .0178)$$

$$\text{CI}\,(b_2) = b_2 \pm\,_{(\alpha/2)}t_{(n-m-1)}\,s(b_2) = b_2 \pm\,_{.025}t_8\,s(b_2) = .4687 \pm 2.306(.0924) = (.2556, .6818)$$

The intervals do not contain zero, the value specified in $H_0$; thus we again conclude that both $b_k$'s are significantly different from zero, at the .05 level of significance.

*Other Tests.* One can also form confidence intervals for the predicted mean of $Y$ and the prediction intervals for individual values of $Y$, as we described in chapter 17.

## 18.2.5 Assumptions

A considerable amount of space in chapter 17 was dedicated to the assumptions of simple linear regression. For the most part, the assumptions of multiple linear regression are the same, and thus we need not devote as much space here. The assumptions are concerned with independence, homogeneity, normality, linearity, fixed $X$, and noncollinearity. This section also mentions those techniques appropriate for evaluating each assumption.

*Independence.* The first assumption is concerned with **independence** of the observations. The simplest procedure for assessing independence is to examine residual plots of $e$ versus $Y'$ and of $e$ versus each $X_k$ (alternatively, one can look at plots of $Y$ versus $Y'$ and of $Y$ versus each $X_k$). If the independence assumption is satisfied, the residuals should fall into a random display of points. If the assumption is violated, the residuals will fall into some sort of pattern. Lack of independence affects the estimated standard errors of the model. For serious violations one could consider generalized or weighted least squares as the method of estimation (e.g., Weisberg, 1985; Myers, 1986), or some type of transformation. The residual plots shown in Fig. 18.1 do not suggest any independence problems for the GGPA example, where Fig. 18.1(a) represents $e$ versus $Y'$, Fig. 18.1(b) represents $e$ versus GRETOT, and Fig. 18.1(c) represents $e$ versus UGPA.

*Homogeneity.* The second assumption is **homogeneity of variance**, where the conditional distributions have the same constant variance for all values of $X$. In the residual plots the consistency of the variance of the conditional distributions may be examined. If the homogeneity

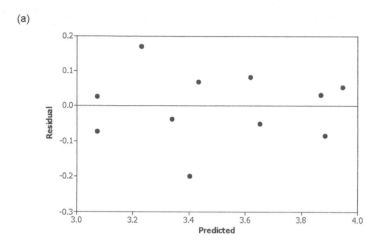

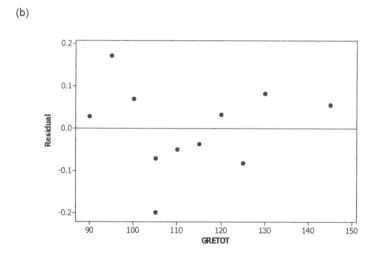

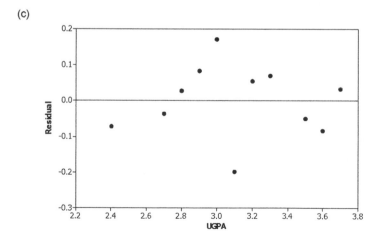

FIG. 18.1    Residual plots for GRE—GPA example: (a), (b), (c).

assumption is violated, estimates of the standard errors are larger, and the conditional distributions may also be nonnormal. As described in chapter 17, solutions include variance stabilizing transformations (such as the square root or log of $Y$), generalized or weighted least squares (e.g., Myers, 1986; Weisberg, 1985), or robust regression (Kleinbaum, Kupper, Muller, & Nizam, 1998; Myers, 1986; Wilcox, 1996, 2003; Wu, 1985). Due to the small sample size, homogeneity cannot really be assessed for the example data.

*Normality.* The third assumption is that the conditional distributions of the scores on $Y$, or the prediction errors, are **normal** in shape. Violation of the normality assumption may be the result of outliers. The simplest outlier detection procedure is to look for observations that are more than two standard errors from the mean. Other procedures were described in chapter 17. Several methods for dealing with outliers are available, such as conducting regression analyses with and without suspected outliers, robust regression (Kleinbaum, Kupper, Muller, & Nizam, 1998; Myers, 1986; Wilcox, 1996, 2003; Wu, 1985), and nonparametric regression (Miller, 1997; Rousseeuw & Leroy, 1987; Wu, 1985). The following can be used to detect normality violations: frequency distributions, normal probability plots, and skewness statistics. For the example data, the normal probability plot is shown in Fig. 18.2, and even with a small sample looks good. Violation can lead to imprecision in the partial slopes and the coefficient of determination. There are also several statistical procedures available for the detection of nonnormality (e.g., Andrews, 1971; Belsley, Kuh, & Welsch, 1980; D'Agostino, 1971; Ruppert & Carroll, 1980; Shapiro & Wilk, 1965; Wu, 1985); transformations can also be used to normalize the data. Review chapter 17 for more details.

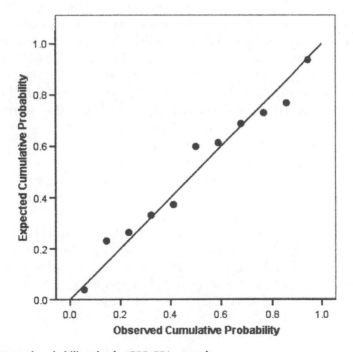

FIG. 18.2    Normal probability plot for GRE-GPA example.

*Linearity.*    The fourth assumption is **linearity**, that there is a linear relationship between $Y$ and the $X_k$'s. If satisfied, then the sample partial slopes and intercept are unbiased estimators of the population partial slopes and intercept, respectively. The linearity assumption is important because regardless of the value of $X_k$, we always expect $Y$ to increase by $b_k$ units for a one unit increase in $X_k$, controlling for the other $X_k$'s. If a nonlinear relationship exists, this means that the expected increase in $Y$ depends on the value of $X_k$; that is, the expected increase is not a constant value. Strictly speaking, linearity in a model refers to there being linearity in the parameters of the model (i.e., $\alpha$ and the $\beta_k$'s).

Violation of the linearity assumption can be detected through residual plots. The residuals should be located within a band of $\pm 2\ s_{res}$ (or standard errors), indicating no systematic pattern of points, as previously discussed in chapter 17. Residual plots for the GGPA example are shown in Figure 18.1. Even with a very small sample, we see a fairly random pattern of residuals, and therefore feel fairly confident that the linearity assumption has been satisfied. Note also that there are other types of residual plots developed especially for multiple regression, such as the added variable and partial residual plots (Larsen & McCleary, 1972; Mansfield & Conerly, 1987; Weisberg, 1985). Procedures to deal with nonlinearity include transformations (of one or more of the $X_k$'s and/or of $Y$ as described in chapter 17) and other regression models (discussed later in this chapter).

*Fixed X.*    The fifth assumption is that the values of $X_k$ are **fixed**, where the $X_k$ are fixed variables rather than random variables. This results in the regression model being valid only for those particular values of $X_k$ that were actually observed and used in the analysis. Thus, the same values of $X_k$ would be used in replications or repeated samples.

Strictly speaking, the regression model and its parameter estimates are only valid for those values of $X_k$ actually sampled. The use of a prediction model developed to predict $Y$, based on one sample of individuals, may be suspect for another sample of individuals. Depending on the circumstances, the new sample of individuals may actually call for a different set of parameter estimates. Expanding on our discussion in chapter 17, generally we may not want to make predictions about individuals having combinations of $X_k$ scores outside of the range of values used in developing the prediction model; this is defined as extrapolating beyond the sample predictor data. On the other hand, we may not be quite as concerned in making predictions about individuals having combinations of $X_k$ scores within the range of values used in developing the prediction model; this is defined as interpolating within the range of the sample predictor data.

It has been shown that when other assumptions are met, regression analysis performs just as well when $X$ is a random variable (e.g., Glass & Hopkins, 1996; Myers & Well, 1995; Pedhazur, 1997; Wonnacott & Wonnacott, 1981). There is no such assumption about $Y$.

*Noncollinearity.*    The final assumption is unique to multiple linear regression, being unnecessary in simple linear regression. A violation of this assumption is known as collinearity where there is a very strong linear relationship between two or more of the predictors. The presence of severe collinearity is problematic in several respects. First, it will lead to instability of the regression coefficients across samples, where the estimates will bounce around quite a bit in terms of magnitude and even occasionally result in changes in sign (perhaps opposite of expectation). This occurs because the standard errors of the regression coefficients become larger, thus making it more difficult to achieve statistical significance. Another result that may occur involves an overall regression that is significant, but none of the individual predictors are significant. Collinearity will also restrict the utility and generalizability of the estimated regression model.

Recall from earlier in the chapter the notion of partial regression coefficients, where the other predictors were held constant. In the presence of severe collinearity the other predictors cannot really be held constant because they are so highly intercorrelated. Collinearity may be indicated when there are large changes in estimated coefficients due to (a) a variable being added or deleted and/or (b) an observation being added or deleted (Chatterjee & Price, 1977). Collinearity is also likely when a composite variable as well as its component variables are used as predictors (e.g., including GRETOT, GRE-Quantitative, and GRE-Verbal as predictors).

How do we detect violations of this assumption? The simplest procedure is to conduct a series of special regression analyses, one for each $X$, where that predictor is predicted by all of the remaining $X$'s (i.e., the criterion variable is not involved). If any of the resultant $R_k^2$ values are close to one (greater than .9 is a good rule of thumb), then there may be a collinearity problem. However, the large $R^2$ value may also be due to small sample size; thus more data would be useful. For the example data, $R_{12}^2 = .0907$ and therefore collinearity is not a concern.

Also, if the number of predictors is greater than or equal to $n$, then perfect collinearity is a possibility. Another statistical method for detecting collinearity is to compute a variance inflation factor (VIF) for each predictor, which is equal to $1/(1 - R_k^2)$. The VIF is defined as the inflation that occurs for each regression coefficient above the ideal situation of uncorrelated predictors. Many suggest that the largest VIF should be less than 10 in order to satisfy this assumption (Myers, 1990; Stevens, 2002; Wetherill, 1986).

There are several possible methods for dealing with a collinearity problem. First, one can remove one or more of the correlated predictors. Second, ridge regression techniques can be used (e.g., Hoerl & Kennard, 1970a, 1970b; Marquardt & Snee, 1975; Myers, 1986; Wetherill, 1986). Third, principal component scores resulting from principal component analysis can be utilized rather than raw scores on each variable (e.g., Kleinbaum et al., 1998; Myers, 1986; Weisberg, 1985; Wetherill, 1986). Fourth, transformations of the variables can be used to remove or reduce the extent of the problem. The final solution, and probably my last choice, is to use simple linear regression, as collinearity cannot exist with a single predictor.

*Summary.* For the GGPA example, although sample size is quite small in terms of looking at conditional distributions, it would appear that all of our assumptions have been satisfied. All of the residuals are within two standard errors of zero, and there does not seem to be any systematic pattern in the residuals. The distribution of the residuals is nearly symmetric and the normal probability plot looks good. A summary of the assumptions and the effects of their violation for multiple linear regression is presented in Table 18.2.

## 18.3 OTHER REGRESSION MODELS

The multiple predictor model we have considered thus far can be viewed as **simultaneous regression**. That is, all of the predictors to be used are entered (or selected) simultaneously, such that all of the regression parameters are estimated simultaneously; here the set of predictors has been selected a priori. There is also another class of models where the predictor variables are entered (or selected) systematically; here the set of predictors has not been selected a priori. This class of models is referred to as **sequential regression** (also known as **variable selection pro-**

**TABLE 18.2**
Assumptions and Violation of Assumptions—Multiple Linear Regression

| Assumption | Effect of Assumption Violation |
| --- | --- |
| 1. Independence | Influences standard errors of the model |
| 2. Homogeneity | Bias in $s_{res}^2$; may inflate standard errors and thus increase likelihood of a Type II error; may result in nonnormal conditional distributions |
| 3. Normality | Less precise slopes and $R^2$ |
| 4. Linearity | Bias in slopes and intercept; expected change in $Y$ is not a constant and depends on value of $X$ variables |
| 5. Values of $X$'s are fixed | (a) Extrapolating beyond the range of $X$ combinations: prediction errors larger, may also bias slopes and intercept |
| | (b) Interpolating within the range of $X$ combinations: smaller effects than in (a); if other assumptions met, negligible effect |
| 6. Noncollinearity of $X$'s | Regression coefficients can be quite unstable across samples (as standard errors are larger); $R^2$ may be significant, yet none of the predictors are significant; restricted generalizability of the model |

**cedures**). This section introduces a brief description of the following sequential regression procedures: backward elimination, forward selection, stepwise selection, all possible subsets regression, and hierarchical regression. We also include introductions to dealing with nonlinear relationships and logistic regression in this section.

*Backward Elimination.* First consider the backward elimination procedure. Here variables are eliminated from the model based on their minimal contribution to the prediction of the criterion variable. In the first stage of the analysis, all potential predictors are included in the model. In the second stage, that predictor is deleted from the model that makes the smallest contribution to the prediction of the dependent variable. This can be done by eliminating that variable having the smallest $t$ or $F$ statistic such that it is making the smallest contribution to $R_{adj}^2$. In subsequent stages, that predictor is deleted that makes the next smallest contribution to the prediction of $Y$. The analysis continues until each of the remaining predictors in the model is a significant predictor of $Y$. This could be determined by comparing the $t$ or $F$ statistics for each predictor to the critical value, at a preselected level of significance. Some computer programs use as a stopping rule the maximum $F$-to-remove criterion, where the procedure is stopped when all of the selected predictors' $F$ values are greater than the specified $F$ criterion. Another stopping rule is where the researcher stops at a predetermined number of predictors (see Hocking, 1976; Thompson, 1978).

*Forward Selection.* In the forward selection procedure variables are added or selected into the model based on their maximal contribution to the prediction of the criterion variable. Initially, none of the potential predictors are included in the model. In the first stage, the predictor is added to the model that makes the largest contribution to the prediction of the dependent variable. This can be done by selecting that variable having the largest $t$ or $F$ statistic such that it is making the largest contribution to $R^2_{adj}$. In subsequent stages, the predictor is selected that makes the next largest contribution to the prediction of $Y$. The analysis continues until each of the selected predictors in the model is a significant predictor of $Y$, whereas none of the unselected predictors is a significant predictor. This could be determined by comparing the $t$ or $F$ statistics for each predictor to the critical value, at a preselected level of significance. Some computer programs use as a stopping rule the minimum $F$-to-enter criterion, where the procedure is stopped when all of the unselected predictors' $F$ values are less than the specified $F$ criterion. For the same set of data and at the same level of significance, the backward elimination and forward selection procedures may not necessarily result in the exact same final model, due to the differences in how variables are selected.

***Stepwise Selection.*** The stepwise selection procedure is a modification of the forward selection procedure with one important difference. Predictors that have been selected into the model can at a later step be deleted from the model; thus the modification conceptually involves a backward elimination mechanism. This situation can occur for a predictor when a significant contribution at an earlier step later becomes a nonsignificant contribution given the set of other predictors in the model. Thus a predictor loses its significance due to new predictors being added to the model.

The stepwise selection procedure is as follows. Initially, none of the potential predictors are included in the model. In the first step, that predictor is added to the model that makes the largest contribution to the explanation of the dependent variable. This can be done by selecting that variable having the largest $t$ or $F$ statistic such that it is making the largest contribution to $R^2_{adj}$. In subsequent stages, the predictor is selected that makes the next largest contribution to the prediction of $Y$. Those predictors that have entered at earlier stages are also checked to see if their contribution remains significant. If not, then that predictor is eliminated from the model. The analysis continues until each of the predictors remaining in the model is a significant predictor of $Y$, while none of the other predictors is a significant predictor. This could be determined by comparing the $t$ or $F$ statistics for each predictor to the critical value, at a specified level of significance. Some computer programs use as stopping rules the minimum $F$-to-enter and maximum $F$-to-remove criteria, where the $F$-to-enter value selected is usually equal to or slightly greater than the $F$-to-remove value selected (to prevent a predictor from continuously being entered and removed). For the same set of data and at the same level of significance, the backward elimination, forward selection, and stepwise selection procedures may not necessarily result in the exact same final model, due to differences in how variables are selected.

***All Possible Subsets Regression.*** Another sequential regression procedure is known as all possible subsets regression. Let us say, for example, that there are five potential predictors. In this procedure, all possible one-, two-, three-, and four-variable models are analyzed (with five predictors there is only a single five-predictor model). Thus there will be 5 one-predictor models, 10 two-predictor models, 10 three-predictor models, and 5 four-predictor models. The best $k$ predictor model can be selected as the model that yields the largest $R^2_{adj}$. For example, the best three-predictor model would be that model of the 10 estimated that yields the largest $R^2_{adj}$. With today's powerful computers, this procedure is easier and more cost efficient than in the past. However, the researcher is not advised to consider this procedure, or for that matter any of the other sequential regression procedures, when the number of potential predictors is large. Here the researcher is allowing number crunching to take precedence over thoughtful analysis. Also, the number of models will be equal to $2^m$, so that for 10 predictors there are 1,024 possible subsets. Obviously examining that number of models is not a thoughtful analysis.

*Hierarchical Regression.*    In hierarchical regression, the researcher specifies a priori a sequence for the individual predictor variables (not to be confused with hierarchical linear models, which is a method for analyzing data collected at multiple levels, such as child, classroom, and school). The analysis proceeds in a forward selection, backward elimination, or stepwise selection mode according to a researcher specified, theoretically-based sequence rather than an unspecified statistically-based sequence. This variable selection method is different from those previously discussed in that the researcher determines the order of entry from a careful consideration of the available research instead of the software dictating the sequence.

A type of hierarchical regression is known as **setwise regression** (also called **blockwise**, **chunkwise**, or **forced stepwise regression**). Here the researcher specifies a priori a sequence for sets of predictor variables. This procedure is similar to hierarchical regression in that the researcher determines the order of entry of the predictors. The difference is that the setwise method uses sets of predictor variables at each stage rather than one individual predictor variable at a time. The sets of variables are determined by the researcher so that variables within a set share some common theoretical ground (e.g., home background variables in one set and aptitude variables in another set). Variables within a set are selected according to one of the sequential regression procedures. The variables selected for a particular set are then entered in the specified theoretically-based sequence.

*Commentary on Sequential Regression Procedures.*    Let me make some comments and recommendations about the sequential regression procedures. First, numerous statisticians have noted problems with stepwise methods (i.e., backward elimination, forward selection, and stepwise selection) (e.g., Derksen & Keselman, 1992; Huberty, 1989; Mickey, Dunn, & Clark, 2004; Miller, 1984, 1990; Wilcox, 2003). These problems include the following: (a) selecting noise rather than important predictors; (b) highly inflated $R^2$ and $R^2_{adj}$ values; (c) confidence intervals for partial slopes that are too narrow; (d) $p$ values that are not trustworthy; (e) important predictors being barely edged out of the model, making it possible to miss the true model; and (f) potentially heavy capitalization on chance given the number of models analyzed. Second, theoretically-based regression models have become the norm in many disciples. Thus hierarchical regression either has or will dominate the landscape of the sequential regression procedures. Thus I strongly encourage you to consider more extended discussions of hierarchical regression (e.g., Bernstein, 1988; Cohen & Cohen, 1983; Pedhazur, 1997; Schafer, 1991; Tabachnick & Fidell, 2001).

If you are dealing in an area of inquiry where research evidence is sparce or non-existant, then you are conducting exploratory research. Thus you are probably trying to simply identify the key variables. Here hierarchical regression is not appropriate, as a theoretically-driven sequence cannot be developed. Here we recommend the use of all possible subsets regression (e.g., Kleinbaum, Kupper, Muller, & Nizam, 1998). For additional information on the sequential regression procedures, see Cohen and Cohen (1983), Weisberg (1985), Miller (1990), Pedhazur (1997), and Kleinbaum, et al. (1998).

*Nonlinear Relationships.*    Here we continue our discussion on how to deal with nonlinearity from chapter 17. We formally introduce several multiple regression models for when the criterion variable does not have a linear relationship with the predictor variables.

First consider polynomial regression models. In polynomial models, powers of the predictor variables are used. In general, a sample polynomial regression model is as follows:

$$Y = b_1 X + b_2 X^2 + \ldots + b_m X^m + a + e$$

where the independent variable $X$ is taken from the first power through the $m^{\text{th}}$ power, and the $i$ subscript for observations has been deleted to simplify matters. If the model consists only of $X$ taken to the first power, then this is a **simple linear regression model** (or **first-degree polynomial**; this is a straight line). A **second-degree polynomial** includes $X$ taken to the second power (or **quadratic model**; this is a curve with one bend in it rather than a straight line). A **third-degree polynomial** includes $X$ taken to the third power (or **cubic model**; this is a curve with two bends in it).

A polynomial model with multiple predictors can also be utilized. An example of a second-degree polynomial model with two predictors would be

$$Y = b_1 X_1 + b_2 X_1^2 + b_3 X_2 + b_4 X_2^2 + a + e$$

For more information on polynomial regression models, see Weisberg (1985), Bates and Watts (1988), Seber and Wild (1989), Pedhazur (1997), and Kleinbaum, et al. (1998). Alternatively, one might transform the criterion variable and/or the predictor variables to obtain a more linear form, as previously discussed.

A final type of model involves the use of an interaction term, as previously discussed in factorial ANOVA (chap. 13). These can be implemented in any type of regression model. We can write a simple two-predictor interaction-type model as

$$Y = b_1 X_1 + b_2 X_2 + b_3 X_1 X_2 + a + e$$

where $X_1 X_2$ represents the interaction of predictor variables 1 and 2. An interaction can be defined as occurring when the relationship between $Y$ and $X_1$ depends on the level of $X_2$. In other words, $X_2$ is a **moderator variable**. For example, suppose one were to use years of education and age to predict political attitude. The relationship between education and attitude might be moderated by age. In other words, the relationship between education and attitude may be different for older versus younger individuals. If age were a moderator, we would expect there to be an interaction between age and education in a regression model. Note that if the predictors are very highly correlated, collinearity is likely. For more information on interaction models, see Cohen and Cohen (1983), Berry and Feldman (1985), Kleinbaum, et al. (1998), Weinberg and Abramowitz (2002), and Meyers, Gamst, and Guarino (2006).

*Logistic Regression.*    There is one final regression model to introduce. If the dependent variable is dichotomous, then none of the regression methods described in this text are appropriate. This is where the method of logistic regression becomes important. Initially used mostly in the hard sciences, this method has become more broadly popular in recent years. Some examples of dichotomous dependent variables are pass/fail, surviving surgery/not, admit/reject, vote for/against, employ/not, or purchase/not. The first condition is indicated by a value of 1 (e.g., pass), whereas a value of 0 indicates the opposite condition (e.g., fail). An important statistic in logistic regression is the odds ratio ($OR$), which is analogous to $R^2$. Conceptually this is the odds for one level (e.g., pass) divided by the odds for the other level (e.g., fail). The null hypothesis to be tested is that $OR = 1$, which indicates that there no relationship between a predictor variable and the dependent variable. Thus we want to find $OR$ to be significantly different from 1. One can also determine $OR_{adj}$ (adjusted $OR$) and confidence intervals for $OR$. Logistic regression utilizes maximum likelihood rather than least squares estimation, and the linear, normality, and homogeneity assumptions are not required. For more information on logistic regression, consider Wright (1995), Glass and Hopkins (1996), Christiansen (1997), Pedhazur (1997), Kleinbaum, et al. (1998), Hosmer and Lemeshow (2000), Pampel (2000), Huck (2004), and Meyers, Gamst, and Guarino (2006).

## 18.4  SPSS

In this section we consider the use of SPSS for the multiple linear regression model, including an APA paragraph of selected results. To conduct a multiple linear regression analysis, go from the "Analyze" pulldown, into "Regression," and then into the "Linear" procedure. Click your dependent variable "GGPA" into the "Dependent:" box and the independent variables "GRE-TOT" and "UGPA" into the "Independent(s):" box. Second, click on the "Statistics" button, where various types of statistics can be requested. At a minimum I suggest the following: estimates, confidence intervals, model fit, and descriptives. Note that part and partial correlations and collinearity diagnostics are also available there. If you click on the "Plots" button, you can generate residual plots and the normal probability plot. Finally, click on the "Save" button if you want to save various results into your dataset (e.g., different types of residuals or values from the confidence intervals). Selected results for the GRE-GPA example are shown in Table 18.3.

Lastly, here is an example paragraph of the results for the GRE-GPA example. From the top panel of Table 18.3, we see that $R^2 = .908$, indicating that 91% of the variation in GGPA was predicted by the set of GRETOT and UGPA. In the middle panel of Table 18.3, the ANOVA summary table indicates that a significant proportion of the total variation in GGPA scores was predicted by GRETOT and UGPA together ($F = 39.291$, $df = 2,8$, $p < .001$). In the bottom panel of Table 18.3 we see the following results: (a) the unstandardized partial slopes are both significantly different from zero (GRETOT: $b = .012$, $t = 5.447$, $df = 8$, $p = .001$; for UGPA: $b = .469$, $t = 5.030$, $df = 8$, $p = .001$); (b) the confidence intervals around the unstandardized partial slopes do not include zero, (c) the intercept was .638, and (d) VIF = 1.100 indicating no collinearity problems. Thus GRETOT and UGPA were shown to be statisticial significant predictors of GGPA, both individually and collectively.

Lastly we note that the more advanced regression models described in the previous section can all be conducted using SPSS. For further information on regression analysis with SPSS, see Morgan and Griego (1998), Weinberg and Abramowitz (2002), and Meyers, Gamst, and Guarino (2006),

## 18.5  WHAT'S NEXT?

As we conclude this text, the natural question to ask is what's next to examine in the field of statistics. There are two likely key alternatives. First, you could consider more advanced regression

**TABLE 18.3**
Selected SPSS Results for the GRE-GPA Example

*Model Summary*[b]

| Model | R | R Square | Adjusted R Square | Std. Error of the Estimate |
|-------|-----|----------|-------------------|----------------------------|
| 1 | .953[a] | .908 | .885 | .11272 |

a. Predictors: (Constant), UGPA, GRETOT

b. Dependent Variable: GGPA

*ANOVA*[b]

| Model | Sum of Squares | df | Mean Square | F | Sig. |
|-------|----------------|-----|-------------|--------|-------|
| 1 Regression | .998 | 2 | .499 | 39.291 | .000[a] |
| Residual | .102 | 8 | .013 | | |
| Total | 1.100 | 10 | | | |

a. Predictors: (Constant), UGPA, GRETOT

b. Dependent Variable: GGPA

*Coefficients*

| | Unstandardized Coefficients | | Standardized Coefficients | | | 95% Confidence Interval for B | | Collinearity Statistics |
|-------|-------|---------------|------|------|------|----------------|----------------|------|
| Model | B | Std. Error | Beta | t | Sig. | Lower Bound | Upper Bound | VIF |
| 1 (Constant) | .638 | .327 | | 1.954 | .087 | −.115 | 1.391 | |
| GRETOT | .012 | .002 | .614 | 5.447 | .001 | .007 | .018 | 1.100 |
| UGPA | .469 | .093 | .567 | 5.030 | .001 | .254 | .684 | 1.100 |

a. Dependent Variable: GGPA

models, along the lines of those introduced toward the end of this chapter. These would also be covered in a regression course. In terms of regression readings, you might consider looking at Cohen and Cohen (1983), Grimm and Arnold (1995), Pedhazur (1997), Kleinbaum, et al. (1998), and Meyers, Gamst, and Guarino (2006).

Alternatively you could consider multivariate analysis methods, either in terms of readings or in a multivariate course. Briefly, the major methods of multivariate analysis include multivariate analysis of variance (MANOVA), discriminant analysis, factor and principal components analysis, canonical correlation analysis, cluster analysis, multidimensional scaling, multivariate regression, and structural equation modeling. For multivariate readings, take a look at Grimm and Arnold (1995, 2000), Marcoulides and Hershberger (1997), Johnson and Wichern (1998),

Kleinbaum, et al. (1998), Stevens (2002), Timm (2002), Manly (2004), and Meyers, Gamst, and Guarino (2006).

## 18.6   SUMMARY

In this chapter, methods involving multiple predictors in the regression context were considered. The chapter began with a look at partial and semipartial correlations. Next, a lengthy discussion of multiple linear regression was conducted. Here we extended many of the basic concepts of simple linear regression to the multiple predictor situation. In addition, several new concepts were introduced, including the coefficient of multiple determination, multiple correlation, and tests of the individual regression coefficients. Finally we examined a number of other regression models, such as forward selection, backward elimination, stepwise selection, all possible subsets regression, hierarchical regression, nonlinear relationship, and logistic regression. At this point you should have met the following objectives: (a) be able to determine and interpret the results of part and semipartial correlations, (b) be able to understand the concepts underlying multiple linear regression, (c) be able to determine and interpret the results of multiple linear regression, (d) be able to understand and evaluate the assumptions of multiple linear regression, and (e) be able to have a basic understanding of other types of regression models. This concludes our statistical concepts text. We wish you the best of luck in your future statistical adventures.

## PROBLEMS

### Conceptual Problems

1.  Variable 1 is to be predicted from a combination of variable 2 and one of variables 3, 4, 5, or 6. The correlations of importance are as follows:

    $r_{13} = .8$      $r_{23} = .2$
    $r_{14} = .6$      $r_{24} = .5$
    $r_{15} = .6$      $r_{25} = .2$
    $r_{16} = .8$      $r_{26} = .5$

    Which of the following multiple correlation coefficients will have the largest value?

    a.  $r_{1.23}$

    b.  $r_{1.24}$

    c.  $r_{1.25}$

    d.  $r_{1.26}$

2.  The most accurate predictions are made when the standard error of estimate equals

    a.  $\overline{Y}$

    b.  $s_Y$

    c.  0

    d.  1

3.  The intercept can take on a positive value only. True or false?

4.  Adding an additional predictor to a regression equation will necessarily result in an increase in $R^2$. True or false?

5.  The best prediction in multiple regression will result when each predictor has a high correlation with the other predictor variables and a high correlation with the dependent variable. True or false?

6.  Consider the following two situations:

    Situation 1     $r_{Y1} = .6$      $r_{Y2} = .5$      $r_{12} = .0$
    Situation 2     $r_{Y1} = .6$      $r_{Y2} = .5$      $r_{12} = .2$

    I assert that the value of $R^2$ will be greater in Situation 2. Am I correct?

7.  Values of variables $X_1, X_2, X_3$ are available for a sample of 50 students. The value of $r_{12} = .6$. I assert that if the partial correlation $r_{12.3}$ were calculated it would be larger than .6. Am I correct?

8.  I assert that the forward selection, backward elimination, and stepwise regression methods will always arrive at the same final model, given the same dataset and level of significance? Am I correct?

9.  I assert the $R^2_{adj}$ will always be larger for the most predictors in the model. Am I correct?

10. In a two-predictor regression model, if the correlation among the predictors is .95 and VIF is 20, then we should be concerned about collinearity. True or false?

## Computational Problems

1.  You are given the following data, where $X_1$ (hours of professional development) and $X_2$ (aptitude test scores) are used to predict $Y$ (annual salary in thousands):

    | $Y$ | $X_1$ | $X_2$ |
    |-----|-------|-------|
    | 40  | 100   | 10    |
    | 50  | 200   | 20    |
    | 50  | 300   | 10    |
    | 70  | 400   | 30    |
    | 65  | 500   | 20    |
    | 65  | 600   | 20    |
    | 80  | 700   | 30    |

    Determine the following values: intercept; $b_1$; $b_2$; $SS_{res}$; $SS_{reg}$; $F$; $s^2_{res}$; $s(b_1)$; $s(b_2)$; $t_1$; $t_2$.

2. Complete the missing information for this regression model ($df = 23$).

$$Y' = 25.1 + 1.2\,X_1 + 1.0\,X_2 - .50\,X_3$$

|  | (2.1) | (1.5) | (1.3) | (.06) | standard errors |
|---|---|---|---|---|---|
|  | (11.9) | ( ) | ( ) | ( ) | $t$ ratios |
|  |  | ( ) | ( ) | ( ) | significant at .05? |

3. Consider a sample of elementary school children. Given that $r$(strength, weight) = .6, $r$(strength, age) = .7, and $r$(weight, age) = .8, what is the first-order partial correlation coefficient between strength and weight holding age constant?

4. For a sample of 100 adults, you are given that $r_{12} = .55$, $r_{13} = .80$, $r_{23} = .70$. What is the value of $r_{1(2.3)}$?

5. A researcher would like to predict salary from a set of four predictor variables for a sample of 45 subjects. Multiple linear regression was used to analyze these data. Complete the following summary table ($\alpha = .05$) for the test of significance of the overall regression model:

| Source | SS | df | MS | F | Critical Value and Decision |
|---|---|---|---|---|---|
| Regression | — | — | 20 | — | — |
| Residual | 400 | — | — |  |  |
| Total | — | — |  |  |  |

6. Calculate the partial correlation $r_{12.3}$ and the part correlation $r_{1(2.3)}$ from the following bivariate correlations: $r_{12} = .5$, $r_{13} = .8$, $r_{23} = .9$.

7. Calculate the partial correlation $r_{13.2}$ and the part correlation $r_{1(3.2)}$ from the following bivariate correlations: $r_{12} = .21$, $r_{13} = .40$, $r_{23} = -.38$.

8. You are given the following data, where $X_1$ (verbal aptitude) and $X_2$ (prior reading achievement) are to be used to predict $Y$ (reading achievement):

| Y | $X_1$ | $X_2$ |
|---|---|---|
| 2 | 2 | 5 |
| 1 | 2 | 4 |
| 1 | 1 | 5 |
| 1 | 1 | 3 |
| 5 | 3 | 6 |
| 4 | 4 | 4 |
| 7 | 5 | 6 |
| 6 | 5 | 4 |
| 7 | 7 | 3 |
| 8 | 6 | 3 |

| | | |
|---|---|---|
| 3 | 4 | 3 |
| 3 | 3 | 6 |
| 6 | 6 | 9 |
| 6 | 6 | 8 |
| 10 | 8 | 9 |
| 9 | 9 | 6 |
| 6 | 10 | 4 |
| 6 | 9 | 5 |
| 9 | 4 | 8 |
| 10 | 4 | 9 |

Determine the following values: intercept; $b_1$; $b_2$; $SS_{res}$; $SS_{reg}$; $F$; $s^2_{res}$; $s(b_1)$; $s(b_2)$; $t_1$; $t_2$.

## Interpretive Problem

Use SPSS to develop a multiple regression model with the example survey data on the CD. Utilize current GPA as the dependent variable to find at least two strong predictors from among the continuous variables in the dataset.

# REFERENCES

Agresti, A. & Finlay, B. (1986). *Statistical methods for the social sciences* (2nd ed.). San Francisco: Dellen.

Agresti, A. & Pendergast, J. (1986). Comparing mean ranks for repeated measures data. *Communications in Statistics—Theory and Methods, 15*, 1417–1433.

Algina, J., Blair, R. C., & Coombs, W. T. (1995). A maximum test for scale: Type I error rates and power. *Journal of Educational and Behavioral Statistics, 20*, 27–39.

Andrews, D. F. (1971). Significance tests based on residuals. *Biometrika, 58*, 139–148.

Andrews, D. F. & Pregibon, D. (1978). Finding the outliers that matter. *Journal of the Royal Statistical Society, Series B, 40*, 85–93.

Applebaum, M. I. & Cramer, E. M. (1974). Some problems in the nonorthogonal analysis of variance. *Psychological Bulletin, 81*, 335–343.

Atiqullah, M. (1964). The robustness of the covariance analysis of a one-way classification. *Biometrika, 51*, 365–373.

Atkinson, A. C. (1985). *Plots, transformations, and regression*. Oxford: Oxford University Press.

Barnett, V. & Lewis, T. (1978). *Outliers in statistical data*. New York: Wiley.

Basu, S. & DasGupta, A. (1995). Robustness of standard confidence intervals for location parameters under departure from normality. *Annals of Statistics, 23*, 1433–1442.

Bates, D. M. & Watts, D. G. (1988). *Nonlinear regression analysis and its applications* . New York: Wiley.

Beal, S. L. (1987). Asymptotic confidence intervals for the difference between two binomial parameters for use with small samples. *Biometrics, 43*, 941–950.

Beckman, R. & Cook, R. D. (1983). Outliers . . . s. *Technometrics*, 25, 119–149.

Belsley, D. A., Kuh, E., & Welsch, R. E. (1980). *Regression diagnostics*. New York: Wiley.

Benjamini, Y. & Hochberg, Y. (1995). Controlling the false discovery rate: A practical and powerful approach to multiple testing. *Journal of the Royal Statistical Society, B, 57*, 289–300.

Bernstein, I. II. (1988). *Applied multivariate analysis*. New York: Springer-Verlag.

Berry, W. D. & Feldman, S. (1985). *Multiple regression in practice*. Beverly Hills: Sage.

Boik, R. J. (1979). Interactions, partial interactions, and interaction contrasts in the analysis of variance. *Psychological Bulletin, 86*, 1084–1089.

Boik, R. J. (1981). A priori tests in repeated measures designs: Effects of nonsphericity. *Psychometrika, 46*, 241–255.

Box, G. E. P. (1954a). Some theorems on quadratic forms applied in the study of analysis of variance problems, I: Effects of inequality of variance in the one-way model. *Annals of Mathematical Statistics, 25*, 290–302.

Box, G. E. P. (1954b). Some theorems on quadratic forms applied in the study of analysis of variance problems, II: Effects of inequality of variance and of correlation between errors in the two-way classification. *Annals of Mathematical Statistics, 25*, 484–498.

Box, G. E. P. & Anderson, S. L. (1962). *Robust tests for variances and effect of non-normality and variance heterogeneity on standard tests*. Technical Report No. 7, Ordinance Project No. TB 2-0001 (832), Dept. of Army Project No. 599-01-004.

Bradley, J. V. (1978). Robustness? *British Journal of Mathematical and Statistical Psychology, 31*, 144–152.

Brown, M. B. & Forsythe, A. (1974). The ANOVA and multiple comparisons for data with heterogeneous variances. *Biometrics, 30*, 719–724.

Brunner, E., Detta, H., & Munk, A. (1997). Box-type approximations in nonparametric factorial designs. *Journal of the American Statistical Association, 92*, 1494–1502.

Bryant, J. L. & Paulson, A. S. (1976). An extension of Tukey's method of multiple comparisons to experimental designs with random concomitant variables. *Biometrika, 63*, 631–638.

Campbell, D. T. & Stanley, J. C. (1966). *Experimental and quasi-experimental designs for research*. Chicago: Rand McNally.

Carlson, J. E. & Timm, N. H. (1974). Analysis of nonorthogonal fixed-effects designs. *Psychological Bulletin, 81*, 563–570.

Carroll, R. J. & Ruppert, D. (1982). Robust estimation in heteroscedastic linear models. *Annals of Statistics, 10*, 429–441.

Chambers, J. M., Cleveland, W. S., Kleiner, B., & Tukey, P. A. (1983). *Graphical methods for data analysis*. Belmont CA: Wadsworth.

Chatterjee, S. & Price, B. (1977). *Regression analysis by example*. New York: Wiley.

Christensen, R. (1997). *Log-linear models and logistic regression* (2nd ed.) New York: Springer-Verlag.

Cleveland, W. S. (1993). *Elements of graphing data*. New York: Chapman & Hall.

Clinch, J. J. & Keselman, H. J. (1982). Parametric alternatives to the analysis of variance. *Journal of Educational Statistics, 7*, 207–214.

Coe, P. R. & Tamhane, A. C. (1993). Small sample confidence intervals for the difference, ratio and odds ratio of two success probabilities. *Communications in Statistics—Simulation and Computation, 22*, 925–938.

Cohen, J. (1988). *Statistical power analysis for the behavioral sciences* (2nd ed.). Hillsdale NJ: Erlbaum.

Cohen, J. & Cohen, P. (1983). *Applied multiple regression/correlation analysis for the behavioral sciences* (2nd ed.). Hillsdale, NJ: Erlbaum.

Coombs, W. T., Algina, J., & Ottman, D. O. (1996). Univariate and multivariate omnibus hypothesis tests selected to control Type I error rates when population variances are not necessarily equal. *Review of Educational Research, 66*, 137–179.

Conover, W. & Iman, R. (1981). Rank transformations as a bridge between parametric and nonparametric statistics. *The American Statistician, 35*, 124–129.

Conover, W. & Iman, R. (1982). Analysis of covariance using the rank transformation. *Biometrics, 38*, 715–724.

Cotton, J. W. (1998). *Analyzing within-subjects experiments*. Mahwah NJ: Lawrence Erlbaum Associates.

Cook, R. D. (1977). Detection of influential observations in linear regression. *Technometrics, 19*, 15–18.

Cook, R. D. & Weisberg, S. (1982). *Residuals and influence in regression*. London: Chapman and Hall.

Cook, T. D. & Campbell, D. T. (1979). *Quasi-experimentation: Design and analysis issues for field settings*. Chicago: Rand McNally.

Cramer, E. M. & Applebaum, M. I. (1980). Nonorthogonal analysis of variance—Once again. *Psychological Bulletin, 87*, 51–57.

D'Agostino, R. B. (1971). An omnibus test of normality for moderate and large size samples. *Biometrika, 58*, 341–348.

Derksen, S. & Keselman, H. J. (1992). Backward, forward and stepwise automated subset selection algorithms: Frequency of obtaining authentic and noise variables. *British Journal of Mathematical and Statistical Psychology, 45*, 265–282.

Duncan, G. T. & Layard, M. W. J. (1973). A Monte-Carlo study of asymptotically robust tests for correlation coefficients. *Biometrika, 60*, 551–558.

Dunn, O. J. (1961). Multiple comparisons among means. *Journal of the American Statistical Association, 56*, 52–64.

Dunn, O. J. (1974). On multiple tests and confidence intervals. *Communications in Statistics, 3*, 101–103.

Dunn, O. J. & Clark, V. A. (1987). *Applied statistics: Analysis of variance and regression* (2nd ed.). New York: Wiley.

Dunnett, C. W. (1955). A multiple comparison procedure for comparing several treatments with a control. *Journal of the American Statistical Association, 50*, 1096–1121.

Dunnett, C. W. (1964). New tables for multiple comparisons with a control. *Biometrics, 20*, 482–491.

Dunnett, C. W. (1980). Pairwise multiple comparisons in the unequal variance case. *Journal of the American Statistical Association, 75*, 796–800.

Durbin, J. & Watson, G. S. (1950). Testing for serial correlation in least squares regression, I. *Biometrika, 37*, 409–428.

Durbin, J. & Watson, G. S. (1951). Testing for serial correlation in least squares regression, II. *Biometrika, 38*, 159–178.

Durbin, J. & Watson, G. S. (1971). Testing for serial correlation in least squares regression, III. *Biometrika, 58*, 1–19.

Educational and Psychological Measurement (October 2000). Special section: Statistical significance with comments by editors of marketing journals. *Educational and Psychological Measurement, 60*, 661–696.

Educational and Psychological Measurement (April 2001). Special section: Colloquium on effect sizes: The roles of editors, textbook authors, and the publication manual. *Educational and Psychological Measurement, 61*, 181–228.

Educational and Psychological Measurement (August 2001). Special section: Confidence intervals for effect sizes. *Educational and Psychological Measurement, 61*, 517–674.

Elashoff, J. D. (1969). Analysis of covariance: A delicate instrument. *American Educational Research Journal, 6*, 383–401.

Feldt, L. S. (1958). A comparison of the precision of three experimental designs employing a concomitant variable. *Psychometrika, 23*, 335–354.

Ferguson, G. A. & Takane, Y. (1989). *Statistical analysis in psychology and education* (6th ed.). New York: McGraw-Hill.

Fidler, F. & Thompson, B. (2001). Computing correct confidence intervals for ANOVA fixed- and random-effects effect sizes. *Educational and Psychological Measurement, 61*, 575–604.

Fink, A. (1995). *How to sample in surveys*. Thousand Oaks CA: Sage.

Fisher, R. A. (1949). *The design of experiments*. Edinburgh: Oliver & Boyd, Ltd.

Friedman, M. (1937). The use of ranks to avoid the assumption of normality implicit in the analysis of variance. *Journal of the American Statistical Association, 32*, 675–701.

Games, P. A. & Howell, J. F. (1976). Pairwise multiple comparison procedures with unequal n's and/or variances: A Monte Carlo study. *Journal of Educational Statistics, 1*, 113–125.

Geisser, S. & Greenhouse, S. (1958). Extension of Box's results on the use of the F distribution in multivariate analysis. *Annals of Mathematical Statistics, 29*, 855–891.

Ghosh, B. K. (1979). A comparison of some approximate confidence intervals for the binomial parameter. *Journal of the American Statistical Association, 74*, 894–900.

Glass, G. V. & Hopkins, K. D. (1996). *Statistical methods in education and psychology* (3rd ed.). Boston: Allyn & Bacon.

Glass, G. V., Peckham, P. D., & Sanders, J. R. (1972). Consequences of failure to meet assumptions underlying the fixed effects analyses of variance and covariance. *Review of Educational Research, 42*, 237–288.

Grimm, L. G. & Arnold, P. R. (Eds.). (1995). *Reading and understanding multivariate statistics.* Washington DC: American Psychological Association.

Grimm, L. G. & Arnold, P. R. (Eds.). (2002). *Reading and understanding more multivariate statistics.* Washington DC: American Psychological Association.

Grissom, R. J. & Kim, J. J. (2005). *Effect sizes for research: A broad practical approach.* Mahwah NJ: Lawrence Erlbaum Associates.

Harlow, L., Mulaik, S., & Steiger, J. (Eds.). (1997). *What if there were no significance tests?* Mahwah NJ: Lawrence Erlbaum Associates.

Harwell, M. (2003). Summarizing Monte Carlo results in methodological research: The single- factor, fixed-effects ANCOVA case. *Journal of Educational and Behavioral Statistics, 28*, 45–70.

Hawkins, D. M. (1980). *Identification of outliers.* London: Chapman and Hall.

Hays, W. L. (1988). *Statistics* (4th ed.). New York: Holt, Rinehart and Winston.

Hayter, A. J. (1986). The maximum familywise error rate of Fisher's least significant difference test. *Journal of the American Statistical Association, 81*, 1000–1004.

Heyde, C. C., Seneta, E., Crepel, P., Feinberg, S. E., & Gani, J. (Eds.) (2001). *Statisticians of the centuries.* New York: Springer.

Hockberg, Y. (1988). A sharper Bonferroni procedure for multiple tests of significance. *Biometrika, 75*, 800–802.

Hochberg, Y. & Tamhane, A. C. (1987). *Multiple comparison procedures.* New York: Wiley.

Hochberg, Y. & Varon-Salomon, Y. (1984). On simultaneous pairwise comparisons in analysis of covariance. *Journal of the American Statistical Association, 79*, 863–866.

Hocking, R. R. (1976). The analysis and selection of variables in linear regression. *Biometrics, 32*, 1–49.

Hoenig, J. M. & Heisey, D. M. (2001). The abuse of power: The pervasive fallacy of power calculations for data analysis. *The American Statistician, 55*, 19–24.

Hoerl, A. E. & Kennard, R. W. (1970a). Ridge regression: Biased estimation for non-orthogonal models. *Technometrics, 12*, 55–67.

Hoerl, A. E. & Kennard, R. W. (1970b). Ridge regression: Application to non-orthogonal models. *Technometrics, 12*, 591–612.

Hogg, R. V. & Craig, A. T. (1970). *Introduction to mathematical statistics.* New York: Macmillan.

Hosmer, D. W. & Lemeshow, S. (2000). *Applied logistic regression* (2nd ed.). New York: Wiley.

Huberty, C. J. (1989). Problems with stepwise methods—better alternatives. In B. Thompson (Ed.), *Advances in social science methodology, Volume 1* (pp. 43–70). Greenwich CT: JAI Press.

Huck, S. W. (2004). *Reading statistics and research* (4th ed.). Boston: Allyn and Bacon.

Huck, S. W. & McLean, R. A. (1975). Using a repeated measures ANOVA to analyze data from a pretest-posttest design: A potentially confusing task. *Psychological Bulletin, 82*, 511–518.

Huitema, B. E. (1980). *The analysis of covariance and alternatives.* New York: Wiley.

Huynh, H. & Feldt, L. S. (1970). Conditions under which mean square ratios in repeated measurement designs have exact F-distributions. *Journal of the American Statistical Association, 65*, 1582–1589.

Jaeger, R. M. (1984). *Sampling in education and the social sciences.* New York: Longman.

James, G. S. (1951). The comparison of several groups of observations when the ratios of the population variances are unknown. *Biometrika, 38*, 324–329.

Jennings, E. (1988). Models for pretest-posttest data: Repeated measures ANOVA revisited. *Journal of Educational Statistics, 13*, 273–280.

Johansen, S. (1980). The Welch-James approximation to the distribution of the residual sum of squares in a weighted linear regression. *Biometrika, 67*, 85–93.

Johnson, P. O. & Neyman, J. (1936). Tests of certain linear hypotheses and their application to some educational problems. *Statistical Research Memoirs, 1*, 57–93.

Johnson, R. A. & Wichern, D. W. (1998). *Applied multivariate statistical analysis* (4th ed.). Upper Saddle River NJ: Prentice Hall.

Kaiser, L. & Bowden, D. (1983). Simultaneous confidence intervals for all linear contrasts of means with heterogeneous variances. *Communications in Statistics—Theory and Methods, 12*, 73–88.

Kalton, G. (1983). *Introduction to survey sampling*. Thousand Oaks CA: Sage.

Keppel, G. (1982). *Design and analysis: A researcher's handbook* (2nd ed.). Englewood Cliffs, NJ: Prentice-Hall.

Keppel, G. & Wickens, T. D. (2004). *Design and analysis: A researcher's handbook* (3rd ed.). Upper Saddle River, NJ: Pearson.

Kirk, R. E. (1982). *Experimental design: Procedures for the behavioral sciences* (2nd ed.). Monterey, CA: Brooks/Cole.

Kleinbaum, D. G., Kupper, L. L., Muller, K. E., & Nizam, A. (1998). *Applied regression analysis and other multivariable methods* (3rd ed.). Pacific Grove CA: Duxbury.

Kramer, C. Y. (1956). Extension of multiple range test to group means with unequal numbers of replications. *Biometrics, 12*, 307–310.

Kruskal, W. H. & Wallis, W. A. (1952). Use of ranks on one-criterion variance analysis. *Journal of the American Statistical Association, 47*, 583–621. (with corrections in *48*, 907–911)

Lamb, G. S. (1984). What you always wanted to know about six but were afraid to ask. *The Journal of Irreproducible Results, 29*, 18–20.

Larsen, W. A. & McCleary, S. J. (1972). The use of partial residual plots in regression analysis. *Technometrics, 14*, 781–790.

Levy, P. S. & Lemeshow, S. (1999). *Sampling of populations: Methods and applications* (3rd ed.). New York: Wiley.

Lomax, R. G. & Surman, S. H. (2007). Factorial ANOVA in SPSS: Fixed-, random-, and mixed-effects models. In S. S. Sawilowsky (Ed.), *Real data analysis*. Greenwich CT: Information Age.

Lord, F. M. (1960). Large-sample covariance analysis when the control variable is fallible. *Journal of the American Statistical Association, 55*, 307–321.

Lord, F. M. (1967). A paradox in the interpretation of group comparisons. *Psychological Bulletin, 68*, 304–305.

Lord, F. M. (1969). Statistical adjustments when comparing preexisting groups. *Psychological Bulletin, 72*, 336–337.

Manly, B. F. J. (2004). *Multivariate statistical methods: A primer* (3rd ed.). London: Chapman & Hall.

Mansfield, E. R. & Conerly, M. D. (1987). Diagnostic value of residual and partial residual plots. *The American Statistician, 41*, 107–116.

Marascuilo, L. A. & Levin, J. R. (1970). Appropriate post hoc comparisons for interactions and nested hypotheses in analysis of variance designs: The elimination of type IV errors. *American Educational Research Journal, 7*, 397–421.

Marascuilo, L. A. & Levin, J. R. (1976). The simultaneous investigation of interaction and nested hypotheses in two-factor analysis of variance designs. *American Educational Research Journal, 13*, 61–65.

Marascuilo, L. A. & McSweeney, M. (1977). *Nonparametric and distribution-free methods for the social sciences*. Monterey, CA: Brooks/Cole.

Marascuilo, L. A. & Serlin, R. C. (1988). *Statistical methods for the social and behavioral sciences*. New York: Freeman.

Marcoulides, G. A. & Hershberger, S. L. (1997). *Multivariate statistical methods: A first course*. Mahwah NJ: Lawrence Erlbaum Associates.

Marquardt, D. W. & Snee, R. D. (1975). Ridge regression in practice. *The American Statistician, 29*, 3–19.

Maxwell, S. E. (1980). Pairwise multiple comparisons in repeated measures designs. *Journal of Educational Statistics, 5*, 269–287.

Maxwell, S. E. & Delaney, H. D. (1990). *Designing experiments and analyzing data: A model comparison perspective*. Belmont, CA: Wadsworth.

Maxwell, S. E., Delaney, H. D., & Dill, C. A. (1984). Another look at ANOVA versus blocking. *Psychological Bulletin, 95*, 136–147.

McCulloch, C. E. (2005). Repeated measures ANOVA, RIP? *Chance, 18*, 29–33.

Mendoza, J. L. & Stafford, K. L. (2001). Confidence intervals, power calculation, and sample size estimation for the squared multiple correlation coefficient under the fixed and random regression models: A computer program and useful standard tables. *Educational and Psychological Measurement, 61*, 650–667.

Meyers, L. S., Gamst, G., & Guarino, A. J. (2006). *Applied multivariate research: Design and interpretation*. Thousand Oaks CA: Sage.

Mickey, R. M., Dunn, O. J., & Clark, V. A. (2004). *Applied statistics: Analysis of variance and regression* (3rd ed.). Hoboken NJ: Wiley.

Miller, A. J. (1984). Selection of subsets of regression variables (with discussion). *Journal of the Royal Statistical Society, A, 147*, 389–425.

Miller, A. J. (1990). *Subset selection in regression*. New York: Chapman and Hall.

Miller, R. G. (1997). *Beyond ANOVA, basics of applied statistics*. Boca Raton, FL: CRC Press.

Morgan, G. A. & Griego, O.V. (1998). *Easy use and interpretation of SPSS for Windows: Answering research questions with statistics*. Mahwah NJ: Lawrence Erlbaum Associates.

Morgan, G. A., Leech, N. L., & Barrett, K. C. (2005). *SPSS for introductory and intermediate statistics*. Mahwah NJ: Lawrence Erlbaum Associates.

Murphy, K. R. & Myors, B. (2004). *Statistical power analysis: A simple and general model for traditional and modern hypothesis tests* (2nd ed.). Mahwah NJ: Lawrence Erlbaum Associates.

Myers, J. L. & Well, A. D. (1995). *Research design and statistical analysis*. Mahwah NJ: Lawrence Erlbaum Associates.

Myers, R. H. (1979). *Fundamentals of experimental design* (3rd ed.). Boston: Allyn and Bacon.

Myers, R. H. (1986). *Classical and modern regression with applications*. Boston: Duxbury.

Myers, R. H. (1990). *Classical and modern regression with applications* (2nd ed.). Boston: Duxbury.

Noreen, E. W. (1989). *Computer intensive methods for testing hypotheses*. New York: Wiley.

O'Grady, K. E. (1982). Measures of explained variance: Cautions and limitations. *Psychological Bulletin, 92*, 766–777.

Olejnik, S. F. & Algina, J. (1987). Type I error rates and power estimates of selected parametric and nonparametric tests of scale. *Journal of Educational Statistics, 21*, 45–61.

Overall, J. E., Lee, D. M., & Hornick, C. W. (1981). Comparison of two strategies for analysis of variance in nonorthogonal designs. *Psychological Bulletin, 90*, 367–375.

Overall, J. E. & Spiegel, D. K. (1969). Concerning least squares analysis of experimental data. *Psychological Bulletin, 72*, 311–322.

Page, M. C., Braver, S. L., & MacKinnon, D. P. (2003). *Levine's guide to SPSS for analysis of variance*. Mahwah NJ: Lawrence Erlbaum Associates.

Pampel, F. C. (2000). *Logistic regression: A primer*. Thousand Oaks CA: Sage.

Pavur, R. (1988). Type I error rates for multiple comparision procedures with dependent data. *The American Statistician, 42*, 171–173.

Pearson, E. S. (Ed.) (1978). *The history of statistics in the 17th and 18th Centuries*. New York: Macmillan.

Peckham, P. D. (1968). *An investigation of the effects of non-homogeneity of regression slopes upon the F-test of analysis of covariance* . Laboratory of Educational Research, Report No. 16, University of Colorado, Boulder.

Pedhazur, E. J. (1997). *Multiple regression in behavioral research* (3rd ed.). Fort Worth: Harcourt Brace.

Pingel, L. A. (1969). *A comparison of the effects of two methods of block formation on design precision*. Paper presented at the annual meeting of the American Educational Research Association, Los Angeles.

Porter, A. C. (1967). *The effects of using fallible variables in the analysis of covariance*. Unpublished doctoral dissertation, University of Wisconsin, Madison.

Porter, A. C. & Raudenbush, S. W. (1987). Analysis of covariance: Its model and use in psychological research. *Journal of Counseling Psychology, 34*, 383–392.

Puri, M. L. & Sen, P. K. (1969). Analysis of covariance based on general rank scores. *Annals of Mathematical Statistic, 40*, 610–618.

Quade, D. (1967). Rank analysis of covariance. *Journal of the American Statistical Association, 62*, 1187–1200.

Ramsey, P. H. (1989). Critical values of Spearman's rank order correlation. *Journal of Educational Statistics, 14*, 245–253.

Ramsey, P. H. (1994). Testing variances in psychological and educational research. *Journal of Educational Statistics, 19*, 23–42.

Reichardt, C. S. (1979). The statistical analysis of data from nonequivalent control group designs. In T. D. Cook & D. T. Campbell (eds.), *Quasi-experimentation: Design and analysis issues for field settings*. Chicago: Rand McNally.

Robbins, N. B. (2004). *Creating more effective graphs*. San Francisco: Jossey-Bass.

Rogosa, D. R. (1980). Comparing non-parallel regression lines. *Psychological Bulletin, 88*, 307–321.

Rosenthal, R. & Rosnow, R. L. (1985). *Contrast analysis: Focused comparisons in the analysis of variance*. Cambridge: Cambridge University Press.

Rousseeuw, P. J. & Leroy, A. M. (1987). *Robust regression and outlier detection*. New York: Wiley.

Rudas, T. (2004). *Probability theory: A primer*. Thousand Oaks CA: Sage.

Ruppert, D. & Carroll, R. J. (1980). Trimmed least squares estimation in the linear model. *Journal of the American Statistical Association, 75*, 828–838.

Rutherford, A. (1992). Alternatives to traditional analysis of covariance. *British Journal of Mathematical and Statistical Psychology, 45*, 197–223.

Sawilowsky, S. S. & Blair, R. C. (1992). A more realistic look at the robustness and type II error properties of the t-test to departures from population normality. *Psychological Bulletin, 111*, 352–360.

Scariano, S. M. & Davenport, J. M. (1987). The effects of violations of independence assumptions in the one-way ANOVA. *The American Statistician, 41*, 123–129.

Schafer, W. D. (1991). Reporting hierarchical regression results. *Measurement and Evaluation in Counseling and Development, 24*, 98–100.

Scheffé, H. (1953). A method for judging all contrasts in the analysis of variance. *Biometrika, 40*, 87–104.

Schmid, C. F. (1983). *Statistical graphics: Design principles and practices*. New York: Wiley.

Seber, G. A. F. & Wild, C. J. (1989). *Nonlinear regression*. New York: Wiley.

Shapiro, S. S. & Wilk, M. B. (1965). An analysis of variance test for normality (complete samples). *Biometrika, 52*, 591–611.

Shavelson, R. J. (1988). *Statistical reasoning for the behavioral sciences* (2nd ed.). Boston: Allyn and Bacon.

Sidak, Z. (1967). Rectangular confidence regions for the means of multivariate normal distributions. *Journal of the American Statistical Association, 62*, 626–633.

Smithson, M. (2001). Correct confidence intervals for various regression effect sizes and parameters: The importance of noncentral distributions in computing intervals. *Educational and Psychological Measurement, 61*, 605–632.

Steiger, J. H. & Fouladi, R. T. (1992). R2: A computer program in interval estimation, power calculation, and hypothesis testing for the squared multiple correlation. *Behavior Research Methods, Instruments, and Computers, 4*, 581–582.

Stevens, J. P. (2002). *Applied multivariate statistics for the social sciences* (4th ed.). Mahwah NJ: Lawrence Erlbaum Associates.

Stigler, S. M. (1986). *The history of statistics: The measurement of uncertainty before 1900.* Cambridge MA: Harvard.

Storer, B. E. & Kim, C. (1990). Exact properties of some exact test statistics for comparing two binomial proportions. *Journal of the American Statistical Association, 85*, 146–155.

Sudman, S. (1976). *Applied sampling.* New York: Academic.

Tabachnick, B. G. & Fidell, L. S. (2001). *Using multivariate statistics.* Boston: Allyn and Bacon.

Tabatabai, M. & Tan, W. (1985). Some comparative studies on testing parallelism of several straight lines under heteroscedastic variances. *Communications in Statistics—Simulation and Computation, 14*, 837–844.

Thompson, M. L. (1978). Selection of variables in multiple regression. Part I: A review and evaluation. Part II: Chosen procedures, computations and examples. *International Statistical Review, 46*, 1–19 and 129–146.

Tiku, M. L. & Singh, M. (1981). Robust test for means when population variances are unequal. *Communications in Statistics—Theory and Methods, A10*, 2057–2071.

Tijms, H. (2004). *Understanding probability: Chance rules in everyday life.* New York: Cambridge University Press.

Timm, N. H. (2002). *Applied multivariate analysis.* New York: Springer-Verlag.

Timm, N. H. & Carlson, J. E. (1975). Analysis of variance through full rank models. *Multivariate Behavioral Research Monographs*, No. 75-1.

Tomarken, A. & Serlin, R. (1986). Comparison of ANOVA alternatives under variance heterogeneity and specific noncentrality structures. *Psychological Bulletin, 99*, 90–99.

Tufte, E. R. (1992). *The visual display of quantitative information.* Cheshire CT: Graphics Press.

Tukey, J. W. (1949). One degree of freedom for nonadditivity. *Biometrics, 5*, 232–242.

Tukey, J. W. (1953). *The problem of multiple comparisons.* Ditto, Princeton University, 396 pp.

Tukey, J. W. (1977). *Exploratory data analysis.* Reading MA: Addison-Wesley.

Wainer, H. (1984). How to display data badly. *The American Statistician, 38*, 137–147.

Wainer, H. (1992). Understanding graphs and tables. *Educational Researcher, 21*, 14–23.

Wainer, H. (2000). *Visual revelations.* Mahwah, NJ: Lawrence Erlbaum Associates.

Wallgren, A., Wallgren, B., Persson, R., Jorner, U., & Haaland, J.-A. (1996). *Graphing statistics & data.* Thousand Oaks: Sage.

Weinberg, S. L. & Abramowitz, S. K. (2002). *Data analysis for the behavioral sciences using SPSS.* Cambridge United Kingdom: Cambridge University Press.

Weisberg, H. I. (1979). Statistical adjustments and uncontrolled studies. *Psychological Bulletin, 86*, 1149–1164.

Weisberg, S. (1985). *Applied linear regression* (2nd ed.). New York: Wiley.

Welch, B. L. (1951). On the comparison of several mean values: An alternative approach. *Biometrika, 38*, 330–336.

Wetherill, G. B. (1986). *Regression analysis with applications.* London: Chapman and Hall.

Wilcox, R. R. (1986). Controlling power in a heteroscedastic ANOVA procedure. *British Journal of Mathematical and Statistical Psychology, 39*, 65–68.

Wilcox, R. R. (1987). *New statistical procedures for the social sciences: Modern solutions to basic problems*. Hillsdale, NJ: Lawrence Erlbaum Associates.

Wilcox, R. R. (1988). A new alternative to the ANOVA F and new results on James'second- order method. *British Journal of Mathematical and Statistical Psychology, 41*, 109–117

Wilcox, R. R. (1989). Adjusting for unequal variances when comparing means in one-way and two-way fixed effects ANOVA models. *Journal of Educational Statistics, 14*, 269–278.

Wilcox, R. R. (1993). Comparing one-step M-estimators of location when there are more than two groups. *Psychometrika, 58*, 71–78.

Wilcox, R. R. (1996). *Statistics for the social sciences*. San Diego: Academic.

Wilcox, R. R. (1997). *Introduction to robust estimation and hypothesis testing*. San Diego: Academic.

Wilcox, R. R. (2002). Comparing the variances of two independent groups. *British Journal of Mathematical and Statistical Psychology, 55*, 169–175.

Wilcox, R. R. (2003). *Applying contemporary statistical procedures*. San Diego: Academic.

Wilkinson, L. (2005). *The grammar of statistics* (2nd ed.). New York: Springer.

Wonnacott, T. H. & Wonnacott, R. J. (1981). *Regression: A second course in statistics*. New York: Wiley.

Wright, R. E. (1995). Logistic regression. In L. G. Grimm & P. R. Arnold (Eds.). (1995). *Reading and understanding multivariate statistics* (pp. 217–244). Washington DC: American Psychological Association.

Wu, L. L. (1985). Robust M-estimation of location and regression. In N. B. Tuma (Ed.), *Sociological methodology, 1985*. San Francisco: Jossey-Bass.

Yu, M. C. & Dunn, O. J. (1982). Robust tests for the equality of two correlation coefficients: A monte carlo study. *Educational and Psychological Measurement, 42*, 987–1004.

Yuan, K.-H. & Maxwell, S. (2005). On the post hoc power in testing mean differences. *Journal of Educational and Behavioral Statistics, 30*, 141–167.

Zimmerman, D. W. (1997). A note of interpretation of the paired-samples t-test. *Journal of Educational and Behavioral Statistics, 22*, 349–360.

Zimmerman, D. W. (2003). A warning about the large-sample Wilcoxon-Mann-Whitney test. *Understanding Statistics, 2*, 267–280.

# APPENDIX TABLES

1. The Standard Unit Normal Distribution

2. Percentage Points of the $t$ Distribution

3. Percentage Points of the $\chi^2$ Distribution

4. Percentage Points of the $F$ Distribution

5. Fisher's $Z$ Transformed Values

6. Orthogonal Polynomials

7. Critical Values for Dunnett's Procedure

8. Critical Values for Dunn's (Bonferroni's) Procedure

9. Critical Values for the Studentized Range Statistic

10. Critical Values for the Bryant-Paulson Procedure

# APPENDIX TABLE 1
## The Standard Unit Normal Distribution

| z | P(z) | z | P(z) | z | P(z) | z | P(z) |
|---|------|---|------|---|------|---|------|
| ·00 | ·5000000 | ·50 | ·6914625 | 1·00 | ·8413447 | 1·50 | ·9331928 |
| ·01 | ·5039894 | ·51 | ·6949743 | 1·01 | ·8437524 | 1·51 | ·9344783 |
| ·02 | ·5079783 | ·52 | ·6984682 | 1·02 | ·8461358 | 1·52 | ·9357445 |
| ·03 | ·5119665 | ·53 | ·7019440 | 1·03 | ·8484950 | 1·53 | ·9369916 |
| ·04 | ·5159534 | ·54 | ·7054015 | 1·04 | ·8508300 | 1·54 | ·9382198 |
| ·05 | ·5199388 | ·55 | ·7088403 | 1·05 | ·8531409 | 1·55 | ·9394292 |
| ·06 | ·5239222 | ·56 | ·7122603 | 1·06 | ·8554277 | 1·56 | ·9406201 |
| ·07 | ·5279032 | ·57 | ·7156612 | 1·07 | ·8576903 | 1·57 | ·9417924 |
| ·08 | ·5318814 | ·58 | ·7190427 | 1·08 | ·8599289 | 1·58 | ·9429466 |
| ·09 | ·5358564 | ·59 | ·7224047 | 1·09 | ·8621434 | 1·59 | ·9440826 |
| ·10 | ·5398278 | ·60 | ·7257469 | 1·10 | ·8643339 | 1·60 | ·9452007 |
| ·11 | ·5437953 | ·61 | ·7290691 | 1·11 | ·8665005 | 1·61 | ·9463011 |
| ·12 | ·5477584 | ·62 | ·7323711 | 1·12 | ·8686431 | 1·62 | ·9473839 |
| ·13 | ·5517168 | ·63 | ·7356527 | 1·13 | ·8707619 | 1·63 | ·9484493 |
| ·14 | ·5556700 | ·64 | ·7389137 | 1·14 | ·8728568 | 1·64 | ·9494974 |
| ·15 | ·5596177 | ·65 | ·7421539 | 1·15 | ·8749281 | 1·65 | ·9505285 |
| ·16 | ·5635595 | ·66 | ·7453731 | 1·16 | ·8769756 | 1·66 | ·9515428 |
| ·17 | ·5674949 | ·67 | ·7485711 | 1·17 | ·8789995 | 1·67 | ·9525403 |
| ·18 | ·5714237 | ·68 | ·7517478 | 1·18 | ·8809999 | 1·68 | ·9535213 |
| ·19 | ·5753454 | ·69 | ·7549029 | 1·19 | ·8829768 | 1·69 | ·9544860 |
| ·20 | ·5792597 | ·70 | ·7580363 | 1·20 | ·8849303 | 1·70 | ·9554345 |
| ·21 | ·5831662 | ·71 | ·7611479 | 1·21 | ·8868606 | 1·71 | ·9563671 |
| ·22 | ·5870644 | ·72 | ·7642375 | 1·22 | ·8887676 | 1·72 | ·9572838 |
| ·23 | ·5909541 | ·73 | ·7673049 | 1·23 | ·8906514 | 1·73 | ·9581849 |
| ·24 | ·5948349 | ·74 | ·7703500 | 1·24 | ·8925123 | 1·74 | ·9590705 |
| ·25 | ·5987063 | ·75 | ·7733726 | 1·25 | ·8943502 | 1·75 | ·9599408 |
| ·26 | ·6025681 | ·76 | ·7763727 | 1·26 | ·8961653 | 1·76 | ·9607961 |
| ·27 | ·6064199 | ·77 | ·7793501 | 1·27 | ·8979577 | 1·77 | ·9616364 |
| ·28 | ·6102612 | ·78 | ·7823046 | 1·28 | ·8997274 | 1·78 | ·9624620 |
| ·29 | ·6140919 | ·79 | ·7852361 | 1·29 | ·9014747 | 1·79 | ·9632730 |
| ·30 | ·6179114 | ·80 | ·7881446 | 1·30 | ·9031995 | 1·80 | ·9640697 |
| ·31 | ·6217195 | ·81 | ·7910299 | 1·31 | ·9049021 | 1·81 | ·9648521 |
| ·32 | ·6255158 | ·82 | ·7938919 | 1·32 | ·9065825 | 1·82 | ·9656205 |
| ·33 | ·6293000 | ·83 | ·7967306 | 1·33 | ·9082409 | 1·83 | ·9663750 |
| ·34 | ·6330717 | ·84 | ·7995458 | 1·34 | ·9098773 | 1·84 | ·9671159 |
| ·35 | ·6368307 | ·85 | ·8023375 | 1·35 | ·9114920 | 1·85 | ·9678432 |
| ·36 | ·6405764 | ·86 | ·8051055 | 1·36 | ·9130850 | 1·86 | ·9685572 |
| ·37 | ·6443088 | ·87 | ·8078498 | 1·37 | ·9146565 | 1·87 | ·9692581 |
| ·38 | ·6480273 | ·88 | ·8105703 | 1·38 | ·9162067 | 1·88 | ·9699460 |
| ·39 | ·6517317 | ·89 | ·8132671 | 1·39 | ·9177356 | 1·89 | ·9706210 |
| ·40 | ·6554217 | ·90 | ·8159399 | 1·40 | ·9192433 | 1·90 | ·9712834 |
| ·41 | ·6590970 | ·91 | ·8185887 | 1·41 | ·9207302 | 1·91 | ·9719334 |
| ·42 | ·6627573 | ·92 | ·8212136 | 1·42 | ·9221962 | 1·92 | ·0725711 |
| ·43 | ·6664022 | ·93 | ·8238145 | 1·43 | ·9236415 | 1·93 | ·9731966 |
| ·44 | ·6700314 | ·94 | ·8263912 | 1·44 | ·9250663 | 1·94 | ·9738102 |
| ·45 | ·6736448 | ·95 | ·8289439 | 1·45 | ·9264707 | 1·95 | ·9744119 |
| ·46 | ·6772419 | ·96 | ·8314724 | 1·46 | ·9278550 | 1·96 | ·9750021 |
| ·47 | ·6808225 | ·97 | ·8339768 | 1·47 | ·9292191 | 1·97 | ·9755808 |
| ·48 | ·6843863 | ·98 | ·8364569 | 1·48 | ·9305634 | 1·98 | ·9761482 |
| ·49 | ·6879331 | ·99 | ·8389129 | 1·49 | ·9318879 | 1·99 | ·9767045 |
| ·50 | ·6914625 | 1·00 | ·8413447 | 1·50 | ·9331928 | 2·00 | ·9772499 |

P(z) represents the area below that value of z.

(continued)

**APPENDIX TABLE 1**   (*continued*)

The Standard Unit Normal Distribution

| z | P(z) | z | P(z) | z | P(z) | z | P(z) |
|---|---|---|---|---|---|---|---|
| 2·00 | ·9772499 | 2·50 | ·9937903 | 3·00 | ·9986501 | 3·50 | ·9997674 |
| 2·01 | ·9777844 | 2·51 | ·9939634 | 3·01 | ·9986938 | 3·51 | ·9997759 |
| 2·02 | ·9783083 | 2·52 | ·9941323 | 3·02 | ·9987361 | 3·52 | ·9997842 |
| 2·03 | ·9788217 | 2·53 | ·9942969 | 3·03 | ·9987772 | 3·53 | ·9997922 |
| 2·04 | ·9793248 | 2·54 | ·9944574 | 3·04 | ·9988171 | 3·54 | ·9997999 |
| 2·05 | ·9798178 | 2·55 | ·9946139 | 3·05 | ·9988558 | 3·55 | ·9998074 |
| 2·06 | ·9803007 | 2·56 | ·9947664 | 3·06 | ·9988933 | 3·56 | ·9998146 |
| 2·07 | ·9807738 | 2·57 | ·9949151 | 3·07 | ·9989297 | 3·57 | ·9998215 |
| 2·08 | ·9812372 | 2·58 | ·9950600 | 3·08 | ·9989650 | 3·58 | ·9998282 |
| 2·09 | ·9816911 | 2·59 | ·9952012 | 3·09 | ·9989992 | 3·59 | ·9998347 |
| 2·10 | ·9821356 | 2·60 | ·9953388 | 3·10 | ·9990324 | 3·60 | ·9998409 |
| 2·11 | ·9825708 | 2·61 | ·9954729 | 3·11 | ·9990646 | 3·61 | ·9998469 |
| 2·12 | ·9829970 | 2·62 | ·9956035 | 3·12 | ·9990957 | 3·62 | ·9998527 |
| 2·13 | ·9834142 | 2·63 | ·9957308 | 3·13 | ·9991260 | 3·63 | ·9998583 |
| 2·14 | ·9838226 | 2·64 | ·9958547 | 3·14 | ·9991553 | 3·64 | ·9998637 |
| 2·15 | ·9842224 | 2·65 | ·9959754 | 3·15 | ·9991836 | 3·65 | ·9998689 |
| 2·16 | ·9846137 | 2·66 | ·9960930 | 3·16 | ·9992112 | 3·66 | ·9998739 |
| 2·17 | ·9849966 | 2·67 | ·9962074 | 3·17 | ·9992378 | 3·67 | ·9998787 |
| 2·18 | ·9853713 | 2·68 | ·9963189 | 3·18 | ·9992636 | 3·68 | ·9998834 |
| 2·19 | ·9857379 | 2·69 | ·9964274 | 3·19 | ·9992886 | 3·69 | ·9998879 |
| 2·20 | ·9860966 | 2·70 | ·9965330 | 3·20 | ·9993129 | 3·70 | ·9998922 |
| 2·21 | ·9864474 | 2·71 | ·9966358 | 3·21 | ·9993363 | 3·71 | ·9998964 |
| 2·22 | ·9867906 | 2·72 | ·9967359 | 3·22 | ·9993590 | 3·72 | ·9999004 |
| 2·23 | ·9871263 | 2·73 | ·9968333 | 3·23 | ·9993810 | 3·73 | ·9999043 |
| 2·24 | ·9874545 | 2·74 | ·9969280 | 3·24 | ·9994024 | 3·74 | ·9999080 |
| 2·25 | ·9877755 | 2·75 | ·9970202 | 3·25 | ·9994230 | 3·75 | ·9999116 |
| 2·26 | ·9880894 | 2·76 | ·9971099 | 3·26 | ·9994429 | 3·76 | ·9999150 |
| 2·27 | ·9883962 | 2·77 | ·9971972 | 3·27 | ·9994623 | 3·77 | ·9999184 |
| 2·28 | ·9886962 | 2·78 | ·9972821 | 3·28 | ·9994810 | 3·78 | ·9999216 |
| 2·29 | ·9889893 | 2·79 | ·9973646 | 3·29 | ·9994991 | 3·79 | ·9999247 |
| 2·30 | ·9892759 | 2·80 | ·9974449 | 3·30 | ·9995166 | 3·80 | ·9999277 |
| 2·31 | ·9895559 | 2·81 | ·9975229 | 3·31 | ·9995335 | 3·81 | ·9999305 |
| 2·32 | ·9898296 | 2·82 | ·9975988 | 3·32 | ·9995499 | 3·82 | ·9999333 |
| 2·33 | ·9900969 | 2·83 | ·9976726 | 3·33 | ·9995658 | 3·83 | ·9999359 |
| 2·34 | ·9903581 | 2·84 | ·9977443 | 3·34 | ·9995811 | 3·84 | ·9999385 |
| 2·35 | ·9906133 | 2·85 | ·9978140 | 3·35 | ·9995959 | 3·85 | ·9999409 |
| 2·36 | ·9908625 | 2·86 | ·9978818 | 3·36 | ·9996103 | 3·86 | ·9999433 |
| 2·37 | ·9911060 | 2·87 | ·9979476 | 3·37 | ·9996242 | 3·87 | ·9999456 |
| 2·38 | ·9913437 | 2·88 | ·9980116 | 3·38 | ·9996376 | 3·88 | ·9999478 |
| 2·39 | ·9915758 | 2·89 | ·9980738 | 3·39 | ·9996505 | 3·89 | ·9999499 |
| 2·40 | ·9918025 | 2·90 | ·9981342 | 3·40 | ·9996631 | 3·90 | ·9999519 |
| 2·41 | ·9920237 | 2·91 | ·9981929 | 3·41 | ·9996752 | 3·91 | ·9999539 |
| 2·42 | ·9922397 | 2·92 | ·9982498 | 3·42 | ·9996869 | 3·92 | ·9999557 |
| 2·43 | ·9924506 | 2·93 | ·9983052 | 3·43 | ·9996982 | 3·93 | ·9999575 |
| 2·44 | ·9926564 | 2·94 | ·9983589 | 3·44 | ·9997091 | 3·94 | ·9999593 |
| 2·45 | ·9928572 | 2·95 | ·9984111 | 3·45 | ·9997197 | 3·95 | ·9999609 |
| 2·46 | ·9930531 | 2·96 | ·9984618 | 3·46 | ·9997299 | 3·96 | ·9999625 |
| 2·47 | ·9932443 | 2·97 | ·9985110 | 3·47 | ·9997398 | 3·97 | ·9999641 |
| 2·48 | ·9934309 | 2·98 | ·9985588 | 3·48 | ·9997493 | 3·98 | ·9999655 |
| 2·49 | ·9936128 | 2·99 | ·9986051 | 3·49 | ·9997585 | 3·99 | ·9999670 |
| 2·50 | ·9937903 | 3·00 | ·9986501 | 3·50 | ·9997674 | 4·00 | ·9999683 |

Percentage Points of the *t* Distribution

| df | $\alpha_1 = .10$ $\alpha_2 = .20$ | .05 .10 | .025 .050 | .01 .02 | .005 .010 | .0025 .0050 | .001 .002 | .0005 .0010 |
|---|---|---|---|---|---|---|---|---|
| 1 | 3·078 | 6·314 | 12·706 | 31·821 | 63·657 | 127·32 | 318·31 | 636·62 |
| 2 | 1·886 | 2·920 | 4·303 | 6·965 | 9·925 | 14·089 | 22·327 | 31·598 |
| 3 | 1·638 | 2·353 | 3·182 | 4·541 | 5·841 | 7·453 | 10·214 | 12·924 |
| 4 | 1·533 | 2·132 | 2·776 | 3·747 | 4·604 | 5·598 | 7·173 | 8·610 |
| 5 | 1·476 | 2·015 | 2·571 | 3·365 | 4·032 | 4·773 | 5·893 | 6·869 |
| 6 | 1·440 | 1·943 | 2·447 | 3·143 | 3·707 | 4·317 | 5·208 | 5·959 |
| 7 | 1·415 | 1·895 | 2·365 | 2·998 | 3·499 | 4·029 | 4·785 | 5·408 |
| 8 | 1·397 | 1·860 | 2·306 | 2·896 | 3·355 | 3·833 | 4·501 | 5·041 |
| 9 | 1·383 | 1·833 | 2·262 | 2·821 | 3·250 | 3·690 | 4·297 | 4·781 |
| 10 | 1·372 | 1·812 | 2·228 | 2·764 | 3·169 | 3·581 | 4·144 | 4·587 |
| 11 | 1·363 | 1·796 | 2·201 | 2·718 | 3·106 | 3·497 | 4·025 | 4·437 |
| 12 | 1·356 | 1·782 | 2·179 | 2·681 | 3·055 | 3·428 | 3·930 | 4·318 |
| 13 | 1·350 | 1·771 | 2·160 | 2·650 | 3·012 | 3·372 | 3·852 | 4·221 |
| 14 | 1·345 | 1·761 | 2·145 | 2·624 | 2·977 | 3·326 | 3·787 | 4·140 |
| 15 | 1·341 | 1·753 | 2·131 | 2·602 | 2·947 | 3·286 | 3·733 | 4·073 |
| 16 | 1·337 | 1·746 | 2·120 | 2·583 | 2·921 | 3·252 | 3·686 | 4·015 |
| 17 | 1·333 | 1·740 | 2·110 | 2·567 | 2·898 | 3·222 | 3·646 | 3·965 |
| 18 | 1·330 | 1·734 | 2·101 | 2·552 | 2·878 | 3·197 | 3·610 | 3·922 |
| 19 | 1·328 | 1·729 | 2·093 | 2·539 | 2·861 | 3·174 | 3·579 | 3·883 |
| 20 | 1·325 | 1·725 | 2·086 | 2·528 | 2·845 | 3·153 | 3·552 | 3·850 |
| 21 | 1·323 | 1·721 | 2·080 | 2·518 | 2·831 | 3·135 | 3·527 | 3·819 |
| 22 | 1·321 | 1·717 | 2·074 | 2·508 | 2·819 | 3·119 | 3·505 | 3·792 |
| 23 | 1·319 | 1·714 | 2·069 | 2·500 | 2·807 | 3·104 | 3·485 | 3·767 |
| 24 | 1·318 | 1·711 | 2·064 | 2·492 | 2·797 | 3·091 | 3·467 | 3·745 |
| 25 | 1·316 | 1·708 | 2·060 | 2·485 | 2·787 | 3·078 | 3·450 | 3·725 |
| 26 | 1·315 | 1·706 | 2·056 | 2·479 | 2·779 | 3·067 | 3·435 | 3·707 |
| 27 | 1·314 | 1·703 | 2·052 | 2·473 | 2·771 | 3·057 | 3·421 | 3·690 |
| 28 | 1·313 | 1·701 | 2·048 | 2·467 | 2·763 | 3·047 | 3·408 | 3·674 |
| 29 | 1·311 | 1·699 | 2·045 | 2·462 | 2·756 | 3·038 | 3·396 | 3·659 |
| 30 | 1·310 | 1·697 | 2·042 | 2·457 | 2·750 | 3·030 | 3·385 | 3·646 |
| 40 | 1·303 | 1·684 | 2·021 | 2·423 | 2·704 | 2·971 | 3·307 | 3·551 |
| 60 | 1·296 | 1·671 | 2·000 | 2·390 | 2·660 | 2·915 | 3·232 | 3·460 |
| 120 | 1·289 | 1·658 | 1·980 | 2·358 | 2·617 | 2·860 | 3·160 | 3·373 |
| ∞ | 1·282 | 1·645 | 1·960 | 2·326 | 2·576 | 2·807 | 3·090 | 3·291 |

$\alpha_1$ is the upper-tail value of the distribution with $\nu$ degrees of freedom, appropriate for use in a one-tailed test; use $\alpha_2$ for a two-tailed test.

Percentage Points of the $\chi^2$ Distribution

| $\alpha$ / $\nu$ | 0·990 | 0·975 | 0·950 | 0·900 | 0·100 | 0·050 | 0·025 | 0·010 |
|---|---|---|---|---|---|---|---|---|
| 1 | 157088.10$^{-9}$ | 982069.10$^{-9}$ | 393214.10$^{-8}$ | 0·0157908 | 2·70554 | 3·84146 | 5·02389 | 6·63490 |
| 2 | 0·0201007 | 0·0506356 | 0·102587 | 0·210721 | 4·60517 | 5·99146 | 7·37776 | 9·21034 |
| 3 | 0·114832 | 0·215795 | 0·351846 | 0·584374 | 6·25139 | 7·81473 | 9·34840 | 11·3449 |
| 4 | 0·297109 | 0·484419 | 0·710723 | 1·063623 | 7·77944 | 9·48773 | 11·1433 | 13·2767 |
| 5 | 0·554298 | 0·831212 | 1·145476 | 1·61031 | 9·23636 | 11·0705 | 12·8325 | 15·0863 |
| 6 | 0·872090 | 1·23734 | 1·63538 | 2·20413 | 10·6446 | 12·5916 | 14·4494 | 16·8119 |
| 7 | 1·239043 | 1·68987 | 2·16735 | 2·83311 | 12·0170 | 14·0671 | 16·0128 | 18·4753 |
| 8 | 1·64650 | 2·17973 | 2·73264 | 3·48954 | 13·3616 | 15·5073 | 17·5345 | 20·0902 |
| 9 | 2·08790 | 2·70039 | 3·32511 | 4·16816 | 14·6837 | 16·9190 | 19·0228 | 21·6660 |
| 10 | 2·55821 | 3·24697 | 3·94030 | 4·86518 | 15·9872 | 18·3070 | 20·4832 | 23·2093 |
| 11 | 3·05348 | 3·81575 | 4·57481 | 5·57778 | 17·2750 | 19·6751 | 21·9200 | 24·7250 |
| 12 | 3·57057 | 4·40379 | 5·22603 | 6·30380 | 18·5493 | 21·0261 | 23·3367 | 26·2170 |
| 13 | 4·10692 | 5·00875 | 5·89186 | 7·04150 | 19·8119 | 22·3620 | 24·7356 | 27·6882 |
| 14 | 4·66043 | 5·62873 | 6·57063 | 7·78953 | 21·0641 | 23·6848 | 26·1189 | 29·1412 |
| 15 | 5·22935 | 6·26214 | 7·26094 | 8·54676 | 22·3071 | 24·9958 | 27·4884 | 30·5779 |
| 16 | 5·81221 | 6·90766 | 7·96165 | 9·31224 | 23·5418 | 26·2962 | 28·8454 | 31·9999 |
| 17 | 6·40776 | 7·56419 | 8·67176 | 10·0852 | 24·7690 | 27·5871 | 30·1910 | 33·4087 |
| 18 | 7·01491 | 8·23075 | 9·39046 | 10·8649 | 25·9894 | 28·8693 | 31·5264 | 34·8053 |
| 19 | 7·63273 | 8·90652 | 10·1170 | 11·6509 | 27·2036 | 30·1435 | 32·8523 | 36·1909 |
| 20 | 8·26040 | 9·59078 | 10·8508 | 12·4426 | 28·4120 | 31·4104 | 34·1696 | 37·5662 |
| 21 | 8·89720 | 10·28293 | 11·5913 | 13·2396 | 29·6151 | 32·6706 | 35·4789 | 38·9322 |
| 22 | 9·54249 | 10·9823 | 12·3380 | 14·0415 | 30·8133 | 33·9244 | 36·7807 | 40·2894 |
| 23 | 10·19567 | 11·6886 | 13·0905 | 14·8480 | 32·0069 | 35·1725 | 38·0756 | 41·6384 |
| 24 | 10·8564 | 12·4012 | 13·8484 | 15·6587 | 33·1962 | 36·4150 | 39·3641 | 42·9798 |
| 25 | 11·5240 | 13·1197 | 14·6114 | 16·4734 | 34·3816 | 37·6525 | 40·6465 | 44·3141 |
| 26 | 12·1981 | 13·8439 | 15·3792 | 17·2919 | 35·5632 | 38·8851 | 41·9232 | 45·6417 |
| 27 | 12·8785 | 14·5734 | 16·1514 | 18·1139 | 36·7412 | 40·1133 | 43·1945 | 46·9629 |
| 28 | 13·5647 | 15·3079 | 16·9279 | 18·9392 | 37·9159 | 41·3371 | 44·4608 | 48·2782 |
| 29 | 14·2565 | 16·0471 | 17·7084 | 19·7677 | 39·0875 | 42·5570 | 45·7223 | 49·5879 |
| 30 | 14·9535 | 16·7908 | 18·4927 | 20·5992 | 40·2560 | 43·7730 | 46·9792 | 50·8922 |
| 40 | 22·1643 | 24·4330 | 26·5093 | 29·0505 | 51·8051 | 55·7585 | 59·3417 | 63·6907 |
| 50 | 29·7067 | 32·3574 | 34·7643 | 37·6886 | 63·1671 | 67·5048 | 71·4202 | 76·1539 |
| 60 | 37·4849 | 40·4817 | 43·1880 | 46·4589 | 74·3970 | 79·0819 | 83·2977 | 88·3794 |
| 70 | 45·4417 | 48·7576 | 51·7393 | 55·3289 | 85·5270 | 90·5312 | 95·0232 | 100·425 |
| 80 | 53·5401 | 57·1532 | 60·3915 | 64·2778 | 96·5782 | 101·879 | 106·629 | 112·329 |
| 90 | 61·7541 | 65·6466 | 69·1260 | 73·2911 | 107·565 | 113·145 | 118·136 | 124·116 |
| 100 | 70·0649 | 74·2219 | 77·9295 | 82·3581 | 118·498 | 124·342 | 129·561 | 135·807 |

## APPENDIX TABLE 4

Percentage Points of the $F$ Distribution, $\alpha = .10$

| $v_2$ \ $v_1$ | 1 | 2 | 3 | 4 | 5 | 6 | 7 | 8 | 9 | 10 | 12 | 15 | 20 | 24 | 30 | 40 | 60 | 120 | $\infty$ |
|---|---|---|---|---|---|---|---|---|---|---|---|---|---|---|---|---|---|---|---|
| 1 | 39.86 | 49.50 | 53.59 | 55.83 | 57.24 | 58.20 | 58.91 | 59.44 | 59.86 | 60.19 | 60.71 | 61.22 | 61.74 | 62.00 | 62.26 | 62.53 | 62.79 | 63.06 | 63.33 |
| 2 | 8.53 | 9.00 | 9.16 | 9.24 | 9.29 | 9.33 | 9.35 | 9.37 | 9.38 | 9.39 | 9.41 | 9.42 | 9.44 | 9.45 | 9.46 | 9.47 | 9.47 | 9.48 | 9.49 |
| 3 | 5.54 | 5.46 | 5.39 | 5.34 | 5.31 | 5.28 | 5.27 | 5.25 | 5.24 | 5.23 | 5.22 | 5.20 | 5.18 | 5.18 | 5.17 | 5.16 | 5.15 | 5.14 | 5.13 |
| 4 | 4.54 | 4.32 | 4.19 | 4.11 | 4.05 | 4.01 | 3.98 | 3.95 | 3.94 | 3.92 | 3.90 | 3.87 | 3.84 | 3.83 | 3.82 | 3.80 | 3.79 | 3.78 | 3.76 |
| 5 | 4.06 | 3.78 | 3.62 | 3.52 | 3.45 | 3.40 | 3.37 | 3.34 | 3.32 | 3.30 | 3.27 | 3.24 | 3.21 | 3.19 | 3.17 | 3.16 | 3.14 | 3.12 | 3.10 |
| 6 | 3.78 | 3.46 | 3.29 | 3.18 | 3.11 | 3.05 | 3.01 | 2.98 | 2.96 | 2.94 | 2.90 | 2.87 | 2.84 | 2.82 | 2.80 | 2.78 | 2.76 | 2.74 | 2.72 |
| 7 | 3.59 | 3.26 | 3.07 | 2.96 | 2.88 | 2.83 | 2.78 | 2.75 | 2.72 | 2.70 | 2.67 | 2.63 | 2.59 | 2.58 | 2.56 | 2.54 | 2.51 | 2.49 | 2.47 |
| 8 | 3.46 | 3.11 | 2.92 | 2.81 | 2.73 | 2.67 | 2.62 | 2.59 | 2.56 | 2.54 | 2.50 | 2.46 | 2.42 | 2.40 | 2.38 | 2.36 | 2.34 | 2.32 | 2.29 |
| 9 | 3.36 | 3.01 | 2.81 | 2.69 | 2.61 | 2.55 | 2.51 | 2.47 | 2.44 | 2.42 | 2.38 | 2.34 | 2.30 | 2.28 | 2.25 | 2.23 | 2.21 | 2.18 | 2.16 |
| 10 | 3.29 | 2.92 | 2.73 | 2.61 | 2.52 | 2.46 | 2.41 | 2.38 | 2.35 | 2.32 | 2.28 | 2.24 | 2.20 | 2.18 | 2.16 | 2.13 | 2.11 | 2.08 | 2.06 |
| 11 | 3.23 | 2.86 | 2.66 | 2.54 | 2.45 | 2.39 | 2.34 | 2.30 | 2.27 | 2.25 | 2.21 | 2.17 | 2.12 | 2.10 | 2.08 | 2.05 | 2.03 | 2.00 | 1.97 |
| 12 | 3.18 | 2.81 | 2.61 | 2.48 | 2.39 | 2.33 | 2.28 | 2.24 | 2.21 | 2.19 | 2.15 | 2.10 | 2.06 | 2.04 | 2.01 | 1.99 | 1.96 | 1.93 | 1.90 |
| 13 | 3.14 | 2.76 | 2.56 | 2.43 | 2.35 | 2.28 | 2.23 | 2.20 | 2.16 | 2.14 | 2.10 | 2.05 | 2.01 | 1.98 | 1.96 | 1.93 | 1.90 | 1.88 | 1.85 |
| 14 | 3.10 | 2.73 | 2.52 | 2.39 | 2.31 | 2.24 | 2.19 | 2.15 | 2.12 | 2.10 | 2.05 | 2.01 | 1.96 | 1.94 | 1.91 | 1.89 | 1.86 | 1.83 | 1.80 |
| 15 | 3.07 | 2.70 | 2.49 | 2.36 | 2.27 | 2.21 | 2.16 | 2.12 | 2.09 | 2.06 | 2.02 | 1.97 | 1.92 | 1.90 | 1.87 | 1.85 | 1.82 | 1.79 | 1.76 |
| 16 | 3.05 | 2.67 | 2.46 | 2.33 | 2.24 | 2.18 | 2.13 | 2.09 | 2.06 | 2.03 | 1.99 | 1.94 | 1.89 | 1.87 | 1.84 | 1.81 | 1.78 | 1.75 | 1.72 |
| 17 | 3.03 | 2.64 | 2.44 | 2.31 | 2.22 | 2.15 | 2.10 | 2.06 | 2.03 | 2.00 | 1.96 | 1.91 | 1.86 | 1.84 | 1.81 | 1.78 | 1.75 | 1.72 | 1.69 |
| 18 | 3.01 | 2.62 | 2.42 | 2.29 | 2.20 | 2.13 | 2.08 | 2.04 | 2.00 | 1.98 | 1.93 | 1.89 | 1.84 | 1.81 | 1.78 | 1.75 | 1.72 | 1.69 | 1.66 |
| 19 | 2.99 | 2.61 | 2.40 | 2.27 | 2.18 | 2.11 | 2.06 | 2.02 | 1.98 | 1.96 | 1.91 | 1.86 | 1.81 | 1.79 | 1.76 | 1.73 | 1.70 | 1.67 | 1.63 |
| 20 | 2.97 | 2.59 | 2.38 | 2.25 | 2.16 | 2.09 | 2.04 | 2.00 | 1.96 | 1.94 | 1.89 | 1.84 | 1.79 | 1.77 | 1.74 | 1.71 | 1.68 | 1.64 | 1.61 |
| 21 | 2.96 | 2.57 | 2.36 | 2.23 | 2.14 | 2.08 | 2.02 | 1.98 | 1.95 | 1.92 | 1.87 | 1.83 | 1.78 | 1.75 | 1.72 | 1.69 | 1.66 | 1.62 | 1.59 |
| 22 | 2.95 | 2.56 | 2.35 | 2.22 | 2.13 | 2.06 | 2.01 | 1.97 | 1.93 | 1.90 | 1.86 | 1.81 | 1.76 | 1.73 | 1.70 | 1.67 | 1.64 | 1.60 | 1.57 |
| 23 | 2.94 | 2.55 | 2.34 | 2.21 | 2.11 | 2.05 | 1.99 | 1.95 | 1.92 | 1.89 | 1.84 | 1.80 | 1.74 | 1.72 | 1.69 | 1.66 | 1.62 | 1.59 | 1.55 |
| 24 | 2.93 | 2.54 | 2.33 | 2.19 | 2.10 | 2.04 | 1.98 | 1.94 | 1.91 | 1.88 | 1.83 | 1.78 | 1.73 | 1.70 | 1.67 | 1.64 | 1.61 | 1.57 | 1.53 |
| 25 | 2.92 | 2.53 | 2.32 | 2.18 | 2.09 | 2.02 | 1.97 | 1.93 | 1.89 | 1.87 | 1.82 | 1.77 | 1.72 | 1.69 | 1.66 | 1.63 | 1.59 | 1.56 | 1.52 |
| 26 | 2.91 | 2.52 | 2.31 | 2.17 | 2.08 | 2.01 | 1.96 | 1.92 | 1.88 | 1.86 | 1.81 | 1.76 | 1.71 | 1.68 | 1.65 | 1.61 | 1.58 | 1.54 | 1.50 |
| 27 | 2.90 | 2.51 | 2.30 | 2.17 | 2.07 | 2.00 | 1.95 | 1.91 | 1.87 | 1.85 | 1.80 | 1.75 | 1.70 | 1.67 | 1.64 | 1.60 | 1.57 | 1.53 | 1.49 |
| 28 | 2.89 | 2.50 | 2.29 | 2.16 | 2.06 | 2.00 | 1.94 | 1.90 | 1.87 | 1.84 | 1.79 | 1.74 | 1.69 | 1.66 | 1.63 | 1.59 | 1.56 | 1.52 | 1.48 |
| 29 | 2.89 | 2.50 | 2.28 | 2.15 | 2.06 | 1.99 | 1.93 | 1.89 | 1.86 | 1.83 | 1.78 | 1.73 | 1.68 | 1.65 | 1.62 | 1.58 | 1.55 | 1.51 | 1.47 |
| 30 | 2.88 | 2.49 | 2.28 | 2.14 | 2.05 | 1.98 | 1.93 | 1.88 | 1.85 | 1.82 | 1.77 | 1.72 | 1.67 | 1.64 | 1.61 | 1.57 | 1.54 | 1.50 | 1.46 |
| 40 | 2.84 | 2.44 | 2.23 | 2.09 | 2.00 | 1.93 | 1.87 | 1.83 | 1.79 | 1.76 | 1.71 | 1.66 | 1.61 | 1.57 | 1.54 | 1.51 | 1.47 | 1.42 | 1.38 |
| 60 | 2.79 | 2.39 | 2.18 | 2.04 | 1.95 | 1.87 | 1.82 | 1.77 | 1.74 | 1.71 | 1.66 | 1.60 | 1.54 | 1.51 | 1.48 | 1.44 | 1.40 | 1.35 | 1.29 |
| 120 | 2.75 | 2.35 | 2.13 | 1.99 | 1.90 | 1.82 | 1.77 | 1.72 | 1.68 | 1.65 | 1.60 | 1.55 | 1.48 | 1.45 | 1.41 | 1.37 | 1.32 | 1.26 | 1.19 |
| $\infty$ | 2.71 | 2.30 | 2.08 | 1.94 | 1.85 | 1.77 | 1.72 | 1.67 | 1.63 | 1.60 | 1.55 | 1.49 | 1.42 | 1.38 | 1.34 | 1.30 | 1.24 | 1.17 | 1.00 |

$v_1$ is the numerator degrees of freedom and $v_2$ is the denominator degrees of freedom.

*(continued)*

# APPENDIX TABLE 4 (continued)

Percentage Points of the $F$ Distribution, $\alpha = .05$

| $\nu_2$ \ $\nu_1$ | 1 | 2 | 3 | 4 | 5 | 6 | 7 | 8 | 9 | 10 | 12 | 15 | 20 | 24 | 30 | 40 | 60 | 120 | ∞ |
|---|---|---|---|---|---|---|---|---|---|---|---|---|---|---|---|---|---|---|---|
| 1 | 161.4 | 199.5 | 215.7 | 224.6 | 230.2 | 234.0 | 236.8 | 238.9 | 240.5 | 241.9 | 243.9 | 245.9 | 248.0 | 249.1 | 250.1 | 251.1 | 252.2 | 253.3 | 254.3 |
| 2 | 18.51 | 19.00 | 19.16 | 19.25 | 19.30 | 19.33 | 19.35 | 19.37 | 19.38 | 19.40 | 19.41 | 19.43 | 19.45 | 19.45 | 19.46 | 19.47 | 19.48 | 19.49 | 19.50 |
| 3 | 10.13 | 9.55 | 9.28 | 9.12 | 9.01 | 8.94 | 8.89 | 8.85 | 8.81 | 8.79 | 8.74 | 8.70 | 8.66 | 8.64 | 8.62 | 8.59 | 8.57 | 8.55 | 8.53 |
| 4 | 7.71 | 6.94 | 6.59 | 6.39 | 6.26 | 6.16 | 6.09 | 6.04 | 6.00 | 5.96 | 5.91 | 5.86 | 5.80 | 5.77 | 5.75 | 5.72 | 5.69 | 5.66 | 5.63 |
| 5 | 6.61 | 5.79 | 5.41 | 5.19 | 5.05 | 4.95 | 4.88 | 4.82 | 4.77 | 4.74 | 4.68 | 4.62 | 4.56 | 4.53 | 4.50 | 4.46 | 4.43 | 4.40 | 4.36 |
| 6 | 5.99 | 5.14 | 4.76 | 4.53 | 4.39 | 4.28 | 4.21 | 4.15 | 4.10 | 4.06 | 4.00 | 3.94 | 3.87 | 3.84 | 3.81 | 3.77 | 3.74 | 3.70 | 3.67 |
| 7 | 5.59 | 4.74 | 4.35 | 4.12 | 3.97 | 3.87 | 3.79 | 3.73 | 3.68 | 3.64 | 3.57 | 3.51 | 3.44 | 3.41 | 3.38 | 3.34 | 3.30 | 3.27 | 3.23 |
| 8 | 5.32 | 4.46 | 4.07 | 3.84 | 3.69 | 3.58 | 3.50 | 3.44 | 3.39 | 3.35 | 3.28 | 3.22 | 3.15 | 3.12 | 3.08 | 3.04 | 3.01 | 2.97 | 2.93 |
| 9 | 5.12 | 4.26 | 3.86 | 3.63 | 3.48 | 3.37 | 3.29 | 3.23 | 3.18 | 3.14 | 3.07 | 3.01 | 2.94 | 2.90 | 2.86 | 2.83 | 2.79 | 2.75 | 2.71 |
| 10 | 4.96 | 4.10 | 3.71 | 3.48 | 3.33 | 3.22 | 3.14 | 3.07 | 3.02 | 2.98 | 2.91 | 2.85 | 2.77 | 2.74 | 2.70 | 2.66 | 2.62 | 2.58 | 2.54 |
| 11 | 4.84 | 3.98 | 3.59 | 3.36 | 3.20 | 3.09 | 3.01 | 2.95 | 2.90 | 2.85 | 2.79 | 2.72 | 2.65 | 2.61 | 2.57 | 2.53 | 2.49 | 2.45 | 2.40 |
| 12 | 4.75 | 3.89 | 3.49 | 3.26 | 3.11 | 3.00 | 2.91 | 2.85 | 2.80 | 2.75 | 2.69 | 2.62 | 2.54 | 2.51 | 2.47 | 2.43 | 2.38 | 2.34 | 2.30 |
| 13 | 4.67 | 3.81 | 3.41 | 3.18 | 3.03 | 2.92 | 2.83 | 2.77 | 2.71 | 2.67 | 2.60 | 2.53 | 2.46 | 2.42 | 2.38 | 2.34 | 2.30 | 2.25 | 2.21 |
| 14 | 4.60 | 3.74 | 3.34 | 3.11 | 2.96 | 2.85 | 2.76 | 2.70 | 2.65 | 2.60 | 2.53 | 2.46 | 2.39 | 2.35 | 2.31 | 2.27 | 2.22 | 2.18 | 2.13 |
| 15 | 4.54 | 3.68 | 3.29 | 3.06 | 2.90 | 2.79 | 2.71 | 2.64 | 2.59 | 2.54 | 2.48 | 2.40 | 2.33 | 2.29 | 2.25 | 2.20 | 2.16 | 2.11 | 2.07 |
| 16 | 4.49 | 3.63 | 3.24 | 3.01 | 2.85 | 2.74 | 2.66 | 2.59 | 2.54 | 2.49 | 2.42 | 2.35 | 2.28 | 2.24 | 2.19 | 2.15 | 2.11 | 2.06 | 2.01 |
| 17 | 4.45 | 3.59 | 3.20 | 2.96 | 2.81 | 2.70 | 2.61 | 2.55 | 2.49 | 2.45 | 2.38 | 2.31 | 2.23 | 2.19 | 2.15 | 2.10 | 2.06 | 2.01 | 1.96 |
| 18 | 4.41 | 3.55 | 3.16 | 2.93 | 2.77 | 2.66 | 2.58 | 2.51 | 2.46 | 2.41 | 2.34 | 2.27 | 2.19 | 2.15 | 2.11 | 2.06 | 2.02 | 1.97 | 1.92 |
| 19 | 4.38 | 3.52 | 3.13 | 2.90 | 2.74 | 2.63 | 2.54 | 2.48 | 2.42 | 2.38 | 2.31 | 2.23 | 2.16 | 2.11 | 2.07 | 2.03 | 1.98 | 1.93 | 1.88 |
| 20 | 4.35 | 3.49 | 3.10 | 2.87 | 2.71 | 2.60 | 2.51 | 2.45 | 2.39 | 2.35 | 2.28 | 2.20 | 2.12 | 2.08 | 2.04 | 1.99 | 1.95 | 1.90 | 1.84 |
| 21 | 4.32 | 3.47 | 3.07 | 2.84 | 2.68 | 2.57 | 2.49 | 2.42 | 2.37 | 2.32 | 2.25 | 2.18 | 2.10 | 2.05 | 2.01 | 1.96 | 1.92 | 1.87 | 1.81 |
| 22 | 4.30 | 3.44 | 3.05 | 2.82 | 2.66 | 2.55 | 2.46 | 2.40 | 2.34 | 2.30 | 2.23 | 2.15 | 2.07 | 2.03 | 1.98 | 1.94 | 1.89 | 1.84 | 1.78 |
| 23 | 4.28 | 3.42 | 3.03 | 2.80 | 2.64 | 2.53 | 2.44 | 2.37 | 2.32 | 2.27 | 2.20 | 2.13 | 2.05 | 2.01 | 1.96 | 1.91 | 1.86 | 1.81 | 1.76 |
| 24 | 4.26 | 3.40 | 3.01 | 2.78 | 2.62 | 2.51 | 2.42 | 2.36 | 2.30 | 2.25 | 2.18 | 2.11 | 2.03 | 1.98 | 1.94 | 1.89 | 1.84 | 1.79 | 1.73 |
| 25 | 4.24 | 3.39 | 2.99 | 2.76 | 2.60 | 2.49 | 2.40 | 2.34 | 2.28 | 2.24 | 2.16 | 2.09 | 2.01 | 1.96 | 1.92 | 1.87 | 1.82 | 1.77 | 1.71 |
| 26 | 4.23 | 3.37 | 2.98 | 2.74 | 2.59 | 2.47 | 2.39 | 2.32 | 2.27 | 2.22 | 2.15 | 2.07 | 1.99 | 1.95 | 1.90 | 1.85 | 1.80 | 1.75 | 1.69 |
| 27 | 4.21 | 3.35 | 2.96 | 2.73 | 2.57 | 2.46 | 2.37 | 2.31 | 2.25 | 2.20 | 2.13 | 2.06 | 1.97 | 1.93 | 1.88 | 1.84 | 1.79 | 1.73 | 1.67 |
| 28 | 4.20 | 3.34 | 2.95 | 2.71 | 2.56 | 2.45 | 2.36 | 2.29 | 2.24 | 2.19 | 2.12 | 2.04 | 1.96 | 1.91 | 1.87 | 1.82 | 1.77 | 1.71 | 1.65 |
| 29 | 4.18 | 3.33 | 2.93 | 2.70 | 2.55 | 2.43 | 2.35 | 2.28 | 2.22 | 2.18 | 2.10 | 2.03 | 1.94 | 1.90 | 1.85 | 1.81 | 1.75 | 1.70 | 1.64 |
| 30 | 4.17 | 3.32 | 2.92 | 2.69 | 2.53 | 2.42 | 2.33 | 2.27 | 2.21 | 2.16 | 2.09 | 2.01 | 1.93 | 1.89 | 1.84 | 1.79 | 1.74 | 1.68 | 1.62 |
| 40 | 4.08 | 3.23 | 2.84 | 2.61 | 2.45 | 2.34 | 2.25 | 2.18 | 2.12 | 2.08 | 2.00 | 1.92 | 1.84 | 1.79 | 1.74 | 1.69 | 1.64 | 1.58 | 1.51 |
| 60 | 4.00 | 3.15 | 2.76 | 2.53 | 2.37 | 2.25 | 2.17 | 2.10 | 2.04 | 1.99 | 1.92 | 1.84 | 1.75 | 1.70 | 1.65 | 1.59 | 1.53 | 1.47 | 1.39 |
| 120 | 3.92 | 3.07 | 2.68 | 2.45 | 2.29 | 2.17 | 2.09 | 2.02 | 1.96 | 1.91 | 1.83 | 1.75 | 1.66 | 1.61 | 1.55 | 1.50 | 1.43 | 1.35 | 1.25 |
| ∞ | 3.84 | 3.00 | 2.60 | 2.37 | 2.21 | 2.10 | 2.01 | 1.94 | 1.88 | 1.83 | 1.75 | 1.67 | 1.57 | 1.52 | 1.46 | 1.39 | 1.32 | 1.22 | 1.00 |

(continued)

APPENDIX TABLE 4  (*continued*)

Percentage Points of the *F* Distribution, $\alpha = .01$

| $v_2 \backslash v_1$ | 1 | 2 | 3 | 4 | 5 | 6 | 7 | 8 | 9 | 10 | 12 | 15 | 20 | 24 | 30 | 40 | 60 | 120 | ∞ |
|---|---|---|---|---|---|---|---|---|---|---|---|---|---|---|---|---|---|---|---|
| 1 | 4052 | 4999.5 | 5403 | 5625 | 5764 | 5859 | 5928 | 5981 | 6022 | 6056 | 6106 | 6157 | 6209 | 6235 | 6261 | 6287 | 6313 | 6339 | 6366 |
| 2 | 98.50 | 99.00 | 99.17 | 99.25 | 99.30 | 99.33 | 99.36 | 99.37 | 99.39 | 99.40 | 99.42 | 99.43 | 99.45 | 99.46 | 99.47 | 99.47 | 99.48 | 99.49 | 99.50 |
| 3 | 34.12 | 30.82 | 29.46 | 28.71 | 28.24 | 27.91 | 27.67 | 27.49 | 27.35 | 27.23 | 27.05 | 26.87 | 26.69 | 26.60 | 26.50 | 26.41 | 26.32 | 26.22 | 26.13 |
| 4 | 21.20 | 18.00 | 16.69 | 15.98 | 15.52 | 15.21 | 14.98 | 14.80 | 14.66 | 14.55 | 14.37 | 14.20 | 14.02 | 13.93 | 13.84 | 13.75 | 13.65 | 13.56 | 13.46 |
| 5 | 16.26 | 13.27 | 12.06 | 11.39 | 10.97 | 10.67 | 10.46 | 10.29 | 10.16 | 10.05 | 9.89 | 9.72 | 9.55 | 9.47 | 9.38 | 9.29 | 9.20 | 9.11 | 9.02 |
| 6 | 13.75 | 10.92 | 9.78 | 9.15 | 8.75 | 8.47 | 8.26 | 8.10 | 7.98 | 7.87 | 7.72 | 7.56 | 7.40 | 7.31 | 7.23 | 7.14 | 7.06 | 6.97 | 6.88 |
| 7 | 12.25 | 9.55 | 8.45 | 7.85 | 7.46 | 7.19 | 6.99 | 6.84 | 6.72 | 6.62 | 6.47 | 6.31 | 6.16 | 6.07 | 5.99 | 5.91 | 5.82 | 5.74 | 5.65 |
| 8 | 11.26 | 8.65 | 7.59 | 7.01 | 6.63 | 6.37 | 6.18 | 6.03 | 5.91 | 5.81 | 5.67 | 5.52 | 5.36 | 5.28 | 5.20 | 5.12 | 5.03 | 4.95 | 4.86 |
| 9 | 10.56 | 8.02 | 6.99 | 6.42 | 6.06 | 5.80 | 5.61 | 5.47 | 5.35 | 5.26 | 5.11 | 4.96 | 4.81 | 4.73 | 4.65 | 4.57 | 4.48 | 4.40 | 4.31 |
| 10 | 10.04 | 7.56 | 6.55 | 5.99 | 5.64 | 5.39 | 5.20 | 5.06 | 4.94 | 4.85 | 4.71 | 4.56 | 4.41 | 4.33 | 4.25 | 4.17 | 4.08 | 4.00 | 3.91 |
| 11 | 9.65 | 7.21 | 6.22 | 5.67 | 5.32 | 5.07 | 4.89 | 4.74 | 4.63 | 4.54 | 4.40 | 4.25 | 4.10 | 4.02 | 3.94 | 3.86 | 3.78 | 3.69 | 3.60 |
| 12 | 9.33 | 6.93 | 5.95 | 5.41 | 5.06 | 4.82 | 4.64 | 4.50 | 4.39 | 4.30 | 4.16 | 4.01 | 3.86 | 3.78 | 3.70 | 3.62 | 3.54 | 3.45 | 3.36 |
| 13 | 9.07 | 6.70 | 5.74 | 5.21 | 4.86 | 4.62 | 4.44 | 4.30 | 4.19 | 4.10 | 3.96 | 3.82 | 3.66 | 3.59 | 3.51 | 3.43 | 3.34 | 3.25 | 3.17 |
| 14 | 8.86 | 6.51 | 5.56 | 5.04 | 4.69 | 4.46 | 4.28 | 4.14 | 4.03 | 3.94 | 3.80 | 3.66 | 3.51 | 3.43 | 3.35 | 3.27 | 3.18 | 3.09 | 3.00 |
| 15 | 8.68 | 6.36 | 5.42 | 4.89 | 4.56 | 4.32 | 4.14 | 4.00 | 3.89 | 3.80 | 3.67 | 3.52 | 3.37 | 3.29 | 3.21 | 3.13 | 3.05 | 2.96 | 2.87 |
| 16 | 8.53 | 6.23 | 5.29 | 4.77 | 4.44 | 4.20 | 4.03 | 3.89 | 3.78 | 3.69 | 3.55 | 3.41 | 3.26 | 3.18 | 3.10 | 3.02 | 2.93 | 2.84 | 2.75 |
| 17 | 8.40 | 6.11 | 5.18 | 4.67 | 4.34 | 4.10 | 3.93 | 3.79 | 3.68 | 3.59 | 3.46 | 3.31 | 3.16 | 3.08 | 3.00 | 2.92 | 2.83 | 2.75 | 2.65 |
| 18 | 8.29 | 6.01 | 5.09 | 4.58 | 4.25 | 4.01 | 3.84 | 3.71 | 3.60 | 3.51 | 3.37 | 3.23 | 3.08 | 3.00 | 2.92 | 2.84 | 2.75 | 2.66 | 2.57 |
| 19 | 8.18 | 5.93 | 5.01 | 4.50 | 4.17 | 3.94 | 3.77 | 3.63 | 3.52 | 3.43 | 3.30 | 3.15 | 3.00 | 2.92 | 2.84 | 2.76 | 2.67 | 2.58 | 2.49 |
| 20 | 8.10 | 5.85 | 4.94 | 4.43 | 4.10 | 3.87 | 3.70 | 3.56 | 3.46 | 3.37 | 3.23 | 3.09 | 2.94 | 2.86 | 2.78 | 2.69 | 2.61 | 2.52 | 2.42 |
| 21 | 8.02 | 5.78 | 4.87 | 4.37 | 4.04 | 3.81 | 3.64 | 3.51 | 3.40 | 3.31 | 3.17 | 3.03 | 2.88 | 2.80 | 2.72 | 2.64 | 2.55 | 2.46 | 2.36 |
| 22 | 7.95 | 5.72 | 4.82 | 4.31 | 3.99 | 3.76 | 3.59 | 3.45 | 3.35 | 3.26 | 3.12 | 2.98 | 2.83 | 2.75 | 2.67 | 2.58 | 2.50 | 2.40 | 2.31 |
| 23 | 7.88 | 5.66 | 4.76 | 4.26 | 3.94 | 3.71 | 3.54 | 3.41 | 3.30 | 3.21 | 3.07 | 2.93 | 2.78 | 2.70 | 2.62 | 2.54 | 2.45 | 2.35 | 2.26 |
| 24 | 7.82 | 5.61 | 4.72 | 4.22 | 3.90 | 3.67 | 3.50 | 3.36 | 3.26 | 3.17 | 3.03 | 2.89 | 2.74 | 2.66 | 2.58 | 2.49 | 2.40 | 2.31 | 2.21 |
| 25 | 7.77 | 5.57 | 4.68 | 4.18 | 3.85 | 3.63 | 3.46 | 3.32 | 3.22 | 3.13 | 2.99 | 2.85 | 2.70 | 2.62 | 2.54 | 2.45 | 2.36 | 2.27 | 2.17 |
| 26 | 7.72 | 5.53 | 4.64 | 4.14 | 3.82 | 3.59 | 3.42 | 3.29 | 3.18 | 3.09 | 2.96 | 2.81 | 2.66 | 2.58 | 2.50 | 2.42 | 2.33 | 2.23 | 2.13 |
| 27 | 7.68 | 5.49 | 4.60 | 4.11 | 3.78 | 3.56 | 3.39 | 3.26 | 3.15 | 3.06 | 2.93 | 2.78 | 2.63 | 2.55 | 2.47 | 2.38 | 2.29 | 2.20 | 2.10 |
| 28 | 7.64 | 5.45 | 4.57 | 4.07 | 3.75 | 3.53 | 3.36 | 3.23 | 3.12 | 3.03 | 2.90 | 2.75 | 2.60 | 2.52 | 2.44 | 2.35 | 2.26 | 2.17 | 2.06 |
| 29 | 7.60 | 5.42 | 4.54 | 4.04 | 3.73 | 3.50 | 3.33 | 3.20 | 3.09 | 3.00 | 2.87 | 2.73 | 2.57 | 2.49 | 2.41 | 2.33 | 2.23 | 2.14 | 2.03 |
| 30 | 7.56 | 5.39 | 4.51 | 4.02 | 3.70 | 3.47 | 3.30 | 3.17 | 3.07 | 2.98 | 2.84 | 2.70 | 2.55 | 2.47 | 2.39 | 2.30 | 2.21 | 2.11 | 2.01 |
| 40 | 7.31 | 5.18 | 4.31 | 3.83 | 3.51 | 3.29 | 3.12 | 2.99 | 2.89 | 2.80 | 2.66 | 2.52 | 2.37 | 2.29 | 2.20 | 2.11 | 2.02 | 1.92 | 1.80 |
| 60 | 7.08 | 4.98 | 4.13 | 3.65 | 3.34 | 3.12 | 2.95 | 2.82 | 2.72 | 2.63 | 2.50 | 2.35 | 2.20 | 2.12 | 2.03 | 1.94 | 1.84 | 1.73 | 1.60 |
| 120 | 6.85 | 4.79 | 3.95 | 3.48 | 3.17 | 2.96 | 2.79 | 2.66 | 2.56 | 2.47 | 2.34 | 2.19 | 2.03 | 1.95 | 1.86 | 1.76 | 1.66 | 1.53 | 1.38 |
| ∞ | 6.63 | 4.61 | 3.78 | 3.32 | 3.02 | 2.80 | 2.64 | 2.51 | 2.41 | 2.32 | 2.18 | 2.04 | 1.88 | 1.79 | 1.70 | 1.59 | 1.47 | 1.32 | 1.00 |

## APPENDIX TABLE 5
Fisher's Z Transformed Values

| r | Z | r | Z |
|---|---|---|---|
| ·00 | ·0000 | ·50 | ·5493 |
| 1 | ·0100 | 1 | ·5627 |
| 2 | ·0200 | 2 | ·5763 |
| 3 | ·0300 | 3 | ·5901 |
| 4 | ·0400 | 4 | ·6042 |
| ·05 | ·0500 | ·55 | ·6184 |
| 6 | ·0601 | 6 | ·6328 |
| 7 | ·0701 | 7 | ·6475 |
| 8 | ·0802 | 8 | ·6625 |
| 9 | ·0902 | 9 | ·6777 |
| ·10 | ·1003 | ·60 | ·6931 |
| 1 | ·1104 | 1 | ·7089 |
| 2 | ·1206 | 2 | ·7250 |
| 3 | ·1307 | 3 | ·7414 |
| 4 | ·1409 | 4 | ·7582 |
| ·15 | ·1511 | ·65 | ·7753 |
| 6 | ·1614 | 6 | ·7928 |
| 7 | ·1717 | 7 | ·8107 |
| 8 | ·1820 | 8 | ·8291 |
| 9 | ·1923 | 9 | ·8480 |
| ·20 | ·2027 | ·70 | ·8673 |
| 1 | ·2132 | 1 | ·8872 |
| 2 | ·2237 | 2 | ·9076 |
| 3 | ·2342 | 3 | ·9287 |
| 4 | ·2448 | 4 | ·9505 |
| ·25 | ·2554 | ·75 | 0·973 |
| 6 | ·2661 | 6 | 0·996 |
| 7 | ·2769 | 7 | 1·020 |
| 8 | ·2877 | 8 | 1·045 |
| 9 | ·2986 | 9 | 1·071 |
| ·30 | ·3095 | ·80 | 1·099 |
| 1 | ·3205 | 1 | 1·127 |
| 2 | ·3316 | 2 | 1·157 |
| 3 | ·3428 | 3 | 1·188 |
| 4 | ·3541 | 4 | 1·221 |
| ·35 | ·3654 | ·85 | 1·256 |
| 6 | ·3769 | 6 | 1·293 |
| 7 | ·3884 | 7 | 1 333 |
| 8 | ·4001 | 8 | 1·376 |
| 9 | ·4118 | 9 | 1·422 |
| ·40 | ·4236 | ·90 | 1·472 |
| 1 | ·4356 | 1 | 1·528 |
| 2 | ·4477 | 2 | 1·589 |
| 3 | ·4599 | 3 | 1·658 |
| 4 | ·4722 | 4 | 1·738 |
| ·45 | ·4847 | ·95 | 1·832 |
| 6 | ·4973 | 6 | 1·946 |
| 7 | ·5101 | 7 | 2·092 |
| 8 | ·5230 | 8 | 2·298 |
| 9 | ·5361 | 9 | 2·647 |

Orthogonal Polynomials

| $J$ | Trend | $j=1$ | 2 | 3 | 4 | 5 | 6 | 7 | 8 | 9 | 10 | $\Sigma c_j^2$ |
|---|---|---|---|---|---|---|---|---|---|---|---|---|
| $J = 3$ | linear | −1 | 0 | 1 | | | | | | | | 2 |
| | quadratic | 1 | −2 | 1 | | | | | | | | 6 |
| $J = 4$ | linear | −3 | −1 | 1 | 3 | | | | | | | 20 |
| | quadratic | 1 | −1 | −1 | 1 | | | | | | | 4 |
| | cubic | −1 | 3 | −3 | 1 | | | | | | | 20 |
| $J = 5$ | linear | −2 | −1 | 0 | 1 | 2 | | | | | | 10 |
| | quadratic | 2 | −1 | −2 | −1 | 2 | | | | | | 14 |
| | cubic | −1 | 2 | 0 | −2 | 1 | | | | | | 10 |
| | quartic | 1 | −4 | 6 | −4 | 1 | | | | | | 70 |
| $J = 6$ | linear | −5 | −3 | −1 | 1 | 3 | 5 | | | | | 70 |
| | quadratic | 5 | −1 | −4 | −4 | −1 | 5 | | | | | 84 |
| | cubic | −5 | 7 | 4 | −4 | −7 | 5 | | | | | 180 |
| | quartic | 1 | −3 | 2 | 2 | −3 | 1 | | | | | 28 |
| | quintic | −1 | 5 | −10 | 10 | −5 | 1 | | | | | 252 |
| $J = 7$ | linear | −3 | −2 | −1 | 0 | 1 | 2 | 3 | | | | 28 |
| | quadratic | 5 | 0 | −3 | −4 | −3 | 0 | 5 | | | | 84 |
| | cubic | −1 | 1 | 1 | 0 | −1 | −1 | 1 | | | | 6 |
| | quartic | 3 | −7 | 1 | 6 | 1 | −7 | 3 | | | | 154 |
| | quintic | −1 | 4 | −5 | 0 | 5 | −4 | 1 | | | | 84 |
| $J = 8$ | linear | −7 | −5 | −3 | −1 | 1 | 3 | 5 | 7 | | | 168 |
| | quadratic | 7 | 1 | −3 | −5 | −5 | −3 | 1 | 7 | | | 168 |
| | cubic | −7 | 5 | 7 | 3 | −3 | −7 | −5 | 7 | | | 264 |
| | quartic | 7 | −13 | −3 | 9 | 9 | −3 | −13 | 7 | | | 616 |
| | quintic | −7 | 23 | −17 | −15 | 15 | 17 | −23 | 7 | | | 2184 |
| $J = 9$ | linear | −4 | −3 | −2 | −1 | 0 | 1 | 2 | 3 | 4 | | 60 |
| | quadratic | 28 | 7 | −8 | −17 | −20 | −17 | −8 | 7 | 28 | | 2772 |
| | cubic | −14 | 7 | 13 | 9 | 0 | −9 | −13 | −7 | 14 | | 990 |
| | quartic | 14 | −21 | −11 | 9 | 18 | 9 | −11 | −21 | 14 | | 2002 |
| | quintic | −4 | 11 | −4 | −9 | 0 | 9 | 4 | −11 | 4 | | 468 |
| $J = 10$ | linear | −9 | −7 | −5 | −3 | −1 | 1 | 3 | 5 | 7 | 9 | 330 |
| | quadratic | 6 | 2 | −1 | −3 | −4 | −4 | −3 | −1 | 2 | 6 | 132 |
| | cubic | −42 | 14 | 35 | 31 | 12 | −12 | −31 | −35 | −14 | 42 | 8580 |
| | quartic | 18 | −22 | −17 | 3 | 18 | 18 | 3 | −17 | −22 | 18 | 2860 |
| | quintic | −6 | 14 | −1 | −11 | −6 | 6 | 11 | 1 | −14 | 6 | 780 |

Critical Values for Dunnett's Procedure

One-tailed, $\alpha = .05$

(The columns represent $J =$ number of treatment means [excluding the control])

| d.f. | 1 | 2 | 3 | 4 | 5 | 6 | 7 | 8 | 9 |
|------|------|------|------|------|------|------|------|------|------|
| 5 | 2.02 | 2.44 | 2.68 | 2.85 | 2.98 | 3.08 | 3.16 | 3.24 | 3.30 |
| 6 | 1.94 | 2.34 | 2.56 | 2.71 | 2.83 | 2.92 | 3.00 | 3.07 | 3.12 |
| 7 | 1.89 | 2.27 | 2.48 | 2.62 | 2.73 | 2.82 | 2.89 | 2.95 | 3.01 |
| 8 | 1.86 | 2.22 | 2.42 | 2.55 | 2.66 | 2.74 | 2.81 | 2.87 | 2.92 |
| 9 | 1.83 | 2.18 | 2.37 | 2.50 | 2.60 | 2.68 | 2.75 | 2.81 | 2.86 |
| 10 | 1.81 | 2.15 | 2.34 | 2.47 | 2.56 | 2.64 | 2.70 | 2.76 | 2.81 |
| 11 | 1.80 | 2.13 | 2.31 | 2.44 | 2.53 | 2.60 | 2.67 | 2.72 | 2.77 |
| 12 | 1.78 | 2.11 | 2.29 | 2.41 | 2.50 | 2.58 | 2.64 | 2.69 | 2.74 |
| 13 | 1.77 | 2.09 | 2.27 | 2.39 | 2.48 | 2.55 | 2.61 | 2.66 | 2.71 |
| 14 | 1.76 | 2.08 | 2.25 | 2.37 | 2.46 | 2.53 | 2.59 | 2.64 | 2.69 |
| 15 | 1.75 | 2.07 | 2.24 | 2.36 | 2.44 | 2.51 | 2.57 | 2.62 | 2.67 |
| 16 | 1.75 | 2.06 | 2.23 | 2.34 | 2.43 | 2.50 | 2.56 | 2.61 | 2.65 |
| 17 | 1.74 | 2.05 | 2.22 | 2.33 | 2.42 | 2.49 | 2.54 | 2.59 | 2.64 |
| 18 | 1.73 | 2.04 | 2.21 | 2.32 | 2.41 | 2.48 | 2.53 | 2.58 | 2.62 |
| 19 | 1.73 | 2.03 | 2.20 | 2.31 | 2.40 | 2.47 | 2.52 | 2.57 | 2.61 |
| 20 | 1.72 | 2.03 | 2.19 | 2.30 | 2.39 | 2.46 | 2.51 | 2.56 | 2.60 |
| 24 | 1.71 | 2.01 | 2.17 | 2.28 | 2.36 | 2.43 | 2.48 | 2.53 | 2.57 |
| 30 | 1.70 | 1.99 | 2.15 | 2.25 | 2.33 | 2.40 | 2.45 | 2.50 | 2.54 |
| 40 | 1.68 | 1.97 | 2.13 | 2.23 | 2.31 | 2.37 | 2.42 | 2.47 | 2.51 |
| 60 | 1.67 | 1.95 | 2.10 | 2.21 | 2.28 | 2.35 | 2.39 | 2.44 | 2.48 |
| 120 | 1.66 | 1.93 | 2.08 | 2.18 | 2.26 | 2.32 | 2.37 | 2.41 | 2.45 |
| ∞ | 1.64 | 1.92 | 2.06 | 2.16 | 2.23 | 2.29 | 2.34 | 2.38 | 2.42 |

*(continued)*

Critical Values for Dunnett's Procedure

One-tailed, $\alpha = .01$

(The columns represent $J$ = number of treatment means [excluding the control])

| d.f. | 1 | 2 | 3 | 4 | 5 | 6 | 7 | 8 | 9 |
|------|------|------|------|------|------|------|------|------|------|
| 5 | 3.37 | 3.90 | 4.21 | 4.43 | 4.60 | 4.73 | 4.85 | 4.94 | 5.03 |
| 6 | 3.14 | 3.61 | 3.88 | 4.07 | 4.21 | 4.33 | 4.43 | 4.51 | 4.59 |
| 7 | 3.00 | 3.42 | 3.66 | 3.83 | 3.96 | 4.07 | 4.15 | 4.23 | 4.30 |
| 8 | 2.90 | 3.29 | 3.51 | 3.67 | 3.79 | 3.88 | 3.96 | 4.03 | 4.09 |
| 9 | 2.82 | 3.19 | 3.40 | 3.55 | 3.66 | 3.75 | 3.82 | 3.89 | 3.94 |
| 10 | 2.76 | 3.11 | 3.31 | 3.45 | 3.56 | 3.64 | 3.71 | 3.78 | 3.83 |
| 11 | 2.72 | 3.06 | 3.25 | 3.38 | 3.48 | 3.56 | 3.63 | 3.69 | 3.74 |
| 12 | 2.68 | 3.01 | 3.19 | 3.32 | 3.42 | 3.50 | 3.56 | 3.62 | 3.67 |
| 13 | 2.65 | 2.97 | 3.15 | 3.27 | 3.37 | 3.44 | 3.51 | 3.56 | 3.61 |
| 14 | 2.62 | 2.94 | 3.11 | 3.23 | 3.32 | 3.40 | 3.46 | 3.51 | 3.56 |
| 15 | 2.60 | 2.91 | 3.08 | 3.20 | 3.29 | 3.36 | 3.42 | 3.47 | 3.52 |
| 16 | 2.58 | 2.88 | 3.05 | 3.17 | 3.26 | 3.33 | 3.39 | 3.44 | 3.48 |
| 17 | 2.57 | 2.86 | 3.03 | 3.14 | 3.23 | 3.30 | 3.36 | 3.41 | 3.45 |
| 18 | 2.55 | 2.84 | 3.01 | 3.12 | 3.21 | 3.27 | 3.33 | 3.38 | 3.42 |
| 19 | 2.54 | 2.83 | 2.99 | 3.10 | 3.18 | 3.25 | 3.31 | 3.36 | 3.40 |
| 20 | 2.53 | 2.81 | 2.97 | 3.08 | 3.17 | 3.23 | 3.29 | 3.34 | 3.38 |
| 24 | 2.49 | 2.77 | 2.92 | 3.03 | 3.11 | 3.17 | 3.22 | 3.27 | 3.31 |
| 30 | 2.46 | 2.72 | 2.87 | 2.97 | 3.05 | 3.11 | 3.16 | 3.21 | 3.24 |
| 40 | 2.42 | 2.68 | 2.82 | 2.92 | 2.99 | 3.05 | 3.10 | 3.14 | 3.18 |
| 60 | 2.39 | 2.64 | 2.78 | 2.87 | 2.94 | 3.00 | 3.04 | 3.08 | 3.12 |
| 120 | 2.36 | 2.60 | 2.73 | 2.82 | 2.89 | 2.94 | 2.99 | 3.03 | 3.06 |
| ∞ | 2.33 | 2.56 | 2.68 | 2.77 | 2.84 | 2.89 | 2.93 | 2.97 | 3.00 |

(*continued*)

Critical Values for Dunnett's Procedure

Two-tailed, $\alpha = .05$

(The columns represent $J$ = number of treatment means [excluding the control])

| d.f. | 1 | 2 | 3 | 4 | 5 | 6 | 7 | 8 | 9 |
|------|------|------|------|------|------|------|------|------|------|
| 5 | 2.57 | 3.03 | 3.29 | 3.48 | 3.62 | 3.73 | 3.82 | 3.90 | 3.97 |
| 6 | 2.45 | 2.86 | 3.10 | 3.26 | 3.39 | 3.49 | 3.57 | 3.64 | 3.71 |
| 7 | 2.36 | 2.75 | 2.97 | 3.12 | 3.24 | 3.33 | 3.41 | 3.47 | 3.53 |
| 8 | 2.31 | 2.67 | 2.88 | 3.02 | 3.13 | 3.22 | 3.29 | 3.35 | 3.41 |
| 9 | 2.26 | 2.61 | 2.81 | 2.95 | 3.05 | 3.14 | 3.20 | 3.26 | 3.32 |
| 10 | 2.23 | 2.57 | 2.76 | 2.89 | 2.99 | 3.07 | 3.14 | 3.19 | 3.24 |
| 11 | 2.20 | 2.53 | 2.72 | 2.84 | 2.94 | 3.02 | 3.08 | 3.14 | 3.19 |
| 12 | 2.18 | 2.50 | 2.68 | 2.81 | 2.90 | 2.98 | 3.04 | 3.09 | 3.14 |
| 13 | 2.16 | 2.48 | 2.65 | 2.78 | 2.87 | 2.94 | 3.00 | 3.06 | 3.10 |
| 14 | 2.14 | 2.46 | 2.63 | 2.75 | 2.84 | 2.91 | 2.97 | 3.02 | 3.07 |
| 15 | 2.13 | 2.44 | 2.61 | 2.73 | 2.82 | 2.89 | 2.95 | 3.00 | 3.04 |
| 16 | 2.12 | 2.42 | 2.59 | 2.71 | 2.80 | 2.87 | 2.92 | 2.97 | 3.02 |
| 17 | 2.11 | 2.41 | 2.58 | 2.69 | 2.78 | 2.85 | 2.90 | 2.95 | 3.00 |
| 18 | 2.10 | 2.40 | 2.56 | 2.68 | 2.76 | 2.83 | 2.89 | 2.94 | 2.98 |
| 19 | 2.09 | 2.39 | 2.55 | 2.66 | 2.75 | 2.81 | 2.87 | 2.92 | 2.96 |
| 20 | 2.09 | 2.38 | 2.54 | 2.65 | 2.73 | 2.80 | 2.86 | 2.90 | 2.95 |
| 24 | 2.06 | 2.35 | 2.51 | 2.61 | 2.70 | 2.76 | 2.81 | 2.86 | 2.90 |
| 30 | 2.04 | 2.32 | 2.47 | 2.58 | 2.66 | 2.72 | 2.77 | 2.82 | 2.86 |
| 40 | 2.02 | 2.29 | 2.44 | 2.54 | 2.62 | 2.68 | 2.73 | 2.77 | 2.81 |
| 60 | 2.00 | 2.27 | 2.41 | 2.51 | 2.58 | 2.64 | 2.69 | 2.73 | 2.77 |
| 120 | 1.98 | 2.24 | 2.38 | 2.47 | 2.55 | 2.60 | 2.65 | 2.69 | 2.73 |
| ∞ | 1.96 | 2.21 | 2.35 | 2.44 | 2.51 | 2.57 | 2.61 | 2.65 | 2.69 |

*(continued)*

Critical Values for Dunnett's Procedure

Two-tailed, $\alpha = .01$

(The columns represent $J$ = number of treatment means [excluding the control])

| d.f. | 1 | 2 | 3 | 4 | 5 | 6 | 7 | 8 | 9 |
|------|------|------|------|------|------|------|------|------|------|
| 5 | 4.03 | 4.63 | 4.98 | 5.22 | 5.41 | 5.56 | 5.69 | 5.80 | 5.89 |
| 6 | 3.71 | 4.21 | 4.51 | 4.71 | 4.87 | 5.00 | 5.10 | 5.20 | 5.28 |
| 7 | 3.50 | 3.95 | 4.21 | 4.39 | 4.53 | 4.64 | 4.74 | 4.82 | 4.89 |
| 8 | 3.36 | 3.77 | 4.00 | 4.17 | 4.29 | 4.40 | 4.48 | 4.56 | 4.62 |
| 9 | 3.25 | 3.63 | 3.85 | 4.01 | 4.12 | 4.22 | 4.30 | 4.37 | 4.43 |
| 10 | 3.17 | 3.53 | 3.74 | 3.88 | 3.99 | 4.08 | 4.16 | 4.22 | 4.28 |
| 11 | 3.11 | 3.45 | 3.65 | 3.79 | 3.89 | 3.98 | 4.05 | 4.11 | 4.16 |
| 12 | 3.05 | 3.39 | 3.58 | 3.71 | 3.81 | 3.89 | 3.96 | 4.02 | 4.07 |
| 13 | 3.01 | 3.33 | 3.52 | 3.65 | 3.74 | 3.82 | 3.89 | 3.94 | 3.99 |
| 14 | 2.98 | 3.29 | 3.47 | 3.59 | 3.69 | 3.76 | 3.83 | 3.88 | 3.93 |
| 15 | 2.95 | 3.25 | 3.43 | 3.55 | 3.64 | 3.71 | 3.78 | 3.83 | 3.88 |
| 16 | 2.92 | 3.22 | 3.39 | 3.51 | 3.60 | 3.67 | 3.73 | 3.78 | 3.83 |
| 17 | 2.90 | 3.19 | 3.36 | 3.47 | 3.56 | 3.63 | 3.69 | 3.74 | 3.79 |
| 18 | 2.88 | 3.17 | 3.33 | 3.44 | 3.53 | 3.60 | 3.66 | 3.71 | 3.75 |
| 19 | 2.86 | 3.15 | 3.31 | 3.42 | 3.50 | 3.57 | 3.63 | 3.68 | 3.72 |
| 20 | 2.85 | 3.13 | 3.29 | 3.40 | 3.48 | 3.55 | 3.60 | 3.65 | 3.69 |
| 24 | 2.80 | 3.07 | 3.22 | 3.32 | 3.40 | 3.47 | 3.52 | 3.57 | 3.61 |
| 30 | 2.75 | 3.01 | 3.15 | 3.25 | 3.33 | 3.39 | 3.44 | 3.49 | 3.52 |
| 40 | 2.70 | 2.95 | 3.09 | 3.19 | 3.26 | 3.32 | 3.37 | 3.41 | 3.44 |
| 60 | 2.66 | 2.90 | 3.03 | 3.12 | 3.19 | 3.25 | 3.29 | 3.33 | 3.37 |
| 120 | 2.62 | 2.85 | 2.97 | 3.06 | 3.12 | 3.18 | 3.22 | 3.26 | 3.29 |
| ∞ | 2.58 | 2.79 | 2.92 | 3.00 | 3.06 | 3.11 | 3.15 | 3.19 | 3.22 |

Critical Values for Dunn's (Bonferroni's) Procedure

| | | Number of contrasts | | | | | | | | | | |
|---|---|---|---|---|---|---|---|---|---|---|---|---|
| $\nu$ | $\alpha$ | 2 | 3 | 4 | 5 | 6 | 7 | 8 | 9 | 10 | 15 | 20 |
| 2 | 0.01 | 14.071 | 17.248 | 19.925 | 22.282 | 24.413 | 26.372 | 28.196 | 29.908 | 31.528 | 38.620 | 44.598 |
| | 0.05 | 6.164 | 7.582 | 8.774 | 9.823 | 10.769 | 11.639 | 12.449 | 13.208 | 13.927 | 17.072 | 19.721 |
| | 0.10 | 4.243 | 5.243 | 6.081 | 6.816 | 7.480 | 8.090 | 8.656 | 9.188 | 9.691 | 11.890 | 13.741 |
| | 0.20 | 2.828 | 3.531 | 4.116 | 4.628 | 5.089 | 5.512 | 5.904 | 6.272 | 6.620 | 8.138 | 9.414 |
| 3 | 0.01 | 7.447 | 8.565 | 9.453 | 10.201 | 10.853 | 11.436 | 11.966 | 12.453 | 12.904 | 14.796 | 16.300 |
| | 0.05 | 4.156 | 4.826 | 5.355 | 5.799 | 6.185 | 6.529 | 6.842 | 7.128 | 7.394 | 8.505 | 9.387 |
| | 0.10 | 3.149 | 3.690 | 4.115 | 4.471 | 4.780 | 5.055 | 5.304 | 5.532 | 5.744 | 6.627 | 7.326 |
| | 0.20 | 2.294 | 2.734 | 3.077 | 3.363 | 3.610 | 3.829 | 4.028 | 4.209 | 4.377 | 5.076 | 5.628 |
| 4 | 0.01 | 5.594 | 6.248 | 6.751 | 7.166 | 7.520 | 7.832 | 8.112 | 8.367 | 8.600 | 9.556 | 10.294 |
| | 0.05 | 3.481 | 3.941 | 4.290 | 4.577 | 4.822 | 5.036 | 5.228 | 5.402 | 5.562 | 6.214 | 6.714 |
| | 0.10 | 2.751 | 3.150 | 3.452 | 3.699 | 3.909 | 4.093 | 4.257 | 4.406 | 4.542 | 5.097 | 5.521 |
| | 0.20 | 2.084 | 2.434 | 2.697 | 2.911 | 3.092 | 3.250 | 3.391 | 3.518 | 3.635 | 4.107 | 4.468 |
| 5 | 0.01 | 4.771 | 5.243 | 5.599 | 5.888 | 6.133 | 6.346 | 6.535 | 6.706 | 6.862 | 7.491 | 7.968 |
| | 0.05 | 3.152 | 3.518 | 3.791 | 4.012 | 4.197 | 4.358 | 4.501 | 4.630 | 4.747 | 5.219 | 5.573 |
| | 0.10 | 2.549 | 2.882 | 3.129 | 3.327 | 3.493 | 3.638 | 3.765 | 3.880 | 3.985 | 4.403 | 4.718 |
| | 0.20 | 1.973 | 2.278 | 2.503 | 2.683 | 2.834 | 2.964 | 3.079 | 3.182 | 3.275 | 3.649 | 3.928 |
| 6 | 0.01 | 4.315 | 4.695 | 4.977 | 5.203 | 5.394 | 5.559 | 5.704 | 5.835 | 5.954 | 6.428 | 6.782 |
| | 0.05 | 2.959 | 3.274 | 3.505 | 3.690 | 3.845 | 3.978 | 4.095 | 4.200 | 4.296 | 4.675 | 4.956 |
| | 0.10 | 2.428 | 2.723 | 2.939 | 3.110 | 3.253 | 3.376 | 3.484 | 3.580 | 3.668 | 4.015 | 4.272 |
| | 0.20 | 1.904 | 2.184 | 2.387 | 2.547 | 2.681 | 2.795 | 2.895 | 2.985 | 3.066 | 3.385 | 3.620 |
| 7 | 0.01 | 4.027 | 4.353 | 4.591 | 4.782 | 4.941 | 5.078 | 5.198 | 5.306 | 5.404 | 5.791 | 6.077 |
| | 0.05 | 2.832 | 3.115 | 3.321 | 3.484 | 3.620 | 3.736 | 3.838 | 3.929 | 4.011 | 4.336 | 4.574 |
| | 0.10 | 2.347 | 2.618 | 2.814 | 2.969 | 3.097 | 3.206 | 3.302 | 3.388 | 3.465 | 3.768 | 3.990 |
| | 0.20 | 1.858 | 2.120 | 2.309 | 2.457 | 2.579 | 2.684 | 2.775 | 2.856 | 2.929 | 3.214 | 3.423 |
| 8 | 0.01 | 3.831 | 4.120 | 4.331 | 4.498 | 4.637 | 4.756 | 4.860 | 4.953 | 5.038 | 5.370 | 5.613 |
| | 0.05 | 2.743 | 3.005 | 3.193 | 3.342 | 3.464 | 3.569 | 3.661 | 3.743 | 3.816 | 4.105 | 4.316 |
| | 0.10 | 2.289 | 2.544 | 2.726 | 2.869 | 2.987 | 3.088 | 3.176 | 3.254 | 3.324 | 3.598 | 3.798 |
| | 0.20 | 1.824 | 2.075 | 2.254 | 2.393 | 2.508 | 2.605 | 2.690 | 2.765 | 2.832 | 3.095 | 3.286 |
| 9 | 0.01 | 3.688 | 3.952 | 4.143 | 4.294 | 4.419 | 4.526 | 4.619 | 4.703 | 4.778 | 5.072 | 5.287 |
| | 0.05 | 2.677 | 2.923 | 3.099 | 3.237 | 3.351 | 3.448 | 3.532 | 3.607 | 3.675 | 3.938 | 4.129 |
| | 0.10 | 2.246 | 2.488 | 2.661 | 2.796 | 2.907 | 3.001 | 3.083 | 3.155 | 3.221 | 3.474 | 3.658 |
| | 0.20 | 1.799 | 2.041 | 2.212 | 2.345 | 2.454 | 2.546 | 2.627 | 2.698 | 2.761 | 3.008 | 3.185 |
| 10 | 0.01 | 3.580 | 3.825 | 4.002 | 4.141 | 4.256 | 4.354 | 4.439 | 4.515 | 4.584 | 4.852 | 5.046 |
| | 0.05 | 2.626 | 2.860 | 3.027 | 3.157 | 3.264 | 3.355 | 3.434 | 3.505 | 3.568 | 3.813 | 3.989 |
| | 0.10 | 2.213 | 2.446 | 2.611 | 2.739 | 2.845 | 2.934 | 3.012 | 3.080 | 3.142 | 3.380 | 3.552 |
| | 0.20 | 1.779 | 2.014 | 2.180 | 2.308 | 2.413 | 2.501 | 2.578 | 2.646 | 2.706 | 2.941 | 3.106 |
| 11 | 0.01 | 3.495 | 3.726 | 3.892 | 4.022 | 4.129 | 4.221 | 4.300 | 4.371 | 4.434 | 4.682 | 4.860 |
| | 0.05 | 2.586 | 2.811 | 2.970 | 3.094 | 3.196 | 3.283 | 3.358 | 3.424 | 3.484 | 3.715 | 3.880 |
| | 0.10 | 2.186 | 2.412 | 2.571 | 2.695 | 2.796 | 2.881 | 2.955 | 3.021 | 3.079 | 3.306 | 3.468 |
| | 0.20 | 1.763 | 1.993 | 2.154 | 2.279 | 2.380 | 2.465 | 2.539 | 2.605 | 2.663 | 2.888 | 3.048 |
| 12 | 0.01 | 3.427 | 3.647 | 3.804 | 3.927 | 4.029 | 4.114 | 4.189 | 4.256 | 4.315 | 4.547 | 4.714 |
| | 0.05 | 2.553 | 2.770 | 2.924 | 3.044 | 3.141 | 3.224 | 3.296 | 3.359 | 3.416 | 3.636 | 3.793 |
| | 0.10 | 2.164 | 2.384 | 2.539 | 2.658 | 2.756 | 2.838 | 2.910 | 2.973 | 3.029 | 3.247 | 3.402 |
| | 0.20 | 1.750 | 1.975 | 2.133 | 2.254 | 2.353 | 2.436 | 2.508 | 2.571 | 2.628 | 2.845 | 2.999 |
| 13 | 0.01 | 3.371 | 3.582 | 3.733 | 3.850 | 3.946 | 4.028 | 4.099 | 4.162 | 4.218 | 4.438 | 4.595 |
| | 0.05 | 2.526 | 2.737 | 2.886 | 3.002 | 3.096 | 3.176 | 3.245 | 3.306 | 3.361 | 3.571 | 3.722 |
| | 0.10 | 2.146 | 2.361 | 2.512 | 2.628 | 2.723 | 2.803 | 2.872 | 2.933 | 2.988 | 3.198 | 3.347 |
| | 0.20 | 1.739 | 1.961 | 2.116 | 2.234 | 2.331 | 2.412 | 2.482 | 2.544 | 2.599 | 2.809 | 2.958 |
| 14 | 0.01 | 3.324 | 3.526 | 3.673 | 3.785 | 3.878 | 3.956 | 4.024 | 4.084 | 4.138 | 4.347 | 4.497 |
| | 0.05 | 2.503 | 2.709 | 2.854 | 2.967 | 3.058 | 3.135 | 3.202 | 3.261 | 3.314 | 3.518 | 3.662 |
| | 0.10 | 2.131 | 2.342 | 2.489 | 2.603 | 2.696 | 2.774 | 2.841 | 2.900 | 2.953 | 3.157 | 3.301 |
| | 0.20 | 1.730 | 1.949 | 2.101 | 2.217 | 2.312 | 2.392 | 2.460 | 2.520 | 2.574 | 2.779 | 2.924 |
| 15 | 0.01 | 3.285 | 3.482 | 3.622 | 3.731 | 3.820 | 3.895 | 3.961 | 4.019 | 4.071 | 4.271 | 4.414 |
| | 0.05 | 2.483 | 2.685 | 2.827 | 2.937 | 3.026 | 3.101 | 3.166 | 3.224 | 3.275 | 3.472 | 3.612 |
| | 0.10 | 2.118 | 2.325 | 2.470 | 2.582 | 2.672 | 2.748 | 2.814 | 2.872 | 2.924 | 3.122 | 3.262 |
| | 0.20 | 1.722 | 1.938 | 2.088 | 2.203 | 2.296 | 2.374 | 2.441 | 2.500 | 2.553 | 2.754 | 2.896 |

(*continued*)

Critical Values for Dunn's (Bonferroni's) Procedure

| | | Number of contrasts | | | | | | | | | | |
|---|---|---|---|---|---|---|---|---|---|---|---|---|
| $v$ | $\alpha$ | 2 | 3 | 4 | 5 | 6 | 7 | 8 | 9 | 10 | 15 | 20 |
| 16 | 0.01 | 3.251 | 3.443 | 3.579 | 3.684 | 3.771 | 3.844 | 3.907 | 3.963 | 4.013 | 4.206 | 4.344 |
| | 0.05 | 2.487 | 2.665 | 2.804 | 2.911 | 2.998 | 3.072 | 3.135 | 3.191 | 3.241 | 3.433 | 3.569 |
| | 0.10 | 2.106 | 2.311 | 2.453 | 2.563 | 2.652 | 2.726 | 2.791 | 2.848 | 2.898 | 3.092 | 3.228 |
| | 0.20 | 1.715 | 1.929 | 2.077 | 2.190 | 2.282 | 2.359 | 2.425 | 2.483 | 2.535 | 2.732 | 2.871 |
| 17 | 0.01 | 3.221 | 3.409 | 3.541 | 3.644 | 3.728 | 3.799 | 3.860 | 3.914 | 3.963 | 4.150 | 4.284 |
| | 0.05 | 2.452 | 2.647 | 2.783 | 2.889 | 2.974 | 3.046 | 3.108 | 3.163 | 3.212 | 3.399 | 3.532 |
| | 0.10 | 2.096 | 2.296 | 2.439 | 2.547 | 2.634 | 2.706 | 2.771 | 2.826 | 2.876 | 3.066 | 3.199 |
| | 0.20 | 1.709 | 1.921 | 2.068 | 2.179 | 2.270 | 2.346 | 2.411 | 2.468 | 2.519 | 2.713 | 2.649 |
| 18 | 0.01 | 3.195 | 3.379 | 3.508 | 3.609 | 3.691 | 3.760 | 3.820 | 3.872 | 3.920 | 4.102 | 4.231 |
| | 0.05 | 2.439 | 2.631 | 2.766 | 2.869 | 2.953 | 3.024 | 3.085 | 3.138 | 3.186 | 3.370 | 3.499 |
| | 0.10 | 2.088 | 2.287 | 2.426 | 2.532 | 2.619 | 2.691 | 2.753 | 2.806 | 2.857 | 3.043 | 3.174 |
| | 0.20 | 1.704 | 1.914 | 2.059 | 2.170 | 2.259 | 2.334 | 2.399 | 2.455 | 2.505 | 2.696 | 2.830 |
| 19 | 0.01 | 3.173 | 3.353 | 3.479 | 3.578 | 3.658 | 3.725 | 3.784 | 3.835 | 3.881 | 4.059 | 4.185 |
| | 0.05 | 2.427 | 2.617 | 2.750 | 2.852 | 2.934 | 3.004 | 3.064 | 3.116 | 3.163 | 3.343 | 3.470 |
| | 0.10 | 2.080 | 2.277 | 2.415 | 2.520 | 2.605 | 2.676 | 2.738 | 2.791 | 2.639 | 3.023 | 3.152 |
| | 0.20 | 1.699 | 1.906 | 2.052 | 2.161 | 2.250 | 2.324 | 2.388 | 2.443 | 2.493 | 2.682 | 2.613 |
| 20 | 0.01 | 3.152 | 3.329 | 3.454 | 3.550 | 3.629 | 3.695 | 3.752 | 3.802 | 3.848 | 4.021 | 4.144 |
| | 0.05 | 2.417 | 2.605 | 2.736 | 2.836 | 2.918 | 2.986 | 3.045 | 3.097 | 3.143 | 3.320 | 3.445 |
| | 0.10 | 2.073 | 2.269 | 2.405 | 2.508 | 2.593 | 2.663 | 2.724 | 2.777 | 2.824 | 3.005 | 3.132 |
| | 0.20 | 1.695 | 1.902 | 2.045 | 2.154 | 2.241 | 2.315 | 2.378 | 2.433 | 2.482 | 2.668 | 2.798 |
| 21 | 0.01 | 3.134 | 3.306 | 3.431 | 3.525 | 3.602 | 3.667 | 3.724 | 3.773 | 3.817 | 3.987 | 4.108 |
| | 0.05 | 2.408 | 2.594 | 2.723 | 2.822 | 2.903 | 2.970 | 3.028 | 3.080 | 3.125 | 3.300 | 3.422 |
| | 0.10 | 2.067 | 2.261 | 2.396 | 2.498 | 2.581 | 2.651 | 2.711 | 2.764 | 2.810 | 2.989 | 3.114 |
| | 0.20 | 1.691 | 1.897 | 2.039 | 2.147 | 2.234 | 2.306 | 2.369 | 2.424 | 2.472 | 2.656 | 2.785 |
| 22 | 0.01 | 3.118 | 3.289 | 3.410 | 3.503 | 3.579 | 3.643 | 3.698 | 3.747 | 3.790 | 3.957 | 4.075 |
| | 0.05 | 2.400 | 2.584 | 2.712 | 2.810 | 2.889 | 2.956 | 3.014 | 3.064 | 3.109 | 3.281 | 3.402 |
| | 0.10 | 2.061 | 2.254 | 2.387 | 2.489 | 2.572 | 2.641 | 2.700 | 2.752 | 2.798 | 2.974 | 3.098 |
| | 0.20 | 1.688 | 1.892 | 2.033 | 2.141 | 2.227 | 2.299 | 2.361 | 2.415 | 2.463 | 2.646 | 2.773 |
| 23 | 0.01 | 3.103 | 3.272 | 3.392 | 3.483 | 3.558 | 3.621 | 3.675 | 3.723 | 3.766 | 3.930 | 4.046 |
| | 0.05 | 2.392 | 2.574 | 2.701 | 2.798 | 2.877 | 2.943 | 3.000 | 3.050 | 3.094 | 3.264 | 3.383 |
| | 0.10 | 2.056 | 2.247 | 2.380 | 2.481 | 2.563 | 2.631 | 2.690 | 2.741 | 2.787 | 2.961 | 3.083 |
| | 0.20 | 1.685 | 1.888 | 2.028 | 2.135 | 2.221 | 2.292 | 2.354 | 2.407 | 2.455 | 2.636 | 2.762 |
| 24 | 0.01 | 3.089 | 3.257 | 3.375 | 3.465 | 3.539 | 3.601 | 3.654 | 3.702 | 3.744 | 3.905 | 4.019 |
| | 0.05 | 2.385 | 2.566 | 2.692 | 2.788 | 2.866 | 2.931 | 2.988 | 3.037 | 3.081 | 3.249 | 3.366 |
| | 0.10 | 2.051 | 2.241 | 2.373 | 2.473 | 2.554 | 2.622 | 2.680 | 2.731 | 2.777 | 2.949 | 3.070 |
| | 0.20 | 1.682 | 1.884 | 2.024 | 2.130 | 2.215 | 2.286 | 2.347 | 2.400 | 2.448 | 2.627 | 2.752 |
| 25 | 0.01 | 3.077 | 3.243 | 3.359 | 3.449 | 3.521 | 3.583 | 3.635 | 3.682 | 3.723 | 3.882 | 3.995 |
| | 0.05 | 2.379 | 2.558 | 2.683 | 2.779 | 2.856 | 2.921 | 2.976 | 3.025 | 3.069 | 3.235 | 3.351 |
| | 0.10 | 2.047 | 2.236 | 2.367 | 2.466 | 2.547 | 2.614 | 2.672 | 2.722 | 2.767 | 2.938 | 3.058 |
| | 0.20 | 1.679 | 1.881 | 2.020 | 2.125 | 2.210 | 2.280 | 2.341 | 2.394 | 2.441 | 2.619 | 2.743 |
| 26 | 0.01 | 3.066 | 3.230 | 3.345 | 3.433 | 3.505 | 3.566 | 3.618 | 3.664 | 3.705 | 3.862 | 3.972 |
| | 0.05 | 2.373 | 2.551 | 2.675 | 2.770 | 2.847 | 2.911 | 2.966 | 3.014 | 3.058 | 3.222 | 3.337 |
| | 0.10 | 2.043 | 2.231 | 2.361 | 2.460 | 2.540 | 2.607 | 2.664 | 2.714 | 2.759 | 2.928 | 3.047 |
| | 0.20 | 1.677 | 1.878 | 2.016 | 2.121 | 2.205 | 2.275 | 2.335 | 2.388 | 2.435 | 2.612 | 2.735 |
| 27 | 0.01 | 3.056 | 3.218 | 3.332 | 3.419 | 3.491 | 3.550 | 3.602 | 3.647 | 3.688 | 3.843 | 3.952 |
| | 0.05 | 2.368 | 2.545 | 2.668 | 2.762 | 2.838 | 2.902 | 2.956 | 3.004 | 3.047 | 3.210 | 3.324 |
| | 0.10 | 2.039 | 2.227 | 2.356 | 2.454 | 2.534 | 2.600 | 2.657 | 2.707 | 2.751 | 2.919 | 3.036 |
| | 0.20 | 1.675 | 1.875 | 2.012 | 2.117 | 2.201 | 2.270 | 2.330 | 2.383 | 2.429 | 2.605 | 2.727 |
| 28 | 0.01 | 3.046 | 3.207 | 3.320 | 3.407 | 3.477 | 3.536 | 3.587 | 3.632 | 3.672 | 3.825 | 3.933 |
| | 0.05 | 2.363 | 2.539 | 2.661 | 2.755 | 2.830 | 2.893 | 2.948 | 2.995 | 3.038 | 3.199 | 3.312 |
| | 0.10 | 2.036 | 2.222 | 2.351 | 2.449 | 2.528 | 2.594 | 2.650 | 2.700 | 2.744 | 2.911 | 3.027 |
| | 0.20 | 1.672 | 1.872 | 2.009 | 2.113 | 2.196 | 2.266 | 2.326 | 2.378 | 2.424 | 2.599 | 2.720 |
| 29 | 0.01 | 3.037 | 3.197 | 3.309 | 3.395 | 3.464 | 3.523 | 3.574 | 3.618 | 3.658 | 3.809 | 3.916 |
| | 0.05 | 2.358 | 2.534 | 2.655 | 2.748 | 2.823 | 2.886 | 2.940 | 2.987 | 3.029 | 3.189 | 3.301 |
| | 0.10 | 2.033 | 2.218 | 2.346 | 2.444 | 2.522 | 2.588 | 2.644 | 2.693 | 2.737 | 2.903 | 3.018 |
| | 0.20 | 1.671 | 1.869 | 2.006 | 2.110 | 2.193 | 2.262 | 2.321 | 2.373 | 2.419 | 2.593 | 2.713 |

(*continued*)

Critical Values for Dunn's (Bonferroni's) Procedure

| | | Number of contrasts | | | | | | | | | | |
|---|---|---|---|---|---|---|---|---|---|---|---|---|
| $v$ | $\alpha$ | 2 | 3 | 4 | 5 | 6 | 7 | 8 | 9 | 10 | 15 | 20 |
| 30 | 0.01 | 3.029 | 3.188 | 3.298 | 3.384 | 3.453 | 3.511 | 3.561 | 3.605 | 3.644 | 3.794 | 3.900 |
| | 0.05 | 2.354 | 2.526 | 2.649 | 2.742 | 2.816 | 2.878 | 2.932 | 2.979 | 3.021 | 3.180 | 3.291 |
| | 0.10 | 2.030 | 2.215 | 2.342 | 2.439 | 2.517 | 2.582 | 2.638 | 2.687 | 2.731 | 2.895 | 3.010 |
| | 0.20 | 1.669 | 1.867 | 2.003 | 2.106 | 2.189 | 2.258 | 2.317 | 2.369 | 2.414 | 2.587 | 2.707 |
| 40 | 0.01 | 2.970 | 3.121 | 3.225 | 3.305 | 3.370 | 3.425 | 3.472 | 3.513 | 3.549 | 3.689 | 3.787 |
| | 0.05 | 2.323 | 2.492 | 2.608 | 2.696 | 2.768 | 2.827 | 2.878 | 2.923 | 2.963 | 3.113 | 3.218 |
| | 0.10 | 2.009 | 2.189 | 2.312 | 2.406 | 2.481 | 2.544 | 2.597 | 2.644 | 2.686 | 2.843 | 2.952 |
| | 0.20 | 1.656 | 1.850 | 1.983 | 2.083 | 2.164 | 2.231 | 2.288 | 2.338 | 2.382 | 2.548 | 2.663 |
| 60 | 0.01 | 2.914 | 3.056 | 3.155 | 3.230 | 3.291 | 3.342 | 3.386 | 3.425 | 3.459 | 3.589 | 3.679 |
| | 0.05 | 2.294 | 2.456 | 2.568 | 2.653 | 2.721 | 2.777 | 2.826 | 2.869 | 2.906 | 3.049 | 3.148 |
| | 0.10 | 1.989 | 2.163 | 2.283 | 2.373 | 2.446 | 2.506 | 2.558 | 2.603 | 2.643 | 2.793 | 2.897 |
| | 0.20 | 1.643 | 1.834 | 1.963 | 2.061 | 2.139 | 2.204 | 2.259 | 2.308 | 2.350 | 2.511 | 2.621 |
| 120 | 0.01 | 2.859 | 2.994 | 3.087 | 3.158 | 3.215 | 3.263 | 3.304 | 3.340 | 3.372 | 3.493 | 3.577 |
| | 0.05 | 2.265 | 2.422 | 2.529 | 2.610 | 2.675 | 2.729 | 2.776 | 2.816 | 2.852 | 2.987 | 3.081 |
| | 0.10 | 1.968 | 2.136 | 2.254 | 2.342 | 2.411 | 2.469 | 2.519 | 2.562 | 2.600 | 2.744 | 2.843 |
| | 0.20 | 1.631 | 1.817 | 1.944 | 2.039 | 2.115 | 2.178 | 2.231 | 2.278 | 2.319 | 2.474 | 2.580 |
| ∞ | 0.01 | 2.806 | 2.934 | 3.022 | 3.089 | 3.143 | 3.188 | 3.226 | 3.260 | 3.289 | 3.402 | 3.480 |
| | 0.05 | 2.237 | 2.388 | 2.491 | 2.569 | 2.631 | 2.683 | 2.727 | 2.766 | 2.800 | 2.928 | 3.016 |
| | 0.10 | 1.949 | 2.114 | 2.226 | 2.311 | 2.378 | 2.434 | 2.482 | 2.523 | 2.560 | 2.697 | 2.791 |
| | 0.20 | 1.618 | 1.801 | 1.925 | 2.018 | 2.091 | 2.152 | 2.204 | 2.249 | 2.289 | 2.438 | 2.540 |

Critical Values for the Studentized Range Statistic, $\alpha = .10$

| $r$ \ $J$ or $r$ | 2 | 3 | 4 | 5 | 6 | 7 | 8 | 9 | 10 |
|---|---|---|---|---|---|---|---|---|---|
| 1 | 8.929 | 13.44 | 16.36 | 18.49 | 20.15 | 21.51 | 22.64 | 23.62 | 24.48 |
| 2 | 4.130 | 5.733 | 6.773 | 7.538 | 8.139 | 8.633 | 9.049 | 9.409 | 9.725 |
| 3 | 3.328 | 4.467 | 5.199 | 5.738 | 6.162 | 6.511 | 6.806 | 7.062 | 7.287 |
| 4 | 3.015 | 3.976 | 4.586 | 5.035 | 5.388 | 5.679 | 5.926 | 6.139 | 6.327 |
| 5 | 2.850 | 3.717 | 4.264 | 4.664 | 4.979 | 5.238 | 5.458 | 5.648 | 5.816 |
| 6 | 2.748 | 3.559 | 4.065 | 4.435 | 4.726 | 4.966 | 5.168 | 5.344 | 5.499 |
| 7 | 2.680 | 3.451 | 3.931 | 4.280 | 4.555 | 4.780 | 4.972 | 5.137 | 5.283 |
| 8 | 2.630 | 3.374 | 3.834 | 4.169 | 4.431 | 4.646 | 4.829 | 4.987 | 5.126 |
| 9 | 2.592 | 3.316 | 3.761 | 4.084 | 4.337 | 4.545 | 4.721 | 4.873 | 5.007 |
| 10 | 2.563 | 3.270 | 3.704 | 4.018 | 4.264 | 4.465 | 4.636 | 4.783 | 4.913 |
| 11 | 2.540 | 3.234 | 3.658 | 3.965 | 4.205 | 4.401 | 4.568 | 4.711 | 4.838 |
| 12 | 2.521 | 3.204 | 3.621 | 3.922 | 4.156 | 4.349 | 4.511 | 4.652 | 4.776 |
| 13 | 2.505 | 3.179 | 3.589 | 3.885 | 4.116 | 4.305 | 4.464 | 4.602 | 4.724 |
| 14 | 2.491 | 3.158 | 3.563 | 3.854 | 4.081 | 4.267 | 4.424 | 4.560 | 4.680 |
| 15 | 2.479 | 3.140 | 3.540 | 3.828 | 4.052 | 4.235 | 4.390 | 4.524 | 4.641 |
| 16 | 2.469 | 3.124 | 3.520 | 3.804 | 4.026 | 4.207 | 4.360 | 4.492 | 4.608 |
| 17 | 2.460 | 3.110 | 3.503 | 3.784 | 4.004 | 4.183 | 4.334 | 4.464 | 4.579 |
| 18 | 2.452 | 3.098 | 3.488 | 3.767 | 3.984 | 4.161 | 4.311 | 4.440 | 4.554 |
| 19 | 2.445 | 3.087 | 3.474 | 3.751 | 3.966 | 4.142 | 4.290 | 4.418 | 4.531 |
| 20 | 2.439 | 3.078 | 3.462 | 3.736 | 3.950 | 4.124 | 4.271 | 4.398 | 4.510 |
| 24 | 2.420 | 3.047 | 3.423 | 3.692 | 3.900 | 4.070 | 4.213 | 4.336 | 4.445 |
| 30 | 2.400 | 3.017 | 3.386 | 3.648 | 3.851 | 4.016 | 4.155 | 4.275 | 4.381 |
| 40 | 2.381 | 2.988 | 3.349 | 3.605 | 3.803 | 3.963 | 4.099 | 4.215 | 4.317 |
| 60 | 2.363 | 2.959 | 3.312 | 3.562 | 3.755 | 3.911 | 4.042 | 4.155 | 4.254 |
| 120 | 2.344 | 2.930 | 3.276 | 3.520 | 3.707 | 3.859 | 3.987 | 4.096 | 4.191 |
| ∞ | 2.326 | 2.902 | 3.240 | 3.478 | 3.661 | 3.808 | 3.931 | 4.037 | 4.129 |

| $r$ \ $J$ or $r$ | 11 | 12 | 13 | 14 | 15 | 16 | 17 | 18 | 19 |
|---|---|---|---|---|---|---|---|---|---|
| 1 | 25.24 | 25.92 | 26.54 | 27.10 | 27.62 | 28.10 | 28.54 | 28.96 | 29.35 |
| 2 | 10.01 | 10.26 | 10.49 | 10.70 | 10.89 | 11.07 | 11.24 | 11.39 | 11.54 |
| 3 | 7.487 | 7.667 | 7.832 | 7.982 | 8.120 | 8.249 | 8.368 | 8.479 | 8.584 |
| 4 | 6.495 | 6.645 | 6.783 | 6.909 | 7.025 | 7.133 | 7.233 | 7.327 | 7.414 |
| 5 | 5.966 | 6.101 | 6.223 | 6.336 | 6.440 | 6.536 | 6.626 | 6.710 | 6.789 |
| 6 | 5.637 | 5.762 | 5.875 | 5.979 | 6.075 | 6.164 | 6.247 | 6.325 | 6.398 |
| 7 | 5.413 | 5.530 | 5.637 | 5.735 | 5.826 | 5.910 | 5.988 | 6.061 | 6.130 |
| 8 | 5.250 | 5.362 | 5.464 | 5.558 | 5.644 | 5.724 | 5.799 | 5.869 | 5.935 |
| 9 | 5.127 | 5.234 | 5.333 | 5.423 | 5.506 | 5.583 | 5.655 | 5.723 | 5.786 |
| 10 | 5.029 | 5.134 | 5.229 | 5.317 | 5.397 | 5.472 | 5.542 | 5.607 | 5.668 |
| 11 | 4.951 | 5.053 | 5.146 | 5.231 | 5.309 | 5.382 | 5.450 | 5.514 | 5.573 |
| 12 | 4.886 | 4.986 | 5.077 | 5.160 | 5.236 | 5.308 | 5.374 | 5.436 | 5.495 |
| 13 | 4.832 | 4.930 | 5.019 | 5.100 | 5.176 | 5.245 | 5.311 | 5.372 | 5.429 |
| 14 | 4.786 | 4.882 | 4.970 | 5.050 | 5.124 | 5.192 | 5.256 | 5.316 | 5.373 |
| 15 | 4.746 | 4.841 | 4.927 | 5.006 | 5.079 | 5.147 | 5.209 | 5.269 | 5.324 |
| 16 | 4.712 | 4.805 | 4.890 | 4.968 | 5.040 | 5.107 | 5.169 | 5.227 | 5.282 |
| 17 | 4.682 | 4.774 | 4.858 | 4.935 | 5.005 | 5.071 | 5.133 | 5.190 | 5.244 |
| 18 | 4.655 | 4.746 | 4.829 | 4.905 | 4.975 | 5.040 | 5.101 | 5.158 | 5.211 |
| 19 | 4.631 | 4.721 | 4.803 | 4.879 | 4.948 | 5.012 | 5.073 | 5.129 | 5.182 |
| 20 | 4.609 | 4.699 | 4.730 | 4.855 | 4.924 | 4.987 | 5.047 | 5.103 | 5.155 |
| 24 | 4.541 | 4.628 | 4.708 | 4.780 | 4.847 | 4.909 | 4.966 | 5.021 | 5.071 |
| 30 | 4.474 | 4.559 | 4.635 | 4.706 | 4.770 | 4.830 | 4.886 | 4.939 | 4.988 |
| 40 | 4.408 | 4.490 | 4.564 | 4.632 | 4.695 | 4.752 | 4.807 | 4.857 | 4.905 |
| 60 | 4.342 | 4.421 | 4.493 | 4.558 | 4.619 | 4.675 | 4.727 | 4.775 | 4.821 |
| 120 | 4.276 | 4.353 | 4.422 | 4.485 | 4.543 | 4.597 | 4.647 | 4.694 | 4.738 |
| ∞ | 4.211 | 4.285 | 4.351 | 4.412 | 4.468 | 4.519 | 4.568 | 4.612 | 4.654 |

$J$ for Tukey, $r$ for Newman-Keuls

(*continued*)

Critical Values for the Studentized Range Statistic, α = .05

| v \ J or r | 2 | 3 | 4 | 5 | 6 | 7 | 8 | 9 | 10 |
|---|---|---|---|---|---|---|---|---|---|
| 1 | 17.97 | 26.98 | 32.82 | 37.08 | 40.41 | 43.12 | 45.40 | 47.36 | 49.07 |
| 2 | 6.085 | 8.331 | 9.798 | 10.88 | 11.74 | 12.44 | 13.03 | 13.54 | 13.99 |
| 3 | 4.501 | 5.910 | 6.825 | 7.502 | 8.037 | 8.478 | 8.853 | 9.177 | 9.462 |
| 4 | 3.927 | 5.040 | 5.757 | 6.287 | 6.707 | 7.053 | 7.347 | 7.602 | 7.826 |
| 5 | 3.635 | 4.602 | 5.218 | 5.673 | 6.033 | 6.330 | 6.582 | 6.802 | 6.995 |
| 6 | 3.461 | 4.339 | 4.896 | 5.305 | 5.628 | 5.895 | 6.122 | 6.319 | 6.493 |
| 7 | 3.344 | 4.165 | 4.681 | 5.060 | 5.359 | 5.606 | 5.815 | 5.998 | 6.158 |
| 8 | 3.261 | 4.041 | 4.529 | 4.886 | 5.167 | 5.399 | 5.597 | 5.767 | 5.918 |
| 9 | 3.199 | 3.949 | 4.415 | 4.756 | 5.024 | 5.244 | 5.432 | 5.595 | 5.739 |
| 10 | 3.151 | 3.877 | 4.327 | 4.654 | 4.912 | 5.124 | 5.305 | 5.461 | 5.599 |
| 11 | 3.113 | 3.820 | 4.256 | 4.574 | 4.823 | 5.028 | 5.202 | 5.353 | 5.487 |
| 12 | 3.082 | 3.773 | 4.199 | 4.508 | 4.751 | 4.950 | 5.119 | 5.265 | 5.395 |
| 13 | 3.055 | 3.735 | 4.151 | 4.453 | 4.690 | 4.885 | 5.049 | 5.192 | 5.318 |
| 14 | 3.033 | 3.702 | 4.111 | 4.407 | 4.639 | 4.829 | 4.990 | 5.131 | 5.254 |
| 15 | 3.014 | 3.674 | 4.076 | 4.367 | 4.595 | 4.782 | 4.940 | 5.077 | 5.198 |
| 16 | 2.998 | 3.649 | 4.046 | 4.333 | 4.557 | 4.741 | 4.897 | 5.031 | 5.150 |
| 17 | 2.984 | 3.628 | 4.020 | 4.303 | 4.524 | 4.705 | 4.858 | 4.991 | 5.108 |
| 18 | 2.971 | 3.609 | 3.997 | 4.277 | 4.495 | 4.673 | 4.824 | 4.956 | 5.071 |
| 19 | 2.960 | 3.593 | 3.977 | 4.253 | 4.469 | 4.645 | 4.794 | 4.924 | 5.038 |
| 20 | 2.950 | 3.578 | 3.958 | 4.232 | 4.445 | 4.620 | 4.768 | 4.896 | 5.008 |
| 24 | 2.919 | 3.532 | 3.901 | 4.166 | 4.373 | 4.541 | 4.684 | 4.807 | 4.915 |
| 30 | 2.888 | 3.486 | 3.845 | 4.102 | 4.302 | 4.464 | 4.602 | 4.720 | 4.824 |
| 40 | 2.858 | 3.442 | 3.791 | 4.039 | 4.232 | 4.389 | 4.521 | 4.635 | 4.735 |
| 60 | 2.829 | 3.399 | 3.737 | 3.977 | 4.163 | 4.314 | 4.441 | 4.550 | 4.646 |
| 120 | 2.800 | 3.356 | 3.685 | 3.917 | 4.096 | 4.241 | 4.363 | 4.468 | 4.560 |
| ∞ | 2.772 | 3.314 | 3.633 | 3.858 | 4.030 | 4.170 | 4.286 | 4.387 | 4.474 |

| v \ J or r | 11 | 12 | 13 | 14 | 15 | 16 | 17 | 18 | 19 |
|---|---|---|---|---|---|---|---|---|---|
| 1 | 50.59 | 51.96 | 53.20 | 54.33 | 55.36 | 56.32 | 57.22 | 58.04 | 58.83 |
| 2 | 14.39 | 14.75 | 15.08 | 15.38 | 15.65 | 15.91 | 16.14 | 16.37 | 16.57 |
| 3 | 9.717 | 9.946 | 10.15 | 10.35 | 10.53 | 10.69 | 10.84 | 10.98 | 11.11 |
| 4 | 8.027 | 8.208 | 8.373 | 8.525 | 8.664 | 8.794 | 8.914 | 9.028 | 9.134 |
| 5 | 7.168 | 7.324 | 7.466 | 7.596 | 7.717 | 7.828 | 7.932 | 8.030 | 8.122 |
| 6 | 6.649 | 6.789 | 6.917 | 7.034 | 7.143 | 7.244 | 7.338 | 7.426 | 7.508 |
| 7 | 6.302 | 6.431 | 6.550 | 6.658 | 6.759 | 6.852 | 6.939 | 7.020 | 7.097 |
| 8 | 6.054 | 6.175 | 6.287 | 6.389 | 6.483 | 6.571 | 6.653 | 6.729 | 6.802 |
| 9 | 5.867 | 5.983 | 6.089 | 6.186 | 6.276 | 6.359 | 6.437 | 6.510 | 6.579 |
| 10 | 5.722 | 5.833 | 5.935 | 6.028 | 6.114 | 6.194 | 6.269 | 6.339 | 6.405 |
| 11 | 5.605 | 5.713 | 5.811 | 5.901 | 5.984 | 6.062 | 6.134 | 6.202 | 6.265 |
| 12 | 5.511 | 5.615 | 5.710 | 5.798 | 5.878 | 5.953 | 6.023 | 6.089 | 6.151 |
| 13 | 5.431 | 5.533 | 5.625 | 5.711 | 5.789 | 5.862 | 5.931 | 5.995 | 6.055 |
| 14 | 5.364 | 5.463 | 5.554 | 5.637 | 5.714 | 5.785 | 5.852 | 5.915 | 5.974 |
| 15 | 5.306 | 5.404 | 5.493 | 5.574 | 5.649 | 5.720 | 5.785 | 5.846 | 5.904 |
| 16 | 5.256 | 5.352 | 5.439 | 5.520 | 5.593 | 5.662 | 5.727 | 5.786 | 5.843 |
| 17 | 5.212 | 5.307 | 5.392 | 5.471 | 5.544 | 5.612 | 5.675 | 5.734 | 5.790 |
| 18 | 5.174 | 5.267 | 5.352 | 5.429 | 5.501 | 5.568 | 5.630 | 5.688 | 5.743 |
| 19 | 5.140 | 5.231 | 5.315 | 5.391 | 5.462 | 5.528 | 5.589 | 5.647 | 5.701 |
| 20 | 5.108 | 5.199 | 5.282 | 5.357 | 5.427 | 5.493 | 5.553 | 5.610 | 5.663 |
| 24 | 5.012 | 5.099 | 5.179 | 5.251 | 5.319 | 5.381 | 5.439 | 5.494 | 5.545 |
| 30 | 4.917 | 5.001 | 5.077 | 5.147 | 5.211 | 5.271 | 5.327 | 5.379 | 5.429 |
| 40 | 4.824 | 4.904 | 4.977 | 5.044 | 5.106 | 5.163 | 5.216 | 5.266 | 5.313 |
| 60 | 4.732 | 4.808 | 4.878 | 4.942 | 5.001 | 5.056 | 5.107 | 5.154 | 5.199 |
| 120 | 4.641 | 4.714 | 4.781 | 4.842 | 4.898 | 4.950 | 4.998 | 5.044 | 5.086 |
| ∞ | 4.552 | 4.622 | 4.685 | 4.743 | 4.796 | 4.845 | 4.891 | 4.934 | 4.974 |

(*continued*)

Critical Values for the Studentized Range Statistic, $\alpha = .01$

| $v$ \ $J$ or $r$ | 2 | 3 | 4 | 5 | 6 | 7 | 8 | 9 | 10 |
|---|---|---|---|---|---|---|---|---|---|
| 1 | 90.03 | 135.0 | 164.3 | 185.6 | 202.2 | 215.8 | 227.2 | 237.0 | 245.6 |
| 2 | 14.04 | 19.02 | 22.29 | 24.72 | 26.63 | 28.20 | 29.53 | 30.68 | 31.69 |
| 3 | 8.261 | 10.62 | 12.17 | 13.33 | 14.24 | 15.00 | 15.64 | 16.20 | 16.69 |
| 4 | 6.512 | 8.120 | 9.173 | 9.958 | 10.58 | 11.10 | 11.55 | 11.93 | 12.27 |
| 5 | 5.702 | 6.976 | 7.804 | 8.421 | 8.913 | 9.321 | 9.669 | 9.972 | 10.24 |
| 6 | 5.243 | 6.331 | 7.033 | 7.556 | 7.973 | 8.318 | 8.613 | 8.869 | 9.097 |
| 7 | 4.949 | 5.919 | 6.543 | 7.005 | 7.373 | 7.679 | 7.939 | 8.166 | 8.368 |
| 8 | 4.746 | 5.635 | 6.204 | 6.625 | 6.960 | 7.237 | 7.474 | 7.681 | 7.863 |
| 9 | 4.596 | 5.428 | 5.957 | 6.348 | 6.658 | 6.915 | 7.134 | 7.325 | 7.495 |
| 10 | 4.482 | 5.270 | 5.769 | 6.136 | 6.428 | 6.669 | 6.875 | 7.055 | 7.213 |
| 11 | 4.392 | 5.146 | 5.621 | 5.970 | 6.247 | 6.476 | 6.672 | 6.842 | 6.992 |
| 12 | 4.320 | 5.046 | 5.502 | 5.836 | 6.101 | 6.321 | 6.507 | 6.670 | 6.814 |
| 13 | 4.260 | 4.964 | 5.404 | 5.727 | 5.981 | 6.192 | 6.372 | 6.528 | 6.667 |
| 14 | 4.210 | 4.895 | 5.322 | 5.634 | 5.881 | 6.085 | 6.258 | 6.409 | 6.543 |
| 15 | 4.168 | 4.836 | 5.252 | 5.556 | 5.796 | 5.994 | 6.162 | 6.309 | 6.439 |
| 16 | 4.131 | 4.786 | 5.192 | 5.489 | 5.722 | 5.915 | 6.079 | 6.222 | 6.349 |
| 17 | 4.099 | 4.742 | 5.140 | 5.430 | 5.659 | 5.847 | 6.007 | 6.147 | 6.270 |
| 18 | 4.071 | 4.703 | 5.094 | 5.379 | 5.603 | 5.788 | 5.944 | 6.081 | 6.201 |
| 19 | 4.046 | 4.670 | 5.054 | 5.334 | 5.554 | 5.735 | 5.889 | 6.022 | 6.141 |
| 20 | 4.024 | 4.639 | 5.018 | 5.294 | 5.510 | 5.688 | 5.839 | 5.970 | 6.087 |
| 24 | 3.956 | 4.546 | 4.907 | 5.168 | 5.374 | 5.542 | 5.685 | 5.809 | 5.919 |
| 30 | 3.889 | 4.455 | 4.799 | 5.048 | 5.242 | 5.401 | 5.536 | 5.653 | 5.756 |
| 40 | 3.825 | 4.367 | 4.696 | 4.931 | 5.114 | 5.265 | 5.392 | 5.502 | 5.599 |
| 60 | 3.762 | 4.282 | 4.595 | 4.818 | 4.991 | 5.133 | 5.253 | 5.356 | 5.447 |
| 120 | 3.702 | 4.200 | 4.497 | 4.709 | 4.872 | 5.005 | 5.118 | 5.214 | 5.299 |
| $\infty$ | 3.643 | 4.120 | 4.403 | 4.603 | 4.757 | 4.882 | 4.987 | 5.078 | 5.157 |

| $v$ \ $J$ or $r$ | 11 | 12 | 13 | 14 | 15 | 16 | 17 | 18 | 19 |
|---|---|---|---|---|---|---|---|---|---|
| 1 | 253.2 | 260.0 | 266.2 | 271.8 | 277.0 | 281.8 | 286.3 | 290.4 | 294.3 |
| 2 | 32.59 | 33.40 | 34.13 | 34.81 | 35.43 | 36.00 | 36.53 | 37.03 | 37.50 |
| 3 | 17.13 | 17.53 | 17.89 | 18.22 | 18.52 | 18.81 | 19.07 | 19.32 | 19.55 |
| 4 | 12.57 | 12.84 | 13.09 | 13.32 | 13.53 | 13.73 | 13.91 | 14.08 | 14.24 |
| 5 | 10.48 | 10.70 | 10.89 | 11.08 | 11.24 | 11.40 | 11.55 | 11.68 | 11.81 |
| 6 | 9.301 | 9.485 | 9.653 | 9.808 | 9.951 | 10.08 | 10.21 | 10.32 | 10.43 |
| 7 | 8.548 | 8.711 | 8.860 | 8.997 | 9.124 | 9.242 | 9.353 | 9.456 | 9.554 |
| 8 | 8.027 | 8.176 | 8.312 | 8.436 | 8.552 | 8.659 | 8.760 | 8.854 | 8.943 |
| 9 | 7.647 | 7.784 | 7.910 | 8.025 | 8.132 | 8.232 | 8.325 | 8.412 | 8.495 |
| 10 | 7.356 | 7.485 | 7.603 | 7.712 | 7.812 | 7.906 | 7.993 | 8.076 | 8.153 |
| 11 | 7.128 | 7.250 | 7.362 | 7.465 | 7.560 | 7.649 | 7.732 | 7.809 | 7.883 |
| 12 | 6.943 | 7.060 | 7.167 | 7.265 | 7.356 | 7.441 | 7.520 | 7.594 | 7.665 |
| 13 | 6.791 | 6.903 | 7.006 | 7.101 | 7.188 | 7.269 | 7.345 | 7.417 | 7.485 |
| 14 | 6.664 | 6.772 | 6.871 | 6.962 | 7.047 | 7.126 | 7.199 | 7.268 | 7.333 |
| 15 | 6.555 | 6.660 | 6.757 | 6.845 | 6.927 | 7.003 | 7.074 | 7.142 | 7.204 |
| 16 | 6.462 | 6.564 | 6.658 | 6.744 | 6.823 | 6.898 | 6.967 | 7.032 | 7.093 |
| 17 | 6.381 | 6.480 | 6.572 | 6.656 | 6.734 | 6.806 | 6.873 | 6.937 | 6.997 |
| 18 | 6.310 | 6.407 | 6.497 | 6.579 | 6.655 | 6.725 | 6.792 | 6.854 | 6.912 |
| 19 | 6.247 | 6.342 | 6.430 | 6.510 | 6.585 | 6.654 | 6.719 | 6.780 | 6.837 |
| 20 | 6.191 | 6.285 | 6.371 | 6.450 | 6.523 | 6.591 | 6.654 | 6.714 | 6.771 |
| 24 | 6.017 | 6.106 | 6.186 | 6.261 | 6.330 | 6.394 | 6.453 | 6.510 | 6.563 |
| 30 | 5.849 | 5.932 | 6.008 | 6.078 | 6.143 | 6.203 | 6.259 | 6.311 | 6.361 |
| 40 | 5.686 | 5.764 | 5.835 | 5.900 | 5.961 | 6.017 | 6.069 | 6.119 | 6.165 |
| 60 | 5.528 | 5.601 | 5.667 | 5.728 | 5.785 | 5.837 | 5.886 | 5.931 | 5.974 |
| 120 | 5.375 | 5.443 | 5.505 | 5.562 | 5.614 | 5.662 | 5.708 | 5.750 | 5.790 |
| $\infty$ | 5.227 | 5.290 | 5.348 | 5.400 | 5.448 | 5.493 | 5.535 | 5.574 | 5.611 |

## Critical Values for the Bryant-Paulson Procedure, $\alpha = .05$

| $v$ | $J = 2$ | $J = 3$ | $J = 4$ | $J = 5$ | $J = 6$ | $J = 7$ | $J = 8$ | $J = 10$ | $J = 12$ | $J = 16$ | $J = 20$ |
|---|---|---|---|---|---|---|---|---|---|---|---|
| | | | | | $X = 1$ | | | | | | |
| 2 | 7·96 | 11·00 | 12·99 | 14·46 | 15·61 | 16·56 | 17·36 | 18·65 | 19·68 | 21·23 | 22·40 |
| 3 | 5·42 | 7·18 | 8·32 | 9·17 | 9·84 | 10·39 | 10·86 | 11·62 | 12·22 | 13·14 | 13·83 |
| 4 | 4·51 | 5·84 | 6·69 | 7·32 | 7·82 | 8·23 | 8·58 | 9·15 | 9·61 | 10·30 | 10·82 |
| 5 | 4·06 | 5·17 | 5·88 | 6·40 | 6·82 | 7·16 | 7·45 | 7·93 | 8·30 | 8·88 | 9·32 |
| 6 | 3·79 | 4·78 | 5·40 | 5·86 | 6·23 | 6·53 | 6·78 | 7·20 | 7·53 | 8·04 | 8·43 |
| 7 | 3·62 | 4·52 | 5·09 | 5·51 | 5·84 | 6·11 | 6·34 | 6·72 | 7·03 | 7·49 | 7·84 |
| 8 | 3·49 | 4·34 | 4·87 | 5·26 | 5·57 | 5·82 | 6·03 | 6·39 | 6·67 | 7·10 | 7·43 |
| 10 | 3·32 | 4·10 | 4·58 | 4·93 | 5·21 | 5·43 | 5·63 | 5·94 | 6·19 | 6·58 | 6·87 |
| 12 | 3·22 | 3·95 | 4·40 | 4·73 | 4·98 | 5·19 | 5·37 | 5·67 | 5·90 | 6·26 | 6·53 |
| 14 | 3·15 | 3·85 | 4·28 | 4·59 | 4·83 | 5·03 | 5·20 | 5·48 | 5·70 | 6·03 | 6·29 |
| 16 | 3·10 | 3·77 | 4·19 | 4·49 | 4·72 | 4·91 | 5·07 | 5·34 | 5·55 | 5·87 | 6·12 |
| 18 | 3·06 | 3·72 | 4·12 | 4·41 | 4·63 | 4·82 | 4·98 | 5·23 | 5·44 | 5·75 | 5·98 |
| 20 | 3·03 | 3·67 | 4·07 | 4·35 | 4·57 | 4·75 | 4·90 | 5·15 | 5·35 | 5·65 | 5·88 |
| 24 | 2·98 | 3·61 | 3·99 | 4·26 | 4·47 | 4·65 | 4·79 | 5·03 | 5·22 | 5·51 | 5·73 |
| 30 | 2·94 | 3·55 | 3·91 | 4·18 | 4·38 | 4·54 | 4·69 | 4·91 | 5·09 | 5·37 | 5·58 |
| 40 | 2·89 | 3·49 | 3·84 | 4·09 | 4·29 | 4·45 | 4·58 | 4·80 | 4·97 | 5·23 | 5·43 |
| 60 | 2·85 | 3·43 | 3·77 | 4·01 | 4·20 | 4·35 | 4·48 | 4·69 | 4·85 | 5·10 | 5·29 |
| 120 | 2·81 | 3·37 | 3·70 | 3·93 | 4·11 | 4·26 | 4·38 | 4·58 | 4·73 | 4·97 | 5·15 |
| | | | | | $X = 2$ | | | | | | |
| 2 | 9·50 | 13·18 | 15·59 | 17·36 | 18·75 | 19·89 | 20·86 | 22·42 | 23·66 | 25·54 | 26·94 |
| 3 | 6·21 | 8·27 | 9·60 | 10·59 | 11·37 | 12·01 | 12·56 | 13·44 | 14·15 | 15·22 | 16·02 |
| 4 | 5·04 | 6·54 | 7·51 | 8·23 | 8·80 | 9·26 | 9·66 | 10·31 | 10·83 | 11·61 | 12·21 |
| 5 | 4·45 | 5·68 | 6·48 | 7·06 | 7·52 | 7·90 | 8·23 | 8·76 | 9·18 | 9·83 | 10·31 |
| 6 | 4·10 | 5·18 | 5·87 | 6·37 | 6·77 | 7·10 | 7·38 | 7·84 | 8·21 | 8·77 | 9·20 |
| 7 | 3·87 | 4·85 | 5·47 | 5·92 | 6·28 | 6·58 | 6·83 | 7·24 | 7·57 | 8·08 | 8·46 |
| 8 | 3·70 | 4·61 | 5·19 | 5·61 | 5·94 | 6·21 | 6·44 | 6·82 | 7·12 | 7·59 | 7·94 |
| 10 | 3·49 | 4·31 | 4·82 | 5·19 | 5·49 | 5·73 | 5·93 | 6·27 | 6·54 | 6·95 | 7·26 |
| 12 | 3·35 | 4·12 | 4·59 | 4·93 | 5·20 | 5·43 | 5·62 | 5·92 | 6·17 | 6·55 | 6·83 |
| 14 | 3·26 | 3·99 | 4·44 | 4·76 | 5·01 | 5·22 | 5·40 | 5·69 | 5·92 | 6·27 | 6·54 |
| 16 | 3·19 | 3·90 | 4·32 | 4·63 | 4·88 | 5·07 | 5·24 | 5·52 | 5·74 | 6·07 | 6·33 |
| 18 | 3·14 | 3·82 | 4·24 | 4·54 | 4·77 | 4·96 | 5·13 | 5·39 | 5·60 | 5·92 | 6·17 |
| 20 | 3·10 | 3·77 | 4·17 | 4·46 | 4·69 | 4·88 | 5·03 | 5·29 | 5·49 | 5·81 | 6·04 |
| 24 | 3·04 | 3·69 | 4·08 | 4·35 | 4·57 | 4·75 | 4·90 | 5·14 | 5·34 | 5·63 | 5·86 |
| 30 | 2·99 | 3·61 | 3·98 | 4·25 | 4·46 | 4·62 | 4·77 | 5·00 | 5·18 | 5·46 | 5·68 |
| 40 | 2·93 | 3·53 | 3·89 | 4·15 | 4·34 | 4·50 | 4·64 | 4·86 | 5·04 | 5·30 | 5·50 |
| 60 | 2·88 | 3·46 | 3·80 | 4·05 | 4·24 | 4·39 | 4·52 | 4·73 | 4·89 | 5·14 | 5·33 |
| 120 | 2·82 | 3·38 | 3·72 | 3·95 | 4·13 | 4·28 | 4·40 | 4·60 | 4·75 | 4·99 | 5·17 |

$X$ is the number of covariates

(*continued*)

Critical Values for the Bryant-Paulson Procedure, $\alpha = .05$

| $v$ | $J = 2$ | $J = 3$ | $J = 4$ | $J = 5$ | $J = 6$ | $J = 7$ | $J = 8$ | $J = 10$ | $J = 12$ | $J = 16$ | $J = 20$ |
|---|---|---|---|---|---|---|---|---|---|---|---|
| | | | | | $X = 3$ | | | | | | |
| 2 | 10·83 | 15·06 | 17·82 | 19·85 | 21·45 | 22·76 | 23·86 | 25·66 | 27·08 | 29·23 | 30·83 |
| 3 | 6·92 | 9·23 | 10·73 | 11·84 | 12·72 | 13·44 | 14·06 | 15·05 | 15·84 | 17·05 | 17·95 |
| 4 | 5·51 | 7·18 | 8·25 | 9·05 | 9·67 | 10·19 | 10·63 | 11·35 | 11·92 | 12·79 | 13·45 |
| 5 | 4·81 | 6·16 | 7·02 | 7·66 | 8·17 | 8·58 | 8·94 | 9·52 | 9·98 | 10·69 | 11·22 |
| 6 | 4·38 | 5·55 | 6·30 | 6·84 | 7·28 | 7·64 | 7·94 | 8·44 | 8·83 | 9·44 | 9·90 |
| 7 | 4·11 | 5·16 | 5·82 | 6·31 | 6·70 | 7·01 | 7·29 | 7·73 | 8·08 | 8·63 | 9·03 |
| 8 | 3·91 | 4·88 | 5·49 | 5·93 | 6·29 | 6·58 | 6·83 | 7·23 | 7·55 | 8·05 | 8·42 |
| 10 | 3·65 | 4·51 | 5·05 | 5·44 | 5·75 | 6·01 | 6·22 | 6·58 | 6·86 | 7·29 | 7·62 |
| 12 | 3·48 | 4·28 | 4·78 | 5·14 | 5·42 | 5·65 | 5·85 | 6·17 | 6·43 | 6·82 | 7·12 |
| 14 | 3·37 | 4·13 | 4·59 | 4·93 | 5·19 | 5·41 | 5·59 | 5·89 | 6·13 | 6·50 | 6·78 |
| 16 | 3·29 | 4·01 | 4·46 | 4·78 | 5·03 | 5·23 | 5·41 | 5·69 | 5·92 | 6·27 | 6·53 |
| 18 | 3·23 | 3·93 | 4·35 | 4·66 | 4·90 | 5·10 | 5·27 | 5·54 | 5·76 | 6·09 | 6·34 |
| 20 | 3·18 | 3·86 | 4·28 | 4·57 | 4·81 | 5·00 | 5·16 | 5·42 | 5·63 | 5·96 | 6·20 |
| 24 | 3·11 | 3·76 | 4·16 | 4·44 | 4·67 | 4·85 | 5·00 | 5·25 | 5·45 | 5·75 | 5·98 |
| 30 | 3·04 | 3·67 | 4·05 | 4·32 | 4·53 | 4·70 | 4·85 | 5·08 | 5·27 | 5·56 | 5·78 |
| 40 | 2·97 | 3·57 | 3·94 | 4·20 | 4·40 | 4·56 | 4·70 | 4·92 | 5·10 | 5·37 | 5·57 |
| 60 | 2·90 | 3·49 | 3·83 | 4·08 | 4·27 | 4·43 | 4·56 | 4·77 | 4·93 | 5·19 | 5·38 |
| 120 | 2·84 | 3·40 | 3·73 | 3·97 | 4·15 | 4·30 | 4·42 | 4·62 | 4·77 | 5·01 | 5·19 |

$\alpha = .01$

| $v$ | $J = 2$ | $J = 3$ | $J = 4$ | $J = 5$ | $J = 6$ | $J = 7$ | $J = 8$ | $J = 10$ | $J = 12$ | $J = 16$ | $J = 20$ |
|---|---|---|---|---|---|---|---|---|---|---|---|
| | | | | | $X = 1$ | | | | | | |
| 2 | 19·09 | 26·02 | 30·57 | 33·93 | 36·58 | 38·76 | 40·60 | 43·59 | 45·95 | 49·55 | 52·24 |
| 3 | 10·28 | 13·32 | 15·32 | 16·80 | 17·98 | 18·95 | 19·77 | 21·12 | 22·19 | 23·82 | 25·05 |
| 4 | 7·68 | 9·64 | 10·93 | 11·89 | 12·65 | 13·28 | 13·82 | 14·70 | 15·40 | 16·48 | 17·29 |
| 5 | 6·49 | 7·99 | 8·97 | 9·70 | 10·28 | 10·76 | 11·17 | 11·84 | 12·38 | 13·20 | 13·83 |
| 6 | 5·83 | 7·08 | 7·88 | 8·48 | 8·96 | 9·36 | 9·70 | 10·25 | 10·70 | 11·38 | 11·90 |
| 7 | 5·41 | 6·50 | 7·20 | 7·72 | 8·14 | 8·48 | 8·77 | 9·26 | 9·64 | 10·24 | 10·69 |
| 8 | 5·12 | 6·11 | 6·74 | 7·20 | 7·58 | 7·88 | 8·15 | 8·58 | 8·92 | 9·46 | 9·87 |
| 10 | 4·76 | 5·61 | 6·15 | 6·55 | 6·86 | 7·13 | 7·35 | 7·72 | 8·01 | 8·47 | 8·82 |
| 12 | 4·54 | 5·31 | 5·79 | 6·15 | 6·43 | 6·67 | 6·87 | 7·20 | 7·46 | 7·87 | 8·18 |
| 14 | 4·39 | 5·11 | 5·56 | 5·89 | 6·15 | 6·36 | 6·55 | 6·85 | 7·09 | 7·47 | 7·75 |
| 16 | 4·28 | 4·96 | 5·39 | 5·70 | 5·95 | 6·15 | 6·32 | 6·60 | 6·83 | 7·18 | 7·45 |
| 18 | 4·20 | 4·86 | 5·26 | 5·56 | 5·79 | 5·99 | 6·15 | 6·42 | 6·63 | 6·96 | 7·22 |
| 20 | 4·14 | 4·77 | 5·17 | 5·45 | 5·68 | 5·86 | 6·02 | 6·27 | 6·48 | 6·80 | 7·04 |
| 24 | 4·05 | 4·65 | 5·02 | 5·29 | 5·50 | 5·68 | 5·83 | 6·07 | 6·26 | 6·56 | 6·78 |
| 30 | 3·96 | 4·54 | 4·89 | 5·14 | 5·34 | 5·50 | 5·64 | 5·87 | 6·05 | 6·32 | 6·53 |
| 40 | 3·88 | 4·43 | 4·76 | 5·00 | 5·19 | 5·34 | 5·47 | 5·68 | 5·85 | 6·10 | 6·30 |
| 60 | 3·79 | 4·32 | 4·64 | 4·86 | 5·04 | 5·18 | 5·30 | 5·50 | 5·65 | 5·89 | 6·07 |
| 120 | 3·72 | 4·22 | 4·52 | 4·73 | 4·89 | 5·03 | 5·14 | 5·32 | 5·47 | 5·69 | 5·85 |

*(continued)*

Critical Values for the Bryant-Paulson Procedure, $\alpha = .01$

| $\nu$ | $J = 2$ | $J = 3$ | $J = 4$ | $J = 5$ | $J = 6$ | $J = 7$ | $J = 8$ | $J = 10$ | $J = 12$ | $J = 16$ | $J = 20$ |
|---|---|---|---|---|---|---|---|---|---|---|---|
| | | | | | $X = 2$ | | | | | | |
| 2 | 23·11 | 31·55 | 37·09 | 41·19 | 44·41 | 47·06 | 49·31 | 52·94 | 55·82 | 60·20 | 63·47 |
| 3 | 11·97 | 15·56 | 17·91 | 19·66 | 21·05 | 22·19 | 23·16 | 24·75 | 26·01 | 27·93 | 29·38 |
| 4 | 8·69 | 10·95 | 12·43 | 13·54 | 14·41 | 15·14 | 15·76 | 16·77 | 17·58 | 18·81 | 19·74 |
| 5 | 7·20 | 8·89 | 9·99 | 10·81 | 11·47 | 12·01 | 12·47 | 13·23 | 13·84 | 14·77 | 15·47 |
| 6 | 6·36 | 7·75 | 8·64 | 9·31 | 9·85 | 10·29 | 10·66 | 11·28 | 11·77 | 12·54 | 13·11 |
| 7 | 5·84 | 7·03 | 7·80 | 8·37 | 8·83 | 9·21 | 9·53 | 10·06 | 10·49 | 11·14 | 11·64 |
| 8 | 5·48 | 6·54 | 7·23 | 7·74 | 8·14 | 8·48 | 8·76 | 9·23 | 9·61 | 10·19 | 10·63 |
| 10 | 5·02 | 5·93 | 6·51 | 6·93 | 7·27 | 7·55 | 7·79 | 8·19 | 8·50 | 8·99 | 9·36 |
| 12 | 4·74 | 5·56 | 6·07 | 6·45 | 6·75 | 7·00 | 7·21 | 7·56 | 7·84 | 8·27 | 8·60 |
| 14 | 4·56 | 5·31 | 5·78 | 6·13 | 6·40 | 6·63 | 6·82 | 7·14 | 7·40 | 7·79 | 8·09 |
| 16 | 4·42 | 5·14 | 5·58 | 5·90 | 6·16 | 6·37 | 6·55 | 6·85 | 7·08 | 7·45 | 7·73 |
| 18 | 4·32 | 5·00 | 5·43 | 5·73 | 5·98 | 6·18 | 6·35 | 6·63 | 6·85 | 7·19 | 7·46 |
| 20 | 4·25 | 4·90 | 5·31 | 5·60 | 5·84 | 6·03 | 6·19 | 6·46 | 6·67 | 7·00 | 7·25 |
| 24 | 4·14 | 4·76 | 5·14 | 5·42 | 5·63 | 5·81 | 5·96 | 6·21 | 6·41 | 6·71 | 6·95 |
| 30 | 4·03 | 4·62 | 4·98 | 5·24 | 5·44 | 5·61 | 5·75 | 5·98 | 6·16 | 6·44 | 6·66 |
| 40 | 3·93 | 4·48 | 4·82 | 5·07 | 5·26 | 5·41 | 5·54 | 5·76 | 5·93 | 6·19 | 6·38 |
| 60 | 3·83 | 4·36 | 4·68 | 4·90 | 5·08 | 5·22 | 5·35 | 5·54 | 5·70 | 5·94 | 6·12 |
| 120 | 3·73 | 4·24 | 4·54 | 4·75 | 4·91 | 5·05 | 5·16 | 5·35 | 5·49 | 5·71 | 5·88 |
| | | | | | $X = 3$ | | | | | | |
| 2 | 26·54 | 36·26 | 42·64 | 47·36 | 51·07 | 54·13 | 56·71 | 60·90 | 64·21 | 69·25 | 73·01 |
| 3 | 13·45 | 17·51 | 20·17 | 22·15 | 23·72 | 25·01 | 26·11 | 27·90 | 29·32 | 31·50 | 33·13 |
| 4 | 9·59 | 12·11 | 13·77 | 15·00 | 15·98 | 16·79 | 17·47 | 18·60 | 19·50 | 20·87 | 21·91 |
| 5 | 7·83 | 9·70 | 10·92 | 11·82 | 12·54 | 13·14 | 13·65 | 14·48 | 15·15 | 16·17 | 16·95 |
| 6 | 6·85 | 8·36 | 9·34 | 10·07 | 10·65 | 11·13 | 11·54 | 12·22 | 12·75 | 13·59 | 14·21 |
| 7 | 6·23 | 7·52 | 8·36 | 8·98 | 9·47 | 9·88 | 10·23 | 10·80 | 11·26 | 11·97 | 12·51 |
| 8 | 5·81 | 6·95 | 7·69 | 8·23 | 8·67 | 9·03 | 9·33 | 9·84 | 10·24 | 10·87 | 11·34 |
| 10 | 5·27 | 6·23 | 6·84 | 7·30 | 7·66 | 7·96 | 8·21 | 8·63 | 8·96 | 9·48 | 9·88 |
| 12 | 4·94 | 5·80 | 6·34 | 6·74 | 7·05 | 7·31 | 7·54 | 7·90 | 8·20 | 8·65 | 9·00 |
| 14 | 4·72 | 5·51 | 6·00 | 6·36 | 6·65 | 6·89 | 7·09 | 7·42 | 7·69 | 8·10 | 8·41 |
| 16 | 4·56 | 5·30 | 5·76 | 6·10 | 6·37 | 6·59 | 6·77 | 7·08 | 7·33 | 7·71 | 8·00 |
| 18 | 4·44 | 5·15 | 5·59 | 5·90 | 6·16 | 6·36 | 6·54 | 6·83 | 7·06 | 7·42 | 7·69 |
| 20 | 4·35 | 5·03 | 5·45 | 5·75 | 5·99 | 6·19 | 6·36 | 6·63 | 6·85 | 7·19 | 7·45 |
| 24 | 4·22 | 4·86 | 5·25 | 5·54 | 5·76 | 5·94 | 6·10 | 6·35 | 6·55 | 6·87 | 7·11 |
| 30 | 4·10 | 4·70 | 5·06 | 5·33 | 5·54 | 5·71 | 5·85 | 6·08 | 6·27 | 6·56 | 6·78 |
| 40 | 3·98 | 4·54 | 4·88 | 5·13 | 5·32 | 5·48 | 5·61 | 5·83 | 6·00 | 6·27 | 6·47 |
| 60 | 3·86 | 4·39 | 4·72 | 4·95 | 5·12 | 5·27 | 5·39 | 5·59 | 5·75 | 6·00 | 6·18 |
| 120 | 3·75 | 4·25 | 4·55 | 4·77 | 4·94 | 5·07 | 5·18 | 5·37 | 5·51 | 5·74 | 5·90 |

# ANSWERS
## TO SELECTED CHAPTER PROBLEMS

## Chapter 1

### Odd-Numbered Answers to Conceptual Problems

1. c (true ratios cannot be formed with interval variables)
3. d (see comment for problem 1)
5. no (see comment for problem 1)
7. false (some characteristics of a sample are constant)
9. false (as this is a population parameter, no inference need be made)
11. yes (although the top 5 scores will be increased, the ranks of every score will remain the same)

### Odd-Numbered Answers to Computational Problems

1.

| Value | Rank |
|-------|------|
| 10    | 7    |
| 15    | 5    |
| 12    | 6    |
| 8     | 8    |
| 20    | 2    |
| 17    | 4    |

| 5 | 9 |
|----|----|
| 21 | 1 |
| 3 | 10 |
| 19 | 3 |

## Chapter 2

### *Odd-Numbered Answers to Conceptual Problems*

1. c (percentile and percentile rank are two sides of the same coin; if the 50th percentile = 100, then $PR(100) = 50$)
3. a (for 96, $crf = .09$ for both $X$ and $Y$ and $crf = .10$ for $Z$)
5. d (ethnicity is not continuous, so only a bar graph is appropriate)
7. c (see Sect. 2.2.3)
9. false (the proportion is .25 by definition)
11. a (eye color is nominal and not continuous)
13. true (with the same interval width, each is based on exactly the same information)
15. no (it is most likely that $Q_1$ will be smaller for the negatively skewed variable)

### *Odd-Numbered Answers to Computational Problems*

1. a–d) Frequency distributions:

| $X$ | $f$ | $cf$ | $rf$ | $crf$ |
|----|----|----|----|----|
| 50 | 3 | 50 | .06 | 1.00 |
| 49 | 5 | 47 | .10 | .94 |
| 48 | 4 | 42 | .08 | .84 |
| 47 | 11 | 38 | .22 | .76 |
| 46 | 8 | 27 | .16 | .54 |
| 45 | 6 | 19 | .12 | .38 |
| 44 | 5 | 13 | .10 | .26 |
| 43 | 4 | 8 | .08 | .16 |
| 42 | 2 | 4 | .04 | .08 |
| 41 | 2 | 2 | .04 | .04 |
|    | 50 |   | 1.00 |   |

e) Frequency polygon

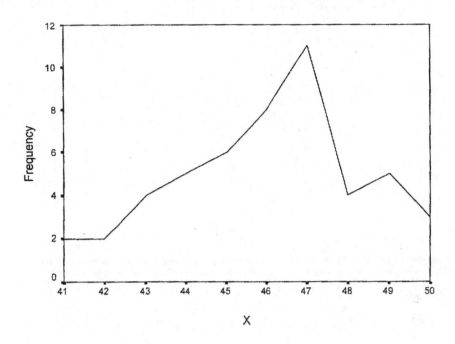

g)  $Q_1 = 44.4, Q_2 = 46.25, Q_3 = 47.4545$

h)  $P_{10} = 42.75, P_{90} = 49.1$

i)  $PR(41) = 2\%, PR(49.5) = 94\%$.

j)  Box-and-whisker plot

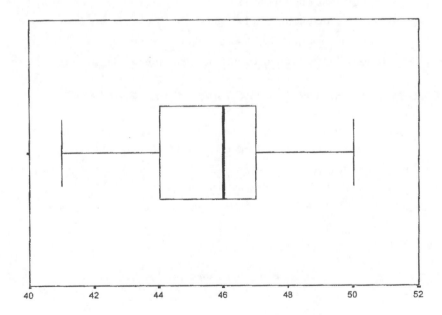

k)   Stem-and-leaf display

| Frequency | Stem | & | Leaf |
|-----------|------|---|------|
| 2.00 | 41 | . | 00 |
| 2.00 | 42 | . | 00 |
| 4.00 | 43 | . | 0000 |
| 5.00 | 44 | . | 00000 |
| 6.00 | 45 | . | 000000 |
| 8.00 | 46 | . | 00000000 |
| 11.00 | 47 | . | 00000000000 |
| 4.00 | 48 | . | 0000 |
| 5.00 | 49 | . | 00000 |
| 3.00 | 50 | . | 000 |

# Chapter 3

## Odd-Numbered Answers to Conceptual Problems

1.  b (will affect variance the most)
3.  d (variance cannot be negative)
5.  false (that proportion is always .25)
7.  no (class rank is ordinal, so mean inappropriate)
9.  yes (middle score still the same)
11. no (will be different for small samples)
13. true (they are based on the same measurement scales)
15. no (impossible as the median must be larger; fire the statistician).

## Odd-Numbered Answers to Computational Problems

1.  mode = 47, median = 46.25, mean = 46, exclusive range = 9, inclusive range = 10, $H$ = 3.0546, variance = 5.28, standard deviation = 2.2978.
3.  mode = 5, median = 5.375, mean = 5.80, exclusive range = 8, inclusive range = 9, $H$ = 2.9334, variance = 4.1655, standard deviation = 2.041.
5.  distribution $X$ (it has more extreme scores than the other distributions)

# Chapter 4

## Odd-Numbered Answers to Conceptual Problems

1.  d (skewness is zero for normal)
3.  b ($\pm 2$ standard deviations)

5. b (only median is a value of $X$)
7. c (positive value = leptokurtic)
9. true (see $z$ score equation)
11. false (mean can be any value)
13. c (where there is the highest concentration of scores in the middle)
15. false (the variance of $z$ is always 1 while the variance of the raw scores can be any value)
17. a (a is 90th percentile, b is 84th percentile, c is 75th percentile, d is 84th percentile)

### Odd-Numbered Answers to Computational Problems

1. a = .0485; b = .6970; c = 10.16; d = 46.31; e = approximately 79.67%; f = approximately 21.48%; g = 76.12%.

## Chapter 5

### Odd-Numbered Answers to Conceptual Problems

1. c (see definition in Sect. 5.2.2)
3. a (2 out of 9)
5. a (see Sect. 5.2.2)
7. true (less sampling error as $n$ increases)
9. false (for symmetric population, a sample mean and median do not have to be the same, as the sample distribution may not be symmetric)
11. b (probability of winning is the same for each hand)
13. false (sampling error decreases with larger samples)

### Odd-Numbered Answers to Computational Problems

1. a, population mean = 5; population variance = 6; b, construct table of possible sample means like Table 5.1; c, mean of the sampling distribution of the mean = 5; variance of the sampling distribution of the mean = 3.
3. 256.

## Chapter 6

### Odd-Numbered Answers to Conceptual Problems

1. c (see definition)
3. a (cannot make Type II error there)
5. e (most extreme value regardless of sign)
7. false (cannot make a Type I error there)

9.  no (cannot tell just from mean difference, need more information)

11.  no (the range will be wider for the 99% CI)

13.  false (the mean is zero for any $t$ distribution)

15.  true (the width of the CI only depends on the critical value and the standard error)

### Odd-Numbered Answers to Computational Problems

1.  a, B may or may not reject; b, A also rejects; c, B also fails to reject; d, A may or may not fail to reject.

3.  a, $t = -1.984$, critical values $= -2.064$ and $+2.064$, fail to reject $H_0$ ; b, (65.84, 74.16), includes hypothesized value of 74 and thus fail to reject $H_0$.

## Chapter 7

### Odd-Numbered Answers to Conceptual Problems

1.  e (if null hypothesis is true and you reject, then you have definitely made a Type I error)

3.  c (see definition)

5.  false (sampling error is less for larger samples)

7.  yes (smaller value when all of critical region is in one tail; see $t$ table)

9.  d (there is no such test; the tests mentioned all deal with means)

11.  no (it will decrease, as shown in Appendix Table 2)

### Odd-Numbered Answers to Computational Problems

1.  a. $t = -2.1097$, critical values are approximately $-2.041$ and $+2.041$, reject $H_0$.
    b. $(-9.2469, -.1531)$, does not include hypothesized value and thus reject $H_0$.

3.  a. $t = -1.9365$, critical values are $-2.262$ and $+2.262$, fail to reject $H_0$.
    b. $(-4.3362, .3362)$, does include hypothesized value and thus fail to reject $H_0$.

5.  $t = 2.4444$, critical value is 1.658, reject $H_0$.

## Chapter 8

### Odd-Numbered Answers to Conceptual Problems

1.  b $(4 \times 6 = 24)$

3.  true (see definition)

5.  no (cannot have a negative proportion)

7. no (reject when test statistic exceeds critical value)

9. d (as the difference between observed and expected increases, the chi-square test statistic increases, and thus we are more likely to reject)

## Odd-Numbered Answers to Computational Problems

1. $p = .75$, $z = 2.1898$, critical values $= -1.96$ and $+1.96$, thus reject $H_0$.

3. $z = -.1644$, critical values $= -1.96$ and $+1.96$, thus fail to reject $H_0$.

5. $\chi^2 = 3.333$, critical value $= 3.84$, thus fail to reject $H_0$.

## Chapter 9

## Odd-Numbered Answers to Conceptual Problems

1. c (see Sect. 9.4)

3. yes (cannot reject if sample variances are equal)

5. no, not enough information (do not know hypothesized variance)

7. b (involves naturally occuring couples or pairs)

## Selected Answers to Odd-Numbered Computational Problems

1. a, sample variance $= 27.9292$, $\chi^2 = 5.5858$, critical values $= 7.2609$ and $24.9958$, thus reject $H_0$. b, $(16.7603, 57.6978)$, thus reject $H_0$ as the interval does not contain 75.

3. $t = 2.3474$, critical values $= -2.042$ and $+2.042$, thus reject $H_0$.

5. $t = -2.6178$, critical values $= -2.756$ and $+2.756$, thus fail to reject $H_0$.

## Chapter 10

## Odd-Numbered Answers to Conceptual Problems

1. d $[2/(3)(2) = .3333]$

3. a (linear relationship will fall into a reasonably linear scatterplot, although not necessarily a perfectly straight line)

5. false (correlation will become smaller; see the correlation equation involving covariance)

7. yes (a perfect relationship implies a perfect correlation, assuming linearity)

9. no (fire the consultant as the correlation cannot be $+2.0$)

11. false (the Pearson is most appropriate for interval/ratio variables, while the Spearman or Kendall's $\tau$ are most appropriate for ordinal variables).

## Odd-Numbered Answers to Computational Problems

1. a, scatterplot shown below; b, covariance = 3.250; c, $r = .631$; d, $r = .400$.

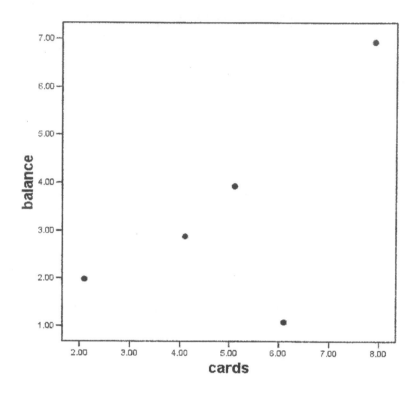

3. $z = -1.6541$, critical values are $-1.96$ and $+1.96$, fail to reject $H_0$.
5. a, $r = -.928$; b, strong effect.

# Chapter 11

## Odd-Numbered Answers to Conceptual Problems

1. a (if the sample means are all equal, then $MS_{betw}$ is 0)
3. c (lose 1 $df$ from each group; $63 - 3 = 60$)
5. a (for between source $= 3 - 1 = 2$ and for within source $= 30 - 3 = 27$)
7. c (an $F$ ratio of 1.0 implies between- and within-groups variation are the same)
9. true (mean square is a variance estimate)
11. true ($F$ ratio must be greater than or equal to 0)
13. no (rejecting in ANOVA only indicates that there is some difference among the means, not that all of the means are different)
15. c (the more $t$ tests conducted, the more likely a Type I error for the set of tests)

17. true (basically the definition of independence)

19. no (find a new statistician as a negative $F$ value is not possible in this context).

### Odd-Numbered Answers to Computational Problems

1. $df_{betw} = 3$, $df_{with} = 60$, $df_{total} = 63$, $SS_{with} = 9.00$, $MS_{betw} = 3.25$, $MS_{with} = 0.15$, $F = 21.6666$, critical value $= 2.76$ (reject $H_0$).

3. $SS_{betw} = 150$, $SS_{total} = 1,110$, $df_{betw} = 3$, $df_{with} = 96$, $df_{total} = 99$, $MS_{betw} = 50$, $MS_{with} = 10$, critical value approximately 2.7 (reject $H_0$).

## Chapter 12

### Odd-Numbered Answers to Conceptual Problems

1. false (requires equal $n$'s and equal variances; we hope the means are different)

3. d (with two groups, no need to follow up the ANOVA)

5. d (see definition of a priori comparisons)

7. b (POC are planned, not post hoc)

9. c (when null is rejected and there are more than two groups, then want to know which means are different)

11. true (see table of critical values for studentized range; easier to reject with more observations)

13. false ($n$'s need not be equal for Dunnett; see characteristics)

15. yes (each contrast is orthogonal to the others as they rely on independent information)

17. d (see Fig. 12.2)

19. no (with equal sample means, the numerator of any $t$ will be zero, thus nothing can possibly be significant).

### Selected Answers to Odd-Numbered Computational Problems

1. contrast $= -5$; standard error $= 1$; $t = -5$; critical value $= 5.10$; fail to reject.

3. a) $\mu_{.1} - \mu_{.2}$, $\mu_{.3} - \mu_{.4}$, $(\mu_{.1} + \mu_{.2})/2 - (\mu_{.3} + \mu_{.4})/2$; b) no as $\Sigma c_j$ not equal to 0; c) $H_0$: $\mu_{.1} - [(\mu_{.2} + \mu_{.3} + \mu_{.4})/3]$

## Chapter 13

### Odd-Numbered Answers to Conceptual Problems

1. c (a plot of the cell means reveals an interaction)

3. a (a nonsignificant interaction results in the greatest generalizability of the main effects)

5.  c (c is one definition of an interaction)

7.  e (3 levels of A, 2 levels of B, thus 6 cells)

9.  b ($170 \times 2 = 340$)

11.  b (interaction $df$ = product of main effects $df$)

13.  d (the effect of one factor depends on the second factor; see definition of inter-
     action as well as example profile plots in Fig. 13.1)

15.  false (when the interaction is significant, this imples nothing about the main effects)

17.  no (the numerator degrees of freedom for factor B can be anything).

### Odd-Numbered Answers to Computational Problems

1.  $SS_{with} = 225$, $df_A = 1$, $df_B = 2$, $df_{AB} = 2$, $df_{with} = 150$, $df_{total} = 155$, $MS_A = 6.15$,
    $MS_B = 5.30$, $MS_{AB} = 4.55$, $MS_{with} = 1.50$, $F_A = 4.10$, $F_B = 3.5333$, $F_{AB} = 3.0333$, critical value for A approximately 3.91, reject $H_0$ for A, critical value for B
    and AB approximately 3.06, reject $H_0$ for B and fail to reject $H_0$ for AB.

3.  $F_A = 14.555$, $F_B = 9.093$, $F_{AB} = .6863$, critical value for A approximately 7.31,
    reject $H_0$ for A, critical value for B and AB approximately 5.18, reject $H_0$ for B, but
    not for AB.

    means: factor A − level 1 = 62, level 2 = 97

    factor B − level 1 = 54.688, level 2 = 81.313, level 3 = 102.5

    with Tukey HSD for factor B, only levels 1 and 3 are different

5.  $F_A = 21.350$, $F_B = 0.133$, $F_{AB} = 21.184$, critical value for A and AB = 3.01,
    reject $H_0$ for A and for AB, critical value for B = 4.26, fail to reject $H_0$ for B.

## Chapter 14

### Odd-Numbered Answers to Conceptual Problems

1.  b (see discussion on homogeneity of regression slopes)

3.  b (14 $df$ per group, 3 groups, 42 $df$ − 2 $df$ for covariates = 40)

5.  c (want covariate having a high correlation with dependent variable)

7.  c (the covariate and dependent variable need not be the same measure; could be
    pretest and posttest, but does not have to be)

9.  b (an interaction indicates that the regression lines are not parallel across the
    groups)

11.  c (a posthoc covariate typically results in an underestimate of the treatment effect,
     due to confounding or interference of the covariate)

13.  no (if the correlation is substantial, then error variance will be reduced in
     ANCOVA regardless of its sign)

15.  b (11 $df$ per group, 6 groups, 66 $df$ − 1 $df$ for covariate = 65)

17.  no (there will be no adjustment due to the covariate and one $df$ will be lost from
     the error term)

### Odd-Numbered Answers to Computational Problems

1. the adjusted groups means are all equal to 150; this resulted because the adjustment moved the mean for Group 1 up to 150 and the mean for Group 3 down to 150.

3. $df_{betw} = 4$, $MS_{betw} = 24$, $F = 3$, critical value 2.78 (reject $H_0$), $df_{with} = 24$, $MS_{with} = 8$, $SS_{cov} = 40$, $df_{cov} = 1$, $MS_{cov} = 40$, $F_{cov} = 5$, critical value 4.26 (reject $H_0$).

## Chapter 15

### Odd-Numbered Answers to Conceptual Problems

1. b (when there are both random and fixed factors, then the design is mixed)
3. c (gender is fixed, order is random, thus a mixed-effects model)
5. false (a repeated measures model can involve fixed and/or random factors)
7. no ($MS_{with}$ is not used as the denominator for all models)
9. b (strategy is a repeated factor)
11. a (interactions require the two factors to be crossed; the other aspects are not relevant)
13. b (review the summary table for that model)

### Odd-Numbered Answers to Computational Problems

1. $SS_{with} = 1.9$, $df_A = 2$, $df_B = 1$, $df_{AB} = 2$, $df_{with} = 18$, $df_{total} = 23$, $MS_A = 1.82$, $MS_B = .57$, $MS_{AB} = 1.035$, $MS_{with} = .1056$, $F_A = 1.7585$, $F_B = 5.3977$, $F_{AB} = 9.8011$, critical value for AB = 6.01 (reject $H_0$ for AB), critical value for B = 8.29 (fail to reject $H_0$ for B), critical value for A = 99 (fail to reject $H_0$ for A).

3. $SS_{time} = 126.094$, $SS_{time \times program} = 2.594$, $SS_{program} = 3.781$, $MS_{time} = 42.031$, $MS_{time \times program} = 0.865$, $MS_{program} = 3.781$, $F_{time} = 43.078$ ($p < .001$), $F_{time \times program} = 0.886$ ($p > .05$), $F_{program} = 0.978$ ($p > .05$).

## Chapter 16

### Odd-Numbered Answers to Conceptual Problems

1. d (subjects are randomly sampled within a range of IQ scores)
3. d (interactions only occur among factors that are crossed)
5. a (this is the notation for teachers nested within methods; see also problem 2)
7. false (cannot be a nested design; must be a crossed design)
9. yes (see the discussion on the types of blocking)
11. c (physician is nested within method)
13. b (there will be two main effects tests and no interaction test)
15. false (IQ cannot be randomly assigned to individuals; IQ must be a blocking factor or a covariate)

### Odd-Numbered Answers to Computational Problems

1.  a) yes; b) at age 4 type 1 is most effective, at age 6 type 2 is most effective, and at age 8 type 2 is most effective.
3.  $F_{section} = 44.385$, $p = .002$; $F_{GRE-Q} = 61.000$, $p = .001$; thus reject $H_0$ for both effects; Bonferroni results: all but sections 1 and 2 are different, and all but blocks 1 and 2 are different.

## Chapter 17

### Odd-Numbered Answers to Conceptual Problems

1.  c (see definition of intercept — a and b refer to the slope and d to the correlation)
3.  a (the predicted value is a constant value of 14 regardless of $X$, thus the variance of the predicted values is 0)
5.  d (linear relationships are best represented by a straight line, although all of the points need not fall on the line)
7.  a (as the slope $= 0$, then the correlation $= 0$)
9.  b (with the same predictor score, they will have the same predicted score; whether the residuals are the same will only depend on the observed $Y$)
11. d (see definition of homogeneity)
13. true (value of $Y$ is irrelevant when correlation $= 0$, so mean of $Y$ is best prediction)
15. false (if the variables are positively correlated, then the slope would be positive and a low score on the pretest would predict a low score on the posttest)
17. no (the regression equation may generate any number of points on the regression line).

### Selected Answers to Odd-Numbered Computational Problems

1.  a, $b = .8571$, $a = 1.9716$, b, $Y' = 7.1142$.
3.  a, $b = .7447$, $a = 1.8136$, b, $F = 14.9431$ $(p < .05)$, $t = 3.8646$ $(p < .05)$.

## Chapter 18

### Odd-Numbered Answers to Conceptual Problems

1.  a (as variable 3 has the largest correlation with variable 1 and the smallest with variable 2)
3.  false (the intercept can be any value)
5.  false (best prediction is when there is a high correlation of the predictors with the dependent variable, and low correlations among the predictors)
7.  no (the partial correlation may be larger than, the same as, or smaller than .6)

9. no (the purpose of the adjustment is to take the number of predictors into account; thus $R^2_{adj}$ may actually be smaller for the most predictors)

## Odd-Numbered Answers to Computational Problems

1. intercept $= 28.0952$, $b_1 = .0381$, $b_2 = .8333$, $SS_{res} = 21.4294$, $SS_{reg} = 1,128.5706$, $F = 105.3292$ (reject at .01), $s^2_{res} = 5.3574$, $s(b_1) = .0058$, $s(b_2) = .1545$, $t_1 = 6.5343$ (reject at .01), $t_2 = 5.3923$ (reject at .01).

3. $r_{12.3} = .0934$.

5. $df_{reg} = 4$, $df_{res} = 40$, $df_{total} = 44$, $SS_{reg} = 80$, $SS_{total} = 480$, $MS_{res} = 10$, $F = 2$, critical value $= 2.61$, fail to reject $H_0$.

7. $r_{13.2} = .5305$, $r_{1(3.2)} = .5187$.

# INDEX

The following typographical conventions are used in the index: *f* and *t* identify figures and tables, respectively

## A

Abramowitz, S. K., 212, 407, 408
Additive effects, ANOVA, 256
Additive model, 346
Agresti, A., 289, 317, 318
Algina, J., 170, 212, 214
All possible subsets regression, 405–406
Analysis of Covariance (ANCOVA)
    adjusted means and related procedures,
        283–285, 284*f*
    assumptions and violations of assumptions,
        286–289, 290*t*
    example, 289–291, 291*t*
    layout of data, 281, 281*t*
    more complex models, 293
    nonparametric procedures, 293
    one-factor fixed-effects model, 278–280
    partitioning the sums of squares, 283
    summary table, 282–283, 282*t*
    without randomization, 292–293
Analysis of variance (ANOVA)
    alternative procedures, 213–214, 317–318
    assumptions and violations of assumptions,
        210–213, 256–257, 257*t*, 305, 306*t*, 308,

        309*t*, 312, 312*t*, 315, 316*t*, 321–322,
        322*t*, 345–346
    characteristics of one-factor model, 198–200
    comparison of models, 351–353
    examples, 208–210, 209–210*t*, 261–265,
        262*t*, 263*f*, 318–319, 318*t*, 323–325,
        324–325*t*, 326*f*, 342–343, 342–343*t*,
        349–350, 349*t*
    factorial, 247–276
    factorial with unequal *n*'s, 267–268
    layout of the data, 200–201
    methods of block formation, 348–349
    model, 206–210
    multiple comparison procedures, 259–260,
        305–306, 308–309, 312–313, 317, 323,
        341–342, 347–348
    one-factor, 196–221, 201*t*
    one-factor random-effects, 303–306
    one-factor repeated measures design,
        313–319, 314*t*
    parameters of the model, 207
    partitioning the sums of squares, 203–204,
        257
    size measures, confidence interval, and power,
        207–208, 260–261

Analysis of variance (ANOVA) (*continued*)
  summary tables, 204–206, 204*t*, 257–259,
    258*t*, 266, 266*t*, 304–305, 307–308,
    311–312, 315, 316*t*, 319*t*, 322–323, 322*t*,
    340–341, 341*t*, 346–347, 346–347*t*
  theory, 201–206
  three-factor and higher-order, 265–267
  triple interaction, 266–267
  two-factor hierarchical model, 336–343,
    337*f*, 339*t*
  two-factor mixed-effects, 309–313, 310*f*
  two-factor model, 249–265, 251*t*, 255*f*, 257*t*
  two-factor random-effects, 306–309
  two-factor randomized block design for $n > 1$,
    350
  two-factor randomized block design for $n = 1$,
    343–350, 345*t*
  two-factor split-plot or mixed design,
    319–325, 320*t*
Anderson, S. L., 287
Andrews, D. C., 377
Andrews, D. F., 378, 401
Applebaum, M. I., 267
A priori power, 108
Arnold, P. R., 409
Assumption of linearity, 186, 186*f*
Asymptotic curve, 64
Atiqullah, M., 287
Atkinson, A. C., 376

### B

Backward elimination, 404
Balanced case, 201
Bar graph, 23–24, 23*f*
Barnett, V., 377
Barrett, K. C., 215
Basu, S., 112
Bates, D. M., 407
Beal, S. L., 147
Beckman, R., 377
Belsley, D. A., 378, 401
Benjamini, Y., 240
Bernstein, I. H., 406
Berry, W. D., 407
Between-groups variability, 202–203, 203*f*
Binomial distribution, proportion, 143
Bivariate analysis, 177–195
Blair, R. C., 125, 126, 170
Blockwise regression, 406
Boik, R. J., 260, 348
Bowden, D., 237
Box, 32–33, 33*f*

Box, G. E. P., 212, 257, 287, 317, 323, 347
Box-and-whisker plot, 32–33, 33*f*
Bradley, J. V., 212
Braver, S. L., 215, 293, 325, 340
Brown, M. B., 212, 213, 214, 237
Brown-Forsythe procedure, 169–171, 171*f*, 213
Brunner, E., 257
Bryant, J. L., 285

### C

Campbell, D. T., 200, 279, 292
Carlson, J. E., 267, 268
Carroll, R. J., 377, 378, 401
Causation, correlation coefficients, 187
Central limit theorem, 87, 88*f*
Chambers, J. M., 29
Chatterjee, S., 403
Chi-square distribution, 151–156, 152*f*
  goodness-of-fit test, 152
  test of association, 154–156
Christensen, R., 408
Chunkwise regression, 406
Clark, V. A., 268, 280, 288, 317, 339, 340, 342,
    376, 377, 406
Cleveland, W. S., 29
Clinch, J. J., 214
Coe, P. R., 147
Coefficient of determination, 369–370
Cohen, J., 108, 109, 123, 130, 134, 145, 153, 158,
    184, 185, 192, 207, 208, 260, 261, 285,
    288, 303, 370, 395, 396, 406, 407, 409
Cohen, P., 288, 406, 407, 409
College Entrance Examination Board (CEEB),
    67–68
Column marginals, 155
Comparisons, 224
Complete factorial design, 337, 337*f*
Completely randomized design, 200
Completely randomized factorial design,
    ANOVA, 250
Complex post hoc contrasts, Scheffé and Kaiser-
    Bowden methods, 236–237
Compound symmetry, 345
Computational formula, 49, 204
Conditional distribution, 376
Conerly, M. D., 402
Confidence intervals, 86, 104–105, 370–375
Conover, W., 129, 132, 293
Constant, definition, 7
Contingency tables
  phi correlation, 190*t*

proportions, 149, 150*t*, 154*t*
Continuous variable, definition, 8
Contrast-based multiple comparison
    procedures, 227
Contrasts, 224–227
Cook, R. D., 376, 377
Cook, T. D., 200, 279
Coombs, W. T., 170, 212, 214
Correlation coefficients, 177
    assumption of linearity, 186, 186*f*
    correlation and causality, 187
    different types, 191*t*
    Pearson product-moment, 182–185
    restriction of range, 187–188, 187*f*
Cotton, J. W., 318, 325
Covariance analysis, relationship among
    variables, 179–182, 181*t*
Covariate
    definition, 279
    independence of, 288
    measured without error, 288
Craig, A. T., 184
Cramer, E. M., 267
Crepel, P., 5
Crossed design, 337, 337*f*
Cumulative frequency distributions, 19*t*, 21–22
Cumulative frequency polygon, 26–27, 27*f*
Cumulative relative frequency distribution, 19*f*,
    22–23
Cumulative relative frequency polygon, 27


**D**

D'Agostino, R. B., 401
DasGupta, A., 112
Data representation, 16–38
    graphical display of distributions, 23–29
    tabular displays of distributions, 18–23
Davenport, J. M., 211, 286
Decision errors, 95–98
Decision-making
    example situation, 95
    full context, 105–108, 106*f*
    overview of steps, 100–101
    table, 96–98, 96*t*
Definitional (conceptual) formula, 49, 204
Degrees of freedom concept, 110
Delaney, H. D., 288, 289, 352
Dependent proportions, 148–151
    contingency table, 150*t*
Dependent samples, 120–121
Dependent *t* test, 129–132, 131*t*, 132*f*, 135*t*

Dependent variable, criterion, 362
Dependent variance, 166–168
Derksen, S., 406
Descriptive statistics, definition, 6
Detta, H., 257
Deviation scores, 48–49, 48*t*
Deviational measures, 48–52
Dichotomous variable, definition, 8
Dill, C. A., 352
Directional alternative hypothesis, 100
Discrete variable, definition, 7–8
Duncan, G. T., 185
Dunn, O. J., 185, 234, 235, 268, 280, 288, 317,
    339, 340, 342, 376, 377, 406
Dunnett, C. W., 233, 234, 240
Durbin, J., 211, 286, 376


**E**

Elashoff, J. D., 280
Equal *n*'s, 201
Exact probability, 104
Expected proportions, 152
Experiment-wise type I error rate, 198
Extrapolation, value of *X*, 380–381


**F**

*F* distribution, variance, 163, 164*f*
Factorial analysis of variance, 247–276
Factorial design, ANOVA, 249
Fail to reject, 96
Family of curves, 61–62
Family-wise multiple comparison
    procedures, 227
Feinberg, S. E., 5
Feldman, S., 407
Feldt, L. S., 315, 317, 323, 346, 347, 349, 352
Ferguson, G. A., 292
Fidell, L. S., 406
Fidler, F., 208, 260, 303
Fink, A., 83
Finlay, B., 289
Fisher, R. A., 239
Fisher's Z transformation, 185
Fixed independent variable, assumption in
    ANCOVA, 287
Fixed *X*, 380–381, 402
Forced stepwise regression, 406
Forsythe, A., 212, 213, 214, 237
Forward selection, 404

Fouladi, R. T., 370, 395
Frequency distributions, 18–21, 18*t*
    shapes of, 27, 28*f*
Frequency polygon, 24–25, 25*f*
Friedman, M., 317, 350
Friedman test, 350–351
Fully crossed design, ANOVA, 249

# G

Games, P. A., 240
Gamst, G., 382, 407, 408, 409, 410
Gani, J., 5
Geisser, S., 316, 323, 347
Ghosh, B. K., 145
Glass, G. V., 125, 154, 211, 212, 268, 289, 325,
    338, 340, 343, 381, 390, 402, 408
Greenhouse, S., 316, 323, 347
Griego, O. V., 382, 408
Grimm, L. G., 409
Grissom, R. J., 109
Grouped frequency distributions, 20–21, 21*t*
Guarino, A. J., 382, 407, 408, 409, 410

# H

*H* spread, 47–48
Haaland, J.-A., 29
Harlow, L., 109
Harwell, M., 286, 287, 289, 293
Hawkins, D. M., 377
Hays, W. L., 346, 390
Hayter, A. J., 239
Heisey, D. M., 108
Hershberger, S. L., 409
Heyde, C. C., 5
Hierarchical design, 337, 337*f*
Hierarchical regression, 406
Hinge, 32–33, 33*f*
Histogram, 24, 25*f*
Hochberg, Y., 240, 285, 317
Hockberg, Y., 240
Hocking, R. R., 404
Hoenig, J. M., 108
Hoerl, A. E., 403
Hogg, R. V., 184
Homogeneity of regression slopes, ANCOVA
    model, 288–289
Homogeneity of variance, 212
    assumption in ANCOVA, 286–287
    assumption in ANOVA, 212

linear regression, 376–377
    multiple regression, 399–400
    tests, 168–172
Homoscedasticity, 212
Hopkins, K. D., 154, 212, 268, 325, 338, 340,
    343, 381, 390, 402, 408
Hornick, C. W., 267, 268
Hosmer, D. W., 408
Howell, J. F., 240
Huberty, C. J., 406
Huck, S. W., 352, 408
Huitema, B. E., 280, 285, 287, 288, 289,
    293, 353
Huynh, H., 315, 317, 323, 346, 347
Hypotheses
    differences between two means, 121
    types, 93–95
Hypothesis testing, 92–118

# I

Iman, R., 129, 132, 293
Incomplete factorial design, 337, 337*f*
Independence
    assumption in ANCOVA, 286
    assumption in ANOVA, 211, 211*f*
    assumptions in linear regression, 375–376
    assumptions in multiple regression, 399, 400*f*
Independent proportions, 146–148
Independent samples, 120–121
Independent *t* test, 122–126, 124*t*, 125*f*, 135*t*
Independent variable
    ANCOVA model, 288
    predictor, 362
Independent variance, 168–172
Inferential statistics, definition, 7, 81
Intact groups, 279, 292
Interaction effect
    ANOVA, 249
    ANOVA model, 253
Interpolation, value of *X*, 380–381
Interval measurement scale, 11, 12*t*
Intervals
    in data sets, 19
    width of, 20
Intuition versus probability, 80–81

# J

Jaeger, R. M., 83
James, G. S., 214

Jennings, E., 352
Johansen, S., 257
Johnson, P. O., 289
Johnson, R. A., 409
Jorner, U., 29


# K

Kaiser, L., 237
Kalton, G., 83
Kennard, R. W., 403
Keppel, G., 208, 211, 226, 234, 236, 240, 260,
        265, 267, 268, 280, 287, 288, 293, 303,
        313, 315, 317, 318, 323, 325, 340, 342,
        343, 346, 349, 352
Keselman, H. J., 214, 406
Kim, J. J., 109
Kirk, R. E., 232, 233, 236, 237, 240, 268, 293,
        315, 317, 323, 325, 339, 346, 347,
        348, 350, 353
Kleinbaum, D. G., 376, 377, 401, 403, 406, 407,
        408, 409, 410
Kleiner, B., 29
Kramer, C. Y., 239
Kruskal, W. H., 213
Kruskal-Wallis, follow-up tests to, 240–241
Kuh, E., 378, 401
Kupper, L. L., 376, 377, 401, 403, 406, 407, 408,
        409, 410
Kurtosis, 71–72, 71$f$
    non-zero, 377


# L

Lamb, G. S., 188
Larsen, W. A., 402
Layard, M. W. J., 185
Least squares criterion, 369
Lee, D. M., 267, 268
Leech, N. L., 215
Lemeshow, S., 83, 408
Leptokurtic distribution, 71$f$
Leroy, A. M., 377, 401
Level of significance, 98–100, 98$f$
Levin, J. R., 260
Levy, P. S., 83
Lewis, T., 377
Linear regression, 361–386
    assumptions and violations of assumptions,
        375–381
    concepts, 362–364, 363$f$

population, 364–365
    sample, 365–381
Linearity
    assumption in ANCOVA, 287
    assumptions in linear regression, 378–379,
        379–380$f$
    assumptions in multiple regression, 402
Logistic regression, 407–408
Lomax, R. G., 326
Lord, F. M., 288, 292


# M

MacKinnon, D. P., 215, 293, 325, 340
Main effect, ANOVA model, 253
Manly, B. F. J., 410
Mansfield, E. R., 402
Marascuilo, L. A., 185, 260, 265, 318, 351
Marcoulides, G. A., 409
Marquardt, D. W., 403
Maxwell, S., 108
Maxwell, S. E., 288, 289, 317, 348, 352
McCleary, S. J., 402
McCulloch, C. E., 325
McLean, R. A., 352
McSweeney, M., 318, 351
Mean, 44–45
    differences between two, 119–139
    inferences about two dependent, 129–133
    inferences about two independent, 122–129
    sampling distribution of the differences, 121
    standard error of the difference between
        two, 122
Mean squares term, 205
Measurement, definition, 8
Measures of association, 177
Measures of central tendency, 41–45
    mean, 44–45
    median, 43–44
    mode, 41–43, 42$t$
Measures of dispersion, 45–52
    deviational measures, 48–52
    $H$ spread, 47–48
    range, 46–47
Median, 43–44
Mendoza, J. L., 370, 395
Meyers, L. S., 382, 407, 408, 409, 410
Mickey, R. M., 268, 280, 288, 317, 340, 377, 406
Midpoint, intervals, 26
Miller, A. J., 406
Miller, R. G., 257, 285, 401
Mixed design, 319

Mode, 41–43, 42*t*
Moments around the mean, 71–72, 71*f*
Morgan, G. A., 215, 382, 408
Mulaik, S., 109
Muller, K. E., 376, 377, 401, 403, 406, 407, 408,
  409, 410
Multiple comparison procedures (MCP), 222–246
  concepts of, 224–228
  Dunn (or Bonferroni) and Dunn-Sidak
    methods, 234–236
  Dunnett method, 233–234
  flowchart, 243*f*
  follow-up test to Kruskal Wallis, 240–241
  Games-Howell, Dunnett T3 and C Tests, 240
  Scheffé and Kaiser-Bowden methods, 236–237
  selected, 228–241
  Tukey HSD, Tukey-Kramer, Fisher LSD and
    Hayter tests, 237–240
Multiple linear regression, 387–413
  assumptions, 399–403, 404*t*
  coefficient of multiple determination and
    correlation, 394–396
  significance tests, 396–399
  standardized regression model, 393–394
  unstandardized regression model, 390–393,
    392*t*
Munk, A., 257
Murphy, K. R., 108, 208, 260, 261, 303,
  313, 396
Myers, J. L., 212, 214, 265, 280, 293, 315, 317,
  318, 325, 342, 349, 352, 381, 402
Myers, R. H., 317, 325, 342, 349, 399, 401, 403
Myors, B., 108, 208, 260, 261, 303, 313, 396

N

Negatively skewed distribution, 27, 28*f*, 70*f*
Nested design, 337, 337*f*
Neyman, J., 289
Nizam, A., 376, 377, 401, 403, 406, 407, 408,
  409, 410
Nominal measurement scale, 8–9, 12*t*
Noncolinearity, assumptions in multiple
  regression, 402–403
Nondirectional alternative hypothesis, 98
Nonlinear models, 379
Nonlinear relationships, 407
Nonparametric tests, 125
Noreen, E. W., 112
Normal distribution, 27, 28*f*
  area, 62–63
  characteristics, 61–65, 61*f*

history, 60–61
  proportions involving, 141–151
  standard scores and, 59–76
Normality
  assumption in ANCOVA, 287
  assumption in ANOVA, 212–213, 213*t*
  assumptions in linear regression, 377–378, 378*f*
  assumptions in multiple regression, 401, 401*f*
Null hypothesis, 94

O

O'Brien procedure, 171*f*, 172
Observed proportions, 152
O'Grady, K. E., 208, 260
Olejnik, S. F., 170
Omnibus test, 199
One-tailed test of significance, 100
Ordinal measurement scale, 9–11, 10*t*, 12*t*
Orthogonal contrasts, 227–228
  planned, 232–233
Ottman, D. O., 212, 214
Outliers, 32–33, 33*f*, 377
Overall, J. E., 267, 268

P

Page, M. C., 215, 293, 325, 340
Pampel, F. C., 408
Parameter, definition, 6
Parametric tests, 125
Partial correlation, 388–389
Partially sequential approach, factorial ANOVA
  with unequal *n*'s, 267
Paulson, A. S., 285
Pavur, R., 229
Pearson, E. S., 5
Pearson product-moment correlation coefficient,
  182–183
  inference for a single sample, 183–184
  inference for two independent samples,
    184–185
Peckham, P. D., 125, 211, 212, 289
Pedhazur, E. J., 288, 367, 377, 381, 390, 394,
  402, 406, 407, 408, 409
Pendergast, J., 317, 318
Percentile rank, 31–32
Percentiles, 29–33
Persson, R., 29
Phi type of correlation, 188–191, 190*t*
Pingel, L. A., 349

Planned analysis of trend, MCP, 229–232, 231*f*
Planned contrasts, 226
    Dunn (or Bonferroni) and Dunn-Sidak
        methods, 234–236
    orthogonal, 232–233
    with reference group, Dunnett method,
        233–234
Platykurtic distribution, 71*f*
Points of inflection, 64
Population, definition, 6
Population parameters
    definition, 6
    estimation of, 83–87
    univariate, 39–58
Population prediction model, 364
Population proportion, 142
Population regression model, 364
Population variance, 49–51
    proportion, 142
Porter, A. C., 288, 293
Positively skewed distribution, 27, 28*f*, 70*f*
Post hoc blocking method, 348
Post hoc contrasts, 227
Post hoc power, 108
Power
    determinants, 107–108
    type II error and, 105–108
Practical significance, versus statistical
        significance, 108–109
Predefined range blocking method, 348
Predefined value blocking method, 348
Prediction errors, 367–369
    scatterplot, 368, 368*f*
Pregibon, D., 377
Price, B., 403
Probability, 77–91
    definition, 79–80
    importance of, 78–79
    intuition versus, 80–81
    sampling and estimation, 81–87
Profile plot, 254
Proof (prove), 97
Proportion of predictable variation, 369–370
Proportions
    binomial distribution, 143
    chi-square distributions, 151–156
    dependent, 148–151
    independent, 146–148
    inferences, 140–161
    normal distribution, 141–151
    sampling distribution, 143
    single, 144–146
    standard error, 143

standard error of difference between two, 147
tests of, 141–144
variance error, 143
Puri, M. L., 293


**Q**

Quade, D., 293
Quartiles, 30–31
Quasi-experimental designs, 279, 292


**R**

Ramsey, P. H., 170, 189
Randomization, definition, 292
Randomized block designs, 344
Range, 46–47
    exclusive, 46
    inclusive, 46
Ratio measurement scale, 11–12, 12*t*
Raudenbush, S. W., 293
Raw residuals, 375
Raw scores, 18
Real limits, in data sets, 19
Regression approach, factorial ANOVA with
        unequal *n*'s, 267
Reichardt, C. S., 288, 353
Relative frequency distribution, 19*t*, 22
Repeated factor, 302
Repeated-measures models, 200
Replacement, simple random sampling with and
        without, 82
Research hypothesis, 94
Restriction of range, 187–188, 187*f*
Robbins, N. B., 29
Rogosa, D. R., 289
Rosenthal, R., 234
Rosnow, R. L., 234
Rousseeuw, P. J., 377, 401
Row marginals, 155
Rudas, T., 78
Ruppert, D., 377, 378, 401
Rutherford, A., 293


**S**

Sample, definition, 6
Sample proportion, 142
Sample size, 19
Sample statistics

definition, 6
   probability and, 77–91
   univariate population parameters and, 39–58
Sample variance, 51–52, 53$t$
Sampled range blocking method, 348
Sampled value blocking method, 348
Sampling distribution
   difference between two means, 121
   full decision-making context, 105–108, 106$f$
   intelligence test case, 107$f$
   of the mean, 83, 84$f$
   proportion, 143
   variance, 163
Sampling error, 84
Sanders, J. R., 125, 211, 212, 289
Sawilowsky, S. S., 125, 126
Scales of measurement, 8, 12$t$
Scariana, S. M., 211, 286
Scatterplots, 177–179, 178$f$, 178$t$, 180$f$, 368, 368$f$
Schafer, W. D., 406
Scheffé, H., 236
Schmid, C. F., 29
Scholastic Achievement Test (SAT), 67–68
Scientific hypothesis, 94
Seber, G. A. F., 407
Semipartial correlation, 389–390
Sen, P. K., 293
Sequential approach, factorial ANOVA with
      unequal $n$'s, 267
Sequential regression model, 403
   commentary on, 406
Serlin, R., 214
Serlin, R. C., 185, 265
Setwise regression, 406
Shapiro, S. S., 126, 213, 287, 401
Shavelson, R. J., 323
Sidak, Z., 235
Significance tests and confidence intervals,
      370–375
Simple post hoc contrasts
   Tukey HSD, Tukey-Kramer, Fisher LSD and
      Hayter tests, 237–240
   for unequal variances, Games-Howell,
      Dunnett T3 and C Tests, 240
Simple random sampling, 82
   with replacement, 82
   without replacement, 82
Simultaneous regression model, 403
Singh, M., 126
Single variance, 164–166
Skewed distribution, 68–70, 79$f$
Skewness, non-zero, 377
Smithson, M., 208, 260, 370, 395

Snee, R. D., 403
Spearman's rank correlation, 188–191
Sphericity, 346
Spiegel, D. K., 267
Split-plot design, 319
SPSS
   central tendency and dispersion, 53–55
   chi-square procedures, 156–158, 157–158$t$
   in data representation, 33–34
   example data sets, 133–134, 134$t$
   MCPs, 241–242, 242$t$
   measures of association, 191–192, 192$t$
   multiple regression, 408, 409$t$
   normal distribution and standard scores,
      72–73, 73$f$
   one-factor ANCOVA model, 293–294, 295–296$t$
   one-factor ANOVA, 215–217, 216$t$, 217$f$
   random- and mixed-effects analysis, 325–331,
      327–329$t$
   simple linear regression, 381–382$t$, 381–383
   statistics quiz data, 54$t$
   testing hypothesis, 113–114, 114$f$
   two-factor ANOVA models, 268–269,
      270–271$t$, 353–356, 354–356$t$
   variances, 172–173
Stafford, K. L., 370, 395
Standard curve, 61, 61$f$
Standard deviation, 49–51, 50
   constant relationship with, 63–64
   sample variance and, 51–52, 53$t$
Standard error
   difference between two means, 122
   difference between two proportions, 147
   of the mean, 85
   proportion, 143
Standard error of estimate, 372
Standard scores, 65–68
   normal distribution and, 59–76
Standard unit normal distribution, 62
Standardized regression model, 367
Standardized residuals, 376
Stanley, J. C., 200, 279, 292
Statistic, definition, 6
Statistical hypothesis, 94
Statistical significance, versus practical
      significance, 108–109
Statistics
   brief history, 5
   definitions, 5–7
   value of, 3–4
Steiger, J., 109
Steiger, J. H., 370, 395
Stem-and-leaf display, 27–29, 28$f$

Stepwise selection, 405
Stevens, J. P., 403, 410
Stigler, S. M., 5
Studentized range test, 237
Sudman, S., 83
Summation notation, 40–41
Surman, S. H., 326
Symmetric around the mean, 68
Symmetric distributions, 27, 28f, 68–69, 69f

**T**

$t$ distribution, 110–111, 111f
$t$ test, 110, 112–113
    correlated samples, 121
    dependent, 129–132, 131t, 132f, 135t
    dependent samples, 120–121
    independent, 122–126, 124t, 125f, 134t
    independent samples, 120
    paired samples, 121
    Welch, 127–128, 213
Tabachnick, B. G., 406
Tabatabai, M., 289
Takane, Y., 292
Tamhane, A. C., 147, 285, 317
Tan, W., 289
Tetrad difference, ANOVA, 259
Thompson, B., 208, 260, 303
Thompson, M. L., 404
Tied ranks, 10t
Tijms, H., 78
Tiku, M. L., 126
Timm, N. H., 267, 346, 410
Tomarken, A., 214
Transformations, 379
Trend analysis, 229
True experimental designs, 279
True experiments, 292
Tufte, E. R., 24, 29
Tukey, J. W., 27, 32, 237, 239, 346, 350
Tukey, P. A., 29
Two-tailed test of significance, 98
Type II error (β), 105–108

**U**

Unbalanced case, 201, 213
Unequal $n$'s, 201, 213
Ungrouped frequency distribution, 18–20, 19t
Unit normal distribution, 62
    areas under, 64–65, 65f

transformation of, 63
Untied ranks, 10t
Univariate analysis
    population parameters, 39–58
    single variable, 177
Unstandardized regression model, 365–367, 366t

**V**

Variable selection procedures, 403–404
Variables
    definition, 7
    types of, 7–8
Variance error
    of the mean, 84–85
    proportion, 143
Variance error of estimate, 371
Variance of the residuals, 371
Variance stabilizing transformations, 377
Variances, 162–175
    Brown-Forsythe procedure, 169–171, 171f, 213
    $F$ distribution, 163, 164f
    homogeneity, 212
    independent, 168–172
    O'Brien procedure, 171f, 172
    sampling distribution of, 163
    single, 164–166
    traditional tests, 168–169
    two dependent, 166–168
Varon-Salomon, Y., 285

**W**

Wainer, H., 29
Wallgren, A., 29
Wallgren, B., 29
Wallis, W. A., 213
Watson, G. S., 211, 286, 376
Watts, D. G., 407
Weinberg, S. L., 212, 407, 408
Weisberg, H. I., 288
Weisberg, S., 376, 377, 399, 401, 402, 403, 406, 407
Welch, B. L., 213, 214, 257
Welch $t$ test, 127–128, 213
Well, A. D., 212, 214, 265, 280, 293, 315, 317, 318, 325, 342, 349, 352, 381, 402
Welsch, R. E., 378, 401
Wetherill, G. B., 403
Whiskers, 32–33, 33f

Wichern, D. W., 409
Wickens, T. D., 208, 211, 212, 234, 236, 240,
        260, 265, 267, 268, 280, 287, 288, 293,
        303, 313, 317, 318, 323, 325, 340, 342,
        343, 349, 352
Wilcox, R. R., 112, 126, 129, 133, 145, 167, 169,
        184, 185, 188, 208, 212, 214, 234, 236,
        237, 240, 257, 260, 289, 293, 303, 305,
        317, 318, 325, 372, 377, 379, 401
Wild, C. J., 407
Wilk, M. B., 126, 213, 287, 401
Wilkinson, L., 29
Within-groups variability, 202–203, 203*f*
Within subjects design, 313
Wonnacott, R. J., 402
Wonnacott, T. H., 402

Wright, R. E., 408
Wu, L. L., 378, 401


**Y**

Yu, M. C., 185
Yuan, K.-H., 108


**Z**

$z$ scores, 65–67
$z$ test, 101–104, 103*f*
Zimmerman, D. W., 126, 129